T0234624

Lecture Notes in Computer Science   9774

Commenced Publication in 1973
Founding and Former Series Editors:
Gerhard Goos, Juris Hartmanis, and Jan van Leeuwen

More information about this series at http://www.springer.com/series/7409

Fernando Bello · Hiroyuki Kajimoto
Yon Visell (Eds.)

Haptics: Perception, Devices, Control, and Applications

10th International Conference, EuroHaptics 2016
London, UK, July 4–7, 2016
Proceedings, Part I

 Springer

Editors
Fernando Bello
Imperial College London
London
UK

Yon Visell
University of California, Santa Barbara
Santa Barbara, CA
USA

Hiroyuki Kajimoto
The University of Electro-Communications
Chofu
Japan

ISSN 0302-9743   ISSN 1611-3349   (electronic)
Lecture Notes in Computer Science
ISBN 978-3-319-42320-3   ISBN 978-3-319-42321-0   (eBook)
DOI 10.1007/978-3-319-42321-0

Library of Congress Control Number: 2016943865

LNCS Sublibrary: SL3 – Information Systems and Applications, incl. Internet/Web, and HCI

This Springer imprint is published by Springer Nature
The registered company is Springer International Publishing AG Switzerland

Preface

These volumes contain the written contributions to the EuroHaptics 2016 conference, which was held at Imperial College London, UK, during July 4–7, 2016. The articles cover key areas of this constantly evolving field: neuroscience, perception and psychophysics, hardware and devices, software, control, and applications.

We received 162 submissions. Each was evaluated by at least three reviewers. Based on these reviews, 36 manuscripts were selected for oral presentations and 64 as posters. The meeting was single track and, in addition to contributed papers, included three keynote speakers, work in progress presentations, and interactive demonstrations. The geographical distribution of the different institutions presenting their research was: Austria, Australia, Belgium, Brazil, Canada, China, Finland, France, Germany, India, Israel, Italy, Japan, The Netherlands, New Zealand, Norway, South Korea, Spain, Turkey, UK, and USA. The quality and breadth of the contributions indicate that the EuroHaptics conference continues to be the primary European conference in the field of haptics, and an important forum for our rapidly growing field attracting researchers from all over the world.

We are very grateful to the Program Committee members and reviewers for volunteering their time to review and discuss the submitted articles and doing so in a timely and professional manner. We are also thankful to all members of the Organizing Committee for their dedication and commitment, the student volunteers for their hard work and always being willing to help, and the Advisory Committee for their assistance throughout the conference. We acknowledge the institutions that supported this event (Bristol Robotics Lab, Imperial College London, University of Birmingham, University College London and University of Reading) and our Gold (CEA, EPSRC UK-RAS Network, Force Dimension, Lofelt, Moog, Shadow Robot, Valeo), Silver (Generic Robotics, Haption, Optoforce Ltd., Prototouch), and Bronze (Actronika, Disney Research, IET Robotics & Mechatronics TPN, Springer, Ocado Technology, Right Hand Robotics, Tactile Labs Inc., Tanvas) sponsors. Last but not least, we would like to thank all authors for presenting their work at the conference. It was a pleasure hosting EuroHaptics 2016 and we hope that all participants enjoyed the intense and stimulating discussions, as well as the opportunity to establish or renew fruitful interactions.

July 2016

Fernando Bello
Hiroyuki Kajimoto
Yon Visell

Organization

General Chair

William Harwin — University of Reading, UK

Local Co-chairs

Fernando Bello — Imperial College London, UK
Etienne Burdet — Imperial College London, UK

Program Chairs

Fernando Bello — Imperial College London, UK
Yon Visell — UC Santa Barbara, USA
Hiroyuki Kajimoto — The University of Electro-Communications, Japan

Finance Co-chairs

Ildar Farkhatdinov — Imperial College London, UK
Ferdinando Rodriguez y Baena — Imperial College London, UK

Industry and Sponsorship Co-chairs

Stuart Bowyer — Imperial College London, UK
Vijay Pawar — University College London, UK
Ferdinando Rodriguez y Baena — Imperial College London, UK

Publicity and Website Co-chairs

Ildar Farkhatdinov — Imperial College London, UK
Angelika Peer — University of Bristol, UK

Workshops Chair

Massimiliano Di Luca — University of Birmingham, UK

Poster and Demos Chair

Yoshikatsu Hayashi — University of Reading, UK

Awards Committee Chair

Jee-Hwan Ryu   KoreaTech, South Korea

Student Volunteers Chair

Ravi Vaidyanathan   Imperial College London, UK

Local Arrangements Co-chairs

Franck Gonzalez   Imperial College London, UK
Alejandro Granados   Imperial College London, UK
Ozan Tokatli   University of Reading, UK

Advisory Committee

Ed Colgate   Northwestern University, USA
Vincent Hayward   University Pierre et Marie Curie, France
Roger Kneebone   Imperial College London, UK
Katherine Kuchenbecker   University of Pennsylvania, USA
Jee-Hwan Ryu   KoreaTech, South Korea
Jan Van Erp   University of Twente, The Netherlands

Program Committee

Kaspar Althoefer   King's College London, UK
Cagatay Basdogan   Koc University, Turkey
Monica Bordegoni   Politecnico di Milano, Italy
Manuel Cruz   Immersion Corporation, Canada
Massimiliano Di Luca   University of Birmingham, UK
Christian Duriez   INRIA, France
Ildar Farkhatdinov   Imperial College London, UK
Antonio Frisoli   Scuola Superiore Sant'Anna, Italy
Ilja Frissen   McGill University, Canada
Matthias Harders   University of Innsbruck, Austria
Jess Hartcher-O'Brien   Universite Pierre et Marie Curie, France
Sandra Hirche   Technical University of Munich, Germany
Seokhee Jeon   Kyung Hee University, South Korea
Astrid Kappers   Vrije Universiteit Amsterdam, The Netherlands
Masashi Konyo ·   Tohoku University, Japan
Ayse Kucukyilmaz   Yeditepe University, Turkey
Yoshihiro Kuroda   Osaka University, Japan
Vincent Levesque   Immersion Corporation, Canada
Anatole Lécuyer   INRIA, France
Monica Malvezzi   University of Siena, Italy
Masashi Nakatani   University of Tokyo, Japan

Miguel Otaduy	Universidad Rey Juan Carlos, Spain
Sabrina Panëels	CEA LIST, France
Betty Semail	Université Lille 1, France
Sriram Subramanian	University of Sussex, UK
Dzmitry Tsetserukou	Skolkovo Institute of Science and Technology, Russia
Jan Van Erp	University of Twente, The Netherlands
Qi Wang	Columbia University, USA
Dangxiao Wang	Beihang University, China
Junji Watanabe	NTT Communication Science Laboratories, Japan
Michael Wiertlewski	Université Aix-Marseille, France
Mounia Ziat	Northern Michigan University, USA
Loes van Dam	University of Essex, UK

Additional Reviewers

Yusuf Aydin	Sylvain Bouchigny	Angela Faragasso
Arsen Abdulali	Luca Brayda	Francesco Ferrise
Merwan Achibet	Anke Brock	Davide Filingeri
Wendy Adams	Domenico Buongiorno	Jeremy Fishel
Marco Aggravi	Martin Buss	Julia Fröhlich
Noman Akbar	John-John Cabibihan	Masahiro Furukawa
Mansoor Alghooneh	Domenico Campolo	Yoren Gaffary
Tomohiro Amemiya	Xi Laura Cang	Florian Gosselin
Margarita Anastassova	Ferdinando Cannella	Yoren Gaffary
Michele Antolini	Francesco Chinello	Alberto Gallace
Arash Arami	Seungmoon Choi	Colin Gallacher
Jumpei Arata	Lewis Chuang	Paolo Gallina
Ferran Argelaguet	Gabriel Cirio	Igor Gaponov
Ahmad Ataka	Ed Colgate	Elia Gatti
Malika Auvray	Daniela Constantinescu	Brent Gillespie
Dennis Babu	Patricia Cornelio Martinez	Marcello Giordano
Marie-Ange Bueno	Mario Covarrubias	Adrien Girard
Carlo Bagnato	Heather Culbertson	Frédéric Giraud
Priscilla Balestrucci	Marco D'Alonzo	Christophe Giraud-Audine
Edoardo Battaglia	Maria Laura D'Angelo	Nicholas Giudice
Gabriel Baud-Bovy	Hein Daanen	Cagatay Goncu
Wael Ben Messaoud	Ravinder Dahiya	Jenna Gorlewicz
Sliman Bensmaia	Marc Dalecki	Danny Grant
Leah Bent	Fabien Danieau	Giorgio Grioli
Wouter Bergmann Tiest	Barbara Del Curto	David Grow
Matteo Bianchi	Benoit Delhaye	Burak Guclu
Hannes Bleuler	Ioannis Delis	Hakan Gurocak
Jeffrey Blum	Aishwar Dhawan	Ahmet Guzererler
Serena Bochereau	Knut Drewing	Quang Ha-van
Christoph Borst	Mohamad Eid	Taku Hachisu

Abdelwahab Hamam
Tracy Hammond
Nobuhisa Hanamitsu
Takeshi Hatanaka
Christian Hatzfeld
Vincent Hayward
Hsin-Ni Ho
Thierry Hoinville
Charles Hudin
Thomas Hulin
Inwook Hwang
Ali Israr
Shuichi Ino
Ekaterina Ivanova
Ardouin Jerome
Nigel John
Lynette Jones
Christophe Jouffrais
Georgiana Juravle
Noriaki Kanayama
Jari Kangas
Abe Karnik
Tomohiro Kawahara
Ryo Kikuuwe
Yeongmi Kim
Seung-Chan Kim
Sang-Youn Kim
Raymond King
Ryo Kitada
Jelizaveta Konstantinova
Katherine Kuchenbecker
Irene Kuling
Yuichi Kurita
Scinob Kuroki
Ki-Uk Kyung
Jean-Claude Leon
Shan Luo
Stephen Laycock
Geehyuk Lee
Seungyon Claire Lee
Laure Lejeune
Daniele Leonardis
Min Li
Tommaso Lisini Baldi
Claudio Loconsole
Pedro Lopes

Rui Loureiro
Karon MacLean
Anderson Maciel
Yasutoshi Makino
Alessandro Mansutti
Maud Marchal
Damien Marchal
Nicolai Marquardt
Giovanni Martino
Luc Maréchal
Troy McDaniel
Sarah McIntyre
Mariacarla Memeo
David Meyer
Makoto Miyazaki
Mostafa Mohammadi
Abdenbi Mohand Ousaid
Arash Mohtat
Alessandro Moscatelli
Mohammadreza
    Motamedi
André Mouraux
Winfred Mugge
Joseph Mullenbach
Selma Music
Abdeldjallil Naceri
Ken Nakagaki
Devika Narain
Frank Nieuwenhuizen
Ilana Nisky
Jean-Paul Noel
Yohan Noh
Takuya Nojima
Shogo Okamoto
Ryuta Okazaki
Victor Adriel Oliveira
Katsuhiko Onishi
Leonie Oostwoud
    Wijdenes
Nizar Ouarti
Claudio Pacchierotti
Cesare Parise
Volkan Patoglu
Vijay Pawar
Dianne Pawluk
Michael Peshkin

Igor Peterlik
Delphine Picard
Thomas Pietrzak
Dario Pittera
Myrthe Plaisier
Roope Raisamo
Jussi Rantala
Nick Reed
Liliana Rincon-Gonzalez
Aurora Rizza
Roberta Roberts
Charles Rodenkirch
Chad Rose
Emanuele Ruffaldi
Alex Russomanno
Jee-Hwan Ryu
Eckehard Steinbach
Hannes Saal
Jamal Saboune
Satoshi Saga
Deepak Sahoo
Gionata Salvietti
Majed Samad
Chad Sampanes
Evren Samur
Massimo Satler
Katsunari Sato
Peter Scarfe
Stefano Scheggi
Oliver Schneider
Brian Schriver
Enzo Pasquale Scilingo
Sue Ann Seah
Riccardo Secoli
Hasti Seifi
Irene Senna
Ali Shafti
Craig Shultz
Anatolii Sianov
Stephen Sinclair
Jeroen Smeets
Massimiliano Solazzi
Florent Souvestre
Daniel Spelmezan
Adam Spiers
Steven Strachan

Ian Summers
Kenjiro Tadakuma
Atsushi Takagi
Shinya Takamuku
Masaya Takasaki
Abdelkrim Talbi
Hong Tan
Yoshihiro Tanaka
Ahmet Murat Tekalp
Alexander Terekhov
Sednaoui Thomas
Ranzani Tommaso
Khalis Totorkulov

Eric Vezzoli
Robert Volcic
Christian Wallraven
Marcelo Wanderley
Qi Wang
Indika Wanninayake
Maarten Wijntjes
Elisabeth Wilhelm
Graham Wilson
Heidi Witteveen
Helge Wurdemann
Hui Xie
Takumi Yokosaka

Shunsuke Yoshimoto
Tao Zeng
Yuru Zhang
Marcello Costantini
Cristina de la Malla
Laurent Grisoni
Charlotte Magnusson
Matjaz Ogrinc
Yasemin Vardar
Wenzhen Yang
Ozan Çaldıran

Contents – Part I

Contents – Part II

Posters 2

Posters 3

Perception of Hardness and Softness

What is the Hardness Perceived by Tapping?

Kosuke Higashi[✉], Shogo Okamoto, and Yoji Yamada

Graduate School of Engineering, Nagoya University, Nagoya, Japan
higashi.kousuke@d.mbox.nagoya-u.ac.jp, okamoto-shogo@mech.nagoya-u.ac.jp

Abstract. A human can perceive the hardness of an object by tapping its surface. We compared the ranked subjective hardness values and physical properties of objects, including their stiffness, viscosity, density, and Shore hardness, and the frequencies and time constants of the natural vibrations caused by tapping. The stiffness, frequency, and viscosity exhibited a relatively strong positive correlation with the perceived hardness. The results show that the viscosity influences the hardness perceived by tapping, as well as the stiffness, whereas the stiffness and elasticity are considered to be major factors in the hardness perceived by pinching or pushing.

Keywords: Hardness perception · Damped natural vibration · Real object

1 Introduction

Hardness is an important characteristic of an object, which humans typically perceive by pinching or pushing the object. Thus far, many researchers have studied how humans perceive the hardness and softness of objects. For example, cutaneous and proprioceptive cues were found to be integrated for the perception of softness [2,3,10]. Because the maximum human force is limited, hardness perception based on the reaction force and deflection of an object caused by pinching or pushing is limited. Indeed, human hardness perception is saturated and less sensitive for harder objects [4]. Similarly, hardness perception using the deformation of a fingertip when contacting an object's surface is not effective for an object that is substantially harder than the fingertip. Hence, humans make use of tapping and the resultant vibrotactile signal to estimate the hardness of an object, for which the perceptual strategy based on the deformation of the object or fingertip is not effective.

Hardness perception by tapping has not yet been thoroughly studied. Okamura et al. [8,9] reported that the frequency and attenuation of the damped natural vibration caused by tapping influence the material perception. This finding has been exploited to allow force display devices with limited output forces to deliver hardness values greater than the device is capable of expressing in a quasi-static manner [6,7]. These studies agree that higher vibratory frequencies lead to the perception of greater hardness. However, few researchers have

© Springer International Publishing Switzerland 2016
F. Bello et al. (Eds.): EuroHaptics 2016, Part I, LNCS 9774, pp. 3–12, 2016.
DOI: 10.1007/978-3-319-42321-0_1

reported the exact physical properties of objects that humans perceive by tapping. In other words, a question is raised about how accurately the hardness perceived by tapping corresponds to the physical hardness.

In a former study, we researched the effects of the mass, viscosity, and stiffness of virtual objects on hardness perception by tapping [5]. The result suggested that an increase in stiffness and decrease in mass lead to the greater perceived hardness. We assume that these parameters are also effective for hardness perception in the case of real objects.

In this study, we investigated the correlations between the hardness perceived by tapping and representative physical parameters related to an object's hardness, including its stiffness, viscosity, density, and Shore hardness, and the frequency and time constant of the natural vibration caused by tapping. Understanding the characteristics of hardness perception by tapping will help us to develop materials or object structures that feel hard or soft, along with a method to render object hardness for virtual reality systems. It can be also linked with a hardness test for industrial products by tapping or hammering.

2   Experiment: Ranking of Perceived Hardness by Tapping

Participants tapped the surfaces of objects and ranked their hardness based on their damped natural vibrations. All of the experimental procedures were approved by the internal review board of the School of Engineering in Nagoya University (#15-12).

2.1   Specimens

We performed an experiment using two types of specimens: spring-damper specimens and material specimens. All of the specimens were hard enough that we could not judge their hardness by pushing on them with a finger. As shown in Fig. 1, the spring-damper specimen was composed of two aluminum plates, a linear spring, and a shock absorber (EMACN1212A, B, and C, MISUMI, Japan). Each aluminum plate was 80×80 mm in size, and the upper and lower plates were 3 mm and 5 mm thick, respectively. Three types of springs and shock absorbers

Table 1. Stiffness and viscosity of spring-damper structures

Sample	Stiffness [N/m]	Viscosity [Ns/m]
I	15700	0.047
II	7830	0.024
III	24700	0.047
IV	15700	0.026
V	15700	0.078

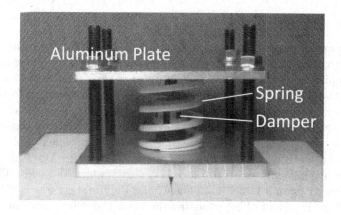

Fig. 1. Spring-damper structure

with different strengths could be used. Thus, as listed in Table 1, there were five types of specimens. The details of the vibration properties of each specimen are described in Sect. 3.

The material specimen was a block formed of a single material ($60 \times 60 \times 30$ mm). We used eight types of materials, including wood, nitril rubber, urethane rubber, modeling wax (ZW-200, Roland DG), ABS resin, acryl, stainless steel, and aluminum. The densities of these specimens are shown in Fig. 2. The density of stainless steel was remarkably higher than those of the other materials. There was a trend for the metal to have a high density and the wood to have a low density. However, there were no significant differences among the others.

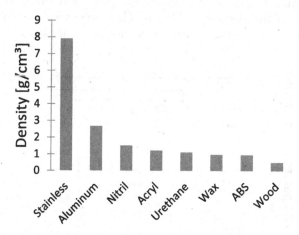

Fig. 2. Ranks of densities of material specimens.

2.2 Tasks and Participants

The participants separately ranked the hardness of each of the five spring-damper specimens and eight material specimens. They evaluated the hardness of a specimen by tapping its surface with the index finger of their dominant hand. It was stressed to the participants that they should tap the specimens with the same speed as much as possible and keep their finger touching a specimen while it was vibrating. The participants could tap each material as many times as they wanted. They ranked the perceived hardness of each specimen, and the same rank could be assigned to multiple specimens. They wore foggy glasses and headphones playing pink noise to block out visual and audio cues. The specimen was placed upon a buffer component, and its vibration was isolated from the ambient environment. They repeated the same task three times at intervals of a few minutes. The participants were five naive outsiders from the research group, who were males in their twenties.

2.3 Results

Figures 3 and 4 show the medians and 25th and 75th percentiles of the perceived hardness ranks. Friedman tests indicated that these ranks significantly varied among the specimens at a significance level of 0.05. In a post hoc manner, we tested the rank differences for all the pairs of specimens using Wilcoxon's rank sum tests, and the results are shown in the figures. As shown in Fig. 3, specimen V, which had a greater viscosity, was ranked first, and specimen III, which had a greater stiffness, was ranked second. Specimen I, which had medium stiffness and viscosity ranks, had a medium rank of perceived hardness. As shown in Fig. 4, the aluminum and stainless steel were ranked first, and the nitril rubber was ranked last among the material specimens. There were no significant differences among the ABS resin, acryl, urethane, modeling wax, and wood.

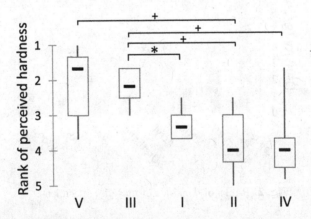

Fig. 3. Perceived hardness ranks of spring-damper specimens, where * and + indicate $p < 0.05$ and $p < 0.10$, respectively.

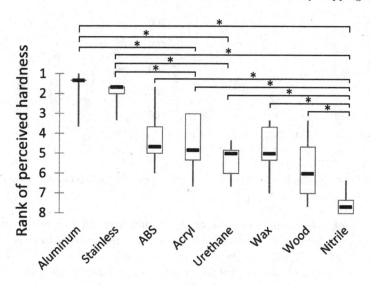

Fig. 4. Perceived hardness ranks of material specimens, where * indicates $p < 0.05$.

3 Physical Characteristics of Hardness Specimens

3.1 Characteristics of Natural Vibration

We tapped the spring-damper specimens and measured their damped natural vibration. An accelerometer (ADXL335, ANALOG DEVICES) was attached to the center part of the upper surface of a specimen. The measurement was repeated 10 times for each specimen with a sampling rate of 10 kHz. The specimen was placed on a buffer component, and its vibration was isolated from the ambient environment, including the table and floor. We specified the main frequency of the damped natural vibration by computing the fast Fourier transform (FFT) of the acceleration signals. The vibration waveform was then band-pass-filtered so as to include the natural frequency to determine the time constant. The time constant was obtained as the time until the amplitude of the filtered waveform was damped to 37 % of the maximum amplitude.

We assumed that the damped natural vibration of a spring-damper specimen was the impulse response of the one-degree-of-freedom spring-mass-damper system. In this assumption, the time constant τ and natural frequency f of the vibration are described as follows:

$$\tau = \frac{2m}{c} \tag{1}$$

$$f = \frac{1}{2\pi}\sqrt{(1 - \zeta^2)\frac{k}{m}} \simeq \frac{1}{2\pi}\sqrt{\frac{k}{m}} \tag{2}$$

where m, c, k, and ζ represent the mass, viscosity, stiffness of the system, and the damping ratio of the vibration, respectively. The stiffness k was defined

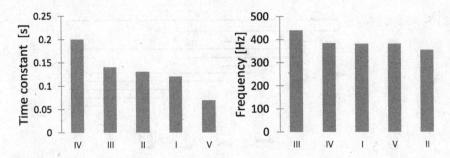

Fig. 5. Time constants and frequencies of vibrations of spring-damper specimens.

as the sum of the spring constants of the spring and damper composing the specimen. The viscosity c listed in Table 2 was obtained by substituting τ and f into Eqs. (1) and (2), respectively.

The time constants and natural frequencies of the damped natural vibrations of the specimens are shown in Fig. 5. The deviations of these values in repeated measurements were negligibly small. Specimens with greater spring constants exhibited greater natural frequencies. In addition, specimens with greater damping ratios had smaller time constants.

We also analyzed the vibration waveform of the material specimens by the same procedure. However, the waveforms contained multiple significant frequency components, which deviated from the damped natural vibration containing a single natural frequency component. Hence, we did not specify the vibration characteristics of the material specimens.

3.2   Shore Hardness

We measured the hardness of each specimen using a method based on the Shore C hardness test. In the original Shore C hardness test, a diamond hammer is dropped on an object, and its rebound height is measured. The Shore hardness is evaluated based on the ratio of the rebound height to the drop height. The Shore hardness may align with a human's hardness perception because both are affected by the physical properties of the object in a momentary contact state. In this experiment, we used a small ball made of hard rubber instead of the diamond hammer to avoid any possible damage to the specimens.

We fixed the specimen in a vise and dropped a rubber ball with a diameter of 22 mm from right above it. The position and initial height of the rubber ball were controlled using a guide frame. We tested each specimen five times, and recorded the drop and rebound heights using a high-speed camera (RX10II, SONY, Japan). We then derived the average rebound ratio for each specimen.

The ranks of the rebound ratios are shown in Fig. 6. Specimen III, which had a greater spring constant, exhibited the highest rebound ratio. Moreover, a specimen with a smaller viscosity had a greater rebound height. Among the material specimens, urethane was ranked first, and nitril rubber was ranked

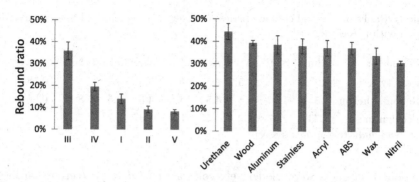

Fig. 6. Percentage of rebound height against falling height. Error bars indicate standard deviations. Left: spring-damper specimens. Right: material specimens.

last. There were no significant differences in the rebound heights of the wood, aluminum, stainless steel, acryl, ABS resin, and modeling wax.

4   Discussion: Comparison Between Perceived Hardness and Physical Characteristics Related to Hardness

We researched the relationships between the hardness perception by tapping and the representative parameters related to hardness. We calculated Spearman's correlation coefficient for the perceived hardness ranks and physical characteristics. The average perceived hardness rank among the participants was used in the calculation. Specimens with physical characteristics with no significant differences or differences that were too small to discriminate were ranked as the same level. Tables 2 and 3 show the ranks of the physical characteristics and their correlation coefficients with the perceived hardness.

It was found that the stiffness and viscosity of an object, and the frequency of the damped natural vibration, exhibited relatively strong correlations with the perceived hardness. Following these parameters, the density of a material and

Table 2. Ranks of physical characteristics of spring-damper specimens and Spearman's correlation with perceived hardness

Parameter	I	II	III	IV	V	Correlation
Stiffness	3	5	1	3	3	0.77
Viscosity	2.5	5	2.5	4	1	0.82
Frequency	3	5	1	3	3	0.77
Time constant	4	2.5	2.5	1	5	0.08
Rebound height	3	4.5	1	2	4.5	0.45
Perceived hardness	3.23	3.77	2.2	3.73	2.13	-

Table 3. Ranks of physical characteristics of material specimens and Spearman's correlation with perceived hardness

Parameter	Alum.	SST*	ABS	Acryl	Ure.	Wax	Wood	Nitril	Correl.
Density	2'	1	6.5	4.5	4.5	6.5	8	3	0.58
Rebound height	4.5	4.5	4.5	4.5	1	4.5	4.5	8	0.50
Per. hardness	1.73	2.07	4.2	4.57	5.37	4.87	5.73	7.47	-

*SST indicates stainless steel

its rebound hardness were moderately correlated with the perceived hardness ($\rho > 0.5$). Here, we discuss the interpretation of these results, although any correlations in the results were insignificant because of the small number of samples.

Stiffness and Frequency. The perceived hardness ranks had a strong correlation with those of the stiffness and the frequency of the damped natural vibration of the specimens. It was experimentally proved that a human has the ability to discriminate the stiffness of an object by tapping. To the best of our knowledge, very few studies have attempted to examine this perceptual mechanism. It was assumed that the effect of the frequency was similar to that of the stiffness because they are related by the vibration property, as shown in Eq. (2). The result, the positive effect of the frequency on the perceived hardness, matches past conclusions on presenting the hardness of a virtual object through vibration stimuli [5, 7–9].

Viscosity. The viscosity was found to be correlated with the perceived hardness as strongly as the stiffness, indicating that the viscosity was not a secondary factor for the perceived hardness. Note that the stiffness and viscosity were fairly independent of each other in our setup, with the correlation between these two types of values being 0.35. The viscosity has a role as important as the stiffness in restraining the amplitude of the vibration caused by tapping. Although the viscosity influences the hardness perception by pushing a compliant virtual object [1], the effect of the viscosity on the hardness perceived by tapping real objects was first confirmed in this study to the best of our knowledge. Because these two types of hardness perception are based on different perceptual mechanisms, we should not simply translate the effect of the viscosity between the hardness perception by pushing and that by tapping.

Density. The density of a material specimen had a moderate correlation with the perceived hardness. Note that the density and mechanical hardness of a material do not necessarily correspond to each other. For example, the hardness of a certain kind of urethane rubber can be changed, while its volume and mass are maintained by changing the ratio of the curing agent. We assumed that this correlation was caused by a change in the vibration properties as a result of a change in the density. The density of an object affects its vibration properties, including the amplitude, time constant, and frequency. The cause of the correlation would become clear by examining the effect of the density on the hardness perception with changes in the vibration properties.

Time Constant. There was no significant correlation between the time constant of the damped natural vibration and the hardness perception. As shown in Eq. (1), the time constant has a relationship with the viscosity. As previously mentioned, the viscosity exhibited a positive correlation with hardness perception. Thus, it seems natural that the time constant may have a negative one. Nonetheless, we are still uncertain about the contribution of the time constant to the perceived hardness, because in another study [5], the time constant of a simulated damped natural vibration influenced the perceived hardness. The effect of the time constant should be examined considering its interaction with other physical parameters and the human ability to discriminate the time change of vibration stimuli in future works.

Rebound Ratio. The rebound ratio was also found to be a secondary parameter affecting the hardness perception. According to the definition of Shore hardness, a harder object exhibits a higher rebound ratio as a result of the lower energy dissipation in the elastic deformation. An object with a higher stiffness whose energy dissipation is lower exhibits a higher rebound ratio. On the other hand, an object with a higher viscosity whose energy dissipation is higher exhibits a lower rebound ratio. Therefore, the hardness based on the rebound ratio has positive and negative correlations with the stiffness and viscosity of the object, respectively. However, as previously mentioned, the hardness perception has positive correlations with both the stiffness and viscosity. It is speculated that the rebound ratio is inferior to the individual use of the stiffness or viscosity as an index of perceived hardness by tapping.

5   Conclusion

We investigated the physical parameters that affect hardness perception based on the tapping of real objects. Through psychophysical experiments and mechanical tests, we compared the hardness perception ranks and six physical properties, including the stiffness, viscosity, density, and Shore hardness values of objects, and the frequencies and time constants of the natural vibrations caused by tapping. Our results suggested that the stiffness and viscosity of an object and the frequency of its damped natural vibration had correlations with the perceived hardness. In contrast with the quasi-static hardness perception by pinching or pushing, the viscosity was also found to be an effective factor, indicating that we should not assume that the perceived hardness is entirely related to the actual hardness of an object. The result suggests that viscosity can compensate for the perceived hardness of objects instead of increasing the stiffness. The findings can be applied to, for example, rendering a hard virtual object by using the powerless displays or the material design of industrial products.

Acknowledgment. This study was partly supported by ImPACT (Tough Robotics Challenge) and MEXT Kakenhi (15H05923).

References

1. van Beek, F.E., Heck, D.J., Nijmeijer, H., Bergmann Tiest, W.M., Kappers, A.M.L.: The effect of damping on the perception of hardness. Proceedings of IEEE World Haptics Conference pp. 82–87 (2015)
2. Tiest, B.: W.M., Kappers, A.M.L.: Cues for haptic perception of compliance. IEEE Trans. Haptics **2**(4), 189–199 (2009)
3. Bicchi, A., Schilingo, E.P., De Rossi, D.: Haptic discrimination of softness in tele-operation: the role of the contact area spread rate. IEEE Transactions on Robotics & Automation **16**(5), 496–504 (2000)
4. Harper, R., Stevens, S.S.: Subjective hardness of compliant materials. Quarterly Journal of Experimental Psychology **16**(3), 204–215 (1964)
5. Higashi, K., Okamoto, S., Nagano, H., Yamada, Y.: Effects of mechanical para-meters on hardness experienced by damped natural vibration stimulation. Proceedings of IEEE International Conference on Systems, Man, and Cybernetics pp. 1539–1544 (2015)
6. Ikeda, Y., Hasegawa, S.: Characteristics of perception of stiffness by varied tapping velocity and penetration in using event-based haptic. Proceedings of 15th Joint Virtual Reality Eurographics Conference on Virtual Environments pp. 113–116 (2009)
7. Kuchenbecker, K.J., Fiene, J., Niemeyer, G.: Improving contact realism through event-based haptic feedback. IEEE Trans. Visual Comput. Graphics **12**(2), 219–230 (2006)
8. Okamura, A.M., Hage, M.W., Cutkosky, M.R., Dennerlein, J.T.: Improving reality-based models for vibration feedback. Proceedings of ASME Dynamic Systems & Control Conference **69**(2), 1117–1124 (2000)
9. Okamura, A.M., Cutkosky, M.R., Dennerlein, J.T.: Reality-based models for vibration feedback in virtual environments. IEEE/ASME Trans. Mechatron. **6**(3), 245–252 (2001)
10. Srinivasan, M.A., LaMotte, R.H.: Tactual discrimination of softness. J. Neurophysiol. **73**(1), 88–101 (1995)

Haptics-1: Preliminary Results from the First Stiffness JND Identification Experiment in Space

André Schiele[1,3](✉), Manuel Aiple[1,3], Thomas Krueger[3], Frank van der Hulst[3], Stefan Kimmer[1,3], Jan Smisek[2,3], and Emiel den Exter[3]

[1] Faculty of Mechanical, Materials and Maritime Engineering,
Delft University of Technology, Delft, The Netherlands
{andre.schiele,manuel.aiple,stefan.kimmer}@esa.int
[2] Faculty of Aerospace Engineering, Delft University of Technology,
Delft, The Netherlands
jan.smisek@esa.int
[3] European Space Agency, Telerobotics & Haptics Laboratory,
Noordwijk, The Netherlands
{thomas.krueger,frank.van.der.hulst,emiel.den.exter}@esa.int

Abstract. On July 28th 2014, 23:47 UTC, the European Space Agency launched the Haptics-1 Kit to the International Space Station (ISS) on its last Automated Transfer Vehicle ATV-5. The Kit reached the station two weeks later, marking the first haptic master device to enter the ISS. The first force-feedback and human perceptual motor performance tests started to take place on December 30th 2014, and are the first of their kind in the history of spaceflight. Three astronauts participated in the Haptics-1 experiment until November 2015, allowing the investigation of the effects of microgravity on various psycho-motor performance metrics related with the usage of haptic feedback. Experiments are conducted following full adaptation to the space environment (after 3 months in space). This paper introduces the Haptics-1 experiment and associated hardware. Detailed experimental results are reported from a first stiffness just noticeable difference (JND) experimental study in space, carried out on the ISS and pre-flight on ground with 3 astronauts. The first findings from the experiment show no major alterations in-flight, when compared to on-ground data, if the manipulandum is secured in flight against a sufficiently stiff reference structure.

Keywords: Micro gravity · Just noticeable difference (JND) · Stiffness discrimination · Space · Haptics

1 Introduction

To enable further human exploration to neighbouring celestial bodies, telerobotic technologies will have to be used extensively. In a scenario that is gaining increasing popularity among the space community, operators will stay in orbiting stations (e.g. around Mars) and control robotic systems on the surface via

© Springer International Publishing Switzerland 2016
F. Bello et al. (Eds.): EuroHaptics 2016, Part I, LNCS 9774, pp. 13–22, 2016.
DOI: 10.1007/978-3-319-42321-0_2

haptic teleoperation [1,5]. This way, they can remotely prepare human outposts for later human arrival, or conduct 'remote-in-situ' geophysical and geoscience research. In order to design haptic teleoperation devices for space, knowledge about potential changes to human motor performance in microgravity is important. The perception thresholds for torque and stiffness, as well as the capability to perform hand-eye coordinated position and torque tracking under long exposure to microgravity, need to be better understood.

Previous studies suggest that microgravity deteriorates human perceptual-motor performance. In [2] the authors showed a deterioration of human arm movement control and stipulate that a decrease in muscle spindle sensitivity in zero-G could be the cause. In general, changes can be related to alterations of cutaneous pressure or with different loading of the joints, muscles and associated sensors. However, often it is unclear whether observed changes are caused by the microgravity itself or by other contributing stressors related with spaceflight [3]. This is especially true for tests performed during short exposure to microgravity, such as during parabolic flight. While existing perceptive motor-performance tests on hand-eye coordination and reaching tasks have been performed in parabolic flights and some during SpaceLab missions with the Space Shuttle, studies involving adapted humans (i.e. at least exposed to microgravity for more than 20 days) to the environment are scarce and limited to the analysis of mental condition and rudimentary hand-eye coordination tasks [4]. Despite the extensive body of literature available on kinaesthetic performance in terrestrial environments, hardly any work is available to date that quantifies such performances under microgravity. The effects of microgravity on torque and stiffness discrimination capabilities in spaceflight are unknown.

It is the goal of this paper to introduce the Haptics-1 experiment of the European Space Agency, which is being conducted on ground (pre-flight) and in-flight on the ISS with multiple ESA, NASA and JAXA astronauts. This paper introduces the Haptics-1 study goals, its hardware Kit consisting of a high resolution force reflective manipulandum (joystick) and its experiment environment for automated in-flight data acquisition. Moreover, it is the goal of the paper to report first results from a stiffness just noticeable difference (JND) identification experiment conducted with 3 astronauts on ground and on-board ISS after full adaptation (> 3 months) to microgravity.

2   Haptics-1 Study Objectives

The Haptics-1 experiment consists of seven individual protocols to measure (a) the mechatronic performance stability of a haptic impedance controlled joystick in space (system self-test), (b) the variations of human impedance during relax, comply and resist tasks, (d) the hand-eye tracking performance and bandwidth for position and force (e) tracking tasks, the just noticeable differences for (f) force and (g) stiffness discrimination with the upper extremity up to the hand and, (h) the detection thresholds for a combined stiffness and damping contact tasks with virtual environments.

The JND experiments are all conducted with the upper limb in a position closely matching a typical 'joystick use case', such as e.g. during aircraft piloting or during robotic operation with a joystick.

All Haptics-1 protocols are performed pre-flight, in-flight on the ISS and if applicable also post-flight, after adaptation to the respective environments. The protocols are performed in 'wall-mount' condition and in 'body-mount' condition. In Fig. 1, the haptic device (1DOF joystick) is depicted in 'wall-mount' configuration on a seat-track interface strip as available also on ISS Columbus module experiment racks. During body-grounded condition, the joystick is worn on a body-vest directly attached to crew (depicted in the inset Fig. 1). The body-mount condition has been added to check whether creating a closed-loop force-path between joystick and the operator hand in space bears perceptive or work-load related advantages. In this case, theoretically, external forces from the joystick should not need to be counteracted by either gravity on ground, or by additional postural control via foot restraints in space. Therefore, this mounting style could be 'easier' to use in space. Haptics-1 is currently not intended as a longitudinal study, mainly due to a limitation of available crew time on-board.

All protocols are trained on ground and conducted in space by the astronauts under the help of an automatically guided experiment App on a touch-screen tablet PC (Fig. 1). The Principal Investigator (PI) monitors the conduct from ground via real-time video stream and is enabled to speak on the space-to-ground voice loop with crew if needed.

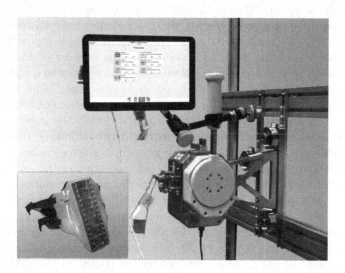

Fig. 1. The Haptics-1 flight model before launch (1DOF haptic joystick and touch-screen tablet PC) installed in wall-mount configuration on two seat track strips in a clean-room. The inset shows the body-vest with the same seat track interface that is used to mount the joystick in a body-grounded manner to crew.

3   The Apparatus: Haptics-1 Kit

The Haptics-1 Kit contains the 1° of freedom joystick, the touch-screen tablet PC with custom experiment software and all required periphery components (LAN Cables, power adapters, launch containers, storage devices, the body-vest, etc.) inside a flame-proof Nomex experiment container.

The joystick receives 28 V from a station portable power supply. The tablet is connected to the joystick's real-time computer via a point to point LAN cable. A reserve LAN interface exists on the joystick, allowing connection to the ISS Joint Station LAN for bilateral control experiments with a ground unit. The Haptics-1 App on the tablet PC is the sole graphical user interface (GUI) for crew. It guides the user through all individual experiment steps and allows the management (save, discard and retrieve) of the experiment data. For re-usability of the Kit, all software is easily exchangeable via file up-load through USB. The Kit is safety certified for human-in-the-loop (medical) data acquisition on-board the ISS and withstands all environmental loads related to ground transport, launch to space and use within the ISS environment.

3.1   The 1DOF Joystick

The 1DOF joystick integrates an Intel Atom 1.6 GHz computer running a Linux operating system with a Xenomai real-time patch. This computer runs the Haptics-1 joystick and experiment control software that interacts with the GUI of the Tablet. Via an EtherCAT bus, the real-time computer connects to a brushless DC motor controller that controls an ILM50x14 RoboDrive direct-drive actuator whose torque ripple is compensated to provide a smooth, ripple-free output to the handle-bar. On the motor shaft, an absolute position encoder provides a 21 bit position signal. The motor is connected via a capstan reducer to a custom built, strain-gauge based, joint-output torque sensor located just before the handle-bar. The actively controlled joystick can act as a pure position or torque source, or can render an impedance through its integrated closed-loop joint torque control running at a cyclic 2 kHz rate. Upstream current inhibitors, thermal fuses (for touch temperature monitoring) and joint limit microswitches as well as handle-bar dead-man microswitches ensure safe operation of the joystick under all circumstances when human-in-the-loop experiments are performed. The joystick has a range of motion of ±60° around the centre position depicted in (Fig. 1). The joystick can render a maximum continuous torque of ±12.0 Nm. The real-time computer running on the joystick encrypts all experiment data with 4096-bit encryption to protect the 'medical rated' data. Data is automatically transmitted via Data Distribution Services (DDS) to the tablet PC for retrieval via USB by crew after the experiment.

3.2   Joint Control Performance

For the Stiffness JND protocol, the joystick enters joint impedance control mode. The joystick can then render stiffnesses in the range from 0–0.286 kNm/rad and

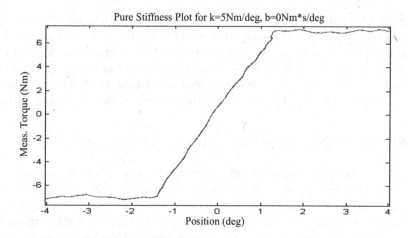

Fig. 2. Stiffness response of the Haptics-1 flight-model joystick during an interaction with an operator (simulated spring with constant $k = 5\,\text{Nm/deg}$).

also damping in the range from 0–1.1 Nms/rad. The achievable torque resolution in closed-loop joint torque control is as low as 7 mNm and torque ripple is less than 6.7 mNm, which is hardly perceivable by an operator. A recording of a rendered virtual spring with stiffness $k = 5\,\text{Nm/deg}$ on the flight-model joystick is depicted in Fig. 2, during interaction with a human operator.

Individual step responses of the position and joint torque controllers are depicted in Fig. 3. For the recording of the position step response, the joystick output was free to move (Fig. 3a). For the torque step response recording it was locked down at its output (Fig. 3b). The joint position controller is intended

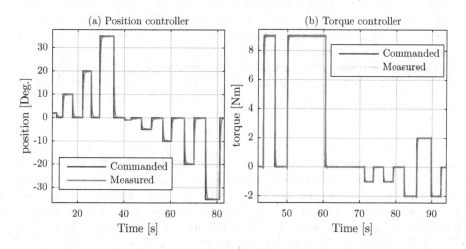

Fig. 3. Varying magnitude step responses of the Haptics-1 joysticks joint position controller (a) and joint torque controller (b). During recordings (a) the joystick was free to move, whereas the joystick output was clamped mechanically in (b). (Color figure online)

mainly for aligning the handle-bar to a reference pose during specific sequences in any of the protocols. This is why it is tuned "soft" to exert appropriately low speeds when the bar is handheld. The rise-time to 90 % output takes 550 ms. The joint torque control is tuned very stiff, in order to allow crisp force feedback to be rendered to the operator and also to enable the high bandwidth joint impedance control. The rise-time to 90 % output for the torque control is less than 180 ms.

4   Stiffness JND Identification Ground vs. Space

Multiple stiffness just noticeable difference (JND) tests have been performed as part of the Haptics-1 experiment campaign on-board the ISS in the time frame between January 5th and November 27th 2015. Three astronauts participated in baseline data collection (BDC) on ground before flight and in-flight data collection on the ISS. Two of the astronauts were trained U.S. air force test pilots and the third one a medical professional with emergency room experience. All study participants have provided signed informed consent via NASA and integrated ISS medical boards, and the study was evaluated by the ethics commission of Delft University of Technology.

4.1   Method

The JND experiment follows a 2-alternative forced choice (2AFC) design with $n = 200$ trials in which a stiffness reference level (e.g. Stimulus A) is compared with one of four modified test levels (e.g. Stimulus B) in multiple binary comparison tests. All trials are randomized with respect to A and B distribution as well as with respect to the reference level locations within the 200 trials. The experiment conduct can be considered double-blinded, since the experiment is hard-coded and automated on the Haptics-1 Tablet PC and 1DOF joystick.

The stiffness reference level is selected to be 1 Nm/deg., and the randomized test levels were at ± 40 %, ± 25 %, ± 15 % and ± 5 % of the reference stimulus (50 repetitions each). The 5 % test value is the lowest threshold that can still be rendered accurately by the Haptics-1 1DOF joystick, which is why this 'lowest possible threshold' series was chosen. During each trial, a pair of two stiffness samples is presented to the crew member via the manipulandum's impedance controller. The astronaut can select which one of the two stimuli (A or B) to probe via the GUI. Following the probing of both stimuli (they are free to choose back and forth between them), the candidate is asked to select the stiffer one of the two (A or B) via a dedicated selection button on the GUI. After selection, the next pair is presented to the astronaut until all 200 repetitions are completed. Each crew member conducts two test sessions on two consecutive days, one for the wall-mount and one for the body-mount data acquisition configurations (Fig. 4). For all trials, the astronauts are instructed to keep their arm parallel to a sagittal plane and similar to operating a joystick for robotic controls.

In space, the experiment was only performed after 3 months into the mission of each crew member. This way, potential dominant effects related with other

(a) wall-mount session   (b) body-mount session

Fig. 4. Astronauts on-board the International Space Station (Butch Wilmore, NASA; Kimiya Yui, JAXA) perform the Stiffness JND protocol of Haptics-1. Joystick in wall-mount setup in (a) and in body-mount (i.e. body-grounded force-feedback) in (b). Experiments done on ISS 3 months in flight.

stressors are minimized. A static design with 200 trials and four levels was chosen in order to present an overview over a large discrimination threshold range (not only a minimum threshold). Moreover, the levels were tailored by ground experiments with non-astronauts. The exact number of 200 trials was also a trade-off between science return and available crew-time on-board ISS. Every participating astronaut received ground training, performed pre-flight BDC and received a de-brief on-board prior to in-flight experiment conduct.

For data post-processing, the crew ratings for each stimuli level are counted and converted into a "percentage correct" for each test level and subject (50 correctly identified 'stronger' stimuli representing 100 % correct). A test subject achieving a percentage of at least 75 % correct estimates in one test level is considered to 'notice the difference' for the scope of this report. The paper reports boxplots for the combined subject data of the 3 astronauts. The test data is additionally checked with 2-way ANOVA and paired t-tests along all dimensions.

5   Stiffness JND Results

5.1   Ground, Body vs. Wall Mount Measurements

The boxplots of Fig. 5 show that the two attachment conditions do not cause stiffness JND results to differ on ground (confirmed by paired t-tests on all tested levels). The stiffness detection threshold lies between 5–15 % for both conditions, which can be seen also without the fitting of a psychometric function. The measurement range is appropriate in both cases to detect the transitioning from above to below the 75 % detection threshold. The difference detection of the 5 % level is more difficult than the 40 % level detection for the entire group ($p < 0.02$, $F = 10.5$) in wall-mount condition. In body-mount condition, the effect is even stronger ($p < 0.001$, $F = 64.1$). While in body-mount condition

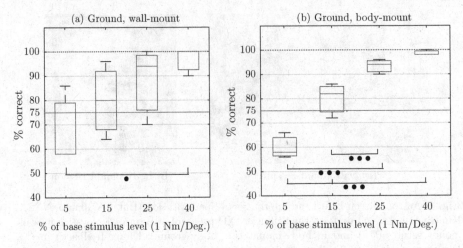

Fig. 5. Group stiffness JND results (three astronauts). Comparison of wall-mount (a) vs. body-mount (b) configuration on ground, obtained during pre-flight baseline data collection ($\bullet : p < 0.02$; $\bullet\bullet : p < 0.01$; $\bullet\bullet\bullet : p < 0.002$). (Color figure online)

there are no significant performance differences between subjects, in wall-mount, one subject performed worse than the other two, which causes more spread of the data.

5.2 Micro-G, Body vs. Wall Mount Measurements

The data presented in Fig. 6 shows slight variations between wall-mount and body-mount JND thresholds in space. Whereas the detection threshold for the wall-mount configuration lies between 5–15 % of the base stimulus, the body-mount configuration indicates a worsening towards the 15–25 % range for the combined subject results. The difference between the detection rates for the individual stimuli levels are more profound in space, with all levels different to each other in wall-mount configuration ($p < 0.01$, $F = 12.7$) and more strongly so in body-mount configuration ($p < 0.002$, $F = 20.72$). Paired t-test performed between equal difference levels of the two mounting conditions reveals no difference between the mounting conditions.

5.3 Ground vs. Micro-Gravity

The only difference detectable between the ground and space data-sets is apparent in the body-mount configuration, in which the 15 % difference level becomes worse in-flight with respect to ground ($p = 0.039$), explaining the apparent worsening of the overall detection threshold for the group in the boxplot in Fig. 6. No overall difference in the combined wall- and body-mount data results can be observed between in-flight and ground measurements.

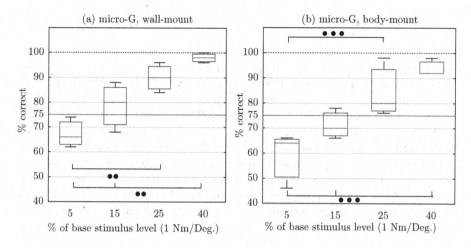

Fig. 6. Group stiffness JND results (three astronauts). Comparison of wall-mount (a) vs. body-mount (b) configuration in-flight on board the International Space Station ($\bullet : p < 0.02$; $\bullet\bullet : p < 0.01$; $\bullet\bullet\bullet : p < 0.002$). (Color figure online)

6 Discussion

It appears from the data above, that humans are very good at adjusting to novel environments, with no overall differences visible in Stiffness discrimination between ground and space after their 3 month adaptation to the micro-gravity environment. Moreover, the results above show strikingly little variation between subjects, considering that the background of test candidates was rather different. This suggests that the protocol automatic conduct, the performance of the hardware and the selection of experiment parameters are appropriate for this experiment. Human palpation from orbit could potentially be performed with the same perceptive capability than on ground, which could be good news for using telerobotics from space (if the teleoperation system itself doesn't limit the perception). Certainly, further analysis with additional subjects is ongoing, however, already the small sample of only 3 test subjects shows consistency. A more detailed analysis with more subjects and psychometric functions will allow to further detail the threshold findings.

One observable effect, however, is apparent in the body-mount configuration data-set with the vest, which seems to make detection of small stiffness differences in space harder. Two of the subjects, when asked during protocol conduct on ISS, reported that the body-vest caused some additional compliance ("sway") in the experiment, which made the stiffness identification much harder in space. This could be due to a sub-optimal design of the vest brace, not having sufficiently well located supporting points on the operator torso. Results show that a rigid support for this task is better. The wall-mount conduct shows no alteration in space compared to ground. The reaction forces imparted to a crew member during this task, however, caused some 'fatigue' in the lower body as reported by one crew member during space-to-ground communication.

7   Conclusion

Stiffness discrimination thresholds in wall-mount configuration show no variation between ground and measurement in space, after long exposure to the space environment. The detection threshold lies between 5–15 % of the 1 Nm/deg. base stimulus level, equalling a threshold of approximately 0.1 Nm/deg. or when expressed as a linear stiffness, approximately 0.9 N/mm (the grip centre point lies 0.113 m from the joint centre). The vest-mount configuration tested in this experiment causes a worsening of the stiffness discrimination threshold to 15–25 % of the base stimulus level in space, likely caused by sway in the mechanical attachment of the body vest. Overall, no deterioration of stiffness detection thresholds can be observed between space and ground for the combined data, if the astronauts are exposed and adjust to 3 months in the microgravity environment.

References

1. Carey, W., Schoonejans, P., Hufenbach, B., Neergard, K., Bosquillon de Frescheville, F., Grenouilleau, J., Schiele, A.: METERON: a mission concept proposal for preparation of human-robotic exploration. In: Global Space Exploration Conference, Washington D.C. (2012)
2. Fisk, J., Lackner, J.R., DiZio, P.: Gravitoinertial force level influences armmovement control. J. Neurophysiol. **69**(2), 504–511 (1993). http://jn.physiology.org/content/69/2/504
3. Fowler, B., Meehan, S., Singhal, A.: Perceptual-motor performance and associated kinematics in space. Hum. Factors J. Hum. Factors Ergon. Soc. **50**(6), 879–892 (2008)
4. Manzey, D., Lorenz, B., Poljakov, V.: Mental performance in extreme environments: results from a performance monitoring study during a 438-day spaceflight. Ergonomics **41**(4), 537–559 (1998). pMID: 9557591
5. Schiele, A.: METERON - validating orbit-to-ground telerobotics operations technologies. In: 11th Symposium on Advanced Space Technologies in Robotics and Automation (ASTRA) (2011)

Haptic Aftereffect of Softness

Anna Metzger$^{(\boxtimes)}$ and Knut Drewing

Justus-Liebig University Giessen, Giessen, Germany
anna.metzger@psychol.uni-giessen.de

Abstract. Past sensory experience can influence present perception. We studied the effect of adaptation in haptic softness perception. Participants compared two silicon rubber stimuli, a reference and a comparison stimulus, by indenting them simultaneously with the index fingers of their two hands and decided which one felt softer. In adaptation conditions the index finger that explored the reference stimulus had previously been adapted to another rubber stimulus. The adaptation stimulus was indented 5 times with a force of >15 N, thus the two index fingers had a different sensory past. In baseline conditions there was no previous adaptation. We measured the Points of Subjective Equality (PSEs) of one reference stimulus to a set of comparison stimuli. We used four different adaptation stimuli, one was harder, two were softer and one had approximately the same compliance as compared to the reference stimulus. PSEs shifted as a function of the compliance of the adaptation stimulus: the reference was perceived to be softer when the finger had been adapted to a harder stimulus and it was perceived to be harder after adaptation to a softer stimulus. We conclude that recent sensory experience causes a shift of haptically perceived softness away from the softness of the adaptation stimulus. The finding that perceived softness is susceptible to adaptation suggests that there might be neural channels tuned to different softness values and softness is an independent primary perceptual quality.

Keywords: Softness · Stiffness · Haptic · Tactile · Perception · Adaptation · Aftereffect

1 Introduction

Prolonged exposure to a stimulus can change neural responses, i.e. physically identical stimuli can be perceived to be dramatically different given different preceding sensory experiences. This form of plasticity (though difficult to be distinguished from other forms, e.g. learning) is usually referred to as perceptual adaptation [1]. One psychophysically measurable effect of adaptation is an aftereffect, which refers to a shift in perception of a test stimulus (reference) along a perceptual dimension after prolonged exposure to another stimulus (adaptation stimulus) with a certain value along this dimension, usually away from the adaptation stimulus [1–3]. A well-known example is the visual aftereffect of motion, which was described as the "waterfall illusion" in 1834 by Robert Addams [4]: He perceived static rocks as moving upwards after prolonged viewing of a waterfall. The established explanation of aftereffects is that a perceptual dimension is represented by the activity of neural channels with narrowly tuned but overlapping sensitivities to the values along this dimension [3, 5]. A stimulus with a

© Springer International Publishing Switzerland 2016
F. Bello et al. (Eds.): EuroHaptics 2016, Part I, LNCS 9774, pp. 23–32, 2016.
DOI: 10.1007/978-3-319-42321-0_3

certain value along a perceptual dimension activates mostly the channel tuned to this value and also a little the channels sensitive for the surrounding values. From the relative activities of the channels the value of the stimulus can be "read out" and it is assumed that this mediates our perception [3]. Prolonged exposure to a narrowband adaptation stimulus would cause a reduction in the sensitivity of the corresponding channel and its neighbors. When a reference stimulus with a value close to the value of the adaptation stimulus is presented afterwards, the channel which should respond maximally would respond less and the activity of the channels sensitive to the neighboring values would be lower at the side close to the value of the adaptation stimulus than on the other side. As a consequence the overall activity would be shifted away from the value of the adaptation stimulus, which would cause a corresponding shift in the perception of the reference - a "repulsion aftereffect" [1]. As neurophysiological studies supported the described model of sensory encoding by providing examples of adaptable cells responding to narrow ranges of a perceptual dimension [6], adaptation became the "psychologist's microelectrode" [3], i.e. revealing how perceptual attributes are encoded in the brain by measuring response changes after adaptation [1]. In the present study we addressed the influence of adaptation in haptic perception of softness.

An early report of an aftereffect in haptic perception was made by John Locke in the seventeenth century. He observed a difference in perceived temperature between his two hands when they were put in a bucket with water: The water felt warm to the hand which had experienced cold water before and cold to the hand, which had been adapted to warm water [7]. Later, haptic aftereffects have been described and studied also in the perception of size, shape and weight of an object, roughness, curvature, vibration and motion. For an extensive overview of aftereffects in the sense of touch see [8]. Most of the observed haptic aftereffects are "repulsion aftereffects", i.e. perception of a reference stimulus shifts away from the adaptation stimulus. This finding is in concordance with the established multichannel model of aftereffects.

Here we study the perception of softness. Softness refers to the subjective measure of an object's compliance. Compliance is defined as the ratio between displacement of the object's surface and the force applied to the object; compliance can be expressed in mm/N. Active exploration of softness usually involves the stereotypical *Exploratory Procedure of Pressure,* meaning that an object is repeatedly squeezed between the fingers or it is repeatedly indented with a finger or a tool usually in direction normal to the object's surface [9, 10]. It has been speculated that SAI fibers are involved in softness perception [11]. However, SAI discharge rates cannot be solely responsible for encoding softness, because these discharge rates also vary with the velocity of skin indentation during exploration, which is not observed for perceived softness [11]. Most authors assume that softness is perceived through a combination of information about the displacement of the object's surface and information about the force being applied to the object [12, 13]. Such information can be obtained from the cutaneous and kinesthetic afferent systems [12–15] and in certain cases even from vision [16, 17] and audition [18].

We hypothesized that perceived softness would also be subject to adaptation effects. We investigated whether the perception of a reference stimulus would change by preceding stimulation with an adaptation stimulus as compared to the case when the reference is explored without previous adaptation. We asked participants to compare a reference and a comparison stimulus by indenting them simultaneously with the two index fingers of their left and right hand. In adaptation trials the index finger that explored the reference stimulus had been previously adapted to another stimulus. The adaptation stimulus was indented 5 times with a force of >15 N. The other index finger that explored the comparison stimulus was not adapted. In baseline trials neither finger underwent previous adaptation. We measured the Points of Subjective Equality (PSEs) between the reference stimulus (0.32 mm/N) and comparison stimuli using a 1-Up-1-Down staircase and an Alternative Forced Choice (AFC) task. We compared the PSEs measured in the adaptation conditions to PSEs measured in the baseline condition. We used different adaptation stimuli: one was harder than the reference (0.16 mm/N), two were softer (0.49 and 0.92 mm/N) and one adaptation stimulus had the same compliance as the reference. One soft adaptation stimulus was chosen to have the same physical difference to the reference stimulus as the hard adaptation stimulus and the other soft adaptation stimulus had a greater difference. Two soft adaptation stimuli were used to account for potential effects of the nonlinearity of the perceptual softness space, which was found to be a power function with a negative exponent (−0.8) of the physical space [19]. Consequently larger physical differences in compliance between the reference and the softer adaptation stimulus might be required to achieve perceived differences in softness which yield well observable adaptation effects.

Given that the dimension of softness is encoded in narrowly tuned channels [3, 5] – as it seems to be the case for other perceptual dimensions – we can expect that the reference stimulus is perceived to be softer with preceding adaptation to a harder stimulus and harder when the finger is adapted to a softer stimulus as compared to the perception without adaptation. In the case of the adaptation to the stimulus with the same compliance, no perceptual shift can be expected.

2   Experiment

2.1   Methods

Participants. 10 right-handed participants were tested (5 males, mean age: 24.2 years, range: 19–30 years). They were naïve to the purpose of the experiment, volunteered to participate and were refunded. None of them reported any sensory or motor impairment of the index fingers at both hands. The study was approved by the local ethics committee LEK FB06 at Giessen University and was in line with the declaration of Helsinki from 1964. Written informed consent was obtained from each participant.

Apparatus. The experiments were conducted at a visuo-haptic workbench, which comprised a PHANToM 1.5A haptic force feedback device, a 22″-computer screen (120 Hz, 1280 × 1024 pixel), stereo glasses, a mirror and a force sensor consisting of a measuring beam (LCB 130) and a measuring amplifier (GSV-2AS, resolution 0.05 N, temporal resolution 682 Hz). Three real silicon rubber stimuli - one adaptation stimulus, the reference and one comparison were placed side-by-side in front of the

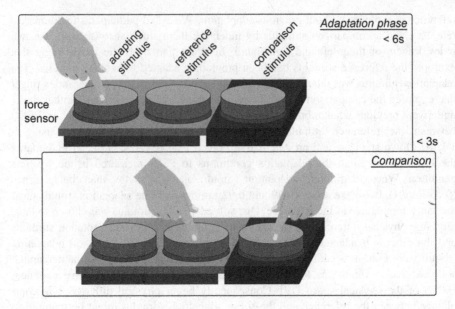

Fig. 1. The arrangement and exploration of the stimuli during the adaptation and the comparison phase.

participant. The adaptation stimulus and the reference were placed on the force sensor, which recorded the force exerted by the participant (Fig. 1). The mirror prevented direct sight on the stimuli. To guide the participants through the experiment, a virtual schematic 3D-representation of the stimuli and the finger (a sphere of 8 mm diameter; hidden during stimulus exploration) were displayed on the monitor, which was positioned over the mirror. Additionally signal tones were displayed via headphones. The virtual representation of the setup, viewed via stereo glasses, was aligned to its real counterpart in a way that the participant had the impression to directly view the real setup. The head was stabilized by a chin rest limiting the viewing distance to 40 cm. The left index finger was connected to the PHANToM which detected its position via a custom-made adapter. The adapter consisted of a pin with a metallic ball affixed to its end and a plastic fingernail with a magnet on its outer surface. The plastic fingernail was affixed to the dorsal side of the finger via an adhesive deformable pad and via the magnet to the metallic pin, which was attached to the PHANToM arm. This way the adapter left the finger pad uncovered and allowed for free finger movements including all six degrees of freedom. A custom-made software controlled the experiment, collected responses and recorded relevant parameters every 3 ms.

Softness Stimuli. We produced stimuli with varying compliance using a two-component silicon rubber solution (AlpaSil EH 10:1), which was mixed with different amounts of a diluent (polydimethylsiloxane, viscosity 50 mPa·s). The stimuli were cast in cylindrical plastic dishes (75 mm diameter × 38 mm high) and had no discriminable differences in size and texture. The compliance was measured using the experimental apparatus. For this purpose instead of the finger-adapter a flat–ended cylindrical probe of 1 cm^2 area ('standard finger') was fixed to the PHANToM arm. This standard finger was pressed 5 times into the stimulus using forces approximately between 15 N and 25 N. To calculate the compliance we fitted regression lines to the measured displacement–force traces for forces of 0–9 N and estimated the slopes. We used only the trajectories caused by the increase of force for analysis, to exclude hysteresis effects during the decrease of force. Possible non-uniformity in data sampling during the measurement due to manual indentation of the stimuli were reduced by calculating mean displacements for every 1 N step over bins of ±0.4 N. For further details and discussion on the measurement method see [10].

We produced two sets of rubber stimuli – a set of adaptation stimuli consisting of three stimuli and a set of test stimuli, consisting of one reference and ten comparison stimuli. In the test set, half of the comparisons had increasingly lower compliance and the other half increasingly higher compliance as compared to the reference. As reference we used a stimulus with 0.32 mm/N compliance. The compliances of the harder comparisons were 0.16, 0.19, 0.23, 0.26 and 0.29 mm/N and of the softer comparisons 0.36, 0.39, 0.43, 0.46 and 0.49 mm/N. The compliance difference between two neighbored comparison stimuli was about 1/2 Weber fraction and the range covered by the comparisons was about 2.5 Weber fractions in each direction. We assumed the Weber fraction to be 20 % (value from [10]). To reduce effects of wear we produced each stimulus of the test set in two similar versions. The use of the two versions was balanced. The adaptation set comprised three stimuli. The hard adaptation stimulus was about 2.5 Weber fractions harder (0.16 mm/N) than the reference stimulus. There were two soft adaptation stimuli, one which had approximately the same difference to the reference as the hard adaptation stimulus but in opposite direction (0.49 mm/N, about 2.5 Weber fractions softer) and another, which was even softer (0.92 mm/N, about 9 Weber fractions softer). Additionally we used a stimulus with approximately the same compliance as the reference as an adaptation stimulus. It was balanced between participants which version of this stimulus served as reference stimulus and which version served as adaptation stimulus.

Design. The experimental design comprised the within-participant variable *Compliance of Adaptation Stimulus* $a \in [0.16, 0.32, 0.49, 0.92] mm/N$. We measured individual Points of Subjective Equality (PSEs) of the reference stimulus which was explored with the index finger that was adapted to one of the adaptation stimulus (adaptation conditions) or not adapted (baseline condition). The PSE was assessed as compared to comparison stimuli which were always explored with the other index finger that was not adapted. We used a two-alternative-force-choice task combined with a 1-Up-1-Down staircase paradigm, to measure the PSEs. We analyzed the differences caused by adaptation as compared to the baseline condition.

Procedure. In total four staircases were performed for each condition: two downwards-directed staircases, which started with the comparison stimulus of highest compliance in the test set and two upward-directed staircases, which started with the comparison stimulus of lowest compliance in the test set. The comparison stimulus for the next trial in the staircase was determined by the response of the participant. In case the participant responded that the comparison felt softer than the reference, the next comparison in the staircase was chosen to be harder (0.03 mm/N step). Whereas, a softer comparison was presented in the next trial of the staircase if the comparison felt harder. In case the participant perceived the softest comparison of the test set as softer or the hardest comparison as harder, the same comparison was presented again in the next trial for this staircase. The estimation of the PSE by one staircase was considered terminated after 10 reversals. A reversal refers to the change of direction in the staircase, which occurs when participants change their judgment from softer to harder and vice versa. The 10 reversals were reached on average after 17.66 trials.

The experiment was split into two sessions. In each session the PSE for each condition was estimated by completion of one downwards and one upwards directed staircases. Each session consisted of blocks in which the current step of each staircase was presented once, in a randomized order. Each block consisted originally of 10 trials (two staircases per condition). Towards the end of one session the number of trials in a block decreased, because the number of terminated staircases increased. There were pauses of 1 min duration after each 45 trials (about every 15 min). Before the first session the participants completed a practice session consisting of 8 trials to familiarize with the setup and the task.

Before each adaptation trial one adaptation stimulus and the reference were placed on the force sensor. The adaptation stimulus was always placed on the left side and the reference was always placed on the right side of the force sensor. The comparison stimulus was placed to the right of the reference (Fig. 1). A tone presented via headphones signaled the beginning of the trial. A visual representation of the adaptation stimulus was displayed and participants were instructed to indent the stimulus 5 times with the left index finger by increasing the force up to 15 N and decreasing it then again down to 3 N. The force was visualized by a schematic level indicator gauge in which the level increased in 3 N steps and turned red when the force exceeded 15 N. Additionally a signal tone indicated when the force had increased to 15 N and decreased to 3 N. If the participant did not reach the threshold of 3 N or 15 N once, the number of required indentations increased. The adaptation phase had to be completed within 6 s. Thereafter visual representations of the reference and the comparison stimuli were displayed. A different signal tone indicated that the participant should start to compare these two stimuli within the next 3 s (a countdown was displayed). Participants indented the reference stimulus with the left index finger and the comparison stimulus with the right index finger simultaneously and only once. Participants were instructed to touch each stimulus in its center and to restrict the contact with the stimuli to the touch of the upper surfaces. After the exploration the participants decided which stimulus had felt softer by pressing a virtual decision button. The participants did not receive any feedback about the correctness of their response. In order to allow for readaptation, the participants had to wait for 20 s before the next trial started. Trials of the baseline condition directly started with comparing the reference and the comparison stimulus. In all other aspects these trials were identical to trials in the adaptation condition including the final period of readaptation. Between trials the experimenter manually changed the stimuli. A trial was repeated later in the block, in case the duration of adaptation exceeded 6 s or if after adaptation more than 3 s passed before the participant started to explore the reference and the comparison stimulus.

Analysis. For each participant and each condition we calculated the PSEs as the mean over all comparisons at which a reversal occurred (40 for each condition). We individually subtracted the baseline PSE from the PSEs with adaptation. These individual PSE shifts entered a one-way repeated measurements ANOVA with the within-participant factor *Compliance of Adaptation Stimulus*. We tested whether the individual adaptation stimuli shifted the PSE significantly away from the baseline with one-sided paired *t*-tests for all adaptation stimuli besides the adaptation stimulus with approximately the same compliance as the reference, for which we used a two-sided *t*-test (in total 4 comparisons). Additionally we performed individual regressions of the log10 of relative PSE shifts (ratio between the PSE with adaptation and the baseline PSE) on the log10 compliance of the adaptation stimulus. The log-log scaling was chosen to account for the power function between physical and perceived softness [19].

2.2 Results

Figure 2 depicts the individual and average PSE shifts of the reference stimulus in the adaptation conditions relative to the baseline condition without adaptation (ratio between the PSE with adaptation and the baseline PSE) in log-log space. The PSE increased with preceding adaptation to a stimulus with lower compliance and decreased after adaptation to a stimulus with higher compliance. That is, the reference was perceived to be softer after the finger had been adapted to a harder stimulus and it was perceived to be harder when a softer stimulus was touched before. The main effect of the factor *Compliance of Adaptation Stimulus* was significant, $F(3,9) = 19.31$, $p < 0.001$. The linear models fitted individually to the log10 relative PSE shifts and log10 compliance of the adaptation stimulus described the individual data quite well (average variance explained $r^2 = 0.81$). Also the overall linear model fit the data well ($r^2 = 0.60$) and, thus, explained well the between participant variance. The slopes of the regression functions were significantly negative as confirmed by a one-sample *t*-test against zero, $t(9) = -4.9$, $p < 0.001$. Comparisons against the baseline, revealed, that adaptation to a harder stimulus induced a significant shift to a softer percept, $t(9) - 5.27$, $p < 0.001$ as also adaptation to a stimulus with approximately the same compliance as the reference stimulus, $t(9) = 4.24$, $p = 0.002$ (two-sided test). The PSEs shifted to a harder percept after the adaptation to the softer stimuli. The shift was significant for the stimulus with the larger difference to the reference stimulus (0.92 mm/N) $t(9) = -2.47$, $p = 0.018$ and not significant for the other softer adaptation stimulus (0.49 mm/N) $t = -1.46$, $p = 0.089$.

2.3 Discussion

In the present study we investigated the impact of adaptation on haptic softness perception. Participants compared two silicon rubber stimuli - a reference and a comparison stimulus - by exploring them simultaneously with their two index fingers. In adaptation trials an adaptation stimulus was indented 5 times with considerable force by one finger before exploring the reference stimulus with the same finger. We found that preceding sensory experience influenced perceived softness. The reference

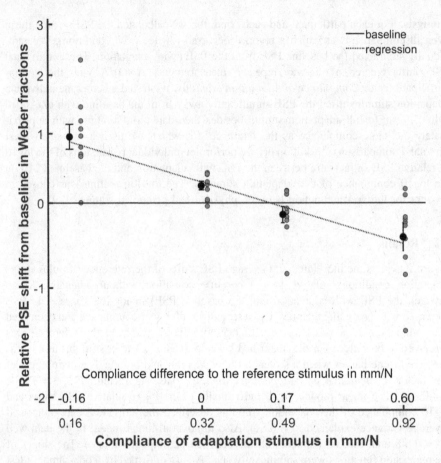

Fig. 2. Average (black dots) and individual (grey dots) shifts of the PSE with adaptation as compared to the baseline PSE without adaptation ($PSE_{with\ adaptation}/PSE_{baseline}$). PSE shifts are plotted as a function of the compliance of the adaptation stimulus in log-log space. Y-axis is spaced in Weber fractions (1 Weber fraction = 20 %).

stimulus was perceived to have different softness, depending on the sensory history of the exploring index finger. After the finger was adapted to a comparably harder stimulus the reference was perceived as being softer and after the finger was adapted to comparably softer stimuli it was perceived as being harder. As could be expected from the properties of the perceptual space [19], a larger perceptual shift (about 1 Weber fraction) was induced by the adaptation to a harder stimulus than by the adaptation to a softer stimulus with the same difference in compliance to the reference. The adaptation stimulus with a difference of about 9 Weber fractions shifted the perception of the reference stimulus by about 1/2 Weber fraction. However, the perceptual shifts fall on a straight line in the log-log space, indicating that adaptation causes shifts along the perceptual dimension of softness. We found "repulsion aftereffects", i.e. perceptual shifts in the opposite direction as compared to the physical difference between the adaptation stimulus and the reference. This was observed for most of the previously studied aftereffects [1] and it is in concordance with the multiple channel model of adaptation.

We found also a significant shift in the perception of the reference's softness after adaptation to a stimulus with approximately the same physical compliance. This finding implies that extended exploration of an object's softness makes it appear softer. The multiple channel model of adaptation does not necessarily predict a shift from self-adaptation. However, there are many examples in visual perception with a similar form of adaptation: prolonged viewing at colors let them fade away, faces appear more average, blurred or sharpened images appear more focused [1]. These aftereffects are referred to as renormalization aftereffects. It is suggested that this kind of aftereffects can be observed when the perceptual dimension is represented in the activity of rather broadly tuned channels and the information is encoded as the difference to a unique neutral status rather than by absolute values [1]. According to this model adaptation would modulate the sensitivity of all channels inducing a shift of the neutral point towards the adaptation stimulus. Consequently after prolonged exploration of a stimulus, the same stimulus would appear closer to the neutral point [1]. A similar mechanism is also imaginable for softness perception, as the compliance of the finger might be the neutral point and thus the division between "hard" and "soft" [20]. Adaptation to our rather hard reference stimulus [20] would hence shift the neutral point to a harder value. When the reference is presented again it would appear to be closer to the neutral point and hence perceived to be softer.

It has also to be mentioned that adaptation likely begins at the receptor level and affects the processing of the stimulus at different sensory and perceptual levels. It was e.g. shown that local adaptation to simple shapes can induce face aftereffects [21]. Hence, the observed perceptual shift in the perception of the adaptation stimulus itself might be the result of a renormalization or similar process at one of the processing levels involved in softness perception.

Taken together our results suggest that, like several haptic properties [8], also softness perception is changed by preceding sensory experience. A physically unchanged stimulus is felt to be softer after adaptation to a comparably harder stimulus and harder after adaptation to a softer stimulus. The bidirectionality of this perceptual shift is in concordance with the multiple channel model of encoding [3, 5]. Changed perception of the adaptation stimulus might be a result of a renormalization process. However, further research is required to reveal perceptual representation of softness.

Acknowledgements. This work was supported by a grant from the Deutsche Forschungsgemeinschaft (SFB/TRR 135, A5).

References

1. Webster, M.A.: Adaptation and visual coding. J. Vis. **11**, 1–23 (2011)
2. Gibson, J.J.: Adaptation, after-effect and contrast in the perception of curved lines. J. Exp. Psychol. **16**, 1–31 (1933)
3. Thompson, P., Burr, D.: Visual aftereffects. Curr. Biol. **19**, R11–R14 (2009)

4. Addams, R.: An account of a peculiar optical phenomenon seen after having looked at a moving body. London Edinb. Philos. Mag. J. Sci. **5**, 373–374 (1834)
5. Graham, N.V.: Visual Pattern Analyzers. Oxford University Press, Oxford (1989)
6. Barlow, H.B., Hill, R.M.: Evidence for a physiological explanation of the waterfall phenomenon and figural aftereffects. Nature **200**, 1345–1347 (1963)
7. Locke, J.: An Essay Concerning Human Understanding. In: Nidditch, P.H. (ed.). Clarendon Press, Oxford (1690/1975)
8. Kappers, A.M., Bergmann Tiest, W.M.: Aftereffects in touch. In: Prescott, T.J., Ahissar, E., Izhikevitch, E. (eds.) Scholarpedia of Touch, pp. 317–326. Atlantis Press, Paris (2016)
9. Lederman, S.J., Klatzky, R.L.: Hand movements: a window into haptic object recognition. Cogn. Psychol. **19**, 342–368 (1987)
10. Kaim, L., Drewing, K.: Exploratory strategies in haptic softness discrimination are tuned to achieve high levels of task performance. IEEE Trans. Haptics **4**, 242–252 (2011)
11. Srinivasan, M.A., LaMotte, R.H.: Tactual discrimination of softness: abilities and mechanisms. In: Franzen, O., Johansson, R., Terenius, L. (eds.) Somesthesis and the Neurobiology of the Somatosensory Cortex, pp. 123–135. Birkhäuser, Basel (1996)
12. Srinivasan, M.A., LaMotte, R.H.: Tactual discrimination of softness. J. Neurophysiol. **73**, 88–101 (1995)
13. Bergmann Tiest, W.M., Kappers, A.M.L.: Cues for haptic perception of compliance. IEEE Trans. Haptics **2**, 189–199 (2009)
14. Matsui, K., Okamoto, S., Yamada, Y.: Relative contribution ratios of skin and proprioceptive sensations in perception of force applied to fingertip. IEEE Trans. Haptics **7**, 78–85 (2014)
15. Metzger, A., Drewing, K.: Haptically perceived softness of deformable stimuli can be manipulated by applying external forces during the exploration. In: 2015 IEEE World Haptics Conference (WHC), Evanston, IL, USA, pp. 75–81 (2015)
16. Kuschel, M., Freyberger, F., Färber, B., Buss, M.: Visual-haptic perception of compliant objects in artificially generated environments. Vis. Comput. **24**, 923–931 (2008)
17. Cellini, C., Kaim, L., Drewing, K.: Visual and haptic integration in the estimation of softness of deformable objects. i-Perception **4**, 516–531 (2013)
18. Avanzini, F., Crosato, P.: Haptic-auditory rendering and perception of contact stiffness. In: McGookin, D., Brewster, S. (eds.) HAID 2006. LNCS, vol. 4129, pp. 24–35. Springer, Heidelberg (2006)
19. Harper, R., Stevens, S.: Subjective hardness of compliant materials. Q. J. Exp. Psychol. **16**, 204–215 (1964)
20. Friedman, R.M., Hester, K.D., Green, B.G., LaMotte, R.H.: Magnitude estimation of softness. Exp. Brain Res. **191**, 133–142 (2008)
21. Xu, H., Dayan, P., Lipkin, R.M., Qian, N.: Adaptation across the cortical hierarchy: lowlevel curve adaptation affects high-level facial expression judgments. J. Neurosci. **28**, 3374–3383 (2008)

Fingertip Recovery Time Depending on Viscoelasticity

Maria Laura D'Angelo[✉], Darwin G. Caldwell, and Ferdinando Cannella

Department of Advanced Robotics, Istituto Italiano di Tecnologia, Genoa, Italy
{marialaura.dangelo,darwin.caldwell,ferdinando.cannella}@iit.it

Abstract. The aim of this paper is to investigate the recovery time of human-fingertip's mechanical properties after indentations cycles. To determine the influencing parameters, three indentation velocities, five recovery times and three subjects were tested. During each experiment, the fingertip of participant was driven against a flat surface, while indentation displacement and velocity were controlled. The results show not only the indentation forces values increase depending on the indentation velocity increment, but also they decrease depending on the number of cycles. While the fingertip recovery depends on the time, but not on the indentation velocity. Finally the recovery time was determined: in 5 min the fingertip restored 99.6 % of the initial mechanical properties.

Keywords: Recovery time · Viscoelasticity effect · Fingertip mechanical properties · Indentation pulp cycles

1 Introduction

The investigation of the mechanisms of the human tactile perception represents an important topic in haptic research. Everyday, the human fingerpad plays an important role in the perception of physical environment to explore surfaces and textures, to grasp and to manipulate objects. Based on this concept and, since tactile sensitivity depends on the tissue strain and hence on the contact area, it is important to characterize the mechanical properties of the human fingertip, when it comes in contact with an object. Several studies have demonstrated that dynamic loading stimulation is affected by the mechanical response of the fingertip, from different points of view. For example, many works focused on the relationship between the mechanical stimuli imposed on fingertip skin and the tactile sensory response of mechanoreceptors [1–4]. Furthermore, from a biomechanics viewpoint, Gulati and Srinivasan [5] applied, with indenters of various shapes and sizes, sinusoidal displacement to the fingerpad. The recorded dynamic force response was measured and it revealed a non-linear dependence of the force on displacement, frequency and contact area. Serina et al. [6] modeled the response of fingerpad, during the tapping task, in a range of frequencies from 0.25 Hz to 3 Hz. Moreover, since the human fingertip has a complex structure [7,8] and it is also considered a non-homogeneous, anisotropic and non linear

© Springer International Publishing Switzerland 2016
F. Bello et al. (Eds.): EuroHaptics 2016, Part I, LNCS 9774, pp. 33–44, 2016.
DOI: 10.1007/978-3-319-42321-0_4

material [9], several studies showed that the human fingertip should be modeled as a structural viscoelastic material [10] based on three main reasons: (i) the force response is only a function of the depth of indentation and the transient response is dependent on the velocity; (ii) the fingertip stress relaxation is evidenced by a decrease from a peak force value to a steady state value and (iii) the hysteresis graph of the human fingertip, subjects to several dynamic loads, indicates that the energy is being dissipated [11–14]. This viscoelasticity influences the human fingertip performances during the tactile tests, in both the initial conditions and during the experiments. In the first case, in order to homogenize the fingertip pulp, the pre-conditioning phase was introduced [6,15]; in the second one, the fingertip stress relaxation was partially balanced with a pre-indentation stage [11]. Although the aforementioned actions, the viscoelastic behavior leads to have final fingertip conditions different to the initial ones. Therefore, to take back the fingertip to initial state, it is necessary a recovery time. Thus this paper aims to determine the minimum time to get this initial state; for instance, to carry out a new experimental test in the same conditions of the previous ones. To do that, we studied the force-displacement relationship on three subjects, during ten load and unload cycles, at three different velocities and five different recovery time values between each experimental test. First of all, the results evidence the viscoelastic effect of the human fingertip during each experimental test and elucidate as the fingertip stress relaxation is related to the number of indentation cycles. Secondly, since we carried out tests at different values of recovery time, we are able to discriminate the minimum time value beyond which the fingertip recovers its initial mechanical properties. Moreover, the fingertip recovery curve is presented and discussed. These results were similar for all three subjects. Last but not least, in this paper we propose an exhaustive and innovative test rig system that allows to measure, contemporary, human finger mechanical properties at contact, in terms of force and deformation (indentation) [16]. This paper is organized as follows: Sect. 2 describes Methods and Materials; the experimental tests carried out with the test rig and the results are depicted in Sect. 3. Finally, Sect. 4 addresses to Discussion and Conclusions with further developments.

2   Methods and Materials

During the screening phase, in order to guarantee the subject's homogeneity, not only in age, sex but also in fingertip dimensions, authors measured their fingerprint area using this innovative optical measurement system. Average and standard deviation value of fingerprint area, between three subjects is $113.78 \pm 7.56 \, mm^2$. Thus, three right-handed female subjects (29 ± 1 years old) participated in this study. Only the right index finger was tested. Their finger pad was free of calluses and each participant gave her informed consent to the experiments.

During the experimental tests, we indented, from 0 to 3 mm, the fingertip against a flat surface in order to study the viscoelastic effect after ten load and unload cycles; indentation parameters such as velocity and displacement have been under control, while the indentation force was recorded. Authors, carried

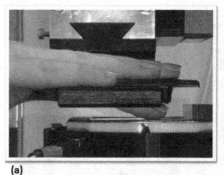 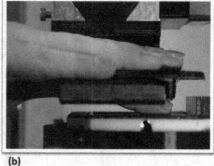

(a)   (b)

Fig. 1. (a) Positioning of the participant finger into the finger-holder barely in contact with the UltraViolet grade Fused Silica window. (b) Participant finger pressed against the UltraViolet grade Fused Silica window, during the experimental test.

out five sets of experimental tests of recovery time (10 min, 5 min, 3 min, 2 min and 1 min) at three different values of velocity (1 mm/s, 2 mm/s and 4 mm/s). Within the same set, we repeated four experimental tests for each velocity. Then, per each subject, we performed 60 experimental tests, and the duration of the whole test was about 2 h. Voluntary movements of the participant fingertip were precluded by gluing the top of the nail to a finger-holder. In this way, we were able to prevent any unwanted and uncontrolled movements and to avoid to loose the contact point during the measurements phase. The finger pad was then centered on the flat window of the test rig; the palm is down, with the fingertip forming with the flat plate an angle of 20°, which is coherent with previous analogous works [6, 17], as shown in Fig. 1(a, b).

2.1 Test Rig

The linear actuator, the finger-holder positioned on the UltraViolet grade Fused Silica window, the sensing part (i.e. the laser, and the force sensors), and the acquisition board, are the five hardware main parts of the test rig, as shown in the Fig. 2; while Labview software was interfaced with device control. The fingertip displacement can be achieved moving the finger holder by a linear stepper actuator (Nanotec Munich, Germany).

The actuator resolution is 0.010 mm/step and the maximum displacement is 50 mm. The flat transparent surface is UV grade Fused Silica (SiO2) window. Three FS20 Low Force Compression load cells, (Measurement Specialties Inc. Hampton, US - VA), with F.S. equal to 7.5 N, can record normal force values with 1 % of accuracy. Moreover, in order to control the effective displacement performed by the linear actuator during the experimental tests, we used an optoNCDT 1302-20 laser (MicroEpsilon Ortenburg, Germany), with a resolution of 10 μm. The stepper linear actuator is controlled using Labview software interface by National Instrument. At the same time, the three force sensors and the laser are acquired via NI PXI-6251 of NI PXIe 1073, at 1 kHz of sampling rate.

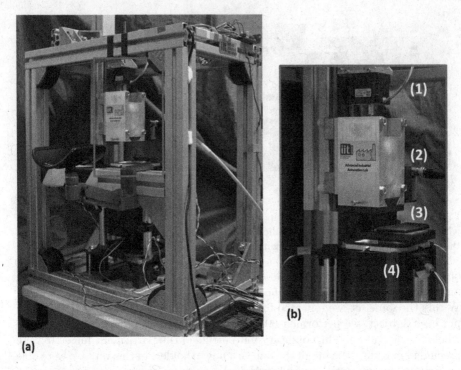

Fig. 2. (a) Test Rig with its main components; (b) Test Rig zoom to the main part: from top to bottom (1) linear actuator, (2) laser, (3) finger-holder on the grade Silica window, (4) force sensor (load cell).

The subject contact area, between the fingertip and the flat surface, was acquired via a acA2000-340 km mono-camera (Basler, Ahrensburg, Germany), with resolution up to 2048 × 1088 and frame rate up to 340 frames per second (fps), connected to a NI PXI-1428 Image Acquisition multifunction DAQ, as shown in Fig. 3. The post-processing of the force signals, displacements and the recorded images was accomplished with Matlab software (Natick, MA).

The optical measurement system, used in order to acquire the contact area, is based on the phenomenon of light reflection/refraction at the interface between two transparent media. Four white light LEDs (light source) were placed at the edges of UV Fused Silica window: in this manner, the glass can act as a light guide preventing the light to escape through the top and/or the bottom surface. During each experimental tests, when the subject fingertip is pressed against the upper surface of the window, the surface of the finger will prevent the complete reflection and, the light will scatter from the interface points where the finger touches the rigid surface. In this way, the high resolution camera, connected to a NI PXI-1428, records the participant fingertip, during the whole experimental test.

Subjects Contact Area at 3 mm of Indentation

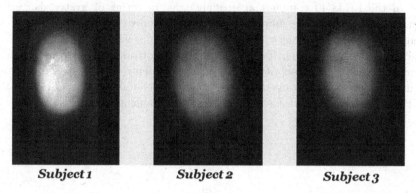

Fig. 3. Subjects contact areas, at 3 mm of indentation, obtained from the optical measurement system.

2.2   Calibration Test Rig

Before proceeding with the experimental tests on the subjects finger, we investigated the structural behavior of the test rig: firstly, the temperature dependence of the deformation, secondly the calibration with a commercial viscoelastic material (Dunlop LR38-40, density 38 Kg/m^3, hardness 40 HRC) [18].

Considering that each experimental test lasts about two hours and they takes several days, the accuracy of the setup in terms of deformations (caused by temperature variations during the hours/days) was checked. The displacements measured by the laser were acquired every minute, consecutively for 72 h. The results show that the displacement is 0.0013 mm $\pm$ 1 % mm. From calibration point of view, a viscoelastic material (LR38-40) was loaded in order to determine the accuracy of the setup in terms of measured force and displacement. During this phase, we considered one level of displacement (8 mm) and four different values of velocity (1 mm/s, 2 mm/s, 4 mm/s and 8 mm/s) and then, we measured the hysteresis area, during 10 trials. First of all, as shown in Fig. 4(a), it is

Table 1. Hysteresis Area values at 8 mm of indentation and 8-4-2-1 mm/s of indentation velocity. From left to right: area of the first hysteresis cycle; averages and STD values of the other nine cycles obtained from experimental tests.

	Hysteresis area [mm^2]	
	1st cycle	Average $\pm$ STD
8 mm/s	30.44	29.56 $\pm$ 0.11
4 mm/s	22.12	21.56 $\pm$ 0.13
2 mm/s	20.74	19.45 $\pm$ 0.08
1 mm/s	19.80	18.77 $\pm$ 0.25

possible to notice the agreement between our experimental results and the data-sheet of the LR38-40 commercial product [18], in terms of hysteresis cycles. Then, Fig. 4(b) shows the subplot of the first hysteresis area cycle, at different indentation velocity. Averages and standard deviations values for hysteresis area, at each velocity, are shown in Table 1. From top to bottom, it is possible to notice, as the area values decreases as the indentation velocity decreases, from 8 mm/s to 1 mm/s. The aforementioned results shown the reliability and accuracy of the test rig in detecting the viscoelastic material mechanical properties [21].

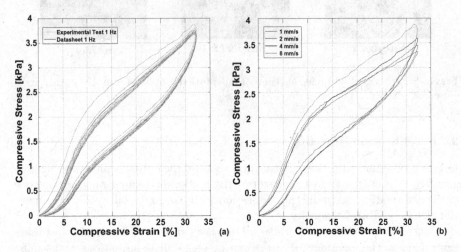

Fig. 4. Viscoelastic comparison: (a) comparison between hysteresis area cycles at 8 mm/s of indentation velocity of LR38-40 with our test rig (magenta solid line) and LR38-40 from Dunlop data-sheet (blue solid line); (b) first hysteresis area cycle of LR38-40, compressed at 30 % at different values of indentation velocity: 1 mm/s, 2 mm/s, 4 mm/s and 8 mm/s. (Color figure online)

3   Experimental Tests and Results

In order to guarantee the same initial conditions, at the beginning of each experimental test, we established the following procedures: (i) all the tests were carried out on early morning at the same time to prevent the daily stress on the finger pulp and skin, (ii) every subject is conveniently and comfortably located in front of the test rig, (iii) each finger of the right hand were positioned on its specific point on the finger-holder using the reference markers and that guaranteed not only the repeatability of the index position and pitch orientation, but also the repeatability of its roll orientation, (iv) the forefinger nail was glued, (v) the finger was preloaded by 0.02 N and the position of the finger-holder was called 'zero position', because was the reference for all the cycles of the all tests. That means that few millimeters square of the skin were in contact with flat glass.

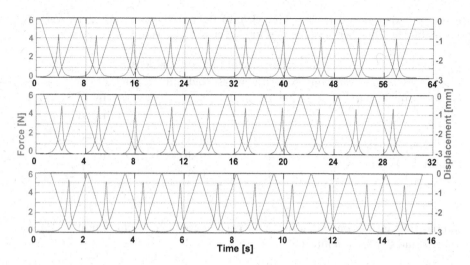

Fig. 5. Averaged force (blue solid line) and displacement (orange solid line) between three subjects. From top to bottom: 1 mm/s, 2 mm/s and 4 mm/s of indentation velocity. (Color figure online)

All experimental tests consist on moving the subject's fingertip against the flat transparent surface from 0 mm to 3 mm. Per each subject, we performed five sets of experimental tests of recovery time (10 min, 5 min, 3 min, 2 min and 1 min), combining randomly the three velocity values. In other words, within the same set, we repeated four experimental tests per each velocity (1 mm/s, 2 mm/s and 4 mm/s), from 0 to 3 mm, on going back to initial position and repeating it for ten cycles. We replicate for ten cycles the fingertip indentation, against the flat surface, because we note that also when the recovery time is equal to 10 min the viscoelastic effects runs out at most after 5 cycles. Each subject carried out 60 experimental tests: 12 per each set of recovery time. In order to better clarify, the combination of various experimental tests, we reported the Table 2.

The results, in term of force and displacement, during the interaction between the finger and the plate, are shown in Fig. 5. Per each indentation velocity, we report the chart of averaged force (blue solid line) and displacement (red solid line) signal, between the three subjects. For the sake of space we report the chart of the results, as shown in Fig. 5, for the set at 1' of recovery time only. In the other sets of experimental tests there is the same trend.

Moreover, to discriminate the time value beyond which the human fingertip restores all its mechanical properties (recovery time), authors waited 10 min, 5 min, 3 min, 2 min and then 1 min, between each experimental test, as shown in Fig. 6. Also in this case, cause of lack of space, we reported the results only for 4 mm/s of indentations velocity, but the trends appear to be the same also for the other two velocities (1 mm/s and 2 mm/s), as shown in Fig. 7. Finally, all the recovery forces (percentage) are plotted in the same chart w.r.t. two input parameters: indentation velocity and recovery time, as shown in the Fig. 8. The

Table 2. Experimental Design. From left to right: Set of recovery time, Velocity, Indentation and number of cycles performed per each subject.

| Set of recovery time | Experimental test combinations | | |
	Velocity [mm/s]	Indentation [mm]	Cycles
10'	1–2–4	0–3	10
5'	1–2–4	0–3	10
3'	1–2–4	0–3	10
2'	1–2–4	0–3	10
1'	1–2–4	0–3	10

standard deviation among subjects for each curve is: 1.2 % for 1 mm/s, 4 % for 2 mm/s and 2.5 % for 4 mm/s.

4   Discussion and Conclusions

To investigate the recovery time of the fingertip, the viscoelasticity influence of the indentation forces was examined. First of all, displacement and force signals were compared, as shown in the Fig. 5. The relationship shows that the indentation and the forces have not any noticeable delay nor any sudden increment; that means 1, 2 and 4 mm/s (0.167, 0.333 and 0.667 Hz) are far away from the fingertip resonance (100–125 Hz) [19]. Another remark is that the force values increase (from 4.3 N to 6.2 N) w.r.t. the indentation velocity increment (from 1 mm/s to 4 mm/s) as demonstrated in [11], always shown in the Fig. 5. That means that the test rig and the experimental tests carrying out are reliable, because the measurements are consistent and aligned with the previous research results on the fingertip mechanical properties studies.

Furthermore the viscoelasticity not only depends on the indentation velocity, but also on the load duration [20], [21]. In Fig. 6, it is possible to notice that when the recovery time is 10 or 5 min, the viscoelastic effect runs out in 5 cycles, while, when the recovery time is 3 min, this effect lasts for 3 cycles and for 2 or 1 min it vanishes in two cycles. The red rectangles highlight the number of cycles affected by viscoelasticity, as shown in Fig. 6. The same phenomena compares in the 1 mm/s and 2 mm/s of indentation velocity, as shown in Fig. 7. Per each indentation velocity, we reported in the column C and column F the number of cycles affected and unaffected by the viscoelasticity. It is possible to notice that the viscoelastic effects lasts the same number of the cycles, w.r.t the indentation velocity and not depends on the time.

Now the question arises when the fingertip recovers the same mechanical properties than the initial conditions. That can be very useful, for instance, to test the same subject several times consecutively. One of the aim of this paper is to determine the relationship of fingertip recovery and the time, as shown in the Fig. 8. From this figure, it is possible to notice that the recovery percentage

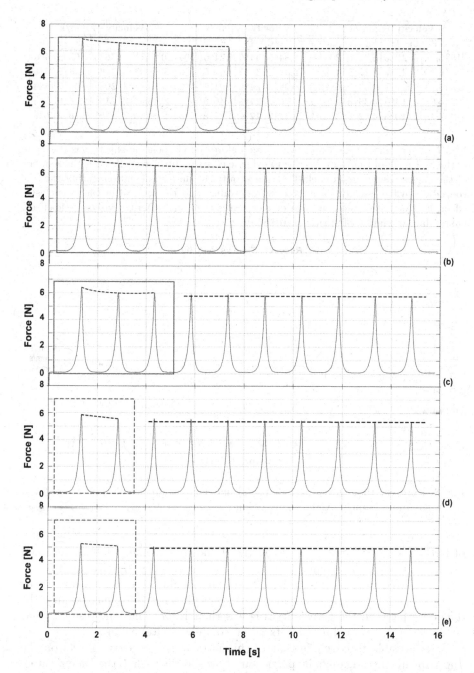

Fig. 6. Averaged force signal among four experimental tests at 4 mm/s of indentation velocity. From the top to the bottom: (a) 10 min, (b) 5 min, (c) 3 min, (d) 2 min and (e) 1 min of recovery time. The red rectangle indicates the cycles involved in the viscoelastic effect and dashed black line evidences the peaks trend of the steady state force. (Color figure online)

Velocity - 1 mm/s							Velocity - 2 mm/s							Velocity - 4 mm/s						
A	B	C	D	E	F	G	A	B	C	D	E	F	G	A	B	C	D	E	F	G
10'	5,78	5	28%	5,21	5	2%	10'	6,84	5	31%	6,21	5	1%	10'	7,37	5	36%	6,65	5	4%
5'	5,70	5	23%	5,20	5	4%	5'	6,83	5	26%	6,06	5	5%	5'	6,93	5	36%	6,33	5	4%
3'	5,24	3	21%	4,69	7	6%	3'	6,08	3	24%	6,01	7	4%	3'	6,56	3	20%	6,06	7	5%
2'	4,88	2	13%	4,39	8	2%	2'	5,76	2	21%	5,46	8	5%	2'	6,32	2	21%	5,76	8	5%
1'	4,48	2	10%	4,22	8	5%	1'	5,21	2	12%	4,82	8	5%	1'	5,56	2	11%	5,16	8	6%

Fig. 7. A-recovery time; B-first peak force before the viscoelastic effect: it is the force of the first peak of the 10 cycles; C-viscoelastic effect number of cycles: it is the number of the cycles where the viscoelasticity runs out; D-standard deviation during the viscoelastic effect; E-steady state force average value: it is the force after the viscoelastic effect; F-steady state force number of cycles: it is the cycles after the viscoelastic effect; G-standard deviation of steady state force.

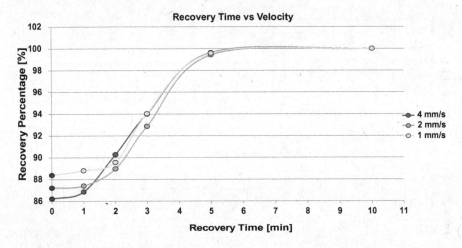

Fig. 8. Recovery time vs velocity. Red solid line 4 mm/s, green solid line 2 mm/s and yellow solid line 1 mm/s. (Color figure online)

of force is almost the same between the 0 and after 1 min, while after 2 and 3 min the recovery is around 90 % and 93 %, respectively. Finally, from 5 and 10 min the recovery is 99.6 % and 100 %. These values are plotted for all the three velocities and it is noticeable that the behavior is the same, because the difference between the three curves is less than 1.5 %. Thus the result is that the fingertip recovers almost all its initial conditions after 5 min.

It is possible to conclude that in this work the viscoelastic effects on the fingertip are investigated; in particular it was verified that the increment of the indentation velocity increases the indentation force, while the increment of the cycles decreases this force; but, after a determined number of the cycles, the viscoelastic effect runs out and the steady state force is constant. To restore the initial forces (99.6 %), it is sufficient to wait 5 min, without any dependence with the indentation velocity. Last not least, a new test rig is shown and tested from point of view of repeatability and reliability for exhausting and long tests. Future work will deal with the following objective: more subjects will be enrolled to statically determine more accurately the recovery time. More indentation displacements and velocities will be investigated. Finally the sequence of the velocities will be evaluated in order to determine the velocity influence between two experimental tests. Last not least the indentation geometry will be evaluated in order to determine the influence in the indentation force on viscoelastic effects.

Acknowledgements. The authors wish to acknowledge Matteo Bianchi, Prof. Gianluca Rossi and Prof. Antonio Bicchi who contributed in test rig development. This work was supported in parts by grants from the EU FP7 (project no. 601165 WEARHAP).

References

1. Maeno, T., Kobayashi, K., Yamazaki, N.: Relationship between the structure of human finger tissue and the location of tactile receptors. JSME Int. J. Ser. C **41**(1), 94–100 (1998)
2. Srinivasan, M.A., LaMotte, R.H.: Encoding of shape in the responses of cutaneous mechanoreceptors. In: Franzén, O., Westman, J. (eds.) Information Processing in the Somatosensory System. Wenner Gren Center International Symposium Series. Macmillan Education, London (1991)
3. Dandekar, K., Srinivasan, M.A.: The Role of Mechanics in Tactile Sensing of Shape. Research Laboratory of Electronics, Massachusetts Institute of Technology, Cambridge (1997)
4. Gerling, G.J., Thomas, G.W.: The effect of fingertip microstructures on tactile edge perception. In: WHC, pp. 63–72. IEEE Computer Society (2005). ISBN 0-7695-2310-2
5. Gulati, R.J., Srinivasan, M.A.: Human fingerpad under indentation I: static and dynamic force response. ASME Publ. Bed **29**, 261 (1995)
6. Serina, E.R., Mote Jr., C.D., Rempel, D.: Force response of the fingertip pulp to repeated compression-effects of loading rate, loading angle and anthropometry. J. Biomech. **30**(10), 1035–1040 (1997)
7. Barbenel, J.C., Evans, J.H.: The time-dependent mechanical properties of skin. J. Invest. Dermatol. **69**, 318–320 (1977)
8. Pereira, J.M., Davis, B.R., Mansour, J.M.: Dynamic measurement of the viscoelastic properties of skin. J. Biomech. **24**(2), 157–162 (1991)
9. Lanir, Y.: Skin mechanics. In: Skalak, R., Chien, S. (eds.) Handbook of Bioengineering. McGraw-Hill, New York (1987)
10. Fung, Y.C.: Biomechanics: Mechanical Properties of Living Tissues. Springer, New York (1993)
11. Pawluk, D.T., Howe, R.D.: Dynamic lumped element response of the human fingerpad. J. Biomech. Eng. **121**(2), 178–183 (1999)
12. Pawluk, D.T., Howe, R.D.: Dynamic contact of the human fingerpad against a flat surface. J. Biomech. Eng. **121**(6), 605–611 (1999)
13. Silver, F.H.: Biological Materials Structure, Mechanical Properties, and Modeling of Soft Tissues. New York University Press, New York (1987)

14. Serina, E.R., Mote, C.D., Rampel, D.M.: Mechanical properties of the finger-tip pulp under repeated, dynamic, compressive loading. ASME Publ. Bed **31**, 245–246 (1995)
15. Hongbin, L., Noonan, D.P., Zweiri, Y.H., Althoefer, K.A., Seneviratne, L.D.: The development of nonlinear viscoelastic model for the application of soft tissue identification. In: IEEE/RSJ International Conference on Intelligent Robots and Systems, pp. 208–213 (2007)
16. D'Angelo, M.L., Cannella, F., Bianchi, M., D'Imperio, M., Battaglia, E., Poggiani, M., Rossi, G., Bicchi, A., Caldwell, D.G.: An integrated approach to characterize mechanical properties of human fingertip. IEEE Trans. Haptics (2015, under press)
17. Wu, J.Z., Dong, R.G., Smutz, W.P., Rakheja, S.: Dynamic interaction between a fingerpad and a flat surface: experiments and analysis. Med. Eng. Phys. **25**(5), 397–406 (2003)
18. http://www.dunlopfoams.com.au/products/medical
19. Wu, J.Z., Welcome, D.E., Krajnak, K., Dong, R.G.: Finite element analysis of the penetrations of shear and normal vibrations into the soft tissues in a fingertip. Med. Eng. Phys. **29**(6), 718–727 (2007)
20. Kumar, S., Liu, G., Schloerb, D.W., Srinivasan, M.A.: Viscoelastic characterization of the primate finger pad in vivo by microstep indentation and three-dimensional finite element models for tactile sensation studies. J. Biomech. Eng. **137**, 6 (2015)
21. Fertis, D.G.: Mechanical and Structural Vibration. Wiley, New York (1995)

Haptic Devices

Rendering Moving Tactile Stroke on the Palm Using a Sparse 2D Array

Jaeyoung Park[1(✉)], Jaeha Kim[1], Yonghwan Oh[1], and Hong Z. Tan[2]

[1] Korea Institute of Science and Technology, Seoul, Korea
{jypcubic,lithium81,oyh}@kist.re.kr
[2] Purdue University, West Lafayette, IN, USA
hongtan@purdue.edu

Abstract. The present study presents a new rendering algorithm for a moving tactile stroke on the palm of the hand placed on a sparse 2D tactor array. Our algorithm utilizes the relation between signal duration and signal onset asynchrony previously proposed for "tactile brush" [1], but extends it by applying 3-actuator phantom sensations and adjusting the sampling rate. We compare our proposed algorithm to the tactile brush algorithm for their similarity in target trajectories and uniformity of tactile stroke motions. The results show that the participants judge the tactile strokes with our algorithm to move significantly closer to target motions and with more uniform velocity than the "tactile brush." The effect of our algorithm is more significant for experimental stimuli with longer travel time and length.

Keywords: Phantom sensation · Tactile brush · Tactile stroke

1 Introduction

One prominent direction in haptic interface design is to increase the quality and the quantity of tactile information through, for example, the use of multiple tactile actuators (tactors). Among various forms of multiple tactors, 2D tactile arrays have been studied to provide users with information such as temporal image, motional or directional cues. The tactile arrays have typically been used on a relatively large skin area including the back, waist or arm, but less commonly found on the glabrous area of hand where haptic sensitivity is high and the skin is easily accessible by devices such as desktop interfaces and wearable devices. In this regard, a 2D tactile array on the hand can be explored in various applications as a means to provide information to a user. We are especially interested in finding effective methods to deliver moving tactile sensations with controllable velocities and a clear start and end (e.g., [1, 2]).

So far, few studies have examined the robustness of rendering methodology for moving tactile strokes. An intuitive way to create a moving tactile stroke is to use a dense tactile tactor array and to activate the tactors around a target trajectory sequentially. Borst and Asutay suggested a rendering method for a dense tactile array to create the sensation of moving tactors for arbitrary paths [3]. The drawback of this approach is that the hardware can be costly and heavy. Relatively sparse arrays of tactors were found to be effective in providing predefined set of cues [4, 5]. Sparse tactile arrays can

© Springer International Publishing Switzerland 2016
F. Bello et al. (Eds.): EuroHaptics 2016, Part I, LNCS 9774, pp. 47–56, 2016.
DOI: 10.1007/978-3-319-42321-0_5

represent motion cues utilizing well-known illusory tactile phenomena such as sensory saltation [6] or phantom tactile sensation [7, 8]. Most of the previous studies can only create the illusion of motion between adjacent physical tactors, limiting target motions to the line segments connecting the adjacent tactors. Schneider et al. recently suggested a method to render a phantom tactor on an arbitrary 2D position with three tactors [9], but did not consider the continuity of the tactile stroke.

The main objective of this paper is to develop an effective rendering method for a tactile stroke moving along an arbitrarily shaped trajectory on the human hand, using a sparse 2D tactor array. Our work is based on the tactile brush algorithm proposed in [1] and seeks to improve its robustness in creating tactile strokes along arbitrary paths. We propose a strategy to overcome the limitations of the tactile brush algorithm and present experimental results that compare our proposed method to the tactile brush.

2 Rendering Moving Tactile Strokes on Sparse 2D Arrays

2.1 A Review of the Tactile Brush Algorithm [1]

The tactile brush algorithm has several notable features including the use of tactile illusions to create the sensation of moving tactile strokes. The authors utilized apparent tactile motion and phantom sensation in their algorithm. Apparent tactile motion is an illusory phenomenon such that two closely-placed vibrotactile stimuli are perceived to come from a single tactor continuously moving between them [10]. The effect can be created by adjusting the stimulus duration and inter-stimulus signal onset asynchrony (SOA), the time interval between the onsets of subsequent actuations. Results of psychophysics experiments indicated that the following relation was optimal for making successive signals feel like a single moving stroke:

$$SOA = 0.32 \cdot duration + 0.0473 \tag{1}$$

where SOA and duration are in seconds.

The tactile brush algorithm removed the restriction that a tactile stroke trajectory can only move along the line segments between physical tactors. It used the phantom tactile sensation that lets a user feel an illusory vibratory tactor between two simultaneously activated physical tactors. A control strategy for the location and intensity of the stimuli was found based on an energy model. When the desired intensity of virtual tactor is A_v and the distance between the virtual tactor and the i-th physical tactor is d_i, the intensity of each physical tactor A_i is controlled by the following equation:

$$A_1 = \sqrt{\frac{d_2}{d_1 + d_2}}A_v, \ A_2 = \sqrt{\frac{d_1}{d_1 + d_2}}A_v \tag{2}$$

The equation assumes that the energy summation model in the Pacinian channel [11] and that the energy moment due to each physical tactor is constant as follows:

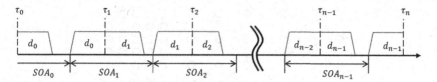

Fig. 1. Timing diagram of the tactile brush algorithm for n + 1 tactors

$$A_v^2 = A_1^2 + A_2^2 \tag{3}$$

$$d_1 \cdot A_1^2 = d_2 \cdot A_2^2 = const. \tag{4}$$

It should be noted that the tactile brush algorithm assumes that the intensities of two successively-activated tactors can be independently modulated.

The tactile brush algorithm renders moving tactile strokes by controlling the SOA and the signal duration of physical/phantom tactors. Once the trajectory and velocity of the tactile stroke are determined, the time τ_i at which the intensity of the i-th tactor is at the maximum can be decided (i = 0, ..., n). The timing diagram of the signals (Fig. 1) shows that $SOA_0 + d_0 = \tau_1$. Then with Eq. (1), SOA_0 and d_0 are decided. For i > 0, the i-th tactor is driven after SOA_{i-1} and is active for $d_{i-1} + d_i$ seconds. Assuming that the i-th tactor is at its maximum intensity d_{i-1} seconds after the activation, then Eq. (1) can be extended to obtain the following relations at the i-th step:

$$SOA_i = 0.32(d_{i-1} + d_i) + 0.0473 \tag{5}$$

$$\sum_{j=0}^{i} SOA_j + d_i = \tau_{i+1} \tag{6}$$

Combining the above two equations results in the following equation for d_i:

$$d_i = 0.76\tau_{i+1} - 0.24d_{i-1} - 0.76\sum_{j=0}^{i-1} SOA_j - 0.036 \tag{7}$$

and SOA_i is derived from Eq. (5).

The tactile brush algorithm restricts the tactile stroke path to move on line-segment paths whose endpoints are on the gridlines defined by physical tactors. Then, to create a tactile stroke along a curved path, a denser array is required as in Fig. 2(a). Another drawback of the algorithm concerns the robustness of the algorithm when the two consecutive tactors share a common physical tactor and the two tactors are supposed to be active simultaneously. Figure 2(b) shows an example where the trajectory of a tactile stroke passes over three phantom tactors. As shown in the timing diagram in the rightmost column, the phantom tactors P_A and P_B can be active at the same time while sharing a common physical tactor P_2. The same problem exists for P_B and P_C. This contradicts the assumption that the phantom tactors can be independently controlled and requires additional handling of the intensity of the overlapping physical tactor. We propose a new method in the next subsection to overcome the two limitations of the tactile brush algorithm.

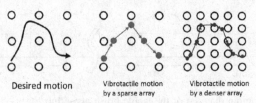

(a) Linear motion constraint

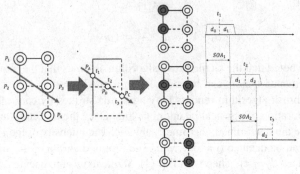

(b) Overlapping physical tactor

Fig. 2. Drawbacks of the tactile brush algorithm

2.2   A New Algorithm for Non-linear Arbitrary 2D Trajectories

In this section, we address the two major limitations of the tactile brush algorithm: (i) linear path constraint and (ii) overlapping physical tactors for consecutive tactors. To avoid the path constraint, we extend the scheme of phantom tactor from two tactors to three tactors forming a triangle out of a rectangular grid as shown in Fig. 3. Then, Eqs. (2) and (3) for the energy summation and the constant energy moment assumptions are extended to the following relations:

$$A_v^2 = \sum_{i=1}^{3} A_i^2 \tag{8}$$

$$d_1 \cdot A_1^2 = d_2 \cdot A_2^2 = d_3 \cdot A_3^2 = const. \tag{9}$$

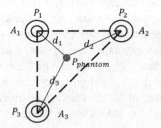

Fig. 3. Phantom tactor at an arbitrary position inside a triangle formed by three tactors

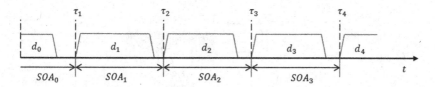

Fig. 4. Timing diagram of the new algorithm that avoids overlapping consecutive tactors

Next, given a phantom tactor $P_{phantom}$ located at an arbitrary position inside of the triangle, the intensity of each tactor is

$$A_i = \sqrt{\frac{1/d_i}{\sum_{j=1}^{3} 1/d_j}} A_v \tag{10}$$

where d_i is the distance between $P_{phantom}$ and the physical tactor P_i and A_v is the target intensity.

The problem of overlapping physical tactor can be avoided by setting the duration of each tactor to be shorter than SOA. Combining it with Eq. (1), we have:

$$SOA = 0.32 \cdot duration + 0.0473 \geq duration \tag{11}$$

which results in the constraint that $duration \leq 0.07$ s. Two consecutive tactors will never overlap in time and the problem of overlapping tactor is avoided (Fig. 4).

Our new algorithm is robust and simple to implement, as follows. Given a desired trajectory as a time constant, points on the path are sampled at a rate less than or equal to 0.07 s following the constraint of Eq. (11). The sampling rate is assumed as the SOA of each tactor and the duration is calculated by Eq. (1). At each point, the three closest physical tactors around the point are selected and the intensity of each tactor is decided by Eq. (10). If the point is aligned on a line segment, the intensity of each physical tactor is decided by Eq. (2). The new algorithm improves upon the tactile brush algorithm in terms of the degrees of freedom in paths and the robustness in handling subsequent tactors.

3   Comparison of Moving Tactile Strokes Generated by the Tactile Brush and the New Algorithm: An Experiment

3.1   Experimental Method

The experimental apparatus consisted of a 3-by-3 sparse array of piezoelectric actuators (a 9-mm ceramic disk mounted concentrically on a 12-mm metal disk; Murata, Inc., Kyoto, Japan). The top of the apparatus has a curvature of 14 cm to ensure that the surface adheres well to a participant's palm during the experiment (Fig. 5). The piezos are arranged with a center-to-center spacing of 20 mm. To create a vibrotactile stimulus, a source signal is generated from an analog output from a multifunction I/O card

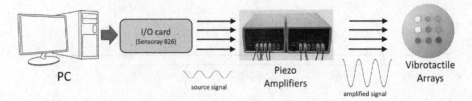

Fig. 5. Block diagram of the experimental setup

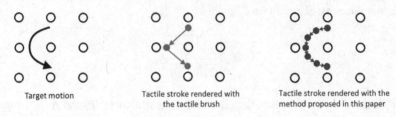

Fig. 6. Target motion and tactile strokes rendered by the tactile brush and our new method

(Model 826, Sensoray Co., Inc, OR, USA) and is sent to a custom-built piezo amplifier (Fig. 5). The source sinusoidal signals had a frequency of 250 Hz around which human sensitivity to vibratory signal is the highest [12]. An amplitude of 7 dB SL (sensation level, dB above human detection threshold) was used.

A haptic stimulus for the experiment is rendered with either the tactile brush algorithm or the new method proposed in Sect. 2 for a target moving at a constant speed. Figure 6 describes an example of comparing the two rendering methods. The tactile brush renders phantom tactors aligned on a line segment on a grid, which creates a piecewise linear motion. Our new algorithm samples points on the target trajectory at a period of 0.07 s and renders each point by adjusting tactor intensities of the nearest three tactors using the relation in Eq. (8).

3.2   Procedures

Twelve participants (nine males) aged between 26 and 36 took part in the experiment. None of them had any known problem with the sense of touch by self-report. The experiment protocol was approved by the KIST IRB.

Each participant conducted four experimental runs. One run tested the perceived similarity between the intended tactile stroke motion and the trajectories rendered by the two algorithms (*similarity test*). Another run tested the perceived uniformity of rendered tactile stroke motions (*uniformity test*). The other two runs asked the participants to rate the similarity of the tactile strokes to the target trajectories (*similarity rating*) and the uniformity of the tactile stroke motion rendered by the two algorithms (*uniformity rating*), both on a 5-point Likert scale. The four target motions shown in Fig. 7 were used in the experiment and the total number of trials for each run was 40.

The participant sat in front of the experiment computer and placed his/her hand over the experimental apparatus. A noise cancelling headphone was worn by the

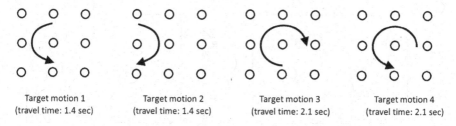

Target motion 1
(travel time: 1.4 sec)

Target motion 2
(travel time: 1.4 sec)

Target motion 3
(travel time: 2.1 sec)

Target motion 4
(travel time: 2.1 sec)

Fig. 7. Four target motions used for the experiment

participant and it played white noise when the piezo actuators were driven. The tactors were sequentially turned on to check if all of them were functioning normally. If no problem was found, the participant could proceed to the experiment. At each trial, one of the trajectories in Fig. 7 was randomly selected. For the similarity test, an animation showing the target motion was displayed visually on the computer screen. Then, the target motion was rendered with the two algorithms sequentially. The order of the rendering method was randomized for each trial. After feeling the two tactile stimuli, the participant was asked to respond which one moved along a trajectory that was felt more similar to that of the animation. For the uniformity test, no animation was shown visually. The participant felt two tactile strokes and had to decide which of the tactile strokes was perceived to have moved with a more uniform velocity. For the similarity rating test, the animation of target motion was shown at the beginning of the trial and one of the two rendering algorithms was randomly selected. After feeling the tactile stimulus, the participant rated the similarity of the sensation to that of the animation on a 5-point Likert scale. For the uniformity rating test, no animation was shown. The participant felt a tactile stroke rendered with one of the methods and rated the uniformity of the perceived stroke velocity on a 5-point Likert scale. It took approximately 30 min for each participant to complete the experiment, including the breaks between subsequent experimental runs.

4   Results

Figure 8 shows the results for the similarity and uniformity tests. The mean percentages of participants' preference for the new rendering method proposed in this paper over the tactile brush algorithm were 79.2 % and 82.3 % for the similarity test and the uniformity test, respectively. When the percentages were compared to 50 % by one-sampled t-tests, significant differences were found for both the similarity test [$t(11) = 6.84$, $p < 0.001$] and the uniformity test [$t(11) = 5.5$, $p < 0.001$]. The mean percentage of preferring the new algorithm was also significantly different from 50 % for all individual target motions. A one-way repeated measure ANOVA for the similarity test with the factor target motion revealed a significant effect [$F(3,33) = 11.428$, $p < 0.001$]. Post-hoc analysis using Tukey's pairwise comparisons indicated that the mean percentage of preferring the new algorithm for target motion 2 is different from those for the other target motions. A one-way repeated measure ANOVA for the uniformity test with the factor target motion also revealed a significant effect [$F(3,33) = 4.4$, $p = 0.01$].

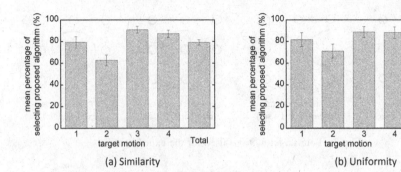

Fig. 8. Mean percentage of preferring the new rendering algorithm for (a) the similarity test and (b) the uniformity test. Error bars indicate standard errors.

Tukey's pairwise comparisons indicated that the mean percentage of preferring the new algorithm for target motion 2 is different from those for target motions 3 and 4, but not target motion 1.

Figure 9 shows the mean ratings for the similarity and uniformity rating tests. The mean ratings for the similarity rating test were 2.65 and 3.89 for the tactile brush and the new algorithm, respectively. For the uniformity rating test, the mean ratings were 2.51 and 3.74 for the tactile brush and the new algorithm, respectively. When pairwise t-test was conducted between the mean ratings of the two rendering methods, significant differences were found for both the similarity ratings [$t(11) = 13.23$, $p < 0.001$] and the uniformity ratings [$t(11) = 8.06$, $p < 0.001$]. A two-way ANOVA for the similarity ratings with the factors algorithm and target motion indicated significant main effects of algorithm [$F(1,11) = 40.66$, $p < 0.001$] and target motion [$F(3,33) = 9.1$, $p < 0.001$]. We also found a significant interaction of algorithm and target motion [$F(3,33) = 7.87$, $p < 0.001$]. Tukey's pairwise comparisons indicated that for the tactile brush algorithm, no significant difference was found for the mean ratings by target motions. When the new algorithm was used, the mean ratings of target motions 3 and 4 did not differ significantly from one another, but were significantly larger than that of target motion 2. The ratings for target motions 1 and 2 did not differ from one another. A two-way

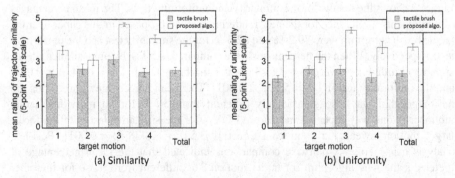

Fig. 9. Mean ratings of the tactile brush and the new algorithm for the similarity and uniformity tests. Error bars indicate standard errors.

ANOVA for the uniformity ratings also indicated significant main effects of algorithm [$F(1,11) = 40.04$, $p < 0.001$] and target motion [$F(3,33) = 6.51$, $p = 0.001$]. A significant interaction of algorithm and target motion was also found [$F(3,33) = 3.91$, $p = 0.02$]. Tukey's pairwise comparisons indicated that for the tactile brush algorithm, no significant difference was found for the mean ratings by target motions. When the new algorithm was used, the mean rating of target motions 3 and 4 did not differ from one another, but were significantly larger than that of target motion 2. The ratings for the target motions 1 and 2 did not differ significantly from one another.

The experimental results indicate that our proposed algorithm led the participants to perceive the tactile stroke to move along paths closer to the target trajectories and with more uniform velocities than the tactile brush algorithm. Also, the effect was more significant for target motions 3 and 4 which are longer in travel length and time duration than target motions 1 and 2.

5   Discussion

The present study proposed and evaluated a rendering method for tactile strokes on the palm of the hand placed on a sparse 2D array. The algorithm utilized the relation between signal duration and signal onset asynchrony derived from the tactile brush algorithm, to create the sensation of moving tactile strokes. Drawbacks of the tactile brush algorithm in linear motion constraint and robustness were addressed in the new rendering method by applying 3-actuator phantom sensations and adjusting the sampling rate. Our new algorithm was compared to the tactile brush algorithm with a user study. The results indicate that the participants perceived the moving tactile stroke rendered with the new method to be significantly better in terms of trajectory shape and velocity uniformity.

The algorithm proposed in the present study is expected to be useful for applications using desktop interfaces and handheld/wearable devices. Future work will include more detailed examination of the effect of tactor parameters (e.g., tactor size and signal frequency) on the perception of tactile strokes. In addition, other factors that can possibly affect human haptic perception of tactile strokes, for example the location of tactile arrays on the body, will be studied to further improve the effectiveness and robustness of our proposed rendering method.

Acknowledgement. This work was supported by the Global Frontier R&D program on < Human-centered Interaction for Coexistence > of the National Research Foundation of Korea funded by the Korean Government (MSIP) (2013M3A6A3078404) and the KIST Institutional Program (2E26460).

References

1. Israr, A., Poupyrev, I.: Tactile brush: drawing on skin with a tactile grid display. In: Proceedings of the SIGCHI Conference on Human Factors in Computing Systems, pp. 2019–2028 (2011)

2. Cholewiak, R.W., Collins, A.A.: The generation of vibrotactile patterns on a linear array: influences of body site, time, and presentation mode. Percept. Psychophys. **62**(2), 1220–1235 (2000)
3. Borst, C.W., Cavanaugh, C.D.: Touchpad-driven haptic communication using a palm-sized vibrotactile array with an open-hardware controller design. In: EuroHaptics Conference, Munich, pp. 344–347 (2004)
4. Tan, H.Z., Gray, R., Young, J.J., Traylor, R.: A haptic back display for attentional and directional cueing. Haptics-e: Electron. J. Haptics Res. **3**(1), 20 (2003)
5. Yatani, K., Truong, K.N.: SemFeel: a user interface with semantic tactile feedback for mobile touch-screen devices. In: Proceedings of the 22nd Annual ACM Symposium on User Interface Software and Technology, pp. 111–120 (2009)
6. Tan, H.Z., Lim, A., Traylor, R.: A psychophysical study of sensory saltation with an open response paradigm. In: Proceedings of the Ninth (9th) International Symposium on Haptic Interfaces for Virtual Environment and Teleoperator Systems, American Society of Mechanical Engineers Dynamic Systems and Control Division, pp. 1109–1115 (2000)
7. Alles, D.: Information transmission by phantom sensations. IEEE Trans. Man-Mach. Syst. **1**(11), 85–91 (1970)
8. Seo, J., Choi, S.: Initial study for creating linearly moving vibrotactile sensation on mobile device. In: 2010 IEEE Haptics Symposium, pp. 67–70 (2010)
9. Schneider, O.S., Israr, A., MacLean, K.E.: Tactile animation by direct manipulation of grid displays. In: Proceedings of the 28th Annual ACM Symposium on User Interface Software & Technology, pp. 21–30 (2015)
10. Sherrick, C.E., Rogers, R.: Apparent haptic movement. Percept. Psychophys. **1**(3), 175–180 (1966)
11. Makous, J.C., Friedman, R.M., Vierck, C.J.: A critical band filter in touch. J. Neurosci. **15**(4), 2808–2818 (1995)
12. Johansson, R.S., Flanagan, J.R.: Coding and use of tactile signals from the fingertips in object manipulation tasks. Nat. Rev. Neurosci. **10**(5), 345–359 (2009)

High Spatial Resolution Midair Tactile Display Using 70 kHz Ultrasound

Mitsuru Ito[1]([✉]), Daisuke Wakuda[2], Seki Inoue[1], Yasutoshi Makino[1], and Hiroyuki Shinoda[1]

[1] Department of Complexity Science and Engineering,
Graduate School of Frontier Science, The University of Tokyo,
5-1-5 Kashiwanoha, Kashiwa City, Chiba, Japan
{ito,inoue}@hapis.k.u-tokyo.ac.jp,
{yasutoshi_makino,hiroyuki_shinoda}@k.u-tokyo.ac.jp
[2] Smart Life Technology Development Center,
Automotive and Industrial Systems Company,
Panasonic Corporation, 1006 Kadoma, Kadoma City, Osaka, Japan
wakuda.daisuke@jp.panasonic.com

Abstract. We fabricated a midair tactile display using a 70 kHz airborne ultrasound. The spatial resolution of the display was improved 1.75 times compared with the conventional 40 kHz ultrasound tactile display. Since the focal spot diameter was smaller than a finger pad, the user could perceive a localized spot on the finger pad. In the experiment determining the physical properties, we found that the ultrasound attenuation at 70 kHz was comparable to that at 40 kHz. The small focal spot was successfully created as expected using the theory. The psychophysical experimental results showed that the minimum perceivable radiation force for the focal spot of 70 kHz was smaller than that for the 40 kHz case in average under 40 or 100 Hz modulations, and the smaller focal spot was easier to perceive. We also conducted a comparison test of the perceived force area with real contacts.

Keywords: Midair haptics · Tactile display · Airborne ultrasound · Acoustic radiation pressure

1 Introduction

Mid-air haptic displays [1] using ultrasound [2–4] provides a convenient tool to stimulate human skins that is not wearing any device. Although the maximum force is weak, tactile sensations can be evoked at any position and time without constraining the human motions in the workspace. Such sensations can be superimposed on visual floating images [5, 6] and enables fully programmable 3D interfaces in midair [7].

However, a significant limitation of the previous midair devices was the low spatial resolution originating from the ultrasound frequency. Since the conventional devices used 40 kHz ultrasound with an 8.5 mm wavelength, the focal spot was comparable to, or larger than, a finger pad. Such spatial resolution is satisfactory in some applications but can be a critical limitation to others. Since the pressure distribution is uniform on

© Springer International Publishing Switzerland 2016
F. Bello et al. (Eds.): EuroHaptics 2016, Part I, LNCS 9774, pp. 57–67, 2016.
DOI: 10.1007/978-3-319-42321-0_6

the finger pad, it cannot stimulate the SAI and SAII receptors effectively [8, 9]. It is impossible to display the local configuration inside the finger pad, which limits the possibility of midair handling and manipulation of floating virtual objects.

In this paper, we fabricate a 70 kHz ultrasound phased array and examine the effect of heightening the spatial resolution. Since the wavelength 5 mm is smaller than a finger pad, it can produce a localized pattern on the finger pad. The rest of the paper is organized as follows. First, we show the specification of the device. Using the device, we measure the physical properties of the generated ultrasound and confirm that high-resolution pressure distribution is achieved. As a critical property of high-frequency ultrasound, we also measure the attenuation in air and confirm the attenuation length is still acceptable for use as a tactile display. Next, we obtain the tactile threshold on a finger pad. We examine whether the smaller focus of the 70 kHz ultrasound improves the threshold for low-frequency vibration compared with the 40 kHz case. Finally, we conduct a comparison test of the perceived force area on a finger pad with real objects.

2 Basic Properties of Acoustic Radiation Pressure

The relation between the sound pressure and radiation pressure [10, 11] is summarized below for the readability of the manuscript. The acoustic radiation pressure P [Pa] is proportional to the sound energy density given by

$$P = \alpha E = \alpha \frac{p^2}{\rho c^2} \tag{1}$$

where E [J/m^3], p [Pa], ρ [kg/m^3], and c [m/s] denote the sound energy density, sound pressure, density of the medium, and sound velocity, respectively. α denotes a constant ranging between 1 and 2 depending on the reflection properties of the object surface. When the ultrasound propagates through the air and is blocked by the surface of an object, almost all of the ultrasound is reflected at the boundary and in this case the coefficient α becomes nearly 2. Thus, we can control the radiation pressure P by controlling the ultrasound pressure p.

The minimum diameter of the focal spot w is estimated as

$$w = 1.22 \frac{\lambda}{\sin \theta}, \quad \sin \theta = \frac{D/2}{\sqrt{R^2 + (D/2)^2}} \tag{2}$$

where λ [m] denotes the wavelength of the acoustic wave, and R [m] and D [m] denote the focal length and the diameter of the aperture, respectively [12]. The spatial resolution of the array is determined by the focal diameter w.

3 Prototype Device

We fabricated two phased arrays of 70 kHz and 40 kHz transducers with an identical arrangement as shown in Fig. 1. The device was an annular phased array with a center transducer and five additional circular layers of transducers. The prototype was

Fig. 1. Prototype devices. Left: 70 kHz phased array. Right: 40 kHz phased array. (Nihon Ceramic T4010B4)

designed to produce a single focus along the center axis perpendicular to the phased array surface. Each circle is driven at an independent phase by a real-time computer to produce a single focus. We used a commercially available 40 kHz transducers (Nihon Ceramic T4010B4) and the 70 kHz types developed for this experiment.

The external diameters of the transducers are 9 mm (70 kHz) and 10 mm (40 kHz). Figure 2(a) shows the schematic diagram of the electrical connections of the transducers. Because of the capacity of the driver IC, the 5th and 6th lines are divided into two parts. Thus, this system is driven by eight signal channels where the maximum number of the transducers connected to a single channel is 18. The output signal from the Digital I/O was amplified by a driving circuit (JRC NJM2670).

The system is shown in Fig. 2. The driving signal was rectangular waves.

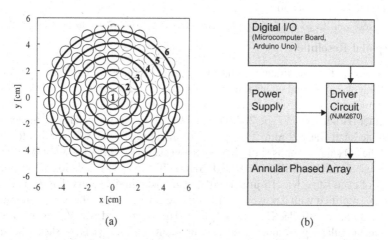

(a)   (b)

Fig. 2. System diagram of annular phased array. (a) Electrical connection and arrangement of transducers. (b) Block diagram of prototype system.

4 Physical Evaluation

4.1 Attenuation in the Air

A critical parameter of high-frequency ultrasound is the attenuation length. The standardized sound pressure of 70 kHz ultrasound is shown in Fig. 3. The case of 40 kHz is also plotted on the same figure. In this experiment, we used a single transmitter as the sound source. For this experiment, the amplitude difference between 40 kHz and 70 kHz ultrasound was within 10 % for the range between 100 and 500 mm. This result shows the 70 kHz ultrasound can be used in a comparable workspace to the 40 kHz case. In the following experiments, the distances between the transducer and the measurement plane are 150 mm and 300 mm.

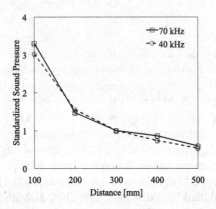

Fig. 3. Attenuation of sound pressure versus distance. The sound pressure level was measured in a range from 100 mm to 500 mm. The measurement data has been standardized by the value of the position of 300 mm. The peak-to-peak voltages of the sinusoidal driving signals at 70 kHz and 40 kHz were 70 V and 30 V, respectively.

4.2 Spatial Resolution

Figure 4 shows the experimental setup to measure the focus of the phased arrays. The phased array was mounted on an aluminum cabinet so that the transducer surface faced a standard microphone. The standard microphone (Brüel&Kjær Type 4138-A-015) with a preamplifier (Brüel&Kjær Type 2670) was mounted on a 3D stage. The diameter of the microphone head was 3.9 mm. The surface of the phased array was parallel to the x-y plane of the 3D stage composed of high-precision stages (SIGMA KOKI SGMV26-200) and a stage controller (SIGMA KOKI SHOT-304GS). The location determination accuracy of each stage was 15 μm. The data were acquired at every 1 mm. The sound signal was amplified with a power amplifier (Brüel&Kjær Type 5935) and calibrated by a sound calibrator (Brüel&Kjær Type 4321). The ultrasound was driven with a continuous rectangular signal during the measurement. Figures 5 and 6 show the spatial distribution of the measured sound pressure along the x-y plane and the x axis.

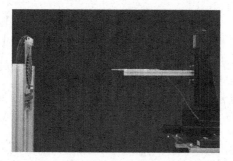

Fig. 4. Experimental setup for the measurement of the sound pressure. A microphone was attached to the 3D stage.

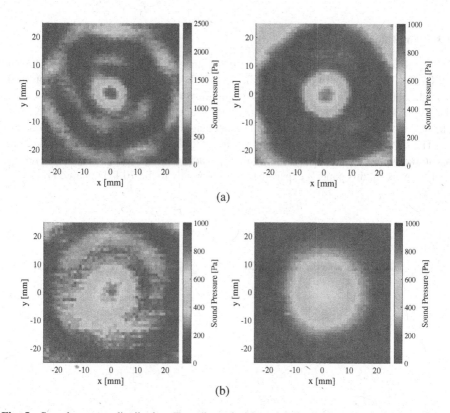

Fig. 5. Sound pressure distribution. Two dimensional spatial distribution of the sound pressure around the focus. Left: 70 kHz phased array. Right: 40 kHz phased array. (a) Focal length: 150 mm. (b) Focal length: 300 mm.

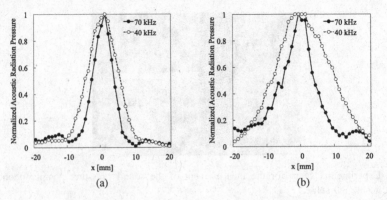

Fig. 6. Radiation pressure distribution along the line $y = 0$. (a) Focal length: 150 mm. (b) Focal length: 300 mm.

4.3   Total Force

The total force was measured using an electronic balance (ViBRA Shinko Denshi AJII-220). The strength of the stimulus in the psychophysical experiments is expressed with the total radiation force obtained in this measurement result. The surface of the phased array is parallel to the measurement plane of the electronic balance. The ultrasound was driven with a continuously rectangular wave during the measurement.

The distance between the radiation surface and the electronic balance was fixed at 150 mm. Figure 7 shows the force value at each driving voltage expressed in the peak-to-peak. In this paper's experiment, power supply to the 70 kHz phased array was 120 W.

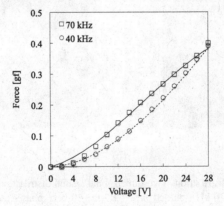

Fig. 7. Total radiation force. We used these relations to control the total acoustic power (total radiation force) from the phased array.

5 Psychophysical Experiment

In this section, we applied vibrotactile patterns to the skin surface and evaluated the threshold value of the stimulus on the finer pad. Next, we evaluated the perceived force area by comparing the stimulation with actual contact to real objects.

5.1 Amplitude Threshold

Experimental Setup and Procedure. The experimental setup is shown in Fig. 8. The experimental procedure was based on the method of limits.

The driving voltage of the phased array was varied in the range specified in Fig. 7. The stimuli were changing in 12 stages between 2 V and 24 V. The focal point was produced below the phased array center with the focal length of 150 mm. The amplitude of the ultrasound was modulated at 40 Hz and 100 Hz for both the 40 kHz and 70 kHz phased arrays. The subjects put their right-hand finger pads at the position of the focal point. The subjects wore the headphones and listened to a white noise to interrupt the audible sound from the phased array corresponding to the driving intensity. The subject gave an answer for tactile sensation on their finger pad. The subjects were allowed only two response alternatives: yes, or no. There was no time limit. The procedure included an ascending series and descending series. These pairs of series were presented three times. The procedure started with the ascending series, where a stimulus was presented at a minimum level, while the start position of descending series was at a maximum level. The subject's absolute threshold was calculated as the average of all obtained thresholds in the pairs of series. There were a total of eight subjects. All subjects were male and their ages were between 22 and 34.

Results. The results of the threshold experiment are shown in Fig. 9. The plots are the averages of the ascending and descending thresholds and the error bars here indicate the averages of the ascending and descending series. The "force" means the peak-to-peak value of the applied radiation force given as a rectangular wave.

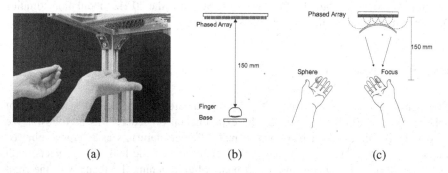

| (a) | (b) | (c) |

Fig. 8. Experimental setup for the psychophysical experiments. We have set up a base for indicating the position of the finger. When the subject places the finger on the base, finger pad and the focus were in the same position.

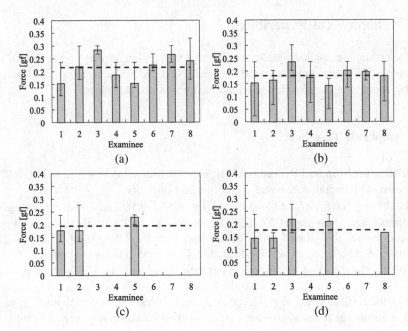

Fig. 9. Absolute detection thresholds for the focal point. (a) 70 kHz phased array, 40 Hz modulation. The average of all examinees was 0.22 gf. (b) 70 kHz phased array, 100 Hz modulation. The average of all examinees was 0.18 gf. (c) 40 kHz phased array, 40 Hz modulation. Examinee 3, 4, 6, 7, and 8 felt no sensation on their finger pad. (d) 40 kHz phased array, 100 Hz modulation. Examinee 4, 6 and 7 felt no sensation on their finger pad.

The maximum stimulus produced by the 70 kHz phased array was perceived on the finger pad for both the modulation frequency of 100 Hz and 40 Hz by all subjects. On the other hand, the maximum stimulus from the 40 kHz phased array was felt on the finger pads of only half of the subjects. Thus, we could not quantify the threshold by the 40 kHz phased array.

We also conducted a similar test for 20 Hz modulation. We did not obtain a quantitative threshold, but all of the subjects could feel the 20 Hz modulation stimulus on their finger pads for the 70 kHz phased array.

5.2   Size Comparison Test

Procedure. In this experiment, the subject compared the perceived size with real spheres for the 70 kHz focal spot. The experimental procedure was as follows. We prepared 11 stainless steel balls, which had different diameters as reference objects. Figure 10(a) shows the appearance of the reference metallic ball. The subjects, with eyes closed, have the sphere in the left hand while touching the focus with the right hand. First, the author put a reference sphere on the palm of the left hand of the subject. Then, the subjects touch the sphere freely with their fingers and compare the sphere

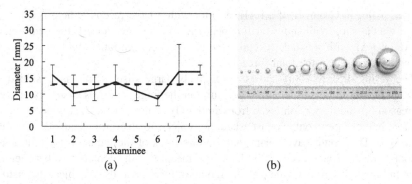

Fig. 10. (a) Perceived focus diameter. The mean value was 13.1 mm. (b) Photograph of the metal spheres used in the comparison test. The diameters of the spheres are 4, 5, 6.35, 7.93, 9.52, 12.7, 15.87, 19.05, 25.4, 30.16, and 41.27 mm.

size with the focus size. After this, the author put the next sphere on the palm of the left hand and repeat this procedure for all the kinds of spheres. All subjects were instructed to sense the stimuli at their finger pads. The subjects compared the size of the ball and the focus. The subjects were allowed multiple choices: larger, smaller, or same. There was no time limit. The experimental procedure is the method of limits similar to the threshold experiment. We started from the smallest ball, and recorded the diameter where the answer switched from the "same" to "larger", while keeping the ultrasound stimulation constant. This was used to obtain the ascending threshold. We also obtain the descending limit in a similar way. We finally obtained the equivalent diameter to the ultrasound stimulation, as the average of the ascending and descending thresholds.

Results. Figure 10 shows the equivalent sphere diameters perceived on the finger pad. In this figure, the error bars indicate the size of the maximum and minimum ball sizes which were judged as being the same as, regardless of whether in the ascending or descending process. The perceived diameter was 13.1 mm for the spot in the condition of the 70 kHz phased array.

6   Discussions

The result of Fig. 9(a), (b) shows comparable thresholds for 40 Hz and 100 Hz vibrations, which seems inconsistent with conventional knowledge. In Ref. [13], the thresholds for 40 Hz and 100 Hz are different by 15 dB for a 2.9 cm^2 contactor. One reason for the difference is that the actual contact area is smaller than this, and the other reason is that the threshold is expressed with "force" not "displacement." In airborne ultrasound tactile displays, the small force spot is effective at stimulating the skin at a low temporal frequency.

In comparison between 40 kHz and 70 kHz stimuli shown in Fig. 9, some subjects (Group A) showed comparable thresholds for 40 or 100 Hz modulations and other subjects (Group B) showed poorer sensitivity to the 40 kHz stimulus. A possible explanation is that FAII was the major (most sensitive) receptor in Group A, and SAI or

FAI was major in Group B. If a FAII receptor with a large receptive field is the main sensor, the threshold will show small dependence on the force area. If the main sensor is SAI or FAI with a small receptive area, force concentration will decrease the threshold expressed in the total force.

The result of Fig. 10(a) shows a relatively large dispersion. As a subjective comment by the authors, a localized pressure on the finger pad was clearly perceived. The reason for the dispersion came from ambiguity in how the subject understood the question. In the experiment, we just asked the subjects to answer the equivalence of the sphere size. This could have meant that the diameters of the radiation force area and the sphere are equivalent, or it could have also meant that the contact area between the finger and the ball was equivalent to the radiation force area. If the subject understood as the former, the equivalent diameter was small, and if it was the latter, the answered diameter become larger. It was the imperfectness of the experiment we noticed after the experiment. Nevertheless, we confirmed the subject could feel a localized force less than 1 cm in diameter on their finger pads.

7 Conclusions

A 70 kHz airborne ultrasound tactile display was fabricated and the effect of the higher spatial resolution was evaluated. The prototype display was composed of 91 transducers and its aperture diameter was 100 mm. In the physical experiment, we confirmed that the radiation force spot diameter of 70 kHz phased array was 43 % smaller than 40 kHz case at 150 mm from the device, comparing the foot width of the pressure distribution. The psychophysical experimental results showed that the minimum perceivable radiation force for the focal spot of 70 kHz was smaller than that for the 40 kHz case in average under 40 or 100 Hz modulations, and the smaller focal spot was easier to perceive. In the psychophysical experiments using the 70 kHz device, we obtained the detection thresholds for 40 Hz and 100 Hz vibrations. They are comparable, and the sensitivity difference was only 2 dB in the applied force. The subject could sense low frequency vibration easily, and perceived a localized sensation where the size could be compared with real objects.

Our future work includes representing fine texture in the tactile display. We will develop a fully controllable two-dimensional phased array.

References

1. Sodhi, R., Poupyrev, I., Glisson, M., Israr, A.: AIREAL: interactive tactile experiences in free air. ACM Trans. Graph. **32**(4), 134 (2013)
2. Iwamoto, T., Tatezono, M., Shinoda, H.: Non-contact method for producing tactile sensation using airborne ultrasound. In: Ferre, M. (ed.) EuroHaptics 2008. LNCS, vol. 5024, pp. 504–513. Springer, Heidelberg (2008)
3. Hoshi, T., Takahashi, M., Iwamoto, T., Shinoda, H.: Noncontact tactile display based on radiation pressure of airborne ultrasound. IEEE Trans. Haptics **3**(3), 155–165 (2010)

4. Long, B., Seah, S.A., Carter, T., Subramanian, S.: Rendering volumetric haptic shapes in mid-air using ultrasound. ACM Trans. Graph. **33**(6), 181 (2014)
5. Monnai, Y., Hasegawa, K., Fujiwara, M., Yoshino, K., Inoue, S., Shinoda, H.: Haptomime: mid-air haptic interaction with a floating virtual screen. In: Proceedings of the 27th Annual ACM Symposium on User Interface Software and Technology, pp. 663–667 (2014)
6. Shinoda, H.: Haptoclone as a test bench of weak force haptic interaction. In: SIGGRAPH Asia 2015 Haptic Media and Contents Design, p. 3 (2015)
7. Ishii, H., Ullmer, B.: Tangible bits: towards seamless interfaces between people, bits and atoms. In: Proceedings of the ACM SIGCHI Conference on Human Factors in Computing Systems, pp. 234–241 (1997)
8. Asamura, N., Yokoyama, H., Shinoda, H.: Selectively stimulating skin receptors for tactile display. IEEE Comput. Graph. Appl. **18**(6), 32–37 (1998)
9. Srinivasan, M.A., Dandekar, K.: An investigation of the mechanics of tactile sense using two-dimensional models of the primate fingertip. J. Biomech. Eng. **118**(1), 48–55 (1996)
10. Awatani, J.: Studies on acoustic radiation pressure. I. (General considerations). J. Acoust. Soc. Am. **27**(2), 278–281 (1955)
11. Hasegawa, T., Kido, T., Iizuka, T., Matsuoka, C.: A general theory of Rayleigh and Langevin radiation pressures. Acoust. Sci. Technol. **21**(3), 145–152 (2000)
12. Born, M., Wolf, E.: Principles of Optics: Electromagnetic Theory of Propagation, Interference and Diffraction of Light. CUP Archive, Cambridge (2000)
13. Gesheider, G.A., Bolanowski, S.J., Hardick, K.R.: The frequency selectivity of information-processing channels in the tactile sensory system. Somatosen. Mot. Res. **18**, 191–201 (2001)

Mid-Air Ultrasonic Pressure Control on Skin by Adaptive Focusing

Seki Inoue[1]([⊠]), Yasutoshi Makino[1,2], and Hiroyuki Shinoda[1,2]

[1] Graduate School of Information Science and Technology,
The University of Tokyo, Tokyo, Japan
seki_inoue@ipc.i.u-tokyo.ac.jp
[2] Graduate School of Frontier Sciences, The University of Tokyo,
Chiba, Japan
{makino,shinoda}@k.u-tokyo.ac.jp

Abstract. Mid-air ultrasound can remotely invoke tactile sensation to bare hand. However, it is difficult to control it precisely because the hand itself scatters ultrasound. In this paper, a scattering model, which can be solved in real-time, is proposed and, this model can create a stronger focal point as compared to the conventional model. The proposed algorithm is based on the boundary element method and is a natural extension of the previously proposed phased array synthesis algorithms. Numerical analysis shows the relationship between the error of the surface model, computation time, and focusing performance. Psychophysical experiment shows that the internal tactile intensity of the focused ultrasound is significantly improved using the proposed adaptive focusing method. The proposed method can be used for mid-air ultrasound as a test bench of precise weak force haptic interaction.

Keywords: Mid-air haptics · Tactile · Scattering problem · Boundary element method

1 Introduction

The attempt to generate haptic sensation in the empty air has attracted people and is actively being researched. It enables an unspecified number of people to freely and actively touch virtual objects cleanly without requesting to wear anything.

Unfortunately, the absolute force generated by mid-air haptics is smaller than that generated by conventional haptic displays, which have rigid contacts and powerful actuators. Therefore, its natural application is tactile display rather than kinesthetic force. A tactile display, in addition to the minimum necessary to stimulate tactile mechanoreceptors, requires time-domain capability, which covers a bandwidth from DC to over 400 Hz, and spatial-domain capability, which can stimulate an exact point or region on the skin.

An air-jet-based tactile display consists of air nozzles or woofer speaks. It is cost-effective and safe, which are crucially important factors for practical applications. However, its time and spatial domain resolution is relatively low [13].

© Springer International Publishing Switzerland 2016
F. Bello et al. (Eds.): EuroHaptics 2016, Part I, LNCS 9774, pp. 68–77, 2016.
DOI: 10.1007/978-3-319-42321-0_7

A laser-based tactile display utilizes very high frequency and short wavelength; thus, its time and spatial resolution is quite high. However, its absolute power is still at a lower level [8, 11].

The use of airborne ultrasound radiation pressure satisfies the temporal requirements since its frequency is much higher than the human haptic frequency band. In addition, the spatial wavelength, 8.5 mm for 40 kHz, and resulting theoretical limit of the spatial resolution are acceptable in many applications.

However, in previous studies, the existence of the objects had not been considered for calculation of the phased array. Therefore, scattering on hand skin deteriorates the precision of both location and intensity of focal points. The surrounded setup of the multi-directional phased array can make the focal point small and enhance the tactile intensity [6, 10]. In addition, a higher ultrasonic frequency may achieve higher spatial resolution. However, these approaches worsen the difficulties of scattering. Our previous finite element analysis showed there are rooms to achieve higher power but it is too high cost for real-time application by FEM approach [4].

In this paper, we propose and analyze an adaptive focusing model and try to generate a stronger focal point than that generated by previous naive distance-based approaches. The proposed model is based on the boundary element method (BEM) and can be calculated in real-time. Furthermore, it is a natural extension of the previously proposed phased array synthesis algorithms. Numerical analysis shows the relationship between an error of surface model, computation time, and focusing performance. Psychophysical experiment shows internal tactile intensity of focused ultrasound is significantly improved using the proposed adaptive focusing method.

2   Scattering Model for Ultrasonic Tactile Display

The scattered acoustic pressure in open space $p(r)$ is calculated by using the boundary integral equation, which is represented by the boundary of the scatterer Ω, and direct sound $q(r)$ as follows [1]:

$$c(r)p(r) = q(r) - \int_{\Omega} p(s)\frac{\partial g(r,s)}{\partial n} - g(r,s)\frac{\partial p(s)}{\partial n}dS \qquad (1)$$

where g is an Helmholtz green function. For 3-dimensional space, it is

$$g(x,y) = \frac{1}{4\pi|x-y|}e^{ik|x-y|}. \qquad (2)$$

$c(r)$ is solid angle. It is $1/2$ on the surface and 1 at the free space.

Here we assume that the admittance ratio between air and skin is zero: $\beta(s) \approx 0$. Then.

$$\frac{\partial p(s)}{\partial n} = -j\omega\rho\frac{1}{\rho c}\beta(s)p(s) = 0. \qquad (3)$$

Therefore, we get a simplified formulation:

$$c(r)p(r) + \int_\Omega \frac{\partial g(r,s)}{\partial n} p(s)dS = q(r). \tag{4}$$

By discretizing the surface, the BEM operator is defined as $B := \frac{1}{2}(I+A)$ where $A_{i,j} = \frac{\partial g(r_i,r_j)}{\partial n} \Delta_j$ and Δ_j is the area of the surface mesh element. Furthermore, the direct sound $q(r)$ is represented by q_i, the complex gains of the transducer at index i, and $G_{i,j} = g(r_{T_i}, r_j)$, transfer from transducer i to surface element j, as: $q(r_j) = Gq$. Therefore, we obtain the discretized phased array scatter equation as follows:

$$Bp = Gq. \tag{5}$$

Similarly, Iwamoto, Carter, Long and Inoue's phased array synthesis method can be represented by the following matrix equation [2,5,7,9].

$$p' = G'q \tag{6}$$

where p' is an acoustic pressure in the air and q' is a phased array drive. p' is a scalar for single focus synthesis or p', G' have multi rows for multi-focus synthesis.

Consequently, the proposed model is a natural extension of the conventional phased array synthesis algorithms. Therefore, it is expected that the integration and application of those algorithms is an easy task.

2.1   Solver for a Single Focus on the Skin

Under the condition that all transducer drive at full power, let us find a phased array drive q to make a focal point at a specified face i on the scatter surface. i.e.,

$$\text{find } q \text{ s.t.} \max_{\forall j \, ||q_j||=1} ||p_i||^2 \tag{7}$$

is our main problem in this paper. If we have inverse matrix of B,

$$p_i = (B^{-1}G)_i q \tag{8}$$

holds. The solution is obviously

$$\hat{q}_j = \frac{(B^{-1}G)_{ij}^H}{||(B^{-1}G)_{ij}^H||} \tag{9}$$

where A^H indicates the Hermitian matrix of A.

Here, $(B^{-1}G)_i$ is denoted by xG where x is a solution of an equation: $B^T x = e_i$, where e_i is i-th basic unit vector.

3 Numerical Analysis

This section shows the numerical analysis by using a finger surface model designed for computer graphics applications[1]. We set a target point at the center of a pad of index finger and the target face element is chosen as the nearest one from the target point. The evaluation is performed by comparing the acoustic pressure of target region, which consists from face elements within 3 mm from target point. As reference baseline method, we employ the distance-based naive method where the transducer drive q_i is denoted by using the distance between focal point and the transducer r_i as follows:

$$q_i = e^{-jkr}. \tag{10}$$

A four-square phased array, which has 996 transducers, is assumed in numerical analyses and psychophysical experiments as shown in Fig. 1.

Figure 2 shows an example of an acoustic pressure distribution on a finger model by using the adaptive focusing and naive methods. The figure shows the pad and nail sides of the adaptive focusing method and the pad and nail sides of the naive method (from left to right). Adaptive focusing method enhances the peak pressure of focus. In addition, an undesired pressure spot is observed using the naive method; however, it is not observed using the adaptive focusing method.

Polygon Size Analysis. Precision of the surface model is an important factor. Therefore, the relationship between the adaptively focused pressure and the mean length of the mesh was investigated. Six surface mesh models having 153 to 5000 faces are prepared, which are gradually simplified. The simplification was done by quadric error-based method [3]. Adaptive focusing was calculated by using each low polygon model, and the finest model was used for evaluation.

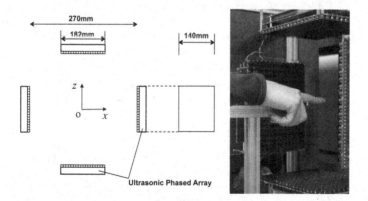

Fig. 1. Left: the geometry of ultrasonic phased array used in numerical and user experiments. Right: a scene of user experiments.

---

[1] Autodesk, Inc. CC License. http://www.123dapp.com/123C-3D-Model/Finger-Index /866442.

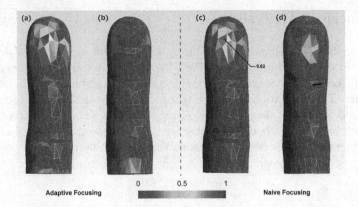

Adaptive Focusing   0   0.5   1   Naive Focusing

Fig. 2. (a): The acoustic pressure distribution of the pad side of the index finger obtained using the adaptive focusing method. (b): The pressure distribution of the nail side of the index finger obtained using the adaptive focusing method. (c): The acoustic pressure distribution of the pad side of the index finger obtained using the naive focusing method. (d): The acoustic pressure distribution of the nail side of the index finger obtained using the naive focusing method. All values are normalized by the maximum value.

Figure 3 shows the pressure ratio of the proposed model to the naive method at the target region with mean length of edges of each models. The proposed method results were worse than that of the naive method when the mean length of the edges was longer than the half of wavelength of the carrier ultrasound.

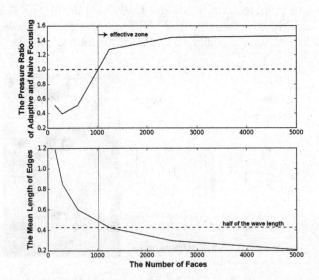

Fig. 3. Top: the pressure ratio of the proposed method to the naive method at the target region. The dashed line shows a constant ratio when the proposed and naive methods result in the same pressure. Down: the mean length of the edges to the total number of faces. The dashed line shows the half of wavelength of the carrier ultrasound.

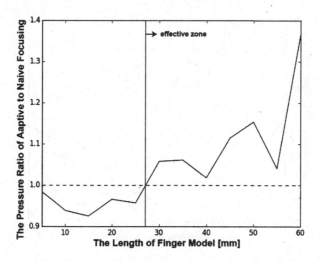

Fig. 4. Effect of modelized length of finger model on the pressure ratio of the proposed method to the naive method at the target region. The dashed line shows a constant ratio when the proposed and naive methods result in the same pressure.

Polygon Region Analysis. Another important question is how far we should modelize the user body. It is practically an important question whether or not the entire arm or body of the user should be captured. Therefore, we intentionally cut a finger model and investigated the relationship between the model region to consider and the focus intensity.

From a 60-mm length finger model, 12 models were cut down in 5 mm intervals. Adaptive focusing was calculated by using each short finger model, and the longest model was used for evaluation. The mean length of the edge of this model was 0.46 mm. Figure 4 shows the relationship between the acoustic pressure ratio of adaptive focusing to naive focusing and the length of the fingers. It is implied that the adaptive focusing method uses the geometry of scatterer within 30 mm, which is 3.5 times longer than the wavelength.

Computation Cost Analysis. Considering real-time applications, the computation time is an important factor. The computation time mainly depends on the number of polygons of the scatter and the number of transducers in the phased array.

The main solver of the algorithm was implemented with CUDA, GPGPU framework. We tested the latency on Intel Xeon E5-2670 and GRID K520 processors.

Figure 5 shows the computation times for the low polygon models used in previous sections. The number of transducers was 1,008. Considering the results of previous sections, the typical and practical number of meshes is given as meshes on a sphere whose diameter is 3.5λ whose edges length is 0.5λ, which is:

$$\frac{4\pi(3.5\lambda)^2}{\sqrt{3}(0.5\lambda)^2/4} \approx 1422. \tag{11}$$

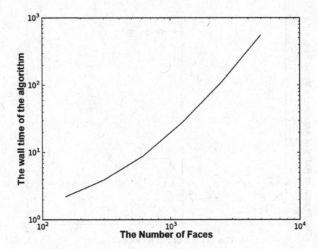

Fig. 5. A log-log plotted computation time against the number of faces on models. Note that the both axes are log scaled.

The computation time in this case is about 28 msec.

Discussion. Adaptive focusing can enhance the acoustic pressure on the skin. The scatterer within a spherical region whose diameter is 3.5 times wavelength should be consideration. In addition, the half wavelength of the carrier ultrasound is enough for the edge length of the meshes.

4   Psychophysical Experiment

To verify that adaptive focusing is psychophysically useful, we conducted an user study.

4.1   Experiment Setup

Four-square phased array is implemented. Each side having 249 transducers, and 996 transducers are equipped in total. To keep the user's finger fixed, an arm rest is mounted to the prescribed point by the index finger. There is a mark to adjust their proximal interphalangeal creases. The subjects for the experiments place their hand on the arm rest under the visual and auditory blind circumstance. A common surface model is used among all subjects in order to examine the effects of the geometric error between the actual finger and calculation model. Diameter of distal interphalangeal crease is measured before the experiments to evaluation. The same surface model as numerical analysis is employed. The number of face elements is 584, mean length of edges is 0.47 mm, and finger is cut at a distance of 40 mm from the target point. The model's diameter of distal interphalangeal crease is 20 mm. The amplitude of ultrasonic wave is modulated to make vibrotactile sensation, which has three peaks at 5 Hz, 40 Hz, and 200 Hz. Eight men in their twenties and a man in his thirty participated in this experiment.

4.2 Subjective Intensity

Protocol. Two ultrasonic stimuli are designed. The "Reference" pattern is generated using the distance-based naive synthesis method, and the "Target" pattern is generated using the adaptive focusing method. Both naive and adaptive method are driven at same amplitudes for all transducers. This phased array system invokes 1.6 gf/cm^2 radiation pressure at free space with naive method. At the beginning, present "Reference" pattern for 5 s and all signals off for 1 s After that, "Reference" or "Target" is randomly chosen and presented. The subjects were requested to answer "Strong" or "Same or Weak" verbally. This procedure repeats 20 times per subject. The number of "Reference" and "Target" for a subject is kept the same (10 times for reference and 10 times for target). The test was performed without any prior knowledge or training.

Results and Discussion. Figure 6 shows the correct answer ratio with diameters on the index fingers. Overall, the ratio was 79.4 %, and it was showed that the adaptive focusing method significantly improved the internal tactile intensity of the ultrasonic stimuli. There was no apparent relations between accuracy and the diameter of the actual finger. Therefore, this result is enough to support that a single common model is sufficient for various users.

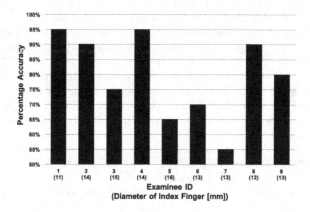

Fig. 6. Percentage accuracy from chance level to full marks against all examinees and the diameters of their index fingers.

5 Conclusion

In this paper, we proposed an adaptive focusing method on the assumption of skin is sound hard boundary. The focusing method overcomes scattering problem by the hand and maximizes the acoustic sound pressure at target point. Numerical analysis gives us a practical guideline to modelize the user body. The psychophysical study proves that the internal tactile intensity significantly improved.

In terms of future work, there are several tasks to explore. Firstly, an inspection and improvement robustness is required. Especially, discussions about geometric errors of surface model and numerical robustness are interesting topics. Secondly, drawing spatial pattern instead of a single point on the skin is also an interesting topic. Certainly, the proposed model is a natural extension of the previously proposed method, but the dimension of the problem is enlarged. Fourthly, actual pressure distribution should be measured. A tiny microphone which does not affect actual pressure field is required to measure it. Finally, a real-time and interactive system is expected. Adaptive focusing system with real-time measurement of the user's hand can become a test bench of weak force haptic interactions.

Acknowledgments. This work was supported in part by JSPS Grant-in-Aid for Scientific Research (A) 25240032, JSPS Grant-in-Aid for Young Scientists (A) 15H05315 and JSPS Grant-in-Aid for JSPS Fellows 15J09604. We thank BEM++ Team for their open source projects from which we got a lot of insights for our implementation [12].

References

1. Bai, M.R., Ih, J.G., Benesty, J.: Acoustic Array Systems: Theory, Implementation, and Application. Wiley, Hoboken (2013)
2. Carter, T., Seah, S.A., Long, B., Drinkwater, B., Subramanian, S.: Ultrahaptics: multipoint mid-air haptic feedback for touch surfaces. In: Proceedings of the 26th Annual ACM Symposium on User Interface Software and Technology, UIST 2013, pp. 505–514. NY, USA (2013). http://doi.acm.org/10.1145/2501988.2502018
3. Garland, M., Heckbert, P.S.: Surface simplification using quadric error metrics. In: Proceedings of the 24th Annual Conference on Computer Graphics and Interactive Techniques, SIGGRAPH 1997, pp. 209–216. ACM Press/Addison-Wesley Publishing Co., New York, NY, USA (1997). http://dx.doi.org/10.1145/258734.258849
4. Inoue, S., Makino, Y., Shinoda, H.: Producing airborne ultrasonic 3D tactile image by time reversal field rendering. In: 2014 Proceedings of the SICE Annual Conference (SICE), pp. 1360–1365, September 2014
5. Inoue, S., Makino, Y., Shinoda, H.: Active touch perception produced by airborne ultrasonic haptic hologram. In: World Haptics Conference (WHC), 2015 IEEE, pp. 362–367, June 2015
6. Inoue, S., Shinoda, H.: A pinchable aerial virtual sphere by acoustic ultrasound stationary wave. In: Haptics Symposium (HAPTICS), 2014 IEEE, pp. 89–92, February 2014
7. Iwamoto, T., Tatezono, M., Shinoda, H.: Non-contact method for producing tactile sensation using airborne ultrasound. In: Ferre, M. (ed.) EuroHaptics 2008. LNCS, vol. 5024, pp. 504–513. Springer, Heidelberg (2008). http://dx.doi.org/10.1007/978-3-540-69057-3_64
8. Lee, H., Kim, J.S., Choi, S., Jun, J.H., Park, J.R., Kim, A.H., Oh, H.B., Kim, H.S., Chung, S.C.: Mid-air tactile stimulation using laser-induced thermoelastic effects: the first study for indirect radiation. In: World Haptics Conference (WHC), 2015 IEEE, pp. 374–380, June 2015

9. Long, B., Seah, S.A., Carter, T., Subramanian, S.: Rendering volumetric haptic shapes in mid-air using ultrasound. ACM Trans. Graph. **33**(6), 181:1–181:10 (2014). http://doi.acm.org/10.1145/2661229.2661257

10. Makino, Y., Furuyama, Y., Inoue, S., Shinoda, H.: Mutual tele-environment: realtime 3D image transfer with force feedback. In: Proceedings of the SIGCHI Conference on Human Factors in Computing Systems, CHI 2016, ACM (2016, to appear)

11. Ochiai, Y., Kumagai, K., Hoshi, T., Rekimoto, J., Hasegawa, S., Hayasaki, Y.: Fairy lights in femtoseconds: aerial and volumetric graphics rendered by focused femtosecond laser combined with computational holographic fields. In: ACM SIGGRAPH 2015 Emerging Technologies, SIGGRAPH 2015, pp. 10:1–10:1. NY, USA (2015). http://doi.acm.org/10.1145/2782782.2792492

12. Śmigaj, W., Betcke, T., Arridge, S., Phillips, J., Schweiger, M.: Solving boundary integral problems with bem++. ACM Trans. Math. Softw. **41**(2), 6:1–6:40 (2015). http://doi.acm.org/10.1145/2590830

13. Sodhi, R., Poupyrev, I., Glisson, M., Israr, A.: Aireal: interactive tactile experiences in free air. ACM Trans. Graph. **32**(4), 134:1–134:10 (2013). http://doi.acm.org/10.1145/2461912.2462007

Characterization of Ultrasound Tactile Display

Georgios Korres and Mohamad Eid[✉]

Department of Engineering, New York University Abu Dhabi,
Saadiyat Island, United Arab Emirates
{george.korres,mohamad.eid}@nyu.edu

Abstract. Traditional haptic interfaces require physical contact between the haptic device and the user. An elegant and novel solution is to provide contactless tactile stimulation via airborne acoustic radiation pressure. However, the characteristics of contactless tactile displays are not well studied in the literature. In this paper, we study the characteristics of the ultrasonic tactile display as a haptic interface. In particular, we examine the effects of increasing the number of ultrasound transducers on four characteristics, namely the maximum producible force, the workspace, the workspace resolution, and the robustness of the simulation. Three rectangular-shaped 2D array configurations are considered: single-tile (10×10 transducers), two-tiles (10×20 transducers), and four-tiles (20×20 transducers). Results show that the maximum producible force remains almost constant as the number of tiles increases, whereas the elevation at which these maxima are generated increases. The workspace increases along the xy-plane as the number of tiles increase almost linearly, however, the elevation of the workspace remains almost the same. Finally, we found that the robustness of tactile display decreases as the number of tiles increases.

Keywords: Haptic interfaces · Ultrasound transducer array · Tactile display

1 Introduction

Haptic-based ultrasonic stimulation relies on an airborne acoustic phased array for giving tactile sensation at the human skin [5]. Dalecki et al. demonstrated that tactile sensations could be evoked from the ultrasound radiated on the skin in water [4]. Subsequent research by Shinoda and colleagues expanded further on this concept, using 2D array of ultrasonic transducers, to produce one focal point on the submerged hand [14]. The study suggested using ultrasound at 40 kHz; higher frequency resulted in higher energy attenuation and degradation in spatial resolution of focusing.

Shinoda and colleagues studied airborne ultrasound tactile stimulation to enhance the quality of the tactile stimulation and integrate it with visual display. A feasibility study with 91 transducers was conducted to generate a fixed focal point [16]. To animate the focal point and produce higher tactile forces

© Springer International Publishing Switzerland 2016
F. Bello et al. (Eds.): EuroHaptics 2016, Part I, LNCS 9774, pp. 78–89, 2016.
DOI: 10.1007/978-3-319-42321-0_8

of around 16 mN (20 mm spatial resolution and 1 kHz vibrations), a subsequent work extended the tactile display to 324 transducers [12]. Experiments showed that users were able to discriminate tactile stimulation movement direction. A further development with 2,241 transducers offered a much larger workspace of 1 m^3 and an improved temporal resolution of 0.5 ms [8]. The system was then integrated with a touch screen to enable noncontact blind touch interaction by adding tactile feedback for notifying the finger location [23,24]. A recent study by Inoue et al. produced a spatially stationary haptic image using ultrasonic waves to construct 3D haptic images without depending on sensor feedback for tracking the hand position [13].

Gavrilov presented a method to display 2D tactile shapes by generating multiple focus ultrasonic focal points [7]. This method led to the development of UltraHaptics; a multi-point tactile feedback system with an interactive visual screen [2]. They further improved the technology for rendering 3D volumetric haptic shapes [19]. A similar work for rendering volumetric tactile shapes via ultrasound is demonstrated in [17]. Displaying haptic texture via ultrasound is demonstrated in [3,21].

Several researchers tried to improve the quality of tactile displays by varying the characteristics of the ultrasonic system (increasing the number of transducers, work-space, producible forces, etc.). For instance, an approach is presented for measuring the strength of the ultrasonic pressure field in [11]. A spatial resolution of less than 0.1 mm with a total force of 16 mN is measured on a 2-D cross-sectional area of 180×180 mm at 200 mm elevation above the array surface, with 18×18 discrete focal point positions. The radiation pressure field of a system comprising of two ultrasonic transducers with different radiation frequencies is analyzed in [18]. Hoshi characterized an aerial tactile system with two arrays of 96 transducers each and a target workspace of $200 \times 200 \times 200$ mm (divided into $5 \times 5 \times 12.5$ mm sub-areas). Each of these sub-areas can be a target focal point that can stimulate tactile feedback in mid-air [9]. The output force for each array is 12 mN.

Existing work has reported varying and sometimes conflicting results about the characteristics of ultrasonic tactile display devices. For instance, [15,16] reported 8 mN of output force at 250 mm elevation, a haptic rendering frequency of 1 KHz, and 20 mm of spatial resolution with 91 transducers. The authors in [10] utilized 364 transducers to achieve 47 mN of output force at 250 mm of elevation, a spatial resolution of 20 mm, and an unmeasured workspace. Hoshi et al. measured 16 mN at 200 mm of elevation, rendering frequency of 1 KHz, and 20 mm of spatial resolution using 324 transducers [11,12]. Multiple ultrasound transducer arrays were deployed in [8,22] with 2241 transducers in total to generate 73 mN of output force at 600 mm elevation, a rendering frequency of 1 kHz, and a spatial resolution of 20 mm. Hoshi reported 12 mN of output force at 300 mm elevation, a rendering frequency of 1 kHz, and 36.4 mm spatial resolution with 384 transducers [9]. Yoshino and Shinoda built a tactile visioacoustic screen with 249 ultrasound transducers to generate 16 mN of output force at 240 mm elevation and a 10 mm spatial resolution [23]. Other research in the acoustic manipulation technology returned similar results. For instance, graphics can be generated using levitated small objects carried by ultrasound pressure [20]. The study reported a spatial resolution of 0.5 mm, a workspace of 270 mm along the z-axis, and a producible force of 20 mN.

In this paper we present an experimental platform for measuring the characteristics that define the quality of the ultrasound tactile display as a haptic interface. The remainder of the paper is organized as follows: Sect. 2 presents an overview of the tile-based Haptogram system that is used in the experimental study. Section 3 presents the experimental setup, procedure, and results along with a discussion of the derived characteristics. Section 4 summarizes our findings.

2 Haptogram System

2.1 Haptogram System Overview

The Haptogram system is presented thoroughly in our previous work [6]. The Haptogram system architecture comprises a software subsystem and a hardware subsystem as shown in Fig. 1(a). The software subsystem has three components: Graphical User Interface (GUI), 3D Point Cloud Representation (PCR) and Focal Point Calculation (FPC). The GUI, shown in Fig. 1(b), enables users to create tactile objects that can be displayed (2D or 3D objects). The PCR component converts the model into a point cloud of focal points, with timestamps representing the order in which these focal points must be displayed. The FPC component calculates the distances between each focal point and the transducers, and the timings to produce the focal point at the desired 3D location. The software subsystem is generalized for N-tiles. The timings for all the $N \times 100$ transducers are calculated automatically.

Three components make up the hardware subsystem, as shown in Fig. 1(a): the FPGA Controller, the Driver Circuit Amplification (DCA) component and the Ultrasound Array (UA). The FPGA Controller produces synchronized pulse signals that feed into the DCA. The DCA component is an amplifier circuit that

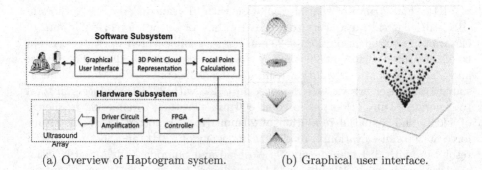

(a) Overview of Haptogram system.   (b) Graphical user interface.

Fig. 1. Haptogram system.

produces sufficient currents to drive the ultrasound transducers. The UA is a composition of tiles of a two-dimensional array of ultrasound transducers (a tile includes 10×10 transducers).

2.2 3D Tactile Rendering

The Haptogram system renders point-cloud 3D tactile objects by switching focal points at a frequency up to 1.34 KHz. The flowchart explaining the haptic rendering is shown in Fig. 2. First of all, the tile configuration is loaded (N number of tiles, n number of transducers along x-axis, and m number of transducers along y-axis) along with the 3D point cloud file that represents the 3D tactile object to be displayed. Then, the coordinates of each focal point (x,y,z) are used to determine all the distances between the given focal point and every transducer of the tiled array ($N \times 100$ transducers). Next, the distances are used to calculate the timings needed by each transducer to produce ultrasound waves. Finally the timings are stored in a HEX memory file that can be uploaded to the FPGA boards.

2.3 The Tile-Based Ultrasonic Array

The fundamental building block of the UA component is a two-dimensional array of ultrasound transducers (10×10 transducers). The MA40S4S 40 kHz Murata ultrasound transducer is used with 10 mm size diameter, 120 dB sound pressure, 80° directivity, and 20 Vpp allowable input voltage. As the number of tiles varies with different Haptogram system configurations, it is imperative for the interaction system to adapt so that users can have a nearly consistent experience regardless of the system configuration. Haptogram is a modular system so that multiple tiles can be connected and used without the need to change the application software.

The hardware architecture for the N-tiles design is shown in Fig. 3(a). The synchronization for the N tiles work as follows: First, the master FPGA will immediately fire the driver circuit to drive its own transducers and create the sequence of focal points. The master FPGA will send a SYNC = 1 pulse to the

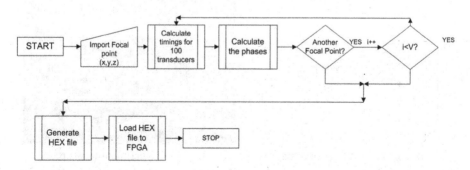

Fig. 2. 3D point cloud haptic rendering for the N tiles Haptogram system.

first slave FPGA once an entire cycle of focal points execution is completed. Then, the first slave FPGA resets the execution of its focal points so that on the next cycle both the master tile and slave tile 1 are synchronized. The same procedure takes place to synchronize slave tile 2 with slave tile 1, and so on.

3 Characterization of the Haptogram System

This section presents an experimental study to determine the haptic characteristics of the tile-based Haptogram system as the number of tiles increases. Specifically, we will focus on characteristics that define the quality of the system as a haptic interface, namely the maximum producible forces, the device workspace, workspace resolution and display robustness. We will compare these characteristics for three configurations: single-tile configuration, two-tiles configuration, and four-tiles configurations.

3.1 Experimental Setup

In order to measure the spatial distribution of the acoustic radiation pressure, we used the experimental setup shown in Fig. 3(b). An ultrasonic sensor probe was attached to the end effector of the robotic arm (ST Robotics R17) whose resolution for movement is 0.1 mm. The sound probe is an MA40S4S 40 kHz Murata ultrasound transducer. Its output was fed to AC-to-DC conversion circuit (a rectifying bridge followed by an array of decoupling capacitors). The resulting DC signal is fed to a 10-bit Analog to Digital Converter (ADC). Finally the digital output is calibrated for force measurement in mN. The following settings were also used in this experiment: the current is limited to 900 mA whereas the voltage is limited to ±12 V.

A simple script is developed to control movement of the robotic arm to measure the force distribution in an arbitrary 3D volume on top of the ultrasound array. Measurement data is acquired at a 1 kHz rate. At every position, 20 sample measurements are taken; the average is stored as the tactile stimulation force at that position to reduce the random noise.

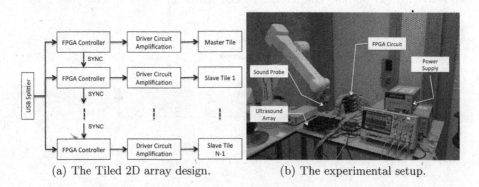

(a) The Tiled 2D array design.   (b) The experimental setup.

Fig. 3. Tile-based Haptogram.

3.2 Maximum Producible Force

The most important characteristic of a haptic device is its ability to produce perceivable forces. In this experiment, the aim is to study how the maximum producible force is affected by an increase in the number of tiles. The robotic arm scans the workspace along the z-axis, starting from an elevation of 20 mm to 350 mm, with a step size of 2 mm. Fourteen (14) focal point stimulations are generated, from an elevation of 40 mm to 300 mm with a step size of 20 mm. For each focal point, for instance (0,0,40 mm), the robotic arm is used to scan the z-axis from 20 mm to 350 mm to measure the acoustic pressure along the z-axis. In total, 14 sets of data are generated where each peak value represents the maximum producible force corresponding to each focal point. The peaks for these data sets are plotted in Fig. 4(a). Similar measurements are made along both the x-axis (from −150 mm to +150 mm) and the y-axis (from −150 mm to +150 mm). The same procedure is performed for the three tile configurations.

Fig. 4(a) shows that as the number of tiles increases, the maximum producible force remains almost the same in terms of amplitude (around 2.73 mN). However the elevation at which the maximum force is produced increases. The maximum forces produced for the one-tile, two-tiles, and four-tiles configurations are found at 76 mm, 120 mm, and 155 mm respectively. The shift in the location of the maximum force is explained by the limited directivity of the transducers. In order for a transducer to contribute to a focal point, the minimum height of the focal point is defined as $h = d \tan \frac{\pi - \theta}{2}$ see Fig. 4(b). In Fig. 4(b), θ is the transducer directivity, d is the distance from the center of the array to transducer, Γ is the focal point location, T is the transducer location, and h is the elevation at which the focal point is formed.

The height at which the furthest transducers contributes are calculated as follows (for the single-tile configuration): $h = \alpha \frac{\sqrt{2}}{2} \tan(50°) = 76$ mm. Similarly, the heights for two tiles are four tiles configurations are 119.0 mm and 151.6 mm. These values are consistent with the experimental results as demonstrated in Figs. 4(a) and 5. As the elevation increases beyond these heights the pressure decreases due to the attenuation of the acoustic waves.

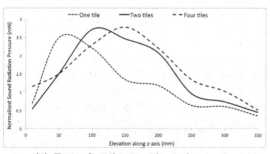

(a) Force distribution along the z-axis.

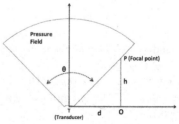

(b) Minimum height for a transducer contribution.

Fig. 4. Acoustic pressure field.

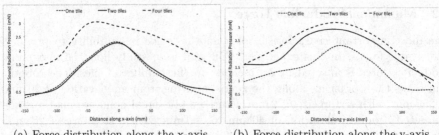

(a) Force distribution along the x-axis.   (b) Force distribution along the y-axis.

Fig. 5. Acoustic pressure field along xy-plane.

Figure 5(a) shows the force distribution along the x-axis and Fig. 5(b) shows the force distribution along the y-axis. These graphs are utilized to derive the effective workspace for the various configurations. For instance, along the x-axis it is clear that the workspace for the one-tile is almost the same as the workspace for the two-tiles configuration since the two-tiles configuration is aligned along the y-axis (workspace of around 100 mm). Table 1 shows the maximum producible forces for each configuration. It is clear that as the number of tiles increase, the maximum producible force remains almost the same. This is justifiable due to the fact that as the number of tiles increases, further transducers would have less contribution due to limited directivity of the transducers.

Table 1. Maximum producible forces for three tile configurations.

	Single-tile	Two-tiles	Four-tiles
Dimensions (transducers)	10×10	10×20	20×20
Maximum Forces (mN)	2.49	2.52	2.55

3.3   Workspace

One of the key characteristics in any haptic device which limits its applicability as a haptic display is the achievable workspace. In order to quantify the tile-based workspace, the robotic arm scanned a volume of $300 \times 300 \times 300$ mm³ on top of the array with a step size of 1 mm³ to measure the effective workspace. For each measurement point, the Haptogram is instructed to generate a focal point at the measurement point, then 20 readings are made and the average value is recorded.

Since a wide variety of parameters could influence stimulus detection at the palm (such as duration, frequency, temporal modulation), we defined the workspace based on the amplitude threshold of the generated force. The detectability of a stimulus is defined as the threshold value above which observers can detect the stimulus more than 50 % of its occurrences. A pilot study is conducted with the experimental setup where the threshold is found to be 2 mN. Therefore, if the average force generated at this measurement point is higher than 2.0 mN, the measurement is plotted onto the workspace graph with a color code proportional to the corresponding intensity.

Figure 6 show the generated graphs of the workspace for the three tile configurations. First of all, we observe that the workspace is symmetrical around the three orthogonal axes, with a workspace in the form of a skewed ellipsoid. Secondly, the workspace volume is increasing linearly as the number of tiles increase. Finally, even though the maximum producible forces remained constant across the three configurations, the workspace volume is elevated along the z-axis as the number of tiles increase. It is clear from Fig. 6 that the center of the workspace is elevated from 76 mm for one-tile configuration to 120 mm for 2-tiles configuration to 155 mm for the 4-tiles configuration. These results are explicitly shown in Table 2. This is mainly due to the fact that the transducers can better reach and contribute to focal point located at higher elevations due to the limited directivity.

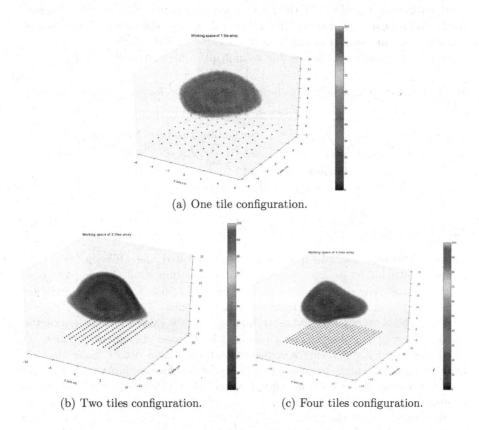

(a) One tile configuration.

(b) Two tiles configuration.   (c) Four tiles configuration.

Fig. 6. Workspace for three tile configurations.

Table 2. Workspace volume for the three configurations.

	Single-tile	Two-tiles	Four-tiles
Number of transducers	10×10	10×20	20×20
Workspace (mm^3)	$110 \times 110 \times 110$	$110 \times 220 \times 180$	$250 \times 270 \times 180$
Workspace center (mm)	(0,0,76)	(0,0,120)	(0,0,155)

3.4   Stimulation Robustness

Another interesting characteristic is the stimulation robustness. The stimulation robustness is defined as the ability of the Haptogram system to display consistently the forces it is instructed to display. To evaluate stimulation robustness, the average and standard deviation of the forces generated within the device workspace are measured (shown in Table 3) for several trials of tactile stimulation. Results show that as the number of tiles increases, the average forces remain almost the same. However, the standard deviation for the generated forces increases as the number of tiles increase. This implies that as the number of tiles increases, the ability of the Haptogram system to reproduce forces consistently and robustly decreases. This is probably due to the increased ultrasound radiation (as the number of transducers increase), which results in a noticeable increase in the ultrasonic noises due to multiple reflections and interference.

Table 3. Average and standard deviation of tactile forces for the three tile configurations.

	Single-tile	Two-tiles	Four-tiles
Average (mN)	2.36	2.26	2.12
Standard Deviation (mN)	0.13	0.26	0.43

3.5   Discussion

The experimental analysis has clearly demonstrated the ability of airborne acoustic radiation to generate perceivable tactile stimulation. The one-tile configuration was able to generate an average force of 2.36 mN (standard deviation of 0.13 mN), over an elevation range of 8 cm to 15 cm.

The airborne acoustic radiation technology has several advantages as a tactile display. First of all, the temporal bandwidth is broad enough to produce 3D tactile feelings by generating a sequence of tactile focal points and switching between them at a high frequency (1.63 KHz for 200 focal points configuration). Secondly, the spatial resolution is good enough (5 mm diameter of a focal point) to produce various 2D and 3D shapes, as reported in a previous study about tactile stimulation at the palm [1].

Even though the maximum producible force marginally increases as the number of tiles increases, the elevation at which these maxima are generated increases

(76 mm for one-tile, 120 mm for 2-tiles, and 150 mm for 4-tiles). This implies that for certain applications where point-based or 2D stimulation is desirable (such as displaying a virtual typing pad), an increase in the number of tiles would shift higher the ideal elevation for tactile stimulation. In case of 3D tactile stimulation, this is less important since any focal point within the stimulation workspace is palpable.

The display workspace increases along the xy-plane almost linearly as the number of tiles increase. However the center of the workspace is shifted higher as the number of tiles increase. This raises a question of whether the utilized transducers are best suited for this kind of application or whether a novel design must be considered to improve the quality of tactile stimulation. The power consumption for the whole tiled system is another factor that must be considered, particularly if applications with mobile devices are to be pondered on.

As for the workspace resolution, the Haptogram system is capable of producing high number of focal points and is thus capable of presenting high-resolution 3D tactile objects. For instance, the single tile configuration is capable of producing a maximum of 10,648 focal points within a workspace of $110 \times 110 \times 110$ mm^3, where the dimensions of one focal point are $5 \times 5 \times 5$ mm^3. As for the two tiles and four tiles configurations, the total number of focal points is 34,848 and 97,200 respectively.

4   Conclusion

In this paper, we presented a study to characterize the airborne ultrasound technology as a tactile display using the Haptogram system. A performance analysis is presented to measure the impact of increasing the number of transducers on the maximum producible forces, the display workspace, the workspace resolution, and stimulation robustness. As a result, it is confirmed that an increase in the number of transducers: (1) does not noticeably increase the maximum producible force but shifts it higher, (2) stretches workspace along the xy-directions, and shift the center of the workspace higher along the z-axis, (3) significantly increases the spatial resolution of the tactile display, and (4) decreases the stimulation robustness.

References

1. Bickley, L., Szilagui, P.: Bates' Guide to Physical Examination and History Taking, 9th edn. Lippincott Williams and Wilkins, Philadelphia (2007)
2. Carter, T., Seah, S., Long, B., Drinkwater, B., Subramanian, S.: Ultrahaptics: multi-point mid-air haptic feedback for touch surfaces. In: 26th Annual ACM Symposium on User Interface Software and Technology, pp. 505–514 (2013)
3. Ciglar, M.: An ultrasound based instrument generating audible and tactile sound. In: Conference on New Interfaces for Musical Expression (NIME 2010), pp. 10–22 (2010)
4. Dalecki, D., Child, S., Raeman, C., Carstensen, E.: Tactile perception of ultrasound. J. Acoust. Soc. Am. **97**, 3165–3170 (1995)

5. Ebbini, E., Cain, C.: Multiple-focus ultrasound phased-array pattern synthesis: optimal driving-signal distributions for hyperthermia. IEEE Trans. Ultrason. Ferroelectr. Freq. Control **36**, 540–548 (1989)
6. Eid, M.: Haptogram: aerial display of 3D vibrotactile sensation. In: IEEE International Conference on Multimedia and Expo Workshops, pp. 1–5 (2014)
7. Gavrilov, L.: The possibility of generating focal regions of complex configurations in application to the problems of stimulation of human receptor structures by focused ultrasound. Acoust. Phys. **54**, 269–278 (2008)
8. Hasegawa, K., Shinoda, H.: Aerial display of vibrotactile sensation with high spatial-temporal resolution using large-aperture airborne ultrasound phased array. In: World Haptics Conference, vol. 2013, pp. 31–36 (2013)
9. Hoshi, T.: Development of aerial-input and aerial-tactile-feedback system. In: IEEE World Haptics Conference, pp. 569–573 (2011)
10. Hoshi, T., Abe, D., Shinoda, H.: Adding tactile reaction to hologram. In: IEEE International Symposium on Robot and Human Interactive Communication, pp. 7–11 (2009)
11. Hoshi, T., Iwamoto, T., Shinoda, H.: Non-contact tactile sensation synthesized by ultrasound transducers. In: Third Joint Symposium on Haptic Interfaces for Virtual Environment and Teleoperator Systems, pp. 256–260 (2009)
12. Hoshi, T., Takahashi, M., Iwamoto, T., Shinoda, H.: Noncontact tactile display based on radiation pressure of airborne ultrasound. IEEE Trans. Haptics **3**, 155–165 (2010)
13. Inoue, S., Makino, Y., Shinoda, H.: Active touch perception produced by airborne ultrasonic haptic hologram. In: IEEE World Haptics Conference (WHC), pp. 362–367 (2015)
14. Iwamoto, T., Shinoda, H.: Two-dimensional scanning tactile display using ultrasound radiation pressure. In: IEEE Proceedings of HAPTICS, vol. 46, pp. 57–61 (2006)
15. Iwamoto, T., Tatezono, M., Hoshi, T., Shinoda, H.: Airborne ultrasound tactile display. In: 35th International Conference and Exhibition on Computer Graphics and Interactive Techniques, p. 1 (2008)
16. Iwamoto, T., Tatezono, M., Shinoda, H.: Non-contact method for producing tactile sensation using airborne ultrasound. In: Ferre, M. (ed.) EuroHaptics 2008. LNCS, vol. 5024, pp. 504–513. Springer, Heidelberg (2008)
17. Long, B., Seah, S., Carter, T., Subramanian, S.: Rendering volumetric haptic shapes in mid-air using ultrasound. ACM Trans. Graph. **33**(6), 181 (2014)
18. Masy, S., Tangen, T., Standal, Ø., Deibele, J., Nasholm, S., Hansen, R., Angelsen, B., Johansen, T.: Nonlinear propagation acoustics of dual-frequency wide-bandexcitation pulses in a focused ultrasound system. J. Acoust. Soc. Am. **128**(5), 2695–2703 (2010)
19. Nishino, H., Goto, R., Kagawa, T., Yoshida, K., Utsumiya, K., Hirooka, J., Osada, T., Nagatomo, N., Aoki, E.: Design with tactile feedback. In: International Conference on Complex, Intelligent and Software Intensive Systems, pp. 53–60 (2011)
20. Ochiai, Y., Hoshi, T., Rekimoto, J.: Pixie dust: graphics generated by levitated and animated objects in computational acoustic-potential field. ACM Trans. Graph. **33**, 85 (2014)
21. Shiokawa, Y., Tazo, A., Konyo, M., Maeno, T.: Hybrid display of realistic tactile sense using ultrasonic vibrator and force display. In: IEEE/RSJ International Conference on Intelligent Robots and Systems, pp. 3008–3013 (2008)
22. Takahashi, M., Shinoda, H.: Large aperture airborne ultrasound tactile display using distributed array units. In: SICE Annual Conference, pp. 359–362 (2010)

23. Yoshino, K., Shinoda, H.: Visio-acoustic screen for contactless touch interface with tactile sensation. In: World Haptics Conference (WHC), pp. 419–423 (2013)
24. Yoshino, K., Shinoda, H.: Contactless touch interface supporting blind touch interaction by aerial tactile stimulation. In: Haptics Symposium (HAPTICS), pp. 347–350 (2014)

Pneumatic Feedback for Wearable Lower Limb Exoskeletons Further Explored

Heidi Muijzer-Witteveen[1](✉), Francisco Guerra[1], Victor Sluiter[1],
and Herman van der Kooij[1,2]

[1] Department of Biomechanical Engineering,
MIRA Institute of Biomedical Technology and Technical Medicine,
University of Twente, Enschede, The Netherlands
h.j.b.witteveen@utwente.nl
[2] Department of Biomechatronics and Human-Machine Control,
Institute of Mechanical, Maritime and Materials Engineering,
Delft University of Technology, Delft, The Netherlands

Abstract. For optimal control of wearable lower limb exoskeletons the sensory information flow should also be (partly) restored, especially when the users are Spinal Cord Injury subjects. Several methods, like electrotactile or electromechanical vibrotactile stimulation, to provide artificial sensory feedback have been studied thoroughly and showed promising results. Pneumatic tactile stimulation might be an alternative to these methods, because the stimulation amplitudes can be larger and in cases of force feedback, the modality of stimulation and sensing can be matched. In this study we have developed a setup that can provide pneumatic feedback with four feedback levels via three stimulation modalities: (1) amplitude modulation, (2) position modulation and (3) frequency modulation. The differences in subject stimulus perception between these three stimulation modalities were evaluated through a magnitude estimation task performed with 10 healthy subjects. Percentages correctly identified feedback levels were significantly higher for frequency modulation than the other two stimulation modalities. Also through questionnaires the subjects indicated that feedback through frequency modulation was the most intuitive and the only method where addition of an extra feedback level was indicated as possible. The results of this study show that pneumatic feedback is feasible, can provide high percentages of feedback level discrimination that are at least comparable to vibrotactile stimulation and therefore encourages further research to optimize the pneumatic setup.

Keywords: Pneumatic feedback · Wearable exoskeleton · Stimulus modulation

1 Introduction

In recent years, a large number of developments has been presented in the field of wearable lower limb exoskeletons. Despite the progress made, the exoskeletons still cannot provide a natural walking pattern and patients depend on crutches for balance. It is hypothesized that the lack of providing sensory information from the exoskeleton to the user could be one of the reasons for this latter shortcoming of the current

© Springer International Publishing Switzerland 2016
F. Bello et al. (Eds.): EuroHaptics 2016, Part I, LNCS 9774, pp. 90–98, 2016.
DOI: 10.1007/978-3-319-42321-0_9

exoskeletons. Furthermore, for Spinal Cord Injury users, also sensory information coming from below the level of the lesion is missing.

Sensory information that is used for human balancing normally comes from three sources: (1) the visual system, (2) the vestibular system and (3) the proprioceptive and exteroceptive system of the lower limbs. The latter source is disturbed in the case of SCI, which increases the burden on the other two sources. The consequence of loss of the proprioceptive and exteroceptive information on balancing is not really clear, but it seems to have a significant effect especially when the surface below the feet changes [1].

Providing artificial sensory feedback can possibly help to (partially) restore the original sensory information flow. It is hypothesized that besides improving balancing, the user will also be more in control, because more information about the behavior of the exoskeleton is provided. Hence, this can eventually increase the embodiment of the exoskeleton and increase the acceptance of the exoskeleton by the user.

One of the most commonly used methods to provide artificial sensory feedback is through vibrotactile stimulation. This method has been used in several studies already for applications in upper limb prostheses [2–6], but also for patients with vestibular deficits to restore their balance [7–9]. Advantages of vibrotactile stimulation are its non-invasive and comfortable application.

However, the amplitude of stimulation and the resulting deflection of the skin is limited for most vibration motors that are commonly used for this application. For the most often used and commercially available C2 tactor (Engineering Acoustics, Inc., Casselberry, Florida, US), the deflection is less than 1 mm. These small stimulation amplitudes may result in less perceivable stimuli, especially when amplitude modulation is used to transfer changing sensory information to the user of the system.

Alternatively, higher stimulation amplitudes can probably be reached through pneumatic stimulation via small balloons that are placed on the skin, providing pressure stimuli to the user. When sensory information that is related to pressure, like ground contact, will be fed back via pressure stimuli, this might be more intuitive compared to vibrotactile feedback as it is modality-matched [10, 11].

There are some examples of the use of pneumatic feedback available for application in lower-limb prostheses [12], balance prostheses [13] and even for wearable exoskeletons [14], but their working principles are not well described, very small actuators are used and no comparison between different control options has been made so far.

In this study we have developed a pneumatic setup with balloon actuators that are comparable in size to the standard vibrotactile C2 tactors. Three different modulation techniques have been compared for differentiation of four different feedback levels. Stimulation was applied at the shoulder region to take into account the possible application for SCI patients, but tested on 10 healthy subjects.

2 Methods

2.1 Development of the Setup

Actuator balloons were made of a PDMS (polydimethylsiloxane) cylindrical housing covered by a 2 mm layer of spin coating silicone (Dragon Skin® high performance

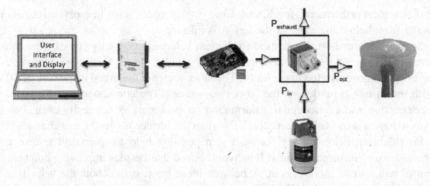

Fig. 1. Overview of the pneumatic setup (from right to left): the silicon balloon actuator that is filled with air coming from a portable tank with pressurized air and its pressure is regulated via a controlled valve. An mbed device is used to allow fast control of the pressure and is controlled via a NI-USB DAQ device, which in turn is controlled by a Labview interface running on a laptop.

silicone rubber). The outer diameter of the balloons is 35 mm and the thickness 18 mm (see Fig. 1), which makes them comparable in size to the C2 tactors (30 mm in diameter, but thickness of only 7 mm). Silicon was chosen because of its large flexibility (large deflections possible) and long-lasting characteristics (withstands many load-cycles).

The air supply was provided through a small air tank with an outlet pressure regulator. The outlet pressure was adjusted (between 1–1.4 bar) for each setup. A MATRIX 750 series air valve with 4 3-3 type valves was used to control the airflow to the actuators with a response time of 5 ms.

For the control of the pressure in the balloons (more precisely the pressure in the outlet tube) a pressure sensor (MPXV5050GP) was incorporated in the setup.

The regulation of the valves, opening and closing, was controlled via a NI DAQ device (NI USB-6218) in combination with Labview 2014 running on a laptop. An embedded platform (ARM mbed FRDM KL25Z) was used for the fast control of the device, which is needed for the stable control of the pressure. See Fig. 1 for a complete overview of the pneumatic setup.

2.2   Stimulation Modulation

Three modulation techniques for pneumatic stimulation, all capable of providing 4 feedback levels, were applied: (1) position modulation, (2) amplitude modulation and (3) frequency modulation. For the first feedback level, the zero level, there is no actuation at all and this is the same for all three modulation techniques. For position modulation three smaller (2.5 cm diameter) balloons were used. For each increase in feedback level, an extra balloon is inflated. So, for level 4 all three balloons are inflated. The level of inflation was kept the same for each balloon, for each feedback level and such that the stimulus was well perceivable, but not maximal. For amplitude modulation the pressure in the balloon is regulated. The maximum pressure that did not cause any membrane tearing during a long period of inflated state was empirically determined to be 0.55 bar and was set for the fourth feedback level. For the other two feedback levels the pressure was set to 0.27 and 0.41 bar. For frequency modulation the time between two periods of inflation was varied. The period of inflation was kept constant for each feedback level at 50 ms. The interval between inflation was 250 ms, 125 ms and 62.5 ms for feedback levels 2, 3 and 4 respectively, which corresponds to frequencies of 3.3 to 8.9 Hz.

2.3   Comparison of the Three Modulation Techniques

10 healthy subjects (students) participated in this study. They were all male subjects who could easily fit the neoprene adjustable chest vest. The balloon actuators were attached with Velcro strips to the interior of the vest and placed directly on the skin of the subjects. For the amplitude and frequency modulation, the exact placement of the actuator at the front side of the shoulder region was selected by searching for the most comfortable location for the subject. For the position modulation the distance between the actuators was at least 4 cm to ensure that the subjects could discriminate between the different stimuli (checked before the start of the experiment and adjusted if necessary).

Subjects were seated behind a desk in a quiet room and wore headphones to cancel out the noise of the valves. To further reduce any auditory clues coming from the valves, a box with isolating foam was placed over the valve setup.

Psychophysical Tests. A basic psychophysical test of magnitude estimation was used to investigate possible differences in stimulus perception between the three modulation techniques. Subjects were asked to indicate the perceived level of the stimulus. The feedback levels were fixed (4 levels including the zero level with no stimulation) and the subjects had to select one of these levels. This is contradictory to the standard method of magnitude estimation where a free scale is used, but in this way we could determine the percentages of correctly identified stimuli.

We did not follow a forced-choice protocol in which a pair of stimuli is presented directly after each other and the subjects have to indicate the stronger stimulus, because this is not representative for the daily situation in which the feedback will be used. However, a stimulus will always be related to the perception of the previous stimulus. Therefore, it was ensured during the tests that each possible transition in feedback levels was present and repeated 5 times. For 4 feedback levels this means that 61 stimuli were provided per modulation technique and thus 183 in total per subject.

Before starting the real tests, subjects were given some time to get familiar with the different feedback levels. They were sitting behind the measurement laptop and by selecting one of the feedback levels, stimulation was provided. The participants were allowed to receive a stimulus as long and often as necessary to get comfortable with the perception of the different levels.

During the tests, the subjects were seated behind the measurement laptop and by pressing "start" the first stimulus was applied. Subjects were instructed to select the perceived feedback level on the computer screen and press the 'confirm' button, after which the next stimulus was presented. This procedure was followed for all three modulation techniques. The order in which the modulation techniques were presented, was randomized between the subjects.

Questionnaire. After finishing the test for each modulation technique, a short questionnaire was presented to the subjects to gather information on their experience with the used modulation technique. The questionnaire consisted of two VAS scales to determine the perceived comfort and intuitiveness. The scale ranges from 'not comfortable at all' or 'not intuitive at all' to 'very comfortable' or 'very intuitive'. Furthermore it was asked whether the subjects thought it would be possible to add another feedback level. This last question could only be answered by yes or no.

Data Analysis. The percentage correctly perceived feedback levels, the accuracy, was determined by comparing the presented feedback level and the selected feedback level by the subjects. Furthermore, it was determined whether the subjects could, regardless of the perceived feedback level, identify the increase or decrease in feedback level (comparable to selecting whether a stimulus was stronger or not in the case of a forced choice procedure). The percentage correctly identified transitions in feedback levels was calculated for each subject for each modulation technique.

Means and standard deviations per modulation technique for both outcome parameters were calculated for the whole group of subjects. A repeated measures ANOVA was used to determine, with a significance level of $p = 0.05$, whether there is a difference between the modulation techniques for both outcome parameters and afterwards a Bonferroni corrected post-hoc test was performed to determine the actual differences between the modulation techniques.

The marked positions on the VAS scales were converted to values between 0 and 10, means and standard deviations were calculated for all three modulation techniques and also for those two parameters an ANOVA test was performed. For the other question the total number of yes and no responses was determined for each modulation technique.

3   Results

In the figures below (Fig. 2) the percentages correctly identified feedback levels and the percentages correctly identified feedback level transitions are shown. ANOVA analysis showed that there is a significant difference between the three feedback modalities for both outcome parameters (the mean accuracy and the mean transition accuracy), with p-values of < 0.001 and 0.002 respectively. Bonferroni corrected post-hoc analysis revealed that frequency modulation resulted in higher accuracies compared to the other two modalities (p-values between < 0.001 and 0.008 for all comparisons and both outcome parameters). No significant differences were found between amplitude and position modulation for both outcome parameters.

The perceived comfort and intuitiveness of the three modulation techniques are presented in the next figure (Fig. 3). For both outcome parameters a significant effect of the modulation technique was found ($p < 0.001$). For the perceived comfort, the amplitude modulation was rated as the most comfortable ($p = 0.001$ compared to

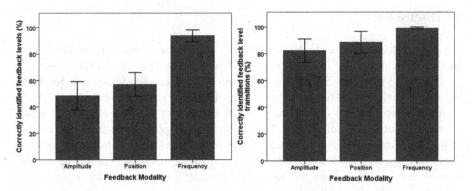

Fig. 2. Percentages correctly identified feedback levels (left chart) and percentages correctly identified feedback level transitions (right chart) for all three feedback modalities. Mean values and standard deviations are given.

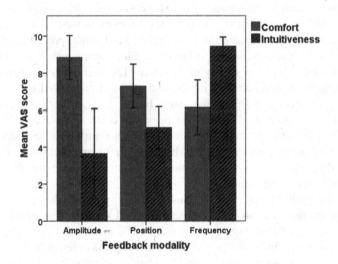

Fig. 3. Mean and standard deviations of the VAS scores for the perceived comfort and intuitiveness of the three modulation techniques.

position as well as to frequency modulation), while no differences in perceived comfort were found between position and frequency modulation. The perceived intuitiveness was rated highest for the frequency modulation ($p < 0.001$ compared to amplitude as well as to position modulation) and no differences between amplitude and position modulation were found.

For both amplitude and position modulation all ten subjects indicated that they believed it is not possible to add another (fourth) feedback level, while for frequency modulation 9 out of the 10 subjects though it would be possible to add an extra level.

4 Discussion

The goal of this study was to develop and test a pneumatic setup that can be used to provide artificial sensory feedback to users of a wearable lower limb exoskeleton.

One of the reasons to investigate pneumatic feedback, while vibrotactile feedback has shown already good results for several applications, was that pneumatic feedback could be more intuitive due to the modality-matching that can be achieved when providing feedback about pressure. Furthermore, the amplitude of stimulation can be larger than with vibrotactile feedback, which would provide more distinctive stimuli. These two aspects have not been addressed explicitly in this study, but will be studied in more detail in future work. In this study a first step towards a pneumatic setup that can compete with the existing feedback methods has been made.

The psychophysical comparison that was made between the three feedback modulation techniques clearly revealed that frequency modulation outperformed amplitude and position modulation in this study. Especially when looking at the percentages correctly identified feedback levels, the performance with frequency modulation was high with an average of almost 94 %.

To be able to compare the results of our study with some other work on pneumatic feedback, the percentages correctly identified level transitions were also calculated. The protocol is not completely the same as used for the forced-choice procedure, but in both cases it can be determined how well subjects can discriminate between an increase or decrease in feedback level. In a study of Fan et al. [12] level transitions between three feedback levels (0, 40 and 100 % of inflation) could be discriminated successfully in a forced choice protocol in 94 % of the cases. In our study, transitions between four feedback levels (pressure amplitudes) were perceived correctly on average in 83 % of the cases. These lower values might be due to the higher number of feedback levels or the more efficient setup used by Fan et al. In our setup the maximal pressure level was empirically determined by trying to avoid tearing of the silicon membrane, which might be optimized in the future.

In the same study by Fan et al. [12] and also in a study by McKinney et al. [15], balloon actuators placed around the leg were used and subjects were asked to identify which balloon was inflated. Subjects succeeded in 95 and 99 % of the cases, respectively, for 4 balloons. This position modulation technique is different from the one used in our study, where balloons were inflated in a cumulative way instead of one by one. Cumulative position modulation was also investigated in the same study of McKinney where they found a performance of 62 %, which is comparable to the 57 % we found in our study. It might be worth looking into position modulation with sequential stimulation for future applications, although the number of actuators is larger compared to amplitude or frequency modulation, which will be more cumbersome for the users.

Frequency or pulse width modulation has, as far as we know, not been described for other studies with pneumatic feedback before. An advantage of using frequency modulation over amplitude modulation would be that the effect of adaptation due to prolonged continuous stimulation will be less or delayed, as was already shown for electrocutaneous stimulation [16]. The main disadvantage of the use of frequency modulation is the inevitable delay that is caused by the time between the two stimuli.

In case of the lowest feedback level, the time between two stimuli was 250 ms, which is the minimum time required by the subject to be able to determine the feedback level. These response times might be a bit larger than the minimum delay between sensing and actuation that can be detected by a subject [17], but is comparable to the reaction times of subjects provided with vibrotactile stimulation [18]. Reduction of the time between stimuli would be one of the first things to improve in a future setup.

From this study it is clear that frequency modulation is superior over amplitude and position modulation for pneumatic feedback. Such a direct comparison between different modulation techniques has not been reported for pneumatic feedback before. For vibrotactile stimulation some more comparisons have been made between different modulation techniques, especially for applications in upper-limb prosthetics. In a study of Stepp and Matsuoka [5] a comparison was made between amplitude and pulse-width modulation and they found a clear preference for amplitude modulation and concluded that this is likely due to the fact that amplitude modulation was more intuitively related to the application they tested, namely feedback about grasping force. Other studies did not show major differences between modulation techniques for vibrotactile stimulation, even when the feedback was modality-matched by relating position modulation to feedback about hand aperture and amplitude modulation to grasping force feedback [6].

In a study of Patterson and Katz [11], a comparison between vibrotactile and pressure (cuff) feedback was made, which showed that pressure feedback scored better, which they related to a more modality-matched application. Based on this latter study and the results of our study, we think that it is worthwhile to further investigate and optimize the pneumatic feedback setup to make it suitable for the application of artificial sensory feedback for users of a wearable lower-limb exoskeleton.

Acknowledgments. This work is part of the SYMBITRON project, supported by EU research program FP7-ICT-2013-10 (contract #611626) and coordinated by the University of Twente.

References

1. Horak, F., Nashner, L., Diener, H.: Postural strategies associated with somatosensory and vestibular loss. Exp. Brain Res. **82**, 167–177 (1990)
2. D'Alonzo, M., Cipriani, C., Carrozza, M.C.: Vibrotactile sensory substitution in multi-fingered hand prostheses: evaluation studies. In: IEEE International Conference on Rehabilitation Robotics (ICORR), pp. 1–6 (2011)
3. Saunders, I., Vijayakumar, S.: The role of feed-forward and feedback processes for closed-loop prosthesis control. J. Neuroeng. Rehabil. **8**, 1 (2011)
4. Cipriani, C., D'Alonzo, M., Carrozza, M.C.: A miniature vibrotactile sensory substitution device for multifingered hand prosthetics. IEEE Trans. Biomed. Eng. **59**, 400–408 (2012)
5. Stepp, C.E., Matsuoka, Y.: Vibrotactile sensory substitution for object manipulation: amplitude versus pulse train frequency modulation. IEEE Trans. Neural Syst. Rehabil. Eng. **20**, 31–37 (2012)
6. Witteveen, H.J.B., Rietman, H.S., Veltink, P.H.: Vibrotactile grasping force and hand aperture feedback for myoelectric forearm prosthesis users. Prosthet. Orthot. Int. **39**, 204–212 (2015)

7. Wall III, C.: Application of vibrotactile feedback of body motion to improve rehabilitation in individuals with imbalance. J. Neurol. Phys. Ther. JNPT **34**, 98 (2010)
8. Goodworth, A.D., Wall III, C., Peterka, R.J.: Influence of feedback parameters on performance of a vibrotactile balance prosthesis. IEEE Trans. Neural Syst. Rehabil. Eng. **17**, 397–408 (2009)
9. Kadkade, P.P., Benda, B.J., Schmidt, P.B., Wall III, C.: Vibrotactile display coding for a balance prosthesis. IEEE Trans. Neural Syst. Rehabil. Eng. **11**, 392–399 (2003)
10. Antfolk, C., D'Alonzo, M., Rosen, B., Lundborg, G., Sebelius, F., Cipriani, C.: Sensory feedback in upper limb prosthetics. Expert Rev. Med. Devices **10**, 45–54 (2013)
11. Patterson, P.E., Katz, J.A.: Design and evaluation of a sensory feedback system that provides grasping pressure in a myoelectric hand. J. Rehabil. Res. Dev. **29**, 1–8 (1992)
12. Fan, R.E., Culjat, M.O., King, C.H., Franco, M.L., Boryk, R., Bisley, J.W., et al.: A haptic feedback system for lower-limb prostheses. IEEE Trans. Neural Syst. Rehabil. Eng. **16**, 270–277 (2008)
13. Wu, S.W., Fan, R.E., Wottawa, C.R., Fowler, E.G., Bisley, J.W., Grundfest, W.S., et al.: Torso-based tactile feedback system for patients with balance disorders. In: Haptics Symposium, 2010 IEEE, pp. 359–362 (2010)
14. Yin, Y.H., Fan, Y.J., Xu, L.D.: EMG and EPP-integrated human–machine interface between the paralyzed and rehabilitation exoskeleton. IEEE Trans. Inf. Technol. Biomed. **16**, 542–549 (2012)
15. McKinney, Z., Heberer, K., Nowroozi, B.N., Greenberg, M., Fowler, E., Grundfest, W.: Pilot evaluation of wearable tactile biofeedback system for gait rehabilitation in peripheral neuropathy. In: Haptics Symposium (HAPTICS), 2014 IEEE, pp. 135–140 (2014)
16. Buma, D.G., Buitenweg, J.R., Veltink, P.H.: Intermittent stimulation delays adaptation to electrocutaneous sensory feedback. IEEE Trans. Neural Syst. Rehabil. Eng. **15**, 435–441 (2007)
17. Englehart, K., Hudgins, B.: A robust, real-time control scheme for multifunction myoelectric control. IEEE Trans. Biomed. Eng. **50**, 848–854 (2003)
18. Yu, J., Möeller, K.: Investigating multimodal displays: reaction times to visual and tactile modality stimuli. In: The 15th International Conference on Biomedical Engineering, pp. 480–483 (2014)

Haptics and Motor Control

A Versatile Robotic Haptic Stimulator
to Study the Influence of Pain
on Human Motor Control and Learning

Maxime Jeanneret, Carlo Bagnato[✉], Alessandro Gabriele Allievi,
and Etienne Burdet[✉]

Department of Bioengineering, Imperial College London, London, UK
{carlo.bagnato12,e.burdet}@imperial.ac.uk

Abstract. This paper presents an inexpensive, versatile and easy-to-install robotic haptic stimulator, capable of delivering computer-controlled innocuous and noxious mechanical stimuli. The system can be coupled with robotic interfaces typically employed to investigate human motor control and learning, and synchronized with the acquisition of relevant physiological measures. The design is based on a modified commercial rotative servomotor that actuates a 1-DOF parallel guiding mechanism connected to an end-effector that applies forces against a subject's target body area. The position of the end-effector and the interaction force with the skin, as well as sensor readings of the subject's movements, can be used by a microcontroller to control the stimulator. The results of experiments to test the stimulator's control and subjects' psychophysical responses show that the device provides robust and consistent mechanical stimulation, which elicits perceptual ratings compatible with previous relevant psychophysical studies. The presented system is the first to allow investigating the effects of painful versus innocuous stimulation on human motor control and learning.

Keywords: Pain · Haptic feedback · Motor control and learning

1   Introduction

The haptic sense allows us to physically interact with the external world [8]; it significantly contributes to shape our motor control and has a considerable impact on motor learning [9]. Despite the plethora of haptic interfaces and experiments to investigate the mechanisms behind human motor control and learning [11], to our knowledge no study has addressed the role of nociception in the context of haptic exploration and manipulation. In everyday life, we are frequently subjected to pain during the execution of physical tasks, such as when carrying a heavy piece of furniture. Through pain, we can identify the location and intensity of the noxious contact and change our motor strategy accordingly, e.g. by shifting the hands away from the sharpest edges of the object being moved, in order to minimize injury whilst successfully accomplishing a task.

© Springer International Publishing Switzerland 2016
F. Bello et al. (Eds.): EuroHaptics 2016, Part I, LNCS 9774, pp. 101–110, 2016.
DOI: 10.1007/978-3-319-42321-0_10

Deciphering the strategies that humans adopt when they explore and manipulate noxious versus innocuous objects represents a fascinating and untested topic. It is also important to understand how we approach/retract from a noxious object, and how pain influences motor learning. Such investigations could give us precious insight into the physiological mechanisms of pain and motor control. Additionally, the identification of human motor strategies adopted to minimize injury, whilst accomplishing a noxious task, may inspire us to implement effective predictive or responsive strategies for damage minimization in robots [1].

Addressing these questions requires devices able to elicit computer-controlled noxious or innocuous tactile stimulation, which can be synchronized with robotic interfaces typically utilized to investigate the processes of human motor control and learning. A large number of electromechanical stimulators have been designed to elicit and study pain [2,3,10,12]. However, none of these systems could be used together with a robotic haptic interface and their controller was not designed to compensate for disturbances caused by subjects' movement. Therefore, to study the influence of pain on motor control and learning, we aimed to develop a versatile custom stimulation device that could be coupled with Hi5, a robotic interface to study the control of wrist flexion/extension movements [7].

We further aimed for the device to be inexpensive, easy-to-install, and capable of delivering innocuous or noxious forces in the range of 0 N to 10 N with a resolution minor than 0.1 N, using an interchangeable (i.e. blunt or pointy) end-effector. In addition to sending and receiving data from a robotic interface for the investigation of human movements, the stimulator should also provide robust and consistent mechanical stimulation, which can be synchronized with the acquisition of relevant physiological measures including electromyography (EMG).

This manuscript describes such a haptic stimulator coupled with a robotic interface for the study of motor control and learning. A bespoke system was developed using fused deposition and an elegant mechatronic design enabling us to use inexpensive actuator and sensor. A validation experiment illustrating the accuracy and correct functioning of the robotic haptic stimulator will be further presented. We also conducted a psychophysical study to examine our participants' perceptual ratings in response to innocuous or noxious forces applied at the level of their forearm. The results of this psychophysical study demonstrates that our robotic haptic stimulator can reliably investigate the peripheral and central mechanisms involved in the processing of innocuous and noxious mechanical contacts.

2 Mechatronics Design

2.1 Hardware

The haptic stimulator consists of a 1-DOF parallel guiding mechanism (Fig. 1) with a longitudinal range of motion of 20 mm and a perpendicular displacement of under 5 %. Figure 2 shows a global CAD view of the device. A modified 25 mNm commercial rotative USB-powered servomotor actuates the mechanism.

(a)   (b)

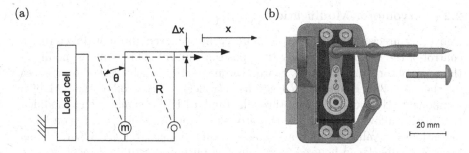

Fig. 1. Hybrid tactile/pain stimulator. (a) Working principle. With a θ rotation, the motor (m) moves the end effector by $x \approx R\theta$. (b) Top view of the haptic stimulator CAD, with the interchangeable end-effector.

As in [2,3,10,12], the stimulation is obtained by pressing the effector against the subject's skin. The device is mounted on a load cell through a single point of contact for continuous resulting force measurement. A pointy or blunt end-effector is interchangeably screwed on the system as shown in Fig. 1b. Pointy tools, shaped as 30° cones with a contact area of $0.1\,\mathrm{mm}^2$, are used to elicit painful sensations whereas blunt tools trigger non-painful tactile sensations.

The safety of the system is guaranteed as the range of motion is mechanically limited. Additional safety measures such as a limit in the effector speed were included, and experimental tests were carried out to ensure the stability of the probe while in contact with the skin, as well as the state machine stability.

The mechanical system was designed using SolidWorks and manufactured via fused deposition of polylactic acid (PLA 3D-printing).

Fig. 2. CAD view of the haptic stimulator and its inner components. Standard aluminium struts are used for the positioning.

2.2   Servomotor Modification

Delivering precise force profiles is more easily achieved through direct torque control of the servomotor rather than position control. This requires modifying the servomotor's driver circuit board. Torque control is achieved by disconnecting the BA 6688 L component (position controller) and controlling the BAL 6686 component (H-Bridge) directly through standard PWM signals. This modification further allows acquiring the actuator's position by reading out the on-board potentiometer value through an analog to digital converter (ADC). Real-time position feedback can be used for monitoring purposes or to implement position control as needed.

3   Control Architecture

A custom designed LabVIEW interface provides and displays the measurements from the haptic stimulator and enables the user to input the desired level of force stimulus. The Hi5 interface communicates with a 16 MHz ATmega32u4-based microcontroller board, which is responsible for the control of the stimulator and the reading of its sensors, via a two-way serial communication protocol using the VISA (Virtual Instrument Software Architecture) LabVIEW standard operating at a sampling rate of 17 ms. The data transfer flowchart is shown in Fig. 3. On the microcontroller, data are sampled at 1 kHz and low-pass filtered for noise reduction. The filtering operation is performed using a digital second order Butterworth filter with a cut-off frequency of 50 Hz. Since the microcontroller sampling frequency is 17 times higher than the frequency of higher-level interface communication, a running average is computed over the most recent 17 values and a single value is provided to the interface. This process contributes to statistical noise reduction, and is carried out for both force and position measurements.

3.1   Force Control

A least square linear fit on the open loop characterization was conducted to identify the conversion factor between the PWM percentage and force delivered,

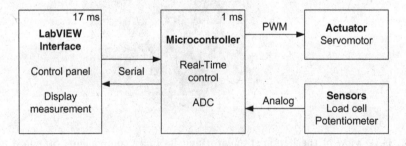

Fig. 3. Data transfer flowchart.

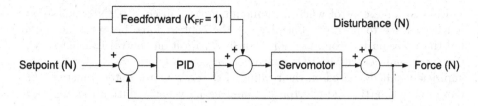

Fig. 4. Block diagram of the PID force controller implemented.

which was calculated as $7.5\%/\text{N}$ (r^2 value: 0.66), and revealed the necessity of closed loop control to compensate for high gear friction. Good performance was obtained by implementing a feedforward controller with proportional-integral-derivative (PID) feedback, presented in Fig. 4. Figure 5 presents 4 different step responses of the controlled system, using the gains $K_p = 12\,\text{N/N}$, $K_i = 30\,\text{N/N/s}$ and $K_d = 0.2\,\text{N\,s/N}$ (empirically tuned).

3.2 Position Control

Force control is exclusively used when the end-effector is in contact with the skin, since during the non-contact phase, the absence of force reading within the force feedback loop would cause the system to undergo a rapid velocity escalation. Therefore, position control is required to softly bridge the contact and non-contact configurations. A state machine controls the switching from

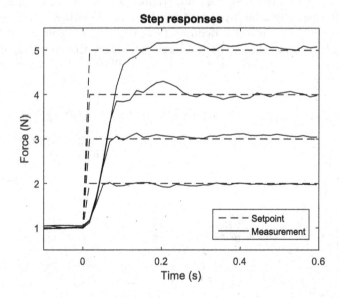

Fig. 5. Step responses of the haptic stimulator when force controlled using the aforementioned gains. The step responses were carried out from $F = 1\,\text{N}$ to ensure that the end-effector was in contact with the subject's skin from the start of recording. For the unitary step response, a 40 ms rise time and 50 ms settling time is observed.

position to force control when a minimum contact force of 0.2 N is measured, and from force to position control when the contact force between the probe and the body part becomes minor than 0.1 N. Position control is achieved via a proportional-derivative (PD) controller ($K_p = 2\,\mathrm{N/mm}$, $K_d = 0.1\,\mathrm{N\,s/mm}$, empirically tuned), based on the reading of the servomotor potentiometer. This allows retracting the end-effector and limiting its velocity during the approach phase to 20 mm/s.

4   Validation

Two aspects of the haptic stimulator were validated: (i) the technical performance of the controller and (ii) the psychophysical responses to the resulting stimulation.

4.1   Technical Performance

The stimulator performance was assessed during a 10 s experiment, run 10 times (Fig. 6). The approach phase can be observed from $t = 0.5\,\mathrm{s}$ to $t = 1.5\,\mathrm{s}$ in Fig. 6b. Force control is then automatically switched on as contact is detected. At $t = 2\,\mathrm{s}$ (Fig. 6a), the desired force is set to 2 N through a rapid step increase and, at $t = 3\,\mathrm{s}$, set back to 1 N, with a $-2\,\mathrm{N/s}$ ramp. The step increase and the ramp are executed with a root mean square error of 0.10 N. At $t = 4\,\mathrm{s}$ (Fig. 6b), a 10 mm step disturbance is intentionally applied against the end-effector; similarly a 10 mm peak-to-peak 1 Hz oscillatory disturbance is applied at $t = 6.5\,\mathrm{s}$. Without force control, these disturbances would have resulted in either loss of contact or in 5 N to 7 N force increases (as deduced from the measurements; skin stiffness is around 0.7 N/mm). Thanks to the force controller, the step disturbance is contained within a range of $\pm 0.2\,\mathrm{N}$ and the oscillatory disturbance within a range of $\pm 0.4\,\mathrm{N}$.

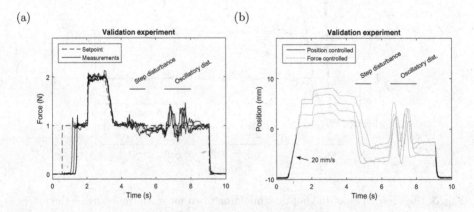

Fig. 6. Four typical measurements of the validation experiment: (a) force setpoint and measurements; (b) position of the end-effector.

4.2   Psychophysical Testing

A total of 18 healthy individuals (aged 26.4 ± 2.9 years, 10 females) participated in a psychophysical test. The subjects gave informed consent to take part in the study, which was approved by the Imperial College Research Ethics Committee. The participants were divided in two groups of 9 subjects (each including 5 females), who were presented with mechanical stimulation at the level of their right posterior forearm by means of either a pointy or a blunt end-effector, according to the group into which they were assigned.

The maximum bearable pain limit was identified by presenting subjects with 10 s constant force levels, starting from 0.5 N and increasing the force test after test. At the end of each test, subjects were asked to report the experimenter whether the force could be increased or not (the force levels would not be increased beyond 3 N to prevent any skin damage). Once the maximum bearable limit was identified, our subjects were asked to refer to the related perception as "level 10" on a 0 to 10 pain scale. Subsequently, three blocks of 5 equally distributed constant forces (between 18 % and 90 % of the force corresponding to "level 10") were applied on the subjects' forearm in a randomized order. After each 10 s stimulus, the subjects were asked to rate the perceived pain from 0 (no pain sensed) to 10 (stimulus as painful as the "level 10" reference).

The same procedure applied for the group whose participants were stimulated by the blunt end-effector. The maximum pressure level (to be referred to as "level 10") was first identified by increasing the forces test after test and making sure that no pain was elicited (for safety reasons, no force levels beyond 5 N were presented). The same psychophysical rating procedure described for the painful condition followed, with our subjects being asked to rate the intensity of the innocuous pressure levels from 0 (no pressure sensed) to 10 (stimulus as intense as the "level 10" reference).

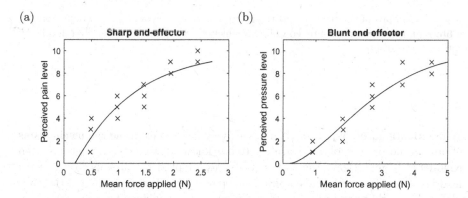

Fig. 7. Set of answers with their fittings, in the two different configurations: (a) eliciting painful sensations; (b) eliciting non-painful tactile sensations.

Figure 7 presents two typical sets of answers. The subjects' answers were consistent and could be fitted using a cumulative Weibull distribution of the form:

$$\text{Perception} = 10 \cdot \left(1 - e^{-\left(\frac{F - F_{\text{offset}}}{\lambda}\right)^k}\right)$$

where F is the force applied on the forearm and λ and k are parameters of the fit. A light $0.2\,\text{N}$ force offset (F_{offset}) was introduced to assign "level 0" to a positive force, so that the stimulator would stay in permanent contact while eliciting sensations ranging from "level 0" to "level 10" during following experiments.

The consistency of the subjects' answers and the quality of the fits can be appreciated from the residuals, i.e. the distance between each answer to its associated point in the fitted curve. Small residual values indicate that a certain force is likely to elicit a similar perception each time that the same force is applied. The boxplots of the residuals of Fig. 8 reveal that the majority of the answers were less than 1 unit of the pain- or pressure-scale apart from the curve.

(a)   (b)

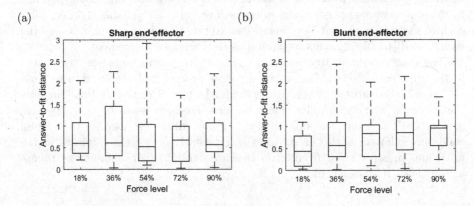

Fig. 8. Residuals of the fits, for: (a) the group stimulated by a pointy end-effector; (b) a blunt end-effector. Each box contains 27 answers (3 stimuli for each force level × 9 subjects per group).

5   Discussion

While robotic interfaces have been extensively used to examine the mechanisms of human motor control and learning, to our knowledge no experiment has been conducted to investigate the motor strategies adopted by humans to deal with noxious tasks. To enable such studies, this paper introduced a novel haptic stimulator device that can apply consistent innocuous or noxious forces and be used conjointly with haptic interfaces for the study of human movements. The system we have designed and implemented consists of a computer-controlled 1-DOF parallel guiding mechanism synchronized with Hi5, a robotic interface to study the control of wrist flexion/extension movements [7]. This system can be used to study how painful versus innocuous feedback provided by the haptic stimulator can affect motor control and learning.

Our robotic haptic stimulator is capable of delivering innocuous or noxious forces in the range of 0 N to 10 N, using an interchangeable (i.e. blunt or pointy) end-effector. Modifications were made to the original servomotor to address the lack of reactivity, precision and stability in delivering forces exhibited by the built-in position controller. Direct torque control of the servomotor proved effective in delivering the haptic stimuli. Over a 10 s dynamic experiment during which the discrepancy between target forces and force measurements was studied, a reasonable root mean square error of 0.10 N could be observed.

Interaction control is based on a state machine switching between position and force control and allowing to softly reach the skin. However, this is achieved within an unpredictable time duration, which is function of the distance that the end-effector has to cover before touching the skin. Combining the haptic stimulator with a contactless distance measurement sensor could overcome this limitation as well as reduce the time required for an effective stimulation. Also, concurrent adaptive control of force, impedance and reference [4,5] may be used to simplify or replace the state machine switching control strategy.

As illustrated in the results of the psychophysical tests, the stability and the small error obtained with the implemented force control permit to elicit consistent perception in response to specific stimuli. In fact, our subjects rated the intensity of a certain stimulus with close perceptual scores at each trial that the same stimulus was presented. Furthermore, the psychophysical values identified for the perception of innocuous pressure and mechanically evoked cutaneous pain are in accordance with those obtained in previous works [6], which indicates that the novel haptic stimulator can be used in psychophysical and physiological experiments.

Remarkably, our solution represents the first haptic stimulator that can be coupled with robotic interfaces typically employed to investigate the processes of human motor control and learning. Additionally, our device can be programmed to deliver any desired force profile; this enables experimenters to test the effect of significant stimulation parameters like peak force magnitude, duration, rise and fall time, and interstimulus interval on the mechanisms of pain and its influence on motor control and learning.

Acknowledgments. This research was supported by the EU-FP7 grants CONTEST (ITN-317488), BALANCE (ICT-601003), SYMBITRON (ICT-661626) and EU-H2020 grant COGIMON (ICT-23-2014).

References

1. Bagnato, C., Takagi, A., Burdet, E.: Artificial nociception and motor responses to pain, for humans and robots. In: 2015 37th Annual International Conference of the IEEE Engineering in Medicine and Biology Society (EMBC), pp. 7402–7405. IEEE, August 2015

2. Baumgärtner, U., Greffrath, W., Treede, R.D.: Contact heat and cold, mechanical, electrical and chemical stimuli to elicit small fiber-evoked potentials: merits and limitations for basic science and clinical use. Clin. Neurophysiol. **42**(5), 267–280 (2012)
3. Cooper, B., Hargens, C.: A stimulator for studies of mechanical nociception based upon a commercially available translation table. J. Neurosci. Methods **47**(3), 199–204 (1993)
4. Ganesh, G., Albu-Schaffer, A., Haruno, M., Kawato, M., Burdet, E.: Biomimetic motor behavior for simultaneous adaptation of force, impedance and trajectory in interaction tasks. In: 2010 IEEE International Conference on Robotics and Automation, pp. 2705–2711. IEEE, May 2010
5. Ganesh, G., Jarrasse, N., Haddadin, S., Albu-Schaeffer, A., Burdet, E.: A versatile biomimetic controller for contact tooling and haptic exploration. In: 2012 IEEE International Conference on Robotics and Automation, pp. 3329–3334. IEEE, May 2012
6. Greenspan, J.D., McGillis, S.L.B.: Stimulus features relevant to the perception of sharpness and mechanically evoked cutaneous pain. Somatosens. Mot. Res. **8**(2), 137–147 (1991)
7. Melendez-Calderon, A., Bagutti, L., Pedrono, B., Burdet, E.: Hi5: a versatile dual-wrist device to study human-human interaction and bimanual control. In: 2011 IEEE/RSJ International Conference on Intelligent Robots and Systems, pp. 2578–2583. IEEE, September 2011
8. Minogue, J., Jones, M.G.: Haptics in education: exploring an untapped sensory modality. Rev. Educ. Res. **76**(3), 317–348 (2006)
9. Rochat, P., Senders, S.J.: Active touch in infancy: action systems in development. In: Infant Attention: Biological Constraints and the Influence of Experience, pp. 412–442 (1991)
10. Schneider, W., Slugg, R., Turnquist, B., Meyer, R., Campbell, J.: An electro-mechanical stimulator system for neurophysiological and psychophysical studies of pain. J. Neurosci. Methods **60**(1–2), 61–68 (1995)
11. Sigrist, R., Rauter, G., Riener, R., Wolf, P.: Augmented visual, auditory, haptic, and multimodal feedback in motor learning: a review. Psychon. Bull. Rev. **20**(1), 21–53 (2013)
12. Slugg, R.M., Meyer, R.A., Campbell, J.N.: Response of cutaneous A- and C-fiber nociceptors in the monkey to controlled-force stimuli. J. Neurophysiol. **83**(4), 2179–2191 (2000)

Weight and Weightlessness Effects on Sensorimotor Performance During Manual Tracking

Bernhard Weber$^{(\boxtimes)}$, Simon Schätzle, Cornelia Riecke,
Bernhard Brunner, Sergey Tarassenko, Jordi Artigas,
Ribin Balachandran, and Alin Albu-Schäffer

German Aerospace Center, Oberpfaffenhofen, Germany
Bernhard.Weber@dlr.de

Abstract. The effects of extra arm weight and weightlessness on sensorimotor performance were investigated in three studies. In all studies, subjects performed two-dimensional tracking tasks with a joystick. Results indicated that extra arm weight did not decrease tracking performance, but decreased acceleration variance. In weightlessness, tracking performance decreased and the control of movement impulses was deteriorated. This result pattern was found during water immersion as well as during spaceflight. The sensorimotor performance losses in weightlessness could be compensated by providing additional haptic cues with the input device.

Keywords: Sensorimotor performance · Weightlessness · Water immersion · Microgravity · Haptic feedback

1 Introduction

For over 15 years, humans have been continually present in space on the International Space Station (ISS), because many missions can only be accomplished by humans. In novel, complex situations human perception, decision-making abilities as well as fine manipulative skills are indispensable and – until now – irreplaceable. Astronauts have to rely on their manipulative skills when working with delicate research equipment, during docking maneuvers or when controlling robotic systems (like the Canadarm). Yet, a large number of studies documented that the precision of motor responses based on sensory input, i.e. the 'sensorimotor performance' is degraded under conditions of weightlessness (see [1] for an overview). Compared to normal gravity conditions, forces are applied less precisely with joysticks [2, 3], aimed arm movements are slower and less accurate [4] and compensatory tracking performance is decreased [5, 6] in weightlessness. These performance decrements have been explained by a distortion of human proprioception [1] and inadequate internal movement models [4].

In weightlessness, anti-gravity stabilization of body and limbs is not necessary. Muscle tone and hence muscle spindle activity is reduced. Limb proprioception and kinesthetic, however, is based on muscle spindle signals [7]. Furthermore, it has been

© Springer International Publishing Switzerland 2016
F. Bello et al. (Eds.): EuroHaptics 2016, Part I, LNCS 9774, pp. 111–121, 2016.
DOI: 10.1007/978-3-319-42321-0_11

discussed that the absence of weight (but not mass) in space leads to an underestimation of hand/arm mass [8]. Consequently, movement impulses are inadequate until the underestimation is noticed and compensated. One potential way to compensate detrimental effects of weightlessness is the provision of additional information about position and kinematics. This can be achieved by haptic feedback. The mechanical properties of a manipulandum (like a joystick) provide different information: in the case of position control, spring stiffness of a joystick provides information about the position (higher resistance equals larger deflection), viscous damping provides information about movement velocity (higher velocity results in higher damping) and similarly inertia (dependent on joystick mass) provides information about acceleration [9]. Indeed, terrestrial studies showed that moderate values of stiffness improve tracking performance [10], damping and inertia help performing smoother movements and attenuate unintended movement impulses during tracking [11]. Yet, for choosing optimal mechanical configuration for weightlessness, we investigated the specific effects of altered arm weight on sensorimotor characteristics like position accuracy and kinematic properties in a novel task paradigm. Furthermore, these effects were explored under terrestrial conditions, under conditions of full body water immersion as well as microgravity during space flight.

We explored the effects of increased and decreased arm weight during a two-dimensional, manual tracking task with a 2-DoF 'isotonic' joystick (allowing free deflection on both axes) as input device. In prior studies [5, 6, 12], researcher used unstable first-order (or rate) control tracking tasks, i.e. subjects had to keep a cursor in a fixed target position by moving a joystick. The task has been denoted as unstable, since the cursor is directed to the periphery by the program and has the tendency to move into the periphery with increasing speed [5]. Thus, unpredictable cursor-target deviations have to be compensated by moving the control device. The cognitive demands of such unstable tracking tasks are relatively high, because the cursor-target deviations have to be perceived and transformed into an appropriate motor response with a first-order transfer function [6, 12]. Using this paradigm, researchers found increased tracking errors in microgravity compared to terrestrial conditions. However, researchers also found evidence that increased workload (unspecific workload and fatigue during space mission [6] as well as secondary task demands [5]) had a negative effect on tracking performance.

We propose a novel tracking task paradigm, with lower cognitive task requirements. Specifically, we suggest a stable, zero-order (or position) control tracking task paradigm, where a target has to be matched along a pre-defined path and with constant speed. Potential changes of kinematics under conditions of changed arm weight should be evident in this task paradigm, but performance should be less dependent on cognitive resources. Moreover, findings with this paradigm are valuable for a wide range of position control tasks (e.g. for telerobotic manipulation) performed with a joystick.

The same tracking experiment was conducted in three different settings: (1) under conditions of normal gravity with vs. without extra arm weight, (2) under conditions of simulated weightlessness induced by water immersion vs. on land, and (3) under conditions of weightlessness in space vs. terrestrial conditions. The motivation of the first study was to investigate the effects of extra arm mass on tracking performance to (a) test the sensitivity of the tracking task paradigm regarding weight changes and

(b) to explore the magnitude and direction of kinematic effects due to additional inertia of the human hand/arm system. We hypothesized that extra weight induces more sluggish movement profiles:

H1: *Movement acceleration is decreased and shows a lower level of variance with extra arm weight compared to normal conditions.*

The subsequent Studies (2 and 3) were devoted to the effects of weightlessness on tracking performance. We chose two different setups: shallow water immersion (5 m depth) and microgravity during spaceflight onboard the ISS. We did this to validate water immersion as a simulation model for microgravity, providing an easy access to experimental data e.g. for future experiments on haptic assistance in weightlessness. Moreover, comparing the result patterns also sheds light on the processes underlying motor deficits in weightlessness. While there is empirical evidence indicating similar sensorimotor effects of degraded proprioception due to weightlessness in both conditions [3], water immersion differs from microgravity in some respects: (1) the effect of water viscosity during joystick deflection, (2) vestibular signals based on the gravito-inertial force is unchanged despite weightlessness, (3) ambient pressure is increased (e.g. 1.5 bar in 5 m depth) compared to normal pressure onboard the ISS (1 bar like on earth). However, it should be noticed that during extravehicular activities (EVAs) the astronaut's suit is also pressurized up to values of 3 bar [13].

Regarding tracking performance we assume negative effects of weightlessness in both settings. In line with prior studies [5, 6] we also assume higher tracking deviations from ideal trajectory in weightlessness, because of the lack of appropriate positional and kinematic cues from the muscles. Besides a larger positional error, we also expect corrective movements to show a higher variance in speed and acceleration due to the proprioceptive deficit.

H2a: *Positional tracking error increases in weightlessness compared to normal conditions.*
H2b: *Kinematic parameters (like speed and acceleration) show a higher level of variance in weightlessness compared to normal conditions.*

Since the differential effects of the water immersion and microgravity setups are not clearly predictable (e.g. ambient pressure in water could degrade performance, availability of vestibular signals should improve it, and laminar flow of water could improve motion regularity while turbulent flow could have other, non-linear effects), the effects will be explored without a formal hypothesis.

In the following Sects. 2, 3 and 4, we will describe the methods and main results of Studies 1, 2 and 3. A synopsis of findings is provided in the last Sect. 5.

2 Study 1: The Effect of Extra Arm Weight

2.1 Methods

Sample. Eight right-handed subjects (two females, six males) with an average age of 30.3 yrs. ranging from 23 to 52 yrs. ($SD = 9.38$) participated in the study.

Fig. 1. Left: experimental GUI; middle: joystick; right: extra weights at arm

Apparatus. The subjects conducted the experiment at a table, sitting on chair. The experimental GUI (see Fig. 1) was displayed on a 21.5 inch monitor connected to a portable computer that controlled the experimental program. A space qualified Joystick developed at the German Aerospace Center ([14], 2 axes, workspace of ±20° in each axis), was connected to the computer and positioned on the table to the right of the subject. Subjects were asked to adjust the chair height so that their right arm could be rested comfortably on the padded armrest of the joystick module. Moreover, for standardization of the arm position on the rest, subjects were told to loosely attach a fixation strap around their right elbow on the armrest (see Fig. 1, middle). The fixation strap allowed movements on both axes without hindering the arm movements at any time. Moreover, movement scaling was doubled, i.e. the complete experimental workspace could be reached with joysticks amplitudes of ±10° on both axes. The angular resolution of the joystick is 0.00318°. Data were recorded with a sampling rate of 50 Hz.

Experimental Tasks and Design. In the experimental GUI, crosshairs were displayed with black lines on a grey background (Fig. 1, left). Each experimental trial had to be started with the cursor positioned exactly in the center of the crosshairs and had to be held for 2 s (indicated by a countdown on the screen). Then, the target ring moved with a constant speed (80 pixels/s) along the vertical or horizontal line. Subjects had to track the target position by moving the cursor with the joystick (zero-order transfer function). In the horizontal tracking task the target moved from the center to the right and left intersection points back to the center. In the vertical task the order was center – upper – lower intersection – center. A full cycle on one axis took 20 s. Prior to each task, the movement axis was indicated by a quick preview of the ring movement. Both tracking tasks had to be completed in random order. Since each participant completed two experimental conditions (with vs. without extra arm weight), we counterbalanced the condition orders.

Procedure. Participants were seated at the experimental workstation and read the instructions displayed on the monitor. In the condition with extra weights, the experimenter attached two 0.5 kg weight cuffs at the right forearm – one near the wrist and one on the middle between wrist and elbow (Fig. 1, right). With both cuffs, the average weight of the human arm (1.02 kg for females and 1.2 kg for males, [15]) was almost doubled. The two experimental conditions (with vs. without extra weight) were started in sequence, interrupted by a short break of 2–3 min. In each condition one experimental block (vertical and horizontal tracking) was performed for training, and then the experiment was started.

Table 1. Performance data without vs. with extra weight; means (SD)

Measure	Unit	No weight	Extra weight	Significance	Effect size
Mean distance	[px]	8.02 (1.05)	8.14 (1.66)	$t = 0.28$; ns.	0.08
Mean speed	[px/s]	0.83 (0.03)	0.84 (0.04)	$t = 0.58$; ns.	0.28
Peak speed	[px/s]	6.11 (1.62)	5.61 (1.68)	$t = 0.66$; ns.	−0.29
SD speed	[px/s]	0.63 (0.09)	0.60 (0.10)	$t = 1.31$; ns.	−0.30
Mean acceleration	[px/s^2]	0.130 (0.01)	0.124 (0.08)	$t = 2.74$; $p < .05$	−0.63
Peak acceleration	[px/s^2]	2.30 (1.22)	2.0 (1.39)	$t = 0.79$; ns.	−0.21
SD acceleration	[px/s^2]	0.139 (0.02)	0.128 (0.02)	$t = 1.50$; $p < .10^a$	−0.52

[a]One-tailed testing

2.2   Results

We analyzed the effects of extra arm weight by performing paired t-tests on the mean distance from target (measured at each time step, in simulation pixel units; each axis measuring 800 px), mean, peak, and standard deviation of speed as well as acceleration[1] during the complete tracking task. Additionally, effect sizes (Hedges' g) were calculated (Table 1).

Paired t-tests revealed no significant effects for the distance variable ($t(7) = .28$; ns.), the speed parameters and the peak acceleration (all ts ≤ 1.31). Yet, the mean acceleration significantly decreased in the extra weight condition ($t = 2.74$; $p < .05$; $g = −.63$), with a similar trend and also a moderate effect size ($g = −.52$) for the SD of acceleration; ($t = 1.5$; $p < .10$, one-tailed testing). Thus, H1 is substantiated. Although subjects maintained tracking performance, movements seemed to be smoother and more sluggish with additional arm weight.

3   Study 2: The Effects of Simulated Weightlessness

3.1   Methods

Sample. In this study $N = 21$ individuals with an average age of $M = 27.8$ yrs. ($SD = 8.0$, range: 21–49 yrs.; 3 females, 18 males; 2 left-handers, 19 right-handers) participated. Except for four individuals, all of them had diving experience (basic diving course). The novices were given a basic theoretical and practical instruction in diving.

Apparatus. An underwater qualified joystick with the same mechanical properties, the same joystick handle and armrest with fixation strap as in Study 1 was used for this study (Fig. 2). Again movement range was restricted to ±10° for each axis. In addition to the conventional version of the joystick, there was a flexible latex gaiter between joystick module and the lower end of the handle, so the module was water proof and at the same time joystick movements were not hindered mechanically. Due to the flexible connection, a pressure regulator was implemented ensuring that the environmental

---

[1] Standard deviation of speed and acceleration across all time steps.

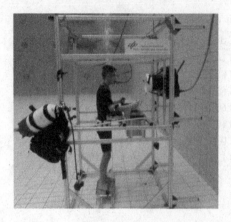 

Fig. 2. Left: underwater setup; right: underwater joystick

pressure and the pressure in the joystick module were identical. Thus, the gaiter did not collapse in the underwater condition (potentially causing friction effects when moving the handle). The joystick and a water proof LCD monitor (15 inch) were installed in an aluminum frame (see Fig. 2, left). Subjects looked on the monitor with a distance of ca. 70 cm. The experiment was conducted in an upright posture, standing on a footrest with a foot strap and an additional holding grip for the left hand. Thus, body stabilization was also ensured for the underwater conditions.

The underwater conditions of the experiment were conducted in a 20 × 20 m pool with 5 m depth, with the frame standing on the bottom of the pool (joystick at 3.6 m depth). Oxygen supply was provided via a hose connected to the compressed air bottle on land. An additional SCUBA jacket with air supply was attached to the frame.

Experimental Task and Design. The participants conducted the identical tracking tasks as in Study 1. Each participant completed a "land" and a "water" condition, while the order of both conditions was counterbalanced across subjects.

Procedure. All participants were instructed regarding the experimental task and procedure on land and underwater. In the underwater condition only, subjects wore 7 mm short sleeved neoprene suits to avoid hypothermia, conventional diving masks (prepared with anti-fog spray) and individually adjusted diving weights to achieve neutral buoyancy. During the whole underwater session, a safety diver was located behind the subject outside the frame. In both the land and the underwater condition, subjects completed an experimental block (vertical and horizontal tracking) for training. In case of any problems they were told to (ascend in the underwater condition and) discuss them with the experimenter before starting the main experiment.

3.2   Results

Again, paired t-tests were performed and effect sizes (Hegdes' g) were computed (Table 2).

Table 2. Performance data on land vs. water; means (SD)

Measure	Unit	Land	Water	Significance	Effect size
Mean distance	[px]	9.73 (1.83)	11.45 (2.39)	$t = 3.73; p < .001$	0.79
Mean speed	[px/s]	0.78 (0.02)	0.80 (0.02)	$t = 3.45; p < .01$	0.98
Peak speed	[px/s]	6.50 (1.53)	7.78 (2.56)	$t = 1.80; p < .10^{a}$	0.60
SD speed	[px/s]	0.71 (0.10)	0.70 (0.08)	$t = 0.26; ns.$	−0.11
Mean acceleration	[px/s^2]	0.17 (0.01)	0.17(0.01)	$t = 0; ns.$	0
Peak acceleration	[px/s^2]	2.58 (1.09)	3.61 (1.52)	$t = 2.35; p < .05$	0.76
SD acceleration	[px/s^2]	0.18 (0.02)	0.20 (0.03)	$t = 1.87; p < .05^{a}$	0.77

[a]One-tailed testing

As hypothesized in H2a, tracking error, i.e. the average distance between cursor and target significantly increased in weightlessness ($t(20) = 3.73$; $p < .001$). Consequently, when trying to maintain target speed during corrective motions, the average and peak speed increased ($t_{M(v)}(20) = 3.45$; $p < .01$; $t_{Peak(v)}(20) = 1.8$; $p < .10$, one-tailed test). However, the movement variance did not change ($t(20) = .26$, $ns.$). Although mean acceleration also did not increase under water ($t(20) = 0$; $ns.$), the opposite was true for peak acceleration ($t(20) = 2.35$; $p < .05$) and SD ($t(20) = 1.87$; $p < .05$; one-tailed testing). Seemingly, acceleration and deceleration impulses were magnified in weightlessness. H2b is only partially corroborated.

4 Study 3: The Effects of Weightlessness in Space

Study 3 was primarily conducted to verify a telerobotic setup, in which a cosmonaut onboard the ISS controlled a robotic system on earth by using the same joystick as in Study 1 [14]. Nevertheless, a physical equivalent of the tracking task was implemented with the same task requirements as the tracking simulation. These data were analyzed for the current work.

4.1 Methods

Sample. The subject of Study 3 was an experienced male cosmonaut (42 years), who participated in his third space mission (with a total of 410 days spent in space). The experiment was conducted on the 45th day after having launched with the Soyuz spacecraft from Baikonur, Kazakhstan.

Apparatus. The experiment was conducted in the Zvezda module of the ISS. The Joystick (same as in Study 1) was installed at a handrail of the module wall. The cosmonaut was working in an upright posture, stabilizing his body with a handle for the left hand and module rails for the feet (see Fig. 3, left). The cosmonaut controlled a two degrees of freedom robot (ROKVISS, [16]), located at the DLR in Oberpfaffen-hofen, with the joystick. At the outermost segment of this robot a 21 cm long metal rod with a ball-shaped end was installed that was used as a pointer during the tracking

Fig. 3. Left: setup onboard the ISS; right: ROKVISS robot and tracking LED screen.

tasks. A camera, right behind the robot focused on a spherical screen with 73 LEDs distributed across four lines (Fig. 3, right). An experimental GUI including the video stream from the robotic site on earth was displayed on a laptop screen onboard the ISS.

Experimental Tasks and Design. As in Studies 1 and 2, tracking tasks were performed. The tracking task was implemented by highlighting the LEDs in sequence, with the same durations for each axis (20 s) as in the former studies. In both tasks, the pointer had to be positioned in the center of the LED star to start the corresponding trial.

Procedure. First, the cosmonaut participated in a terrestrial experiment session, conducted 29 days before launch. The cosmonaut was located at the Gagarin Cosmonaut Training Center (GCTC) in Moscow and remotely controlled the robot at the DLR via Internet. After general instruction by the GCTC, he performed two experimental blocks (each with vertical and horizontal tracking) for training and then one experimental block as main experiment. The same was done in the ISS session under conditions of microgravity (μG).

4.2   Results

First, the communication parameters were analyzed. The average round-trip delay during the ISS sessions was $M = 24$ ms with an average packet loss of 0.35 %. During the terrestrial training sessions conducted via Internet the delay was $M = 65$ ms with packet losses up to 7 % [17]. Please note that worse telecommunication values should theoretically decrease performance in the terrestrial compared to the ISS sessions. The means and the relative changes from 1G to μG are reported in Table 3; robot movement (i.e. rotatory motion) was measured in radian units.

The average distance was more than doubled (+113 %), average speed increased by 19.4 %, peak speed by 130.6 % and SD of speed by 56.3 % in μG compared to the 1G

Table 3. Performance data in 1G and μG conditions; means and relative change

Performance measure	Unit	1G	μG	% Change
Mean distance	[rad]	0.104	0.222	+113.5 %
Mean speed	[rad/s]	0.031	0.037	+19.4 %
Peak speed	[rad/s]	0.258	0.595	+130.6 %
SD speed	[rad/s]	0.032	0.050	+56.3 %
Mean acceleration	[rad/s^2]	0.050	0.049	−2.0 %
Peak acceleration	[rad/s^2]	67.04	71.34	+6.4 %
SD acceleration	[rad/s^2]	5.40	7.57	+40.2 %

session. Furthermore, μG led to higher peak and SD of acceleration (+6.4 and +40.2 %). Obviously, H2a and H2b are confirmed.

5   Discussion

In a series of studies we investigated sensorimotor performance during a novel two-dimensional tracking task performed with a joystick. The main research objective of this empirical work was to better understand how weightlessness alters position accuracy and kinematic characteristics. In a first step, we explored the effects of extra arm weight under terrestrial condition. Here, positional accuracy was not impaired and tracking performance did not change with extra weights. As expected (H1), however, extra arm weight had an effect on the kinematic profile: additional inertia smoothened movements with lower acceleration values and acceleration variation.

Under conditions of weightlessness, we expected decreased positional accuracy (H2a) and more variance in speed and acceleration profiles (H2b) due to degraded proprioception and kinesthetic. Indeed, data for both studies in weightlessness documented a higher average tracking error that had to be compensated with higher average speed to hold the continuously moving target position. Furthermore, weightlessness induced higher acceleration variance. Seemingly, the human capability to trigger adequate movement impulses deteriorates, leading to higher acceleration/deceleration amplitudes. The kinematic changes found during weightlessness with a stable and predictable tracking task are partially in contrast to prior research. In line with the assumption that limb weight is underestimated in microgravity, leading to mis-calibrated movement impulses, researchers documented decreased peak velocity as well as peak acceleration and more sluggish movements [5, 12, 18]. In these studies, using aiming, discrete tracking and unstable tracking tasks, movement paths and speed were not pre-defined like in our task paradigm. Thus, the more unstable kinematic profiles when correcting tracking errors in the current studies might be better explained by distorted proprioception (as reported in studies on force production [3]) and correspondingly inadequate motor programs and not by the weight underestimation approach.

Comparing the underwater and the space experiment revealed congruent findings. Seemingly, the overall effect directions seem to be induced primarily by the weightlessness aspect and resulting proprioceptive distortion. Consistent with prior findings on force production with an isometric joystick [19], shallow water immersion also seems to be a valid analog environment to simulate and estimate the effects of microgravity when using an isotonic, minimal deflection joystick. Noteworthy, the higher average and peak speed during water immersion did not provide any indication that water viscosity might have played a relevant role during the tracking task.

Nevertheless, the effects in both settings are not identical and differ in magnitude. In contrast to the microgravity study, the speed variance is not increased during water immersion. Individuals are able to pursue the target with relatively constant speed. In microgravity, performance degradation effects are stronger and trajectory profiles revealed significant and more uncontrolled deviations, resulting in higher speed variance. The higher effect magnitude in space might be explained by altered vestibular information (absence of a gravito-inertial force), which could also degrade manipulative performance [1, 2].

Conclusion and Outlook. Altogether, the above findings allow thinking about potential solutions of the sensorimotor degradation in weightlessness when performing precise, continuous movements. In the light of Study 1, it is a promising approach to attenuate unintended or exaggerated movement impulses by increasing the inertia of the input device. Force feedback joysticks, e.g. allow adjusting the virtual inertia of the system. Impaired perception of limb position could be compensated by spring stiffness and the reported speed deviations by viscous damping. With an optimally adjusted force feedback joystick, the specific effects of weightlessness could be compensated.

In Study 1, we did not find any significant impairment of the overall tracking performance in terms of mean cursor-target deviations. However, it should be further investigated whether a change of the weight of the hand, but not only the weight of the arm would affect tracking performance.

In future studies, the optimal mechanical parameters for different task requirements (smooth vs. quick; precise vs. large-scale motions) will be investigated in weightlessness. Furthermore the promising results of the current work will be validated with the same simulation paradigm we used for terrestrial experiments (without any network delay and without a teleoperated robot) in microgravity, with additional subjects and with repeated measurements in different mission phases.

Acknowledgements. We want to express our gratitude to Prof. Stefan Schneider, Vanja Zander and Sebastian Dern from the German Sport University in Cologne as well as Jonas Schäffler and Henning Mende from the German Aerospace Center for their excellent support during the underwater study.

References

1. Lackner, J.R., DiZio, P.: Human orientation and movement control in weightless and artificial gravity environments. Exp. Brain Res. **130**, 2–26 (2000)
2. Mierau, A., Girgenrath, M., Bock, O.: Isometric force production during changed Gz episodes of parabolic flight. Eur. J. Appl. Physiol. **102**(3), 313–318 (2008)
3. Dalecki, M., Dräger, T., Mireau, A., Bock, O.: Production of finely graded forces in humans: effects of simulated weightlessness by water immersion. Exp. Brain Res. **218**, 41–47 (2012)

4. Crevecoeur, F., McIntyre, J., Thonnard, J.L., Lefèvre, P.: Movement stability under uncertain internal models of dynamics. J. Neurophysiol. **104**, 1301–1313 (2010)

5. Bock, O., Abeele, S., Eversheim, U.: Sensorimotor performance and computational demand during short-term exposure to microgravity. Aviat. Space Environ. Med. **74**(12), 1256–1262 (2003)

6. Manzey, D., Lorenz, B., Heuer, H., Sangals, J.: Impairments of manual tracking performance during spaceflight: more converging evidence from a 20-day space mission. Ergonomics **43**(5), 589–609 (2000)

7. Jones, L.A., Hunter, I.W.: Human operator perception of mechanical variables and their effects on tracking performance. Proc. ASME Winter Annu. Meet. Adv. Robot. **42**, 49–53 (1992)

8. Bock, O., Arnold, K.E., Cheung, B.S.: Performance of a simple aiming task in hypergravity: I. overall accuracy. Aviat. Space Environ. Med. **67**(2), 127–132 (1996)

9. Howland, D., Noble, M.E.: The effect of physical constants of a control on tracking performance. J. Exp. Psychol. **46**(5), 353 (1953)

10. Jones, L.A., Hunter, I.W.: Influence of the mechanical properties of a manipulandum on human operator dynamics. Biol. Cybern. **62**(4), 299–307 (1990)

11. Jones, L.A., Hunter, I.W.: Influence of the mechanical properties of a manipulandum on human operator dynamics. II. Viscosity. Biol. Cybern. **69**(4), 295–303 (1993)

12. Heuer, H., Manzey, D., Lorenz, B., Sangals, J.: Impairments of manual tracking performance during spaceflight are associated with specific effects of microgravity on visuomotor transformations. Ergonomics **46**, 920–934 (2003)

13. Patrick, N., Kosmo, J., Locke, J., Trevino, L., Trevino, R.: Extravehicular activity operations and advancements. Wings Orbit Sci. Eng. Legacies Space Shuttle **2010**, 110–129 (1971)

14. Riecke, C., Artigas, J. Balachandran, R., Bayer, R., Beyer, A., Brunner, B., Buchner, H., Gumpert, T., Gruber, R., Hacker, F., Landzettel, K., Plank, G., Schätzle, S., Sedlmayr, H.-J., Seitz, N., Steinmetz, B.-M., Stelzer, M., Vogel, J., Weber, B., Willberg, B., Albu-Schäffer, A.: KONTUR-2 mission: the DLR force feedback joystick for space telemanipulation from the ISS. In: Proceedings of i-SAIRAS 2016, Peking, China (2016)

15. Jürgens, H.W.: Körperteilgewichte des lebenden Menschen: Ergonomische Studien Nr. 13. Bundesamt für Wehrtechnik u. Beschaffung (1985)

16. Hirzinger, G., Landzettel, K., Reintsema, D., Preusche, C., Albu-Schäffer, A., Rebele, B., Turk, M.: Rokviss-robotics component verification on ISS. In: Proceedings of 8th International Symposium on Artificial Intelligence, Robotics and Automation in Space (iSAIRAS) (2005)

17. Artigas, J., Balachandran, R., Riecke, C., Stelzer, M., Weber, B., Ryu, J.-H, Albu-Schäffer, A.: KONTUR-2: force-feedback teleoperation from the international space station. In: Proceedings of the IEEE International Conference on Robotics and Automation, ICRA 2016, Stockholm, Sweden (2016, in press)

18. Sangals, J., Heuer, H., Manzey, D., Lorenz, B.: Changed visuomotor transformations during and after prolonged microgravity. Exp. Brain Res. **129**, 378–390 (1999)

19. Dalecki, M.: Human fine motor control and cognitive performance in simulated weightlessness by water immersion (Doctoral dissertation, German Sport University Cologne) (2013)

Individuals with Chronic Hemiparetic Stroke Correctly Match Forearm Position Within a Single Arm: Preliminary Findings

Erik J. Euving[1]([✉]), Netta Gurari[2], Justin M. Drogos[2], Stuart Traxel[2],
Arno H.A. Stienen[1,2], and Julius P.A. Dewald[1,2,3,4]

[1] Faculty of Engineering Technology, Department of Biomechanical Engineering,
University of Twente, Enschede, The Netherlands
e.j.euving@student.utwente.nl
[2] Department of Physical Therapy and Human Movement Sciences,
Northwestern University, Chicago, USA
netta.gurari@northwestern.edu
[3] Department of Biomedical Engineering, Northwestern University, Chicago, USA
[4] Department of Physical Medicine and Rehabilitation, Northwestern University,
Chicago, USA

Abstract. According to between arms position matching assessments,
more than 50 % of individuals with stroke may have moderate to severe
proprioceptive deficits. This study is the first of a series of studies designed
to investigate the reason for observed between arms position matching
deficits. In this work, we quantified the ability of five participants with
chronic hemiparetic stroke (participants with stroke) and five age-matched
participants without neurological impairments (controls) to match forearm positions within a single arm. According to the revised Nottingham
Sensory Assessment, the participants with stroke all had impaired forearm position sense and unimpaired forearm movement direction sense,
while the controls had unimpaired forearm position and movement direction sense. A custom robotic device was used to quantify each participant's
task performance during active movements when performing a single arm
memory matching task. Participants were asked to match the location of
the forearm with a remembered target location. Results show that the participants with stroke identified the target location just as well as the controls. Based on our findings, we suggest that our participants with chronic
hemiparetic stroke, who have deficits in matching forearm positions across
both arms, may not have impaired forearm position sense within a single
arm, and we suggest that the position matching deficits may arise for non-
sensory related reasons. Future work will continue to use such behavioral
studies to investigate possible central neural mechanisms that may be contributing to the observed between arms position matching deficits.

1 Introduction

In the absence of proprioception, coordinated movements are nearly impossible
for an individual to perform [2]. According to between arms position matching

---

Erik J. Euving and Netta Gurari equally contributed to this work.

© Springer International Publishing Switzerland 2016
F. Bello et al. (Eds.): EuroHaptics 2016, Part I, LNCS 9774, pp. 122–133, 2016.
DOI: 10.1007/978-3-319-42321-0_12

assessments, more than 50 % of individuals with stroke may have proprioceptive deficits [3,4,13,14] that may be contributing to their movement disabilities [23]. In this study, we use a single arm robotic assessment to investigate the reason for position matching deficits during a between arms position matching clinical assessment.

Currently available clinical proprioceptive assessments face a number of limitations including that they: (1) lack sensitivity to identify the degree of a deficit (e.g., rating options are unimpaired, mildly impaired, severely impaired), (2) may not be reliable (e.g., ratings may differ depending on the rater and testing session), and (3) may be confounded by additional impairments [1,4,20]. Assessments that rely on single arm tasks to characterize an individual's ability to sense limb movement can be insensitive to position sense and motor impairments [24], while assessments that do characterize an individual's ability to sense limb position generally rely on between arms tasks, where results can be confounded by non-sensory related deficits including compromised interhemispheric transfer of information [9]. The aim of this work was to identify whether sensory deficits within the paretic arm of individuals with chronic hemiparetic stroke may be contributing to forearm position matching deficits that are observed during a between forearms position matching clinical assessment.

We employed the revised Nottingham Sensory Assessment (rNSA) as the between forearms position matching clinical assessment [14]. During this assessment, the examiner characterizes an individual's forearm proprioception by using a between forearms position matching task and by providing an ordinal rating of the individual's task performance based on visual inspection.

We also characterized forearm position matching performance during a single arm task by using a within-arm memory position matching robotic assessment. For this single arm assessment, a robotic system automated and standardized the testing procedures. Each participant's tested forearm was attached to a custom robotic device, which was equipped with an encoder that provided a highly precise assessment of measured angular positions. The device supported the weight of the participant's arm, and the participant actively rotated the forearm about the elbow joint. The participant's position matching capabilities at the forearm were quantified based on measurements from a high-resolution position sensor.

Human subject testing was conducted on five individuals with chronic hemiparetic stroke and moderate to severe motor impairments (see Table 1) and five individuals without neurological impairments. Our results provide evidence that, even though these individuals with stroke demonstrate between forearms position matching deficits, their within forearm position sense in the paretic arm may be intact. Scientific and clinical implications of these finding will be discussed.

2   Participants

The Northwestern University Institutional Review Board granted approval to run this study, and each participant provided informed consent. Five individuals with chronic hemiparetic stroke, i.e., *participants with stroke*, and five individuals without neurological impairments, i.e., *controls*, partook in this study. All participants were dominantly right handed based on the Edinburgh Handedness

Inventory [15]. Inclusion criteria for this experiment included that the individual had the capacity to provide informed consent, the ability to understand the task, the absence of upper extremity injury that may impact task performance and the absence of a polyneuropathy (and, thus, proprioceptive deficits). For participants with stroke, criteria were also that the paresis was confined to one side of the body and that the brain lesion occurred at least one year prior to participation in this study.

Participants were screened by a licensed physical therapist for forearm proprioception impairments using the rNSA. A score of 3 was given if participants were able to successfully match forearm positions, and a score of 2 was given if participants were unable to correctly match forearm positions but still had a correct sense of direction of movement. Controls all had a score of 3, and participants with stroke all had a score of 2. The same physical therapist also conducted the Upper-Extremity Fugl-Meyer Motor Assessment (FMA) to identify the level of motor impairments in all participants with stroke [6]. Motor impairments were moderate to severe in the participants with stroke (FMA scores between 12 to 35), and arm paresis was observed at the left arm for three of these participants and at the right arm for the remaining two participants.

Demographic and clinical information about each of the five participants with stroke are summarized in Table 1. The five controls are comprised of 4 males and 1 female, and ages range between 55 and 66 years (mean ± standard deviation of age: 60 ± 4 years), a similar age range as our participants with stroke (see Table 1).

Table 1. Demographic and clinical information about the participants with chronic hemiparetic stroke.

Participant	Gender	Age	Paretic arm	Years since stroke	Upper-extremity FMA
Stroke 1	M	61	L	4	20
Stroke 2	M	61	L	7	15
Stroke 3	M	46	L	14	35
Stroke 4	F	63	R	29	13
Stroke 5	M	69	R	21	12

3   Experimental Setup and Protocol

The experimental setup is shown in Fig. 1.

3.1   Robotic System

A custom one-degree-of-freedom robotic device, derived from Stienen et al.'s device [21], controlled and guided movements of the participant's forearm about the elbow joint. The forearm was rotated by a Harmonic Drive FHA-17C-100 motor with an attached US250 encoder (Peabody, MA, USA). Angular position was measured by the encoder, and torque was measured by an OMEGA Engineering Inc. LCM201-500N load sensor (Stamford, CT, USA) located 5.25 cm from the axis of rotation.

The robotic system rendered a virtual haptic environment that had little inertia and damping using an admittance controller. To create this virtual haptic environment, a virtual mass-damper model transformed the measured interaction force (i.e., load sensor measurement) into a desired angular velocity and position. Then, the desired angular velocity, with a proportional feedback loop on position to reduce positional drift, was sent as an input to the motor to control the velocity and position of a user's forearm. The virtual haptic environment had a moment of inertia of $0.16 \, \text{kg} \cdot \text{m}^2$ and a damping constant of $0.84 \times 10^{-2} \text{Nm} \cdot \text{s}/°$. These values were selected based on pilot testing so that the individuals with chronic hemiparetic stroke could easily start and stop their movements. The control loop rendering the virtual haptic environment ran at 4 kHz, and data were stored at 1 kHz.

3.2   Forearm Position Matching Task

The participant's goal during the position matching task was to rotate the forearm to a *reference target location*, to remember the forearm position based on haptic cues, and then to return to this forearm position after a series of random movements (see Fig. 2). The participant wore a blindfold and white-noise canceling headphones throughout the task, so that angular positions could not be determined based on visual and auditory cues.

The task started with the participant's forearm at the *central location* of 90°. At the start of a trial, the participant was instructed by an automated

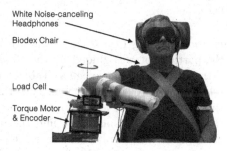

Fig. 1. Experimental Setup. Participants were seated in the Biodex chair with the tested forearm casted and attached to the custom robotic device. Participants wore a blindfold and white noise-canceling headphones.

auditory recording to hold the tested forearm still for 1.5 s ("*Hold*"). Subsequently, the participant was instructed in which direction to rotate the forearm by a recorded command playing "*In*" or "*Out*". Once the participant reached the reference target location, the participant heard the command "*Remember this target location*" and had to hold his or her forearm stationary for four seconds. A hold time of four seconds was selected to provide enough time for the participant to stop the movement and to memorize the forearm position [8], while being short enough to avoid possible positional drift of the forearm [7]. See Sect. 3.4 for a discussion about the positional drift when each participant held the forearm at the reference target location and matched target location. Next, the participant moved to the *first randomized location* and the *second randomized*

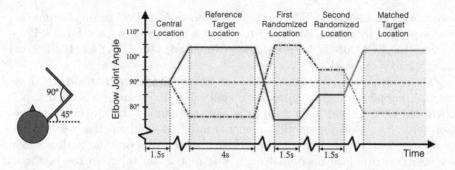

Fig. 2. Trial Timeline. (Left) A participant began the trial with the forearm at the central location of 90°. (Right) For the extension target (i.e., red line), the participant extended the forearm to the reference target location, flexed toward the first randomized location and extended toward the second randomized location, before matching the forearm position with the reference target location. For the flexion target (i.e., blue dashed line), the participant flexed the forearm to the reference target location, then moved to the randomized locations (that mirrored the directions of movement for the extension target) and last matched the forearm position with the reference target location. Table 2 gives the randomized locations for each reference target location. (Color figure online)

location, holding 1.5 s at each location. For each of these additional movements, the participant was guided by the commands "*In*", "*Out*" and "*Hold*". These extra randomized movements (Table 2) ensured that the participant could only rely on haptic position cues, and not timing cues (e.g., counting), to remember the reference target location. After moving to the second randomized location, the participant was asked to find the reference target location ("*Find the target location*") and to indicate when he or she had reached the reference target location by saying out loud "*Target*". Once the participant verbally indicated that the reference target location had been reached, the experimenter pressed the keyboard key programmed to indicate that the matched target location had been reached. The participant held the forearm still for four more seconds, and this location was saved as the *matched target location*. This last step marked successful completion of the trial.

To ensure that position sensing [16] and haptic environment rendering was comparable across participants [11], the maximum speed at which a participant was allowed to rotate the forearm during a trial was set to 10°/s. The participant repeated all trials where he or she exceeded the maximum speed. Additionally, the participant could repeat a trial if he or she forgot the reference target location.

Table 2. Randomized angles for each reference target location.

Reference target location	First randomized location	Second randomized location
102.5°	75° or 80°	85° or 90°
77.5°*	100° or 105°	90° or 95°

*The flexion reference target location for Stroke 4 and Stroke 5 was set to 85° rather than 77.5°, since each of these participants had a limited range of motion in flexion.

3.3 Experimental Protocol

Clinical assessments (i.e., rNSA, upper-extremity FMA) were administered during a 60 to 90 min session on a separate day prior to the testing with the robotic system. The experiment with the robotic system spanned one 2 to 3 h session. The participant's forearm position sense was measured within the paretic arm of the participants with stroke and within the non-dominant arm of the controls.

At the beginning of the first session, the non-paretic arm of a participant with stroke or dominant arm of a control was placed loosely inside the robotic device, and the participant was instructed how to perform the forearm position matching task. Training was considered finished once the participant successfully completed two practice trials.

Next, the participant's testing forearm (paretic forearm in participants with stroke or non-dominant forearm in controls) was outfitted with a Techform® Premium 204WH cast (Reykjavik, Capital Region, Iceland) that extended from approximately 10 cm distally from the medial epicondyle to beyond the fingertips. The cast ensured that the participant's hand posture was consistent between controls and participants with stroke, because individuals with chronic hemiparetic stroke may naturally have a flexed hand posture and may face difficulty extending the fingers. The cast also ensured that forces transmitted by the robotic device spread evenly across the participant's forearm and that torques produced about the elbow joint were accurately measured by the load cell.

The participant was positioned in a System 3 Pro™ Biodex chair (Shirley, NY, USA), and his or her shoulder and waist regions were strapped to the chair to minimize trunk and shoulder movements. The participant's casted forearm was rigidly fixed to and fully supported by the robotic device (Fig. 1), and his or her elbow joint was situated in the robotic device's cup such that the rotational axis of the elbow joint shared the rotational axis of the motor. The location of the Biodex chair was adjusted so that the participant was in the following configuration: shoulder abduction at 90°, shoulder flexion angle at 45° and elbow joint angle at 90° (see Fig. 2).

First, we investigated whether the participant had movement impairments relevant to this experiment by asking the participant to flex and extend the testing forearm about the full experimental range of motion (70° to 110°). Then, the participant performed the motor assessment task. The participant was required to successfully reach and hold the forearm still for four seconds at four locations. The locations were 75° (minimum angle that participants had to actively reach), 105° (maximum angle that participants had to actively reach), 77.5° (flexion target location) and 102.5° (extension target location); these angles were unknown to the participant. One reference target location (77.5°) was adjusted for two participants with stroke (i.e., Stroke 4 and Stroke 5) who showed a limited range of motion (see Table 2). They were able to reach 75°, but not flex much further. To give these participants the freedom to overshoot past the flexion target location of 77.5°, it was decided to change its value to 85°.

Following the motor assessment, the participant practiced the allowable range of speeds by extending and flexing his or her forearm once about the full range of motion (70° to 110°) at $<10°/s$. For Stroke 4 and Stroke 5 the minimal angle was approximately 75°. The participant repeated trials in which the threshold speed was exceeded. After two successful trials, the participant was finished with the speed training.

Next, the participant completed the position matching trials. The participant moved to one of two potential reference target locations that were situated equidistant from the central location – an *extension target* of 102.5° and a *flexion target* of 77.5° (Fig. 2). These two target locations were selected to identify potential differences in task performance (such as biases) due to target location. The *flexion target* was adjusted for Stroke 4 and Stroke 5 to 85° since these two participants had a limited range of motion. Participants performed eight trials for each reference target location (16 trials total), with a mandatory minimum break of one minute after every eight successive trials. Additional breaks were given if trials were repeated or if the participant requested.

3.4 Data Analysis

Task performance was measured using three metrics: constant error, absolute error, and variable error [12,19]. Constant error identified how accurately the participant identified the reference target location by determining whether the participant overshot, undershot or matched the reference target location across all trials; a smaller value indicates that the participant was better able to judge the location of the reference target location, a positive value indicates that the participant overshot the reference target location and a negative value indicates that the participant undershot the reference target location. Absolute error also identified how accurately the participant identified the reference target location by determining the magnitude of the matching errors across all trials without taking into account the direction of the errors; again, a smaller value indicates that the participant was better able to judge the location of the reference target location. Variable error identified how precisely the participant selected the matching target location, or how well the participant could distinguish between two positions; a larger variable error indicates a poorer ability to differentiate between locations (or possibly a working memory deficit [8]). Constant error, absolute error and variable error were calculated for each participant and for every condition.

To obtain these metrics, the reference target location, $\theta_{\text{ref,i}}$, and matched target location, $\theta_{\text{match,i}}$, were identified for each trial i. The participant may have made small movement adjustments when initially instructed to hold the forearm still, so $\theta_{\text{ref,i}}$ and $\theta_{\text{match,i}}$ were defined as the mean angular position based on the last two seconds (of four seconds) of holding the forearm still at each respective location. We verified that the forearm was held still for each analyzed data segment by looking at the variability of the position data. The standard deviation in the angular position for each analyzed segment had a mean $\pm$ standard deviation of 0.076° $\pm$ 0.062° (range: 0.004° to 0.405°) at the reference target location and a mean $\pm$ standard deviation of 0.076° $\pm$ 0.079° (range: 0.005° to 0.664°) at the matched target location.

Next, the target error was calculated for every trial. Target error is defined as the difference between the matched target location, $\theta_{\text{match},i}$, and reference target location, $\theta_{\text{ref},i}$. Flexion target errors were multiplied by -1, so that a positive and negative target error corresponds to the target location being overshot and undershot, respectively.

Then, the constant error, absolute error and variable error were calculated. The constant error is defined as the mean target error across all extension or all flexion trials for each participant, or

$$CE = \frac{\sum_{i=1}^{n} \left(\theta_{\text{match},i} - \theta_{\text{ref},i} \right)}{n}. \tag{1}$$

The absolute error is defined as the mean absolute target error across all extension or all flexion trials for each participant, or

$$AE = \frac{\sum_{i=1}^{n} \left| \theta_{\text{match},i} - \theta_{\text{ref},i} \right|}{n}. \tag{2}$$

The variable error is defined as the standard deviation across the same extension or flexion trials for each participant and each arm, or

$$VE = \sqrt{\frac{\sum_{i=1}^{n} \left(\theta_{\text{match},i} - CE \right)^2}{n}}. \tag{3}$$

We ran a between subjects two-way ANOVA with the fixed factors of reference target location (extension target, flexion target) and group (participants with stroke, controls) to determine the impact of these main factors and their interaction on task performance, as determined by the constant error, absolute error and variable error. A significant effect was based on $\alpha = 0.05$.

4 Results

The main finding of this study is that the five participants with stroke performed the within forearm position matching task as accurately and precisely as the five controls. Results are summarized in Fig. 3.

The magnitude of the target errors, or absolute error, was slightly less in the participants with stroke than in the controls ($F(1,16) = 7.91, \eta_p^2 = 0.33, p = 0.01$), with a mean absolute error (95 % confidence interval (CI): [lower limit, upper limit]) of $2.36°$ (95 % CI: [1.55, 3.18]) and $3.88°$ (95 % CI: [2.84, 4.93]), respectively. The main effect of group also significantly affected the constant error ($F(1,16) = 13.24, \eta_p^2 = 0.45, p < 0.01$), where the mean constant error for the participants with stroke was $-1.14°$ (95 % CI: [-2.44, 0.15]) and for the controls was $2.12°$ (95 % CI: [0.19, 4.06]). Additionally, group significantly affected the variable error ($F(1,16) = 6.99, \eta_p^2 = 0.30, p = 0.02$), where the mean variable error for the participants with stroke, $2.20°$ (95 % CI: [1.68, 2.73]), was less than the mean variable error for the controls, $3.30°$ (95 % CI: [2.60, 4.17]). While the results for the participants with stroke were significantly different from the results for the controls, the difference in the magnitude of the target errors was only on the order of $1.10°$ (variable error) to $3.26°$ (constant error).

Reference target location was found to have a significant effect on participant task performance, where performance was better at the flexion target than at the extension target. The mean absolute error was significantly greater at the extension target, 4.06° (95 % CI: [3.03, 5.10]), than at the flexion target, 2.18° (95 % CI: [1.53, 2.84]) $(F(1,16) = 12.08, \eta_p^2 = 0.43, p < 0.01)$. Additionally, the mean variable error was significantly greater at the extension target, 3.21° (95 % CI: [2.46,3.96]), that at the flexion target, 2.30° (95 % CI: [1.76,2.83]) $(F(1,16) = 4.87, \eta_p^2 = 0.23, p = 0.04)$.

Last, the interaction of group and reference target location was found to significantly affect the constant error $(F(1,16) = 13.71, \eta_p^2 = 0.46, p = 0.002)$, suggesting that the difference in participants accuracy at the flexion target and extension target was greater for the controls than for the participants with stroke.

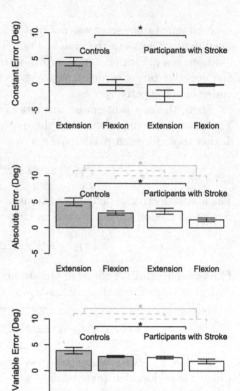

Fig. 3. Task Performance. (Top) Constant error, (Middle) absolute error and (Bottom) variable error are given as a function of reference target location and group. A significant main effect of group is indicated by a solid black line with a star above, and a significant main effect of reference target location is indicated by a solid gray line with a star above. Group had a significant effect on the constant error, absolute error and variable error, reference target location had a significant effect on the absolute error and variable error and the interaction of group and reference target location had a significant effect on the constant error.

5   Discussion

Findings from this study indicate that deficits occurring when an individual with chronic hemiparetic stroke matches forearm positions across both arms may not arise due to sensory deficits occurring within the paretic arm. The individuals with chronic hemiparetic stroke who participated in this study all exhibited forearm position matching deficits according to the clinical revised Nottingham Sensory Assessment between forearms proprioception task [14], but these individuals did not perform significantly worse than the individuals without neurological impairments during a robotic single forearm position matching assessment when using the paretic arm. Rather, our results indicate that the participants with stroke identified the reference target locations just as accurately and precisely as the controls.

Our results indicate that participants with stroke were significantly more accurate and precise in identifying the reference target locations. We point out that Stroke 4 and Stroke 5 had a different flexion reference target location, which might have affected their performance and, in turn, the results. An individual's ability to accurately and precisely identify positions may change depending on the limb's location [5, 22] (this point is further supported by our finding that task performance significantly differed depending on whether an individual was matching a flexion target or an extension target). Additionally, we note that differences in task performance were relatively small, being on the order of $1.10°$ for the variable error and $3.26°$ for the constant error.

Position sense arises from numerous mechanoreceptors located within the body, including muscle spindles, joint mechanoreceptors and cutaneous mechanoreceptors [17]. Moreover, literature suggests that position judgment may be better during active movements when compared to passive movements (in individuals without neurological impairments), for reasons including that muscle spindles may become more sensitive (via the gamma motor system) and motor commands may provide additional position-related information [10] (although another body of work indicates that differences during active and passive position sensing tasks may occur due to muscle thixotropy, worded by Proske et al. as the dependence of a muscle's passive mechanical property on its previous history of contraction and length changes [17, 18]). Based on our findings, it is possible that the peripheral mechanoreceptors, peripheral sensory tracts and muscle spindle sensitivity may not be impaired in our tested individuals with chronic hemiparetic stroke despite the damage occurring in their central nervous systems (CNS). In turn, we propose that the deficits occurring during between forearms position matching tasks may arise due to non-sensory related deficits (i.e., deficits arise due to central processing impairments and not damage to the peripheral mechanoreceptors).

During a between forearms position matching task, intact sensory information may reach the CNS. However, this sensory information may not be processed correctly due to compromised central neural mechanisms, resulting in the observed deficits. Various arguments may explain at which part of the central processing the observed errors arise. Stroke-induced changes to the diencephalon (i.e., thalamus) may result in cross-talk in the sensory pathways from the dorsal column and contribute to the observed between forearms position matching deficits. Additionally, the between forearms position matching deficits may arise due to compromised cross-hemispherical communication between the sensorimotor cortices. Moreover, an altered body schema [17] of positions for each arm could be another explanation for the observed deficits. During a between forearms position matching task the absolute positions (in the global coordinate frame) of both forearms may not match, whereas during a single forearm position matching task the CNS may support the participants to match the forearm to the same relative position. If there was indeed an altered body schema for either arm with respect to the global coordinate frame, between forearms position matching errors may occur. Further research could be conducted to investigate whether any of these potential changes may explain the observed forearm position matching errors in our participants with stroke during the between forearms position matching assessments.

Implications of this work include that more targeted and effective rehabilitation assessments, and, in turn, treatments are needed. New approaches for assessing forearm position sense deficits in the clinic include using the rNSA task (or a different between arms perceptual task) in conjunction with our single arm task to determine whether a participant exhibits position sensing deficits within the paretic arm. Based on our findings, we can suggest that sensory rehabilitation may not be needed for a single arm task for a subpopulation of individuals with chronic hemiparetic stroke; rather, rehabilitation treatments for this group of individuals may be improved by focusing on exercises or activities of daily living that require individuals to coordinate movements across both arms.

Acknowledgements. We thank Arvid Keemink for his assistance with the software, Paul Krueger and Di Zhang for their assistance with the hardware, Carolina Carmona for her assistance with the data collection, the participants who partook in the experiment and the anonymous reviewers for their feedback.

References

1. Carey, L.M., Matyas, T.A., Oke, L.E.: Evaluation of impaired fingertip texture discrimination and wrist position sense in patients affected by stroke: comparison of clinical and new quantitative measures. J. Hand Ther. **15**(1), 71–82 (2002)
2. Cole, J.: Pride and a Daily Marathon. MIT Press, Cambridge (1995)
3. Connell, L.A., Lincoln, N., Radford, K.: Somatosensory impairment after stroke: frequency of different deficits and their recovery. Clin. Rehabil. **22**(8), 758–767 (2008)
4. Dukelow, S.P., Herter, T.M., Moore, K.D., Demers, M.J., Glasgow, J.I., Bagg, S.D., Norman, K.E., Scott, S.H.: Quantitative assessment of limb position sense following stroke. Neurorehabil. Neural Repair **24**(2), 178–187 (2010)
5. Fuentes, C.T., Bastian, A.J.: Where is your arm? Variations in proprioception across space and tasks. J. Neurophysiol. **103**(1), 164–171 (2010)
6. Fugl-Meyer, A.R., Jääskö, L., Leyman, I., Olsson, S., Steglind, S.: The post-stroke hemiplegic patient. 1. A method for evaluation of physical performance. Scand. J. Rehabil. Med. **7**(1), 13–31 (1974)
7. Ghez, C., Gordon, J., Ghilardi, M., Christakos, C., Cooper, S.: Roles of proprioceptive input in the programming of arm trajectories. In: Cold Spring Harbor Symposia on Quantitative Biology, vol. 55, pp. 837–847. Cold Spring Harbor Laboratory Press (1990)
8. Goble, D.J., Aaron, M.B., Warschausky, S., Kaufman, J.N., Hurvitz, E.A.: The influence of spatial working memory on ipsilateral remembered proprioceptive matching in adults with cerebral palsy. Exp. Brain Res. **223**(2), 259–269 (2012)
9. Goble, D.J., Brown, S.H.: Task-dependent asymmetries in the utilization of proprioceptive feedback for goal-directed movement. Exp. Brain Res. **180**(4), 693–704 (2007)

10. Gritsenko, V., Krouchev, N.I., Kalaska, J.F.: Afferent input, efference copy, signal noise, and biases in perception of joint angle during active versus passive elbow movements. J. Neurophysiol. **98**(3), 1140–1154 (2007)

11. Gurari, N., Baud-Bovy, G.: Customization, control, and characterization of a commercial haptic device for high-fidelity rendering of weak forces. J. Neurosci. Methods **235**, 169–180 (2014)

12. Henry, F.M.: Variable and constant performance errors within a group of individuals. J. Mot. Behav. **6**(3), 149–154 (1974)

13. Hirayama, K., Fukutake, T., Kawamura, M.: 'Thumb localizing test' for detecting a lesion in the posterior column-medial lemniscal system. J. Neurol. Sci. **167**(1), 45–49 (1999)

14. Lincoln, N., Jackson, J., Adams, S.: Reliability and revision of the Nottingham sensory assessment for stroke patients. Physiotherapy **84**(8), 358–365 (1998)

15. Oldfield, R.C.: The assessment and analysis of handedness: the Edinburgh inventory. Neuropsychologia **9**(1), 97–113 (1971)

16. Proske, U., Wise, A., Gregory, J.: The role of muscle receptors in the detection of movements. Prog. Neurobiol. **60**(1), 85–96 (2000)

17. Proske, U., Gandevia, S.C.: The proprioceptive senses: their roles in signaling body shape, body position and movement, and muscle force. Physiol. Rev. **92**(4), 1651–1697 (2012)

18. Proske, U., Morgan, L., Gregory, J.E., Morgan, D.L., Gregory, J.E., Morgan, L., Gregory, J.E.: Thixotropy in skeletal muscle and in muscle spindles; a review. Prog. Neurobiol. **41**(6), 705–721 (1993)

19. Schutz, R.W., Roy, E.A.: Absolute error: the devil in disguise. J. Mot. Behav. **5**(3), 141–153 (1973)

20. Simo, L., Botzer, L., Ghez, C., Scheidt, R.A.: A robotic test of proprioception within the hemiparetic arm post-stroke. J. Neuroeng. Rehabil. **11**(1), 1 (2014)

21. Stienen, A.H., McPherson, J.G., Schouten, A.C., Dewald, J.: The ACT-4D: a novel rehabilitation robot for the quantification of upper limb motor impairments following brain injury. In: 2011 IEEE International Conference on Rehabilitation Robotics (ICORR), pp. 1–6. IEEE (2011)

22. Tan, H.Z., Srinivasan, M.A., Reed, C.M., Durlach, N.I.: Discrimination and identification of finger joint-angle position using active motion. ACM Trans. Appl. Percept. (TAP) **4**(2), 10 (2007)

23. Vidoni, E.D., Boyd, L.A.: Preserved motor learning after stroke is related to the degree of proprioceptive deficit. Behav. Brain Funct. **5**(1), 1 (2009)

24. Winward, C.E., Halligan, P.W., Wade, D.T.: The Rivermead Assessment of Somatosensory Performance (RASP): standardization and reliability data. Clin. Rehabil. **16**(5), 523–533 (2002)

Shape Features of the Search Target Modulate Hand Velocity, Posture and Pressure During Haptic Search in a 3D Display

Kathrin Krieger[✉], Alexandra Moringen, Robert Haschke, and Helge Ritter

Neuroinformatics, CITEC, Bielefeld University,
Inspiration 1, 33619 Bielefeld, Germany
{kkrieger,abarch,rhaschke,helge}@techfak.uni-bielefeld.de

Abstract. We have investigated spontaneous haptic search in a scenario in which both the search target and the search field are represented by a random composition of different primitive shapes. In our experiment, blindfolded sighted individuals were asked, firstly, to learn a complex search target and, secondly, to find this search target embedded in a larger, encompassing search field. Our goal was to examine, how different shape characteristics of the complex search target influenced the overall search behaviour.

We have evaluated data of eight participants by correlating the features, representing the search behaviour, with the features, representing the target object. This approach showed that the number of vertices, the curvature and the height of the target may have a global impact on the hand posture, velocity and pressure during the haptic search.

Keywords: Haptic search · Haptic shape exploration · Salient form features · Multimodal data · Human movement

1 Introduction

The processes underlying haptic learning and haptic search of a complex shape are still not well understood. In an unstructured 3D display, no clear strategy, such as serial or parallel search, was observed (e.g. [5]). In our scenario (see Fig. 1), in which both the target object and the search field have been represented by a random composition of primitive shapes, our main goal has been to find factors that contribute to the efficiency of the haptic search. One application can be found in robotics: our long-term goal is to generate motion instructions for a robotic arm and hand to perform a search task based on tactile feedback, exploiting the findings of this research.

In our analysis we adapt the traditional approach of analyzing the relationship between the search target and the search dynamics. This results in the following question: how does the target object shape influences the search strategy?

K. Krieger and A. Moringen—Both authors contributed equally to this paper.

© Springer International Publishing Switzerland 2016
F. Bello et al. (Eds.): EuroHaptics 2016, Part I, LNCS 9774, pp. 134–145, 2016.
DOI: 10.1007/978-3-319-42321-0_13

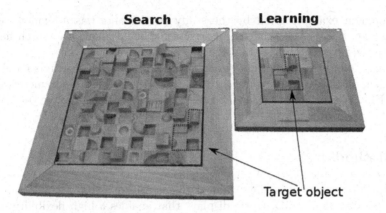

Fig. 1. Haptic display consisting of two boards: a learning board (right) with the search target object, and a search board (left) containing the search field with an integrated search target.

Our work focused on two main directions: representation of a target object and representation of the search strategy. Regarding the target object representation, we base our approach on haptic saliency. In simple scenarios of haptic search, salient features of the search target are characterized by their influence on the search strategy and, consequently, the overall search performance [3]. Features, such as movability [10], vertices and edges [9], have been considered as salient to touch in certain scenarios. Here we extend the simple approach for salient feature extraction [9] to complex shapes.

Regarding the representation of search, we based our approach on the previous work done on parameterization of exploratory procedures (EPs) during different tasks. Exploratory procedures [4] are used during execution of any haptic exploration task, such as identification of an object, discrimination between objects or haptic search. Although a lot is known about the types of the exploratory patterns used (lateral motion, unsupported holding, etc.), not a lot is known about their parameterization, especially in the case of shape exploration [2]. Tanaka et al. [14] compared parameterization of lateral motion in different tasks – a discrimination and an identification task – and showed that different tasks invoked different levels of velocity and pressure during the execution of the same EP. To this end they averaged their feature values over the whole time series of the task. We adopt this approach, assuming that in our search task such an average of the feature values roughly captures the overall search strategy w.r.t. a particular target.

Our main hypothesis is that during search, certain target object features influence the prevailing parameterization of the executed EPs, independent of their type. This hypothesis is congruent with the feedback that we received from our study participants in the interview conducted after they performed the experimental tasks. Such common parameterization of movement, independent of the executed EPs, was one of the main descriptions of the search strategy.

One common example given by the study participants was a shallow search strategy, i.e. a fast search movement with a flat hand above the search field in the case the target object contained a higher shape element.

In an exploratory evaluation of our data we use features, such as hand configuration, velocity and pressure of the hand to represent the parameterization of the EPs. We correlate their mean values, taken over the complete time series, with the target object features in a hypothesis-generating approach.

2   Methods

In this section we will describe (1) our data acquisition setup[1], (2) our approach to the construction of 3D haptic displays that enables a high flexibility of the experimental design, and can serve as a framework for a large number of haptic shape exploration scenarios, (3) the search task posed to participants, (4) the proposed object and motion features, and the data evaluation method.

2.1   Experimental Setup

Haptic Displays. We employed two tactile displays: the target display used for memorizing the target pattern, and the search display, in which the target pattern was embedded in complex shape landscape (see Fig. 1). Both displays were assembled from wooden bricks 3×3 cm in size. The current set of bricks consists of 360 elements comprising 55 distinct elementary shapes (plus a flat brick type). Wooden frames with a capacity of 5×5 (target display) and 10×10 bricks (search display) were designed to fix the bricks within the displays. The frames also provided a border of the shape environment to the study participants. In our experiments both the search field and the search target were composed of randomly chosen bricks from the above-mentioned set. Nine search targets used in the experiment contained elementary shape combinations of different number and spatial distribution of bricks within a 3×3 grid (see Fig. 2).

Data Capture. For data capture we have used a comprehensive recording setup comprising a Basler camera for video recording, a microphone, a 14-camera Vicon setup for hand tracking, and a tactile data glove [1] for recording interaction forces (see Fig. 3 left). Using a glove during haptic search is highly controversial. On the one hand it allows us to obtain the most detailed information about force profiles during interaction – in comparison to all other alternatives, like using a haptic table underneath the haptic displays. On the other hand, the glove may interfere with a natural execution of motion. For the sake of our future work directed towards teaching robots to perform haptic exploration and search, we have decided to use the glove and record the data in this pilot experiment. The haptic data may be used in the future for inverse reinforcement learning or learning by demonstration.

---

[1] The experimental setup has been previously described in [6].

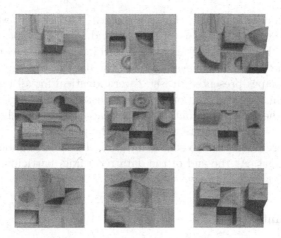

Fig. 2. Nine target objects employed in different trials.

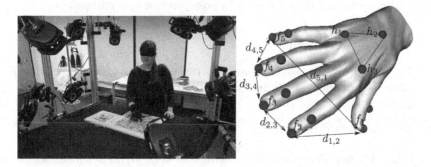

Fig. 3. Left: data acquisition setup. Right: visualization of marker placement and distance feature calculation.

In order to be able to calculate features, such as velocity of the fingers and hand, thirteen Vicon markers have been placed on fingers and the hand (see Fig. 3 right). Three markers were positioned on the back of the hand to track the orientation of the hand, and two Vicon marker were positioned on each finger[2].

2.2   Task and Procedure

Participants were instructed to put on the haptic glove and were blindfolded. Following this, participants performed a training run to become familiar with the task and the experimental layout. Each one of the following nine trials started with a *learning phase*, during which the participants took an unconstrained amount of time to get familiar with the target object on the right display (see Fig. 1). Afterwards they had to search for the same shape embedded in the search

---

[2] A video of one experimental run is available on http://www.techfak.uni-bielefeld.de/persons/abarch/s2t7.avi.

display in the same orientation, the *search phase*. Participants were allowed to return to the target display whenever they wanted. After they located the target, they had to say "Found". The start of this word in the audio recording has been used to mark the end of the relevant part of the data recording.

The target shapes presented in Fig. 2 were identical for all participants but were presented in a randomized order. The location of the target in the search field as well as the remaining content of the search field were chosen randomly in each trial. No time constraints were put on the participants to find the target object. They were instructed to search until absolutely sure about the location of the search target. At the end of the data recording, participants were asked to describe their search strategy.

2.3   Participants

We processed data of 8 participants (3 males, 5 females). Their age varied between 22–30 and all of them were right-handed. We recorded data on five more participants, but their Vicon data post-processing is still pending.

2.4   Feature Extraction

Complex target objects features used on the one side of the correlation are inspired by the previous work on haptic saliency [9]. Hand and finger features used on the other side of the correlation were motivated by previous work in [2,7–10,13]. A detailed description is given in the section below.

Hand and Finger Features. Because in this work we do not focus on movement strategy of the hand in 3D space, our main approach to feature extraction for the raw 3D kinematic trajectories of the hand and fingers consists of making the data invariant w.r.t. affine transforms. The feature set Φ that has been used as a foundation of our analysis consists of multimodal features: distances between fingers, velocities, heights and pressure values of the fingers. It is defined as follows:

$$\Phi := (d_{1,2}, d_{2,3}, d_{3,4}, d_{4,5}, d_{5,1}, v_{f,1}, \dots, v_{f,5}, v_{h,1}, v_{h,2}, v_{h,3},$$
$$h_{f,1}, \dots, h_{f,5}, h_{h,1}, h_{h,2}, h_{h,3}, p_{f,1}, \dots, p_{f,5}) \in \mathbb{R}^{26}_{\geq 0},$$

where

- $d_{i,j}$ represent the **distances between adjacent fingertips** i and j, e.g. the distance between the thumb and the index finger is denoted by $d_{1,2}$, the distance between the index finger and the middle finger is denoted by $d_{2,3}$ (see Fig. 3 right).
- $v_{f,i}$ represent the absolute values of the **fingertip velocities** $i \in \{1, \dots, 5\}$ w.r.t. the hand coordinate system. Hence, these values do not comprise the velocity induced by arm motion.

- $v_{h,i}$ represent the **velocity of the hand**. Using all three values corresponding to the hand markers, we can capture the hand dynamics in 3D space.
- $h_{f,i}$ and $h_{h,k}$ denote the vertical distance between the Vicon markers at fingertips and hand to the board, referred to as the **heights**.
- Finally $p_{f,i}$ denote the average **pressure** recorded by fingertip sensors. We have used Grubbs' test to detect outliers ($\alpha = 0.05$) corresponding to sensor short-circuits.

All features of the set Φ were z-standardized per participant.

Shape Features. The set of all target object shape features can be divided into four groups: (1) edges and vertices, (2) surface area and curved surface area, (3) height and volume, as well as (4) the spatial extension in the x-y plane.

All shape features (see Fig. 4) were calculated based on the CAD models of the component bricks. The feature extraction builds upon the work of Plaisier [9], who studied the saliency of various shape features. We extend this work with a feature-extraction method for **complex shapes**.

A vertex is one of the most salient shape features for touch. Because it is not known yet, how vertices of recessed shapes influence haptic search, we consider only the vertices of the raised shapes. Since all vertices of our stimuli had the same acuteness, we have chosen the **number of raised vertices** to represent the target shape. Like vertices, edges are also salient to touch. Nearly all edges of our stimuli have the same acuteness so based on previous work [9] we counted the **number of raised edges** in the complex target shape. For the same reason as mentioned above, we have only included edges of raised shape elements. Finally, the overall **length of edges** has been calculated as a sum over all raised edges.

Maximal curvature has been previously used as a shape feature [9]. In order to adapt this feature to the complex shapes studied here, we propose to use the **mean weighted curvature** value. The calculation of this feature consists of two parts: (i) calculation of the maximal curvature per curved area n by

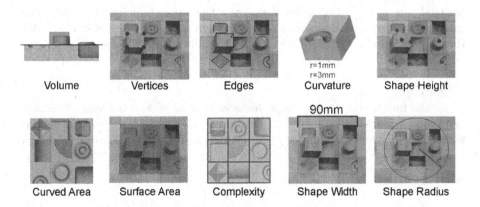

Volume   Vertices   Edges   Curvature   Shape Height

Curved Area   Surface Area   Complexity   Shape Width   Shape Radius

Fig. 4. Illustration of the shape feature.

determining the smallest radius r_n and (ii) calculation of the corresponding weight. Standard averaging over the number N of curved areas would consider uniform weights for each curvature, ignoring the fact that the corresponding surface areas are different in size. This motivated us to use the area of each curved surface $\tilde{A}_n$ as a weight to the selected maximum curvature k_n resulting in an average $\bar{k} = \left(\sum_{n=1}^{N} k_n \tilde{A}_n \right) / \sum_{n=1}^{N} \tilde{A}_n$.

The **curved area** feature measures the overall amount of curved surfaces by summing up the area of all curved surfaces in the target object. Finally, the **surface area** feature measures the overall surfaces area within the target, comprising both, curved and planar surfaces.

Based on the insights that we gained from participant interviews concerning their search strategy, we have augmented the set of the features listed in [9] by some height-related features: **Mean height** was calculated based on the maximum depth of recessed components (negative values) and the maximum height of raised components (positive values). Figure 4 (Shape Height) illustrates the selected extreme values with blue and red points. Because the negative and positive effects will cancel out when summing up, we additionally consider the **standard deviation of the shape height** as a feature. Finally, the **volume** feature has been calculated analogously to the height feature as the sum of recessed and raised shape volumes, where recessed shapes contribute with a negative values and raised shapes with positive values.

We measure the **complexity** of the target pattern by the number of bricks (1 to 9) in the target object. Because this measure does not provide information about the spatial distribution of the target object in the x-y plane, we also consider **shape width** (extension along the x-axis) and **shape radius** (see Fig. 4).

2.5   Data Evaluation

Our data evaluation is based on Pearson's correlations between the target object shape features and the mean (or standard deviation) of the hand feature vector per trial (e.g. $1/T \sum_{t=1}^{T} v_t$, where T denotes the number of points in a trial). The correlations were tested against zero and a significance level of $p < 0.001$ was chosen. The discovered correlations may contain false positives, because during our preliminary hypothesis-generating evaluation, we have not performed any corrections, such as Bonferroni, to counteract the problem of multiple comparisons.

In the future text we use *shape features* instead of *search target shape features*, and *hand features* instead of *mean over the hand feature time series* for simplicity. We use the wording of *finger features* analogously to the *hand features*.

3   Results

In the following subsection we present several exemplary findings. The correlations between all hand features and all shape features can be found in [12].

In the following figures significant correlations against zero with $p < 0.001$ are marked with hatched bars.

3.1 Height and Velocity

Figure 5 presents an overview of how different shape features correlate with the features height (left) and velocity (right) during the search phase. The height of the bars indicates the correlation values. The x-axis illustrates the object features, such as volume, vertices, edges, etc. Both plots in Fig. 5 compare the correlations between the finger features (blue) and the hand features (yellow).

The left part of the figure shows three significant correlations for the movement features *height*. Firstly, the height of the hand above the display plane and the volume exhibit a positive significant correlation. The intuition behind this result is: the larger the part of the target object volume located above the board, the higher the hand height above the board on average. Secondly, the height of the fingertips and the hand correlate positively with the number of vertices. We assume that staying higher above the display reflects less detailed search and a greater search simplicity. This demonstrates that the saliency of the vertices has a strong effect on the movement of the fingers and the hand, even in our complex setting.

The right plot in Fig. 5 shows the relation between all shape features and the *velocity* of search. For the hand velocity positive significant correlations can be observed for the mean curvature and the height of the object. The higher the target, the higher the curvature of the target, the faster the hand movement along the board on average. The plot illustrates positive significant correlation of finger velocity and the shape feature mean height. The higher the object elements w.r.t. the board, the faster both the hand and the fingers move during search.

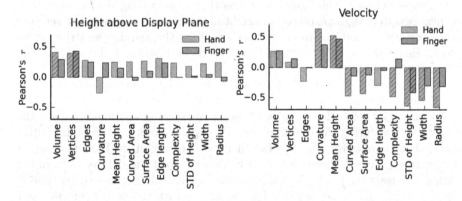

Fig. 5. Correlations between shape features and hand/finger features in the search phase. Left: hand and finger height. Right: hand and finger velocity. (Color figure online)

All other significant correlations between the hand velocity and the shape features (the surface of the target, the curved surface of the target, the standard deviation of the height, the width and the radius of the target) are negative. Larger curved areas and larger overall area of the target object slow down the movement of the hand. Similarly the radius and the width of the target object showed a significant negative correlation with the velocity of the hand. The more is the spatial extension of the target object, the slower the search speed on average. High standard deviation of the height of the target object also showed a strong negative impact on the velocity. The more diverse the height profile of the target object, the slower the movement of both the fingers and the hand.

3.2   Hand Posture

Among all shape features, only the mean height of the target correlated significantly with the hand feature *average distance between fingers*. The negative relation indicates that the higher the elements of the target, the closer the finger-tips to each other during search. Together with the previously outlined results describing a positive relationship of both the hand and the finger velocity with the mean height, this results may illustrate a very specific search strategy in case of a higher target object: fast movement of the hand, and the fingers that quickly explore only the peaks of the shapes. These results are conform with the information that we have received from the study participants after the experiment.

3.3   Search vs. Learning Phase

Next we compare correlations during the learning phase (LP) and search phase (SP) (see Fig. 6). Figure 6 (left) shows significant positive correlations between the number of vertices and the finger height for both phases. The slope is steeper in the learning phase. This figure also shows that an increasing number of vertices correlates with a higher exploration height of the hand as well as finger velocity. Since vertices are salient, more vertices simplifies the learning and the search phase. However, the effect of this features on the learning is larger than the effect on the search.

Figure 6 (right) shows a significant positive correlation between the standard deviation of the finger velocity and the curvature feature during search. This means that the more the complex shape is curved, the less homogeneous the finger velocity during the search phase. The figure shows a significant positive correlations between the velocity of the hand and the curvature: Higher curvature in the target object is associated with higher velocity and velocity variance during the learning phase, and the highest velocity during the search phase. Because traditionally, higher speed is associated with simpler search, we infer that high curvature also facilitates search.

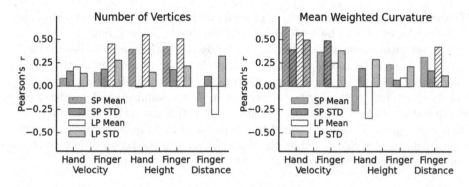

Fig. 6. Correlations between shape features and hand features during the search phase (SP) and the learning phase (LP). Left: number of vertices Right: mean weighted curvature. (Color figure online)

3.4 Pressure

Our preliminary examination of the fingertip pressure showed only one significant correlation of the thumb with the mean weighted curvature. The higher the mean weighted curvature, the higher is the applied pressure of the thumb. An overview of other results and less significant correlations can be found in [12].

4 Discussion

In our evaluation, we have found that *local* shape features like curvature, number of vertices and height, correlate with a wide range of finger and hand features. However, the *global* shape features describing the complexity or the spatial extension of the target (e.g. area, radius), correlate just with the velocity the hand.

Based on previous work [11], we assume that the features that increase velocity or the height of the hand or fingers facilitate search. Therefore, our findings imply that more vertices, larger curvature and higher targets simplify search. This is conform with the previous research (e.g. [3,9]).

We associate the features that decrease the velocity of the hand and fingers with a harder search. Most of the shape features that decrease the velocity describe the spatial extension of the target, e.g. complexity. A high standard deviation of the height, which also decreases the velocity, might correlate with the complexity: a target consisting of more basic shapes usually has a higher height variance.

Through averaging and element-wise maximum calculation during feature extraction relevant information about the target object is lost, e.g. the exact order of elementary shapes in space. All of our shape features are invariant to the order of elements. Developing a feature extractor that takes the spatial order into account is a direction of our future research.

For the particular set of target objects used in our experiment, some shape features, e.g. spatial shape features, may exhibit correlation among each other.

However, this is not the case in a general scenario. In the future experiments this correlation should be avoided by a careful design of the target objects.

In our future work we would like to analyze the data on a more fine-grained level. Although the method showed good preliminary results, interesting local phenomena are lost through temporal averaging. We would like to consider segments generated by the method described in [6] to examine our hypothesis on a more detailed level[3]. The most promising direction for future work is a multivariate regression model, trained to output hand and finger parameters (such as velocity and height) based on the shape features of the target object. Such a model could then be used to inform a robot hand during haptic search.

5 Summary

We have investigated a scenario of a spontaneous haptic search in a 3D display. The task has been to learn a previously unknown complex target shape and to find it embedded in a more complex shape landscape. The goal of this work has been to establish a connection between the shape features of the search target and the global characteristics of the search behaviour. We have posed a hypothesis that suggests a prevailing parameterization of the executed exploratory procedures influenced by the shape features of the target object.

In order to generate the hypothesis, our preliminary method consisted of three steps. Firstly, in order to represent the characteristics of the hand during the task, we have extracted multimodal features from the kinematic and haptic trajectories of the hand and fingers. Secondly, we have calculated characteristic shape features of the complex search target objects. Finally, we have calculated correlations between the hand and the object features. Our results imply significant correlations between shape features and the hand and finger parameters. This suggests that a common parameterization of the EPs during search may take place.

Acknowledgments. We would like to thank Rebecca Förster for very helpful discussions. This research was supported by the Cluster of Excellence Cognitive Interaction Technology 'CITEC' (EXC 277) at Bielefeld University, which is funded by the German Research Foundation (DFG).

References

1. Büscher, G., Koiva, R., Schürmann, C., Haschke, R., Ritter, H.: Tacile dataglove with fabric-based sensors. In: Proceedings of Humanoids, pp. 204–209 (2012)
2. Jansen, S., Bergmann, T., Kappers, A.: Identifying haptic exploratory procedures by analyszing hand dynamics and contact force. IEEE Trans. Haptics 6(4), 464–472 (2013)

---

[3] Our paper (in press) outlining this method is available http://www.techfak.uni-bielefeld.de/persons/abarch/abstract.pdf.

3. Kappers, A., Bergmann, T.: Feature saliency and integration in haptic perception. J. Robot. Soc. Jpn. **30**(5), 456–459 (2012)
4. Lederman, S., Klatzky, R.: Hand movements - a window into haptic object recognition. Cogn. Psychol. **19**(3), 342–368 (1987)
5. Morash, V.S.: Detection radius modulates systematic strategies in unstructured haptic search. In: World Haptics (2015)
6. Moringen, A., Haschke, R., Ritter, H.: Search procedures during haptic search in an unstructured 3D display. In: 2016 IEEE Haptics Symposium (HAPTICS), pp. 192–197 (2016)
7. Overvliet, K., Smeets, J., Brenner, E.: Haptic search with finger movements: using more fingers does not necessarily reduce search times. Exp. Brain Res. **182**, 427–434 (2007)
8. Plaisier, M., Bergmann, T., Kappers, A.: Haptic pop-out in a hand sweep. Acta Psychol. **128**, 368–377 (2008)
9. Plaisier, M., Bergmann, T., Kappers, A.: Salient features in 3-D haptic shape perception. Attention Percept, Psychophysics **71**(2), 421–430 (2009)
10. van Polanen, V., Bergmann, T., Kappers, A.: Haptic pop-out of movable stimuli. Attention Percept. Psychophysics **74**, 204–215 (2012)
11. van Polanen, V., Bergmann, W.M.T., Kappers, A.M.L.: Movement strategies in a haptic search task. In: Proceedings of World Haptics (2011)
12. All correlations. http://www.techfak.uni-bielefeld.de/persons/abarch/overview.pdf
13. Smith, A., Gosselin, G., Houde, B.: Deployment of fingertip forces in tactile exploration. Exp. Brain Res. **147**(2), 209–218 (2002)
14. Tanaka, Y., Bergmann, T., Kappers, A., Sano, A.: Contact force and scanning velocity during active roughness perception. PloS ONE **9**(3), e93363 (2014)

Haptic SLAM: An Ideal Observer Model for Bayesian Inference of Object Shape and Hand Pose from Contact Dynamics

Feryal M. P. Behbahani[1](✉), Guillem Singla–Buxarrais[2], and A. Aldo Faisal[1,2,3]

[1] Department of Computing, Imperial College London, London, UK
{feryal,a.faisal}@imperial.ac.uk
[2] Department of Bioengineering, Imperial College London, London, UK
[3] MRC Clinical Sciences Centre, Imperial College London, London, UK

Abstract. Dynamic tactile exploration enables humans to seamlessly estimate the shape of objects and distinguish them from one another in the complete absence of visual information. Such a blind tactile exploration allows integrating information of the hand pose and contacts on the skin to form a coherent representation of the object shape. A principled way to understand the underlying neural computations of human haptic perception is through normative modelling. We propose a Bayesian perceptual model for recursive integration of noisy proprioceptive hand pose with noisy skin–object contacts. The model simultaneously forms an optimal estimate of the true hand pose and a representation of the explored shape in an object–centred coordinate system. A classification algorithm can, thus, be applied in order to distinguish among different objects solely based on the similarity of their representations. This enables the comparison, in real–time, of the shape of an object identified by human subjects with the shape of the same object predicted by our model using motion capture data. Therefore, our work provides a framework for a principled study of human haptic exploration of complex objects.

Keywords: Tactile sensing · Haptic exploration · Internal representation · Ideal observer · Object recognition · Normative model

1 Introduction

Enabled by the remarkable dexterity of our hands and the multi–modal tactile sensors of our skin, 3–dimensional objects can be effortlessly detected and categorised from among thousands of possibilities. This is possible even in the absence of visual feedback and despite the presence of variability in our sensory and motor pathways introducing uncertainty in the true pose of our hands and the precise location of contacts on our skin [5,12]. This uncertainty complicates the localisation of tactile contact sensations in forming the internal representation of object shape and its location within the environment. Consider using

© Springer International Publishing Switzerland 2016
F. Bello et al. (Eds.): EuroHaptics 2016, Part I, LNCS 9774, pp. 146–157, 2016.
DOI: 10.1007/978-3-319-42321-0_14

a single finger to haptically explore an unknown object. The finger moves in space and we register contact locations on our skin. From the information of our finger's pose and the location of contacts, we can estimate where in space with respect to our hand the surface of the object lies. This is complicated as due to the presence of proprioceptive noise, the precise location of the finger within the space is not known. Also, the exact location where the contact between the object and the skin has occurred is ambiguous. Tactile exploration involves repeatedly exploring the space and piecing together out of the multiple contacts a tactile representation of how the object may look like. Here, a recursive Bayesian estimator can help us overcome the ambiguities assuming that the object has not changed during the exploration. Thus, we can correlate consistent object contacts with each–other which helps us reduce the uncertainty of our finger pose and the contacts locations.

The ease of our haptic object recognition abilities relies mainly on the computational magnitude of this feat. The study of human haptic perception and object recognition is complicated by the challenges of measuring rich contact dynamics in fingers and palm while manipulating objects, without occluding the tactile surfaces. The human hand can take advantage of rich dynamics in object interaction, but capturing the data and interpreting it with regards to well–defined physics models is challenging and has not been done in a systematic way. This explains perhaps why relatively little is known about the computational strategies that the brain employs to determine, represent and identify objects through pure haptic interaction, in contrast to the considerable literature on cross–modal visuo-haptic object recognition [1, 8]. While direct experimental investigation on the integration of contact and pose information is complicated, indirect measurements, e.g. through object discrimination tasks combined with an ideal observer model, can provide a pathway to novel insight. An ideal observer is a hypothetical device that performs optimally in a perceptual task given the available information. The theory of ideal observers has proven to be a powerful paradigm for investigating assumptions regarding human perceptual information processing and has been applied to a wide range of problems in neuroscience. We present here a Bayesian ideal observer model for haptic object shape representations. Our computational model of haptic object perception follows the normative theory of Simultaneous Localisation and Mapping (SLAM) developed for robotic vision [3, 11]. Our computational strategy solely relies on the knowledge of contact points on finger surfaces, noisy proprioceptive information of the finger joint configuration, and by setting torque control signals to the finger joints to drive active perception.

We present a proof–of–principle reconstruction of object shape from multi–finger exploration and propose a straightforward extension to a full hand model with realistic properties. Crucially our model assumes no visual or prior information about object shape or hand pose. We use a simple voxel–based representation of the space in reach of our fingers to represent tactile contact experiences. In a noise–free setting and without drift in our joint angle sensors, we should be able to perfectly reconstruct shapes given hand pose and contact dynamics,

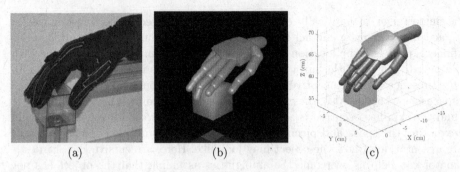

Fig. 1. 1(a) Blind haptic object exploration of a cube using CyberGlove to track finger kinematics while exploring a cube. 1(b) Our hand model simulated using the controls directly sent via the human hand CyberGlove data in the MuJoCo physics engine. 1(c) Reconstruction of finger dynamics and surface contacts on veridical hand model and cube derived from the cutaneous and kinaesthetic information extracted from the simulation.

however, both proprioceptive information and motor commands are subject to variability. This is exacerbated by the multi–joint nature of our fingers, will additively perturb our estimate of finger–tip endpoints and hence contact information and location.

The brain can improve on noisy sensory and motor information, so–called sensorimotor integration, through internal forward models [13] that predict the sensory consequences of motor actions. Such models have been successfully employed in predicting human reaching movements under visual perturbations and can be implemented algorithmically through Kalman filter observer that can provide an estimate of hand position by integrating sensory and motor signals. However, in explaining active haptic perception, visual information is not necessary or always available, and thus, tactile contact information becomes crucial. Contacts can significantly perturb motor commands resulting in deflection or prevention of desired movements that cannot be easily predicted. We use a more complex type of Bayesian inference models that enable us to exploit the fact that contact information has to be self-consistent, assuming we keep touching an object of constant shape, which enables us to iteratively refine an internal shape representation of the object. Once we have a method of inferring how tactile experience leads to a 3–dimensional representation of object surfaces, we can make experimentally testable predictions (see Fig. 1) about human ability to discriminate different shapes given known contact locations and duration of exploration.

2   Haptic SLAM Theory

We hypothesise that the underlying computational strategy for visual SLAM can be used as the basis for a model of optimal statistical inference of object shape from haptic perception. Such an ideal observer's optimal inference goals are to form dynamically an estimate of the hand configuration and shape of

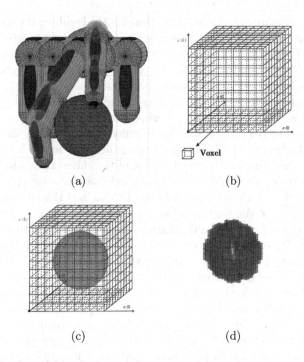

(a)   (b)

(c)   (d)

Fig. 2. 2(a) Hand model exploring a sphere, noise in proprioceptive sensory information is represented by rendering the many possible poses weighted by their probability
(blurred appearance of fingers) ?(b) Simple occupancy grid based internal representation of the contact map. We assume here a minimum resolution represented by the
nervous system of one voxel. 2(c) True position of object sphere in contact map. 2(d)
The region of occlusion by the object (empty grid cells not shown).

objects manipulated by the hand given noisy proprioceptive and tactile contact
information. We represent the physical occlusion of voxels in the space around
the hand using a contact map (see Fig. 2). This contact map of the environment
is built using the occupancy grid method [4]. In our model, we track the log–odds
representation of the probability that a grid cell is occupied. The advantage of
using a contact map model based on simple occupancy grid maps is that it is
not necessary to extract complex geometrical features from the sensor data, nor
to make hypotheses on the geometry of the surrounding environment [6] – which
will depend on the relatively little explored nature of the coordinate system
and resolution of our internal representations. During haptic exploration, the
state of the contact map is iteratively estimated. To build a spatially accurate
contact map of the hand exploring the environment (in the absence of non–tactile
information) we need to infer where in space contacts have occurred, which is
complicated by our noisy perception of the hand pose.

To simplify notation, we present here the discrete time and discrete space
version of our Haptic SLAM model. These can be thought of as straightforward approximations of continuous models. All variables have a time index k.

The contact points are mathematically speaking the result of the hand touching occupied regions of space $\mathbf{m}$, i.e. producing contacts. Thus, $\mathbf{z}(k)$(vector of contact points) is the result of a function Θ which takes the current pose of the hand ($\mathbf{q}(k)$, vector of joint angles) and the true map of contacts of the environment $\mathbf{m}$ (3–dimensional map of the explored space): $\mathbf{z}(k) = \Theta(\mathbf{q}(k), \mathbf{m})$. For simplicity, we assume here the vector to be binary (contact vs no–contact) and reflect contacts in a discrete set of patches covering the surface of our hand model (ultimately one could increase the resolution to reflect individual mechanoreceptors). We also assume here that the contact regions are sufficiently large, so that is practically no uncertainty as to which region of the surface was stimulated when a contact occurred – of course in the real hand contact point resolution varies considerably and it would be straightforward to include this in our model.

We want to infer the best possible reconstruction of $\mathbf{m}$ given noisy pose $\hat{\mathbf{q}} = \mathbf{q} + \epsilon$ and contacts $\mathbf{z}(k)$ information. $\hat{\mathbf{m}}(k)$ is the hypothesised internal representation of the physical environment at time step k which is a probability vector representing the belief (probability) that a volume element is occupied by an object (G possible grid elements). In practical terms $\hat{\mathbf{m}}$ is implemented as a 3–dimensional array reflecting a regular lattice of occupancy elements (however our models allows for any regular or amorphous parcellisation of space). We define a tupel $s(k) = (\mathbf{q}(k), \hat{\mathbf{m}}(k))$, as the current estimate of the pose and the associated contact map. We assume that proprioception (our perception of the current pose of our hand) is corrupted by a zero mean Gaussian noise with standard deviation σ and hence we can never perceive the true pose $\mathbf{q}$ and instead we perceive $\hat{\mathbf{q}}(k) = \mathbf{q}(k) + \epsilon$:

$$p(\hat{\mathbf{q}}(k)|\mathbf{q}(k)) = \mathbb{N}(0, \sigma) \tag{1}$$

Motor commands, $\mathbf{u}(k)$ continuous control vector, result in a change of hand pose configuration under the constraints of physically excluded volumes $\mathbf{m}$, thus motion is only possible if there is no hard contact. These physical and contact dynamics are represented by a function f that takes pose and true physical occlusion map $\mathbf{m}$.

$$\mathbf{q}(k) = \mathbf{q}(k-1) + f(\mathbf{u}(k-1), \mathbf{m}) \tag{2}$$

The complexity of the SLAM problem is constrained by the strong correlation between the pose and the mapping tasks: on one side, the hand pose has to be estimated with respect to the contact map of the environment which includes any objects within the explored space; on the other side, the map itself is built with from estimates of the hand pose and the current locations in physical space.

The aim of our Haptic SLAM algorithm is to infer the position of the fingers, $\mathbf{q}$, together with a map of the environment, $\hat{\mathbf{m}}$, given a set of observed contacts $\mathbf{z}$. In order to account for uncertainty in pose, contact location and motor commands in a principled manner, we frame the problem as a Bayesian inference task. In a probabilistic framework, our uncertainty of the pose is expressed as a belief in terms of a probability density function. We assume that measurements are obtained sequentially over time (tactile exploration) and previous estimates of $\mathbf{q}$ can be integrated up to time step $k - 1$ by solving the recursive Bayesian estimation problem:

$$p(\mathbf{s}(k)|\mathbf{z}(1)\ldots\mathbf{z}(k)) = \frac{p(\mathbf{z}(k)|\mathbf{s}(k))\ p(\mathbf{s}(k)|\mathbf{z}(1)\ldots\mathbf{z}(k-1))}{p(\mathbf{z}(k)|\mathbf{z}(1)\ldots\mathbf{z}(k-1))}, \qquad (3)$$

There are several computational solution approaches to this estimation problem subject to the underlying representation of the environment and the uncertainty with respect to the hand's pose. To implement it numerically, we have translated the FastSLAM algorithm from visual SLAM [7] to haptic perception, which provides a very efficient numerical computation, making it suitable for real–time applications of haptic object reconstruction such as context–aware prosthetic [2]. FastSLAM is an instance of the Rao–Blackwellised Particle Filters for a state-space approach to the SLAM problem [6]. The key idea of particle filters is to approximate $p(\mathbf{s}(k)|\mathbf{z}(1)\ldots\mathbf{z}(k))$ with sets of weighted samples from that distribution. Each sample (our particles) are a hypothesis on the state of the system $\mathbf{s}$ (pose and contact map) and the attached weight (described below) is our degree of belief that the actual state is equal to the hypothesis. Crucially, particle filtering has been used to explain human biases in a variety of sequential tasks and we believe that it can implicitly model the human ability to simultaneously consider multiple hypotheses about the shape of an object, and ultimately its identity throughout the exploration process. Using this model on real–life haptic exploration data thus allows us to infer an ideal internal representation $\hat{\mathbf{m}}$ and compare this to the true haptic environmental shape $\mathbf{m}$. These can be experimentally tested in haptic object exploration experiments where by tracking finger pose we can reconstruct our ideal observer's contact map for different objects. We can then test the ability to discriminate different objects in human subjects which should be equal or worse to using our ideal observer model.

3   Methods

In order to compute and predict the contact map given noisy proprioceptive and haptic contact information, we have adopted the FastSLAM 2.0 algorithm combined with the Occupancy Grid Mapping using Rao–Blackwellized particle filters [7]. Within our model, the uncertainty in the finger pose is represented with a set of weighted samples, where each sample is a hypothesis of the finger trajectory and has its occupancy grid map attached. This enables the Haptic SLAM problem to be decomposed into the separate problem of finger localisation and the problem of cell occupancy estimation for the G cells within the map. Each particle includes both the finger's state and an occupancy grid map. The map for each particle is updated according to the occupancy grid mapping algorithm outlined earlier, with the joint configuration of the finger fixed at the configuration of the particle. This separation allows the occupancy grid algorithm to work with a guaranteed joint measurements while still allowing for uncertainty in the finger's pose. By looking at the highest probability particle, we determine the current best guess of the finger's pose relevant to the environment's map.

The set of all particles is represented as $S_k = \mathbf{s}_k^{[1]}, \mathbf{s}_k^{[2]}, \ldots, \mathbf{s}_k^{[N]}$ where N is the number of particles used. At each time step, k, each particle is given a weight depending on how well its estimate of the state agrees with the observed measurements. Within each iteration, the set of all particles is re–sampled and replaced by randomly drawing new particles from the previous distribution based on calculated weights creating a new distribution. Particles whose predictions match the measurements are given a high weight and thus, have a higher chance of being resampled.

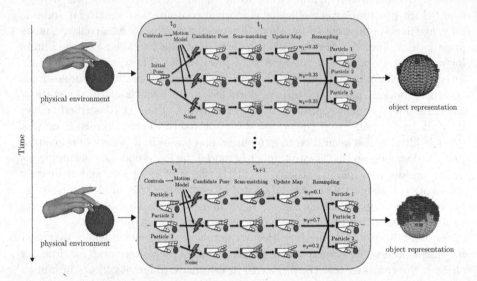

Fig. 3. Illustration of the haptic SLAM computational model. (Left) haptic exploration of objects yields both noisy proprioceptive signals and contact locations. This information is integrated (middle) by multiple concurrent particle filters implementing simultaneous hypothesis about the true pose of the hand and the contact map associated with that pose. This information is integrated and updated with incoming contact and pose information and the weighting between the various particles (hypotheses) are calculated according to their plausibility. (Right) the information is thus integrated into an internal representation of the contact locations – the contact map (see text for details).

Computing the dynamic updates during haptic exploration is possible with the following algorithm that implements the haptic SLAM model:

(1) The set of particles $S(k)$ is initialised with all particles having the same hand pose (i.e., all joint angles set to a particular pose) and holding its occupancy grid map where all cells have a 50 % probability of occupancy. We hypothesise that humans, in the absence of other sensory signals, start exploring the environment with this prior: cells have an equal probability of being occupied.

(2) Motor commands, $\mathbf{u}(k)$, are sent to the hand (or in our model implementation torque commands to the physics simulation of hand and environment) to move the fingers to the next pose. It has been shown that the correlation structure of finger movements suggests that their motion is controlled in a lower–dimensional space [9]. For simplicity here we have only used random torques as control signals for individual joint actuation. However, such movement synergies can be easily integrated into our model for the generation of more natural control signals and more efficient computations.

(3) A simple motion model is used to propagate the particles in the model. This is the equivalent step to having an internal forward model predicting the consequences of a motor action. The difference between the old and noisy perception of the new pose, delta pose, is used to draw samples from the proposal distribution.

(4) Scan–matching is performed for each particle. To perform scan–matching, by small perturbations to the particle pose, several hypothesised poses centred on and close to the candidate pose are generated. Each scan–matching pose will evaluate the current sensory information on different locations of the contact map of the particle based on their pose. Within these new set of poses, the scan–matching procedure finds the pose that best explains the new measurements and thus the copy of the full internal map that the particle currently holds. Consequently, the scan–matching procedure improves the candidate pose by maximising the likelihood of the measurements given the pose and the contact map.

(5) The particle weight is calculated. Each particle is given an importance weight according to how well its estimate of the state agrees with the measurements (i.e. proportional to the likelihood of the current sensory information given the contact map): $w^{[i]}(k) = p(\mathbf{z}(k)|\hat{\mathbf{q}}^{[i]}(k), \hat{\mathbf{m}}^{[i]}(k-1))$. Notice that this weight has already been computed during the scan-matching procedure. In addition, we use the occupancy grid mapping algorithm fixed on the particle pose to update the contact map based on the measurements perceived in this step. In this manner, each particle starts building their self–consistent map of the environment.

(6) The new set of particles are resampled. Particles are drawn with replacement chance proportional to their importance weight. In conditions where all the samples have equal weights, all particles will be resampled and continue to the next set. However, for an intermediate step where particles are given different weights, the new particle set will contain copies of the particles that have higher weights while particles with low weights that do not represent the target distribution will be depleted. This can be thought of as the survival of the fittest approach to selecting the best–competing hypothesis (particles) and it is crucial to the success of the algorithm as we are approximating a multidimensional continuous distribution only through a finite number of particles [6]. The resampling step generates a new set of particles whose weights are set to be equal.

Furthermore, we have also adopted the adaptive resampling method [10] which instead of resampling the particle set in every time step, uses a criterion for deciding on the necessity of the resampling procedure. Thus, at each time step k an effective sample size is estimated which reflects how well the current particle set represents the target distribution. The calculation of the effective sample size is approximated as $\hat{N}_{\text{eff}} = \frac{1}{\sum_{i=1}^{N} (w^{(i)})^2}$ where $w^{[i]}(k)$ refers to the normalised weight of particle i. This measure captures the variance of particle likelihoods and increases as the approximation of uncertainty of the hand pose by the particle set becomes worse. In the haptic SLAM algorithm, we resample each time N_{eff} drops below the threshold of $N/2$, where N is the number of particles, as experimentally shown to significantly reduce the risk of replacing good particles.

Following the resampling step, the new set of particles are propagated from t_k to t_{k+1}, controls are sent to the simulation engine and the motion model with normally distributed noise is used to obtain the next candidate hand pose for each particle and the loop begins anew. Our Haptic SLAM algorithm goes through this iteration loop until exploration is completed (see Fig. 3).

4   Results and Discussion

We explore four different geometric primitives using two–finger tactile exploration and present the results of our model's reconstruction of the object shapes. Given defined shape and location of these primitives, we can directly line up the non–zero entries in the true occupancy map of space $\mathbf{m}$ with the geometric primitives. In the absence of proprioceptive noise, the model builds over time an internal representation $\hat{\mathbf{m}}$ that accurately replicates $\mathbf{m}$ (see Fig. 4). This is expected, given that there is no uncertainty in the pose of the hand and so as to the spatial location that the contact points are registered during exploration.

The more interesting scenario is exploration in the presence of proprioceptive noise. We evaluated haptic exploration for a number of different levels of additive proprioceptive noise (see Fig. 5). Here, independent Gaussian distributed noise with zero mean and standard deviation σ was added to each joint's proprioceptive feedback so as to model perceptual uncertainty. Inferred contact maps for the same tactile experience reflect differences in internal representation due to sensory variability of $\sigma = 1°$, $2°$, $3°$, and $5°$. Note how the use of an internal

$t = 1\,\text{sec}$ $t = 10\,\text{sec}$ $t = 60\,\text{sec}$

Fig. 4. The contact map updates throughout tactile exploration can be seen here. We show here only voxels with contact evidence (red voxels) superimposed on the true shape and location of the object. (Color figure online)

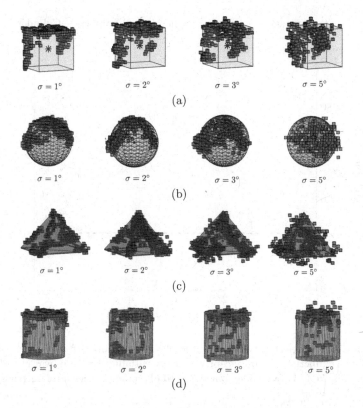

$\sigma = 1°$ $\sigma = 2°$ $\sigma = 3°$ $\sigma = 5°$

(a)

$\sigma = 1°$ $\sigma = 2°$ $\sigma = 3°$ $\sigma = 5°$

(b)

$\sigma = 1°$ $\sigma = 2°$ $\sigma = 3°$ $\sigma = 5°$

(c)

$\sigma = 1°$ $\sigma = 2°$ $\sigma = 3°$ $\sigma = 5°$

(d)

Fig. 5. The inferred contact map, superimposed on the true object shape, of the four object categories after 30 s of tactile exploration and varying levels of noise (zero mean and standard deviation $\sigma = 1°, 2°, 3°, 5°$) in proprioceptive information.

model enables to reasonably contain perceptual uncertainty to reliably estimate 3–dimensional contact locations – consider that the cumulative proprioceptive joint uncertainty in the left most simulation is the reconstruction of an object with a cumulative uncertainty of the finger tip end–points with 5° standard deviation *per* joint of which each finger has four.

Finally, we evaluated the ability to use the occupancy grid representation of our contact map to estimate the ability of observers to distinguish between four geometric primitives (cube, sphere, pyramid, cylinder). We report here as accuracy the ability to identify the correct object out of the four presented objects. The discrimination rule for the ideal observer model was, in this case, the nearest neighbour classification – we computed the Hamming distance between an inferred contact map $\hat{m}$ obtained from tactile exploration with 1 instance of exploration for each of the four objects resembling supervised one–shot learning capability in humans, however, within our framework different categorisation models can be incorporated and compared in performance. We performed repeated exploration trials and determined the accuracy with which we were

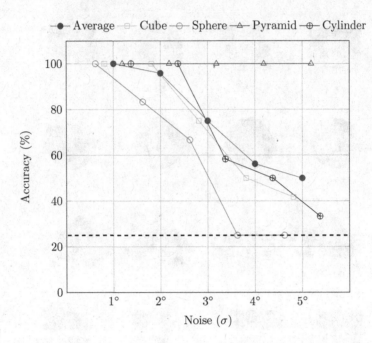

Fig. 6. Classification performance of haptic object recognition from inferred contact maps varies as a function of proprioceptive sensory variability σ. Four–way classification (chance level is 25 %) between the four depicted object categories after 72 trials of 10 s of haptic exploration for each shape.

able to correctly identify the object (see Fig. 6). While the spiky pyramid was even in a high noise regime perfectly classifiable, cube, sphere and cylinder were increasingly more difficult to discriminate. The lack of defined edge features in the contact map of the sphere may explain the poor performance at identifying this smooth object correctly from others – bearing in mind that tactile exploration was subject to random motions and not the smooth pursuit of surface features which we may employ. These results can be directly compared to human performance once single joint sensory uncertainty has been reliably characterised. Moreover, by using sensorised gloves and computer physics engines to approximatively reconstruct the contact experience of human tactile exploration (see Fig. 1) we can obtain more realistic exploration motions and thus further improve our predictions.

In conclusion, we presented a normative model for forming spatially embedded object representations from blind tactile exploration in the presence of sensory noise. Our proposed ideal observer model for haptic object exploration and shape reconstruction is based on the well–known Fast SLAM algorithm from computer vision but is translated here to 3–dimensional haptic perception. In the visual setting we have noisy estimates of camera location (Cartesian coordinates) and pixels reflecting the associated camera image, while in the haptic setting, we have noisy estimates of hand pose (in joint angles) and contact points reflecting the associated haptic feedback. Our Haptic SLAM model provides a framework for a principled study of natural human haptic exploration. Moreover, in conjunction with tactile–enabled prostheses, our model allows for real–time object recognition with direct implications for the design and control of context–aware prosthetic devices.

References

1. Amedi, A., Malach, R., Hendler, T., Peled, S., Zohary, E.: Visuo-haptic object-related activation in the ventral visual pathway. Nature Neurosci. **4**(3), 324–330 (2001)
2. Behbahani, F.M., Taunton, R., Thomik, A.A., Faisal, A.A.: Haptic slam for context-aware robotic hand prosthetics-simultaneous inference of hand pose and object shape using particle filters. In: 2015 7th International IEEE/EMBS Conference on Neural Engineering (NER), pp. 719–722. IEEE (2015)
3. Dissanayake, M., Newman, P., Clark, S., Durrant-Whyte, H.F., Csorba, M.: A solution to the simultaneous localization and map building (slam) problem. IEEE Trans. Robot. Autom. **17**(3), 229–241 (2001)
4. Elfes, A.: Using occupancy grids for mobile robot perception and navigation. Computer **22**(6), 46–57 (1989)
5. Faisal, A.A., Selen, L.P., Wolpert, D.M.: Noise in the nervous system. Nat. Rev. Neurosci. **9**(4), 292–303 (2008)
6. Grisetti, G., Stachniss, C., Burgard, W.: Improved techniques for grid mapping with rao-blackwellized particle filters. IEEE Trans. Robot. **23**(1), 34–46 (2007)
7. Montemerlo, M., Thrun, S., Koller, D., Wegbreit, B., et al.: Fastslam: a factored solution to the simultaneous localization and mapping problem. In: AAAI/IAAI, pp. 593–598 (2002)
8. Newell, F.N., Ernst, M.O., Tjan, B.S., Bülthoff, H.H.: Viewpoint dependence in visual and haptic object recognition. Psychol. Sci. **12**(1), 37–42 (2001)
9. Santello, M., Flanders, M., Soechting, J.F.: Postural hand synergies for tool use. J. Neurosci. **18**(23), 10105–10115 (1998)
10. Smith, A., Doucet, A., de Freitas, N., Gordon, N.: Sequential Monte Carlo Methods in Practice. Springer Science & Business Media, Berlin (2013)
11. Smith, R.C., Cheeseman, P.: On the representation and estimation of spatial uncertainty. Int. J. Robot. Res. **5**(4), 56–68 (1986)
12. Van Beers, R., Sittig, A.C., van der Gon, J.J.D.: The precision of proprioceptive position sense. Exp. Brain Res. **122**(4), 367–377 (1998)
13. Wolpert, D.M., Ghahramani, Z., Jordan, M.I.: An internal model for sensorimotor integration. Science **269**(5232), 1880 (1995)

The Influence of Motor Task on Tactile Suppression During Action

Nienke B. Debats[1,2(✉)], Marieke Rohde[2,3], Catharina Glowania[1,2], Anna Oppenborn[1], and Marc O. Ernst[2,4]

[1] Department of Cognitive Neuroscience, University of Bielefeld,
Bielefeld, Germany
nienke.debats@uni-bielefeld.de
[2] Center for Cognitive Interaction Technology (CITEC), University of Bielefeld,
Bielefeld, Germany
[3] AFFS Affective Signals GmbH, Berlin, Germany
[4] Department of Applied Cognitive Psychology, University of Ulm,
Ulm, Germany

Abstract. Movement of a limb substantially decreases the intensity and sensitivity with which tactile stimuli on that limb are perceived. This movement-related tactile suppression likely interferes with performance in motor tasks that require the precise evaluation of tactile feedback, such as the adjustment of grip forces during grasping. Therefore, we hypothesise that suppression might be stronger for stimuli that are irrelevant to successful performance in a given motor task. To test this hypothesis, we measured participants' perception of tactile intensity while performing different motor tasks. We investigated perception of both supra-threshold stimuli (Exp. 1: intensity discrimination) and of stimuli close to the detection threshold (Exp. 2: detection). We compared tactile perception between two grasping conditions (active, tactile inputs relevant), a condition where participants pointed in the air (active, tactile inputs irrelevant) and a static condition (baseline). In both experiments, we observed tactile suppression in all three movement conditions but not the predicted attenuation of tactile suppression in the grasp conditions. Contrary to our hypothesis, there was even an amplification of tactile suppression in the grasping conditions of Exp. 1, which might be related to the movement velocity. In conclusion, we did not find evidence that motor tasks modulate the strength of tactile suppression. Our results further suggest that it is important to control for possibly confounding variables, such as movement velocity and laterality, in this line of research.

Keywords: Tactile suppression · Active touch · Motor behaviour

1 Introduction

Haptic perception is inherently active and task-dependent. For instance, the selection of motor strategies for haptic exploration depends on the estimated

© Springer International Publishing Switzerland 2016
F. Bello et al. (Eds.): EuroHaptics 2016, Part I, LNCS 9774, pp. 158–167, 2016.
DOI: 10.1007/978-3-319-42321-0_15

object property [13]. This is likely because exploratory movements modulate the precision with which properties such as the height of a Braille-like dot [7] or an object's moment of inertia [5] can be haptically estimated. Indeed, exploratory strategies have been shown to optimise the precision of haptic estimates (e.g., [6, 15]).

Research on tactile suppression during movement, also commonly referred to as movement-related tactile gating, has generated a body of results that are difficult to reconcile with the above-mentioned literature. Comparing the tactile sensation between an active (movement) and a passive (no movement) condition, the active condition is found to reduce the perceived intensity and the tactile sensitivity (e.g., [8, 10, 14, 17]). This effect occurs robustly both for electrical stimuli applied directly in the afferent nerves, for electrical stimuli applied to the skin, and for vibrotactile stimuli applied to the skin; it was found to occur for near-threshold as well as for supra-threshold stimuli (e.g., [2, 17]); and its magnitude was found to increase with movement speed (e.g., [16]). It is puzzling that our brains, on the one hand, fine-tune the exploratory movements to maximise tactile precision while, on the other hand, suppressing the tactile sensation during movement.

One key question is: Is tactile suppression under some form of top-down neural control that enables the brain to selectively suppress only the task-irrelevant tactile stimuli? Recent research by Brozzoli et al. [1] has shown such a task-related modulation of tactile processing for visuo-tactile integration. Moreover, a recent study by Colino et al. [3] suggests that similar modulatory effects might also occur in tactile suppression: The authors studied tactile suppression during grasping, and found that stimuli were only suppressed when applied to the forearm, where they are irrelevant for grasping. Stimuli were not suppressed when they were applied to the index finger, where they are important to adjust grip forces and avoid slip of the object. However, this study might be confounded by comparably high stimulus intensities (i.e., 'readily detectable a rest' [3]) that caused ceiling effects for the measure of tactile sensitivity in the detection task (d' of approximately four). This makes it difficult to assess the strength of this attenuation. Moreover, the effect was observed when comparing stimulation in different (relevant and irrelevant) skin locations. To quantify the strength of the possible modulation of tactile suppression, one would ideally have a baseline for both suppressed and unsuppressed tactile sensation for a given stimulus location.

The current study set out to test the hypothesis that tactile suppression during movement occurs predominantly in motor task-irrelevant skin locations, using a different experimental paradigm. We studied the perceived sensation of tactile stimuli delivered to the ring finger in two different psychophysical tasks (Experiment 1: intensity discrimination, supra-threshold stimuli; Experiment 2: detection, stimuli at threshold). We compared four different movement conditions: A baseline condition for unsuppressed sensation (Condition *Static*; right arm resting), a baseline condition for suppressed sensation (Condition *Point*: right arm moving without an additional motor-task), and two different object grasping conditions (Condition *Power*: power grip; Condition *Pinch*: pinch grip). We hypothesised that tactile suppression during grasping (Conditions Pinch and Power) would be attenuated compared to baseline (Condition Point), as tactile stimuli to the fingers are relevant for grasping. The additional contrast between the two grasp conditions (Pinch and Power) might reveal how localised such effects of task might be, as tactile inputs to the ring finger are more relevant to performing a power grip than a pinch grip.

2   Methods

2.1   Participants

Ten participants (3 male; age range 20–28 years) volunteered to participate in Exp. 1, and ten participants (1 male; age range 23–26 years) volunteered to participate in Exp. 2. All participants were right-handed and naïve with respect to the purpose and theoretical background of the experiments. They were compensated with a payment of 6 Euro per hour. The Bielefeld University ethics committee approved the study, and participants gave written informed consent prior to their participation.

2.2   Apparatus

Participants were seated on a height-adjustable chair at a desk with a board (task surface) mounted 15 cm above the desk surface (see Fig. 1). They faced a computer monitor (approximately 60 cm viewing distance) that displayed trial instructions. At the beginning of a trial, participants rested both hands on the surface. Movement onsets were detected using a self-made contact sensor with a sampling frequency of 60 Hz. The task surface was transparent on the right side to allow tracking of the right hand's movement by a LEAP infrared motion sensor that was located under the task surface. A cylindrical object for grasping stood centrally 30 cm in front of participants' wrists (see Fig. 1 and Sect. 2.3).

The vibratory stimuli were applied using the Haptuator Original (Tactile labs). These stimulators were attached to the proximal phalanx of the left and right ring

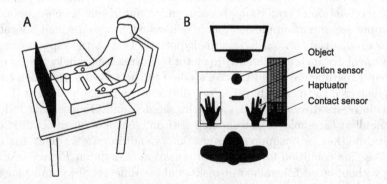

Fig. 1. The experimental apparatus as illustrated from a side view (A) and in top view (B).

fingers (Exp. 1), or to the right ring finger only (Exp. 2). The timing of stimulus delivery in response to movement onset (see Sect. 2.4) was controlled using the Psychophysics Toolbox for Matlab [12]. Participants' responses were submitted after a trial using the right hand by pressing a key on a keyboard that was located next to the right hand's resting position. Participants wore over-the-ear earmuffs to avoid that they might hear activation of the vibrotactile stimulators.

2.3   Motor Tasks

At the beginning of each trial, the computer monitor displayed the instruction to put both hands in the start position (i.e., flat on the task surface). When the contact sensor detected the right hand in the correct position, the task instruction for the motor task was displayed on the monitor. In both experiments, we compared four movement conditions:

1. In the *Static* condition, both hands were lying flat on the task surface throughout a trial to record participants' unsuppressed tactile sensitivity (instruction on screen: "Rest").
2. In the *Point* condition, the participants made an out-and-back movement to the location of the cylinder with their right hand. There is no relevant tactile input during this pointing movement, so this condition gives a baseline for the participant's suppressed tactile sensation (instruction on screen: "Point").
3. In the *Pinch* grip condition, participants reached and grasped the cylinder with the thumb and index finger of their right hand. In this condition, the stimulated ring finger was not relevant for successful grasping (instruction on screen: "Grasp thumb & index").
4. In the *Power* grip condition, participants grasped the cylinder with all fingers of the right hand. Here, the stimulated ring finger was relevant for execution of the grasping task (instruction on screen: "Grasp whole hand").

From the recorded hand movements we computed for each trial the ring finger velocity in the horizontal plane. We centred these velocity profiles at the time of movement onset, averaged across trials, and defined the velocity during stimulation as the average velocity over the 6 time samples (i.e., 100 ms) at which the stimulation was given. Unfortunately, we had unnoticed technical issues with the tracking system after approximately 250 trials were recorded. We excluded 4 participants (Exp. 1) and 1 participant (Exp. 2) from the velocity analysis because they had fewer than 25 useable movement traces. For the remaining 6 and 9 participants we discarded on average 54.8 % (Exp. 1) and 22.9 % (Exp. 2) of the trials.

2.4   Perceptual Tasks

In both experiments, vibrotactile stimuli that consisted of a 100 ms long 80 Hz pure sine wave vibration were applied to participants' ring fingers. The stimulus intensity was modulated by varying the sine wave amplitude. In the active conditions (Point, Pinch, Power), the stimuli were applied right after the contact sensor registered a movement onset. In the rest condition (Static), the stimuli were delivered one second after the instruction to rest was displayed.

In Exp. 1 we used an intensity discrimination task. Supra-threshold stimuli were applied simultaneously to the ring fingers of both hands. One hand received a standard stimulus with a fixed intensity, the other hand received a comparison stimulus with one of seven predefined levels of stimulus intensity (Method of Constant Stimuli). When prompted, participants had to judge (forced choice) which of these two stimuli felt more intense by responding with a key press of the right hand. The seven levels of comparison stimulus intensity were spaced equidistant on a logarithmic scale which was centred at the intensity of the standard stimulus. In total there were 7 (intensity pairs) × 20 (repetitions) = 140 trials for each of the four movement conditions (see Sect. 2.3), i.e., 560 trials in total. In half the trials, the standard stimulus was applied to the left hand; in the other half, it was applied to the right hand. We fitted a cumulative Gaussian psychometric function with two free parameters (μ, σ) to the responses using the Matlab function glmfit.m. The 50 % cut gave our estimate of the point of subjective equality (PSE) of left and right hand stimulus intensity.

In Exp. 2 we used a detection task with a single near-threshold stimulus intensity, whose intensity we had determined in pilot experiments. Stimuli were applied only to the right ring finger. When prompted, participants had to judge whether there had been a stimulus or not by pressing a key with the right hand. For each condition, we presented 40 trials in which the stimulus was present and 40 trials in which the stimulus was absent. Thus there were 2 (stimulus present vs. absent) × 40 (repetitions) = 80 trials per movement condition, so 320 trials in total. As some participants had either full coverage (no false rejections) or full specificity (no false alarms), we analysed the results using the loglinear approach [9] to estimate d' from the confusion matrix.

In both experiments, the order of stimulus presentation and movement condition was randomised within a repetition block. Participants had the option to label a trial as invalid if they were inattentive or thought there might have been a technical mistake (e.g., stimulus too early). These trials (Exp. 1: 2.2 %; Exp. 2: 0.75 %) were discarded and repeated at the end of the experiment. At the beginning of an experimental session, participants performed between 5 and 20 practice trials to get familiar with the task. There were no scheduled breaks, but participants were encouraged to take breaks autonomously after every 100 trials. Exp. 1 took approximately 90 min, Exp. 2 approximately 45 min to complete.

3   Results

3.1   Experiment 1

Figure 2(A) depicts the result of a representative participant. Compared to the Static baseline condition (black), the psychometric functions from the three movement conditions (Point, Power, Pinch) are shifted to the right, i.e., the PSE is larger and tactile suppression occurred. In addition, there is a leftward

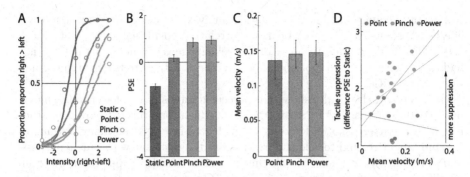

Fig. 2. Results experiment 1. A: Psychometric curves for an example participant. B: Population results PSE (mean and standard error). C: Population results movement velocity (mean and standard error). D: Tactile suppression (difference in PSE from Static) against mean velocity for individual participants (with least squares regression lines). (Color figure online)

shift in the Static baselines condition psychometric function relative to the standard intensity (vertical striped line), suggesting that stimuli applied to the right hand were perceived as more intense than stimuli applied to the left hand.

The same result is observed also on the population level (Fig. 2(B)). Paired-sample t-tests confirm that tactile suppression occurred in all movement conditions, i.e., there are significant differences between PSEs in the Static condition and all of the movement conditions (Point: $t(9) = 7.3, p < 0.001$; Pinch: $t(9) = 10.5, p < 0.001$; Power: $t(9) = 16.1, p < 0.001$). Furthermore there are significant differences between the Point condition and the two grip conditions (Pinch: $t(9) = 3.3, p = 0.002$; Power: $t(9) = 5.4, p < 0.001$) but not between the two grip conditions ($t(9) = 0.8, p = 0.434$). The differences between the Point condition and the two grip conditions (Pinch, Power) were in the opposite direction as we had predicted. That is, in the two grip conditions (Power, Pinch) where tactile inputs are deemed important, tactile suppression was stronger compared to the Point condition (Fig. 2(B)). Additionally, the PSE results of the Static condition are significantly smaller than 0 (two-tailed t-test: $t(9) = 23.9, p < 0.001$), which indicates that stimuli applied to the left hand were perceived as less intense than stimuli applied to the right hand. This is an unexpected result that we return to in our Discussion (Sect. 4).

Figure 2(C) shows the velocity of the ring finger at the time of stimulation. Previous studies have shown that the strength of tactile suppression depends on movement velocity [4,16], so differences in velocity might explain the differences between conditions that we observe. Qualitatively, differences in velocity between conditions follow the same pattern as differences in PSEs, i.e., on average movement velocity is a bit lower in the Point condition than in the Pinch and Power conditions. However, these differences are not significant (Point vs. Pinch $t(5) = -1.0, p = 0.247$; Point vs. Power $t(5) = -1.1, p = 0.321$; Power vs. Pinch $t(5) = -0.5, p = 0.607$). We assessed whether there was a positive relationship between velocity and tactile suppression effects (i.e., the increase in PSE relative to the static condition), but a correlation analysis did not reveal any significant effects (Absolute value of all Pearson correlation coefficients $|r| \leq 0.6$; Fig. 2 (D)). This might be due to noise in the velocity measurements, as many trials had to be discarded from motion analysis (cf. Sect. 2.3), or to the relatively small range of velocities.

In summary, the results show that perceived intensity was lower in the movement conditions than in the Static condition, which conforms with previous studies on this matter [14,17]. There is no evidence that task-relevancy attenuates this movement-related tactile suppression, in disagreement with our hypothesis and the results by Colino et al. [3]. On the contrary, tactile suppression was even amplified in the grasping conditions (Pinch, Power) compared to the Point condition. This unexpected effect might be explained by differences in motor planning, muscle activation, or movement velocity between the movement conditions, even if an effect of velocity is not evident in our results.

A possible explanation of why our results differ from those reported by Colino et al. [3] is that we used a different perceptual task. Wrongly assessing the intensity of a supra-threshold stimulus is not the same as detecting whether a stimulus occurred in the first place. We therefore performed a second experiment, where we measured perceptual sensitivity (yes/no detection task) for weaker vibrotactile stimuli.

3.2   Experiment 2

Figure 3(A) depicts the population results of Experiment 2 on tactile sensitivity (d'). Here, suppression corresponds to a lower d' in the movement conditions (Point, Power, Pinch) relative to the Static condition. Tactile suppression relative

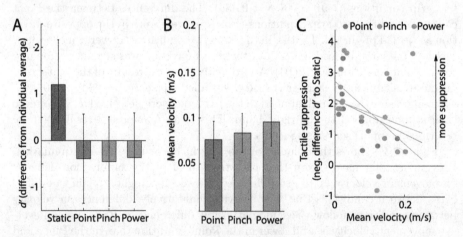

Fig. 3. Results experiment 2. A: Population results d' (normalised for visualisation by subtracting average individual d' values; mean and standard error). B: Population results movement velocity (mean and standard error). C: Tactile suppression (negative difference in d' from Static) against mean velocity for individual participants (with least squares regression lines). (Color figure online)

to the Static condition was observed in all movement conditions: the Point condition ($t(9) = 4.8, p = 0.001$), Pinch condition ($t(9) = 3.7, p = 0.005$), and the Power condition ($t(9) = 3.4, p = 0.008$). We found no effect of motor task on tactile suppression, as indicated by t-tests comparing movement conditions: Point vs. Pinch: $t(9) = 0.3, p = 0.751$; Point vs. Power: $t(9) = -0.1, p = 0.898$; Pinch vs. Power: $t(9) = -0.5, p = 0.646$.

In Exp. 2, there was a significantly lower movement velocity in the Point condition than in the Power condition ($t(8) = -2.4, p = 0.041$), but no differences between the other conditions (Point vs. Pinch $t(8) = -1.3, p = 0.234$; Power vs. Pinch $t(8) = -1.4, p = 0.213$). We again performed a regression analysis to investigate whether the strength of tactile suppression between participants might be explained by differences in velocity, in which case we would expect a positive correlation between velocity and the decrease in d' relative to Static condition (Fig. 3(C)). However, we found no significant relationship in any of the three movement conditions (all $|r| \leq 0.52$).

4   Discussion

In this study we examined whether tactile suppression might be modulated by a 'clever', centrally controlled mechanism that knows whether tactile sensory inputs at a specific location are relevant to behavioural success in a given task. This presumed mechanism would process relevant stimuli at the regular, unsuppressed intensity but would attenuate the perceived intensity of task-irrelevant stimuli. Such task-dependent processing of tactile stimuli has been reported in other contexts [1] and preliminary results in the literature [3] suggested that also tactile suppression might be modulated in such a way. However, the results here do not indicate the existence of such mechanism. We tested participants' intensity discrimination performance (Exp. 1) and detection performance (Exp. 2) for vibrotactile stimuli comparing two grasping conditions (Pinch, Power), where tactile inputs to the finger were presumed relevant to avoid slip, with a pointing-in-the-air condition (Point), where tactile inputs are irrelevant. The results show no effect of task on detection (Sect. 3.2) and even the opposite effect of task than hypothesised on intensity discrimination (Sect. 3.1), i.e., more suppression for the grasping conditions. We therefore conclude that movement related tactile suppression is likely not modulated in a top-down manner by task-relevancy.

Of course, it is possible that such a modulation does indeed exist and that our experimental design was unsuitable to detect it. For instance, we investigated suppression early on during the outward hand movement and in one skin location. Instead, the task-relevancy in tactile suppression might be specific in both space and time. As for the spatial aspect, it might be that only a highly specific part of the moving limb is considered task-relevant and that in our grasping task the proximal part of the finger was not included. Similarly, the task-relevancy effect might occur later during the movement, close to the time of grasping contact. It is also possible that motor-task relevancy alone is not sufficient to cause attenuation of movement-related tactile suppression. A study by Juravle et al. [11] suggests that there might be an interaction between motor tasks and the ecological validity of the corresponding perceptual task.

However, given the influence of movement velocity on tactile suppression [4,16], one has to also bear a different explanation in mind for why differences between tasks were observed in some studies but not in ours. Different motor tasks can lead to differences in muscle activation and movement velocity, which then might modulate the strength of tactile suppression effects recorded. In our design, we picked actions that were very similar (i.e., grasping and pointing) and we chose to compare very early stages of movement (i.e., movement onset) where no larger velocity differences were expected. Nevertheless, even in our experiments there is a tendency for slower movements in the Point condition than in the Grasp conditions (Figs. 2C and 3B). This finding illustrates how hard it is to obtain equivalent experimental conditions when comparing tactile suppression between movement conditions. It is therefore essential to control for such low-level confounds when assessing the effect of task-relevancy (or other task-related factors) on tactile suppression.

An additional unexpected result is the difference in perceived tactile intensity between the right and left hands (Static condition in Exp. 1, Sect. 3.1 and in Fig. 2B). We included only right-handed participants, so this unexpected laterality effect might have been caused by hand dominance. Alternatively, there might have been attentional effects on perceived tactile intensity, as the right hand was active in 75 % of the trials, whereas the left hands was always passive. This might have shifted attention to the right hand. Irrespective of the nature of this laterality effect, it is also a possible confound in experiments that compare perceived intensity between an active and a passive hand (e.g., [3]).

In summary, while we cannot rule out that the motor task modulates tactile suppression, our results suggest that such an influence is minor. Instead, we found that tactile suppression is modulated more by low-level factors, such as laterality and possibly also movement velocity, which have to be controlled when performing this kind of experiment.

Acknowledgments. NBD was supported by the German Research Foundation (DFG) grant HE 1187/19-1. MR, CG and MOE were supported by the Cluster of Excellence Cognitive Interaction Technology 'CITEC' (EXC 277), which is funded by the DFG. MOE was additionally supported by the FP7/2007-2013 project n8 601165 WEARHAP. We would like to thank Irene Senna for fruitful discussions and Miriam Henning for her work on pilot experiments.

References

1. Brozzoli, C., Pavani, F., Urquizar, C., Cardinali, L., Farnè, A.: Grasping actions remap peripersonal space. NeuroReport **20**(3), 913–917 (2009)
2. Chapman, C.E., Bushnell, M.C., Miron, D., Duncan, G.H., Lund, J.P.: Sensory perception during movement in man. Exp. Brain Res. **68**(3), 516–524 (1987)

3. Colino, F.L., Buckingham, G., Cheng, D.T., van Donkelaar, P., Binsted, G.: Tactile gating in a reaching and grasping task. Physiol. Rep. **2**(3), e00267 (2014)
4. Cybulska-Klosowicz, A., Meftah, E.M., Raby, M., Lemieux, M.L., Chapman, C.E.: A critical speed for gating of tactile detection during voluntary movement. Exp. Brain Res. **210**(2), 291–301 (2011)
5. Debats, N.B., Kingma, I., Beek, P.J., Smeets, J.B.J.: Moving the weber fraction: the perceptual precision for moment of inertia increases with exploration force. PLoS ONE **7**(9), e42941 (2012)
6. Drewing, K.: After experience with the task humans actively optimize shape discrimination in touch by utilizing effects of exploratory movement direction. Acta Psychol. **141**(3), 295–303 (2012)
7. Drewing, K., Kaim, L.: Haptic shape perception from force and position signals varies with exploratory movement direction and the exploring finger. Attention Percept. Psychophys. **71**(5), 1174–1184 (2009)
8. Garland, H.T., Angel, R.W.: Modulation of tactile sensitivity during movement. Neurology **24**(4), 361 (1974)
9. Hautus, M.J.: Corrections for extreme proportions and their biasing effects on estimated values of d'. Behav. Res. Methods Instrum. Comput. **27**(1), 46–51 (1995)
10. Juravle, G., Deubel, H., Tan, H.Z., Spence, C.: Changes in tactile sensitivity over the time-course of a goal-directed movement. Behav. Brain Res. **208**(2), 391–401 (2010)
11. Juravle, G., McGlone, F., Spence, C.: Context-dependent changes in tactile perception during movement execution. Front. Psychol. 4(913) (2013)
12. Kleiner, M., Brainard, D., Pelli, D.: What's new in psychtoolbox-3? In: Abstract Supplement of the 30th European Conference on Visual Perception (ECVP), vol. 36, p. 14 (2007)
13. Lederman, S.J., Klatzky, R.L.: Hand movements: a window into haptic object recognition. Cogn. Psychol. **19**(3), 342–368 (1987)
14. Milne, R.J., Aniss, A.M., Kay, N.E., Gandevia, S.C.: Reduction in perceived intensity of cutaneous stimuli during movement: a quantitative study. Exp. Brain Res. **70**(3), 569–576 (1988)
15. Plaisier, M.A., van Dam, L.C.J., Glowania, C., Ernst, M.O.: Exploration mode affects visuohaptic integration of surface orientation. J. Vis. **14**(13), 22 (2014)
16. Schmidt, R.F., Torebjörk, H.E., Schady, W.J.L.: Gating of tactile input from the hand. Exp. Brain Res. **79**(1), 103–108 (1990)
17. Williams, S.R., Chapman, C.E.: Time course and magnitude of movement-related gating of tactile detection in humans. II. Effects of stimulus intensity. J. Neurophysiol. **84**(2), 863–875 (2000)

Tactile Cues

Ultrasonic Friction Modulation While Pressing Induces a Tactile Feedback

Jocelyn Monnoyer[1,2](✉), Emmanuelle Diaz[2], Christophe Bourdin[1], and Michaël Wiertlewski[1]

[1] Aix-Marseille Université, CNRS, ISM UMR 7287, 13009 Marseille, France
{christophe.bourdin,michael.wiertlewski}@univ-amu.fr,
jocelyn.monnoyer@mpsa.com
[2] PSA Peugeot Citroën, Paris, France
emmanuelle.diaz@mpsa.com

Abstract. Current touchscreen technology makes for intuitive human-computer interactions but often lacks haptic feedback offered by conventional input methods. Typing text on a virtual keyboard is arguably the task in which the absence of tactile cues imparts performance and comfort the most. Here we investigated the feasibility of modulating friction via ultrasonic vibration as a function of the pressing force to simulate a tactile feedback similar to a keystroke. Ultrasonic vibration is generally used to modulate the sliding friction which occurs when a finger moves laterally on a surface. We found that this method is also effective when the exploratory motion is normal to the surface. Psychophysical experiments show that a mechanical detent is unambiguously perceived in the case of signals starting with a high level of friction and ending to a low friction level. A weaker effect is experienced when friction is increasing with the pressure exerted by the finger, which suggests that the mechanism involved is a release of the skin stretch accumulated during the high-friction state.

Keywords: Surface-haptics · Finger friction · Keyclick · Virtual keyboard

1 Introduction

Typing text on flat glass panel is a much more difficult task than using a conventional keyboard. The absence of tactile cues in virtual keyboard decreases the users efficiency and increases the cognitive load [1,2], making the interaction uncomfortable and slow. In addition, when no haptic cues are available, the user has to rely on visual cues, which might interfere with other tasks. Providing tactile feedback resembling a mechanical keyclick on flat glass, would allow for programmable and tangible touch-screen interfaces.

Mechanical switches, such as those found in computer keyboards are based on various mechanisms that provide haptic cues which notify the user that the

© Springer International Publishing Switzerland 2016
F. Bello et al. (Eds.): EuroHaptics 2016, Part I, LNCS 9774, pp. 171–179, 2016.
DOI: 10.1007/978-3-319-42321-0_16

pressure exerted is sufficiently strong and the action has been successfully performed. One possible embodiment, which is illustrated in Fig. 1a, involves a spring and a linear cam to create a region in the trajectory of the keys where the apparent stiffness becomes negative. Because of the negative stiffness, the key is accelerated downward, and the reaction force applied the pulp of the finger is momentarily reduced, leading to a distinct feeling of keyclick [3,4]. Other technical implementation such as those that use buckling of a coiled spring [5], a flexible dome [6] or a scissor linkage [7] have increased reliability, reduced noise and minimized the size.

The mechanical displacement of the surface contacted by the finger is often not compatible with touchscreen technology, and vibrotactile stimulation can therefore be used to simulate the feeling of a keyclick. The method mainly used for this purpose is based on a short vibratory signal, which is triggered when force reaches a programmed threshold. The signal is usually a short sine-wave burst, which emulates the finger contact with a rigid material [8]. The vibration can be transmitted to the user using piezoelectric actuators [9], voice-coils [1] or electromagnets [10]. Adding vibrotactile feedback to this kind of virtual keyboard has been shown to increase the typing speed and user's comfort [11]. In addition, vibrotactile feedback can be used in a interactive way to influence the perceived compliance of an object. Visell et al. have reported that if the amplitude of a vibration is modulated according to the rate of change in the force while a user steps onto a actuated tile, the assembly appears to be more compliant [12]. While very effective, touchscreen interaction mediated by vibrotactile feedback generaly needs a flexible mounting for the screen, because of the large amplitude of the vibrations, which is often an engineering challenge.

The user's interactions with a glass plate can be altered when it is subjected to ultrasonic transverse vibrations. The vibration induces a non-linear compression of the film of air trapped between the skin and the glass surface, called squeeze-film, which reduces the friction. Increasing the amplitude of the ultrasonic wave results in a monotonic decrease of the friction force [13]. This effect

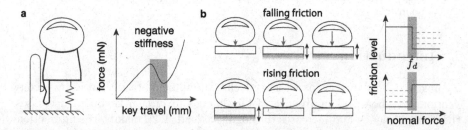

Fig. 1. a. Schematic of a mechanical switch. The detent of the switch is triggered by a reversal of the stiffness at a pre-defined travel threshold. The negative stiffness region relieves some of the interface stretch built up while pressing the key. **b.** Similar skin-stretch relief is achieved by decreasing or increasing friction once the normal force reaches a threshold f_d. Dashed lines show the various friction levels used in this experiment.

has been exploited to create interfaces that produce virtual bumps and textures while the finger is laterally sliding on the surface [14–16].

The working hypothesis adopted in this study, hinges on the observation that at the first contact between the one's finger and a surface, enough information is acquired to be able to estimate the frictional properties and the compliance of the object [17]. Although the compliance is likely to be extracted from the contact area spread rate and the relation between the force and the deformation of the finger pulp [18,19], the mechanism used by the central nervous system to estimate frictional properties of the surface seems to be based on the distribution of tangential stress created in the contact area by the friction between the surface and the skin [20]. We focus here on the skin-stretch induced by the friction at the interface between the subjects' skin and a glass plate. As illustrated in Fig. 1b, a sudden change in the friction coefficient induced ultrasonic transverse waves evokes a sensation corresponding to the detent of a switch, such as that typically experienced when using mechanical buttons.

2   Experimental Procedures

2.1   Apparatus

The friction reduction device used in the present experiment based on a similar rectangular glass plate to that presented in [16], vibrating in the 1×0 mode. The frame is mounted on a strain-gauge force sensor that measures the normal force exerted by the finger. The sensor is able to resolve 10 mN of force in a 3.5 N range. The normal force is acquired with a 12 bits resolution by the onboard analog-to-digital converter of the micro-controller and processed via a lookup table containing the profile of excitation. The value is then converted back to analog, smoothed by means of a 1 kHz reconstruction filter and multiplied to the carrier to produce the amplitude-modulated signal. The reconstruction filter ensures that the signal is smooth and devoid from vibrotactile artifacts. The analog signal is then amplified 20 times with a maximum voltage of 160 V and fed to the piezoelectric actuators bonded to the plate. The whole assembly is able to reach peak-to-peak amplitudes up to 4 μm at the 35 kHz resonant frequency. A picture of the apparatus and the functional scheme involved is presented in Fig. 2.

2.2   Participants

Fourteen right-handed volunteers (5 females and 8 males), ranging from 21 to 43 years of age, participated in the study. They were naive to the aim of the study and had no experience with surface-haptic devices. None of them reported having any skin conditions or perceptual deficits. The study was conducted in line with the recommendations of Aix-Marseille University's ethics committee and the participants gave their informed consent to the procedure.

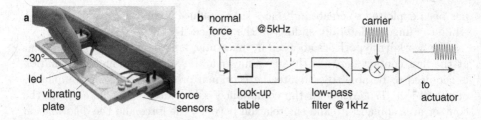

Fig. 2. a. Picture of the apparatus showing the glass plate used for friction modulation, mounted on normal force sensors. **b**. Rendering scheme. The force is fed into a lookup table controlling the envelope of the ultrasonic vibration.

2.3   Protocol

Participants sat in a chair in darkness and wore noise-canceling headphones to prevent any visual or auditory cues. They were asked to press on the device with their index finger, using their dominant hand. The location on the device where the participants had to press was indicated by a LED placed below the glass plate. Subjects first found a comfortable position, which amount roughly to placing their finger at a 30° angle to the surface. They were instructed to press with a similar force "to that exerted when using a tablet, or typing on a keyboard" and to restrict their motion in the vertical direction. When the measured force reached the threshold f_d, the led turned off to indicate they could answer. A constant stimuli single interval paradigm protocol was used. Participants are asked if "they felt a mechanical detent", i.e. a key click sensation. They answered pressing on YES or NO buttons, with other hand.

Preliminary trials showed that fast transient from one level of friction to another resembled the perceptual substance of a mechanical switch most closely. Signals of two kinds were delivered in the this study. In the first case, friction varied from high-to-low values (falling edge condition) and in the second case increased from low-to-high values (rising edge condition), see Fig. 1b. The force threshold used to trigger the transition from one state to the other was set at 0.3 N, based on previous informal experiments. Each signal is derived with 10 different levels of reduced friction, the higher friction being set by the glass plate at rest. Each condition was repeated 10 times, for a total of $2 \times 10 \times 10 = 200$ trials. Each of them was presented randomly and the session lasted 15 to 20 minutes.

3   Results

The effects of the frictional keyclick on both the participants responses and the behavioral changes in the force production levels were analyzed.

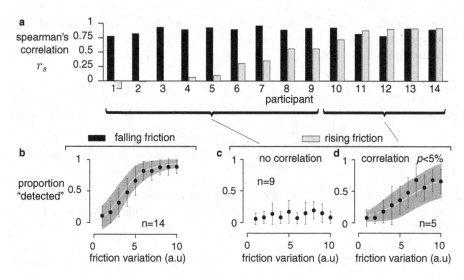

Fig. 3. a. Spearman's rank correlations calculated from each participant's psychometric data. **b.** In the case of rapidly decreasing friction, every single participant response follows a psychometric curve, showing that the keyclick has been unambiguously detected. **c,d.** In the condition starting with low friction, two groups emerged. The one group obtained a low detection rate and no correlation was observed between the responses and the friction level (**c**, n = 9). The other group detected the largest difference of friction and followed a psychometric curve (**c**, n = 5). Light gray line shows the averaged results of the fitting procedure with a logistic function. The dark gray are show the one standard deviation of the logistic regression. Error bars represent one standard deviation of the data

3.1   Detection Thresholds

The participants' responses to the single interval paradigm procedure were aggregated. The proportion of "keyclick detected" answers were compared with the intensity of the stimulus presented using non-parametric Spearman's coefficients r_s. Figure 3 presents the value of the coefficient obtained by each participant in each condition test. In the condition where the friction levels switched from high-to-low, the correlation is always greater than 0.75, with a p-value $p < 0.05$, indicating that the data are statistically correlated. On the other hand, in the condition in which the friction increased from low to high level, the correlation depended strongly on the participant. The response of five participants out of the fourteen were significantly correlated with the level of friction ($p < 0.05$).

In each case where significant correlation was found to exist between friction variation and the detection rate, a logistic function $f(x) = 1/(1 + \exp(\frac{-x+\mu}{\sigma}))$ was fitted using non-linear least-square methods, where μ is the absolute threshold and σ is the standard deviation. The values of the detection threshold are presented in Fig. 4. It can be noted here that the detection threshold when the friction increases is greater (average $\langle \mu_{rising} \rangle = 8$ a.u.) than for the decreasing friction condition (average $\langle \mu_{falling} \rangle = 3$ a.u.). Two-sample t-test rejected the null hypothesis of a correlation between the distribution across participant of absolute threshold in both cases ($p = 0.03$).

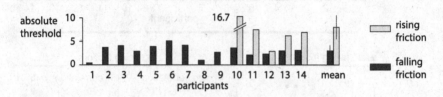

Fig. 4. Each participant's absolute detection threshold in both conditions. Only the trials in which responses are statistically correlated to the amplitude of friction variation are shown.

3.2   Behavioral Changes

The time-related evolution of the normal force suggests how the haptic feedback provided via ultrasonic vibration influences the exploratory behavior of the participants. We selected only the trials in which the responses were unambiguous, i.e., those in which friction values of less than 1 were used in the "undetected" cases and more than 9 in for the "detected" cases, regardless of the condition. Two datasets were excluded because participants 1 and 6 repeatedly saturated the force sensor.

The typical force profile follows a bell shaped curve, as can be seen from Fig. 5a. The duration and level of the peak force delivered varied from one trial to another, see Fig. 5b. The largest forces took longer time to develop. In order to find a unique descriptor, we used principal component analysis (PCA) was performed to obtain the average and standard deviation of the locus of the maximum force delivered of in each trial in the force/time space, along the first eigenvector. The relative change is computed on the basis of $(\sigma_{detected} - \sigma_{undetected})/\sigma_{detected}$ where σ is either the average value or the standard deviation along the first eigenvector. Figure 5c indicates that the relative change in the locus between the detected and the undetected response is positive for a majority of the participant and trial. In other words, the presence of a tactile feedback significantly reduced the peak force and the time taken to produce the keyclick by 14 % on average. In addition, the variability of the force delivered from one trial to another also decreased by 36 % in the cases where the keyclick was detected.

4   Discussion and Possible Mechanisms Involved

Friction modulation devices operate on the basis that the finger explores the surface laterally and the relative movement of the two surfaces in contact gives rise to friction forces. However, fast changes in the frictional force occurring during a

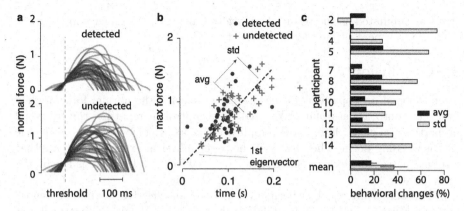

Fig. 5. a. Typical force traces obtained with participant 8 when he detected or did not detect the keyclick. **b.** Locus of the maximum force exerted in each trial by participant 8. The average and standard deviation were measured along the first eigenvector.**c.** Average and standard deviation of the maximum force locus along the principal axis for each participant. When the keyclick was not detected the maximum force was greater and the variability across trial increased.

normal pressing movement suffice to produce haptic feedback, even without any lateral motion. The results of the psychophysical and behavioral experiments performed here indicate that this effect is stronger when the friction is initially high and then decreases, which provides clues to the mechanism underlying the perception of changes in friction occurring during normal finger motion.

The results support the idea that the feeling of a keyclick is achieved by suddenly releasing stretching of the skin, built up during the initial contact with an adherent surface. The skin is a membrane that progressively sticks to the surface as the finger is pressing down. The edge of the contact area pulls on the rest of the skin that is already in contact, creating an interfacial shear stress that is radially distributed around the initial point of contact. Evidence of this lateral stress field has been presented in [17] and used in a robotic finger in [20].

In the opposite case, where the friction level changes from low to high, the skin will not undergo any stretching, because the surface is almost frictionless. The transition was therefore not so clearly perceived by the subjects. Some of the participants did feel a detent, but the absolute threshold was higher in this case and the effect was not as strong. The perception was probably due here to an acute sensitivity to frictional changes. It could also be due to undesirable lateral movement, leading to slight gross slippage of the participant's finger. Future investigation will control the deployment of lateral forces.

During the contact with a real mechanical keyboard, however, the depression of the keys temporarily reduces the normal force and thus releases some of the accumulated stretch in the contact area. With the present device, the tangential stretching of the skin was relieved when the ultrasonic vibration was turned on, breaking the contact between the plate and the skin. The sudden release of the stress accumulated as the result of the friction between the finger and the plate gave rise to a perceptible tactile transient.

5   Conclusion

We developed an apparatus for accurately measuring the normal force applied by a user onto a glass plate. We used it to control in real-time the frictional properties of a glass plate, via the application of ultrasonic vibrations, while the user is pressing down. The results of the psychophysical experiment shows that a robust perceptual experience, resembling the effect of a keyclick, is felt by the user.

Ultrasonic vibration has been proven to be an effective method to render tactile texture and shape by modulating the friction of the user's finger while it slides onto a surface. In this study, it was established that even in the absence of lateral motion, a tactile stimulus can be vividly perceived. This study extends the range of potential application of friction modulation, by showing that it is possible to leverage changes in friction in cases where no relative lateral movements have occurred between the finger and the plate. Moreover, this method can create virtual switches on flat surface-haptic devices without requiring any additional vibratory actuators.

The frictional signals delivered in this study were transient and therefore relatively easy to detect. Future studies will look into the effect of more complex signals such as ramp, noise and periodic wave, in order to investigate the full rendering capabilities of this approach. In addition, the results of the psychophysics experiment suggest the existence of a mechanism based on the release of residual skin stretch. High-speed imaging will help quantify the temporal evolution of the tangential stress field under various ultrasonic vibration patterns, and the results obtained will predictably shed light on the exact mechanisms at work.

Acknowledgments. The authors wish to thank Stéphane Viollet for valuable insights. They are also grateful for the technical support provided by Marc Boyron and Julien Diperi. This research was partly supported by the Openlab PSA-Aix- Marseille University and partly by CNRS basic funding.

References

1. Hoggan, E., Brewster, S.A., Johnston, J.: Investigating the effectiveness of tactile feedback for mobile touchscreens. In: Proceedings of the SIGCHI Conference on Human Factors in Computing Systems, pp. 1573–1582. ACM (2008)
2. Ma, Z., Edge, D., Findlater, L., Tan, H.Z.: Haptic keyclick feedback improves typing speed and reduces typing errors on a flat keyboard. In: 2015 IEEE World Haptics Conference (WHC), pp. 220–227. IEEE (2015)
3. Murmann, G., Bauer, G.: Low profile switch. US Patent 4,467,160, 21 August 1984
4. Weir, D.W., Peshkin, M., Colgate, J.E., Buttolo, P., Rankin, J., Johnston, M.: The haptic profile: capturing the feel of switches. In: Proceedings of 12th International Symposium on Haptic Interfaces for Virtual Environment and Teleoperator Systems, HAPTICS 2004, pp. 186–193. IEEE (2004)

5. Harris, R.H.: Catastrophically buckling compression column switch and actuator. US Patent 3,699,296, 17 October 1972
6. English, G.: Computer keyboard with flexible dome switch layer. US Patent 5,212,356, 18 May 1993
7. Chen, P.C.: Computer keyboard key switch. US Patent 5,457,297, 10 October 1995
8. Poupyrev, I., Maruyama, S.: Tactile interfaces for small touch screens. In: Proceedings of the 16th Annual ACM Symposium on User Interface Software and Technology, pp. 217–220. ACM (2003)
9. Kaaresoja, T., Brown, L.M., Linjama, J.: Snap-crackle-pop: tactile feedback for mobile touch screens. In: Proceedings of Eurohaptics, vol. 2006, pp. 565–566. Citeseer (2006)
10. Zoller, I., Lotz, P., Kern, T.A.: Novel thin electromagnetic system for creating pushbutton feedback in automotive applications. In: Isokoski, P., Springare, J. (eds.) EuroHaptics 2012, Part I. LNCS, vol. 7282, pp. 637–645. Springer, Heidelberg (2012)
11. Kim, J.R., Tan, H.Z.: Haptic feedback intensity affects touch typing performance on a flat keyboard. In: Auvray, M., Duriez, C. (eds.) EuroHaptics 2014, Part I. LNCS, vol. 8618, pp. 369–375. Springer, Heidelberg (2014)
12. Visell, Y., Giordano, B.L., Millet, G., Cooperstock, J.R.: Vibration influences haptic perception of surface compliance during walking. PLoS ONE **6**(3), e17697 (2011)
13. Watanabe, T., Fukui, S.: A method for controlling tactile sensation of surface roughness using ultrasonic vibration. In: IEEE ICRA, pp. 1134–1139, May 1995
14. Biet, M., Giraud, F., Lemaire-Semail, B.: Squeeze film effect for the design of an ultrasonic tactile plate. IEEE Trans. Ultrason. Ferroelectr. Freq. Control **54**(12), 2678–2688 (2007)
15. Winfield, L., Glassmire, J., Colgate, J.E., Peshkin, M.: T-pad: Tactile pattern display through variable friction reduction. In: World Haptics Conference, pp. 421–426. IEEE (2007)
16. Wiertlewski, M., Leonardis, D., Meyer, D.J., Peshkin, M.A., Colgate, J.E.: A high-fidelity surface-haptic device for texture rendering on bare finger. In: Auvray, M., Duriez, C. (eds.) EuroHaptics 2014, Part II. LNCS, vol. 8619, pp. 241–248. Springer, Heidelberg (2014)
17. Johansson, R.S., Flanagan, J.R.: Coding and use of tactile signals from the fingertips in object manipulation tasks. Nat. Rev. Neurosci. **10**(5), 345–359 (2009)
18. Bicchi, A., Scilingo, E.P., De Rossi, D.: Haptic discrimination of softness in teleoperation: the role of the contact area spread rate. IEEE Trans. Robot. Autom. **16**(5), 496–504 (2000)
19. Di Luca, M., Knörlein, B., Ernst, M.O., Harders, M.: Effects of visual-haptic asynchronies and loading-unloading movements on compliance perception. Brain Res. Bull. **85**(5), 245–259 (2011)
20. Maeno, T., Kawamura, T., Cheng, S.C.: Friction estimation by pressing an elastic finger-shaped sensor against a surface. IEEE Trans. Robot. Autom. **20**(2), 222–228 (2004)

Perception of Skin Stretch Applied to Palm: Effects of Speed and Displacement

Ahmet Guzererler[1]([✉]), William R. Provancher[2],
and Cagatay Basdogan[3]

[1] Department of Design, Technology and Society,
Koc University, Istanbul, Turkey
aguzererler@ku.edu.tr
[2] Tactical Haptics, Inc., Santa Clara, USA
william.provancher@tacticalhaptics.com
[3] Department of Mechanical Engineering, Koc University, Istanbul, Turkey
cbasdogan@ku.edu.tr

Abstract. Skin stretch is a powerful haptic effect with a great potential as a feedback mechanism for digital gaming applications. For example, it has been shown to communicate directional information accurately to game players. However, the existing devices apply stretch to the tip of index finger except the Reactive Grip game controller by Tactical Haptics, which applies skin stretch to a user's palm and finger pads. We have designed a compact hand-held haptic device that applies skin stretch to the palm via an actuated tactor. Compared to the fingertip, the palm is slightly less sensitive to skin stretch but affords larger stretch area. The stretch area of the palm enables us to control both tactor displacement and speeds for a broader range, resulting in richer haptic feedback. Using this device, we conduct experiments with 8 participants to investigate the effects of tactor displacement, speed, direction and hand orientation on perceived magnitude of skin stretch. The results of the study show that not only the tactor displacement but also the speed has a significant effect on the perceived intensity of skin stretch and the mapping function between them is nonlinear. Moreover, it appears that the tactile sensitivity of human palm to skin stretch is not homogeneous and stretch applied to the radial aspect of palm (towards the thumb) results in higher intensity than that of ulnar aspect.

Keywords: Haptics · Gaming · Tactile feedback · Skin stretch · Palm

1 Introduction

The gaming industry is one of the fastest growing industries, reaching a $91.5 billion US dollar market worldwide value with 9.4 % growth rate in 2015 [14]. Great effort is paid to enhance the gaming experience of users by the industry. Research shows that multi-modal stimuli significantly augments user experience and engagement in digital gaming [15]. In this regard, researchers have already exploited the visual and auditory channels, but relatively little attention has been paid to the haptic channel. However, this may change in time with the recent progress in tactile haptics leading to more compact and low-cost interfaces that stimulate our fingertip and/or palm in new ways.

© Springer International Publishing Switzerland 2016
F. Bello et al. (Eds.): EuroHaptics 2016, Part I, LNCS 9774, pp. 180–189, 2016.
DOI: 10.1007/978-3-319-42321-0_17

For example, *skin stretch* is a new form of tactile feedback that has a great potential in displaying directional information and has recently been implemented in gaming applications [1, 8, 9, 17, 18]. Skin stretch feedback simulates the skin deformation as it happens when our extremities are in tactile interaction with the real objects. For this purpose, skin is deformed by moving a tactor (pin), which is in contact with the skin, in the tangential direction. Bark et al. show that skin stretch is superior to vibrational feedback, which is the most common haptic feedback in the gaming industry, on communicating directional cues [2]. Moreover, it is suggested that skin stretch can convey sensory substituted force information better than traditional audiovisual feedback [19, 20]. Arasan et al. convey rotational direction via skin stretch applied to a finger holding an active stylus that is embedded with a DC motor [1].

Skin stretch has been investigated in the forearm, foot, palm, and fingers [2–4, 6, 7, 12, 16]. In the context of this paper, we focus on the skin stretch applied to palm and fingers. In fact, the earlier research on tangential skin stretch has primarily focused on fingertips. Paré et al. [16] conduct magnitude estimation experiments with 7 participants for tangential and normal skin deformation applied to fingertip. The participants are asked to assign values for the stimulus intensity varying from 0.15 N to 0.64 N under 3 different loading rates (0.1, 0.2, 0.3 N/s). Their results show that perceived stretch intensity is in a linear relationship with the applied force magnitude regardless of the rate and direction. Gleeson et al. explore the effects of displacement, speed and movement direction of the tactor on identifying the direction of stretch applied to fingertip [6]. The authors have conducted a user study with 11 participants. The participants are asked to identify the direction of stretch (north, south, west, east) for the tactor displacements varying from 0.05 mm to 1 mm at speeds varying from 0.5 mm/s to 4 mm/s. The results show that (a) participants identified the directional cues with almost 100 % accuracy for 1 mm displacement, (b) an increase in tactor speed, up to 4 mm/s, significantly improves the perception of direction, (c) direction of the cue also affects the accuracy.

A number of studies investigating the skin stretch or shear applied to palm [5, 10, 11] are much less than those of the fingertips. Moreover, to our knowledge, all of these studies are in the area of neuroscience and have focused on identifying the mechanoreceptor locations and recording their action potentials rather than human tactile perception. Johansson and Vallbo conducted experiments with 40 healthy adults to determine locations and distribution of low-threshold mechanoreceptors in human hand via recording impulses from median nerve during von Frey hair indentation [11]. They derived the density map of each type of mechanoreceptors (FAI, FAII, SAI, SAII) in hand (see Fig. 1). Edin et al. conducted a 4-month long experiment with 14 participants. In the experiments, they recorded mechanoreceptor response data from the right median, right radial, right inferior alveolar and left inferior alveolar nerves during skin stretch stimuli that are applied with 3 different brushes. Their results show that the mechanoreceptor response to skin stretch depends on the stimulus displacement, speed, and direction [5].

Compared to the fingertip, the palm is less sensitive to skin stretch but affords larger stimulation area. Since biomechanics research shows that human skin displays strain-dependent and rate-dependent viscoelastic behavior [2], having a broader range of tactor displacement and speed can potentially lead to richer haptic effects. In this study, we have investigated the effect of tactor speed, displacement, direction and hand

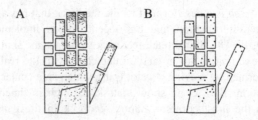

Fig. 1. A. Receptive fields in a human hand, B. Locations of SAII receptors, which are highly sensitive to lateral skin stretch and directional information, in human hand [10, 11].

orientation on the perceived magnitude of skin stretch applied to the palm. For this purpose, we have designed a compact, hand-held haptic interface that stretches the skin of the palm for tactile feedback and conducted magnitude estimation experiments with 8 participants under two different grasp orientations (horizontal and vertical) of the device.

2 Device Design

We have developed a compact, cable-driven, and hand-held haptic device that stretches palm skin with a tactor having one degree of freedom movement capability. The device is originally designed to provide independent tactile feedback to the fingers and palm simultaneously via 2 tactors separated by 180°. The device is made of two symmetrical half cylinders; each can house a motor and a cable-driven mechanism with a moving tactor for applying skin stretch to the palm and the fingers independently (see Fig. 2).

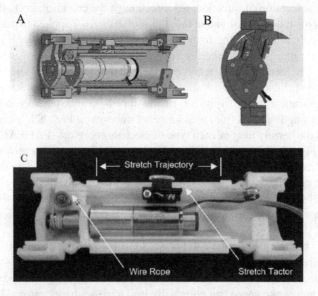

Fig. 2. A. and B. CAD model of the hand-held haptic device enabling skin stretch to palm. C. Realization of the design

However, at the time of this study, only the part applying stretch to the palm has been implemented. When assembled, the device has a diameter of 36 mm and is suitable to grip by an average person. The cylinders and the tactor are 3D-printed (uPrint SE, Stratasys). The top surface of the tactor is a half ellipsoid for smoother tactile inter- action (width: 14 mm, depth: 7 mm and height: 1 mm, surface area: 86 mm^2) and made of silicone rubber for a more natural tactile feel. The tactor has a total travel range of 64 mm. The power is transmitted to the tactor from a DC motor (DCX16S EB KL 6 V, Maxon) via a coated steel wire rope of 0.5 mm thickness and three pulleys. The rotational speed of the motor and the resulting trajectory of the tactor are controlled by Maxon EPOS2 24/2 Positioning Controllers. The actuation system is capable of reaching a maximum speed of 68 mm/s with an acceleration of 38 mm/ms^2 and positional resolution of 0.05 mm under no-load conditions. In our design, we have targeted to reach relatively larger displacements with higher tactor velocities compared to earlier on fingertip [6, 9, 16]. Our aim is to take advantage of a relatively larger area of the palm for investigating the interplay between displacement and speed to augment the perceived intensity of skin stretch.

3 Experiment

We have designed a magnitude estimation experiment (as in [16, 21]) to investigate the effect of tactor displacement, speed, direction, and hand orientation (orientation of the grasped haptic device) on perceived magnitude of stretch applied to the palm.

3.1 Participants

8 volunteers (seven males, one female; the average 26.2 ± 2 years) participated in the experiment. All participants are right-handed with no known sensorimotor problems.

3.2 Stimuli

A stretch stimulus is a combination of 4 different tactor displacements (2, 4, 8 and 16 mm), 5 different tactor velocities (4, 8, 16, 32 and 64 mm/s), 2 different movement directions of the tactor with respect to the palm (radial, towards thumb and ulnar, away from thumb), and 2 different device orientations (horizontal and vertical). A total of 320 stimuli (5 displacements × 4 velocities × 2 directions × 2 holding orienta- tions × 4 repetitions) is applied to the right palm of the participants in two sessions. Each stimulus is a half stroke of the tactor (one-way movement). During each stimulus, the tactor starts its movement from the center position (the midpoint of the travel range) and terminates after the desired displacement has achieved. It follows a trapezoidal velocity profile in which the acceleration and deceleration periods are much shorter than the total travel time. After the desired position is reached and the subject enters her/his response to perceived magnitude and direction, the tactor is moved back to the center position with a speed of 40 mm/s.

3.3   Experimental Procedure

Before the experiment starts, the participants are informed about the nature of the experiments and the experimental procedures. They are instructed to sit on a chair in front of the experimental setup, which includes the skin stretch device mounted on a fixture (see Fig. 3). This fixture ensures horizontal and vertical holding orientations for the device. Participants are asked to grasp the device with a certain amount of force in a comfortable manner. The grasp force applied by the participants is not recorded and adjusted manually during the demonstration session by trial and error such that the participants could feel the stimuli comfortably. Participants are asked to apply same grasp force across the trials, but obviously each may apply a different amount of force individually due to the difference in her or his tactile sensitivity levels. We eliminate possible variances in perceived magnitude due to grasp force and individual sensitivity levels via normalizing data across participants in our analysis. During the experiments, participants are asked to wear headphones playing white noise to block the noise coming from the motor. They are also provided with a soft pad to place their elbow to reduce fatigue. Before the actual experiments, the participants are presented with a training session displaying all possible combinations of the stimuli once in the vertical orientation of the device (40 stimuli). During the experiments, the participants are asked to estimate the direction of the stimuli (left/right and up/down for the horizontal and vertical orientations respectively) and its stretch magnitude. They are allowed to enter any positive number up to four digits for the magnitude. The participants enter their responses using a small keypad and their left hand. The stimuli are displayed to the participants in random order while the same order is used for each subject. The experiments are completed in two sessions, each taking approximately 30 min.

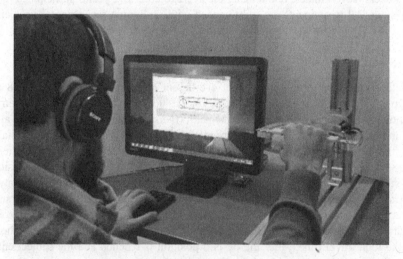

Fig. 3. Experiment setup

3.4 Results

The participants have successfully identified the direction of the tactor movement with a high accuracy of 98.12 % ± 1 %. The minimum accuracy in identifying the direction (93.75 % ± 6 %) was observed for stretch stimuli with 2 mm displacement at 4 mm/s speed in the ulnar direction.

We applied a normalization to the magnitude data based on the method suggested by Murray et al. [13]. For this purpose, we first computed the geometric mean of all responses, MG, and then the geometric mean of each subject, MG_P. Finally, the normalized value for each subject is calculated by MG/MG_P.

We applied 4-way ANOVA analysis to investigate the effect of tactor displacement, speed, direction, and holding orientation of the device on normalized skin stretch magnitude. The analysis shows that holding orientation has no significant effect on magnitude (hence, the data collected from the vertical and horizontal device orientations can be merged). Then, we combined participant data from both orientation conditions and calculated mean intensity values across trials for each participant. And, we apply 3-way repeated measures ANOVA analysis using [23]. As expected, speed ($F_{4,28} = 15.301$, $p < 0.0001$) and displacement ($F_{3,21} = 43.566$, $p < 0.0001$) have significant effects on the stretch intensity. Unexpectedly, stretch direction also has a significant effect on the perceived intensity ($F_{1,7} = 17.295$, $p < 0.005$). Our results also show that there is an interaction effect between displacement and speed ($F_{12,84} = 4.268$, $p < 0.0001$) and direction ($F_{3,21} = 8.761$, $p < 0.001$).

ANOVA analysis showed that stretch intensity is a function of speed and displacement and it also shows that interaction between speed and displacement is significant. In the light of this information, we fit a first order model to the averaged intensity data across participants (Eq. 1). The R^2 values of the fit functions are 0.994 and 0.989 for radial and ulnar directions, respectively (see Table 1 for the coefficients). Statistical analysis shows that all coefficients of the model are significant.

$$I(v, x) = Ax + Bv + Cxv + D \qquad (1)$$

In the equation, I is the perceived stretch magnitude while x and v represent the displacement and speed of the tactor, respectively.

Table 1. The coefficients of the fit function.

	A	B	C	D
I_{Radial}	0.37	0.016	0.0033	1.26
I_{Ulnar}	0.26	0.0096	0.0034	1.40

3.5 Discussion

In the experiment, 16 mm is the longest displacement condition. Stimuli with 16 mm displacement, applies stretch and some slip together to the palm. The earlier research showed that slip has no adverse effect on movement direction estimation [22]. Moreover, the same study also shows that humans could not detect slip applied to fingertips

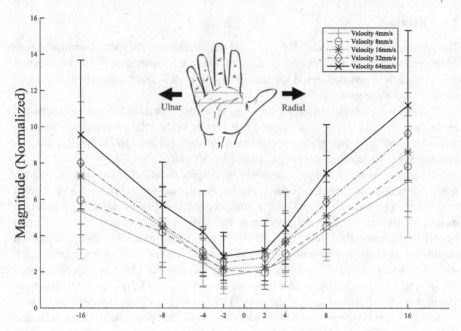

Fig. 4. Perceived stretch intensity as a function of tactor displacement and speed. (Color figure online)

by a smooth surface that is displaced for 14 mm. In the light of this information, we do not believe that slip has a significant effect on our results since our tactor has a smooth surface and palm is less sensitive than fingertips.

Figure 4 shows that an increase in the tactor speed results in an increase in the perceived stretch magnitude in movement directions, left and right, on the palm. The earlier neuroscience studies performed on human palm [5, 24] supports our finding. On the other hand, [16] who suggests that speed has no effect on the perceived stretch magnitude does not agree our finding on the effect of movement speed on perceived stretch magnitude. However, the rate of loading in [16] was quite low, so it is not surprising that they did not observe this effect, as is observed herein for the palm and previously for fingertips [13]. Furthermore, it appears that the relation between perceived magnitude and the tactor displacement and speed are nonlinear (see Eq. 1).

Finally, it appears that tactile sensitivity of the human palm to skin stretch is not homogeneous and stretch applied to the radial aspect of palm (towards thumb, up) results in higher intensity than that of ulnar aspect (away from the thumb, down). It is known that mechanoreceptors are not distributed uniformly in the palm. In general, there are more receptors (see Fig. 1A), in particular, more SAII receptors (see Fig. 1B) in the radial direction. Also, the topography of the palm could be another reason for asymmetry in skin stretch perception. In the radial direction, the index finger's metacarpophalangeal joint creates bump towards the palm, which increases pressure on the tactor on this region. For this reason, we present the data for the radial and ulnar stimuli in two separate plots for perceived stretch magnitude (see Fig. 5). In these plots, perceived stretch magnitude of the participants is presented as a function of both

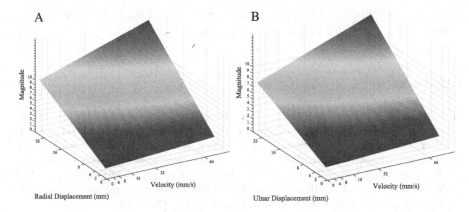

Fig. 5. Perceived stretch intensity as a function of tactor displacement and speed based on a surface fit using Eq. (1) to our experiment data: A. Lower perceived magnitudes observed for ulnar direction (away from the thumb, down). B. Higher perceived magnitudes observed for radial direction (towards thumb, up). See ulnar/radial diagram in Fig. 4.

displacement and speed. Moreover, a first order equation has been shown as a fit model for perceived skin stretch intensity in terms of tactor displacement and speed. Color coding is used to display iso-regions of the same perceived magnitude. As observed from these plots, the same haptic effect via stretch can be obtained by the combinations of different tactor displacement and speeds. For example, in the radial direction, a stretch intensity perceived by 10 mm displacement at 4 mm/s can be also achieved by 5 mm displacement at 64 mm/s speed. Therefore, our results virtually extend the limited travel distance of the tactor.

4   Conclusion and Future Work

We have designed a hand-held haptic device that applies tangential skin stretch to the palm via a tactor. We paid particular attention to making our device compact and ergonomic and achieve large tactor displacements and speeds. We then investigated the effects of tactor speed, displacement, direction and device orientation on the perceived magnitude of skin stretch. Due to the anatomy of the human palm, we were able to consider larger tactor displacements and speeds in our study compared with the previous studies of skin stretch applied to fingertip [6, 16]. The earlier studies in the palm have mainly focused on the effect of tactor displacement and showed that the perceived magnitude of skin stretch increases with the displacement. On the other hand, our results show that not only the tactor displacement but also its speed has a significant effect on the perceived magnitude of skin stretch. Furthermore, due to the asymmetrical distribution of mechanoreceptors in the palm, we observed a significant difference between the perceived stretch magnitudes of the radial (up) and ulnar (down) aspects (directions). In the future, we plan to conduct more experiments to investigate the individual effects of stimulus location and direction on the perceived stretch magnitude for multiple locations on the human palm. Our result, could be used in skin stretch interfaces, especially for gaming, to virtually extend the physical travel distance of tactor/s on the skin stretch device to produce haptic richer effects.

References

1. Arasan, A., Basdogan, C., Sezgin, T.M.: HaptiStylus: a novel stylus for conveying movement and rotational torque effects. IEEE Comput. Graph. Appl. **36**(1), 30–41 (2016)
2. Bark, K., Wheeler, J.W., Premakumar, S., Cutkosky, M.R.: Comparison of skin stretch and vibrotactile stimulation for feedback of proprioceptive information. In: 2008 Symposium on Haptic Interfaces Virtual Environment Teleoperator System, pp. 71–78 (2008)
3. Bark, K., Wheeler, J., Shull, P., Savall, J.: Rotational skin stretch feedback: a wearable haptic display for motion. IEEE Trans. Haptics **3**(3), 166–176 (2010)
4. Caswell, N.A., Yardley, R.T., Montandon, M.N., Provancher, W.R.: Design of a forearm-mounted directional skin stretch device. In: Haptics Symposium 2012, HAPTICS 2012 – Proceedings, pp. 365–370 (2012)
5. Edin, B., Essik, G.K., Trulsson, M., Olsson, K.A.: Receptor encoding of moving tactile stimuli in humans. I. Temporal pattern of discharge of individual low-threshold mechanoreceptors. J. Neurosci. **15**(1 Pt 2), 830–847 (1995)
6. Gleeson, B.T., Horschel, S.K., Provancher, W.R.: Perception of direction for applied tangential skin displacement: effects of speed, displacement, and repetition. IEEE Trans. Haptics **3**(3), 177–188 (2010)
7. Guinan, A.L., Caswell, N.A., Drews, F.A., Provancher, W.R.: A video game controller with skin stretch haptic feedback. In: Digest Technical Papers - IEEE International Conference on Consumer Electronics, pp. 456–457 (2013)
8. Guinan, A.L., Koslover, R.L., Caswell, N.A., Provancher, W.R.: Bi-manual skin stretch feedback embedded within a game controller. In: 2012 IEEE Haptics Symposium, pp. 255–260 (2012)
9. Guinan, A.L., Montandon, M.N., Caswell, A., Provancher, W.R.: Skin stretch feedback for gaming environments. In: 2012 IEEE International Workshop on Haptic Audio Visual Environment Games (HAVE 2012) Proceedings, pp. 101–106 (2012)
10. Johansson, R.S.: Tactile sensibility in the human hand: receptive field characteristics of mechanoreceptive units in the glabrous skin area. J. Physiol. **281**, 101–125 (1978)
11. Johansson, R.S., Vallbo, A.B.: Tactile sensibility in the human hand: relative and absolute densities of four types of mechanoreceptive units in glabrous skin. J. Physiol. **286**, 283–300 (1979)
12. Kennedy, P.M., Inglis, J.T.: Distribution and behaviour of glabrous cutaneous receptors in the human foot sole. J. Physiol. **538**(3), 995–1002 (2002)
13. Murray, A.M., Klatzky, R.L., Khosla, P.: Psychophysical characterization and testbed validation of a wearable vibrotactile glove for telemanipulation. Presence Teleoperators Virtual Environ. **12**(2), 156–182 (2003)
14. Newzoo: Global Games Market Will Reach $102.9 Billion in 2017. http://www.newzoo. com/insights/global-games-market-will-reach-102-9-billion-2017-2/
15. Orozco, M., Silva, J., Saddik, A.E.: The role of haptics in games. In: El Saddik, A. (ed.) Haptics Rendering and Applications, pp. 953–978 (2012)
16. Paré, M., Carnahan, H., Smith, A.M.: Magnitude estimation of tangential force applied to the fingerpad. Exp. Brain Res. **142**(3), 342–348 (2002)
17. Provancher, W.: Creating greater VR immersion by emulating force feedback with ungrounded tactile feedback. IQT Q. **6**(2), 18–21 (2014)

18. Provancher, W.R., Montandon, M.N., Doxon, A.J., Caswell, N.A., Gwilliam, L.T.: Skin stretch feedback devices, systems and methods. US patent 9, 317, 123 (2016)

19. Quek, Z.F., Schorr, S.B., Nisky, I., Provancher, W.R., Okamura, A.M.: Sensory substitution of force and torque using 6-DoF tangential and normal skin deformation feedback. In: 2015 IEEE International Conference on Robotics Automation (ICRA) (2015)

20. Quek, Z.F., Schorr, S.B., Nisky, I., Provancher, W.R., Okamura, A.M.: Sensory substitution using 3-degree-of-freedom tangential and normal skin deformation feedback. IEEE Haptics Symp. **8**(2), 27–33 (2014)

21. Ryu, J.: Psychophysical model for vibrotactile rendering in mobile devices. Presence Teleoperators Virtual Environ. **19**(4), 364–387 (2010)

22. Srinivasan, M.A., Whitehouse, J.M., LaMotte, R.H.: Tactile detection of slip: surface microgeometry and peripheral neural codes. J. Neurophysiol. **63**(6), 1323–1332 (1990)

23. Trujillo-Ortiz, A., Hernandez-Walls, R., Trujillo-Perez, F.A.: RMAOV33: three-way analysis of variance with repeated measures on three factors test (2006). http://www. mathworks.com/matlabcentral/fileexchange/9638-rmaov33

24. Vallbo, A.B., Johansson, R.S.: Properties of cutaneous mechanoreceptors in the human hand related to touch sensation. Hum. Neurobiol. **3**(1), 3–14 (1984)

Effect of Waveform in Haptic Perception of Electrovibration on Touchscreens

Yasemin Vardar[1]([✉]), Burak Güçlü[2], and Cagatay Basdogan[1]

[1] College of Engineering, Robotics and Mechatronics Laboratory,
Koç University, Rumeli Feneri Yolu, 34450 Sarıyer, Istanbul, Turkey
{yvardar13,cbasdogan}@ku.edu.tr
[2] Institute of Biomedical Engineering, Tactile Research Laboratory,
Boğaziçi University, Kandilli Campus, 34335 Çengelköy, Istanbul, Turkey
burak.guclu@boun.edu.tr

Abstract. The perceived intensity of electrovibration can be altered by modulating the amplitude, frequency, and waveform of the input voltage signal applied to the conductive layer of a touchscreen. Even though the effect of the first two has been already investigated for sinusoidal signals, we are not aware of any detailed study investigating the effect of the waveform on our haptic perception in the domain of electrovibration. This paper investigates how input voltage waveform affects our haptic perception of electrovibration on touchscreens. We conducted absolute detection experiments using square wave and sinusoidal input signals at seven fundamental frequencies (15, 30, 60, 120, 240, 480 and 1920 Hz). Experimental results depicted the well-known U-shaped tactile sensitivity across frequencies. However, the sensory thresholds were lower for the square wave than the sinusoidal wave at fundamental frequencies less than 60 Hz while they were similar at higher frequencies. Using an equivalent circuit model of a finger-touchscreen system, we show that the sensation difference between the waveforms at low fundamental frequencies can be explained by frequency-dependent electrical properties of human skin and the differential sensitivity of mechanoreceptor channels to individual frequency components in the electrostatic force. As a matter of fact, when the electrostatic force waveforms are analyzed in the frequency domain based on human vibrotactile sensitivity data from the literature [15], the electrovibration stimuli caused by square-wave input signals at all the tested frequencies in this study are found to be detected by the Pacinian psychophysical channel.

Keywords: Waveform · Electrovibration · Perception · Electrostatic forces · Square · Sinusoidal waves

1 Introduction

Surface haptics has recently gained a growing interest by the haptics community due to the popularity of touch screens used in a variety of electronic devices.

F. Bello et al. (Eds.): EuroHaptics 2016, Part I, LNCS 9774, pp. 190–203, 2016.
DOI: 10.1007/978-3-319-42321-0_18

The current studies on surface haptics have focused on displaying efficient tactile feedback to a user as the user moves her/his finger on the screen. One approach to generating tactile effects through a touch surface is to control the friction force between fingertip of the user and the surface using electrostatic actuation [20,26,28]. If an alternating voltage is applied to the conductive layer of a touchscreen, an attraction force is created between the finger and the surface. This force modulates the friction between the surface and the skin of the moving finger. By controlling the amplitude, frequency and waveform of this input voltage, different texture feelings can be generated on the touchscreen [11,26].

Creating haptic effects using electrostatic attraction was first utilized by Strong and Troxel [27]. In their study, they developed an electrotactile display consisting of an array of pins insulated with a thin layer of dielectric. Using friction induced by electrostatic attraction force, they generated texture sensations on the display surface. Their experimental results showed that the intensity of texture sensation was primarily due to the peak intensity of the applied voltage rather than to the current density. Later, Beebe et al. [13], developed a polyimide-on-silicon electrostatic fingertip tactile display using lithographic microfabrication. They were able to create texture sensations using 200–600 V pulse excitations on this thin and durable display and reported perception at the fingertip as "sticky". In a following study, Tang and Beebe [18] performed experiments of detection threshold, line separation and pattern recognition on visually impaired subjects. Although they encountered problems such as dielectric breakdown and sensor degradation, the subjects were able to differentiate simple tactile patterns by haptic exploration. Agarwal et. al [1] continued these human detection threshold experiments and tested the effect of dielectric thickness in haptic perception during electrostatic stimulation. Their results showed that variations in dielectric thickness did not have a linear impact on the threshold voltage. Following this study, Kaczmarek et al. [21] explored the perceptual sensitivity to positive and negative input pulses. Their results showed that the subjects perceived negative or biphasic pulses better than positive ones. In all of these studies, electrovibration was obtained using opaque patterns of electrodes on small scale surfaces. However, in the recent works of Bau et al. [26] and Linjama et al. [20], electrovibration was delivered via a transparent electrode on a large and commercial touch surface, which demonstrates the viability of this technology on mobile applications. Wijekoon et al. [11], followed the work of [20], and investigated the perceived intensity of modulated friction created by electrovibration. Their experimental results showed that the perceived intensity was logarithmically proportional to the amplitude of the applied signal and dependent on the frequency.

Although electrovibration can provide rich tactile sensation opportunities, little work has been done on creating realistic texture sensations using this method. One of the main reasons for this is the difficulty of measuring the electrostatic force between the human fingertip and the touch surface. Due to its small magnitude, it is difficult to measure the electrostatic attraction force using the force transducers commercially available today. To understand how mechanical forces develop at the fingertip-surface interface, Meyer et al. [10], developed a tribometer and measured the lateral force to estimate the electrostatic attraction force for the applied voltage. They showed the effect of actuation frequency on the lateral frictional force despite some subject-dependent variability. They reported that this person to person variability depends on varying environmental impedances which are caused by voltage controlled electrovibration. Later, Vezzoli et al. [14] improved the model of electrovibration by including frequency-dependent electrical properties of human skin as documented in [30]. Recently, Kim et al. [16], developed a current control method to solve the non-uniform intensity perceived by the subjects, reported in the earlier studies. The results of their user study show that the proposed current control method can provide significantly more uniform perceived intensity of electrovibration than voltage controlled one.

The earlier studies showed that displaying textures realistically on a touch screen is not straightforward since the human finger show complex frequency-dependent mechanical and electrical properties. Moreover, human to human variability of these properties further complicates the problem. For example, both the electrical and mechanical impedances of the human finger are frequency-dependent and the coupling between them has not been well understood yet. The existing model explaining the electrostatic forces developed between fingertip and touchscreen shows that electrostatic force depends on the amplitude and frequency of the input voltage (see Sect. 2.1). Even though the effects of these two parameters on human tactile perception have already been investigated using pure sine waves, there is no early study on how our perception changes when another waveform is used. Therefore, we explore how input voltage waveform alters human haptic perception in this paper. This work was particularly motivated by our initial observation that square-wave excitation causes stronger tactile sensation than the sine-wave excitation, although the electrostatic force generated by square-wave appears to be constant according to the existing model (see Sect. 2.1). In this model, the electrostatic force is a function of the square of the input voltage signal, hence the electrostatic force becomes constant when the input voltage is a square wave. Since DC (constant) excitation voltages and constant electrostatic forces do not cause vibration sensation (although they cause adhesion sensation [9]), the square wave excitation is expected to be filtered electrically by the stratum corneum as suggested as in the previous work [10,14].

In this paper using a simulation model developed in Matlab-Simulink, we first show that the forces transmitted to the human finger by electrovibration are very different for square and sinusoidal input voltages at low fundamental frequencies due to electrical filtering. We then support this claim by presenting the results of psychophysical experiments conducted with 8 human subjects. The results indicate that the human finger is more sensitive to a square wave than sinusoidal wave at fundamental frequencies lower than 60 Hz. We conclude that the Fourier frequency components in the electrostatic force, generated by the filtered square wave excitation signal, are typically high (> 200 Hz) and activate the Pacinian psychophysical channel [2,25].

2 Electrovibration with Waveform Analysis

2.1 Reinterpretation of Electrostatic Force

Based on the parallel plate capacitor theory, the attractive force between two plates is expressed as

$$F = \frac{\epsilon_0 \epsilon_i A V^2}{2d^2},\tag{1}$$

where ϵ_0 is permittivity of vacuum, ϵ_i is relative permittivity of the insulator, V is applied voltage (can be time varying), A area of the plates and d is the thickness of the insulator, [12]. Electrostatic forces are developed at the boundaries of the two dielectrics: stratum corneum and insulator. If a human finger on a touch surface is represented in Fig. 1a, the electrostatic force which effects the fingertip can be expressed as

$$F_e = \frac{\epsilon_0 \epsilon_{sc} A}{2}\left(\frac{V_{sc}}{d_{sc}}\right)^2,\tag{2}$$

where ϵ_{sc} is relative permittivity of the stratum corneum, A the area of the fingertip, d is the thickness of the stratum corneum and V_{sc} is the voltage to across the stratum corneum. V_{sc} can be expressed in terms of the applied voltage as

$$V_{sc} = V\frac{Z_{sc}}{Z_{body} + Z_{sc} + Z_{surface}},\tag{3}$$

where Z_{body}, Z_{sc} and $Z_{surface}$ represents the impedances of the human body, stratum corneum, and tactile surface respectively. Even though Shultz et al. state in [9] that the air gap between the fingertip and the touch surface has a substantial effect in the created electrostatic force, we neglect the impedance of the air in this model for simplification purposes.

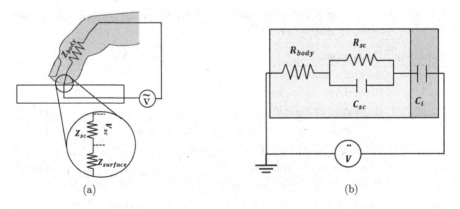

(a)   (b)

Fig. 1. a. Equivalent circuit model of human finger on a touch surface. b. The simplified equivalent circuit model of human finger on a touch surface.

Equation 2 may look slightly different than the electrostatic force formulas defined in [10,14]. In those articles, the total electrostatic force created between the conductive layer of the touch surface and the conductive layer of the finger is represented as the perceived electrostatic force. However, in our opinion, it is more reasonable to represent the perceived effects due to the electrostatic force at the inner boundary of the stratum corneum, because the mechanoreceptors are located close to the epidermal junction or in the dermis, [3,5,8]. Therefore, V_{sc} and not V is used in our calculations. For more information related to the derivation of the electrostatic force created on the boundaries of two parallel or series dielectrics, the reader may refer to [22].

2.2   Waveform Analysis of Electrovibration

To investigate the effect of waveform in electrovibration, we develop an equivalent circuit model of human finger (see Fig. 1a) in Matlab-Simulink environment. The model here is simplified, and the capacitance of the human body and the internal resistance of the touch surface are neglected. Also, the finger is simply modelled as resistance and capacitance in parallel as shown in Fig. 1b. The parameters used in Fig. 1b and their values used in the Matlab simulation are given in Table 1. The human resistance is approximated as $1\,\mathrm{k\Omega}$ [16]. Vezzoli et al. show that intensity of electrovibration is highly frequency-dependent [14]. In their model, they use frequency-dependent values of resistivity, ρ_{sc}, and dielectric constant, ϵ_{sc}, of human stratum corneum as reported in [30]. Likewise, we fit mathematical functions to the experimental data reported by [30] and use these functions in our Matlab simulations (see Fig. 2a). Using Eq. 3, the relation between input voltage, V, and the voltage across stratum corneum, V_{sc}, is written as

$$\frac{V_{sc}}{V} = \frac{R_{sc}C_i s}{s^2(R_{body}C_i R_{sc}C_{sc}) + s(R_{body}C_i + R_{sc}C_i + R_{sc}C_{sc}) + 1}. \tag{4}$$

Table 1. The description of parameters used in the circuit model shown in Fig. 1b and their values used in the Matlab simulations.

Parameter	Explanation	Value	Unit
A	Area of human fingertip	1	cm^2
ϵ_0	Permittivity of vacuum	8.854×10^{-12}	F/m
R_{body}	Resistance of human body	1	$\mathrm{k\Omega}$
C_i	Capacitance of the insulator of 3M MicroTouch	$C_i = \frac{\epsilon_0 \epsilon_i A}{d_i}$	F
ϵ_i	Relative permittivity of the insulator	3.9	-
d_i	Thickness of the insulator	1	$\mathrm{\mu m}$
R_{sc}	Resistance of stratum corneum	$R_{sc} = \frac{\rho_{sc} d_{sc}}{A}$	Ω
C_{sc}	Capacitance of stratum corneum	$C_{sc} = \frac{\epsilon_0 \epsilon_{sc} A}{d_{sc}}$	F
ρ_{sc}	Resistivity of stratum corneum	Figure 2a	Ωm
ϵ_{sc}	Relative permittivity of stratum corneum	Figure 2a	-

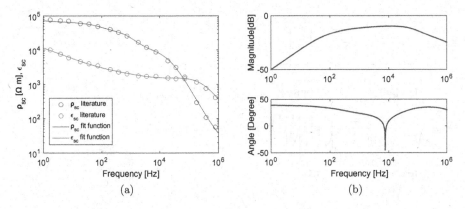

(a)   (b)

Fig. 2. a. The resistivity and dielectric constant of epidermal stratum corneum by [30] and the polynomial functions fitted by us on the experimental data points. b. Bode plot of the transfer function $\frac{V_{sc}}{V}$. (Color figure online)

Figure 2b represents the Bode plot of the system. It appears that the system shows the behaviour of a bandpass filter with cut-off frequencies, f_{low}, and, f_{high}, at approximately 1 kHz and 20 kHz. Hence, the system shows first order high pass filter behaviour at low frequencies. To test the effects of signal filtering, we perform simulations with two different input waveforms (sinusoidal and square) at two fundamental frequencies (15 and 480 Hz). Figure 3a shows the applied input voltage signals in simulations. Figure 3b shows the filtered signals, in other words, the voltage across the stratum corneum. When the input is a low frequency (15 Hz) sinusoidal signal, the output signal is phase-shifted and its amplitude drops significantly, whereas the drop in the output amplitude is much

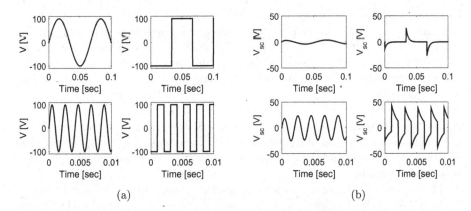

(a)   (b)

Fig. 3. a. The input voltage signals used in Matlab/Simulink simulations; sinusoidal and square signals at 15 Hz (first row) and 480 Hz (second row). b. The resulting voltage on the stratum corneum, V_{sc}, for the four cases.

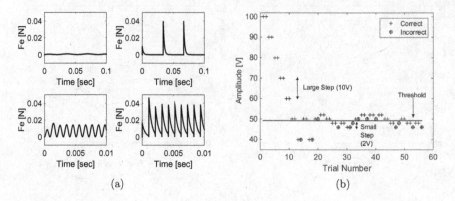

(a)   (b)

Fig. 4. a. The resulting electrostatic force across stratum corneum, F_e, for the four cases, calculated by Eq. 2. b. Illustration of absolute detection threshold experiment utilizing one-up/two-down adaptive staircase method. The large and small steps and the estimated threshold are marked on the figure.

less for the high frequency sinusoidal signal at 480 Hz, as expected from high pass filtering. For the square wave at a low fundamental frequency of 15 Hz, the output has exponentially decaying low amplitude transients. As the fundamental frequency of the square wave is increased to 480 Hz, the output resembles the input more because the signal alternates fast enough that the exponential decay is not complete. The results show that, even though the touch screen is excited with an input having a certain amplitude and waveform, our mechanoreceptors may be stimulated with a different waveform and amplitude (see Fig. 4a).

3   Experiments

To investigate how the detection of electrovibration varies with input waveform and fundamental frequency, we conduct psychophysical experiments. As explained above, due to the electrical filtering of the system, different waveforms induce different output voltages on the stratum corneum of the user. Absolute detection threshold experiments determine the minimum stimulus amplitude that the observer can barely detect, [2,6,24,31]. According to the filtering model explained in Sect. 2.2, this threshold is expected to be different especially at low frequencies for square and sinusoidal signals. However, since human sensitivity also changes as a function of frequency [2,7,24], one must also study the Fourier (frequency) components in the resultant force waveform to better interpret the experimental results.

The experimental setup used for the absolute threshold experiment is shown in Fig. 4a. A touchscreen (SCT3250, 3M Inc.) is placed on top of an LCD screen. There is a computer monitor in front of the subjects to enter their response. On top of the 3M glass, an IR frame is placed to determine the location of the finger. The 3M screen is excited with a signal generated by a DAQ card (PCI-6025E, National Instruments Inc.). The voltage from the card is amplified by an amplifier (E-413, PI Inc.) before transmitted to the touch screen. The subjects' arms are supported by the arm rest during the experiments. Subjects are asked to put on head phones displaying white noise.

Absolute detection thresholds are estimated for seven input frequencies: 15, 30, 60, 120, 240, 480 and, 1920 Hz. The frequency interval is chosen specifically to show the perception differences caused by input waveform for a large range of fundamental frequencies. The two-alternative-forced-choice method is used to determine the threshold levels. This method enables bias-free experimental results [2]. Two regions are displayed to the subjects on the LCD screen and they are asked to find the region where there is a tactile stimulus. The amplitude of the tactile stimulus is changed by using one-up/two-down adaptive staircase method. This procedure decreases the number of trials and duration of the experimentation [2,7,17,23,24]. Levitt et al. state in [17] that, one-up/two-down procedure tracks thresholds at 70 % correct probability of detection.

The experiments are conducted with 8 subjects (4 female, 4 male) with an average age of 27.5 (SD: 1.19). Only one of the subjects is left-handed. All of them are engineering Ph.D. students and have some experience with electrovibration.

As seen in Fig. 5a, the touch screen is divided into two marked areas as A and B. The tactile stimulus is presented only in one of the two areas. The stimulus location is randomized. The finger position of the subject (whether her/his finger is in the area A or B) is detected via the IR frame. The subject is asked to explore both areas consecutively and choose the one which has a tactile stimulus.

Each session starts with the stimulus amplitude of 100 V. This initial voltage amplitude provides sufficiently high intensity stimulus for all the subjects. If the subject gives two consecutive correct answers, the voltage amplitude is decreased by 10 V. If the subject has one incorrect response, the stimulus intensity is increased by 10 V. The change of the responses from correct to incorrect or the opposite is counted as one reversal. After four reversals, the step size

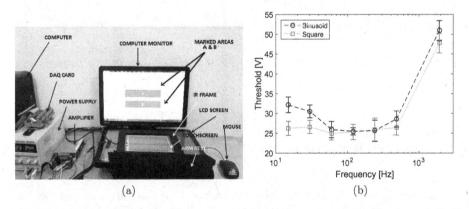

(a)   (b)

Fig. 5. a. Illustration of the experimental setup used in absolute threshold detection experiments. b. Absolute detection thresholds for seven fundamental frequencies and two waveforms, sinusoidal (black) and square (red), with their mean and standard deviation errorbars. (Color figure online)

is decreased by 2 V to have more precise threshold value as suggested in [26]. The experiment is stopped after 18 reversals. The average of the last 15 reversals gives the estimated absolute detection threshold value. For an illustration of this procedure, see Fig. 4b. Each session takes approximately 15–20 min. The total duration of the experiment for each subject is approximately 4 h.

4   Results

The absolute detection thresholds for seven fundamental frequencies (15, 30, 60, 120, 240, 480, 1920 Hz) and two different waveforms (sinusoidal and square) are shown in Fig. 5b.

The results were analyzed by using two-way ANOVA with repeated measures. There was statistically significant main effects of both frequency and waveform on the threshold levels ($F(6,42) = 306.7$, $p < 0.001$ and $F(1,7) = 80$, $p < 0.001$). These results indicate that the threshold levels depended on both stimulus frequency and waveform. Also, there was a statistically significant interaction between frequency and waveform ($F(6,42) = 7.4$, $p < 0.001$). Therefore, the amount of differences in measured thresholds for different waveforms changed at different frequencies.

Additionally, the effect of waveform for each frequency was analyzed by using Bonferroni corrected paired t-tests. The results showed that there was a statistically significant effect of the waveform on our haptic perception for fundamental frequencies less than 60 Hz. At frequencies greater than and equal to 60 Hz, the difference between square and sinusoidal waves were not significant. The corrected p-values for each frequency (15, 30, 60, 120, 240, 480, 1920 Hz) were 0.008, 0.016, 1, 1, 1, 0.168, 0.128 respectively.

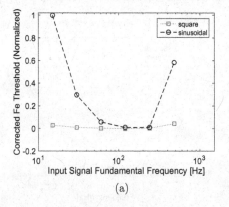
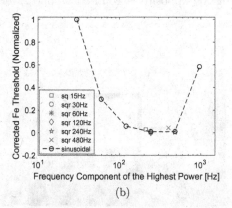

(a)   (b)

Fig. 6. The electrostatic force detection thresholds (F_e is first corrected with human sensitivity curve taken from [15] and then normalized) for sinusoidal (black) and square (red) waveforms. a. The data is plotted as a function of fundamental frequency. b. The data is plotted as a function of the frequency component with the highest power. Note: The detection thresholds for 1920 Hz are not plotted because there is not any data for this frequency in the human sensitivity curve in [15]. (Color figure online)

To investigate which psychophysical tactile channel was activated during each stimulus, the corresponding electrostatic forces, F_e, were calculated using measured mean threshold values and Eq. 2. In other words, the voltage waveform with amplitudes equal to the threshold values was first filtered by Eq. 3 and then the electrostatic force was calculated. Then, the Fast Fourier Transform (FFT) magnitude of the corresponding F_e was weighted by the normalized human sensitivity curve taken from [15]. The maximum peak of this corrected FFT magnitude represents the frequency component detected by the psychophysical channel with the lowest threshold at that frequency. Figures 6a and b show normalized electrostatic force threshold values (corrected for the human sensitivity curve) for sinusoidal and square input signals. In Fig. 6a, the threshold values are plotted as a function of the fundamental frequency of the input. In Fig. 6b, they are plotted as a function of the frequency component with the highest power.

5 Discussion

The absolute detection threshold values for both waveforms resemble the well known U-shaped human sensitivity curve as shown in Fig. 5b. Here, the threshold values are low between 60 Hz and 240 Hz, and higher for the rest. The results are consistent with the existing literature [2,15,24,29]. In these studies, vibratory stimulus detection thresholds of the index or middle finger were measured as a function of frequency by using various contactors. However, our experimental results should be interpreted based on the frequency components with the highest power in the corrected electrostatic force signal [15,29]. Vibrotactile studies in the literature used sinusoidal displacement stimuli with slow onsets and offsets, which created mechanical excitation with a single frequency component. However, the excitation voltage applied to the touchscreen is first filtered electrically by Eq. 3 and the filtered voltage across the stratum corneum (or possibly the entire epidermal layer) generates an electrostatic force according to Eq. 2. This nonlinear transformation of the signal introduces frequency components not presented in the filtered signal. Specifically, when a pure sine wave is applied to the touchscreen, the force waveform will have twice the frequency of the sine wave due to the second power in Eq. 2. Therefore, when we plotted the thresholds with the sinusoidal excitation according to 2ω (Fig. 6b), we obtained almost a perfect match with the human sensitivity curve [2,15,24,29]. This U-shaped region originates from the activation of the Pacinian psychophysical channel.

In [26], Bau et al. measured absolute detection thresholds for sinusoidal inputs. Their results also show a U-shaped trend, but their detection threshold values for sinusoidal inputs were slightly lower than our results. This difference may be caused by environmental factors, the number of the test subjects and the person-to-person variability in the physical factors as explained in Sect. 2.1. Maintaining good stimulus control is essential in psychophysical experiments. Although the excitation voltage was well controlled in our experiments, contact force was not controlled. Higher contact forces would increase contact area and decrease thresholds due to spatial summation in the Pacinian channel [4].

Another limitation was regarding the simulations of the electrical filtering step. We used the values of the human skin parameters (ρ_{sc} and ϵ_{sc}) at the fundamental frequency of the input signals. Although this is valid for the sine wave, it is a simplification for the square wave, since square wave contains many frequency components. We plan to correct this in our future work by measuring the electrical impedance directly.

If a complex waveform, i.e. one which has many frequency components, is applied to the touchscreen, the frequency components in the range of 100–150 Hz would be mostly effective in psychophysical detection due to the high sensitivity of Pacinian channel at twice these frequencies. For example, due to the electrical filtering of a square wave excitation at the touchscreen-biological tissue interface, low-frequency components would be suppressed. Therefore, the voltage across the dielectric layer would include exponentially decaying transients. The electrostatic force generated based on these transients is rather complex, including twice the frequencies and distortion products of the filtered signal components. The frequency components in the force waveform would not be equally effective because human sensitivity changes as a function of frequency. We found these resultant components by Fourier analysis and weighted them according to human sensitivity. When the data was plotted as a function of the frequencies of these components in the force waveform, and not as a function of the fundamental frequency of the excitation voltage applied to the touchscreen, the results were remarkable (compare Figs. 6a and b). All the square wave excitation stimuli used in our experiments generated force waveforms which have frequency components of the highest power in the range of 200–500 Hz. This frequency interval again is in the detection range of Pacinian channel. Therefore, all our stimuli tested in psychophysical experiments were detected mainly by the Pacinian channel [2,24]. Pacinian channel is the most sensitive psychophysical channel in that range, compared to the remaining three non-Pacinian channels mediated by the mechanoreceptors in the skin [15,29]. It should be noted that the mechanical stimuli induced by electrovibration are not exactly like vibrotactile stimuli used in the previous psychophysical experiments. For example, Summers et al. [19], found that vibrotactile sine waves and monophasic/tetraphasic pulses at supra-threshold levels resulted in similar identification scores in a frequency identification task. They concluded that temporal cues are more important than spectral cues in that particular task. Although their psychophysical task is very different, the ineffectiveness of spectral cues and their variation somewhat supports our argument that the strongest frequency component in complex waveforms (after correction for human sensitivity) determines the psychophysical channel for detection. The spectral contents of the stimuli used in their study would activate the Pacinian channel mostly as well.

6   Conclusion

In this paper, we conducted psychophysical studies with 8 human subjects and showed that human finger is more sensitive to a square wave than sinusoidal wave at fundamental frequencies lower than 60 Hz. Using equivalent circuit model of finger-surface system developed in Matlab-Simulink, we showed that sensation difference of waveforms in low fundamental frequencies could be explained by frequency-dependent electrical properties of human skin and human tactile sensitivity. The tactile sensation generated by electrovibration depends on the frequency components in the input waveform. This input waveform passes through a filter and a nonlinear transfer function (see Eq. 2) and arrives into mechanoreceptors. Since this resultant waveform is rather complex and contains many frequency components, it may activate different psychophysical channels at different threshold levels [15,29]. These four psychophysical channels (NPI, NPII, NPIII, P) are mediated by four corresponding mechanoreceptors which enable the tactile perception. To predict tactile sensitivity to a complex stimulation, the Fourier components of the stimulation should be weighted by the inverse of human sensitivity curve [15]. The tactile perception occurs at the channel in which the maximum of this weighted function located. In our study, we found that the Fourier frequency components in the electrostatic force, generated by the filtered square-wave excitation signal, are typically high (>200 Hz) and activate the Pacinian psychophysical channel [2,25] for tactile detection.

Even though our approach can predict the experimental results qualitatively, the correct electrostatic force can be calculated with a proper measurement of the electrical impedances in the entire system. Moreover, we have not investigated the effect of normal force and finger velocity on our results. When there is no relative movement between the surface and the finger, the electrostatic force, albeit varying in time with sinusoidal excitation, does not generate a vibration sensation. It is generally accepted that the electrostatic force changes the normal force, and thus friction during movement. The mechanoreceptors in the skin are probably excited by shear forces modulated by friction. Therefore, a physically accurate explanation of electrovibration can only be obtained by an electromechanical model linking the electrostatic force generation at the tissues and the mechanical forces during movement. For future work we aim to (1) measure the electrical impedance of subjects who participated in the experiments and estimate the resulting electrostatic force more accurately, (2) investigate the effect of normal force and finger velocity during experiments, and (3) extend our electrical model by combining it with the mechanical properties of the finger.

Acknowledgements. The Scientific and Technological Research Council of Turkey (TUBITAK) supported this work under Student Fellowship Program BIDEB-2211. Also, Y.V would like to first thank Prof. Dr. Ozgur Birer for his valuable comments during discussions. Moreover, Y.V would like to acknowledge Ozan Caldiran, Gokhan Serhat, Amir Reza Aghakhani, Omer Sirin, and Utku Boz for their valuable comments and technical help during this study. Moreover, Y.V would like to acknowledge the initial help and support given by Ezgi Emgin and Enes Selman Ege. They introduced electrovibration to Y.V. and provided a quick start for her study. Also, Y.V would like to thank all subjects who participated in the experiments.

References

1. Agarwal, A.K., Namni, K., Kaczmarek, K.A., Tyler, M.E., Beebe, D.J.: A hybrid natural/artificial electrostatic actuator for tactile stimulation. In: Proceedings of the 2nd Annual Conference on Microtechnologies in Medicine and Biology, Madison, Wisonsin, USA, pp. 341–345 (2002)
2. Güçlü, B., Öztek, C.: Tactile sensitivity of children: effects of frequency, masking, and the non-pacinian I psychophysical channel. J. Exp. Child Psychol. **98**, 113–130 (2007)
3. Güçlü, B., Schepis, E.A., Yelke, S., Yücesoy, C.A., Bolanowski, S.J.: Ovoid geometry of the pacinian corpuscle is not the determining factor for mechanical excitation. Somatosens. Mot. Res. **23**, 119–126 (2006)
4. Güçlü, B., Gescheider, G.A., Bolanowski, S.J., İstefanopulos, Y.: Population model for vibrotactile spatial summation. Somatosens. Mot. Res. **22**, 239–253 (2005)
5. Güçlü, B., Mahoney, G.K., Pawson, L.J., Smith, R.L., Bolanowski, S.J.: Localization of merkel cells in the skin: an anatomical model. Somatosens. Mot. Res. **25**, 123–138 (2008)
6. Güçlü, B., Bolanovski, S.J.: Vibrotactile thresholds of the non-pacinian I channel: I. Methodological issues. Somatosens. Mot. Res. **22**, 49–56 (2005)
7. Güçlü, B., Bolanowski, S.J.: Frequency responses of cat rapidly adapting mechanoreceptive fibers. Somatosens. Mot. Res. **20**, 249–263 (2003)
8. Güçlü, B., Bolanowski, S.J., Pawson, L.: End-to-end linkage (EEL) clustering algorithm: a study on the distribution of meissner corpuscles in the skin. J. Comput. Neurosci. **15**, 19–28 (2003)
9. Shultz, C.D., Peshkin, M.A., Colgate, E.: Surface haptics via electroadhesion: expanding electrovibration by Johnsen and Rahbek. In: Proceedings of the IEEE World Haptics Conference (WHC 2015), Evanston, USA, pp. 57–62, June 2013
10. Meyer, D., Peshkin, M., Colgate, E.: Fingertip electrostatic modulation due to electrostatic attraction. In: Proceedings of the IEEE World Haptics Conference (WHC 2013), Daejeon, South Korea, pp. 43–48, April 2013
11. Wijekoon, D., Cecchinato, M.E., Hoggan, E., Linjama, J.: Electrostatic modulated friction as tactile feedback: intensity perception. In: Isokoski, P., Springare, J. (eds.) EuroHaptics 2012, Part I. LNCS, vol. 7282, pp. 613–624. Springer, Heidelberg (2012)
12. Cheng, D.K.: Fundamentals of Engineering Electromagnetics. Addison-Wesley, Reading (1994)
13. Beebe, D.J., Heymel, C.M., Kaczmarek, K.A., Tyler, M.E.: A polyimide-on-silicon electrostatic fingertip tactile display. In: Proceedings of the IEEE 17th Annual Conference on Engineering in Medicine and Biology Society, Montreal, Que, pp. 1545–1546 (1995)
14. Vezzoli, E., Amberg, M., Giraud, F., Lemaire-Semail, B.: Electrovibration modeling analysis. In: Auvray, M., Duriez, C. (eds.) EuroHaptics 2014, Part II. LNCS, vol. 8619, pp. 369–376. Springer, Heidelberg (2014)
15. Gescheider, G.A., Bolanovski, S.J., Pope, J.V., Verrillo, R.T.: A four-channel analysis of the tactile sensitivity of the fingertip: frequency selectivity, spatial summation, and temporal summation. Somatosens. Mot. Res. **19**(2), 114–124 (2002)
16. Kim, H., Kang, J., Kim, K., Lim, K., Ryu, J.: Method for providing electrovibration with uniformed density. IEEE Trans. Haptics **8**(4), 492–496 (2015)
17. Levitt, H.: Transformed up-down methods psychoacoustics. J. Acoust. Soc. Am. **49**(2), 467–477 (1971)

18. Tang, H., Beebe, D.J.: A microfabricated electrostatic haptic display for persons with visual impairments. IEEE Trans. Rehabil. Eng. **6**(3), 241–248 (1998)
19. Summers, I.R., Cooper, P.G., Wright, P., Gratton, D.A., Milnes, P.M., Brown, B.H.: Information from time-varying vibrotactile stimuli. J. Acoust. Soc. Am. **102**(6), 3686–3696 (1997)
20. Linjama, J., Mkinen, V.: E-sense screen: novel haptic display with capacitive electrosensory interface. In: Proceedings of the 4th Workshop for Haptic and Audio Interaction Design (HAID 2009), Dresden, Germany (2009)
21. Kaczmarek, K., Nammi, K., Agarwal, A., Tyler, M., Haase, S., Beebe, D.: Polarity effect in electrovibration for tactile display. IEEE Trans. Biomed. Eng. **53**(10), 2047–2054 (2006)
22. Demarest, K.R.: Engineering Electromagnetics. Prentice Hall, Upper Saddle River (1998)
23. Leek, M.R.: Adaptive procedures in psychophysical research. Percept. Psychophys. **63**(8), 1279–1292 (2001)
24. Yıldız, M.Z., Güçlü, B.: Relationship between vibrotactile detection threshold in the pacinian channel and complex mechanical modulus of the human glabrous skin. Somatosens. Mot. Res. **30**, 37–47 (2013)
25. Yıldız, M.Z., Toker, İ., Özkan, F.B., Güçlü, B.: Effects of passive and active movement on vibrotactile detection thresholds of the pacinian channel and forward masking. Somatosens. Mot. Res. **32**(4), 262–272 (2015)
26. Bau, O., Poupyrev, I., Israr, A., Harrison, C.: Teslatouch: electrovibration for touch surfaces. In: Proceedings of the 23nd Annual ACM Symposium on User Interface Software and Technology (UIST 2010), NewYork, USA, pp. 283–292 (2010)
27. Strong, R.M., Troxel, D.E.: An electrotactile display. IEEE Trans. Man-Mach. Syst. **11**(1), 72–79 (1970)
28. Kim, S.C., Israr, A., Poupyrev, I.: Tactile rendering of 3D features on touch surfaces. In: UIST 2013, St. Andrews (2013)
29. Bolanovski, S.J., Gescheider, G.A., Verrillo, R.T., Checkosky, C.M.: Four channels mediate the mechanical aspects of touch. Acoust. Soc. Am. **84**(5), 1680–1694 (1988)
30. Yamamoto, T., Yamamoto, Y.: Dielectric constant and resistivity of epidermal stratum corneum. Med. Biol. Eng. **14**, 494–500 (1976)
31. Ehrenstein, W.H., Ehrenstein, A.: Psychophysical methods. In: Windhorst, U., Johansson, H. (eds.) Modern Techniques in Neuroscience Research, pp. 1211–1241. Springer, Heidelberg (1999)

Temporal Integration of Tactile Inputs
from Multiple Sites

Sarah McIntyre[1,2(✉)], Ingvars Birznieks[1,2,3], Robin Andersson[4],
Gabriel Dicander[4], Paul P. Breen[1], and Richard M. Vickery[2,3]

[1] MARCS Institute, Western Sydney University, Sydney, Australia
s.mcintyre@westernsydney.edu.au
[2] Neuroscience Research Australia, Sydney, Australia
[3] School of Medical Sciences, Faculty of Medicine,
UNSW Australia, Sydney, Australia
[4] The Faculty of Medicine and Health Sciences,
Linköping University, Linköping, Sweden

Abstract. We investigated the perceived frequency elicited by two vibrating probes on the skin. Participants (n = 11) compared two probes vibrating in counter-phase (25 Hz), with comparison stimuli of in-phase vibration (18–54 Hz). They indicated which had the higher perceived frequency. Skin sites on the palm (glabrous) and arm (hairy) were tested with a range of probe separations (1–16 cm) and amplitudes (10–120 μm). Perceived frequency increased with decreasing separation of the probes ($F_{1,10} = 182.8$, $p < 0.001$). The two skin sites did not significantly differ ($F_{1,10} = 3.6$, $p = 0.087$). Perceived frequency was only minimally affected by amplitude changes between 40 and 120 μm ($F_{2,20} = 6.4$, $p = 0.007$, $\eta_G^2 = 0.06$). Both phase and spatial separation strongly influence vibrotactile interaction between two skin locations in a manner largely independent of changes in amplitude, and of skin type.

Keywords: Touch · Vibration · Frequency · Psychophysics · Human

1 Introduction

Fast adapting mechanoreceptors in the skin are uniquely adapted to respond to mechanical vibration. Recordings of FA1 and FA2 primary afferents show that their responses are precisely phase-locked to each cycle of sinusoidal vibration, providing highly reliable temporal information [1, 2]. In this study, we investigated how temporal features of vibrotactile stimulation are processed for perception of frequency for inputs that are spatially separated. It is not obvious to what extent the precise temporal information available in primary afferent trains is processed in later neural pathways, nor are the perceptual consequences of any such processing understood.

During vibrotactile stimulation, some afferents with receptive fields furthest from the center of stimulation will be poorly activated and fail to respond on some cycles [2]. This does not give rise to a lower apparent frequency in that zone, however [3], and frequency perception appears to rely on an integrated population response. Units with receptive fields close to the center of stimulation that respond on every cycle of

© Springer International Publishing Switzerland 2016
F. Bello et al. (Eds.): EuroHaptics 2016, Part I, LNCS 9774, pp. 204–213, 2016.
DOI: 10.1007/978-3-319-42321-0_19

vibration may effectively 'fill-in' the missing spikes from poorly activated units that respond intermittently, resulting in integrating inputs from multiple units [1]. If no one afferent is adequately stimulated, multiple weakly responding afferents might fill-in for each other, preserving the stimulus frequency in the population response.

A challenge for central nervous system (CNS) neurons to preserve the precise timing present in the periphery is that these higher order neurons receive multiple converging peripheral inputs, which travel along axons varying in conduction velocity [4]. Responses in multiple afferents caused by the same mechanical event reach the first synapse with slightly different delays (up to 15 ms), reducing the temporal precision with which the vibratory signal is encoded [5].

The main goal of this study was to test to what extent frequency perception integrates temporal inputs from separate sources of afferent sub-populations. To do this, we applied vibration to the skin with two probes simultaneously, and asked participants to judge the overall frequency of the vibration. Both probes vibrated at 25 Hz, in counter-phase with each other. When two probes are located close to each other, a considerable number of afferents would be recruited by both probes, responding to indentations from each alternately, encoding a frequency of 50 Hz. Other afferents are likely to be recruited by only one probe, encoding a frequency of 25 Hz. When a greater distance separated the probes, fewer (and eventually no) primary afferents are likely to be recruited by both probes (Fig. 1).

When the probes are separated enough that no primary afferents are activated by both of them, some higher order neurons with their larger receptive fields [6] may still receive inputs from afferents responding to each of the probes. In this case, filling-in due to phase differences may still occur, but because this process is subject to varying

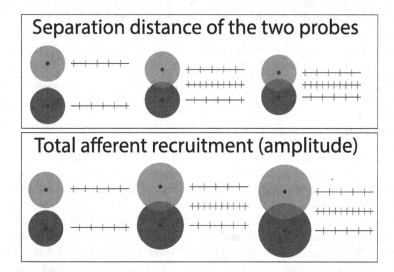

Fig. 1. Illustration of activation regions: primary afferents with their receptive fields in the shaded areas will be activated by a probe. *Top*: as the probes move closer together, more afferents respond to both. *Bottom*: as the amplitude is increased, activation areas increase. This causes more afferents to respond to both probes, but also recruits more afferents that respond to just one.

delays of peripheral inputs, the signal may be degraded. Instead, if higher order neurons are unable to sufficiently preserve the temporal precision of the periphery, neural filters may serve to temporally align the inputs to produce a perceived frequency of 25 Hz. By systematically varying the distance between the probes, we tested to what extent integration is preserved over these distances.

A secondary goal of this study was to test how the properties of different skin regions influence the integration of peripheral frequency signals. The glabrous skin of the hands and in the hairy skin of the arms differ in spatial resolution [7], sensitivity thresholds, elasticity and receptor types (e.g. hair sensitive units not found in glabrous skin) [8]. It seems likely that these differences may lead to different strategies for integrating peripheral inputs for frequency perception.

In addition, we wanted to test how the number of recruited afferents affects perceived frequency. Higher amplitude vibration will recruit additional afferents, with receptive fields further from the center of stimulation compared to a lower amplitude stimulus [2]. This increases the number of afferents responding to both probes, but also increases the number responding to only one (Fig. 1). If perceived frequency is dominated by the highest frequency (double the frequency of individual probes) (maximal filling-in), we might expect to see an upwards frequency shift at increasing spatial separations as amplitude increases.

2   Method

2.1   Participants

Eleven participants volunteered for the two main experiments (8 male, aged 19–33), 6 for the hairy-glabrous direct comparison experiment (all male, aged 21–43), and 8 for the double probe control experiment (7 male, aged 18–34). All participants were healthy, with no history of neurological dysfunction. The experimental protocol was approved by the human research ethics committee of Western Sydney University and conformed to the Declaration of Helsinki.

2.2   Apparatus

Vibration was delivered to the skin via two spherical probes (diameter 5 mm), attached to V4 shakers (Data Physics, San Jose, USA). Vibration waveforms were generated in Spike2 (v7.07) software and converted to an analog voltage signal using a Power 1401 MkII (CED, Cambridge, UK) and a 30 W amplifier to drive the shakers.

The vibration was measured using an OptocoNCDT 2200 displacement laser (Micro-Epsilon, Ortenburg, Germany). Two push buttons recorded participants' responses. These signals were acquired by the Power 1401 and recorded in Spike2.

Participants were seated with their right arm on a bench-top, supported by a pillow filled with polystyrene balls molded to the arm, which holds its shape when the air is pumped out. The probes were lowered until they just contacted the skin (causing a displacement of the probes of approximately 20 μm) and locked into position with a

Mini Salon 190 Studio Stand (Manfrotto, Cassola, Italy). To mask the sound of the shakers, participants wore earplugs and listened to white noise played through noise-isolating headphones.

2.3   Vibrotactile Stimuli

We used a pulsatile waveform, with each indentation having a fixed wavelength of approximately 4 ms, independent of the indentation rate (vibration frequency). Unlike with sinusoidal waveforms, even when our stimuli varied in frequency, they recruited approximately the same primary afferents. Recordings from both types of fast adapting primary afferents in glabrous skin have validated this, showing that pulsatile stimuli similar to what we used produced a reliable stereotyped response for each cycle of vibration, independent of frequency [9, 10].

We wanted to test how vibration cues, provided at spatially separated locations on the skin, influences the processing of temporal phase information present in the vibrations. To do this, we measured perceived frequency of two probes contacting nearby skin locations. The probes each vibrated at a frequency of 25 Hz, 180° out-of-phase with each other. Simply adding the signals together produces a frequency of 50 Hz, and we tested whether this occurs in frequency perception. The participants compared the frequency of this stimulus to the two probes vibrating in-phase at 18–54 Hz (Fig. 2A). One probe always stimulated a reference location, and the other stimulated a location 1–16 cm from the reference location (Fig. 2B). The distances were measured center-to-center, and at a separation of 1 cm, the probes were almost touching. Participants were aware that two probes contacted their skin, but regardless of the separation, the vibration felt diffuse and was difficult to perceptually separate.

To measure perceived frequency, we used the method of constant stimuli with a 2-interval forced choice paradigm (Fig. 2A). Participants felt a pair of vibrating stimuli, presented one after the other. For each pair, they were asked to say which stimulus felt higher frequency, the first or second (20 repeats). If they were unsure, they were told to

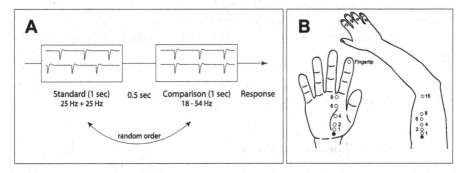

Fig. 2. A: Two-interval forced choice procedure, with the vibration waveforms of the double-probe standard and comparison stimuli. **B:** The reference location (filled circles) was always used, while the other probe varied in location (unfilled circles, cm). The 'fingertip' location on the hand, nominally 16 cm, varied between 13 and 16 cm due to differences in hand size.

guess. In each pair, one stimulus was the 'standard' stimulus, the two probes vibrating out-of-phase. The other stimulus in the pair was the 'comparison' stimulus, the two probes vibrating in-phase, which varied in frequency from trial to trial. The order of the standard and comparison stimuli was randomized for each trial.

For each comparison frequency, we calculated the proportion of times the participant responded that it was higher in frequency than the standard stimulus. Logistic regression was applied to produce a psychometric function. Perceived frequency was given by the PSE (point of subjective equality), the 50 % point on the regression line. This is the value of the comparison frequency that is equally likely to be judged higher as judged lower frequency than the standard.

2.4   Spatial Separation in Glabrous and Hairy Skin

We wanted to determine whether glabrous and hairy skin, with their different mechanical and receptor properties, resulted in different effects on frequency integration from spatially separated vibratory inputs (1, 2, 4, 6, 8 and 16 cm). We measured frequency perception of the two out-of-phase probes on both the glabrous skin of the palm of the hand and the hairy skin of the upper arm (Fig. 2B). The amplitude of vibration was always 40 μm on the hand, and 120 μm on the upper arm. These amplitudes were well above threshold and were determined in piloting to have approximately the same perceived intensity.

We also tested whether perceived frequency of vibration is the same for glabrous and hairy skin by having participants directly compare the frequency of a single probe applied to each skin region. The standard stimulus of a single probe vibrating at 23 Hz was applied to the glabrous skin of the index finger pad, and the comparison stimulus (15–38 Hz) was applied to the hairy skin of the arm.

2.5   Spatial Separation and Afferent Recruitment via Amplitude of Vibration

We varied the amplitude of vibration to manipulate the number of afferents recruited by the stimulus, and the area of skin over which afferents were likely to respond. We wanted to test how the number of recruited afferents influenced the temporal integration of vibration cues. We measured perceived frequency for the two probes applied to the palm of the hand, with a variety of vibration amplitudes (10, 40, 80, 120 μm). A subset of the probe distances from the first experiment was used (4, 8, 16 cm).

2.6   Double-Probe Control Experiment

In our two main experiments, we used a standard stimulus of two out-of-phase vibrating probes, and a comparison stimulus of two in-phase vibrating probes. We chose to use two in-phase probes for the comparison instead of a single probe so that the standard and comparison stimuli would have a similar subjective intensity and so that attention would be drawn to an area of the skin of similar spatial extent. In doing this, we assumed that the simultaneous stimulation of the two, in-phase probes results in near-simultaneous afferent responses propagated through to the CNS, with little effect on perceived frequency. However, given that the two probes were sometimes as far apart as 16 cm, there could be a delay of up to ~ 5 ms between the afferent inputs to the CNS from the two probes [11], 12 % the period between indentations of the vibration. This might lead to a higher perceived frequency of the comparison stimulus than anticipated, and result in an under-estimation of the true perceived frequency of the out-of-phase standard stimulus.

To address this issue, we conducted a control experiment on both glabrous and hairy skin, comparing two in-phase vibrating probes located 16 cm apart, to a single probe at one of the two locations (randomly varied trial-to-trial). We interleaved two experimental protocols, one in which the double-probe stimulus was the standard (25 Hz) and the single probe was the comparison (19–31 Hz), and vice versa.

3 Results

3.1 Spatial Separation

Our results show that perceived frequency of the pair of out-of-phase probes was generally higher than the base frequency of the individual probes of 25 Hz, but lower than 50 Hz, which would have resulted from a simple combination of the two signals (Fig. 3).

In general, perceived frequency was higher when the probes were closer to each other than when they were further apart. Repeated measures ANOVA analyses revealed a significant main effect of separation distance on PSE in both the skin type ($F_{5,50} = 77.0$, $p < 0.001$, $\eta_G^2 = 0.66$) and amplitude ($F_{2,20} = 95.118$, $p < 0.001$, $\eta_G^2 = 0.33$) experiments. Between 1 cm and 8 cm probe separation the skin type experiment, the PSE decreased linearly such that for each 1 cm increase, there was a

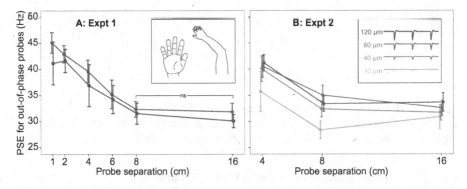

Fig. 3. Mean PSE (point of subjective equality) with 95 % confidence intervals. PSE is a measure of perceived frequency for the two probes vibrating out of phase (25 Hz + 25 Hz), and is given for different probe separations. Data points are shifted horizontally to avoid overlap. **A**: Data for the glabrous skin of the hand (green) and the hairy skin of the arm (blue). **B**: Data for different vibration amplitudes (separate lines). (Color figure online)

decrease in mean PSE of 1.8 Hz (post-hoc linear contrast: $F_{1,107} = 210.3$, $p < 0.001$, $R^2 = 0.56$). There was no significant difference between PSE at 8 and 16 cm distances (post-hoc pair-wise comparison: mean diff. = 0.7 Hz, $t_{21} = 1.2$, $p = 0.248$).

3.2   Integration of Afferent Inputs in Glabrous and Hairy Skin

Skin type did not appear to impact perceived frequency of the out-of-phase probes. A repeated measures ANOVA revealed no significant main effect of skin type ($F_{1,10} = 3.6$, $p = 0.087$, $\eta_G^2 = 0.08$), nor was there a significant interaction between skin type and separation distance ($F_{5,50} = 0.7$, $p = 0.593$, $\eta_G^2 = 0.01$). Although the mean PSE for hairy skin appears lower than for glabrous skin (Fig. 3A), this difference was not significant, and it was not consistently the case for individual participants (Fig. 4A). These results indicate that the mechanical and neural differences in the two skin regions have negligible influence on how temporal phase of the two probes is combined at different separations.

Similarly, when vibration applied to hairy and glabrous skin sites was directly compared, perceived frequency was similar (Fig. 4B). A 23 Hz stimulus applied to the glabrous skin produced a PSE of 22.2 ± 1.2 Hz (mean $\pm$ 95 % CI) when compared to various vibration frequencies on the hairy skin.

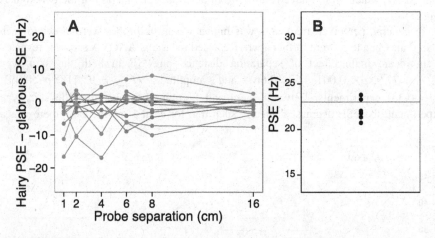

Fig. 4. A: Difference in perceived frequency between hairy and glabrous skin for the two out-of-phase probes. Separate lines for each participant (n = 11). **B:** PSE for a single probe vibrating at 23 Hz on glabrous skin when directly compared to vibration on hairy skin (n = 6).

3.3   Afferent Recruitment via Amplitude of Vibration

We found that amplitude had a small influence of perceived frequency of the out-of-phase probes. A repeated measures ANOVA found a significant main effect of amplitude on PSE ($F_{3,30} = 17.5$, $p < 0.001$, $\eta_G^2 = 0.42$), and a significant interaction effect with probe separation ($F_{9,60} = 4.3$, $p = 0.001$, $\eta_G^2 = 0.13$).

The effect of amplitude appears to be primarily due to lower perceived frequencies at amplitudes of 10 μm compared to higher amplitudes (Fig. 3B). The vibration at 10 μm is close to detection thresholds, and this is reflected in the higher variance of PSE measurements (SD = 5.2 Hz) compared to higher amplitudes (SD = 4.7, 4.3 and 4.3 Hz for 40, 80 and 120 μm, respectively). For this reason, we conducted a contrast analysis comparing PSE at 10 μm to all higher amplitudes. This revealed a significant difference ($F_{1,10} = 20.5$, $p = 0.001$) with a moderate effect size ($\eta_G^2 = 0.24$). When we excluded the 10 μm data to evaluate the effect of varying amplitude between 40 and 120 μm, amplitude was still significant ($F_{2,20} = 6.4$, $p = 0.007$), but with a considerably smaller effect size ($\eta_G^2 = 0.06$).

3.4   Double Probe Control Experiment

If the double probe stimulus were perceived as higher frequency than a single probe, we would expect that when the double probe was used as the standard, that the PSE would be higher than when the single probe was used as the standard. However, this wasn't the case and the PSE was close to the 25 Hz standard stimulus, regardless of whether it was delivered with double or single probes (Fig. 5). On the glabrous skin, the difference in PSE was 1.2 ± 4.5 Hz (mean diff ± 95 % CI). On the hairy skin, it was 3.5 ± 5.9 Hz. Pooling data from both sites to maximize statistical power, a paired samples t-test revealed no significant difference between PSE for a double-probe standard vs. a single-probe standard ($t_{11} = 1.6$, $p = 0.139$).

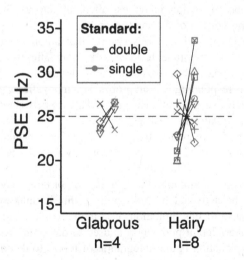

Fig. 5. PSE measured either with a standard stimulus composed of two probes vibrating in phase (double) compared to a single probe vibrations (red); or with a single-probe standard stimulus compared to double-probe stimuli (blue). The black lines link each participant's PSEs (different symbols) for the double and single probe standards. A dashed line indicates the 25 Hz frequency of the standard stimulus. (Color figure online)

4 Discussion

We showed that frequency perception integrates temporal cues from spatially separated sources of afferent inputs, provided by two probes vibrating out-of phase. As expected, perceived frequency of the out-of-phase probes was higher for smaller separations. Spike trains of individual primary afferents encode stimulus information with very precise timing [1, 2]. However, the temporal dispersion of spikes from different afferents when they reach the next synapse on the pathway to cortex may cause a reduction in temporal resolution [4]. We anticipated that perceived frequency would reflect the maximal stimulus integration, depending on whether or not any individual primary afferents were activated by both probes.

However, our results indicate that common activation of primary afferents by the two probes was not a critical determinant of perceived frequency. Firstly, there were no differences between glabrous and hairy skin. With different mechanical properties, receptor types, thresholds and response properties, it is surprising that perceived frequency decreased with increasing separation in a nearly-identical fashion for the different skin types. Secondly, even when the two probes were undoubtedly activating many of the same primary afferents at the shortest separation of 1 cm, perceived frequency did not reach 50 Hz, which would be the result if the signals from the two probes were fully combined with maximal filling-in.

One possible explanation is that perceived frequency may be a result of combining competing frequency channels related to primary afferent inputs that contribute to the encoding of one or another frequency. Even at the closest separation of the probes, some afferents with receptive fields at the far edges of the stimulated area would have been activated by only one probe, providing a relatively low frequency input signal (25 Hz). As the probe separation increases, afferents activated by only one probe contribute a greater proportion of the input signals.

This is also consistent with our observation that amplitude has little effect on perceived frequency. As amplitude is increased, more afferents are recruited with receptive fields further apart from the centre of stimulation [2]. This simultaneously leads to more afferents responding to both probes, and more afferents responding to just one probe. This wouldn't substantially change the balance between frequency channels and thus would have a relatively small net effect.

One limitation of the competing frequency channels explanation is that even at separation distances up to 16 cm, perceived frequency was typically higher (>30 Hz) than the frequency with which the individual probes vibrated (25 Hz). Although it's possible that transmission of vibration through the skin or bone may have caused some primary afferents to be activated by both probes, this is unlikely to be a strongly weighted input. Because of this limitation, it is unlikely that a simple average of the discharge rate from the afferent population is used to determine perceived frequency.

An alternative explanation is that integration of inputs to determine the perceived frequency may occur after processing that localises the two probes. Top-down processes may contribute to the separation of inputs as having different origins [12]. This is consistent with the smooth decline in perceived frequency as probe separation increased. As the distance between the probes increases, it becomes less plausible that these out-of-phase sensory input signals are caused by the same real-world event.

In conclusion, some central summation of vibration frequency occurs for separately stimulated sub-populations of primary afferents. The degree of summation is insensitive to mechanical and peripheral features irrelevant to the vibration frequency, except spatial separation. This may reflect top-down filters that use the degree of spatial and temporal coincidence to determine the extent to which peripheral inputs are integrated.

Acknowledgments. This work was supported by NHMRC Project Grant APP1028284 to IB & RMV and NHMRC Project Grant APP1067353 to PB & IB.

References

1. LaMotte, R.H., Mountcastle, V.B.: Capacities of humans and monkeys to discriminate vibratory stimuli of different frequency and amplitude: a correlation between neural events and psychological measurements. J. Neurophysiol. **38**(3), 539–559 (1975)
2. Johnson, K.O.: Reconstruction of population response to a vibratory stimulus in quickly adapting mechanoreceptive afferent fiber population innervating glabrous skin of the monkey. J. Neurophysiol. **37**(1), 48–72 (1974)
3. Kuroki, S., Watanabe, J., Nishida, S.: Contribution of within- and cross-channel information to vibrotactile frequency discrimination. Brain Res. **1529**, 46–55 (2013)
4. Ferrington, D., Rowe, M.: Differential contributions to coding of cutaneous vibratory information by cortical somatosensory areas I and II. J. Neurophysiol. **43**, 310–331 (1980)
5. Johansson, R.S., Birznieks, I.: First spikes in ensembles of human tactile afferents code complex spatial fingertip events. Nat. Neurosci. **7**(2), 170–177 (2004)
6. Gardner, E.P., Palmer, C.I., Hämäläinen, H.A., Warren, S.: Simulation of motion on the skin. V. Effect of stimulus temporal frequency on the representation of moving bar patterns in primary somatosensory cortex of monkeys. J. Neurophysiol. **67**(1), 37–63 (1992)
7. Essick, G.K., Bredehoeft, K.R., McLaughlin, D.F., Szaniszlo, J.A.: Directional sensitivity along the upper limb in humans. Somatosens. Mot. Res. **8**(1), 13–22 (1991)
8. Vallbo, Å.B., Olausson, H., Wessberg, J., Kakuda, N.: Receptive field characteristics of tactile units with myelinated afferents in hairy skin of human subjects. J. Physiol. **483**(3), 783–795 (1995)
9. Gardner, E.P., Palmer, C.I.: Simulation of motion on the skin. I. Receptive fields and temporal frequency coding by cutaneous mechanoreceptors of OPTACON pulses delivered to the hand. J. Neurophysiol. **62**(6), 1410–1436 (1989)
10. Birznieks, I., Vickery, R.M.: The role of temporal features of the afferent spike train in the perception of vibrotactile stimulus frequency. Program No. 644.19/NN8. 2013 Neuroscience Meeting Planner. Society for Neuroscience, San Diego, CA (2013)
11. Buchthal, F., Rosenfalck, A.: Evoked action potentials and conduction velocity in human sensory nerves. Brain Res. **3**(1), 1–122 (1966)
12. Orchard-Mills, E., Van der Burg, E., Alais, D.: Poorer resolution for audiotactile than for audiovisual synchrony detection in cluttered displays. J. Exp. Psychol. Hum. Percept. Perform. (2016). Advance online publication

Control of Haptic Interfaces

Improved Control Methods for Vibrotactile Rendering

Ha-Van Quang$^{(\boxtimes)}$ and Matthias Harders

Institute of Computer Science, University of Innsbruck,
6020 Innsbruck, Austria
{Ha-Van.Quang,matthias.harders}@uibk.ac.at

Abstract. Many applications in the domain of haptics make use of vibrotactile rendering. One means for the delivery of the signals is employing voice coil actuators. However, existing control strategies for these exhibit limitations, for instance their dynamic characteristic is often not taken into account leading to output distortion. We propose two new control methods to improve vibrotactile rendering – once based on data-driven spline interpolation and once on following power spectral density. Both approaches rely on the idea of first decomposing a desired signal into a combination of harmonic components of different frequencies. For these, separate optimal gains are then employed to achieve a flat frequency response. The behavior of these controllers is examined in experiments and compared to a constant gain strategy. Both proposed methods result in improvements, such as lower spectral dissimilarity scores.

1 Introduction

A desired and important goal of haptic rendering is the faithful reproduction of tool-object interactions. A typical strategy to generate high-fidelity feedback for such contacts is to separate the required haptic signals into two components: low-frequency kinesthetic forces and high-frequency vibrotactile contact transients (see e.g. [1]). Low-frequency signals can be rendered reasonably well by traditional impedance-type haptic interfaces, however, these devices are often not tailored for presenting higher-frequency content [2]. Instead, such signal components are better displayed via vibration actuators attached appropriately to handles of the kinesthetic device (see e.g. [3])

Several types of actuators exist to deliver vibrotactile feedback to a user's hand. In our current work, we focus on employing voice-coil actuators (VCAs). The traditional method to control these in a haptic rendering system is to employ a constant gain strategy for mapping the desired accelerations to the actual command signals (controller structure visualized in inset of Fig. 2). However, this method ignores the large underdamped resonance of the actuator and thus cannot compensate for amplitude changes across the frequency band. Therefore, we targeted the design and development of improved controllers for vibrotactile rendering with VCAs.

© Springer International Publishing Switzerland 2016
F. Bello et al. (Eds.): EuroHaptics 2016, Part I, LNCS 9774, pp. 217–228, 2016.
DOI: 10.1007/978-3-319-42321-0_20

The core idea followed in this paper is to decompose the desired signal into a combination of harmonic components with different frequency, and then employ separate gains for each frequency to achieve a flat frequency response. We propose two new methods along this line to control a VCA to reproduce the acceleration profile – a data-driven spline interpolation technique and a power spectral density method. The former relies on interpolation of pre-recorded signals. In the latter, signal distortion is reduced and fidelity improved by trying to follow the desired power spectrum. In addition, for both methods, a further goal was to ensure stability as well as straightforward parameter setting.

2 Related Work

Vibrotactile displays come in various different shapes and flavors [4] and have been applied in diverse application domains, ranging for instance from electronic travel aids to improving surgical simulation [5]. As an example, voice coil actuators have been widely used to effectively transfer vibrotactile signals to a user in many haptic applications, including telerobotic systems [6], haptic recreation of virtual textures [7], augmented reality [8], enhancing realism of walking simulation [9], surgical training simulation [10], and telesurgery [11]. In most of those applications, the VCA has been controlled without considering system dynamics.

In several projects only a constant gain control is applied. In order to avoid the resulting acceleration output distortions in this case, McMahan et al. proposed a feedforward dynamic compensation method [12]. It showed better performance than the constant gain strategy, however, suffered from high sensitivity to system nonlinearities. Their proposed controller compensates the frequency-dependent response of a VCA by inverting the system's dynamics model. The model must be carefully picked to avoid actuator saturation due to the infinite gain at steady-state and high gain at lower frequency. As reported, the uncertainty in the system parameters reduces the applicability of the technique. The nonlinear stiffness of the suspension led to the nonlinear behavior of the system. In our own work we initially also implemented a similar feed-forward compensation method, but also observed saturation problems with the estimated model.

Another related work is active noise control (ANC) in which digital control systems are designed to cancel out unwanted acoustic pressure [13] for instance to create a silence zone. Adaptation algorithms (e.g. FxLMS) have been developed to adjust the ANC controllers. However, FxLMS and its variants suffer from either slow convergence rate or computational complexity. It was suggested that frequency domain ANC algorithms can be used to overcome those problems. For instance, in [14], reference and error signals are first stored in buffers and then transformed to the frequency domain using the Fast Fourier Transform. The elements of the frequency domain reference vector are multiplied by filter weights to generate a frequency-domain control vector. The later is then fed to an inverse FFT to create a time-domain control signal. The filter weights are updated via the complex FxLMS algorithm [15]. Another technique recently proposed in [16] tries to reduce computational complexity, effectively canceling out non-stationary noise via the short-time Fourier Transform. In general, in the ANC field, generated signals are combined with noise. However, the focus is then on measuring error signals and designing filters to minimize the latter in the time-domain. Thus, this class of algorithms may not be readily applicable to our setting, since our focus is directly on signals in the frequency domain.

Our approach is inspired by the control of electrodynamic shakers in vibration tests. The general goal of these is to reproduce a specified acceleration profile at the shaker table that is close to the device under test. The time-domain sine control solution proposed in [17] reduces the delay in updating the drive signal. The controller is implemented in response to the input accelerations on a sample-by-sample basis. Good experimental performance is achieved in typical frequency ranges of automotive and aerospace vibration testing, between 10 Hz and 2 kHz. However, this method requires knowledge of the dynamic model of the shaker, and controller stability is sensitive to resonances. Related to this, the frequency-domain self-tuning method [18] has been proposed to control the random vibration of a payload. It consists of a power spectrum estimator to determine the spectrum of the shaker output and an equalization algorithm to force the output spectrum to converge to the reference spectrum.

In general, in the field of vibration testing, the acceleration profile and its power spectrum density are static and can be pre-computed. In contrast to this, in haptic rendering the desired acceleration is dynamically changing in real-time. Therefore, existing approaches in vibration testing are not readily applicable in our case.

3   Hardware

For our developments and experiments, we employed the Haptuator Mark II [19], and its amplifier (Haptu Amp), developed by Tactile Labs[1]. The haptuator was enclosed in a plastic box and suspended in the air by sewing thread as shown

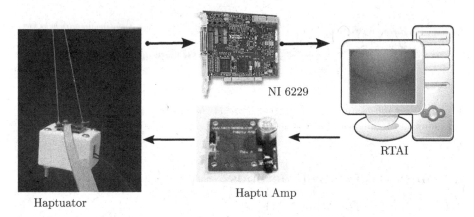

Haptuator   Haptu Amp

Fig. 1. Data recording setup

---

[1] http://tactilelabs.com.

in Fig. 1. Vibration signal recordings were performed via a 3-axis accelerometer (ADXL335), tightly attached to the Haptuator holder with a screw. The sensor was connected to a National Instruments NI-6229 acquisition board in a PC running the Real-Time Application Interface (RTAI) Linux at a frequency of 10 kHz. To investigate the frequency-dependent response of the VCA, experiments have been performed employing the constant gain method. Gains were chosen in the range [0.05, 0.4], at a resolution of 0.05. For each selected constant gain, sinusoidal signals with frequency from 50 to 500 Hz, step of 5 Hz, over the course of 0.5 s were used as desired signals. Gravitational acceleration was removed from the data. Acceleration output is calculated as the mean of measured accelerations in three directions. The largest magnitudes were observed along the main axis of the linear actuator. The mean of the maximum magnitude of the acceleration output was divided by the magnitude of the input signal to compute the amplification ratio for each frequency. Figure 2 shows the results; each line represents the changes of the amplification ratio across the frequency band for a specific constant gain. As can be seen, the amplification ratio changes with frequency and gain. Due to this, we explored strategies of selecting tailored gains for separate frequencies to ensure a fl at frequency response.

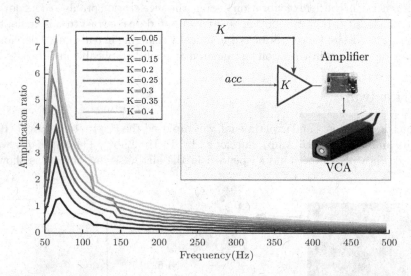

Fig. 2. Constant gain method – controller structure and amplification ratios for different gains and frequencies ($acc = \sin(2\pi ft)$)

4   Improved Control Methods

4.1   Spline Interpolation Method

The general idea of this controller is to employ interpolation of the pre-recorded data shown in Fig. 2. Separate gains are computed as the inverse of the amplification ratios, each according to a frequency. Thus, a method is required to decompose the input signal into a combination of harmonic components with known frequencies. The standard technique for spectral analysis is the discrete Fourier transform (DFT), typically implemented as the FFT algorithm. However, in our method, a new DFT output spectrum is desired for each new sample. Therefore, a computationally more efficient method than traditional FFT is needed. Thus, we employ for this purpose the sliding DFT (SDFT) method proposed in [20], and later updated in [21]. Initially, the N-point DFT (i.e. with a window size of N samples) is computed. Thereafter, each new DFT sample is efficiently obtained directly from the old DFT by shifting the previous $S_k(n-1)$ components, dropping sample $x(n-N)$, and adding the current sample $x(n)$:

$$S_k(n) = e^{j2\pi k/N}[S_k(n-1) + x(n) - x(n-N)]. \tag{1}$$

While the SDFT is computationally simpler than the traditional FFT, this advantage is reduced for the inverse case (inverse sliding DFT – ISDFT) due to the sliding window. Nevertheless, as mentioned in [22], if we are only attempting to reconstruct the first sample of the shifting window, it can simply be obtained as the average of the frequency components:

$$f_{acc}(n) = \frac{1}{N} \sum_{k=1}^{N-1} S_k(n), \tag{2}$$

where $S_k(n)$ is the kth component of the DFT which has been computed in the signal decomposition step. Returning to the idea of using separate gains for each frequency, we update Eq. (2) for reconstructing the signal:

$$u(n) = \frac{1}{N} \sum_{k=1}^{N-1} K_{f_k} S_k(n), \tag{3}$$

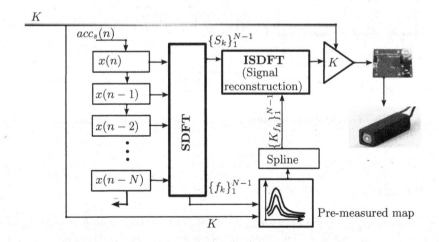

Fig. 3. Controller structure of spline interpolation method

where K_{f_k} is the specific separate gain spline interpolated at the frequency corresponding to the k_{th} component of the DFT. The output $u(n)$ is the signal to be sent to the VCA using the same optimal gain as in the constant gain method. The overall controller architecture is shown in Fig. 3.

4.2 Power Spectral Density Method

While the previously introduced spline interpolation method is simple to be implemented, its precision depends on the resolution and quality of the measured data. Moreover, the pre-measured data need to be updated whenever the system dynamic changes. Therefore, we examined as an alternative the computation of separate gains according to the difference between the power spectra of the desired (acc_s) and the actual acceleration (acc_m) signal. In this approach, both the desired and the measured signals are decomposed using the SDFT (via Eq. (1)). The power spectra are estimated for each via the square of the corresponding DFT's magnitude. A PID controller is designed to compute the gain for each frequency based on the error between the power spectra of the desired and the measured signal. The acceleration signal is then reconstructed via applying Eq. (3). The overall architecture of the Power Spectral Density (PSD) method is depicted in Fig. 4.

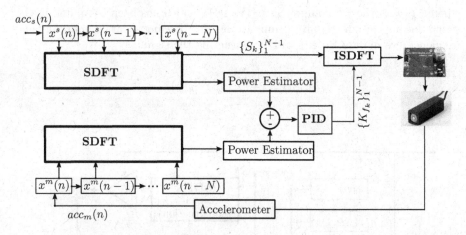

Fig. 4. Controller structure of power spectral density method

5 Results

Quantitative experiments have been performed to examine the performance of the proposed control methods. Both are compared to the widely-used constant gain method. The behavior is examined for three types of input signals: artificial

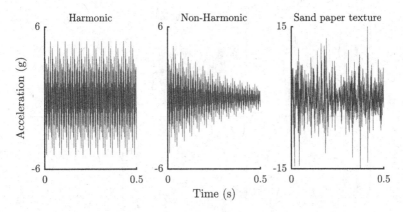

Fig. 5. Test acceleration profiles (period of 0.5 s)

harmonic (h) and non-harmonic (nh) signals, as well as actual recorded data. The former two are generated via the following equations so that the signal has the largest power in both low frequencies (75 Hz, 100 Hz) and high frequencies (300 Hz, 400 Hz):

$$f_{acc}^h(t) = \sin(150\pi t) + \sin(200\pi t) + 2\sin(600\pi t) + 1.5\sin(800\pi t)$$
$$f_{acc}^{nh}(t) = e^{-3t} f_{acc}^h(t).$$

In addition, actual acceleration datasets obtained from sample materials, published in [23], were also examined. Figure 5 depicts parts of these signals (example of actual data recording stemming from sand paper) for a time interval of 0.5 s. In all experiments, signals are decomposed using SDFT with a sliding window of 400 samples and a sampling frequency of 10 kHz.

Figure 6 shows the experimental results of the three methods for the harmonic and the non-harmonic signal in the time-domain. Only a short portion of the overall signal is shown for better visual comparison. In case of the harmonic signal, it can be seen that spline interpolation and PSD are more responsive to signal changes, while the constant gain method filters out high-frequency components. In case of the non-harmonic signal, the spline interpolation method helps to improve the response of the actuator for all frequencies. The performance of the PSD is worse, however, it still yields better behavior than the constant gain method. As a shifting window is used for Fourier transform computation, the proposed methods introduce time delay to the system. Therefore, examining acceleration errors in time domain is not optimal for comparison. Instead, we employ a frequency-based metric which will be addressed in more detail below.

Since human perception of vibrotactile signals relies significantly on the spectral power of a signal [24], we also examined the power spectra of the measured and desired signals for all methods. It is not feasible to show the frequency performance of the full spectrum. Moreover, the artificial signal has largest power at specific frequencies and is almost zero at others. Therefore, only the power

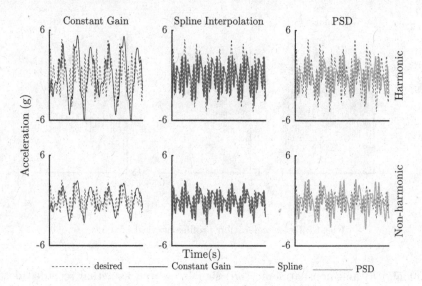

Fig. 6. Time-domain performance (harmonic and non-harmonic signals) (Color figure online)

spectra of the four highest power frequencies over time with different control approaches are displayed in Fig. 7. Note that for the spline interpolation method power is adjusted according to frequency (i.e. reducing it in case of 75 Hz and 100 Hz, while increasing it for 300 Hz and 400 Hz). Thus, its actual power follows more closely the desired one than the constant gain method. However, a drawback of the method is the overshoot visible at the beginning of the measured power. This is due to the start-up time connected to initializing the first window of the SDFT, during which the same gain as for the constant gain method was employed. In addition, subsequent deviations from the desired signal are due to interpolation errors. The overshoot could be reduced by decreasing the size of the sliding window, however, interpolation error would be increased as the frequency resolution is decreased. Another option could be to employ a smaller gain during start-up, instead of a constant gain, but as a result the power of the output signal would be reduced in all frequencies.

In contrast to this, the PSD method allows for – in theory – tuning the PID controller for optimal performance for each frequency in order to minimize the steady state error. However, in practice this turned out to be difficult. Traditionally, PID controllers are tuned, for instance, manually or via rule-based methods [25]. However, the former is iterative and time-consuming, while the latter are only applicable for certain operating conditions. Moreover, PID auto-tuning methods (see e.g. [26]) are incapable of running in real-time and complicated to apply. For now, only the manual tuning method was employed.

In the next experiment we compared the performance of the three control methods with various recorded vibration signals. First, Fig. 8 shows resulting acceleration profiles in the time-domain, again using the sand paper data as

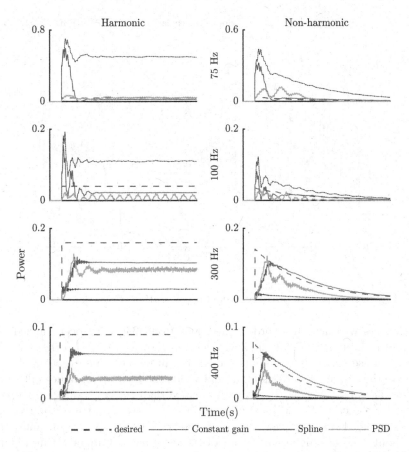

Fig. 7. Frequency-domain performance (harmonic and non-harmonic signals) (Color figure online)

example input. Qualitatively the spline interpolation and PSD method allow for a better reconstruction of high-frequency signals, while the constant gain method tends to filter them out. However, the power spectra in this experiment cover a considerably larger number of frequencies than the small number of known frequencies in the previous experiment.

A different method of analysis was needed next to quantitatively examine the performance in the frequency domain. One option is employing the spectra dissimilarity metric derived in [24], given as

$$D_{S_1 S_2} = \frac{\sum_f |P_{S_1}(f) - P_{S_2}(f)|}{\frac{1}{2}\sum_f |P_{S_1}(f) + P_{S_2}(f)|}, \tag{4}$$

where $P_S(f)$ is the power spectrum of signal S at frequency f. The metric varies between 0 (perfect match) and 2 (complete mismatch), and was developed to compare the spectra of desired and measured accelerations. Additional

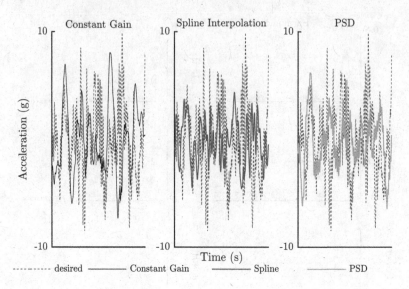

Fig. 8. Acceleration profiles for sand paper texture (Color figure online)

experiments with actual recorded data, also from [23], have been carried out. Part of the data yields the dissimilarity metrics shown in Table 1 (other recorded sample datasets exhibited similar trends). It can be seen that according to this measure the spline interpolation method yields the best performance. The PSD method also mostly shows better performance than the constant gain method, except for the case of sand paper. Analyzing the power spectra of the recorded signals revealed that the mean speed of change in power spectra of sand paper was about 33 times higher than that of tissue paper and about 8 times higher than that of wood, respectively. In general, the reduced performance of PSD can be attributed to the fast change of powers for each frequency, which renders the PID unable to control the actual power to follow closely.

Table 1. Spectral dissimilarity, ranging from 0 (perfect match) to 2 (complete mismatch)

	Harmonic	Non-harmonic	Sand paper	Wood	Tissue paper
Constant gain	1.53	1.52	1.23	1.48	1.13
Spline	0.66	0.45	1.12	0.99	0.9
PSD	1.13	1.13	1.34	1.34	1.09

6 Conclusion and Future Work

Motivated by creating high-fidelity vibration feedback, this paper proposed two methods, spline interpolation and power spectral density, for controlling the widely-used VCA in haptic applications. The core idea was to decompose the desired acceleration signal into a combination of harmonic components with different frequency and employ separate gains for each frequency to avoid distortion of the output signal due to the frequency-dependent response of the VCA. Experiments have been carried out to compare the two methods with the constant gain approach. The spline interpolation method yielded the best performance in all cases. However, a drawback is the error that depends on the pre-recorded data. In actual use, the system dynamic changes when a tool with a mounted haptuator is held by different users. As a result, it would become necessary to update the database for the spline interpolation approach to maintain performance. Instead, the PSD method, which requires the use of an accelerometer during runtime shows promise to reduce the steady state error. Moreover, the PSD method is independent from user hand dynamics, while the spline interpolation method requires an update of the pre-recorded data for different users and devices. In future work, we will explore methods for designing appropriate PID controllers for PSD as well as implementing the algorithm in DSP as a standalone control board. Moreover, we will explore the application of the proposed control methods in the context of surgical training simulators.

References

1. McMahan, W., Romano, J.M., Abdul Rahuman, A.M., Kuchenbecker, K.J.: High frequency acceleration feedback significantly increases the realism of haptically rendered textured surfaces. In: 2010 IEEE Haptics Symposium, pp. 141–148. IEEE (2010)
2. Campion, G., Hayward, V.: Fundamental limits in the rendering of virtual haptic textures. In: World Haptics Conference, pp. 263–270 (2005)
3. Wall, S.A., Harwin, W.: A high bandwidth interface for haptic human computer interaction. Mechatronics 11(4), 371–387 (2001)
4. Choi, S., Kuchenbecker, K.J.: Vibrotactile display: perception, technology, and applications. Proc. IEEE 101(9), 2093–2104 (2013)
5. Tenzer, Y., Davies, B., et al.: Investigation into the effectiveness of vibrotactile feedback to improve the haptic realism of an arthroscopy training simulator. Stud. Health Technol. Inform. 132, 517–522 (2007)
6. Dennerlein, J.T., Millman, P.A., Howe, R.D.: Vibrotactile feedback for industrial telemanipulators. In: Sixth Annual Symposium on Haptic Interfaces for Virtual Environment and Teleoperator Systems, ASME International Mechanical Engineering Congress and Exposition, vol. 61, pp. 189–195 (1997)
7. Culbertson, H., Unwin, J., Kuchenbecker, K.J.: Modeling and rendering realistic textures from unconstrained tool-surface interactions. IEEE Trans. Haptics 7(3), 381–393 (2014)
8. Hachisu, T., Sato, M., Fukushima, S., Kajimoto, H.: Augmentation of material property by modulating vibration resulting from tapping. In: Isokoski, P., Springare, J. (eds.) EuroHaptics 2012, Part I. LNCS, vol. 7282, pp. 173–180. Springer, Heidelberg (2012)
9. Turchet, L., Burelli, P., Serafin, S.: Haptic feedback for enhancing realism of walking simulations. IEEE Trans. Haptics 6(1), 35–45 (2013)
10. Olsson, P., Nysjö, F., Singh, N., Thor, A., Carlbom, I.: Visuohaptic bone saw simulator: combining vibrotactile and kinesthetic feedback. In: SIGGRAPH Asia 2015 Technical Briefs, p. 10. ACM (2015)

11. L'Orsa, R., Zareinia, K., Gan, L.S., Macnab, C., Sutherland, G.: Potential tissue puncture notification during telesurgery. In: Oakley, I., Brewster, S. (eds.) HAID 2013. LNCS, vol. 7989, pp. 30–39. Springer, Heidelberg (2013)

12. McMahan, W., Kuchenbecker, K.J.: Dynamic modeling and control of voice-coil actuators for high-fidelity display of haptic vibrations. In: Haptics Symposium, pp. 115–122. IEEE (2014)

13. Tabatabaei Ardekani, I., Abdulla, W.H.: FxLMS-based active noise control: a quick review. In: Proceedings of Asia Pacific Signal and Information Processing Association Annual (APSIPA) Submit and Conference, pp. 1–11 (2011)

14. Shen, Q., Spanias, A.: Time and frequency domain X block LMS algorithms for single channel active noise control. In: Proceedings of 2nd International Congress on Recent Developments in Air-and Structure-Borne Sound Vibration, pp. 353–360 (1992)

15. Reichard, K.M., Swanson, D.C.: Frequency-domain implementation of the filtered-x algorithm with on-line system identification. In: Proceedings of Recent Advances in Active Control of Sound Vibration, pp. 562–573 (1993)

16. Tang, X.L., Lee, C.-M.: Time-frequency-domain filtered-x LMS algorithm for active noise control. J. Sound Vib. **331**(23), 5002–5011 (2012)

17. Della Flora, L., Grundling, H.A.: Time domain sinusoidal acceleration controller for an electrodynamic shaker. IET Control Theory Appl. **2**(12), 1044–1053 (2008)

18. Wellstead, P., Zarrop, M.: Self-tuning Systems: Control and Signal Processing. Wiley, New York (1991)

19. Yao, H.-Y., Hayward, V.: Design and analysis of a recoil-type vibrotactile transducer. J. Acoust. Soc. Am. **128**(2), 619–627 (2010)

20. Jacobsen, E., Lyons, R.: The sliding DFT. IEEE Sig. Process. Mag. **20**(2), 74–80 (2003)

21. Jacobsen, E., Lyons, R.: An update to the sliding DFT. Sig. Process. Mag. **21**(1), 110–111 (2004)

22. Bradford, R., Dobson, R., Ffitch, J.: Sliding is smoother than jumping. In: International Computer Music Conference, pp. 287–290 (2005)

23. Culbertson, H., Lopez Delgado, J.J., Kuchenbecker, K.J.: One hundred data-driven haptic texture models and open-source methods for rendering on 3D objects. In: IEEE Haptics Symposium, pp. 319–325. IEEE (2014)

24. Bensmaïa, S., Hollins, M.: Pacinian representations of fine surface texture. Percept. Psychophysics **67**(5), 842–854 (2005)

25. Kasilingam, G., Pasupuleti, J.: Coordination of PSS and PID controller for power system stability enhancement-overview. Indian J. Sci. Technol. **8**(2), 142–151 (2015)

26. Yoon, M.-H., Shin, C.-H.: Design of online auto-tuning pid controller for power plant process control. In: Proceedings of SICE Annual Conference, pp. 1221–1224. IEEE (1997)

Co-actuation: Achieve High Stiffness and Low Inertia in Force Feedback Device

Jian Song, Yuru Zhang$^{(\boxtimes)}$, Hongdong Zhang,
and Dangxiao Wang$^{(\boxtimes)}$

Beihang University, No. 37 Xueyuan Rd., Haidian, Beijing, China
{yuru,hapticwang}@buaa.edu.cn

Abstract. Achieving high stiffness, low inertia and friction is a big challenge in the design of a haptic device. Admittance display is a common solution to obtain high stiffness but is difficult to achieve low inertia and friction. We describe a new concept of co-actuation to overcome this difficulty. The co-actuation approach disconnects the actuators and joints of a haptic device, making the two components work cooperatively according to characteristics of simulated environment. In free space, the joints are tracked and followed by the actuators. Users can move the joints freely without feeling resistance from the actuators. In constraint space, physical constraints driven by the actuators apply impedance to the joints. By producing a direct physical contact between the joints and the physical constraints, users can feel a hard virtual surface. The paper describes the mechanical and control design and implementation of a one degree-of-freedom (DOF) co-actuation module. Stiffness of 40 N/mm and friction force of less than 0.3 N was achieved on the module. By effectively reducing inertia and friction, the proposed approach demonstrates its potential advantage over conventional admittance displays. The co-actuation approach can be applied to multi-DOF haptic devices to achieve high stiffness, low inertia and friction.

Keywords: Co-actuation · Haptic device · High stiffness · Low inertia

1 Introduction

It is well known that impedance displays and admittance displays are two distinct classes of haptic devices. Impedance displays usually have low inertia and friction, and are highly back-drivable [1, 2]. Admittance displays usually contain a transmission of significant reduction, and are therefore non-back-drivable due to high inertia and friction [3, 4]. The essential control paradigm of impedance displays is displacement in, and force out. Admittance control is the inverse of impedance control. Although well-engineered admittance devices may have a higher dynamic range than their counterparts, most successful commercial haptic displays are impedance devices [5].

Impedance displays and admittance displays are dual not only in their cause-and-effect structure, but also in their performance and limitation. Impedance devices typically are able to display low-inertia, low-damping environments, but have difficulty rendering stiff constraints. Notable impedance devices, Phantom models, have a maximum stable stiffness range from 1 to 3.5 N/mm [6]. Admittance devices on the other hand are capable of rendering high stiffness and high force. However, they are

© Springer International Publishing Switzerland 2016
F. Bello et al. (Eds.): EuroHaptics 2016, Part I, LNCS 9774, pp. 229–239, 2016.
DOI: 10.1007/978-3-319-42321-0_21

often not capable of rendering low inertia. Notable admittance device, Haptic Master, has a stable stiffness range from 10–50 N/mm and the nominal/max force are 100/250 N, while the minimal tip inertia is 2 kg [3]. In some applications, such as dental surgery simulation [7], both low inertia and high stiffness are required to render light dental tools and rigid tooth surfaces. Either conventional impedance display or admittance display are difficult to achieve the required performances.

Our goal is to develop a new haptic device that can render both low inertia and high stiffness for potential application in dental simulation. To achieve the goal, we need to overcome the limitations of impedance displays in rendering high stiffness and admittance displays in rendering low inertia. We adopt the principle of admittance display to achieve high stiffness. To overcome the limitation of high inertia and friction, we introduce a new concept of co-actuation. The basic idea of co-actuation is to disconnect the joints with their actuators in a haptic device. The actuators will follow the motion of the joints and apply required force when necessary. Because the actuators and the joints are separated, the inertia and friction in the actuators and its transmission will not be reflected to the device. Therefore, it is possible for the co-actuation approach to achieve high stiffness at the level of admittance displays while keep low inertia and friction at the level of impedance displays. In this paper, we describe the co-actuation approach by the design and construction of a single DOF haptic interface prototype. Our work is primarily inspired by the prior work on dynamic physical constraint (DPC) [8].

2 Related Works

The emulation of hard virtual surface has led to numerous research efforts. Different concepts have been tried in order to implement a truly "hard" constraint. Several researchers studied the maximum stiffness that an impedance display can stably render. Colgate and Schenkel developed a relationship between damping, stiffness, and update rate from which the maximum stiffness of a virtual wall can be estimated [9]. More recently, the relationship was generalized by considering more factors including sensor quantization and coulomb friction [10–12].

To render stiff environments over a large workspace, Zinn et al. [13] addressed the limitation of traditional impedance devices by introducing a new actuation approach based on parallel actuation concept. They divided the torque generation into separate low and high-frequency actuators whose torque sum in parallel. A high-power, high-torque actuator was used to provide the low frequency torques while a small, fast actuator was used to provide the high frequency torques. They also distributed the low and high-frequency actuators to locations on the device so that their effect on device transparency was minimized while their contribution to force dynamic range was maximized. Experimental data showed that the approach was able to achieve a high stiffness of 57 N/mm for a three DOF prototype and reduce the output friction to less than 1.5 N within a large workspace of 0.6 m^3.

Since brakes are dissipative by nature, they are ideally suited to provide physical damping for a haptic device. Several researchers have investigated the use of brakes to achieve high impedance and thus improve stability. Different types of brakes were used

[14–18]. It was found that some characteristics of the brakes, such as slow to actuate and nonlinear relationship between velocity and torque, limit the fidelity of the rendering. To improve the performance, Gosline and Hayward proposed to use eddy current brakes (ECBs) as linear, fast actuating, programmable viscous dampers for haptic rendering. They found that virtual walls rendered using the physical dampers do not have the characteristic "sticky" feel that is typical of walls rendered using conventional programmable brakes. However, the use of dampers in brakes leads to increase in the inertia and power consumption of the device [19]. In an alternative approach, the dissipative properties of a DC motor were taken as an advantage to realize programmable electrical damping [20].

Another concept to provide a convincingly hard surface is to use mechanical constraints. A typical example was Cobot, which used parallel linkage to build a 6 DOF device [4]. Although controlled as an admittance device, the Cobot does not suffer from the high inertia, friction and backlash that normally exist in a highly geared admittance device. By using a rotational-to-linear continuously variable transmission (CVT), the Cobot enhanced dynamic range that extends continuously from a completely clutched state to a highly back drivable state. With the novel mechanical design, the Cobot achieved a force transmission capabilities exceeding 50 N, structural stiffness ranging from 20–400 N/mm, a motion control bandwidth of 40 Hz, and near zero power requirements for sustaining high output loads.

A further variation on mechanical constraints is dynamic physical constraints (DPC) introduced recently by [8]. The DPC is adjusted depending on the user's current position in space. When not in contact with the virtual surface, the user can move the device with complete freedom as all joints are unimpeded. Once the virtual surface is reached, the DPC creates a unidirectional physical barrier to limit the movement of partial joints. The DPC concept can produce a realistic sensation of hard surface contact because of the real physical contact between the user and the DPC. However, the DPC concept was proposed to emulate a virtual surface that is approximately concentric with the central pivot point. The extension of this idea to arbitrary virtual surfaces needs further investigation.

3   Principle of Co-actuation

To render realistic virtual environments, the difference between desired and rendered dynamics must be small. We focus on a virtual environment in surgical simulation in which a light surgical tool is required to interact with a stiff object. To simulate the light tool and stiff object contact, a haptic device should be able to display low inertia and high stiffness. Impedance displays are good at simulating low inertia, but suffer from instability and surface penetration problems commonly experienced with high stiffness values. In contrast, admittance displays can provide high stiffness, but are difficult to simulate low inertia. In the following, we present a new concept of co-actuation for achieving high stiffness and low inertia of a haptic device.

The key point of the co-actuation concept is to disconnect the actuators with the joints of linkage in order to reduce the inertia of the device. Figure 1 shows the concept using a one DOF co-actuation module which works in two modes: free motion and

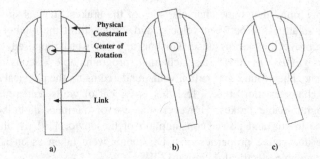

Fig. 1. One DOF co-actuation module: (a) home position; (b) free motion; (c) constrained motion.

constrained motion. In free motion mode, the rotation of link is free but tracked by the physical constraint. The motion of link is unimpeded because the physical constraint is not in contact with the link, but continually keeps a short distance with the link. In constrained motion mode, the motion of the link is impeded by the physical constraint through the physical contact between them. Because of mechanical decoupling between the joint and the motor, high stiffness can be achieved by adopting large gear reductions without affecting users' feeling in free space.

4   Mechanical Structure of a One DOF Co-actuation Module

To illustrate how the co-actuation concept can be implemented, we designed a mechanical structure for the co-actuation module of Fig. 1. As shown in Fig. 2a, two optical encoders are placed on the joint axis and the motor axis respectively. A force sensor is mounted at the tip of the link to measure the force applied by the user. The physical constraint is actuated by a motor connected to a high-ratio gear reducer and controlled by a two-mode controller described in the next section. During free motion, the joint angle of the link is measured to command the tracking motion of the physical

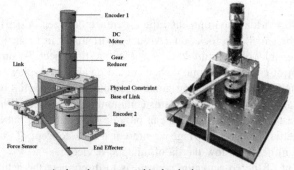

a) virtual prototype b) physical prototype

Fig. 2. Structure of a one DOF co-actuation module

constraint. During constraint motion, the user's force is measured to command the reactive force of the physical constraint.

A clearance between the link and the physical constraint is designed to obtain decouple between the link and the actuator, and also to allow the encoder of the joint to detect the link motion. The amount of the clearance depends on the speed of the link and the frequency response of the motor. In general, the higher the speed and the lower the frequency response, the larger the clearance should be. However, if the clearance is bigger, the switch between free space and constrained space requires a longer time, which may decrease the performance of stiff object simulation. For high stiffness performance, it is ideal that the clearance is zero so that the switch between free space and constrained space requires no time. Therefore, the critical problem in the design of the co-actuation module is to find a minimum clearance by making a tradeoff between the performances in free space and constraint space. This problem will be addressed in the next section on the control approach of co-actuation.

5   Control Approach of Co-actuation

5.1   Control Structure for Co-actuation

Figure 3 shows the control structure for the co-actuation module. By decomposing the actuator and joint, the co-actuation module can achieve a high transparency in free space and high stiffness in constraint space. Users can move the link freely when in free space as the joint is unimpeded by friction and inertia of the motor and reducer. In constraint space, users can feel a hard virtual surface due to the direct physical contact between the link and the physical constraint. The co-actuation module can apply bidirectional impedance to the joint, which is different from the DPC concept [8]. This characteristic

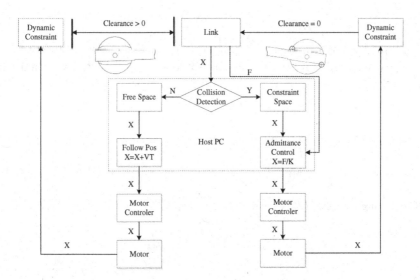

Fig. 3. Control architecture of co-actuation

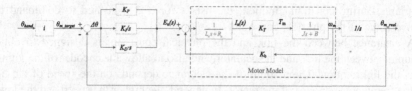

Fig. 4. Block diagram of the control loop

makes the co-actuation concept capable of emulating arbitrary hard surfaces and extended to broaden the range of applications. Force sensors are needed to predict the user's intent, which means that admittance control method is used in constraint space.

5.2 Clearance Model

The diagram shown in Fig. 4 illustrated the control law in the free space, which was used to derive the clearance model to maintain the movement of the actuator to follow the movement of the link. i refers to the gear ratio.

The transfer function of the control loop can be derived as

$$H(s) = [\theta_{m\_real}(s)]/[\theta_{hand}(s)] = \frac{PID(s)M(s)}{PID(s)M(s) + s} \cdot i \tag{1}$$

where $PID(s)$ and $M(s)$ refers to the transfer function of the PID controller and the motor model respectively.

Suppose the performance of the PID controller is perfect and $La \ll Ra$ for typical DC servo motors, the function becomes

$$H(s) = \frac{K_T \cdot i}{JR_a s^2 + (BR_a + K_T K_b)s + K_T} \tag{2}$$

Suppose the hand moves at the maximum velocity ω_{max}, and then we can derive

$$\theta_{hand} = \frac{\omega_{max}}{s^2} \tag{3}$$

The maximal steady-state following error $\Delta\theta_{max}$ should be

$$\Delta\theta_{max} = \lim_{s \to 0} s \cdot (\theta_{hand}(s) - \theta_{m\_real}(s)/i) \tag{4}$$

Combining with Eq. (2), we can derive

$$\Delta\theta_{max} = \frac{BR_a + K_T K_b}{K_T} \cdot \omega_{max} \tag{5}$$

In order to ensure no contact between the link and the physical constraint, the minimal clearance δ_{min} should follow

$$\delta_{min} > \Delta\theta_{max} \tag{6}$$

This model implicates that the minimal clearance is correlated with the maximal interaction velocity, the impedance of the structure, and the performance of the motor.

6 Performance Experiments

Table 1 shows the values of main parameters in the physical prototype (Fig. 2b).

Table 1. Values of main parameters in the one DOF prototype

Parameter	Value	Parameter	Value
Motor	MAXON RE30 268214	Gear reducer	Harmonic drive, Ratio 50
Res. of the motor's encoder	0.036°	Force sensor	ATI NANO17, Max F_z 70 N
Res. of the link's encoder	0.005°	Servo rate	1 kHz

6.1 Free Motion Performance

In the prototype, the clearance between the link and the physical constraint was set as 1.62°. To validate the performance of simulating free space, the user rotated the link back and forth for three times. The motor was driven to follow the motion of the link. From Fig. 5, the constraint angle followed the link angle in a responsive way, and the clearance was maintained above zero at all time. Correspondingly, the real-time back driving force measured by the force sensor was shown in Fig. 6. The average force is about 0.1 N, and the maximal force is less than 0.3 N. These results demonstrated that the prototype produced satisfied free space performance.

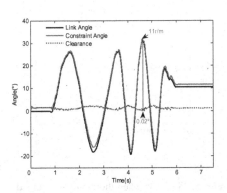

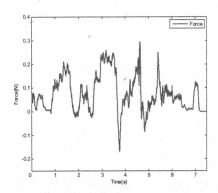

Fig. 5. High frequency accurate tracking (Color figure online)

Fig. 6. Back driving force (Color figure online)

As shown in Fig. 5, the clearance between the link and the physical constraint was about 0.02° when the moving velocity of the link approached 11 rpm. Considering the model in Eq. (5), the theoretical value of $\Delta\theta_{max}$ is 1.65° when the maximum moving velocity ω_{max} is 11 rpm. The small error between the theoretical and measured value of the clearance illustrated the accuracy of the theoretical model.

6.2   Constrained Motion Experiment

To validate the performance of simulating constraint space, the user rotated the link to collide with a pre-defined virtual wall. Figure 7 illustrated the measured contact force versus the penetration distance of the link into the virtual wall. The parameter r refers to the distance (i.e. the rotating radius) from the force exerting point to the rotating center of the link. The results showed that a higher stiffness of the virtual wall can be achieved with the cost of reducing workspace of the end-effector. For the shorter rotating radius ($r = 0.08$ m), the workspace is sufficient for some fine manipulations such as the movement of a dental tool in an oral cavity. The measured contact stiffness (40 N/mm) provides a promising solution for simulating stiff contacts.

Another interesting finding is there existed two slopes of the stiffness for a given rotating radius. To investigate the possible reasons leading to this two-phase stiffness, we performed another experiment in which the motor was turned off in the constraint space. Therefore, when the user rotated the link to collide the actuator, he/she felt the pure mechanical resistance produced by the mechanical damping and the gear reduction system, instead of the servo-controlled virtual wall. The shaft of the motor did not rotate until the active force from the user was big enough to back-drive the motor and the gear-box. As shown in Fig. 8, the stiffness of the pure mechanical contact was identical to the first phase stiffness in the Fig. 7. This coincidence implied that the stiffness of the first phase was produced by the mechanical contact and the second phase was produced by both the mechanical and electrical impedances.

Based on above analysis, we can infer the two phase stiffness was caused by the mechanical clearance. The servo-controlled algorithm did not work until the clearance was eliminated by the increasing contact force from the user.

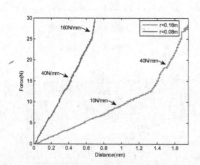

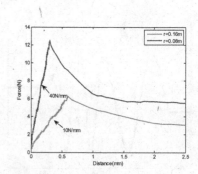

Fig. 7. Stiffness of simulating a virtual wall (Color figure online)

Fig. 8. Stiffness when the motor was turned off (Color figure online)

From the human perception side, Lawrence and Chapel [21] reported that stiffness greater than 10 N/mm would be difficult for humans to differentiate between, suggesting that the proposed method could be used for the realistic perception of hardness. Theoretically speaking, the first phase stiffness should be much larger as both the link and the physical constraint was made of Aluminum, which should produce large mechanical contact stiffness. However, there existed clearance in the bearing of the link's shaft, actual stiffness was greatly reduced. In the next step, a smaller tolerance in the mechanical design and assembly may help to reduce the influence of this issue.

7   Co-actuation in Multi-DOF Devices

The concept of co-actuation can be extended to multi-DOF devices. Figure 9 illustrates two examples of 3-DOF haptic devices in the cases of parallel and serial linkages. In each case, we can obtain a multi-DOF haptic device by simply use the co-actuation module described in Sect. 4 for each active joint of the linkage. A particular issue needs to be considered is the increase in inertia of a multi-DOF haptic device. In the case of parallel linkage, even though the effective inertia of the device does not include the inertia of actuation, the linkage itself might be too heavy due to a large number of links. The same problem is more sever in the case of serial linkage, because most co-actuation modules are located in the moving links and their inertia will affect the effective inertia of the haptic device. Although the problem of increased inertia may limit the application of the co-actuation method, it is possible to include gravity compensation in the co-actuation module to obtain good transparency in free space. When the gravity compensation is necessary, the co-actuation module works like an admittance-controlled device.

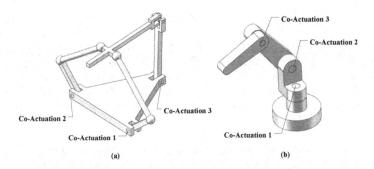

Fig. 9. Multi-DOF haptic devices with co-actuation: (a) parallel linkage; (b) serial linkage

8   Conclusion

We have presented a new concept of co-actuation for reducing inertia and friction in conventional admittance displays. The effectiveness of the approach was tested on a physical prototype of 1-DOF haptic device. The experimental data showed that the proposed approach can achieve high stiffness while effectively reduce inertia and friction, thus has potential advantage over conventional admittance display.

The clearance between the physical constraint and the link depends on the speed of device and parameters of motor, gear train and controller. A large speed of device requires a large clearance. On the other hand, a small clearance is required for small surface penetration. A key design issue in co-actuation approach is to balance the conflict between fast moving in free space and small penetration in constraint space. Optimal solution to the tradeoff between the two conflict requirements needs to be explored in future study. Concerning our target application of dental simulation, penetration of less than what we obtained in the test may be expected. Our future work will try to find out if the co-actuation approach can achieve the smallest penetration depth required and if haptic illusion can be used to obtain desired performance. In the future, it is also needed to measure the force generation error of the proposed approach. As we adopted the admittance control approach in the constrained space, the error might depend on the force sensing accuracy of the force sensor, the accuracy of the position control of the physical constraint during the constrained space, and the value of the stiffness of the simulated virtual wall.

In the co-actuation approach, because joints are separated from actuators, the compensation of link gravity and inertia is not as easy as in conventional admittance display. Therefore, the approach is suited to the application requiring small workspace, such as VR-based dental simulator. The approach is also applicable to the cases that are more sensitive to large stiffness or force, but less sensitive to device gravity and inertia. Such applications may include virtual fixture in orthopedic surgery, where preventing surface penetration is the most import performance, and rehabilitation, where large force may be required for arm or leg training.

References

1. Massie, T., Salisbury, J.: The PHANTOM haptic interface: a device for probing virtual objects. In: ASME Winter Annual Meeting, Symposium on Haptic Interfaces for Virtual Environment and Teleoperator Systems, vol. DSC 55, Chicago, IL, pp. 295–302 (1994)
2. Salisbury, K., Eberman, B., Levin, M., Townsend, W.: The design and control of an experimental whole-arm manipulator. In: The Fifth International Symposium on Robotics Research, pp. 233–241 (1990)
3. Van der Linde, R., Lammertse, P., Frederiksen, E., Ruiter, B.: The haptic master, a new high-performance haptic interface. In: Proceedings of Euro-Haptics, Edinburgh, U.K. (2002)
4. Faulring, E., Colgate, J., Peshkin, M.: The cobotic hand controller: design, control and performance of a novel haptic display. Int. J. Robot. Res. **25**(11), 1099–1119 (2005)
5. Arata, J., Kondo, H., Ikedo, N., Fujimoto, H.: Haptic device using a newly developed redundant parallel mechanism. IEEE Trans. Robot. **27**(2), 201–214 (2011)
6. http://www.geomagic.com/en/products-landing-pages/haptic
7. Wang, D., Zhang, Y., Hou, J., Wang, Y., Lv, P., Chen, Y., Zhao, H.: iDental: a haptic-based dental simulator and its preliminary evaluation. IEEE Trans. Haptics **5**(4), 332–343 (2012)
8. Hungr, N., Roger, B., Hodgson, A.J., Plaskos, C.: Dynamic physical constraints: emulating hard surfaces with high realism. IEEE Trans. Haptics **5**(1), 48–57 (2012)

9. Colgate, J.E., Schenkel, G.: Passivity of a class of sampled data systems: application to haptic interfaces. In: Proceedings of the American Control Conference, pp. 3236–3240 (1994)
10. Abbott, J.J., Okamura, A.M.: Effects of position quantization and sampling rate on virtual wall passivity. IEEE Trans. Robot. **21**(5), 952–964 (2005)
11. Diolaiti, N., Niemeyer, G., Barbagli, F., Salisbury, J.K.: Stability of haptic rendering: discretization, quantization, time delay, and coulomb effects. IEEE Trans. Robot. **22**(2), 256–268 (2006)
12. Mahvash, M., Hayward, V.: High fidelity passive force reflecting virtual environments. IEEE Trans. Robot. **21**(1), 38–46 (2005)
13. Zinn, M., Khatib, O., Roth, B., Salisbury, J.K.: Large workspace haptic devices: a new actuation approach. In: Symposium on Haptic Interfaces for Virtual Environment and Teleoperator Systems, pp. 185–192 (2008)
14. Cho, C., Song, J.-B., Kim, M.: Energy-based control of a haptic device using brakes. IEEE Trans. Syst. Man Cybern. Part B Cybern. **37**(2), 341–349 (2007)
15. Conti, F., Khatib, O., Baur, C.: A hybrid actuation approach for haptic devices. In: World Haptics 2007, pp. 367–372 (2007)
16. An, J., Kwon, D.S.: Stability and performance of haptic interfaces with active/passive actuators theory and experiments. Int. J. Robot. Res. **25**(11), 1121–1136 (2006)
17. Kwon, T.B., Song, J.B.: Force display using a hybrid haptic device composed of motors and brakes. Mechatronics **16**, 249–257 (2006)
18. Swanson, D.K., Book, W.J.: Path-following control for dissipative passive haptic displays. In: Proceedings of the 11th Symposium on Haptic Interfaces for Virtual Environment and Teleoperator Systems, pp. 101–108, March 2003
19. Gosline, A.H.C., Hayward, V.: Eddy current brakes for haptic interfaces: design, identification, and control. IEEE/ASME Trans. Mechatron. **13**(6), 669–677 (2008)
20. Weir, D.W., Colgate, J.E., Peshkin, M.A.: Measuring and increasing Z-width with active electrical damping. In: Proceedings of the Symposium on Haptic Interfaces for Virtual Environment and Teleoperator Systems, pp. 169–175 (2008)
21. Lawrence, D.A., Chapel, J.D.: Performance trade-offs for hand controller design. In: Proceedings of the IEEE International Conference on Robotics and Automation, vol. 4, pp. 3211–3216, May 1994

Comparing Series Elasticity and Admittance Control for Haptic Rendering

Takamasa Horibe[1,2], Emma Treadway[2(✉)], and R. Brent Gillespie[2]

[1] Aerospace Engineering, Nagoya University, Furo-cho, Chikusa-ku, Nagoya, Japan
horibe.takamasa@j.mbox.nagoya-u.ac.jp
[2] Mechanical Engineering, University of Michigan, Ann Arbor, MI, USA
{etreadwa,brentg}@umich.edu

Abstract. While feedback control can be used to cause a motorized device to render the dynamic behavior of a virtual environment, this capacity inevitably breaks down at high frequencies where the rendered impedance reverts to the impedance of the device hardware. This situation amounts to a disadvantage for admittance display, for which hardware impedance is high. Series elastic actuators offer an attractive alternative with lower impedance at high frequencies, though stability considerations impose limits on the stiffest virtual environment that may be rendered. In this paper we explore the tradeoffs between admittance control and series elastic actuation with the use of analytical comparisons in the frequency domain backed up by experiments and complemented with a passivity analysis that accounts for an excess of passivity contributed by human biomechanics.

Keywords: Series elastic actuator · Admittance display · Passivity

1 Introduction

The design of a haptic device and its controllers is invariably a study in tradeoffs. In theory, rendering a programmable immitance[1] simply requires sourcing force in a certain relationship to sensed motion or sourcing motion in the inverse of that same relationship to sensed force. But pure force and motion sources cannot be found on the shelf and cannot even be built in a lab. Above a certain frequency, the mass used to build the device will necessarily foil any efforts to source force or motion, and the inherent dynamics of the device will dominate the immitance rendered at high frequencies.

Haptic display devices fall into two basic families: impedance display devices that function as force sources (sensing motion) and admittance display devices that function as motion sources (sensing force). An impedance display device usually employs motors with low rotor inertia in direct drive so that free space

---

[1] *Immitance* is a term that can be used to refer to the relationship between force and motion without specifying input and output, whereas admittance implies motion response to force and impedance implies force response to motion.

© Springer International Publishing Switzerland 2016
F. Bello et al. (Eds.): EuroHaptics 2016, Part I, LNCS 9774, pp. 240–250, 2016.
DOI: 10.1007/978-3-319-42321-0_22

may be rendered without feedback compensation—freespace impedance generally defaults to the inherent device impedance. As a consequence of using lower inertia motors in direct drive, however, force capacity is limited, and rendering a virtual wall is often hampered by force saturation. An admittance display device, on the other hand, uses powerful motors often outfitted with transmissions to render crisp and stiff virtual walls, but as a result, free space motion is in fact not very free. At high frequencies the rendered impedance reverts to the inherent device impedance, which is relatively high.

In this paper we explore the promise of series elasticity as an intermediate option between an impedance and an admittance device. We aim for a device design capable of rendering much free-er free space than a typical admittance device yet capable of sourcing higher forces than a typical impedance device.

A series elastic actuator (SEA) features a physical spring introduced between a geared motor and the load [8]. A SEA can be considered a special class of variable impedance actuator (VIA), but with a fixed compliance. VIAs use software control and hardware to render varying impedances [14]. SEAs have found wide acceptance in applications such as legged robotics, where tolerance to shock loading is of paramount concern. Other significant advantages to SEA have been pointed out in the literature, including filtering and masking of motor- and gear-induced nonlinearities to produce a clean force output, masking of high inertia, low inherent impedance, and conversion of a force-control problem into a position-control one [9,10,13]. Series elastic actuators inherently feature energy-storage as well [8].

A number of papers treating series elasticity have suggested its application to haptic interfaces because of the clean force output [9,10]. Our group explored free-space rendering using a series elastic interface with possible fluid power applications [5]. But SEA has not been widely adopted within the haptics community to date. SEA does involve compromises introduced by the elastic element. Perhaps most significantly, SEA devices are unable to passively render virtual environments stiffer than the series elastic element [11,13].

In this paper we undertake a side by side comparison of admittance display and what we shall call SEA display, with a focus on the range of impedances that may be displayed by either device across the frequency range. The advantage at high frequencies afforded by SEA display, where rendered impedance defaults to a lower inherent impedance, must be evaluated in parallel with the range of impedances that can be rendered at low frequencies. We first evaluate the fidelity with which either display can render freespace or a stiff virtual object. Our evaluation is presented in the frequency domain. We compare analytical results to experimental results produced with a platform that can be configured either for admittance display or SEA display. In the second part of the paper, we consider the upper limits on stiffness rendering imposed by an analysis of passivity. In our analysis of passivity we adopt an approach that accounts for an excess of passivity contributed by the biomechanics of the human user [2].

2 Model Description

2.1 Admittance Control Devices

Let us begin by describing admittance control in detail. A schematic model and block diagram model of an admittance-controlled device are shown in Fig. 1. Let M designate the effective mass of the rotor inertia reflected through the transmission to the stage which is grasped by the human user, and let B describe damping to ground. The user applies force F_u and a motor applies force F_m through a transmission with gear ratio n. A feedback controller $C(s)$ is used to close a loop so as to cause sensed force F_u to track the desired force F_{des}, which is specified as a response of the virtual environment Z_{VE} to $\dot{x}$. The inherent impedance of the haptic device is abbreviated as $Z_h = Ms + B$.

Since we care about what the user *feels*, it is appropriate to analyze the device in terms of driving point impedance $\mathcal{Z}$, the force-velocity relationship at the interface between the human and the haptic device. In terms of the variables used here, we therefore have $\mathcal{Z} \equiv F_u/\dot{X}$. Hence the closed-loop (powered - "P") driving point impedance in this architecture may be expressed as:

$$\mathcal{Z}^P_{ADM} = \frac{nC(s)Z_{VE} + Z_h}{nC(s) + 1}. \tag{1}$$

In this expression, we can see that the driving point impedance is shaped by tuning the feedback gain $C(s)$. As $C(s) \to \infty$, the driving point impedance converges to the virtual environment impedance: $\mathcal{Z}^P_{ADM} \to Z_{VE}$.

We also define the open loop driving point impedance (unpowered - "U"). This is found by substituting $C(s) = 0$ into Eq. (1), and is expressed as

$$\mathcal{Z}^U_{ADM} = Z_h. \tag{2}$$

As previously mentioned, the inherent open loop impedance Z_h is usually large (non-backdrivable) when admittance control is used. Inevitably, the rendered impedance will approach this mechanical impedance at high frequencies.

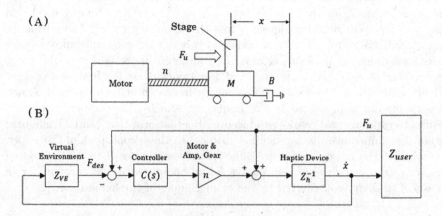

Fig. 1. Schematic model (A) and block diagram (B) of admittance control device

2.2 Series Elastic Actuator Device

We now introduce the control architecture of a haptic device that features a series elastic element. A schematic model and block diagram are presented in Fig. 2. As depicted in the diagram in part A, an elastic element (physical spring) is placed between the stage and end-effector. The force F_u applied by the user can be approximated if the relative displacement of the spring is measured and the spring constant is known: $F_u \simeq k(y - x)$. Thus a force sensor is not required.

The impedance of the end effector is $Z_e = ms$, and k and b are the stiffness and damping of the physical spring placed between stage and end-effector. The driving point impedance (powered - "P"), $\mathcal{Z} \equiv F_u/\dot{Y}$, can be found from this diagram to be:

$$\mathcal{Z}_{SEA}^P(s) = \frac{Z_e(Z_h + knC(s)/s + k') + k'(Z_h + nC(s)Z_{VE})}{Z_h + knC(s)/s + k'} \tag{3}$$

where $k' = k/s + b$. It should be noted that the rendered impedance does not converge to the virtual environment as feedback gain increases to infinity.

$$\mathcal{Z}_{SEA}^P \rightarrow Z_e + Z_{VE}\left(1 + \frac{b}{k}s\right), \quad (C(s) \rightarrow \infty). \tag{4}$$

This is because F_u has been approximated by neglecting the end-effector mass and damping. Since the end-effector is usually designed with a small mass compared to that of the stage ($m \ll M$) and the force is dominated by the spring k rather than damping b, this error between desired and rendered impedance is negligible.

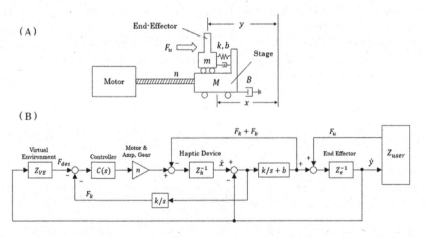

Fig. 2. Schematic model (A) and block diagram (B) of SEA haptic device.

By virtue of the physical spring, the SEA device has a low inherent (unpowered - "U") impedance:

$$Z_{SEA}^U = Z_e + \frac{Z_h k'}{Z_h + k'}. \tag{5}$$

Visible here is the series coupling of two impedances, Z_e and $Z_h k'/(Z_h+k')$. The second impedance is essentially the parallel coupling of Z_h and k'. The elastic element masks Z_h, resulting in a smaller unpowered impedance than Z_{ADM}^U.

2.3 Comparative Analysis

In the following, the virtual environment Z_{VE} is set to a constant stiffness, $Z_{VE}(s) = K_{VE}/s$, and the controller is set as a proportional gain, $C(s) = C_p$ for the sake of simplicity. One can examine the behaviors by analyzing Z in different extreme cases, as shown in Table 1.

Table 1. Comparative values of driving point impedance.

	$\omega \ll 1, K_{VE} \neq 0$	$\omega \ll 1, K_{VE} = 0$	$\omega \gg 1$
Z_{ADM}^P	$\dfrac{nC_p}{nC_p+1}\dfrac{K_{VE}}{\omega}$	$\dfrac{B}{nC_p+1}$	$\dfrac{M}{1+nC_p}\omega$
Z_{SEA}^P	$\dfrac{nC_p}{nC_p+1}\dfrac{K_{VE}}{\omega}$	$\dfrac{B}{nC_p+1}$	$m\omega$

At low frequencies, the apparent impedances for the admittance and SEA devices converge to the same values, while the impedances at high frequency diverge. The mass of the end-effector is very small compared to the stage ($m \ll M$), so generally the impedance in the SEA architecture is smaller than in the admittance architecture at high frequencies ($\omega \gg 1$).

These differences can also be viewed graphically. Figure 3 shows frequency plots of the driving point impedance magnitude for both the admittance display and SEA devices in both unpowered ($C(s) = 0$) and powered ($C(s) = C_p$)

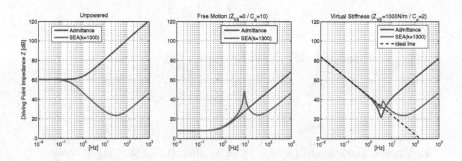

Fig. 3. Driving point impedance theoretical results. (Color figure online)

conditions. At low frequency both devices behave similarly for all three cases, but there is a large difference at high frequencies. Clearly for free motion (center figure), the lines should be as low as possible at all frequencies; except for a resonant spike, the SEA device achieves lower impedances as frequency increases. For rendering a virtual stiffness (right figure), both devices fail to achieve the desired stiffness as frequency increases, but the SEA device is able to render "spring-like" behavior up to a higher frequency.

3   Apparatus Description

We devised a single-axis system that could be configured either as an admittance display device or a Series Elastic Actuator. Figure 4 shows a CAD rendering of the apparatus and Fig. 5 shows a photograph of the device. As is typical in admittance- and SEA-display devices, a high gear ratio ball screw (5 mm pitch, SFU series 1605) is attached to the motor (Maxon RE65 #353295). While this allows large forces to be sourced, it makes the apparent mass of the motor and ballscrew shaft n^2 times higher and friction on the screw n times higher. These values reflected through the gear ratio, along with other relevant parameters estimated through system identification, are provided in Table 2. These large friction and inertia values render the carriage totally non-backdrivable — when the motor is unpowered, a human pushing on the stage cannot move the motor at all. An encoder (US Digital E2-1024) attached to the back shaft of the motor measures the shaft angle. A linear encoder (US Digital EM1-0-500-N) measures the relative displacement (x y) between the stage and end effector, which yields the compression of the physical spring. For the admittance display setup, the proximal side of a beam load cell (Transducer Techniques LSP-10) is attached to the stage. The distal side of this load cell is grasped by the user. Control and data acquisition are performed with Visual Studio/C++, using a Sensoray Model 626 card.

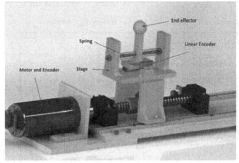

Fig. 4. SolidWorks design rendering

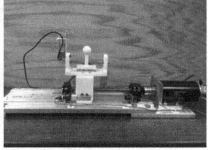

Fig. 5. Apparatus for haptic rendering

Table 2. Physical device parameter values from system ID.

	Symbol	Value	Units
Stage and motor inertia	M	176	[kg]
Stage damping	B	1051	[kg/s]
End-effector mass	m	0.035	[kg]
End-effector damping	b	15.05	[kg/s]
Physical spring stiffness	k	1300	[N/m]
Gear ratio	n	41.8	[-]

4   Experimental Results

Using the two configurations of the apparatus described in the previous section (SEA and admittance), we ran a number of experimental tests to validate the analytical findings. For each configuration, data was collected in three conditions, matching those simulated in the analytical work: unpowered, powered rendering free space, and powered rendering a stiffness. In each case, manual excitation of the device was performed. The results of these tests are shown in Fig. 6 in the frequency domain, along with the analytical curves previously shown in Fig. 3.

The left pane of Fig. 6 shows the open-loop impedance $\mathcal{Z}^U$ ($C_p = 0$). The SEA device response matched the model fairly well, but the admittance device had a significant offset from the modeled impedance. In reality, the stage is not backdrivable at all, largely due to unmodeled stiction.

The middle pane of Fig. 6 shows the driving point impedance for both devices rendering free motion. At low frequencies, both devices performed similarly, comparable with the analytical prediction. As the frequency increased, the two device configurations' responses diverged. At high frequencies, the SEA device rendered lower admittances when trying to achieve free space; this effect is visible at the high end of human motion generation, up to about 20 Hz [12].

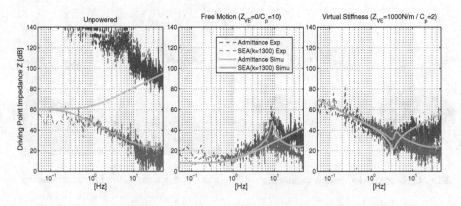

Fig. 6. Driving point impedance experimental results. (Color figure online)

The same situation is visible in the right pane of Fig. 6 which shows the two devices rendering a virtual spring ($K_{VE} = 1000N/m$). Again, the devices are comparable at low frequencies. As frequency increases, both devices diverge from the ideal stiffness, but the SEA device exhibits higher fidelity (the desired and achieved responses are more similar).

As is evident from both analytical and experimental results, SEA holds an advantage over the admittance display device in terms of backdrivability and high frequency performance. While this analysis has allowed us to compare free space rendering and fidelity, we have not yet examined the upper limits of stiffness rendering for each device. These limits follow from a loss of stability of the coupled human-device system; thus, we take up the topic of stability.

5   Passivity Limits on Rendered Springs

One method for guaranteeing the coupled stability of the system comprising human user and haptic interface is to assume the human user is passive and require the haptic device to adhere to strict passivity [4]. Justification for the assumption of human passivity is made with reference to the literature [6]. Necessary and sufficient conditions for passivity of a 1-port system are

1. $\mathcal{Z}(s)$ has no poles in the right half plane, and   (6)
2. $Re(\mathcal{Z}(j\omega)) > 0$,   (7)

where $\mathcal{Z}(s)$ is the driving point impedance [3].

Under ideal conditions (linearity holds, without sampling or saturation effects), the admittance control device is passive. SEA on the other hand is not passive, even under ideal conditions. Consider first the passivity of the transfer function $\dot{Y}/F_u$ for SEA Display. If $b = 0$ is assumed for simplicity, the condition that places the poles of this transfer function in the left-half plane is found by application of the Routh-Hurwitz criterion:

$$K_{VE} < \frac{1 + nC_p}{nC_p}k.$$ (8)

In general, nC_p has a large value by hardware and control design. Therefore, the virtual stiffness must be smaller than the physical spring stiffness to achieve passivity. This was observed by Vallery et. al. [13], who also applied passivity analysis to series elastic actuators. This challenge was recently discussed in [11], where coupled stability analysis was undertaken for sampled-data SEA devices, resulting in a calculation of the minimum necessary coupled mass to achieve stability above the physical spring stiffness.

The sampling and zero order hold (ZOH) processes, inherent in any sampled-data controller, may have an effect on stability, so we take them into account for our passivity analysis. We rewrite the motor command as a sampled and held signal and approximate the Laplace representation of a ZOH, $(1 - e^{-sT})/(sT)$ (where T is the sampling time step), with a first order Padé approximation as

$1/(\tau s + 1)$ where $\tau = 1/2T$. From this form it is clear that sampling introduces a time delay of τ. Thus, the maximum stiffness K_{VE} that can be rendered by an admittance device at any given frequency is a function of the sampling rate T and the feedback gain C_p. For an SEA device, the upper stability limit on K_{VE} depends on C_p and T, as well as the physical spring stiffness k.

It has been shown that in the presence of any delay/sampling, an admittance display device without a virtual coupling to limit the virtual environment is no longer unconditionally passive [1]. One way to address this challenge is to introduce a model of the human that includes a minimum and maximum impedance, reducing the conservativeness of the analysis. Limits on the maximum impedance Z_{max} and minimum impedance Z_{min} of the human were handled in [2] by placing two constant impedances $Z_1 = Z_{min}$ and $Z_2 = Z_{max} - Z_{min}$ respectively in series and in parallel with a variable human impedance Z_p. If Z_p is zero, the presented impedance is $Z_1 = Z_{min}$ and if Z_p is infinity, the impedance becomes $Z_2 - Z_1 = Z_{max}$. To reduce the conservativeness of the passivity analysis, the driving point impedance can be re-written to absorb these constant limiting portions of this human arm model, yielding:

$$\mathcal{Z}' = \left(\frac{1}{Z_2} + \frac{1}{Z_1 + \mathcal{Z}} \right)^{-1} = \frac{Z_2(Z_1 + \mathcal{Z})}{Z_1 + Z_2 + \mathcal{Z}}. \tag{9}$$

In this paper we adopt the approach introduced in [1] and apply it to both Admittance Display using Eq. 1 for $\mathcal{Z}$, and to SEA Display using Eq. 3 for $\mathcal{Z}$.

We do not limit the minimum impedance — we use $Z_{min} = 0$ so as to cover cases with no contact. For maximum impedance, we borrow from [2] again and set $Z_{max}(s) = 300 + 1000/s$. This was in turn based on previous research [7], which shows that human arm impedance can be approximated as a damper and spring. These values pertained to the whole arm, whereas our device is only grasped with the fingers, so we acknowledge that our results may not be sufficiently conservative.

Our objective is to render an arbitrary virtual environment to the user, but here we only assess the range of virtual stiffnesses that can be rendered passively by the Admittance and SEA Display devices. We assess passivity by checking the expression for $\mathcal{Z}'$ against the conditions in Eqs. 6 and 7 for a range of values for the following parameters: control gain C_p, sampling time T, stiffness k of the series elastic element for SEA Display, and virtual environment stiffness K_{VE}.

The sampling rate imposes an upper limit on what virtual environment stiffness K_{VE} may be rendered passively for both the SEA and admittance devices, as shown in Fig. 7A. Values for the control gain $C_p = 2$ and compliant element stiffness $k = 1300$ N/m were chosen to match the values used in the experiments described above. The limiting effects of stiffness k on virtual stiffness rendering for SEA can be seen in Fig. 7B. When a systematic search of T and C_p (and k for SEA) is performed, an upper limit on the virtual stiffness that can be passively rendered may be found. For our device, the sampling time was variable, but averaged about 1 ms, as indicated.

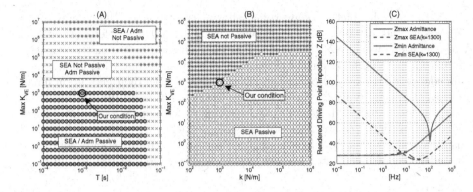

Fig. 7. (A) Effect of sampling rate on passivity for SEA ($k = 1300$) and admittance devices, both at $C_p = 2$. Approximate experimental condition indicated. Blue circles indicate passivity-satisfying conditions for SEA, green x's indicate passivity for admittance, and red stars indicate non-passive conditions. (B) Effect of SEA physical stiffness k on passivity. Approximate experimental condition indicated. (C) Limits of passively renderable K_{VE}/s for SEA and admittance devices. (Color figure online)

On the other hand, the minimum virtual stiffness does not come from the stability analysis, but is achieved when $Z_{VE} = 0$. To realize an accurate virtual environment, high feedback gain is needed. Thus in our allowed feedback gain range, the minimum impedance is rendered by setting $Z_{VE} = 0$ and $C_p = 10$.

Figure 7C shows the limits on the range of virtual stiffnesses which can be rendered by our device while maintaining passivity. At low frequencies, the advantage of the admittance device is clear: it can render higher stiffness passively. However, as frequency increases, the rendering of pure stiffness breaks down, and both devices revert to an impedance that feels like a mass — a small mass with the SEA device, and a large mass with the admittance device.

6   Conclusion

In this work, we made a direct comparison between the limitations, performance, and stability of admittance and series elastic haptic devices. By employing a reconfigurable experimental platform, we were able to make this comparison not only analytically, but also experimentally. For free-space rendering, SEA and admittance devices perform comparably at low frequencies, but at the high end of the human motor generation frequency range the user feels only the mass of the end effector with SEA, while the admittance device reflects the rotor inertia through the gear ratio and results in higher impedances. The "free-er" free space of the SEA device, however, comes at the expense of stiff virtual walls, since passivity analysis shows that SEA cannot render walls as stiff as admittance can. However, since applications exist for which impedance-controlled devices are currently considered stiff enough, this trade-off may be desirable in some applications.

Naturally, the picture concerning all the trade-offs in the design of an impedance, admittance, or SEA display device is still incomplete. Additional considerations would include force and speed saturation by the electromagnetic actuators, and perhaps effects of stiction. Admittance-controlled devices and impedance-controlled devices are generally designed with their end-use in mind, and as such they typically use drastically different hardware designs. However, valuable insight might be gained from experiments with an "intermediate" hardware design (lightly geared, but still possible to backdrive, trading off force and backdrivability) that could be configured for use with admittance control or impedance control, or fitted with springs to realize a series elastic actuator.

Acknowledgments. This research was supported by NIH grant R01-EB019834 and NSF grant DGE 1256260.

References

1. Adams, R.J., Hannaford, B.: Stable haptic interaction with virtual environments. IEEE Trans. Robot. Autom. **15**(3), 465–474 (1999)
2. Adams, R.J., Hannaford, B.: Control law design for haptic interfaces to virtual reality. IEEE Trans. Control Syst. Technol. **10**, 3–13 (2002)
3. Colgate, E., Hogan, N.: An analysis of contact instability in terms of passive physical equivalents. In: Proceedings of IEEE International Conference on Robotics and Automation, pp. 404–409 vol.1, May 1989
4. Colgate, J.E., Hogan, N.: Robust control of dynamically interacting systems. Int. J. Control **48**(1), 65–88 (1988)
5. Gillespie, R.B., Kim, D., Suchosk, J.M., Bo, Y., Brown, J.D.: Series elastic for free free-space motion for free. In: IEEE Haptic Symposium, pp. 609–615 (2014)
6. Hogan, N.: Controlling impedance at the man/machine interface. In: International Conference on Robotics and Automation (ICRA), pp. 1626–1631 (1989)
7. Mussa-Ivaldi, F.A., Hogan, N., Bizzi, E.: Neural, mechanical, and geometric factors subserving arm posture in humans. Neuroscience **5**, 2732–2743 (1985)
8. Pratt, G.A., Williamson, M.M.: Series elastic actuators. In: IEEE/RSJ International Conference on Intelligent Robots and Systems. Human Robot Interaction and Cooperative Robots, vol. 1, pp. 399–406 (1995)
9. Pratt, J., Krupp, B., Morse, C.: Series elastic actuators for high fidelity force control. Ind. Robot Int. J. **29**(3), 234–241 (2002)
10. Robinson, D.W.: Design and analysis of series elasticity in closed-loop actuator force control. Ph.D. thesis (2000)
11. Sergi, F., O'Malley, M.K.: On the stability and accuracy of high stiffness rendering in non-backdrivable actuators through series elasticity. Mechtronics **26**, 54–75 (2015)
12. Tan, H.Z., et al.: Human factors for the design of force-reflecting haptic interfaces. Dyn. Syst. Control **55**(1), 353–359 (1994)
13. Vallery, H., Veneman, J., van Asseldonk, E., Ekkelenkamp, R., Buss, M., van Der Kooij, H.: Compliant actuation of rehabilitation robots. IEEE Robot. Autom. Mag. **15**(3), 60–69 (2008)
14. Vanderborght, B., Albu-Schaeffer, A., et al.: Variable impedance actuators: a review. Robot. Auton. Syst. **61**(12), 1601–1614 (2013)

Texture Rendering Strategies with a High Fidelity - Capacitive Visual-Haptic Friction Control Device

Eric Vezzoli[1(✉)], Thomas Sednaoui[1,2], Michel Amberg[1],
Frédéric Giraud[1], and Betty Lemaire-Semail[1]

[1] Univ. Lille, Centrale Lille, Arts et Metiers ParisTech, HEI,
EA 2697 - L2EP – Laboratoire d'Electrotechnique et d'Electronique de
Puissance, 59000 Lille, France
eric.vezzoli@ed.univ-lille1.fr, thomas.
sednaoui@st.com, Michel.Amberg@univ-lille1.fr,
{frederic.giraud,betty.semail}@polytech-lille.fr
[2] STMicroelectronics, 38920 Crolles, France

Abstract. Ultrasonic vibrations of a plate can modify the perception of the friction between a surface and a sliding finger. This principle, coupled with modern position sensing techniques, is able to reproduce textured materials. In this paper, an open loop control through model inversion of the friction force between the finger and the plate is presented. The device incorporating the control system is described, and two different reproduction strategies are formalized to address the reproduction of objects and textures. In the end, a psychophysical experiment evaluating the two control strategies is described.

Keywords: Ultrasonic · Tactile device · Ultrasonic vibrations · Friction control

1 Introduction

In recent years, a lot of interest raised around the implementation of haptic stimulation and simulation. Many technologies are available to provide stimulation on a finger touching or sliding on a surface. However, few of those shown a promising opportunity for a coupling with touchscreen and the consequent aim for integration in the mobile world. Friction modulation techniques, namely electrovibration [1, 2], electroadhesion [3] and ultrasonic vibrations [4] are among this group. Their principle relies on the modulation of the friction between a finger sliding on an active surface. Electrovibration and electroadhesion exploit the electrostatic attraction generated between the finger and the plate, the first through the application of a voltage and the second through the application of a current. Both of them enhance the friction between the finger and the plate. On the other hand, ultrasonic vibrations of a plate reduce the friction between the finger and the surface. The reduction of friction was firstly explained through the squeeze film effect [4], later, a more mechanical explanation of the phenomenon was introduced [5], but a reliable modelling is yet to be developed. With the availability of finger detection techniques, the possibility to actively change the friction as a function of the finger position led to the ability to simulate textures [6]. This study focused on the

© Springer International Publishing Switzerland 2016
F. Bello et al. (Eds.): EuroHaptics 2016, Part I, LNCS 9774, pp. 251–260, 2016.
DOI: 10.1007/978-3-319-42321-0_23

reproduction of a squared grating, but it is lacking a broader approach on object reproduction. As introduced in [7], force plays a fundamental role on the reproduction of shapes, and a similar approach on texture reproduction has not been introduced yet.

In this paper, the development and the control of a device able to simulate textures thanks to the friction coefficient modulation between the finger and the vibrating plate is described.

The paper is organized as follows: initially the characteristics of the friction reduction provided by ultrasonic devices are recalled, following, an analysis of previously developed strategies for friction coefficient control is performed. The structure and the open loop control scheme of the device are then described followed by the formalization of the two haptic signal rendering schemes. In the end, a psychophysical experiment exploring the advantages of the two rendering techniques is proposed and the results discussed.

2 Ultrasonic Lubrication

The first explanation for the friction reduction in ultrasonic devices was found in the squeeze film effect [8]. The effect relied on the generation of an overpressured film of gas between the ultrasonic vibrating plate in the range of micrometres and the interface of the finger. The underlying physical phenomenon was firstly modelled by Biet et al. [4]. The presence of the squeeze film effect in these devices was lately questioned by Sednaoui et al. [9]. The extended study on the characteristics of the friction reduction, reported in [9], identified an empirical model to describe the evolution of the friction modulation. The friction coefficient reduced by the ultrasonic vibration is unable to reach the zero value, and it is reduced with an exponential decay in function of the vibration amplitude. The friction coefficient reaches an asymptotic value for high vibration amplitude where 90 % of the maximum reduction is reached for an amplitude around 2 µm, Fig. 1. It is possible to define the relative friction coefficient μ' as:

$$\mu'(w) = \frac{\mu(w)}{\mu(0)} \tag{1}$$

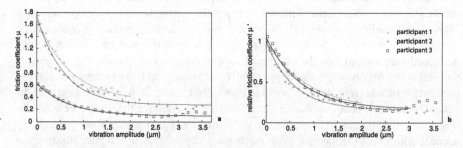

Fig. 1. Experimental results measured for the friction reduction in ultrasonic device. On the left, the friction coefficient measured through the tribological assessment. On the right, the relative friction coefficient of the same measures.

Where $\mu(w)$ is the friction coefficient for a given vibration amplitude w. In the reported study, μ' was identified as the invariant for similar conditions between different subjects, Fig. 1b. The height of the asymptote of the friction reduction is linearly dependent on the normal force applied. The reduction of relative friction coefficient, $\Delta\mu$, in function of the vibration amplitude can be expressed as:

$$\Delta\mu(w) = (1 - \Delta\mu_1)e^{-bw} + \Delta\mu_1$$
$$\text{With } \Delta\mu_1 = 1.13F_n$$

$$(2)$$

where b is an empirical constant with $1.67 \ \mu m^{-1}$ as value, F_n is the normal force applied by the finger.

3 Friction Coefficient Control

In the present section, an analysis of previous implementation of friction coefficient control in ultrasonic devices is presented.

The friction felt by the finger while exploring different surfaces is greatly variable for different subjects: many different parameters influence this force, like the nature of the surface, lipid and water content or the mechanics properties of the finger. Moreover, the friction coefficient may dramatically change within seconds after the contact due to generated occlusion and non-Coulomb friction [10]. A closed loop approach of the friction coefficient control was previously developed with the SMARTTAC [11]. This device incorporated a broad bandwidth tribometer around an ultrasonic tactile plate. The lateral and normal force sensors implemented allowed the real time recording and processing of the normal and friction force permitting the implementation of a closed-loop control of the friction coefficient. The system works smoothly for a step of friction coefficient and it is able to maintain the control in the steady state. In this device, the participants' friction coefficient is recorded along the first stroke over the plate and then controlled based on the previous measure.

One issue with this architecture is that a relevant change of the friction due to the generated occlusion or deposited moisture could lead to the saturation of the control. Moreover, the bandwidth of the device is intrinsically limited by the mechanical properties of the fingertip. To effectively control the friction coefficient, the lateral force sensor needs to be able to measure the friction force. Based on the measurements performed in the cited work on different participants, an average rise time of the lateral force of 3.84 ms was recorded. This value is reflected in a bandwidth of around 90 Hz for the signal reproduction. The reported value matches the mechanical properties of the fingertip highlighted in [12] and it is in accord with similar measurements performed in [13] and validated for both electrovibration and ultrasonic vibrations in the cited work. The elastic response of the fingertip imposes a bandwidth limit to the closed loop friction coefficient control far below the perceptual bandwidth of the finger. Due to the intrinsic limitation of a direct measurement and control of the lateral force, an open-loop approach will be described in the following sections.

4 High Fidelity Texture Rendering

In this section, the developed device is described and the strategies of texture reproduction are introduced.

4.1 Device

The device is built around the banana pi (Shenzhen LeMaker Technology Co. Ltd, China) single board computer featuring a 1 GHz ARM Cortex-A7 dual-core CPU with 1 GB of ram working in parallel with a microcontroller (stm32f4, STMicroelectronics, France). The single board computer is connected to a 5 in. flat capacitive touch screen (Banana-LCD-5″-TS, Marel, China) providing the finger position input and display output, where the sampling frequency of the finger position is 50 Hz. The communication between the microcontroller and the single board pc is provided by an SPI bus working at 10 kframes/s. 4 flat resistive force sensors (CP 150, IEE, Luxemburg) are placed under the corners of the display and provide the normal force value to the microcontroller. The microcontroller synthesizes a PWM signals to pilot a voltage inverter the motor piezoceramics. In Fig. 2, the structure of the device is represented.

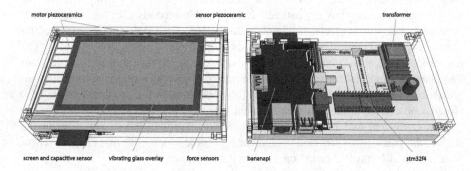

Fig. 2. Device structure.

4.2 Ultrasonic Vibrating Plate

The ultrasonic vibrating plate implemented in the device is a glass plate $154 \times 81 \times 1.6$ mm^3 resonating at 60750 Hz, where the half wavelength of the vibration mode is 8 mm. 22 piezoceramics, $14 \times 6 \times 0.5$ mm^3, are mounted on the sides of the plate along a full wavelength, 20 of which are used as motors and 2 as vibration sensors. Their unglued electrode was split along the nodal line and both halves connected to 2 complementary outputs of the voltage inverter. This setup avoids the needing of electrical access to the glued electrode, while maintaining it at ground voltage in order to reduce perturbations to the capacitive sensor. The cartography of the vibration amplitude of the plate is reported in Fig. 3a. A closed loop control on the vibration amplitude, running at 60 kHz, is implemented on the microcontroller acquiring the value of the vibration from two piezoceramics used as sensors. The controller is a PI and its parameters were tuned

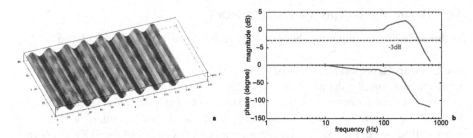

Fig. 3. (a) Cartography of the ultrasonic vibrating plate. (b) Bode diagram of the vibration response of the plate. The dashed line at −3 dB indicates the bandwidth of the plate up to 400 Hz.

with the Ziegler-Nichols method. In Fig. 3b, the bode diagram of the controlled system is reported. The system exhibits a bandwidth of 400 Hz at 2 μm. The closed loop control allows the stability of the vibration amplitude within a tolerance of 50 nm for a normal force applied lower than 3 N by the fingertip.

4.3 Model Inversion

In this subsection, the open loop control of the friction coefficient implemented in the device is described.

The identification of the invariance of the relative modulation of the friction coefficient allows the implementation of an inverse model on the control chain of the device. Once selected the desired percentage of friction modulation, the related vibration amplitude can be determined through an inversion of (2):

$$w = -\frac{1}{b}\ln\frac{\Delta\mu - \Delta\mu_1}{1 - \Delta\mu_1} \tag{3}$$

where the constant $\Delta\mu_1$ is dependent on the normal force applied by the finger, Fig. 4.

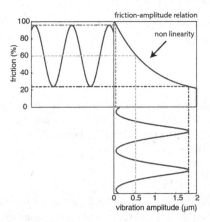

Fig. 4. Relation between reduction of friction coefficient and vibration amplitude for a given normal force and exploration speed.

4.4   Haptic Signal Representation Strategies

In this section, two different strategies for texture reproduction are introduced.

4.4.1   Map Representation – SHO
In this subsection, the definition of the surface haptic object (SHO) is reported.

The classical strategy to reproduce texture and object on a flat surface through friction modulation relies on the comparison of the detected position with a map previously selected, Fig. 5a. It is possible to introduce a concept of the SHO to describe this control strategy. We shall define as SHO a spatially located haptic activated area. The reproduction of SHO relies on the accuracy and the bandwidth of the position acquisition system to reproduce textures. This leads to the implementation of different solutions to maximize the bandwidth of the position acquisition with an optical [14] or force based [15] position detection solutions, effective, but hardly implementable on mass produced devices. A noisy or low bandwidth system cannot reproduce accurately the desired signal; e.g. a 50 Hz capacitive touch screen is only able to reproduce a grating up to 25 Hz. This value corresponds in the spatial domain to a grating of 1 mm period for a finger velocity of 2 mm/s.

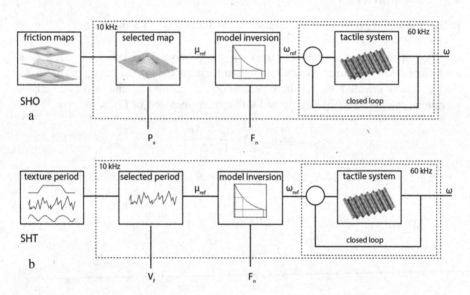

Fig. 5. (a) Structure of the control chain for friction coefficient modulation through map representation (SHO). (b) Structure of the control chain for friction coefficient modulation through period synthesis (SHT). The rate of reproduction of the selected period is dependent on the speed of exploration of the finger.

4.4.2   Signal Synthesis – SHT
In this subsection, the definition of the surface haptic texture (SHT) is introduced.

A different approach on the texture reproduction is implemented through a synthesis of the haptic signal based on a single period. It has been shown that the interaction with a spatially periodical texture of the fingertip leads to a periodical spatial pattern of the lateral force [16]. Through a synthesis based on the periodic force signal it is possible to avoid the limitations imposed by a low bandwidth position sensor, Fig. 5b. As SHT, we define a spatial frequency haptic pattern independent on the finger position. The reproduction rate of the identified friction period is determined by the velocity of the finger, which is updated to the new value at each cycle of acquisition. By implementing this approach, it is possible to reproduce the full bandwidth of a periodical tactile signal with capacitive touch sensor. The drawback of this approach is the error in the spatial phase of the signal, which is related to the reintegration of the velocity without considering the position of the finger at contact, and the difference between the measured and real velocity of the finger. This is not problematic for an opaque tactile stimulator, where there is not a visual clue given by a screen of the local placement of the friction interface. However, for a transparent stimulator coupled with a screen, the errors introduced for a low spatial frequency, e.g. 1 interface/cm, may be easily perceivable.

4.4.3   Composed Control

The definition of two conceptually different surface haptic signals, SHO and SHT, allows us to theoretically define a merged control. A control composed by the linear superposition of SHT and SHO allows to obtain a broad spatial reproduction bandwidth. Following [17], the spatial bandwidth separation between SHO and SHT can be attested by the single object separation of 3–4 mm. A greater spatial frequency is identified as texture, whereas a smaller is identified as single objects scattered on a flat surface. A psychophysical experiment validating this limit will be proposed in the next section.

5   Texture Rendering Strategies Validation

A psychophysical experiment was developed to validate the advantages and disadvantages of the rendering strategies SHO and SHT. It was asked to 6 participants to freely evaluate, with a number from one to ten, the accuracy of reproduction of three different spatialized tactile signals, which gave their informed consent to the participation to the experiment. During the exploration, a visual grating was shown on the screen of the device with the same spatial frequency as the tactile grating, Fig. 6a. The tactile signals were programmed to provide a step friction change at the interface between a black and white line, Fig. 6b. The participants were free to accustom themselves with the sensation provided by the device before the beginning of the experiment with a simple visual and tactile interface in the middle of the screen. The three analyzed cases were, respectively, composed by a spatial grating of 15, 5 and 0.6 mm, all of them reproduced with both strategies. The signals were presented randomly to the users which were allowed to explore them freely. At the end of each exploration, it was asked to the users to rate, with the number from one to ten, the accuracy of reproduction of the signals. The results are reported in Fig. 6c. The difference between the control strategies was tested with an unpaired t-test. For the lowest spacing, the SHT performs significantly better than SHO ($p = 0.0001$). Whereas for the higher spacing SHO performs better than SHT ($p = 0.0232$). No significant difference between the two strategies was found for the intermediate case ($p = 0.8$).

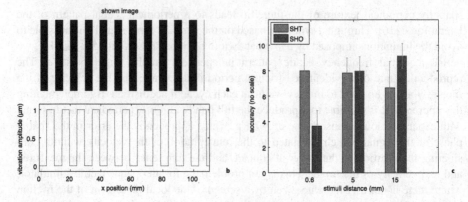

Fig. 6. (a) Image shown on the screen, (b) envelope of the vibration amplitude in function of the x position of the finger, (c) given rate of reproduction accuracy for SHO and SHT. (Color figure online)

6 Discussion

The empirical model describing the behaviour of the friction reduction is included in the control scheme of the friction force of an ultrasonic friction modulation device. This inclusion allows to overcome the limitations of a closed loop approach of the friction coefficient control in terms of bandwidth and a robust friction coefficient control up to 400 Hz is designed.

The approach to texture simulation on friction control devices used to be based on the comparison of the finger position with a precompiled map of friction. This approach is effective, but the bandwidth of the position sensor determines the maximum reproduction bandwidth of the device. In the case of capacitive touchscreen, this value is in the order of 50 Hz, largely insufficient to reproduce real textures. By defining two different signals, the SHO, spatially located, and the SHT, spatially periodical, it is possible to overcome the limitation of the slow position acquisition through the introduced texture rendering strategy.

The advantages of the different control strategies in function of the spatial frequency of the stimulus were investigated with a psychophysical experiment. The SHT approach performs significantly better than the SHO for a large spatial frequency (17 stimuli/cm) resolving the undersampling problem of the finger position. The SHO approach is better than the SHT for a spatial frequency around (0.7 stimuli/cm) where the phase error accumulated by SHT becomes noticeable. No statistical difference was found for the intermediate case. This allows us to set a spatial frequency boundary between SHO and SHT, located around 2 stimuli/cm in accord with perception separation described in [17].

This results here shown present a fundamental difference to a related experience introduced by Meyer et al. [18]. In the cited work, the interest of the author was on the identification of the smallest spatial gap impossible to identify by the user as different from the provided noise. The aim of their experience was to highlight the passage from a spatial encoded regime, to a fully vibrational regime. The present work is totally focussed on the spatial texture perception provided by periodic signals. In this work, the participants were not able to perceive the difference between a spatial signal where the tactile stimulation was provided on the white/black interface or consistently in another spatial phase of the period, accordingly with the hypothesis at the basis of the SHT definition.

The boundary between SHO and SHT placed around a spatial density of 5 mm is understandable by considering that the friction modulation device does not provide a localisable stimulus under the fingerpad, but provide a change of the frictional boundary condition of the whole area in contact. The inability to place the stimulus in a determined area of the finger induce the inability to distinguish the spatial phase error of the SHO signal when at least two expected stimuli are present under the fingerpad area.

The results confirm that the necessity of a high bandwidth position recording is not necessary to provide dense spatial stimuli information, provided that the reproduced spatial signal can be described as a periodic signal. This result is consistent with the [16] and do provide a direct experimental proof of the introduced concept.

The developed decomposition of the haptic signal is implementable in every friction-based technique, and can overcome low fidelity of texture reproduction currently implemented in these devices for periodical signals.

7 Prospective

A future work with the developed device will be to identify a joint control strategy and digital texture representation unifying the advantages of SHO and SHT. The device itself is a versatile tool that will be employed in multiple works on the interaction with haptic devices. The advantages of the synthesis-based rendering approach will be shown with a demonstrator at the conference.

8 Conclusion

A device incorporating an open loop control of the friction force between the finger sliding on an ultrasonic vibrating plate is proposed. Two different texture rendering schemes are introduced, a classic one for object representation and a digital synthesis for texture representation. To conclude, the advantages of the two texture rendering techniques are analysed through a psychophysical experiment.

Acknowledgement. This work was founded by the FP7 Marie Curie Initial Training Network PROTOTOUCH, grant agreement No. 317100 and supported by IRCICA USR 3380 Univ. Lille - CNRS (www.ircica.univ-lille1.fr).

References

1. Mallinckrodt, E., Hughes, A.L., Sleator Jr., W.: Perception by the skin of electrically induced vibrations. Science **118**, 277–278 (1953)
2. Vezzoli, E., Amberg, M., Giraud, F., Lemaire-Semail, B.: Electrovibration modeling analysis. In: Auvray, M., Duriez, C. (eds.) EuroHaptics 2014, Part II. LNCS, vol. 8619, pp. 369–376. Springer, Heidelberg (2014)

3. Shultz, C.D., Peshkin, M.A., Colgate, J.E.: Surface haptics via electroadhesion: expanding electrovibration with Johnsen and Rahbek. In: 2015 IEEE World Haptics Conference (WHC), pp. 57–62 (2015)
4. Biet, M., Giraud, F., Lemaire-Semail, B.: Squeeze film effect for the design of an ultrasonic tactile plate. IEEE Trans. Ultrason. Ferroelectr. Freq. Control **54**(12), 2678–2688 (2007)
5. Vezzoli, E., Dzidek, B.M., Sednaoui, T., Giraud, F., Adams, M., Lemaire-Semail, B.: Role of fingerprint mechanics and non-Coulombic friction in ultrasonic devices. In: WHC (2015)
6. Biet, M., Casiez, G., Giraud, F., Lemaire-Semail, B.: Discrimination of virtual square gratings by dynamic touch on friction based tactile displays. In: Symposium on Haptic Interfaces for Virtual Environment and Teleoperator Systems, Haptics 2008, pp. 41–48 (2008)
7. Robles-De-La-Torre, G., Hayward, V.: Force can overcome object geometry in the perception of shape through active touch. Nature **412**(6845), 445–448 (2001)
8. Watanabe, T., Fukui, S.: A method for controlling tactile sensation of surface roughness using ultrasonic vibration. In: Proceedings of the 1995 IEEE International Conference on Robotics and Automation, vol. 1, pp. 1134–1139 (1995)
9. Sednaoui, T., Vezzoli, E., Dzidek, B.M., Lemaire-Semail, B., Chiappaz, C., Adams, M.: Experimental evaluation of friction reduction in ultrasonic devices. In: World Haptics Conference (WHC) (2015)
10. Dzidek, B.M., Adams, M., Zhang, Z., Johnson, S., Bochereau, S., Hayward, V.: Role of occlusion in non-Coulombic slip of the finger pad. In: Auvray, M., Duriez, C. (eds.) EuroHaptics 2014, Part I. LNCS, vol. 8618, pp. 109–116. Springer, Heidelberg (2014)
11. Ben Messaoud, W., Lemaire-Semail, B., Bueno, M.-A., Amberg, M., Giraud, F.: Closed-loop control for squeeze film effect in tactile stimulator. In: Actuator, Bremen (2014)
12. Wiertlewski, M., Hayward, V.: Mechanical behavior of the fingertip in the range of frequencies and displacements relevant to touch. J. Biomech. **45**(11), 1869–1874 (2012)
13. Vezzoli, E., Ben Messaoud, W., Amberg, M., Lemaire-Semail, B., Giraud, F., Bueno, M.-A.: Physical and perceptual independence of ultrasonic vibration and electrovibration for friction modulation. IEEE Trans. Haptics **8**, 235–239 (2015)
14. Wiertlewski, M., Leonardis, D., Meyer, D.J., Peshkin, M.A., Colgate, J.: A high-fidelity surface-haptic device for texture rendering on bare finger. In: Auvray, M., Duriez, C. (eds.) EuroHaptics 2014, Part II. LNCS, vol. 8619, pp. 241–248. Springer, Heidelberg (2014)
15. Amberg, M., Giraud, F., Semail, B., Olivo, P., Casiez, G., Roussel, N.: STIMTAC: a tactile input device with programmable friction. In: Proceedings of the 24th Annual ACM Symposium Adjunct on User Interface Software and Technology, New York, NY, USA, pp. 7–8 (2011)
16. Wiertlewski, M., Lozada, J., Hayward, V.: The spatial spectrum of tangential skin displacement can encode tactual texture. IEEE Trans. Robot. **27**(3), 461–472 (2011)
17. Klatzky, R.L., Lederman, S.J.: Touch. In: Handbook of Psychology. Wiley (2003)
18. Meyer, D.J., Peshkin, M.A., Colgate, J.E.: Modeling and synthesis of tactile texture with spatial spectrograms for display on variable friction surfaces. In: IEEE - World Haptics Conference (2015)

Successive Stiffness Increment Approach for High Stiffness Haptic Interaction

Harsimran Singh[✉], Aghil Jafari, and Jee-Hwan Ryu

School of Mechanical Engineering, Korea University of Technology and Education,
1600 Chungjeolno, Cheonan, Chungnam, Republic of Korea
{harsimran,jhryu}@koreatech.ac.kr, jafari_aghil@kut.ac.kr

Abstract. This paper proposes a method to further enlarge the displayed stiffness range of the impedance-type haptic interfaces. Numerous studies have been done for a stable haptic interaction in a wide impedance range. However, most of the approaches sacrifice the actual displayed stiffness as a cost of stability. A novel approach, which successively increases the stiffness as the number of interaction cycle increase, is presented. The stiffness is sequentially modulated from a low value to a high value, close to the desired stiffness while maintaining stability. This sequential stiffness increment was possible because the proposed approach guarantees the convergence of the penetration distance and increases the feedback force with every successive interaction cycle. The main advantage of the proposed approach over conventional approaches is that this approach allows much larger actual displayed stiffness than any other approach, such as time-domain passivity approach, force bounding and energy bounding approach. Experiments with PHANToM Premium 1.5 evaluate the performance of the proposed approach, and compare the actual displayed stiffness with other approaches.

1 Introduction

Haptic interaction results in bidirectional energy flow between the human operator and haptic display. The generation and flow of energy depends on the rendering of the virtual environment (VE). When the haptic interface is used to render contact with a stiff virtual wall, oscillatory and unstable behavior of the haptic display is observed. Such a behavior may damage the haptic display, distract or in a worse case scenario, injure the human operator. The stability analysis is therefore a non trivial task and something that can't be overlooked.

The two particular aspects that are responsible for system instability are discretization and zero order sample and hold. It is certain that when a controller designed for a continuous domain is implemented to a discrete domain, the performance will be degraded. Interactions in the real and virtual world are completely different. The latter is an approximation model of the real world. These approximations depend on the sampling rate, greater the sampling rate better will be the approximations. However, even small errors can add up and the implications can be profound. A haptic interaction may diverge due to instability

© Springer International Publishing Switzerland 2016
F. Bello et al. (Eds.): EuroHaptics 2016, Part I, LNCS 9774, pp. 261–270, 2016.
DOI: 10.1007/978-3-319-42321-0_24

and limit cycle oscillations, both of which result from non-passivity. Small limit cycles distorts the transparency or 'feel' of the VE, as human tactile perception is extremely sensitive to vibrations in the range of 100 Hz to 1 kHz [1].

There have been numerous studies to achieve stable haptic interaction, and most of the researches were based on passivity constraint. Passivity criterion has several valuable properties, such that, it only uses input/output information independent of system parameters, it is a sufficient condition for stability, and it is generally applicable to linear and nonlinear systems. Inspired from passivity theorem, several approaches have been proposed for stable haptic interaction, *i.e.* time-domain passivity approach, energy bounding algorithm, force bounding algorithm and wave variable approach [2]. Hannaford and Ryu [3] proposed time domain passivity approach, which injects an adaptive virtual damping to satisfy the passivity constraint. Inspired from graphical interpretation of passivity in a position vs. force graph, Ryu and Yoon [4] proposed a concept to increase the dynamic range of impedance in which a haptic interface can passively interact using passivation method. Kim and Ryu [5] proposed an energy bounding algorithm, which blocks out the generated energy from a sample and hold operator so that it makes the haptic system not to have the excessive energy. Recently, a less conservative version of force bounding approach was proposed to bound the interaction force such that only the forces passively can be displayed [6]. Although passivity constraint guarantees stable haptic interaction, it is only a small set of sufficient condition for stability, and has been suffering from intrinsic conservatism. Jafari and Ryu [7] proposed a less conservative control approach for stable haptic interaction inspired from the analogy between virtual environments systems with hysteresis nonlinearity.

Several other studies have been done to reduce the conservativeness of passivity criterion. A two-port network is said to be absolutely stable if there exist no set of passive terminating one-port impedances for which the system is unstable. Therefore, only as long as human operator and virtual environment are passive, the haptic interaction remains stable. Llewellyns stability criterion provides both necessary and sufficient conditions for absolute stability of linear two-ports networks [8]. However, the sufficient condition for absolute stability is represented in frequency domain and also includes system parameters, which may not always be available.

Even though, there exist several approaches to guarantee stability of haptic interfaces, most of the approaches either cover a limited range of stiffness or sacrifice the actual displayed stiffness at the cost of stability. This paper presents an approach to further enlarge the achievable stiffness range. A novel approach which increases the displayed stiffness with each pressing interaction cycle is presented. The haptic interaction starts by displaying a small value of stiffness which later increases close to the desired value in a couple of cycles. This is achieved by gradually increasing the feedback force with every successive cycle. The proposed approach guarantees the convergence of the penetration distance and increment of the force feedback with every consecutive cycle. This allows for a much larger displayed stiffness than any other approach while maintaining interaction stability.

This paper is organised as follows: Sect. 2 describes the general concept of hapic interaction with low and high stiffness virtual environment. Section 3 gives an in depth look into the successive stiffness increment (SSI) approach and explains in detail the functions used to compute the force for pressing and releasing paths. Section 4 shows the experimental setup used and experimental evaluation for (SSI) approach, it also compares our approach with force bounding approach. Section 5 concludes and discusses the future work.

2   Haptic Interaction with Low and High Stiffness Virtual Environment

In case of interacting with high stiffness virtual environment, the generated energy will be more than the energy which can be dissipated by the intrinsic friction of the haptic device. Therefore, after the first cycle, the remaining energy from the first cycle acts as the initial stored energy for the second cycle. Therefore, the haptic probe has more energy to penetrate into the virtual Environment with the same stiffness gain. As a result, the system oscillates more and the position response diverges as time goes.

Conversely, when the generated energy is smaller than the energy dissipated by the physical damping of the system, the interaction can be stable. After the haptic probe penetrates the virtual environment, it moves back and forth for some cycles while converging to a point where the human force is almost equal to the force from the virtual environment. Even after converging, there will be small vibrations around the point of convergence due to sampling and zero-order-hold.

3   Successive Increment of Force Approach

To maintain stability and increase the displayed stiffness, we propose an approach whereby the stiffness is increased gradually starting from a small value in successive cycles. We named it SSI (Successive Stiffness Increment) approach, because the stiffness is sequentially modulated starting from a low value, the generated energy at each cycle would be small. Moreover with a couple of cycle this produced energy at each cycle would finally converge to a small enough value to be dissipated by the intrinsic physical damping of the haptic display since the proposed SSI approach guarantees the convergence of the penetration distance, and increases the feedback force with each successive interaction cycle.

3.1   Overview of the Successive Stiffness Increment Approach

For an intuitive understanding, the approach is explained conceptually one cycle at a time using the position vs force graph, Fig. 1. The proposed approach can be broken down into two sections, namely the pressing path and the releasing path. The force for the pressing path is a function of a smaller stiffness (K_s) than the

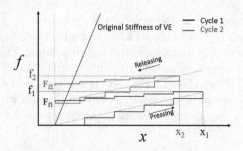

Fig. 1. Basic principle of the SSI approach. (Color figure online)

original stiffness of the VE, and the stiffness is selected such that the generated energy is lower than the dissipated energy by inherent damping. Considering that the interaction of haptic probe with the virtual environment is modeled as a simple virtual spring, the force is:

$$f(n) = \begin{cases} K_s x(n) + F_r, & \text{for} \quad x(n) \geq 0 \\ 0, & \text{for} \quad x(n) < 0 \end{cases} \tag{1}$$

where, K_s is the selected small stiffness, $x(n)$ is the penetration distance and F_r is the last force value of the previous releasing path. It is important to note that the pressing path begins from the point where the previous releasing path ended. In case of first cycle F_r would be 0.

The releasing path does not follow Eq. 1. The function for releasing path is chosen so that the value of force is some finite value even when penetration distance is 0. This is shown in Fig. 1 as F_{f1} and F_{f2}, which are the finite force values at zero penetration after first and second cycle, respectively. Thus, the function for releasing path is:

$$f(n) = \begin{cases} \mu x(n) + F_f, & \text{for} \quad x(n) \geq 0 \\ 0, & \text{for} \quad x(n) < 0 \end{cases} \tag{2}$$

where, μ is the slope of the releasing path, $x(n)$ is the penetration distance and F_f is the chosen finite value of force when penetration is 0. It is shown in Eq. 1 that pressing path starts from a point where the previous releasing path ended, therefore, F_f after the first releasing path will be the F_r for the second pressing path.

When the first cycle ends, the total output energy in the system is:

$$Output_1 = Input_1 + GeneratedEnergy_1 - E_{b1} \tag{3}$$

where, E_{b1} is the energy dissipated by the physical damping of the haptic display during first cycle, which is given by $E_{b1} = \sum_{k=1}^{n} [b_m (\Delta \dot{x}(k))^2] \Delta T$.

This output energy is transferred to the human operator, who is passive in the range of frequencies of interest in haptics [9], which is then transferred back to the system. So the output energy at the end of the first cycle is the input energy to the second cycle. The pressing path for the second cycle follows Eq. 1 with F_r equal to the F_f of the first cycle. The haptic probe should penetrate the VE until the input energy for the second cycle is equal to or greater than the output energy of the first cycle. Therefore, the following equation must be satisfied:

$$output_1 \leq input_2$$
$$\leq \sum_{k=1}^{n} \left[f(k-1)\, \Delta x(k) \right] \tag{4}$$
$$\leq \sum_{k=1}^{n} \left[(K_s x(k-1) + F_r)\, \Delta x(k) \right]$$

Since the pressing cycle starts from a finite value, F_r, and not 0, we can draw the conclusion that the penetration distance for the second cycle would be smaller than the penetration distance for the first cycle based on Eq. 4. Also from Eq. 1, the force at the end of the second pressing path (f_{p2}) would be greater than the force at the end of the first pressing path (f_{p1}). Moreover, greater the value of F_r, greater would be the force and smaller the penetration distance for the second cycle and vice versa.

Thus, the penetration distance would converge and the force increase after every cycle even though the system is generating energy. Also as the penetration distance decreases with each cycle, the generated energy after each cycle becomes smaller than previous. This explains that the displayed stiffness increases with every successive cycle with the system being stable.

3.2 Detailed Description for Successive Stiffness Increment Approach

Previous subsection explains the proposed idea conceptually, and demonstrated that the penetration distance get smaller and the interaction force get larger as the number of interaction cycle increases. However, Eqs. 1 and 2 do not take into account the desired stiffness of the VE. In order to realize the aforementioned concept, based on the stiffness of the VE, two different functions are defined for calculating forces for pressing and releasing paths (Fig. 2).

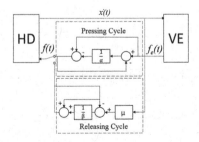

Fig. 2. Control structure for the proposed SSI approach.

Pressing Path. The function for calculating force during pressing path is:

$$f(k) = f_e(k) - \left(\frac{f_e(k) - f_p(k)}{\alpha} \right) \tag{5}$$

where, $f_e(k)$ is the force from the VE, $f_p(k)$ is previous value of $f(k)$ and α will determine how steep the pressing path rises. Greater value of α denotes steeper pressing path and vice versa.

Releasing Path. The releasing path starts after the pressing path ends. A local slope, μ, is calculated of the line joining the last force and the position values of the pressing path to the boundary of the VE, as depicted in Fig. 3. This local slope is calculated only once per cycle after the end of pressing path.

$$\mu = f_{Top}/x_{Top} \tag{6}$$

where, f_{Top} is last value of f and $x_{Top}(k)$ is the last value of x on the pressing path.

The force on the releasing path should follow this local slope, μ. As explained in Sect. 3.1, the force should have a finite value after the end of releasing path. The following function defines the force during releasing path:

$$f(k) = f_p(k) + \left(\frac{f_r(k) - f_p(k)}{\beta} \right) \tag{7}$$

where, β will determine how steep the releasing path will be. Greater value of β means greater value of force at the end of the releasing path and vice versa.

And,

$$f_r(k) = \mu x(k). \tag{8}$$

Selection of α and β. The value of stiffness for which the generated energy is dissipated by the physical damping of the haptic display for a linear relation between force and position is given by the passivity condition in [10]:

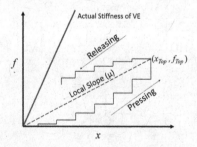

Fig. 3. Schematic showing calculation of local slope (μ).

$$K_v \leq \frac{2b_m}{\Delta T} \qquad (9)$$

where, b_m is the physical damping of the haptic display and ΔT is the sampling time.

When the system converges after a couple of cycles, there exists a small back and forth motion around the point of convergence due to the sampling and zero-order-hold, as explained in Sect. 2. This back and forth motion generates some energy, which should be dissipated by the physical damping of the haptic display to ensure smooth haptic interaction without any jittering.

The feedback force for the first sample at the beginning of each pressing path should follow Eq. 9 and is given by:

$$f(k) = K_v x(k) + [f_p(k) - K_v x_p(k)] \qquad (10)$$

where, $x(k)$ is the current penetration distance, f_p is the value for previous feedback force and x_p is the previous penetration distance.

The value for α is thus deduced using Eqs. 5 and 10:

$$\alpha = \frac{f_e(k) - f_p(k)}{f_e(k) - [K_v x(k) + (f_p(k) - K_v x_p(k))]} \qquad (11)$$

Similarly, the feedback force for the first sample at the beginning of each releasing path should be same as Eq. 10. Therefore, the value for β is deduced using Eqs. 7 and 10:

$$\beta = \frac{f_r(k) - f_p(k)}{K_v x(k) + (f_p(k) - K_v x_p(k)) - f_p(k)} \qquad (12)$$

4   Experiments

4.1   Experimental Setup

To demonstrate the performance of the proposed approach on a single-DOF impedance-type haptic display, commercially available PHANToM Premium 1.5 was used. The basic specification of which are: maximum force output of 8.5 N, continuous exertable force of 1.4 N, physical damping, (b_m), is selected as 0.0002 Ns/mm, therefore according to Eq. (9) K_v is 0.4 N/mm, encoder resolution of 0.03 mm and sampling rate of 1 kHz.

The interaction of haptic probe with VE is modeled as a simple virtual spring

$$f_e(n) = \begin{cases} kx(n), & \text{for} \quad x(n) \geq 0 \\ 0, & \text{for} \quad x(n) < 0 \end{cases} \qquad (13)$$

where, $x(n)$ is the penetration depth of the haptic probe in the VE and k is the stiffness of the VE.

4.2   Experimental Evaluation

The experiments were carried out for virtual walls of varying stiffness, with and
without control law. Figure 4 shows the unstable haptic interaction for a virtual
wall having stiffness of 5 N/mm. Since the generated energy was much greater
than what could be dissipated by the physical damping of the system, therefore,
the response shows unstable behavior.

Figure 5 shows the results for conducting the same experiment by implementing the SSI approach. The position and force response were stable and the
operator did not feel any vibrations as shown in Fig. 5a. Figure 5c shows the generated energy during the interaction. Although the generated energy was greater
than what could be dissipated by the haptic display, still the haptic interaction
was stable as the penetration distance converged and the generated energy after
a couple of cycles became small enough that could be dissipated by the physical
damping of the system. Figure 5d shows the displayed stiffness, which was close
to the desired stiffness of the virtual wall.

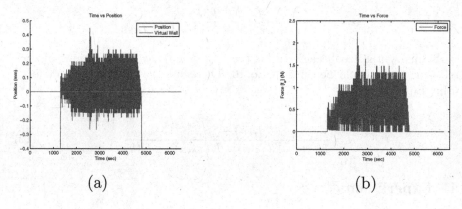

Fig. 4. Virtual wall stiffness 5 N/mm. (a) Position response, (b) force response (Color
figure online)

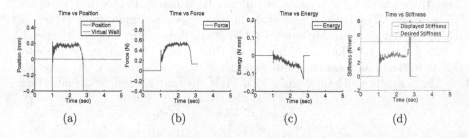

Fig. 5. SSI approach with virtual wall stiffness 5 N/mm. (a) Position response, (b) force
response, (c) energy, (d) displayed stiffness. (Color figure online)

4.3 Comparison with Force Bounding Approach

The proposed SSI approach was compared with Force Bounding Approach for displaying the desired stiffness. The experiments were carried out on PHANToM Premium 1.5 for both of the approaches and the value of physical damping, b_m was selected as $0.0002\,\mathrm{Ns/mm}$. It can be seen from Fig. 6a that the maximum displayed stiffness for FBA was around $0.4\,\mathrm{N/mm}$ when the stiffness of VE was $5\,\mathrm{N/mm}$. On the other hand, the displayed stiffness of the SSI approach was around $3\,\mathrm{N/mm}$. Also when the stiffness for the VE was increased to $100\,\mathrm{N/mm}$, the displayed stiffness increases to around $10\,\mathrm{N/mm}$. There are fluctuations for displayed stiffness because the force increases after couple of cycles and so even small changes in penetration distance causes shifts in the value of displayed stiffness. Please note that Time Domain Passivity Approach [3] was not able to stabilize such a high stiffness VE.

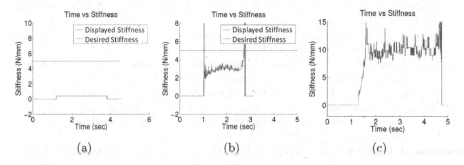

Fig. 6. Comparison of displayed stiffness for SSI approach with FBA approach. (a) FBA with $5\,\mathrm{N/mm}$, (b) SSI with $5\,\mathrm{N/mm}$, (c) SSI with $100\,\mathrm{N/mm}$. (Color figure online)

5 Conclusions and Future Works

This paper proposes a new concept of stable haptic interaction method for further enlarging the achievable stiffness range of impedance-type haptic displays. In order to successively increase the displayed stiffness, two separate functions for each pressing and releasing region were defined in such a way that the stiffness get gradually increased as close as possible to the desired value while the produced energy can be dissipated by the inherent physical damping of the device. Because the proposed method allows continuous increment of the displayed force in every consecutive cycle of interaction without any sudden change of the force, the operator do not notice the change of the stiffness. The biggest advantage of the proposed method over conventional approaches is that this approach allows much larger actual displayed stiffness to a human operator than any other approaches, such as time-domain passivity approach, force bounding and energy bounding approach. Experiments with Phantom proved the enlarged stiffness range of the proposed approach, and compared the actual displayed stiffness with other approaches.

As a future work, we are working on extending this approach to multi-DOF interaction and to teleoperation systems.

Acknowledgment. This paper is supported by the project (Development of core teleopertion technologies for maintaining and repairing tasks in nuclear power plants) funded by the Ministry of Trade, Industry & Energy of S. Korea.

References

1. Bolanowski, S.J., Gescheider, G.A., Verrillo, R.T.: Hairy skin: psychophysical channels and their physiological substrates. Somatosens. Mot. Res. **11**(3), 279–290 (1994)
2. Niemeyer, G., Slotine, J.-J.E.: Stable adaptive teleoperation. IEEE J. Oceanic Eng. **16**(1), 152–162 (1991)
3. Hannaford, B., Ryu, J.-H.: Time-domain passivity control of haptic interfaces. IEEE Trans. Robot. Autom. **18**(1), 1–10 (2002)
4. Ryu, J.-H., Yoon, M.-Y.: Memory-based passivation approach for stable haptic interaction. IEEE/ASME Trans. Mechatron. **19**(4), 1424–1435 (2014)
5. Kim, J.-P., Ryu, J.: Energy bounding algorithm based on passivity theorem for stable haptic interaction control. In: 12th International Symposium on Haptic Interfaces for Virtual Environment and Teleoperator Systems, 2004, HAPTICS 2004, Proceedings, pp. 351–357, March 2004
6. Kim, J.-P., Baek, S.-Y., Ryu, J.: A force bounding approach for multi-degree-of-freedom haptic interaction. IEEE/ASME Trans. Mechatron. **20**(3), 1193–1203 (2015)
7. Jafari, A., Ryu, J-H.: Input-to-state stable approach to release the conservatism of passivity-based stable haptic interaction. In: 2015 IEEE International Conference on Robotics and Automation (ICRA), pp. 285–290, May 2015
8. Llewellyn, F.B.: Some fundamental properties of transmission systems. Proc. IRE **40**(3), 271–283 (1952)
9. Hogan, N.: Controlling impedance at the man/machine interface. In: 1989 IEEE International Conference on Robotics and Automation, 1989, Proceedings, vol. 3, pp. 1626–1631, May 1989
10. Colgate, J.E., Stanley, M.C., Brown, J.M.: Issues in the haptic display of tool use. In: 1995 IEEE/RSJ International Conference on Intelligent Robots and Systems 1995, Human Robot Interaction and Cooperative Robots, Proceedings, vol. 3, pp. 140–145. IEEE (1995)

Thermal Perception

A Century Later, the Hue-Heat Hypothesis: Does Color Truly Affect Temperature Perception?

Mounia Ziat[(✉)], Carrie Anne Balcer, Andrew Shirtz,
and Taylor Rolison

Psychology Department, Northern Michigan University,
Marquette, MI 49855, USA
mziat@nmu.edu

Abstract. The present study aims to determine whether color has an impact on temperature perception, a paradigm known as the hue-heat hypothesis. Our results shows that a color-temperature association exists since the participants hold a hot vessel longer when associated with blue and similarly a cold vessel longer when paired with red. Participants' ratings of the perceived temperature were also influenced by crossmodal interaction between color and temperature confirming the effect of color on temperature perception. These findings are consistent with previous studies and validates the hue-heat hypothesis that was first investigated almost a century ago.

Keywords: Hue-heat hypothesis · Temperature perception · Color perception · Multimodal integration

1 Introduction

Our perceptual knowledge of the world not only relies on past experiences but is affected by how our sensory inputs interact and affect each other [1–3]. More specifically, in both visual and tactile domains, several interactions have been reported [4, 5] and we are interested in the effect of color on temperature perception, which has been known, for almost a century, as the hue-heat hypothesis [6]. The hue-heat hypothesis (HHH) considers the change in the subjective feeling of the temperature based on the color of the object. As indicated by its name it is mainly related to heat and has been reported first by Morgensen and English in 1926 who showed no evidence of such interaction [6]. The subject regained attention almost forty years later with similar results [7, 8] or effects too small [9] to be considered as interactive. More recently, several research groups showed that color can actually affect temperature and pain perception [11–13]. For instance, Moseley and Arntz [10] showed that the perception of noxious stimuli paired with a red visual cue is perceived hotter and more painful as opposed to the same thermal stimulus when paired with blue. In a different study [11], red light decreased cold pain thresholds compared to white and green light that increased the detection of pain thresholds for warm stimulus. However, the effects remain small.

© Springer International Publishing Switzerland 2016
F. Bello et al. (Eds.): EuroHaptics 2016, Part I, LNCS 9774, pp. 273–280, 2016.
DOI: 10.1007/978-3-319-42321-0_25

Because of the divergent results with old studies showing no effect and more recent ones showing an effect of the HHH, we took a different approach by focusing on a meticulous synchronization between color and temperature. In this study, we tested the HHH using an experimental apparatus [14–16] that allows precise spatial and temporal congruencies. Based on multisensory integration principles, the integration is more likely or stronger if the two stimuli are closer in time and space [17]. Our hypothesis is that under color-temperature congruent conditions participants would have shorter contact times compared to incongruent trials. We also expected that participants' rating for cold stimuli would increase when paired with a red color cue and would decrease for hot stimuli paired with a blue color cue.

2 Experiment

Participants. Fourteen (11 females and 3 males) Northern Michigan University students, aged between 18 and 27 (Mean 19.5, SD 2.28), took part in this experiment and received a course credit for their participation. Participants were screened through a short non-invasive questionnaire for any known abnormalities in tactile or thermal sensory systems. They all reported that they were not suffering from any temperature altering illness or skin disorder. Participants were all right-handed and gave their informed consent upon participation. This research was approved by the Institutional Review Board.

Apparatus and Stimuli. The stimulus consisted of touching a steel cup that was either warm or cold while displaying a virtual hand touching a vessel that was either blue or red. The virtual environment was created using the UNITY game engine that was connected to the Oculus Rift SDK1, a head-mounted display (HMD) that has a 7-inch screen. Mounted to the Oculus Rift, a CREATIVE interactive gesture camera was used to track participants' hand movements, using the iisu middleware, a platform for tracking gestures. Hand movements were synchronized with the movements of the virtual hand in the UNITY environment. The interactive camera was attached to the Oculus using a holder (Fig. 1) printed on a 3D printer (MakerBot® Replicator™ 2X).

Two Winco stainless steel bar shakers (cups) were utilized to present thermal stimuli to the participants' hand. The thermal properties of stainless steel allow for a larger heat flux out of skin contact than other materials [18]. Thermal stimuli were maintained at a mean of 17°C, SD = .24°C for the cold cup and a mean 36.9°C, SD = .8°C for the warm cup. To ensure that this study measured temperature perception and not pain perception, temperatures were kept in the non-noxious stimulus range, above 16.6°C for painful cold stimuli and below 42.1°C for painful heat stimuli [19]. The cups were put on a support that delivered either cold or warm temperatures. The cold temperature was controlled by a 12 V Peltier thermo-electric cooler mounted to a heatsink and 12 V fan. The warm temperature was controlled by an electric heating pad 10 cm × 5 cm, powered by a 5VDC. The temperature of each cup was recorded by a TMP-36 temperature sensor, which provided an accuracy of ± 2°C for temperatures between −40°C and +125°C. The contact duration, i.e. grasp duration, was measured by using an

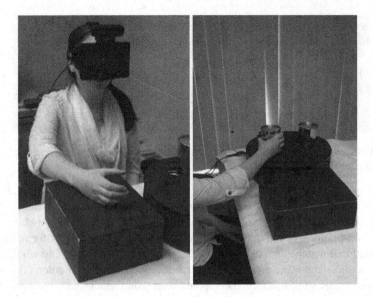

Fig. 1. Participant with her right hand: left: on the resting box; right: reaching for one of the temperature-controlled steel cups.

Infrared Proximity Sensor (Short Range - Sharp GP2Y0A41SK0F) that was attached at the exterior bottom of each cup and was controlled by an Arduino board.

The support consisted of a custom-made noise-free rotating device to conceal all modes of thermal cooling or heating and to present one cup at a time. Because we are manipulating temperature, this method allowed changing the cups quickly without the participants' knowledge, as they were wearing the HMD and therefore were only perceiving the virtual world. The experiment was carried out in a quiet room under normal lighting and temperature conditions.

Procedure. Participants were asked to wash their hands before entering the testing room. They answered a short non-invasive health questionnaire about any peripheral vascular diseases or illnesses that may interfere with temperature perception. A Veridian Healthcare digital thermometer (Model 08-350) with protective probe covers, were used to measure the oral temperature of each participant. The participant's initial oral temperatures ranged from 33.3°C to 37.0°C (Mean 35.6, SD 1.1). Palm temperature was assessed using the Fluke 62 Max+ an infrared thermometer ranged from 26.4°C to 35.7°C (Mean 33.2, SD 2.46). During the first set of twenty-four trials (training phase) skin temperature ranged between 26.2°C and 36.8°C (Mean 33.8, SD 2.4). During the second set of forty-eight trials (test phase) skin temperature ranged between 26.5°C and 36.6°C (Mean 33.9, SD 2.1). Room temperature was maintained at approximately 22.4° C for the entirety of the experiment.

Participants' were then seated at a table with the rotating device, cups and thermo-components covered from sight. Before starting the experiment, participants were introduced to the apparatus and were instructed to practice grasping the cup with their right full hand to insure an accurate contact time recording. Once participants

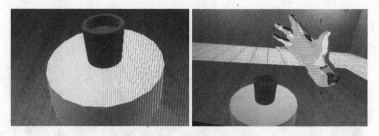

Fig. 2. Virtual environment: left: red cup on a rotating platform; right: real-time tracked hand reaching for a blue cup in the virtual world

were confident with grasping instructions, the HMD was fitted to their head to accustom to the virtual environment that consisted of a room containing a chair, a table with a round platform, a red or blue cup that would appear on the platform, and their virtual hand that matches the movements of their real hand (Fig. 2). The whole system creates a spatio-temporal congruent/incongruent feedback between color (virtual) and temperature (real) stimuli. Once participants were comfortable with the virtual hand grasp, the experiment began. They were instructed to place their right-hand on the provided resting box situated to the right of the rotating table (that was hidden from their view), while the left hand was placed below the real table (see Fig. 1).

Training Phase. For the training, participants were informed that a red cup in the virtual environment indicates a warm cup in the real environment and a blue cup in the virtual environment indicates a cold cup in the real environment. Once either a red or blue cup appeared, participants grasped the cup, assessed the temperature by giving a numerical rating of 1–5 (with 1-cold, 2-cool, 3-neurtral or room temperature, 4-warm and 5-hot), released the cup and returned their hand to the resting box. This was repeated twenty-four times, counterbalanced across trials and participants, with a 30 s pause between each trial. Contact times and cup temperature were recorded for each grasp and palm temperature was reassessed after each grasp. After the forth and twelfth trials, participants were asked whether the thermal stimuli were painful or uncomfortable. After all twenty-four trials were completed, the rotating temperature device was hidden from view, and the HMD was removed.

Test Phase. Participants were given a 10 min break before starting the test phase. This phase included four stimuli combination in total (congruent red/cold, blue/warm and incongruent blue/warm, and red/cold, see Fig. 3). Participants were not informed of these combinations. After wearing the HMD, participants had to grasp either a virtual red or blue cup and at the same time grasp the real steel cup, assessed the temperature by giving a numerical rating of 1–5, released the cup, and returned their hand to the resting box. This was repeated randomly forty-eight times using a counterbalanced ABC-CBA scheme (12 trials of each pattern), with a 30 s pause between each trial in which the experimenter recorded palm temperature. Contact times and cup temperature were recorded for each cup grasp. We asked the participants whether the thermal stimuli were painful or uncomfortable after the forth trial and the twenty-forth trial. Once the trials had been completed the rotating temperature device was hidden from

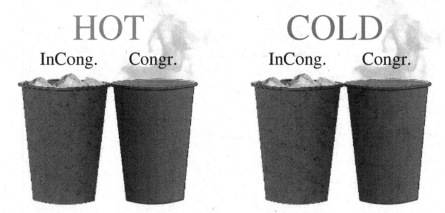

Fig. 3. Congruent (Co.) and Incongruent (InCo.) conditions for each temperature (hot and cold).

view and the HMD was removed. The participants then filled out a short questionnaire asking about their perception of the temperature experience.

3 Results

Data Analysis. A two way repeated measure ANOVA was used to assess the effect of temperature (cold, hot) and color (blue, red) on participant's contact time (CT) and temperature ratings. According to whether contact times were significant or not, we conducted simple pairwise comparison using one-way ANOVA on each subset of the data. Only significant effects ($p < .05$) are reported.

Contact Duration. There was a significant interaction between the two factors temperature and color [$F(1,13) = 23.50$, $p < .001$]. To break down this interaction, we conducted simple effect tests using one-way ANOVA. Cold-blue and cold-red conditions were significantly different [$F(1,13) = 32.75$, $p < .001$]. Hot-blue and hot-red conditions were also significantly different [$F(1,13) = 9.7$, $p < .008$]. Figure 4 shows that participants hold the cup longer for incongruent trials, i.e. cold temperatures when associated with red and hot temperatures when blue was presented. This suggests two possible explanations: (1) when conflict arises between color and temperature, participants' require longer time for processing the information; (2) they actually perceived the temperature as being less cold/hot when color stimulus was incongruent. We also explored which one of the two temperatures creates a larger effect. A paired t-test revealed ($t = 2.04$, $p < 0.05$) that this temperature bias is higher for cold temperatures when associated with red than hot temperatures when associated with blue.

Participants' Ratings. Using participants' rating as a dependent variable we conducted a repeated measures ANOVA with color cue (blue/red) and temperature of cup

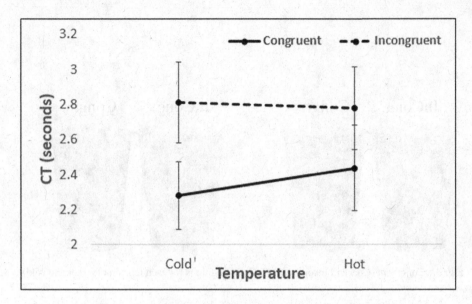

Fig. 4. Average CTs and error bars for congruent and incongruent conditions.

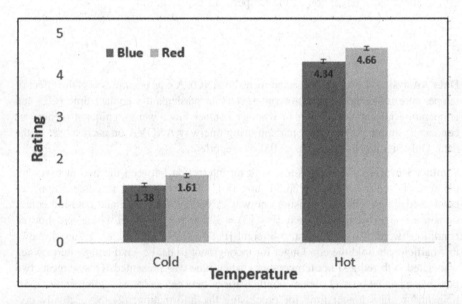

Fig. 5. Participants' ratings for congruent (cold-blue, hot-red) and incongruent (cold-red, hot-blue) stimuli.

(cold/hot) as factors. There was a significant effect of the main factors temperature [$F(1,167) = 2586.96$, $p < .001$] and color [$F = (1,167) 61.25 p < .001$]. This result is not surprising and as shown is Fig. 5, participants' ratings were significantly higher for cold temperatures when red was presented and were significantly lower for hot temperatures when associated with blue. Participants' ratings support the second explanation, i.e. that the perceived temperature is biased by the color stimulus.

4 Discussion and Conclusion

Results revealed that congruent presentation of stimuli is associated with shorter CTs than incongruent stimuli. Our results corroborate previous findings by Ho et al. [13] that indicated that red-warm and blue-cold congruency influences participants' response speed. Other recent studies showed also similar results [11, 12] for temperature and pain perception. It also seems that colder temperatures, when associated with red, have a larger effect than hot temperatures associated with blue. This finding in itself is interesting as it could suggest: (1) heat is more resistant to color effects than cold, or (2) red is more deceptive than blue. That said, both temperature-color showed a significant effect and the interesting question is why very early studies showed no or insignificant effect of HHH? This can be explained by the fact that previous studies used colorful ambient lights to assess object or room temperatures as opposed to most recent studies that used patch of color or virtual reality with control over stimuli synchronization, temperature accuracy, and hue-heat congruency. The only recent study that used ambient light reported very small effects and were not significant for all colors (for instance cold perception was not affected by color) [11]. This aspect was probably accentuated by the fact that first HHH experiments tested only heat that is, according to our results, more resistant to color effects and could have contributed to the absence of interaction. The results of our study showed an interaction effect of CTs when participants were required to discriminate a thermal stimulus presented with a color stimulus, which could suggest a slight domination of color over temperature when a conflict arises [13]. Participants' ratings confirmed the notion that color has an effect on temperature perception, with cold stimuli rated warmer when paired with a red color cue and a warm stimulus rated cooler when paired with a blue color cue. Finally, some incongruent temperature-color associations (cold-red) have stronger effect that other incongruent associations (hot-blue). In the future, we would like to add additional stimuli such as neutral temperatures (32° C) and color (i.e., white) to extend the findings to other color and temperature ranges.

References

1. Ziat, M., Gapenne, O., Rouze, M.O., Delwarde, A.: Recognition of different scales by using a haptic sensory substitution device. In: Proceeding of the 6th International Conference EuroHaptics 2006 (2006)
2. Ziat, M., Lenay, C., Gapenne, O., Stewart, J., Ammar, A.A.B., Aubert, D.: Perceptive supplementation for an access to graphical interfaces. In: Stephanidis, C. (ed.) HCI 2007. LNCS, vol. 4554, pp. 841–850. Springer, Heidelberg (2007)
3. Ziat, M., Gapenne, O., Stewart, J., Lenay, C.: A comparison of two methods of scaling on form perception via a haptic interface. In: Proceedings of the 7th International Conference on Multimodal Interfaces, pp. 236–243 (2005)

4. Kennett, S., Eimer, M., Spence, C., Driver, J.: Tactile-visual links in exogenous spatial attention under different postures: convergent evidence from psychophysics and ERPs. Cogn. Neurosci. J. **13**(4), 462–478 (2001)
5. Ziat, M., Savord, A., Frissen, I.: The effect of visual, haptic, and auditory signals perceived from rumble strips during inclement weather. In: IEEE World Haptics Conference (WHC) 2015, pp. 351–355 (2015)
6. Mogensen, M.F., English, H.B.: The apparent warmth of colors. Am. J. Psychol. **37**, 427–428 (1926)
7. Berry, P.C.: Effect of colored illumination upon perceived temperature. J. Appl. Psychol. **45**(4), 248 (1961)
8. Bennett, C.A., Rey, P.: What's so hot about red? Hum. Factors J. Hum. Factors Ergon. Soc. **14**(2), 149–154 (1972)
9. Fanger, P.O., Breum, N.O., Jerking, E.: Can colour and noise influence man's thermal comfort? Ergonomics **20**(1), 11–18 (1977)
10. Moseley, G.L., Arntz, A.: The context of a noxious stimulus affects the pain it evokes. Pain **133**(1), 64–71 (2007)
11. Landgrebe, M., Nyuyki, K., Frank, E., Steffens, T., Hauser, S., Eichhammer, P., Hajak, G., Langguth, B.: Effects of colour exposure on auditory and somatosensory perception–hints for cross-modal plasticity. Neuroendocrinol. Lett. **29**(4), 518 (2008)
12. Michael, G.A., Galich, H., Relland, S., Prud'hon, S.: Hot colors: the nature and specificity of color-induced nasal thermal sensations. Behav. Brain Res. **207**(2), 418–428 (2010)
13. Ho, H.N., Van Doorn, G.H., Kawabe, T., Watanabe, J., Spence, C.: Colour-temperature correspondences: when reactions to thermal stimuli are influenced by colour. PLoS ONE **9**(3), e91854 (2014)
14. Balcer, C.A., Schirtz, A., Rolison, T., Ziat, M.: Is seeing warm, feeling warm? In: IEEE Haptics Symposium 2014, Houston, TX (2014)
15. Balcer, C., Shirtz, A., Rolison, T., Ziat, M: Visual cues effects on temperature perception. In: Psychonomic Society Meeting, Long Beach, CA (2014)
16. Ziat, M., Rolison, T., Shirtz, A., Wilbern, D., Balcer, C.A.: Enhancing virtual immersion through tactile feedback. In: Proceedings of the Adjunct Publication of the 27th Annual ACM Symposium on User Interface Software and Technology, pp. 65–66 (2014)
17. Calvert, G., Spence, C., Stein, B.E.: The Handbook of Multisensory Processes. MIT Press, Cambridge (2004)
18. Galie, J., Jones, L.: Thermal cues and the perception of force. Exp. Brain Res. **200**(1), 81–90 (2010)
19. Kuhtz-Buschbeck, J.P., Andresen, W., Gobel, S., Gilster, R., Stick, C.: Thermoreception and nociception of the skin: a classic paper of Bessou and Perl and analyses of thermal sensitivity during a student laboratory exercise. Adv. Physiol. Educ. **34**, 25–34 (2010)

Influence of Object Material Properties and Geometry on Skin Temperature Responses During Contact

Hsin-Ni Ho[✉]

NTT Communication Science Laboratories,
Nippon Telegraph and Telephone Corporation, 3-1 Morinosato Wakamiya,
Atsugi, Kanagawa 243-0198, Japan
ho.hsinni@lab.ntt.co.jp

Abstract. When the hand makes contact with an object, the changes in skin temperature provide information about not only the object's material composition but also its geometry. Consider, for example, the temperature difference felt when touching an aluminum block and a piece of aluminum foil. To study the thermal cues associated with material properties and object thickness, we measured the changes in skin temperature elicited when touching objects with varying material properties and geometries, and compared them to the theoretical predictions obtained from two thermal models, of which one assumes the object having an infinite thickness and the other takes into consideration the actual object thickness. The comparison results indicate that the former model is effective in capturing the rapid temperature changes at the moment of contact and the latter model is better at predicting the total change in skin temperature at the end of contact. These findings provide a knowledge basis for the development of thermal displays for material simulation and automatic object identification systems that identify an object's material composition and thickness based on thermal feedback.

Keywords: Object identification · Hand-object interactions · Thermal modeling · Thermal displays

1 Introduction

Thermal cues that are used to assist in identifying an object arise from changes in skin temperature during hand-object interactions. They provide information about the object's temperature and material properties and are important when the object must be identified with ambiguous or absent visual information. Accordingly, integrating thermal feedback into haptic interfaces has been gaining interest, because such an interface is expected to create a more realistic image of an object and to facilitate object recognition in virtual environments and teleoperated robotic systems [1].

The resting temperature of the skin is generally higher than the temperature of the objects encountered in the environment [2], so upon touching an object the skin temperature decreases and typically takes a form similar to an exponential decay [3], with a rapid temperature drop at the moment of contact and approaching an asymptote as time

© Springer International Publishing Switzerland 2016
F. Bello et al. (Eds.): EuroHaptics 2016, Part I, LNCS 9774, pp. 281–290, 2016.
DOI: 10.1007/978-3-319-42321-0_26

increases. The changes in skin temperature have been shown to depend on the thermal properties of the object [3–5]. Objects that have higher thermal conductivities and heat capacities in general elicit higher initial rates of change and lower end temperatures as compared to those that are small in those properties. This explains why a metallic object feels colder than a wooden object of the same physical temperature. Besides the thermal properties of the object, the changes in skin temperature also provide information about the object's geometry. It has been shown that people were able to discriminate between stimuli of different thickness based on thermal cues. Thicker objects were found to feel colder than thin objects [6, 7]. These findings indicate that thermal cues could assist in the identification of an object's material composition and geometry.

While a number of studies have investigated the influence of material properties on skin temperature responses upon contact (for review see [1]), there are few studies focus on the influence from object geometry. To study the thermal cues associated with material properties and object thickness, we measured the changes in skin temperature elicited by touching objects with varying materials and geometries and compared them to the theoretical predictions obtained from two thermal models. One is the classical Semi-R model proposed by Ho and Jones [8, 9], which assumes the object in contact is a semi-infinite body (i.e. the object has an infinite thickness) and the other is the LC model, which is newly developed in the present study and takes into consideration the actual object geometry. The comparison results are expected to give insight into the thermal cues for object identification and to provide a knowledge basis for the development of thermal displays for material simulation and automatic object identification systems that can be used in teleoperated robotic systems to identify the material and the geometry of an object based on thermal feedback.

2 Skin Temperature Response Measurement

2.1 Methods

Participants. Seven normal healthy adults (two men) aged between 23 and 44 years participated in this experiment. There were no calluses on their right index fingerpads. The experiment was approved by the local ethics committee.

Apparatus. A thermistor (457 µm in diameter and 3.18 mm in length; 56A1002-C8, Alpha Technics, CA, USA) was attached to the center of the right index fingerpad to measure the changes in skin temperature at a sampling rate of 30 Hz. The thermistor was chosen for its small size and rapid response. It was connected to a data acquisition unit (AIO-160802AY-USB, Contec Co., Osaka, Japan). A program written in VB.NET was used to control the measurement and log the temperature data.

Four materials that covered a broad range of thermal properties were selected: Aluminum, glass, plastic (acrylic), and foam. Their thermal properties are listed in Table 1. For each material, samples with a width of 80 mm, a length of 80 mm and a thickness of 1 mm, 3 mm, 10 mm and 100 mm were prepared, which gave 16 material samples in total. The 80 mm × 80 mm surfaces of the samples (except foam) were polished to provide a flat, smooth contact surface. Their surface roughness was

Table 1. Thermal and surface properties of the material samples

Material	Aluminum	Glass	Acrylic	Foam	Skin
Thermal conductivity k (W/mK)	237	1.4	0.2	0.2	0.37
Heat capacity ρc (J/m^{3}K)	$1.9*10^6$	$1.6*10^6$	$1.7*10^6$	$0.2*10^6$	$3.7*10^6$
Contact coefficient $(k\rho c)^{1/2}$ (J/m^{2}s$^{1/2}$K)	$24*10^3$	$1.5*10^3$	$0.6*10^3$	$0.2*10^3$	$1.2*10^3$
RMS roughness Rq (μm)	0.27	1.68	0.03	12.13	21.69

measured with a surface roughness tester (SJ-400, Mitutoyo Co., Kanagawa, Japan) and the values are listed in Table 1. The samples were stored at a room temperature of 25 °C and the initial skin temperature of the right hand was maintained at 34 °C with a commercial hotplate (Yagami Inc., Nagoya, Japan).

Procedure. The 16 material samples were presented to the participants in a randomized order. At the beginning of the experiment, a thermistor was attached to the center of the right index fingerpad with a thin thread. The participants then placed their hand on the hotplate to adapt their skin temperature to 34 °C for 3 min. The temperature measurement for each sample began with the participants placing their right hand on the hotplate. Upon hearing a sound cue, the participants moved their right hand from the hotplate to a preparation position, which was 3 cm above the material sample. 15 s after the first sound cue, a second sound cue was presented and the participants made contact with the material sample with the right index fingerpad for 20 s. At the end of the contact, another sound cue was presented, and the participants returned their hand to the hotplate to await the start of the next measurement. The intertrial interval was around 60 s. Note that the 15 s spent in the preparation position was included to ensure that the skin temperature was stabilized before making contact with the sample and that the 60 s intertrial interval was chosen to ensure that the skin temperature was stabilized at the adapting temperature of 34 °C before the next measurement started.

2.2   Results and Discussion

The average skin temperature responses recorded during 20 s of contact as a function of material and sample thickness are shown in Fig. 1(a). The data indicate that both material and sample thickness had an effect on the changes in skin temperature during contact. Materials with high contact coefficients, such as metal and glass, elicited larger total change in skin temperature as compared to those with low contact coefficients, such as plastic and foam (see Fig. 1(c)). The sample thickness affected both the initial rate of temperature change and the total change in skin temperature. In general, thick samples tended to elicit higher initial rate of temperature change and larger total change in skin temperature as compared to thin samples (see Fig. 1(b), (c)).

Depending on the material and the thickness of the sample, there are three possible responses in the late phase of contact. In general, for samples that have high contact coefficients, such as aluminum and glass, the skin temperature tended to continue decreasing at a lower rate or approach an asymptote as time increases. On the other hand, for samples that are very thin (e.g. 1 mm) or have low contact coefficients, such

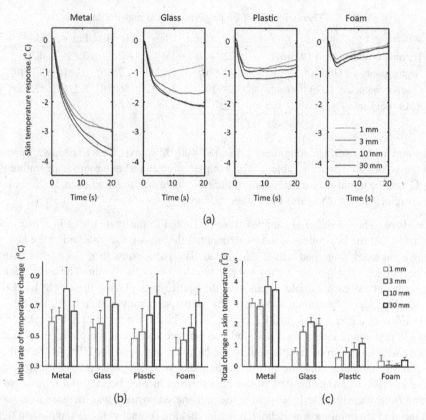

Fig. 1. Average skin temperature responses during 20 s of contact (a), the group mean ($\pm$ SEM) initial rate of temperature change (b) and the total change in skin temperature (c) are shown as a function of material and sample thickness. (Color figure online)

as plastic or foam, the skin temperature tended to start to increase again after it reached its lowest level, resulting in a V-shaped temporal profile.

The V-shaped temporal profile reflects that a sample was heated up during contact. The whole process can be considered as a point contact heat source, i.e. the finger, is brought into contact with an object. During contact, the heat was transferred from the finger to the sample. The heat accumulated in the sample and caused the sample temperature to elevate as time increased. At some point, the temperature of the sample at the contact interface would exceed that of the finger and caused the skin temperature to increase again. For materials that have low contact coefficients (e.g. foam), the heat accumulation would be limited to the region near the contact interface and therefore the V-shaped temperature responses of foam were similar among the 4 thickness used even they spanned a 30-fold range. As for materials that have high contact coefficients (e.g. metal), they require much more energy and therefore much more time for the heat up effect to reflect on the skin temperature responses and therefore the V-shaped temperature responses were not observed within 20 s of contact.

Besides material properties and sample thickness, surface roughness of the object has also been suggested to influence on the skin temperature responses through thermal contact resistance [8]. Among the materials used in the present study, foam had a surface roughness that is 1-2 order higher than those of the other materials. However, its skin temperature response was not dramatically different from that of plastic. This is because the thermal contact resistance is a function of the effective surface roughness, $(R_{q,skin}^2 + R_{q,object}^2)^{0.5}$. Given that the R_q of the skin is higher than those of the materials (see Table 1), the effective surface roughness is in fact not so different among these 4 materials. Under such condition, the thermal conductivity of the object becomes the major determinant of the thermal contact resistance and materials with similar thermal conductivity would result in similar skin temperature responses.

In sum, the temperature data measured in the present study indicate a strong dependence of the skin temperature responses on both material properties and object thickness. This finding combined with the previous finding that people are able to discriminate between different thickness based on subjective coldness [7] suggest that the thermal sense, unlike vision, could penetrate solid objects and retrieve thickness information. This points out the potential of automatic object identification based on thermal feedback.

3   Comparison to Theoretical Predictions

To have further insight into the influence of material and object geometry on the skin temperature responses during hand-object interactions, the temperature data were compared to the theoretical predictions obtained from two thermal models. One is the classical Semi-R model proposed by Ho and Jones [8, 9], which assumes the object in contact is a semi-infinite body (i.e. the object has an infinite thickness). The other is the LC model, which is newly developed in the present study and takes into consideration the actual object thickness.

3.1   The Lumped Capacitance (LC) Model

While the thermal cues associated with material properties have been modeled in numerous studies [1], few studies have studied the thermal cues associated with object geometry. One exception is a numerical model that predicts the influence of object geometry on the heat transfer rate during contact, with the assumption that the finger temperature is constant during contact [6]. As the aim of this study is to characterize the thermal cues in terms of skin temperature changes, a new model was developed to allow the estimation of skin temperature responses at various skin depth. In this model, the object is assumed to be a lumped system, that is, the temperature of the object is spatially uniform at any instant during the process and the skin is modeled as a semi-infinite body whose temperature variation is only significant in the direction perpendicular to the contact surface [10]. The schematic representation of this model is shown in Fig. 2 and the governing equations of the skin and object are:

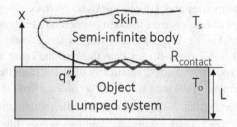

Fig. 2. Schematic representation of the lumped capacitance (LC) model

$$\frac{\partial^2 T_s}{\partial x^2} = \frac{1}{\alpha_s}\frac{\partial T_s}{\partial t}, \quad \left\{ \begin{array}{l} t = 0, \ T_s = T_{s,i} \\ x = \infty, \ T_s = T_{s,i} \end{array} \right\} \tag{1}$$

$$(\rho c)_o L \frac{dT_o}{dt} = -k_s \frac{dT_s}{dx}\bigg|_{x=o,} \quad \{ t = 0, \ T_o = T_{o,i} \} \tag{2}$$

The boundary condition at the interface is given by:

$$q''(t) = \frac{T_s(x = 0, t) - T_o(t)}{R_{contact}} \tag{3}$$

Where T is temperature (°C), α is thermal diffusivity (m²/s), x is the skin depth (m), with $x = 0$ indicating the skin surface, t is time (s), ρc is heat capacity (J/m³K), k is thermal conductivity (W/mK), L is the thickness of the object in contact (m), q'' is the heat flux exchanged during contact (W/m²), and $R_{contact}$ is the thermal contact resistance (m²K/W). Subscripts s, o, and i represent the skin, object and initial conditions, respectively.

The thermal contact resistance depends on a number of variables that are related to the contact force and the thermal and surface properties of the surfaces in contact. For details please refer to [8, 9]. By determining and the initial temperatures of the skin $T_{s,i}$ and object $T_{o,i}$, the temperature response of the skin during contact, T_s, can be solved as a function of t and x:

$$T_s(x,t) = \frac{A}{(b-a)} \left\{ \begin{array}{l} \alpha_s e^{-bx + \alpha_s \cdot (-b)^2 \cdot t} \cdot \mathrm{erfc}\left(\frac{x}{2(\alpha_s t)^{\frac{1}{2}}} - b \cdot (\alpha_s t)^{\frac{1}{2}}\right) \\ \\ -\alpha_s e^{-ax + \alpha_s \cdot (-a)^2 \cdot t} \cdot \mathrm{erfc}\left(\frac{x}{2(\alpha_s t)^{\frac{1}{2}}} - a \cdot (\alpha_s t)^{\frac{1}{2}}\right) \end{array} \right\} + T_{s,i}$$

$$A = \frac{(T_{o,i} - T_{s,i})}{R_{contact} k_s \alpha_s}, \ a = \frac{-\beta + \sqrt{\beta^2 - 4\lambda}}{2}, \ b = \frac{-\beta - \sqrt{\beta^2 - 4\lambda}}{2}, \tag{4}$$

$$\beta = \frac{1}{R_{contact} k_s}, \ \lambda = \frac{1}{\alpha_s R_{contact} L (\rho c)_o},$$

The Biot number, *Bi*, can be used to check whether an object is valid for the lumped system assumption and in turn whether it can be well-predicted by the LC model. The Biot number provides a measure of the temperature difference within the object relative to the temperature difference at the skin-object interface and can be defined as:

$$\text{Bi} = \frac{R_{int}}{R_{ext}} = \frac{L/2k_o}{R_{contact}} \tag{5}$$

where R_{ext} is the thermal contact resistance and R_{int} is the internal thermal resistance of the object and can be approximated as $L/2k_o$. Here L is the thickness and k_o is the thermal conductivity of the object. A small Biot number (i.e. Bi < 0.1) indicates that the temperature difference within the object is negligible and therefore the lumped system assumption is valid [11]. Thus, objects that are very thin or made from materials with high thermal conductivities (e.g. metal) are generally valid for this assumption. For situations in which *Bi* > 1, since the lumped system assumption is not valid, the model will not be able to describe the skin temperature responses well.

3.2   Results and Discussion

Previous studies have shown that a thermal sensor's thermal mass and the extra thermal contact resistance introduced at the skin-sensor and sensor-object interfaces may result in their insensitivity to the instantaneous change in skin temperature and so they are unable to capture the full extent of the temperature change during contact [12]. As the temperature data obtained in the present study were measured under this inevitable limitation, the influence from the thermal sensor was taken into account by modeling it as a part of the skin, so the predictions of the skin temperature response at $x = 0.4$ mm, which corresponds to the size of the sensor used in this study, were used to compared with the temperature responses measured by the thermal sensor. In addition, the extra thermal contact resistance introduced by the sensor was modeled by doubling the thermal contact resistance.

The comparisons between the temperature data and the theoretical predictions from the Semi-R model and the LC model are shown in Fig. 3. These theoretical predictions were calculated based on the thermal and surface properties listed in Table 1. As previous studies indicate that initial rate of temperature change, dT/dt, and total change in temperature, ΔT, are important thermal cues for material discrimination [3], the performance of the models were evaluated with prediction errors of the total change in skin temperature during 20 s of contact, defined as $|\Delta T_{data} - \Delta T_{model}|$ and the initial rate of temperature change, defined as $|dT/dt_{data} - dT/dt_{model}|$. As shown in Fig. 3(b), in general the Semi-R model was better at predicting initial rate of temperature change while the LC model gave better predictions for the total change in skin temperature.

For the material-thickness combinations whose Bi < 0.1, the LC model gave good predications for both the total change in skin temperature and the initial rate of temperature change (solid bars in Fig. 3(b)). However, for material-thickness combinations, whose Biot numbers are larger than 1, the skin temperature responses were not well described by both models. The LC model tended to predict a gradual decrease in

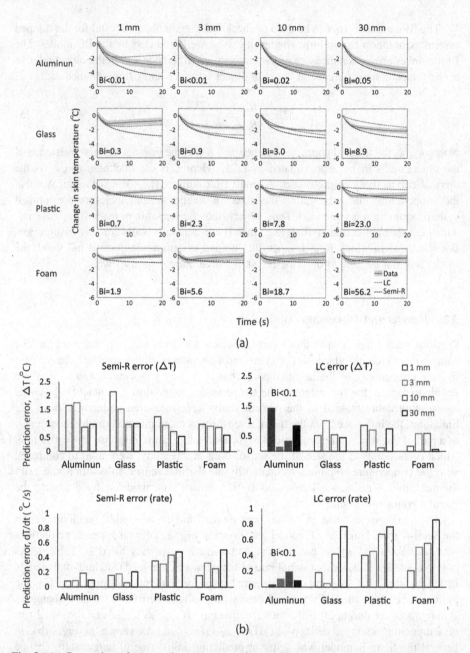

Fig. 3. (a) Comparisons between the temperature data (red line) and theoretical predictions from the Semi-R model (black dashed line) and the LC model (green dashed line). The shaded area represents the standard error of mean. The Biot number of each material-thickness combination is noted. (b) Prediction errors of total change in skin temperature and the initial rate of temperature change for Semi-R model and LC model are shown as a function of material and sample thickness. The solid bars indicate material-thickness combinations that have Bi < 0.1. (Color figure online)

the skin temperature throughout the contact period, so the prediction error of the initial rate of change was large. On the other hand, although the Semi-R model was better at capturing the initial rate of temperature change, it either overestimated the total change or did not predict the V-shaped temperature responses. Therefore, further improvement of the LC model is required to cover broader range of material properties.

Previous psychophysical studies have shown that human used both initial rate of temperature change and total change in skin temperature for material discrimination [3]. Although the initial rate of change seems to be the most important cue, the total change in skin temperature also contains information of material properties and object thickness. These findings suggest that for applications that aim to present the thermal image or recognize the material properties of an object during brief, incidental contact, the Semi-R model would be sufficient for the purpose. However, for applications that involve prolong contact and intend to provide/retrieve thickness information, the LC model would be useful for thin objects or objects made from materials with high thermal conductivity. However, further improvement of the LC model is required if the applications involve objects with broader range of material properties.

4   Conclusion

The present study measured and analyzed the empirical data of skin temperature responses elicited when touching objects of various material composition and thickness. The temperature data indicate a strong dependence of the skin temperature responses on both material properties and object thickness and point out the potential of presenting and retrieving an object's material composition and thickness based on thermal feedback. The comparison between the temperature data and the theoretical predictions indicate that the thermal models can predict the thermal cues used for material identification, with the classic Semi-R model being effective in predicting the rapid temperature changes at the moment of contact and the LC model having better performance in predicting the total change in skin temperature. These findings provide a knowledge basis for the development of thermal displays for material simulation and automatic object identification systems that can identify the material and the geometry of an object based on thermal feedback.

Acknowledgements. The author would like to thank Dr. Junji Watanabe and Dr. Warrick Roseboom for their valuable comments on the manuscript. This research was supported by Grants-in-Aid for Scientific Research on Innovative Areas (15H05915) from the Japanese Ministry of Education, Culture, Sports, Science, and Technology.

References

1. Jones, L.A., Ho, H.-N.: Warm or cool, large or small? The challenge of thermal displays. IEEE Trans. Haptics **1**, 53–70 (2008)
2. Verrillo, R.T., Bolanowski, S.J., Checkosky, C.M., McGlone, F.P.: Effects of hydration on tactile sensation. Somatosens. Mot. Res. **15**, 93–108 (1998)

3. Bergmann Tiest, W.M., Kappers, A.M.L.: Tactile perception of thermal diffusivity. Attention Percept. Psychophysics **71**, 481–489 (2009)
4. Ho, H.-N., Jones, L.A.: Contribution of thermal cues to material discrimination and localization. Percept. Psychophys. **68**, 118–128 (2006)
5. Jones, L.A., Berris, M.: Material discrimination and thermal perception. In: Proceedings of the 11th International Symposium on Haptic Interfaces for Virtual Environment and Teleoperator Systems, pp. 171–178 (2003)
6. Bergmann Tiest, W.M.: An experimentally verified model of the perceived 'Coldness' of Objects. In: Proceedings of World Haptics Conference 2007, pp. 61–65 (2007)
7. Bergmann Tiest, W.M., Kappers, A.M.L.: Thermosensory reversal effect quantified. Acta Psychologica **127**, 46–50 (2008)
8. Ho, H.-N., Jones, L.A.: Thermal model for hand-object interactions. In: Proceedings of the IEEE Symposium on Haptic Interfaces for Virtual Environment and Teleoperator Systems, pp. 461–467 (2006)
9. Ho, H.-N., Jones, L.A.: Modeling the thermal responses of the skin surface during hand-object interactions. J. Biomech. Eng. **130**, 21005-1–21005-8 (2008)
10. Sarda, A., Deterre, R., Vergneault, C.: Heat perception measurements of the different parts found in a car passenger compartment. Measurement **35**, 65–75 (2004)
11. Incropera, F.P., DeWitt, D.P.: Fundamentals of Heat and Mass Transfer. Wiley, New York (1996)
12. Ho, H.-N., Jones, L.A.: Infrared thermal measurement system for evaluating model-based thermal displays. In: Proceedings of World Haptics Conference, pp. 157–162 (2007)

Space-Time Dependencies and Thermal Perception

Anshul Singhal and Lynette Jones[(✉)]

Department of Mechanical Engineering, Massachusetts Institute of Technology,
Cambridge, MA 02139, USA
{anshuls,ljones}@mit.edu

Abstract. This experiment was focused on determining whether the spatial representation of thermal stimuli is influenced by the temporal parameters of stimulation as has been demonstrated for tactile stimuli. Four warm thermal pulses within the innocuous range of temperatures were presented on the forearm in varying spatial and temporal sequences. Participants indicated the perceived location of the first two pulses in the four-pulse sequence after each trial. The results indicate that the perceived position of the second pulse changed substantially in the direction of the third pulse when the interval between the pulses was brief (0.2 s). At longer intervals there was no change in perceived location. These results indicate that despite the limitations in the spatial and temporal processing of thermal stimuli, somatotopic information appears to be integrated similarly for tactile and thermal stimuli.

1 Introduction

Perceptual illusions have often been studied to reveal the mechanisms involved in perceiving the external environment and to understand the conditions under which discrepancies emerge between a physical stimulus and its corresponding percept. Much of the research on perceptual illusions has focused on vision, although tactile and haptic illusions have been of interest to those involved in the design of haptic displays [1, 2] For these devices it has been shown that by selecting particular spatial and temporal sequences of motor activation it is possible to create a display with a higher perceived spatial resolution than is implied by the number of actuators actually present [3, 4]. Haptic illusions have also been used to evaluate the degree of realism in virtual environments by measuring the strength of an illusion in the real and simulated environment [5].

A number of tactile illusions involve distortions in the spatial representation of tactile stimuli applied to the skin, such as the perceived location of the stimulus or the perceived distance between points of stimulation. Such illusions typically result from interactions between the temporal and spatial properties of the stimuli and show how the spatial representation of stimuli on the skin critically depends on the temporal properties of stimulation. One of the classic demonstrations of these effects involves presenting three equally spaced tactile stimuli successively on the skin of the forearm

F. Bello et al. (Eds.): EuroHaptics 2016, Part I, LNCS 9774, pp. 291–302, 2016.
DOI: 10.1007/978-3-319-42321-0_27

and asking subjects to judge whether the distance between the first and second stimulus is equal to, or shorter or longer than the distance between the second and third stimulus. Subjects overwhelmingly judge the distance to be shorter when the temporal interval between the first and second stimulus is brief (250 ms) and longer with greater temporal intervals (500 ms). This illusion which demonstrates the dependence of space on time in estimations of tactile space is known as the tau effect and has also been shown to occur in vision and audition [6]. It is often not observed at very short time intervals, but it can occur tactually when there are long delays (1500 ms) between the two pairs of comparison stimuli. It has been suggested that the ratio between the two temporal intervals should not be greater than 3 to 4 to 1 for the illusion to occur [7].

In contrast to the considerable research on tactile spatial illusions, there have been relatively few reports of spatio-temporal illusions involving the thermal sensory system. A serendipitous observation was reported by Rózsa and Kenshalo [8] during their experiments on spatial summation of cooling pulses delivered to each forearm. They noted that when there was a delay of about 250 ms between the onsets of the temperature change in the two arms, subjects reported that a cool sensation appeared to move from one forearm to the other. This apparent movement persisted until the onset interval between the two stimuli was less than 100 ms. In an earlier study by Békésy [9] on heat sensations on the skin he noted that when two stimuli with no time delay between them were applied to two fingers spaced apart, a sensation of heat could occur outside the skin as if it was "floating in the air" between the fingers. He also observed that the sensation of heat arising from two stimuli spaced 140 mm apart could move from one stimulus to the other as a function of the delay between the stimuli. These studies suggest that the spatio-temporal interactions reported for other sensory modalities also apply to thermal sensory processing. However, the boundary conditions that define when these illusions occur thermally have not been specified. In contrast to the sense of touch, the ability to localize precisely thermal stimulation is limited and as compared to other sensory systems the thermal senses are relatively sluggish [10].

In a recent study Singhal and Jones [11] demonstrated that when four cooling pulses were presented on the forearm in varying spatial and temporal sequences, the perceived position of the second pulse changed as a function of temporal interval and distance between the pulses. When the onset interval between the second and third pulse was brief (0.2 s) and the distance between them greater, the perceived position of the second pulse moved by up to 43–59 mm in the direction of the third pulse which was delivered 150 mm from the second pulse. At longer intervals and shorter distances there was no change in its perceived location.

The present experiment was designed to evaluate whether the perceived location of a warm stimulus also changes as a function of the temporal parameters of stimulation. It was hypothesized that spatio-temporal interactions for warm stimuli may be less robust and more variable than those found for cold because of the decreased sensitivity of all body regions for warmth as compared to cold [12, 13]. In addition, the time to detect warm sensations is longer than that for cold which is presumably a consequence of the slower conduction velocity of warm afferent fibers (1–2 m/s) as compared to cold fibers (10–20 m/s) [14, 15].

2 Experimental Design

Thermal stimuli in the form of short pulses were delivered to the forearm using a thermal display. These stimuli varied with respect to the location at which they were presented on the arm and the delays between pulses.

2.1 Participants

Ten normal healthy males ranging in age from 24 to 36 years old (mean: 28 years) participated in the experiments. They had no known abnormalities of the skin or peripheral sensory or vascular systems. None of the participants had any significant experience in thermal perception studies. They all signed an informed consent form that was approved by the MIT Committee on the Use of Humans as Experimental Subjects.

2.2 Apparatus

A thermal display based on Peltier devices provided the thermal inputs to the skin. The display consisted of three thermoelectric modules (Model TE-83-1.0-1.5, TE Technology, Inc.) 22 mm × 19 mm × 3.8 mm, with a center-to-center distance between the modules of 75 mm. The contact area on the skin for each module was 418 mm^2. Laser-cut acrylic sheets enclosed the display and on the top surface the acrylic sheet was flush with the Peltier devices so that the locations of the Peltier modules were tactually imperceptible. Fans were mounted in the display to provide convection cooling. Figure 1 shows the assembled thermal display with the Peltier modules, heat sink and fans.

Five thermistors (Model 56A1002-C8, Alpha Technics; 457 μm in diameter and 3.18 mm in length) recorded the temperature of the Peltier modules and the skin during the experiment. The display temperature was controlled using a feedback loop with temperature input from the thermistors placed on each Peltier surface. Two other

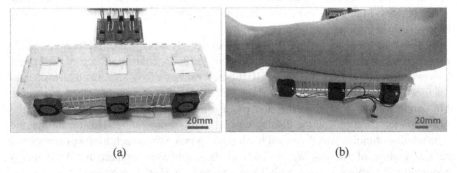

Fig. 1. (a) Thermal display assembly with three Peltier modules, heat sink and fans. (b) The position of the forearm on the thermal display.

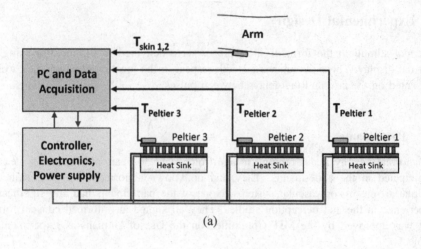

(a)

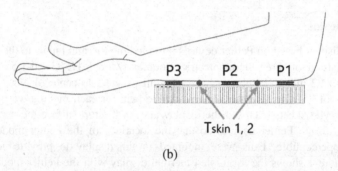

(b)

Fig. 2. (a) Schematic illustration of the thermal display with the Peltier modules mounted on heat sink. Thermistors measured the temperature of the modules and skin on the forearm. (b) The numbering of the Peltier modules in contact with the forearm, and the position of thermistors measuring skin temperature.

thermistors measured the temperature of the skin in regions not in contact with the Peltier devices. Figure 2 provides a schematic illustration of the position of the Peltier devices and thermistors on the arm.

National Instruments modules (Model NI cDAQ-9174, NI 9263, NI 9474, NI9205) were used for data acquisition and independent feedback control of each of the Peltier devices. A graphical user interface (GUI) based on LabVIEW (National Instruments) was used to control the temperature of the Peltier modules and continuously record the skin temperature at 1 kHz. At the start of each trial skin temperature was used as the calibration temperature and the display was set to this temperature. This meant that the same relative stimulus was delivered to all participants. When each trial was completed the temperature of the display returned to the calibration temperature. Participants recorded their responses using a GUI running on a separate computer.

2.3   Thermal Patterns

The thermal stimuli were composed of four short temperature pulses (A, B, C and D), all of which had the same amplitude (ΔT) of 6°C and pulse duration (t_p) of 2 s. There was a fixed interval of 4 s which is twice the pulse duration ($2t_p$), between the onset of Pulse A and B, and between Pulse C and D. A schematic illustration of the different parameters of the patterns is shown in Fig. 3. Prior to the start of Pulse A, the temperature of all three Peltier modules (P1, P2 and P3 as numbered from the elbow) was set at the mean skin temperature (T_{skin}) for 5 s (t_C) as measured simultaneously at two locations on the arm not in contact with the Peltier modules. The first location was midway between Peltier 1 and 2 (P1 and P2), and the second was between P2 and P3.

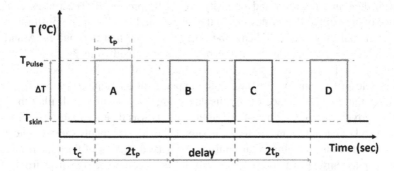

Fig. 3.   Different parameters of the four temperature pulses used to create the patterns.

Eight different thermal patterns were created by varying the delay between Pulse B and C, the direction of activation of the Peltier devices and the specific Peltier modules warmed as shown in Table 1. In the first sequence (AB-C-D), all the Peltier modules (P1, P2, P3) were activated with at least one pulse whereas in the second sequence (AB-CD) the second Peltier (P2) was maintained at the mean skin temperature and two pulses were delivered to P1 (or P3) and then to P3 (or P1). With a delay of 4 s between Pulse B and C, the pulses were evenly distributed in time. A shorter onset delay of 0.2 s

Table 1.   Thermal patterns created based on varying the Peltier modules (P) activated, the direction of activation and the delay (in s) between Pulse B and C.

Pattern	Sequence	Delay	Direction	P1	P2	P3
1	AB-C-D	4	P1 P2 P3	AB	C	D
2	AB-C-D	0.2	P1 P2 P3	AB	C	D
3	AB-C-D	4	P3 P2 P1	D	C	AB
4	AB-C-D	0.2	P3 P2 P1	D	C	AB
5	AB-CD	4	P1 - P3	AB	-	CD
6	AB-CD	0.2	P1 - P3	AB	-	CD
7	AB-CD	4	P3 - P1	CD	-	AB
8	AB-CD	0.2	P3 - P1	CD	-	AB

was chosen to determine whether the perceived position of the second pulse changed as a function of the delay between the pulses. Depending on the direction of activation, Pulses A, B, and D were always presented at either the first (P1) or third Peltier (P3) module. Similarly, the direction of activation also determined the location of Pulse C. Each pattern was presented 5 times, giving a total of 40 trials for each participant. The order of presentation of the trials was randomized.

2.4 Procedure

The procedure was initially explained to participants and they were familiarized with the temperature pulses that would be delivered. They were told that four warm pulses each with the same duration and intensity would be presented. The pulses could be presented on any of the Peltier devices in the display and start from any position. At the end of each trial they had to indicate the positions of the first two pulses, A and B.

The initial skin temperatures of the participants ranged from 30 to 32°C with a mean of 31°C. The ambient temperature was maintained at 25°C, as measured with a thermocouple in free air. At the start of the experiment participants placed their right forearm on the contact surface of the display using markers on the display that indicated the correct placement. One of the eight patterns was then presented (see Table 1) and at the end of each trial an auditory cue signaled that participants should indicate the locations of the first two temperature pulses. A visual depiction of the forearm and the thermal display surface was presented in a GUI on a computer screen in front of the participants (see Fig. 4). They moved a cursor to indicate the locations of each pulse. Responses had to be made within 10 s and on most trials participants indicated the location within a couple of seconds. After every two trials, participants switched the forearm that was on the display in order to avoid any adaptation effects. A rest break was provided when requested.

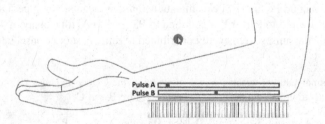

Fig. 4. Screen shot of the GUI presented on the computer screen in front of participants used to record their responses.

3 Results

Temperatures were measured during each trial on the Peltier modules and at two locations on the skin not in contact with the Peltier modules. The temperatures measured during presentation of Patterns 1 and 2 are illustrated in Fig. 5. The skin

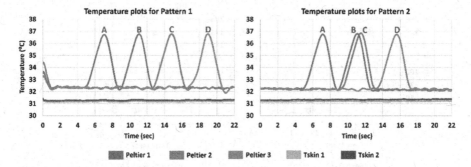

Fig. 5. Group mean temperature recordings throughout two trials from the three Peltier devices and from the skin on the forearm not in contact with the Peltier devices. (Color figure online)

temperature at the two locations not in contact with the Peltier modules remained constant, indicating that the temperature change was localized to the contact region.

The participants indicated the perceived locations of Pulses A and B using the GUI shown in Fig. 4; these data were then digitized using the Image Processing Toolbox in MATLAB (Mathworks, Inc.). The position of each pulse was measured from the wrist. A format devised by Goldreich [16] to conceptualize tactile length illusions has been used to illustrate the perceived location of pulses A and B. The schematic illustration shown in Fig. 6 depicts graphically the temporal and spatial properties of the physical stimuli and the perceived position of pulses A and B on the forearm for each of the eight patterns. Each adjacent pair of patterns (1 and 5, 2 and 6 etc.) differs only with respect to where the third stimulus (pulse C) in the sequence was delivered. This representation illustrates quite vividly how the position of pulse B was perceived to move in the direction of pulse C when the delay between the onset of pulses B and C was 0.2 s. When the delay between pulses B and C was longer (4 s) as in patterns 1, 3, 5 and 7, participants perceived the first and second pulses as being close together. Figure 6 also illustrates that at the longer delay participants were more accurate at localizing pulses A and B when they were presented near the elbow as compared to the wrist (1 and 5 as compared to 3 and 7). The elbow may have served as an anatomical landmark to facilitate localization, which has been reported for vibrotactile stimuli [17].

Figure 7 shows the perceived location of pulses A and B for the eight patterns, averaged across the 10 participants. When the sequence began at the elbow and moved distally the mean perceived location of the first pulse varied across patterns by 15 mm. For sequences that started at the wrist the position varied by 19.8 mm. Pulse B was always delivered at the same location as pulse A, but as is evident in Fig. 7, its perceived position changed substantially when there was a short delay between it and pulse C. On average the position of pulse B changed by 40 mm when the delay was 0.2 s and by only 7.5 mm when the delay was 4 s. The spatial sequence of stimulation (AB-C-D or AB-CD) did not have a marked effect on the perceived position of pulse B.

The effect of the various parameters used to create the warm stimuli on perceived position was evaluated by analyzing the absolute difference in perceived location for pulses A and B. A three-way repeated-measures analysis of variance (ANOVA) was

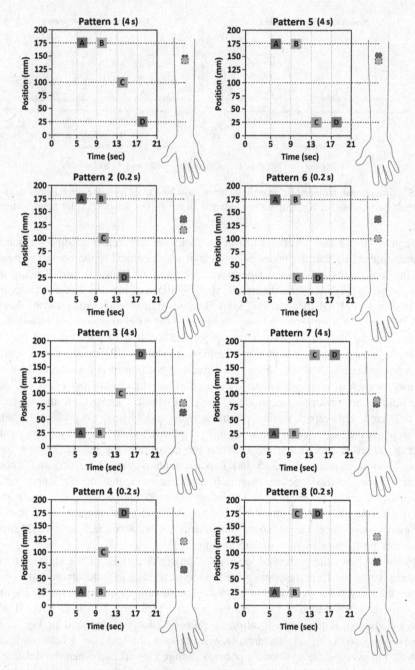

Fig. 6. Schematic illustration of the physical stimuli depicted graphically and the group mean perceived position of those stimuli on the forearm. The horizontal dashed lines indicate the positions of the Peltier modules.

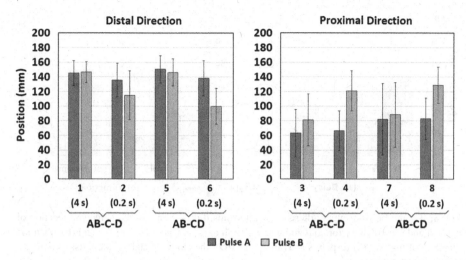

Fig. 7. The group mean perceived position of pulse A and B for each pattern when the direction of the thermal display's activation was either distal (from the elbow) or proximal (from the wrist). Standard deviations are shown. (Color figure online)

performed on these data with spatial sequence (AB-C-D and AB-CD), delay (0.2 and 4 s) and direction (proximal or distal) as factors. The results indicated a main effect of delay ($F(1,9) = 21.56$, $p = 0.001$) and of direction ($F(1,9) = 8.19$, $p = 0.019$), but no effect of sequence. None of the interactions was significant. These findings reveal that the perceived distance between pulses A and B was significantly greater for stimuli with the shorter delay of 0.2 s and was greater for sequences that began at the wrist as compared to the elbow.

The results from the present experiment were compared to those from an earlier study using the same stimulus parameters except that cooling rather than warming stimuli were delivered to the skin [11]. A comparison of the results from these two experiments which involved different participants is presented in Fig. 8. The absolute difference in the perceived locations of pulses A and B for cold and warm stimuli is shown as a function of delay and direction. It is evident that the perceived location of both cold and warm thermal stimuli can change as a function of the temporal parameters of stimulation. Figure 8 also illustrates that for both parameters cold stimuli resulted in a larger change in the perceived position of pulse B than warm stimuli. For cold and warm stimuli, sequences that started near the elbow and sequences with a shorter delay between pulses B and C resulted in a greater change in the perceived position of pulse B. The difference as a function of direction of stimulation was 34 mm for cold stimuli and 15 mm for warm stimuli. However, the change in perceived position with delay was more pronounced for warm stimuli, with a difference of 32 mm as compared to 24 mm for cold stimuli.

A repeated-measures analysis of variance (ANOVA) was performed on the combined dataset from both experiments, with thermal stimuli as a between-subjects factor and sequence, delay and direction as within-subjects factors. The results indicated a main effect of thermal stimuli ($F(1,18) = 141.80$, $p < 0.001$), of sequence ($F(1,18) = 10.99$,

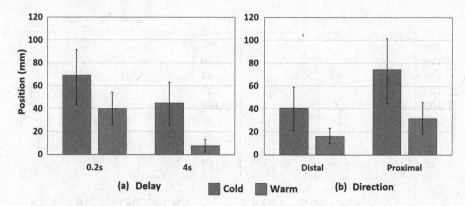

Fig. 8. Group mean absolute difference (with standard deviations) in the perceived location of the first and second pulse for cold and warm stimuli at (a) a delay of 0.2 or 4 s and (b) when the direction of the thermal display's activation was from the elbow (distal) or the wrist (proximal). (Color figure online)

p = 0.004), of delay (F(1,18) = 34.57, p < 0.001), and of direction (F(1,18) = 18.48, p < 0.001). The interactions between sequence and thermal stimuli (F(1,18) = 6.07, p = 0.02) and between sequence, delay and thermal stimuli (F(1,18) = 10.27, p = 0.005) were also significant. The interaction between sequence and thermal stimuli reflects the effect of the spatial sequence (AB-C-D and AB-CD) on the perceived location of pulse B for the cold stimuli which did not occur with warm stimuli. The three-way interaction is consistent with the greater change in perceived location for cold stimuli at shorter delays in the AB-CD sequence.

4 Discussion

The results from this experiment indicate that the spatio-temporal illusions that have been reported for tactile stimuli also occur for warm stimuli within the innocuous range of temperatures. In this experiment the second pulse was always delivered at the same location as the first pulse, but its perceived position changed as a function of the delay between it and the third pulse. When the delay was short (0.2 s) its position was perceived to move by 40 mm on average towards the location of the third pulse. This occurred independently of whether the third pulse was close to (75 mm, Patterns 2 and 4) or further away (150 mm, patterns 6 and 8) from the second pulse. At longer delays (4 s) the position of the second pulse was perceived accurately, that is, at the same location as the first pulse. These findings provide strong evidence that for the thermal modality, similar to touch, the temporal interval between warm stimuli delivered to the skin can influence their perceived location. The optimal interval for such effects to occur is probably around 200 ms, although this needs to be further studied. For tactile stimuli, intervals between 200 and 250 ms are optimal [18].

A comparison of the results from the present experiment with those from an earlier experiment with cold stimuli [11] reveals some interesting differences between the thermal senses. First, the magnitude of the change in perceived position was greater for cold than warm stimuli (see Fig. 8); second, at short delays the change in the perceived position of a cold, but not warm, stimulus was affected by the distance between the stimuli (i.e. pulses B and C). Consistent with previous studies that have shown that there is better localization for cooling than for warming stimuli on the forearm [19], in the present research there was more accurate localization when the first stimulus was cold. In summary, these results indicate that despite the limitations in the spatial and temporal processing of thermal stimuli, somatotopic information appears to be integrated similarly for tactile and thermal stimuli.

These interactions between the temporal and spatial properties of thermal stimuli offer an opportunity to enhance the representation of information in thermal displays. They show that in addition to the quality (warm or cold), amplitude and rate of change of thermal stimuli it is possible to vary the perceived location of stimulation by changing the inter-stimulus interval. In the context of social touch such thermal cues may provide information related proximity or separation.

References

1. Lederman, S.J., Jones, L.A.: Tactile and haptic illusions. IEEE Trans. Haptics **4**, 273–294 (2011)
2. Seo, J., Choi, S.: Initial study for creating linearly moving vibrotactile sensation on mobile device. In: IEEE Haptics Symposium, pp. 67–70 (2010)
3. Cholewiak, R.W., Collins, A.A.: The generation of vibrotactile patterns on a linear array: influences of body site, time, and presentation mode. Percept. Psychophys. **62**, 1220–1235 (2000)
4. Tan, H., Lim, A., Traylor, R.: A psychophysical study of sensory saltation with an open response paradigm. In: Proceedings of the 9th International Symposium on Haptic Interfaces for Virtual Environment and Teleoperator Systems, vol. 69, pp. 1109–1115 (2000)
5. IJsselsteijn, W.A., de Kort, Y.A.W., Haans, A.: Is this my hand I see before me? The rubber hand illusion in reality, virtual reality, and mixed reality. Presence **15**, 455–464 (2006)
6. Jones, B., Huang, Y.L.: Space-time dependencies in psychophysical judgment of extent and duration: algebraic models of the tau and kappa effects. Psychol. Bull. **91**, 128–142 (1982)
7. Helson, H.: The tau effect – an example of psychological relativity. Science **71**, 536–537 (1930)
8. Rózsa, J., Kenshalo, D.R.: Bilateral spatial summation of cooling of symmetrical sites. Percept. Psychophys. **21**, 455–462 (1977)
9. Békésy, G.V.: Lateral inhibition of heat sensations on the skin. J. Appl. Physiol. **17**, 1003–1008 (1962)
10. Jones, L.A., Ho, H.-N.: Warm or cool, large or small? The challenge of thermal displays. IEEE Trans. Haptics **1**, 53–70 (2008)
11. Singhal, A., Jones, L.A.: Space-time interactions and the perceived location of cold stimuli. In: Proceedings of the IEEE Haptics Symposium, pp. 92–97 (2016)
12. Stevens, J.C., Choo, K.C.: Temperature sensitivity of the body surface over the life span. Somatosens. Mot. Res. **15**, 13–28 (1998)
13. Harding, L.M., Loescher, A.R.: Adaptation to warming but not cooling at slow rates of stimulus change in thermal threshold measurements. Somatosens. Mot. Res. **22**, 45–48 (2005)

14. Darian-Smith, I.: Thermal sensibility. In: Darian-Smith, I. (ed.) Handbook of Physiology: The Nervous System, vol. I, pp. 879–913. American Physiological Society, Bethesda (1984)
15. Yarnitsky, D., Ochoa, J.L.: Warm and cold specific somatosensory systems. Brain **114**, 1819–1826 (1991)
16. Goldreich, D.: A Bayesian perceptual model replicates the cutaneous rabbit and other spatiotemporal illusions. PLoS ONE **2**, e333 (2007)
17. Cholewiak, R.W., Collins, A.A.: Vibrotactile localization on the arm: effects of place, space, and age. Percept. Psychophys. **65**, 1058–1077 (2003)
18. Geldard, F.A.: The mutability of time and space on the skin. J. Acoust. Soc. Am. **77**, 233–237 (1985)
19. Lee, D.K., McGillis, S.L.B., Greenspan, J.D.: Somatotopic localization of thermal stimuli: 1. a comparison of within- versus across-dermatomal separation of innocuous thermal stimuli. Somatosens. Mot. Res. **13**, 67–71 (1996)

Posters 1

A Study on Control of a Phantom Sensation by Visual Stimuli

Arinobu Niijima[1](✉) and Takefumi Ogawa[2]

[1] Graduate School of Engineering, The University of Tokyo, Bunkyō, Japan
a.niijima@ogawa-lab.org
[2] Information Technology Center, The University of Tokyo, Bunkyō, Japan
ogawa@nc.u-tokyo.ac.jp

Abstract. In this paper, we present a notable study to control occurrence of a phantom sensation by visual stimuli. A phantom sensation is one of tactile illusion caused by vibration stimuli. Some previous works employed vibration motors for a tactile display, and utilized a phantom sensation to present tactile stimuli in a large area with a few vibration motors. However, there are few studies to investigate the influence of visual stimuli on a phantom sensation. Our previous works showed that visual stimuli influenced localization of vibrotactile perception. From the results, we considered that visual stimuli also influence on a phantom sensation. We made a visual-tactile display, and conducted some experiments. The results showed that visual stimuli influenced a phantom sensation and it seemed to be possible to control the occurrence of a phantom sensation by changing visual stimuli.

Keywords: Phantom sensation · Cross modal perception · Visual-tactile display

1 Introduction

In virtual reality, haptics is important for interaction with virtual objects and environment. For example, some studies used wire actuators to present tactile feedback as touching virtual objects [2,15]. In our study, we make augmented reality applications in which virtual characters move on user's body and the user can feel the movement by tactile sensation as shown in Fig. 1. However, there is a big problem about a tactile display that when virtual characters move around in a large area on user's body, s/he has to equip many actuators for tactile feedback. To solve it, we focus on cross modal perception of visual sensation and tactile sensation. Some studies showed the cross modal perception on stiffness perception and tactile motion perception [4,14,16]. Based on these studies, we supposed that visual stimuli have influence on localization of vibrotactile perception and the location will be shifted toward that of visual stimuli. In our previous study, we conducted some experiments, and the results showed that it is possible to control localization of vibrotactile perception by visual stimuli [11,12]. Our

F. Bello et al. (Eds.): EuroHaptics 2016, Part I, LNCS 9774, pp. 305–315, 2016.
DOI: 10.1007/978-3-319-42321-0_28

study will contribute to design a visual-tactile display with a few actuators for presenting tactile feedback in a large area. In this paper, we investigated the influence of visual stimuli on a tactile illusion to enhance our proposal method.

There are various tactile stimuli for tactile feedback such as vibration [7,8], electrical stimuli [9], and ultrasound [6]. Some tactile display with vibration motors utilizes a phantom sensation to present tactile stimuli where vibration motors are not attached [3,13,17]. A phantom sensation is one of tactile illusions, which presents tactile stimuli between two spatially separated vibration motors [1]. Both location and intensity of a phantom sensation can be controlled by changing the intensities of the vibration motors. If the intensities of two motors are different, the location of a phantom sensation will be shifted toward that of the motor with higher intensity. This tactile illusion is useful to extend the presentable area of tactile feedback.

However, previous works investigated the characteristic of a phantom sensation in case that only tactile stimuli were presented [1,3,13], and there are few works which investigated the influence of visual stimuli on a phantom sensation. From our previous studies, we supposed that visual stimuli have influence on the occurrence rate of a phantom sensation. In other words, it is possible to cause a phantom sensation or not to cause a phantom sensation by controlling visual stimuli. Therefore, if a visual-tactile display is designed without consideration of the influence, it will be difficult to present a phantom sensation on intended locations in visual-tactile applications.

In this paper, we investigated the influence of visual stimuli on the occurrence of a phantom sensation by some experiments with a primitive visual-tactile display. Though they were under the limited condition, our contribution is to show an example of visual stimuli which promote a phantom sensation or not, and to suggest that the occurrence rate of a phantom sensation is influenced by not only current stimuli but also past stimuli.

2   Hypothesis

Our hypothesis is that the occurrence of a phantom sensation can be controlled by visual stimuli. The patterns of visual stimuli for the control are as follows.

1. When a visual stimulus is presented between two vibration motors, a phantom sensation will occur.
2. When visual stimuli are presented on two vibration motors, a phantom sensation will not occur.

To verify our hypothesis, we made a primitive visual-tactile display which employed LED tapes (Adafruit Industries, NeoPixel Digital RGB LED Strip) for visual stimuli and vibration motors (Tokyo Parts Industrial Co. Ltd., FM34F) for tactile stimuli as shown in Fig. 2. The center position of each LED and that of each vibration motor were the same. The diameter of a vibration motor was about 10 mm. The interval of each actuator was about 17 mm. LEDs and vibration motors were controlled by a microcomputer (Arduino, Arduino Uno).

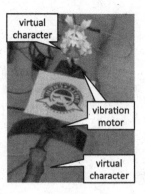

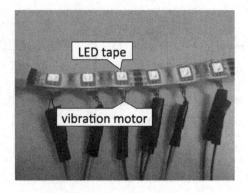

Fig. 1. An augmented reality application

Fig. 2. A primitive visual-tactile display

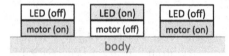

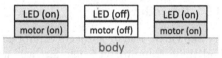

Fig. 3. An example pattern of visual stimuli and tactile stimuli to cause a phantom sensation

Fig. 4. An example pattern of visual stimuli and tactile stimuli not to cause a phantom sensation

The motors were supplied with 3.0 V and the frequency of them was about 200 Hz at which Pacinian corpuscle, which is a receptor for vibration, fires well [1].

Figure 3 shows an example pattern of visual stimuli and tactile stimuli to cause a phantom sensation based on our hypothesis. We suppose that when two vibration motors are vibrating and a LED on the middle of two motors is turned on, the location of vibrotactile perception will be on the middle lighted LED. In this case, the user feel a phantom sensation, and the number of the location of vibrotactile perception is only one. Figure 4 shows an example pattern of visual stimuli and tactile stimuli not to cause a phantom sensation based on our hypothesis. We suppose that when two vibration motors are vibrating and two LEDs on the same position as the motors are turned on, the locations of vibrotactile perception are on the both ends lighted LEDs. In this case, the user does not feel a phantom sensation, and the number of the locations of vibrotactile perception is two. In next section, we showed the experiment to verify our hypothesis.

3　Experiment 1: The Investigation of the Influence of Visual Stimuli on a Phantom Sensation

35 subjects (20s–60s years old) participated in this experiment. We investigated how visual stimuli influence the occurrence of a phantom sensation with a visual-tactile display.

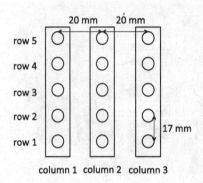

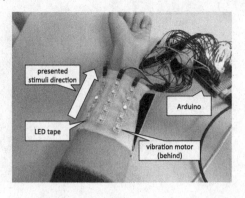

Fig. 5. Layout of the visual-tactile display

Fig. 6. The experimental environment

3.1 Procedure

As shown in Fig. 5, subjects equipped with the visual-tactile displays which had three columns on a left forearm where a phantom sensation occurs easily [1,3,13]. The interval of each LED tape was 20 mm which is short enough to control the location of vibrotactile perception by visual stimuli [10–12]. There were five LEDs and five vibration motors in each column.

Figure 6 shows the experimental image. Visual stimuli and tactile stimuli were presented from the elbow (row 1) to the wrist (row 5) one by one. This experiment was conducted in noisy environment, so it was no need to present white noise to subjects for preventing bias.

The experimental procedure was as follows. First, visual stimuli and tactile stimuli were presented as a demonstration. We explained how to answer with a check sheet. We didn't explain the relationship of visual stimuli and tactile stimuli. Next, subjects looked at their own left forearm, then visual stimuli and tactile stimuli were presented. They answered the location of vibrotactile perception in each row. If they felt vibration on more than two locations in one row, they answered all locations of vibrotactile perception. After one trial, the pattern of presenting stimuli was changed. We conducted three trials for each subject. From Figs. 7, 8 and 9 show the patterns of presenting stimuli. The red circles and blue circles mean the locations of stimuli. The presentation pattern of tactile stimuli was common in all trials; vibration motors in column 1 and column 3 vibrated simultaneously. Figure 7 shows the presentation pattern of stimuli in the first trial. The LEDs in column 2 were turned on in each row. Figure 8 shows the presentation pattern of stimuli in the second trial. The LEDs on column 1 and column 3 were turned on in each row. Figure 9 shows the presentation pattern of stimuli in the third trial. In row 1, row 3 and row5, the LEDs in column 1 and column 3 were turned on. In row 2 and row 4, the LEDs in column 2 were turned on. In all trials, the timing of presenting stimuli of three columns was synchronized. The time of presenting stimuli in each row was 500 ms which was set via a preliminary experiment. After stimuli in row 5 were

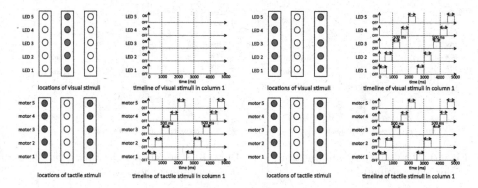

Fig. 7. The stimuli pattern in trial 1 (Color figure online)

Fig. 8. The stimuli pattern in trial 2 (Color figure online)

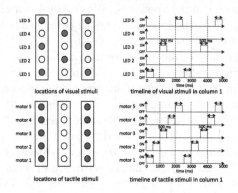

Fig. 9. The stimuli pattern in trial 3 (Color figure online)

presented, repeated from row 1. Three cycles of stimuli from row 1 to row 5 were set as one trial.

When subjects answered the location of vibrotactile perception was in column 2, it means they felt a phantom sensation. When they answered the locations of vibrotactile perception were in column 1 and column 3, it means they didn't feel a phantom sensation. In our hypothesis, the rate of where they answered would be different from each trial though the tactile stimuli are the same.

3.2   Results

We classified the answers as follows.

1. the location in column 2 only
2. the locations in both of column 1 and 3
3. the other locations

"1" means subjects felt a phantom sensation, and "2" means they didn't feel a phantom sensation. The answer rate in each trial is shown in Figs. 10, 11 and 12.

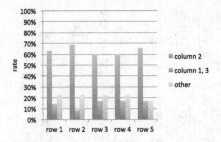

Fig. 10. The answer rate in trial 1 (Color figure online)

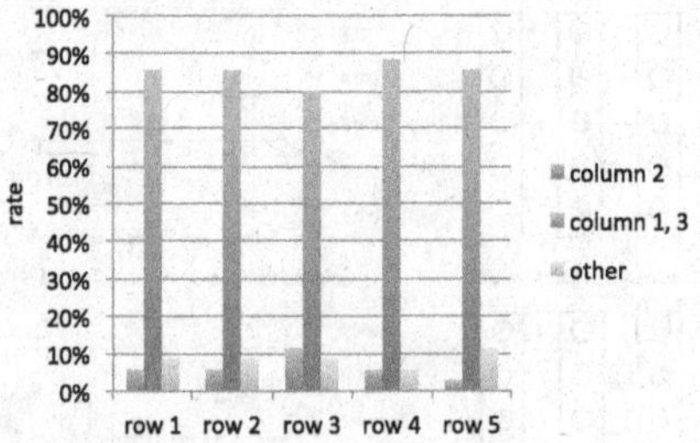

Fig. 11. The answer rate in trial 2 (Color figure online)

The rate was calculated from the number of answers divided by 35 as the total number of subjects.

The results supported our hypothesis. We conducted a chi-square test. As shown in Fig. 10, in trial 1, the rate of answer in column 2 only was the highest because LEDs in column 2 were turned on ($\chi^2(8) = 217, p < .01$). As shown in Fig. 11, in trial 2, the rate of answer in both column 1 and 3 was the highest because LEDs in both of column 1 and 3 were turned on ($\chi^2(8) = 418, p < .01$). As shown in Fig. 12, in trial 3, the rate of answer in column 2 only was the highest in row 2 and 4, and the rate of answer in both column 1 and 3 was the highest in row 1, 3, and 5 ($\chi^2(8) = 432, p < .01$). From these results, when the LED in column 2 was turned on, subjects tended to feel a phantom sensation. When the LEDs in both column 1 and 3 were turned on, subjects tended not to feel a phantom sensation. In trial 1 and 2, the answer rate had no significant difference between each rows (trial 1: $\chi^2(8) = 2.04, p = .98$, trial 2: $\chi^2(8) = 3.01, p = .93$).

Compared with the result in trial 1 and that in trial 3, the occurrence rate of a phantom sensation (the answer rate of column 2 in row 2 and 4) in trial 3 was higher than that in trial 1 ($\chi^2(1) = 6.21, p < .05$) as shown in Fig. 13. This result suggested that the occurrence rate of a phantom sensation depends on not only current stimuli but also past stimuli. On the other hand, compared with the result in trial 2 and that in trial 3, the false alarm rate of a phantom sensation (the answer rate of column 2 in row 1, 3, and 5) were almost the same ($\chi^2(1) = 0.35, p = .55$).

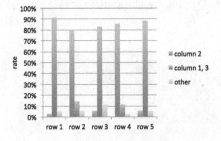

Fig. 12. The answer rate in trial 3 (Color figure online)

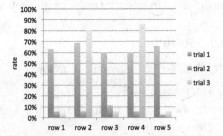

Fig. 13. The rate of a phantom sensation (Color figure online)

3.3   Discussion

In each trial, the patterns of tactile stimuli were the same, but the locations of vibrotactile perception were different from each other. This is because the patterns of visual stimuli were different in each trial. Some previous works suggested that users feel a phantom sensation more clearly with visual stimuli than that without visual stimuli, and the location of a phantom sensation can be shifted toward that of visual stimuli [5,11,12]. This experimental result suggested another influence of visual stimuli on a phantom sensation. It means that the occurrence of a phantom sensation is influenced by visual stimuli, and it seems to be possible to control by visual stimuli.

In addition, the results show that the locations of vibrotactile perception are decided by not only the locations of visual stimuli and those of tactile stimuli at that time. The before and after locations of visual stimuli and those of tactile stimuli also seem to be important for the locations of vibrotactile perception. We suppose that it is important to convince subjects that the locations of visual stimuli and those of tactile stimuli are the same. Compared with the results in trial 1 and trial 2, the rate of answer in trial 2 had more bias than that in trial 1. Subjects tended to to feel the locations of visual stimuli and those of tactile stimuli were the same when LEDs in column 1 and column 3 were turned on. In trial 3, subjects recognized the location of visual stimuli and that of tactile stimuli were the same because of stimuli in row 1, row 3 and row5. Because of it, they tended to feel the location of visual stimuli and that of tactile stimuli were the same in row 2 and row 4. This hypothesis is not yet confirmed, thus we will investigate the mechanism in the future.

In this section, we presented a novel study about the influence of visual stimuli on a phantom sensation. However, this experiment was under limited conditions such as the pattern of stimuli and the order of stimuli. To enhance this experimental results, we conducted an additional experiment as experiment 2 in which the pattern and the order were changed.

4   Experiment 2: The Study on the Influence of Visual Stimuli on a Phantom Sensation Under Other Conditions

6 males (20s–30s), who were not in experiment 1, participated in this experiment. In this experiment, we presented various patterns of visual stimuli to verify the influence on a phantom sensation.

4.1   Procedure

We used the same visual-tactile display as experiment 1. The patterns of tactile stimuli were the same; vibration motors in column 1 and 3 vibrated simultaneously. The patterns of visual stimuli were shown in Table 1. It showed the number of rows where LEDs in column 1 and 3 were turned on and the number of rows where a LED in column 2 was turned on among 5 rows. For example, in case of the pattern of Fig. 9, the former is 3 and the latter is 2. Our hypothesis is that the occurrence rate of a phantom sensation depends on not only current stimuli but also past stimuli. Therefore, we assumed that the occurrence would be different from each pattern.

In this experiment, we presented white noise to subjects to prevent bias from vibration sounds. To prevent other bias, we presented 17 dummy patterns of visual and tactile stimuli in the trial, and the order of stimuli was random. The dummy patterns were shown in Table 2.

Table 1. The patterns of visual stimuli

No. of rows where LEDs in column 1, 3 were turned on	No. of rows where a LED in column 2 was turned on	No. of total cases in each pattern
4	1	5
3	2	10
2	3	10
1	4	5
0	5	1

Table 2. The dummy patterns of visual and tactile stimuli

Columns of visual stimuli	Columns of rows of tactile stimuli	No. of total cases
1 or 2 or 3	1 or 3	6
1&2 or 1&3 or 2&3	1 or 3	6
1 or 3	1&3	2
1&2 or 1&3 or 2&3	1&3	3

4.2   Results

Figure 14 showed the occurrence rate of a phantom sensation (subjects felt vibration in column 2 when a LED in column 2 was turned on) and the false alarm rate (subjects felt vibration in column 2 when LEDs in column 1 and 3 were turned on). The occurrence rate was about 60–80 %. It suggested that a phantom sensation was occurred whenever a LED in column 2 was turned on. On the other hand, in case that the number of rows where a LED in column 2 was turned on was 5, there was a significant difference of the occurrence rate from other cases with a chi-square test ($\chi^2(4) = 17.9, p < .01$). We also investigated about false alarm rate, but there was no significant difference between each pattern ($\chi^2(3) = 3.30, p = .35$). It suggested that once LEDs in column 1 and 3 were turned on, subjects tended to feel a phantom sensation.

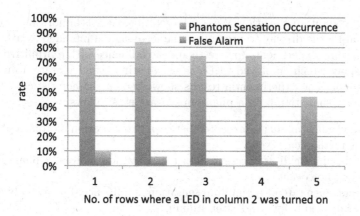

Fig. 14. The occurrence rate of a phantom sensation for each pattern (Color figure online)

4.3   Discussion

From the results, it seemed to be possible to control occurrence of a phantom sensation by visual stimuli which is independent of stimuli pattern and order. The number of rows where a LED in column 1 and 3 was turned on among 5 rows would be one of factors for controlling a phantom sensation.

In experiment 1 and 2, the interval between each stimuli was nothing, so it might occur apparent movement of tactile stimuli. We investigated the influence of apparent movement by an experiment with 3 subjects to compare two cases, one was with apparent movement, and the other was without it by setting 1 second interval between each stimuli. The result was that no one described the difference between the two cases. Therefore, we think that apparent movement didn't influence a phantom sensation.

Finally, we found some characteristics about the cross modal perception between visual stimuli and a phantom sensation. Though we conducted the experiments only on a forearm, our previous works suggest that the similar influence of visual stimuli on a phantom sensation will occur on other body parts such as a hand [12]. However, we did not reveal the mechanism of the influence of visual stimuli on a phantom sensation. In future work, we will conduct more experiments under other conditions to show the characteristic and the mechanism.

5   Coclusions

We presented a notable study on the influence of visual stimuli on a phantom sensation. Some previous works employed vibration motors for tactile display and utilized a phantom sensation to present tactile stimuli in a large area with a few motors. However, there are few studies to investigate the influence of visual stimuli on a phantom sensation. We considered this study is important for designing a visual-tactile display to present tactile feedback on intended locations. We conducted some experiments to investigate the influence with a primitive visual-tactile display which employed LEDs as visual stimuli and vibration motors as tactile stimuli. The experimental results showed some characteristics about the influence of visual stimuli on a phantom sensation as follows.

1. When a visual stimulus is presented between two vibration motors, a phantom sensation will occur.
2. When visual stimuli are presented on two vibration motors, a phantom sensation will not occur.
3. The occurrence rate of a phantom sensation is influenced by not only current stimuli but also before and after stimuli.

In future works, we will conduct more experiments under other conditions to reveal the mechanism of the cross modal perception clearly.

Acknowledgments. This research was supported in part by a Grant-in-Aid for Scientific Research (C) numbered 16K00266 by the Japan Society for the Promotion of Science (JSPS).

References

1. Alles, D.: Information transmission by phantom sensations. IEEE Trans. Man-Mach. Syst. **1**(11), 85–91 (1970)
2. Aoki, T., Mitake, H., Keoki, D., Hasegawa, S., Sato, M.: Wearable haptic device to present contact sensation based on cutaneous sensation using thin wire. In: Proceedings of the International Conference on Advances in Computer Enterntainment Technology, pp. 115–122. ACM (2009)
3. Barghout, A., Cha, J., El Saddik, A., Kammerl, J., Steinbach, E.: Spatial resolution of vibrotactile perception on the human forearm when exploiting funneling illusion. In: IEEE International Workshop on Haptic Audio visual Environments and Games, HAVE 2009, pp. 19–23. IEEE (2009)
4. Craig, J.C.: Visual motion interferes with tactile motion perception. Perception **35**(3), 351 (2006). London
5. Hashiguchi, S., Shibata, F., Kimura, A.: Psychophysical influence on phantom sensation of temperature perception by mixed-reality visual stimulation. In: Proceedings of ASIAGRAPH 2016, vol. 11, pp. 63–64 (2016)
6. Hoshi, T., Takahashi, M., Iwamoto, T., Shinoda, H.: Noncontact tactile display based on radiation pressure of airborne ultrasound. IEEE Trans. Haptics **3**(3), 155–165 (2010)
7. Israr, A., Poupyrev, I.: Tactile brush: drawing on skin with a tactile grid display. In: Proceedings of the SIGCHI Conference on Human Factors in Computing Systems, pp. 2019–2028. ACM (2011)
8. Jin, M.S., Park, J.I.: Interactive mobile augmented reality system using a vibrotactile pad. In: 2011 IEEE International Symposium on VR Innovation (ISVRI), pp. 329–330. IEEE (2011)

9. Kajimoto, H.: Electrotactile display with real-time impedance feedback using pulse width modulation. IEEE Trans. Haptics **5**(2), 184–188 (2012)
10. Lederman, S.J., Klatzky, R.L.: Haptic perception: a tutorial. Attention Percept. Psychophysics **71**(7), 1439–1459 (2009)
11. Niijima, A., Ogawa, T.: A study of changing locations of vibrotactile perception on a forearm by visual stimulation. In: Yuizono, T., Zurita, G., Baloian, N., Inoue, T., Ogata, H. (eds.) CollabTech 2014. CCIS, vol. 460, pp. 86–95. Springer, Heidelberg (2014)
12. Niijima, A., Ogawa, T.: Visual stimulation influences on the position of vibrotactile perception. In: Kajimoto, H., Ando, H., Kyung, K.-U. (eds.) Haptic Interaction. LNEE, vol. 277, pp. 29–36. Springer, Heidelberg (2015)
13. Rahal, L., Cha, J., Saddik, A.E., Kammerl, J., Steinbach, E.: Investigating the influence of temporal intensity changes on apparent movement phenomenon. In: IEEE International Conference on Virtual Environments, Human-Computer Interfaces and Measurements Systems, VECIMS 2009, pp. 310–313. IEEE (2009)
14. Sano, Y., Hirano, Y., Kimura, A., Shibata, F., Tamura, H.: Dent-softness illusion in mixed reality space: further experiments and considerations. In: 2013 IEEE Virtual Reality (VR), pp. 153–154. IEEE (2013)
15. Sawada, H., Jiang, C., Takase, H.: Tactoglove: displaying tactile sensations in tacto-gestural interaction. In: 2011 International Conference on Biometrics and Kansei Engineering (ICBAKE), pp. 216–221. IEEE (2011)
16. Spence, C., Pavani, F., Driver, J.: Spatial constraints on visual-tactile cross-modal distractor congruency effects. Cogn. Affect. Behav. Neurosci. **4**(2), 148–169 (2004)
17. Ueda, S., Uchida, M., Nozawa, A., Ide, H.: A tactile display using phantom sensation with apparent movement together. Electron. Commun. Jpn. **91**(12), 29–38 (2008)

Integrating Measured Force Feedback in Passive Multilateral Teleoperation

Michael Panzirsch[1,2]($\boxtimes$), Thomas Hulin[1], Jordi Artigas[1], Christian Ott[1], and Manuel Ferre[2]

[1] Institute of Robotics and Mechatronics, DLR, Wessling, Germany
[2] Centre for Automation and Robotics (CAR) UPM-CSIC,
Universidad Politécnica de Madrid, Madrid, Spain
michael.panzirsch@dlr.de

Abstract. In teleoperation systems, the master robot receives force feedback from the remote slave side. Thus, the human operator can perceive the contact between the slave robot and its environment. Application of a force sensor at the slave robot improves the performance of the telepresence system in terms of transparency. Still, so far no approach allowing measured force feedback in time delayed multilateral systems that allow the interaction of multiple agents can be found in literature. To this end, this paper presents a multilateral setup with passive measured force feedback based on the time domain passivity approach. Besides this solution to measured force feedback in multilateral systems, the presented approach promises improvements compared to other time invariant and model based approaches for measured force feedback also when applied to bilateral systems. Experiments are presented to allow for a performance analysis of the proposed system design.

Keywords: Teleoperation · Measured force feedback · Passivity · TDPA

1 Introduction

The enhancement of robot technology in the past few years increased the quality of teleoperation systems that couple a slave robot with a master input device by a controller. Besides former application in space and the nuclear industry, new markets, e.g. in medicine and industrial maintenance evolved. Impedance controlled light weight robots, higher computational performance and modern control techniques improved the transparency of teleoperation systems, i.e. the quality of immersion into the slave's environment that the human operator perceives via his/her interaction device.

The focus of the present work lies on teleoperation systems that incorporate measurement of the slave contact forces in its environment For instance, in the classical Position-Force measured architecture (PF_{meas}) a position P or velocity respectively is sent from master to slave and a measured force F_{meas} from slave

© Springer International Publishing Switzerland 2016
F. Bello et al. (Eds.): EuroHaptics 2016, Part I, LNCS 9774, pp. 316–326, 2016.
DOI: 10.1007/978-3-319-42321-0_29

to master through the communication channel [3, 4, 7]. Measured force feedback eases the remote control of the slave's motion in free environment as the slave robot's dynamics are completely masked and only the interaction force with the environment is perceived by the operator. Furthermore, forces of higher bandwidth are transmitted in the PF_{meas} architecture compared to the Position-Force computed (PF_{comp}) architecture. In this type of architecture the force of the PI controller is fed back to the master which can have a damping effect during free motion, i.e. transparency is reduced. Tavakoli et al. studied in [12] the benefits of a 4-Channel architecture that consists of two controllers on each side of the communication channel and feedback of the measured human and environmental interaction forces. In theory, a perfectly transparent system can be achieved through this architecture.

The motivation of this paper originates from multilateral systems that are currently of high interest for training and cooperative scenarios [10]. In particular, multilateral control approaches that consider time delay are based on the principle of passivity. Willaert et al. [14] showed that bilateral control structures which contain force sensors are non-passive. Passivity could be established by representing the system created by the slave robot and the environment through a 1-port network. However, in that approach, the force feedback path is considerably downscaled and a maximmal environment impedance is assumed. In [6], Khademian et al. designed a 4-Channel system for multilateral control. In [8], the Raisbeck passivity criterion was applied. Kanno and Yokokohji [5], Quang and Ryu [11] and Panzirsch et al. [9] presented multilateral teleoperation systems considering time delay. The passivity of the communication channels were guaranteed by the wave variables method and the time domain passivity approach (TDPA) respectively. In [9], a generic approach based on passive modules was developed which serve as the basic multilateral framework for the present work.

In [2], Artigas et al. applied the TDPA in order to handle the effect of time delay in a bilateral PF_{meas} architecture by representing the system through time domain passivity networks (TDPN). Tobergte and Albu-Schaeffer [13] implemented a full state feedback controller for bilateral teleoperation of a surgical robot. The approach allowed stable interaction with hard and soft environments. The TDPA guaranteed passivity of the overall bilateral teleoperator. In contrast to the present work [2, 13] applied the TDPA to the time delay in the communication channel.

The main contribution of this paper is the enhancement of passivity based nonlinear multilateral teleoperation via a new control approach guaranteeing passivity despite use of measured force feedback. Note that this approach is not meant to overcome the effects of time delay. Still, the presented framework can be combined with passivity-based methods tackling time delay like wave variables or time domain control methods. The novel method does not rely on imprecise model parameters and as, furthermore, the passivity is enforced by an additional variable damper in time domain, no conservative controller parametrization is necessary. Thus, the proposed approach also brings benefit when applied in bilateral systems.

Section 2 provides an overview of our modular multilateral architecture [9] and the related challenges of measured force feedback. The model-free control approach for measured force feedback architectures as the main contribution of the paper is presented in Sect. 3. Experiments are presented in Sect. 4 and Sect. 5 summarizes the results.

2   Multilateral Structure

The signal flow diagram of a 1DoF (Degree of Freedom) bilateral PF_{meas} architecture is depicted in Fig. 1. The human operator is controlling a slave robot in a remote or unaccessible environment (Env)

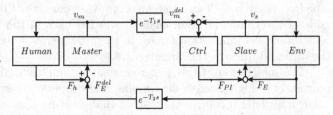

Fig. 1. Signal flow for measured force feedback architecture

through a master input device. The slave's position is controlled by a position/velocity controller ($Ctrl$) - acting as a virtual spring - to match the master's position. The measured interaction force between slave and environment is fed back to the master. The communication channel is represented by the Laplace transformation of a pure constant delay $e^{-T_1 s}$ and $e^{-T_2 s}$. A virtual damping can be added as a proportional part in the controller ($Ctrl$) or as local dampers at master and slave devices.

Anderson proposed in [1] the application of the network representation to the analysis of teleoperation systems. The network representation divides a system into several n-ports that are connected by power-conjugated ports. Port i is an interface of flow v_i and effort F_i such that a power $P_i(t) = F_i(t)v_i(t)$ can be defined at port i.

Figure 2 shows an exemplary network representation of a PF_{meas} architecture without time delay. The generalized multilateral system developed in [9] can be analyzed in Fig. 3. The human operator at the master and the slave in its environment are represented as agent subsystems conjointly. Those are connected

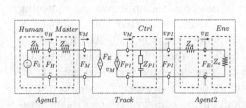

Fig. 2. Network representation of a PF_{comp} architecture without time delay

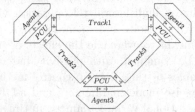

Fig. 3. Network representation of a multilateral teleoperation system

via power control units (PCU) and tracks containing e.g. controller and communication channel. Figure 4 presents the bilateral network representation for the 1-port passivity approach presented in [14]. This approach for passive measured force feedback cannot be straightforwardly applied to multilateral systems as no 1-port teleoperation subsystem integrating the devices, controllers and the environment can be defined for the multilateral network. This problem is the main motivation for the present work.

3   Control Design

Another approach has to be investigated for multilateral systems with measured force feedback. The TDPA for a passive PF_{meas} module is suggested as a solution and designed in the following. Figure 5 can be considered as a generalization of a bilateral 2-channel teleoperation system (the subsystems $PC_{L/R}$ have to be neglected first).

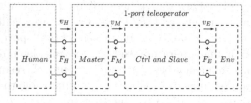

Fig. 4. Network representation of the 1-port teleoperator proposed in [14]

The setup is split up into two channels representing the two directions of energy flow (compare [2]). Energy sent from master to slave is flowing from left to right (L2R) and the energy sent from slave to master flows in right to left (R2L) direction. In R2L direction a dependent effort source F_{FB} injects energy that is sent from slave to master. The dependent flow source v_1 injects the energy introduced by the master in L2R direction. The power flowing in the R2L part of the track in direction to the slave is dissipated by the effort source and the power flowing in direction to the flow source in the L2R part of track is dissipated by the flow source. The power at the ports flowing in the different directions can be easily distinguished:

$$P_{8b}^{L2R}(t) = \begin{cases} 0, & \text{if } P_{8b}(t) < 0 \\ P_{8b}(t), & \text{if } P_{8b}(t) > 0 \end{cases} \quad \text{and} \quad P_{8b}^{R2L}(t) = \begin{cases} 0, & \text{if } P_{8b}(t) > 0 \\ -P_{8b}(t), & \text{if } P_{8b}(t) < 0 \end{cases}$$

with $P_{8b}(t) = v_{8b}(t)F_{8b}(t)$. The same computation of power flow holds for all other ports.

In the case of open loop teleoperation where the master receives no feedback the dependent effort source does not inject energy, as F_{FB} is zero. The system is stable, as the L2R can be proven to be passive. The PI-controller acting as spring and damper is passive and the terminations (i.e. the environment, human operator and their representative effort and flow source) are generally assumed to behave passive in their interactions.

In a PF_{comp} architecture (compare Fig. 2) F_{FB} is equal to F_{8b}. Every network subsystem is passive in that case.

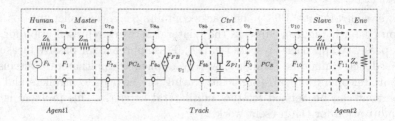

Fig. 5. Network representation of passive PF_{meas} architecture without time delay

The effort source depends on F_{11} (i.e. the measured force F_E in the slave environment) in a PF_{meas} architecture. Willaert et al. [14] showed that then passivity can only be guaranteed if the 1-port including every subsystem despite the human operator (see Fig. 4) is considered in a frequency-based analysis. Since this frequency-based passivity approach results in a conservative non-adaptive gain parametrization and is not applicable to multilateral systems, time domain control is applied to guarantee passivity of the measured force feedback. The concept is based on the following observations: The system is passive for the PF_{comp} architecture as the PI has a passive behavior:

$$\int_0^t P_{8b}^{L2R}(\tau) + P_9^{R2L}(\tau) \, d\tau \geq \int_0^t P_{8b}^{R2L}(\tau) + P_9^{L2R}(\tau) \, d\tau. \tag{1}$$

At port 8b and 8a the same power is flowing in the PF_{comp} architecture.

Therefore, as long as the measured force feedback ($F_{FB} = F_{11}$) does not inject more energy via the effort source in R2L direction compared to the computed force feedback ($F_{FB} = F_{8b}$), the control architecture remains passive also for PF_{meas} architecture. The L2R part of the track is not influenced by the measured force feedback.

The resulting concept can be realized by the following implementation:

The energy injected into the PI controller has to be observed and stored.

The energy leaving the PI controller to the slave at port 10 (compare Fig. 5 neglecting PC subsystems) and the energy sent to the master by the independent force source F_{FB} have to be limited depending on the energy storage of the PI controller. This can be solved by dissipative impedance type passivity controllers PC_L and PC_R. Note that impedance type PCs don't cause position drift.

When a power should leave at port 8a or 9 (P_{8a}^{R2L} or P_9^{L2R}) it has to be checked if enough energy has entered the controller beforehand. The energy content of the controller can be computed (see Fig. 5) in each time step:

$$\Delta E_C(k) = \Delta E_C(k-1) + P_{8b}^{L2R}(k) + P_9^{R2L}(k). \tag{2}$$

At first the desired output P_{out}^{dem} in both direction of energy flow has to be calculated:

$$P_{out}^{dem}(k) = P_{8a}^{R2L}(k) + P_9^{L2R}(k). \tag{3}$$

If this power P_{out}^{dem} is smaller than ΔE_C, this power may exit. The PCs are only active if excess power needs to be dissipated:

$$P_{diss}^{PC_L}(k) = \begin{cases} (\Delta E_C(k)P_{8a}^{R2L}(k))/(P_{out}^{dem}(k)T_s), & \text{if } \Delta E_C(k) < P_{out}^{dem}(k)T_s \\ 0, & \text{if } \Delta E_C(k) > P_{out}^{dem}(k)T_s \end{cases},$$

$$P_{diss}^{PC_R}(k) = \begin{cases} (\Delta E_C(k)P_{9}^{L2R}(k))/(P_{out}^{dem}(k)T_s), & \text{if } \Delta E_C(k) < P_{out}^{dem}(k)T_s \\ 0, & \text{if } \Delta E_C(k) > P_{out}^{dem}(k)T_s \end{cases},$$

with the system sample time T_s. The impedance type PC_L e.g. dissipates the power $P_{diss}^{PC_L}$ with the variable damping α_{PC_L} via the force F_{PC_L} reducing the measured force feedback force ($F_{7a} = F_{FB} + F_{PC_L}$):

$$F_{PC_L}(k) = \alpha_{PC_L}(k)v_{7a}(k), \quad \text{with} \quad \alpha_{PC_L}(k) = -P_{diss}^{PC_L}(k)/v_{7a}^2(k).$$

The track in Fig. 5 is passive, if the 4-port of PC_L, PI and PC_R is passive:

$$E_{7a}^{10}(k) = \sum_0^k (P_{8b}^{L2R}(k) + P_9^{R2L}(k) - P_{7a}^{R2L}(k) - P_{10}^{L2R}(k)) \geq 0.$$

This holds, since the power at those 4 ports are monotonously increasing and the passivity controllers assure that the output energy is lower or equal to the input energy:

$$\int_0^t P_{8b}^{L2R}(\tau) + P_9^{R2L}(\tau)\,d\tau \geq \int_0^t P_{8b}^{R2L}(\tau) + P_9^{L2R}(\tau)\,d\tau, \tag{4}$$

$$P_{7a}^{R2L}(t) \leq P_{8a}^{R2L}(t) \quad \text{and} \quad P_{10}^{L2R}(t) \leq P_9^{L2R}(t) \tag{5}$$

Through this design the biggest benefits of measured force feedback are maintained: If there's no contact with the environment (free motion) the operator's motion will not be hindered by a force, as desired. When the operator steers the slave into a collision, power is flowing from master to slave. Therefore PC_L will not vary the force feedback to the master such that the dynamics of the impact can be well perceived.

The measured force feedback will only be varied if the environment injects energy. E.g. in case of an external impact on the slave robot the force feedback may be affected by the PC_L as there can be an excess energy output at port $8a$. The dissipation in the PI controller determines how high this effect is.

The delay free setup of Fig. 5 can be combined with the approach presented in [2], in which the time delay in the communication channel is represented by two Time Domain Power Networks (TDPN, Fig. 6). The energy generated by the time delay in L2R direction e.g. can be observed at port 7a and 5a of TDPN1. The passivity controllers PC1 and PC2 terminating the TDPNs dissipate the energy generated by the time delay and thus guarantee passivity of the communication channel. The resulting track of Fig. 6 can be straightforwardly applied to the multilateral systems proposed in [9,10].

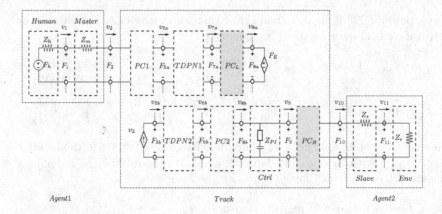

Fig. 6. Network representation of passive PF_{meas} architecture with time delay

4   Experiments

The following experiments were performed with three 1DoF rotatory devices (see Fig. 7) which are equipped with torque sensors in the rotatory center of the grip. The control software was implemented in Matlab/Simulink and running on a QNX-machine in real-time with 1kHz sampling rate. At first the performance of teleoperation with measured force feedback is compared with computed force feedback in free motion and during a wall contact. The later experiments consider a time delay in the communication channel and a multilateral setup. A local

Fig. 7.   1DoF   master-slave-system (courtesy of sensodrive)

damping was applied to each device, but in order to test the most critical case for the approach, the damping in the PI controllers of the tracks was set to zero.

In the first experiments the master is controlling the slave at different speeds with computed (see Fig. 8) and measured force feedback (see Fig. 9). During free motion power is flowing mainly from master to slave (compare P_9^{L2R} in Fig. 8). Comparing Figs. 8 and 9, it is obvious that during low speeds (Fig. 8: 2.5 s–4 s; Fig. 9: 4.2 s–5.6 s), the master receives a higher feedback force when computed force feedback is active. Figure 9 shows that the passivity controllers $PC_{L/R}$ do not need to dissipate energy though the dissipative damping in the controller was set to zero. E_{7a}^{10} - the sum of input and output energy measured between port $7a$ and port 10 - is never negative which proofs that the subsystem consisting of PI, PC_L and PC_R behaves passive. During faster motion (Fig. 8: 1.5 s–2.5 s; Fig. 9: 3 s–4 s) the grip mass leads to a measured feedback force due to high acceleration of the tool mass. The position tracking is satisfactory in all experiments and at all speeds. In the next part of the experiment the operator moves the slave device such that it contacts a wall. Figure 8 shows that energy

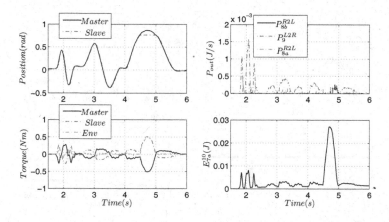

Fig. 8. Free motion and wall contact with computed force feedback

flows from slave to master when the master leaves out of the penetrated wall (4.8 s–5 s). This amount of energy was injected before when the master moved into the wall (4.4 s–4.8 s). As the slave velocity is zero at that time, no energy is leaving to the slave. Figure 9 shows a torque peak (6.4 s) measured by the sensor during the impact into the wall. This torque is fed back unaltered to the master device. It is obvious that other approaches that demand a constant high down-scaling of the feedback force would result in a worse perception of the environment for the operator in this situation.

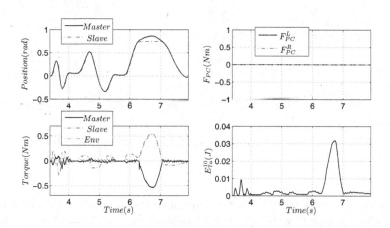

Fig. 9. Free motion and wall contact with measured force feedback

The following experiment considers time delay (compare Fig. 6). Figure 10 depicts the behavior under symmetric 100 ms roundtrip delay. Comparing Figs. 9 and 10 it can be seen that the position following is of course better in the

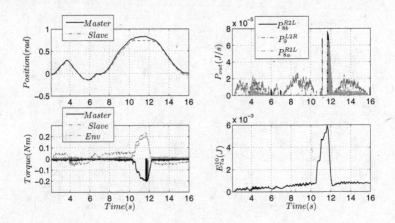

Fig. 10. Wall contact with measured force feedback at 100 ms roundtrip delay

experiment without delay. E_{7a}^{10} (Fig. 10) is always positive, i.e. the subsystem consisting of PI, PC_L and PC_R is still passive.

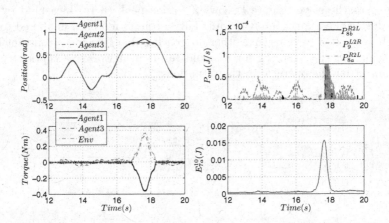

Fig. 11. Position tracking in a multilateral setup (forces and energy behaviour of track2)

A multilateral system as designed in Fig. 3 can be analyzed in Fig. 11. The Agent1 and Agent2 - grasped by the operator's hands - receive measured force feedback from Agent3 (track2,3) whereas Agent1 and Agent2 receive computed force feedback from each other (track1). Note that the plot considers for the sake of clarity only track2. Agent1 has the authority and steers the Agent3 against a wall. The position tracking of the three devices is satisfactory. The energy plot proofs passivity of the subnetwork of concern.

5 Conclusion

A passive module for PF_{meas} architecture based on the TDPA has been designed for multilateral architectures in the presented work. It could be shown that the system is not conservative as it is designed in the time domain. As other approaches aiming at absolute stability or passivity of measured force feedback systems consider physical model parameters and therefore limit the force feedback more gravely and as the PCs dissipate rarely, the proposed approach can be assumed to provide better performance also for general bilateral systems. Furthermore, the module can be used in combination with other passivity based approaches as e.g. the wave variables method. Experiments with time delay proved the system's adequacy for the classical teleoperation tasks. Subjectively rated, the performance with respect to transparency could be improved substantially in free motion and at fast collisions compared to a PF_{comp} architecture. In future work the presented approach will be extended to a 4-Channel architecture.

References

1. Anderson, R.J., Spong, M.W.: Asymptotic stability for force reflecting teleoperators with time delay. Int. J. Robot. Res. **11**(2), 135–149 (1992)
2. Artigas, J., Ryu, J.H., Preusche, C., Hirzinger, G.: Network representation and passivity of delayed teleoperation systems. In: IEEE International Conference on Intelligent Robots and Systems (IROS), pp. 177–183 (2011)
3. Daniel, R., McAree, P.: Fundamental limits of performance for force reflecting teleoperation. Int. J, Robot. Res **17**(8), 811 830 (1998)
4. Hannaford, B., Anderson, R.: Experimental and simulation studies of hard contact in force reflecting teleoperation. In: Proceedings of 1988 IEEE International Conference on Robotics and Automation, pp. 584–589. IEEE (1988)
5. Kanno, T., Yokokohji, Y.: Multilateral teleoperation control over time-delayed computer networks using wave variables. In: Haptics Symposium, pp. 125–131 (2012)
6. Khademian, B., Hashtrudi-Zaad, K.: A four-channel multilateral shared control architecture for dual-user teleoperation systems. In· IEEE International Conference on Intelligent Robots and Systems, pp. 2660–2666 (2007)
7. Lawrence, D.A.: Stability and transparency in bilateral teleoperation. IEEE Trans. Robot. Autom. **9**(5), 624–637 (1993)
8. Mendez, V., Tavakoli, M.: A passivity criterion for n-port multilateral haptic systems. In: 2010 49th IEEE Conference on Decision and Control (CDC), pp. 274–279 (2010)
9. Panzirsch, M., Artigas, J., Ryu, J.H., Ferre, M.: Multilateral control for delayed teleoperation. IEEE International Conference on Advanced Robotics, pp. 1–6 (2013)
10. Panzirsch, M., Balachandran, R., Artigas, J.: Cartesian task allocation for cooperative, multilateral teleoperation under time delay. In: IEEE International Conference on Robotics and Automation, pp. 312–317 (2015)
11. Quang, H.V., Ryu, J.H.: Stable multilateral teleoperation with time domain passivity approach. In: IEEE International Conference on Intelligent Robots And Systems, pp. 5890–5895 (2013)

12. Tavakoli, M., Aziminejad, A., Patel, R., Moallem, M.: Enhanced transparency in haptics-based master-slave systems. In: IEEE American Control Conference (ACC), pp. 1455–1460 (2007)

13. Tobergte, A., Albu-Schaeffer, A.: Direct force reflecting teleoperation with a flexible joint robot. In: IEEE International Conference on Robotics and Automation, pp. 4280–4287 (2012)

14. Willaert, B., Corteville, B., Reynaerts, D., Brussel, H.V., Poorten, E.B.V.: Bounded environment passivity of the classical position-force teleoperation controller. In: IEEE International Conference on Intelligent Robots and Systems, pp. 4622–4628 (2009)

Enhancement of Virtual Simulator for Marine Crane Operations via Haptic Device with Force Feedback

Yingguang Chu[1](✉), Houxiang Zhang[1], and Wei Wang[2]

[1] Norwegian University of Science and Technology,
Postboks 1517, 6025 Aalesund, Norway
{yingguang.chu,hozh}@ntnu.no
[2] Beihang University, Xueyuanlu 37, Haidian, 100191 Beijing, China
wangweilab@buaa.edu.cn

Abstract. This paper presents simulations of marine crane operations using a haptic device with force feedback. Safe and efficient marine crane operations are challenging under adverse environmental conditions. System testing and operation training on physical systems and prototypes are time-consuming and costly. The development of virtual simulators alleviates the shortcomings with physical systems by providing 3D visualization and force feedback to the operator. Currently, haptic technology has limited applications in heavy industries, due to the system stability and safety issues related to the remote control of large manipulators. As a result, a novel 6-DoF haptic device was developed for crane operations allowing for a larger workspace range and higher stiffness. The employment of the haptic device enlarges the interaction scope of the virtual simulator by sending feedback forces to the operator. In the case study, simulations of marine crane anti-sway control suggested that the load sway time and amplitude were reduced with force feedback. Using the haptic device, it also helps the crane operator to prevent problematic operations.

Keywords: Marine crane operations · Virtual simulation · Force feedback

1 Introduction

Compared to land-based cranes, marine cranes are even harder to operate when considering both safety and working efficiency. The movements of the vessel cause many problems in offshore and subsea applications. As a result, it is difficult to achieve stable and accurate positioning of the heavy pendulum load via remote control devices. The load sway results in high safety risks for the object, equipment and personnel on board. In marine crane operations, direct visual information including monitors and sensors in the control room tends to be insufficient for the operators to make quick and adequate response in practice. It demands a lot of experience from the operators, and intensive concentrations during the operation. Haptic device with force feedback can help

F. Bello et al. (Eds.): EuroHaptics 2016, Part I, LNCS 9774, pp. 327–337, 2016.
DOI: 10.1007/978-3-319-42321-0_30

convey information directly to the operators, leaving them to concentrate on the task in hand. The employment of force feedback in virtual simulations improves the effectiveness of training for operational skill acquisition [1].

Haptic technology has so far few applications in marine industry compared to other engineering fields, such as robotics, medical surgery, and gaming. This is partly due to the remote-controlled mechanisms in offshore and subsea applications are usually much larger and heavier. What's more, the inertial effects of the heavy pendulum create tremendous impacts on the stability of the crane. As a result, the velocity and force mapping between the haptic device and the controlled mechanism are more difficult to achieve. In addition, the operational environment, which is hard to predict, is as equally complex to cope with.

Previous studies on the effects of force feedback in suppressing the load sway during crane teleoperation show that both the sway amplitude and time for stabilizing the load are reduced with force feedback [2–4]. These studies performed experiments on sway suppressing of 1-DoF overhead crane operations, specifically the initiative sway due to the acceleration at start. Takemoto et al. [5, 6] presented control system for obstacle avoidance and load sway suppressing using a proposed haptic joystick. The joystick with 2-DoF rotates about X-axis and Y-axis controlling the first rotary joint and the hoisting boom of the crane. However, the flexibility of the proposed system is limited to certain types of crane applications. Load sway in marine crane operations exists in three dimensions, which changes constantly due to the environmental effects. As a result, safe and efficient marine crane operations is highly dependent on the experience and skills of the operators.

In this paper, we present a virtual simulator for marine crane operation with force feedback using a Novel Haptic Device (NHD). The 6-DoF haptic device was developed for large slave mechanisms providing a large working space and high stiffness [7]. Modeling of the crane's physical systems is developed using Bond Graph (BG) method, which is a modeling technique based on identifying the energetic structure of the physical system [8]. A typical 3-DoF offshore Knuckle Boom Crane (KBC) is implemented for the simulations [10]. A special type of bond graph called IC-field is provided for the implementation of the Lagrange's equations, which are used to describe the multi-body dynamics of the KBC [9]. The manipulation of the crane is realized using inverse velocity control instead of joint-by-joint control, i.e., control of the crane end tip movements by solving the inverse kinematics of the joystick and the crane [11]. This provides more flexibility for different types of cranes, and the possibility of implementing the heave compensation and anti-sway algorithms.

The implementation and simulation of the modeling is done by a software tool called 20-sim [12]. A static-link DLL is used in order to connect the haptic device to the virtual crane simulator. The virtual crane simulator alleviates the shortcomings of operating physical systems in terms of time and cost for system testing and operation training purposes. With the employment of force feedback in the simulations, the control algorithms can be tested for the improvement of the working efficiency and safety of operations. Human interaction applications can also be studied to reduce the working stress of the operators.

2 Mapping of the Haptic Device and the Crane

According to the architecture, industrial joystick type of devices for remote-controlled equipment can be divided into two categories, i.e., serial type devices and parallel type devices. Parallel type devices with closed-loop architectures provide higher stiffness and accuracy, but smaller workspace. Application practices of parallel type haptic devices are mostly found in medical surgery, aerospace, micromanipulation and gaming in controlling small manipulators and robots [13]. Parallel type devices are with more compact architectures, hence allow for smaller workspace, more positioning precision, and smaller feedback force to the operator. These are, however, not suitable for controlling of large slave mechanisms with heavy loads like marine cranes, where the requirement on positioning precision is less crucial than on safety and working efficiency. The other category, i.e., serial type of devices are with higher force capability and comparatively larger workspace [14]. As a result, the control of serial type haptic devices usually requires the movements from the forearm of the operator instead of only the waist and fingers. Serial type devices have simpler architectures, which makes it easier to solve the kinematics and more convenient for the installation of sensors and actuators. However, serial type devices have the drawbacks in singularities, low system stiffness and large momentum inertias due to their open architectures.

Based on the above considerations, the NHD was developed for marine operations with the Robotics Institute of Beihang University. The NHD has 6-DoF allowing for the adaption to different types of cranes, as shown in Fig. 1. Marine cranes are usually with serial type architectures; hence it is easier for the velocity and force mapping to serial types of devices and more intuitive for the operators to manipulate the cranes. In order to increase the operational stability of the device, a parallel four-bar mechanism is designed at the second link [15]. The spring wheel mechanism is used to achieve static self-balance of the device at any position. This also means that joint two and three are dependent on each other. From the kinematic point of view, the first three joints determine the positions of the end effector, and the last three joints determine the

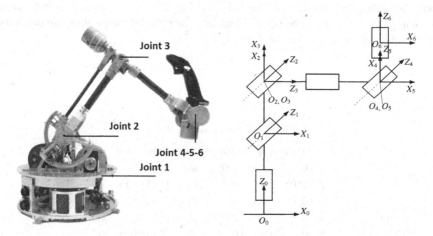

Fig. 1. The NHD prototype and its kinematic coordinates based on the DH method

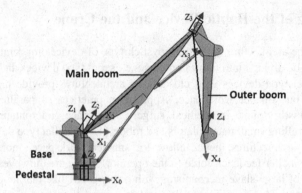

Fig. 2. The KBC and its kinematic coordinates based on DH method

orientations. The origins of the last three joints are intersecting at the same point in order to make it easier for getting explicit solutions of the inverse kinematics and the allocation of the motors and encoders for static self-balance.

The controlled slave mechanism in the case study is a typical 3-DoF offshore crane with a compact size for storage and maneuvering objects on the deck, as shown in Fig. 2. It consists of a crane base seated via the slew bearing at the pedestal. The two booms bend like the finger knuckles actuated via two hydraulic cylinders. Traditional control of cranes using joysticks is joint-by-joint control, which lacks the flexibility for the adaption to different types of cranes. Through the inverse control of the crane, the NHD can be employed regardless of the types of the cranes, hence more intuitive for the operator to position the load.

The Denavit-Hartenberg (DH) method is a systematic approach in robotics describing the mapping from the end tip to the joints of a kinematic chain. The kinematic coordinates of the NHD and the KBC are shown in Figs. 1 and 2. The DH tables of the DH parameters are given in Tables 1 and 2. The transformation matrix and the Jacobian can be derived accordingly. Due to the size limitation of the paper, the computations of the kinematics of the NHD and the KBC are not presented, but can be found in reference [7, 10]. The velocity and force mapping of the joystick and the crane can then be obtained, as given by Eqs. (1) and (2).

$$\dot{\theta} = J^{-1}v \tag{1}$$

$$\tau = J^T F \tag{2}$$

Table 1. DH parameters of the NHD

i	a_i(mm)	α_i(°)	d_i(mm)	θ_i(°)	Range of θ_i
1	0	−90	197	θ_1	[−40,40]
2	250	0	0	θ_2	[−135,−45]
3	0	−90	0	θ_3	[−45,45]
4	0	90	250	θ_4	[−80,80]
5	0	90	0	θ_5	[35,135]
6	0	0	0	θ_6	[−80,80]

Table 2. DH parameters of the KBC

i	a_i(mm)	α_i(°)	d_i(mm)	θ_i(°)
1	0	0	2560	θ_1
2	0	90	0	θ_2
3	7010	0	0	θ_3
4	3500	0	0	0

Where J is the Jacobian matrix, $\dot{\theta}$ is the joint angular velocity vector, v is the e end tip velocity vector, τ is the joint torque vector, and F is the end tip force vector.

3   The Virtual Crane Simulator with Force Feedback

The architecture of the control diagram of the virtual crane simulator with force feedback is shown as in Fig. 3. The force feedback of the NHD uses impedance control, i.e. the operator moves the joystick to control the crane in the virtual simulator, where the feedback joint torques are calculated and sent back to the joystick controller. More specifically, the NHD controller calculates the end tip position according to the joint position increment obtained by the sensor at each joint using the forward kinematics. By a coefficient, the crane simulator calculates the positions of the crane joints using the inverse kinematics. The virtual crane simulator calculates the acting force on the crane end tip and sends it to the NHD. By a coefficient, the NHD controller calculates joint torques from the force on the joystick end tip, and sends them to the joint servo motors of the NHD,

Modeling of the crane are developed using BG method and implemented in 20-sim. The complete model is shown in Fig. 4 using a combination of bond graphs for representing the crane dynamics and block disgrams for the control algorithms. The development of the component sub-models in detail can be found in the reference [11], including the multi-body dynamics of the crane, the wire and the pendulum load, the actuators with PID-controllers, and the kinematic control of the crane. All the bond graphs and sub-model blocks arc equation-based implementations of the physical laws.

A static-link DLL, i.e., the pmacDLL sub-model, is implemented in order to connect the haptic device to the virtual crane simulator. The static DLL calls a "pmac" function at each simulation time-step to read the end position of the NHD, and record the force on the crane end tip to calculate the torques of the servo motors. The input for

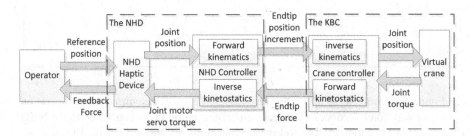

Fig. 3. The control architecture of the virtual crane simulator with force feedback

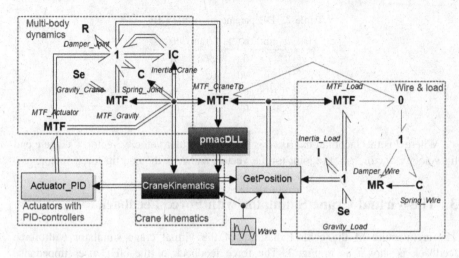

Fig. 4. BG model of the KBC with the NHD

the controller sub-model is the end tip force for the NHD, and the output is the end tip velocity for the KBC. The program code of calling the pmac.dll in 20-sim is presented. The frequency for the discrete signals is set at 20 Hz, in consideration of the real-time performance and computation accuracy of the simulations.

```
//This sub-model calls a function called 'pmac'
parameters
   string dll_name = 'pmac.dll';
   string function_name = 'pmac';
variables
   real dll_input[6], dll_output[6];
code
//Prepare the DLL function inputs
   dll_input = [ feedback_fx; feedback_fy; feedback_fz;
   feedback_gamma; feedback_beta; feedback_alpha ];
//Call the 'my_custom_20simfunction' function in the DLL
   dll_output = dll(dll_name, function_name, dll_input);
//Read the DLL function outputs
   [tip_delta_pos_px; tip_delta_pos_py; tip_delta_pos_pz;
   tip_delta_pos_gamma; tip_delta_pos_beta;
   tip_delta_pos_alpha] = dll_output;
```

Figure 5 shows the setup of the physical systems of the virtual crane operation simulator with force feedback. The crane simulator on the PC is connected to the NHD controller via the Ethernet. The following control modes are implemented to increase

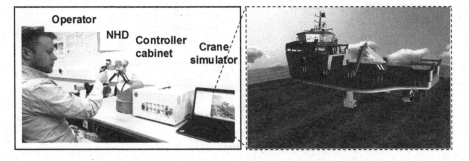

Fig. 5. The virtual marine crane simulator with force feedback

the usability and stability of the system. Switching between the alternative modes is realized using buttons on the joystick, and indicated by LED lights on the NHD controller cabinet.

- Check mode: The NHD controller checks all the safety factors of the system, including the joint positions and velocity, the servo motor current, the communication to the virtual crane simulator, etc. The end tip position and feedback force are both set at zero. The servo motors remain at open-loop until all the checking conditions are passed.
- Idle mode: The servo motors are switched to close-loop after all checking conditions passed at the check mode. The end tip position and feedback force remain at zero. The virtual crane doesn't follow the control of the joystick. The joystick doesn't receive feedback force from the crane.
- Work mode: Work mode includes Uni-direction and Bi-direction control, i.e., the crane in the virtual simulator is controlled either with or without feedback forces sent to the joystick.
- Emergency mode: In case of emergency, the stop button on the controller can be pressed down. The end tip position and feedback force are set to zero. The servo motors are set to open-loop. The controller remains at check mode until the emergency stop button is released.

4 Load Anti-sway Control Using the NHD

Load sway is one of the most challenging problems in offshore lifting operations. Inteligent control algorithms have been proposed in order to reduce the sway of the pendulum load caused by the movements of the vessel, external forces, system instability and problematic human operations. However, load sway in offshore operations is hard to be predicted or effectively avoided in practice as many external factors affect the sway. As a result, it requires the interference of the operators whenever the sway occurs. Experience and skills from practice is an essential part of the crane operator training. Virtual crane simulators for training have been used and proved of great

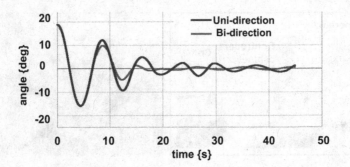

Fig. 6. Load sway angles of crane anti-sway control using the NHD (Color figure online)

values in the aspects of improving the operators' skills, hence improving the operation safety and efficiency. The following experimental setup presents simulations of using the NHD for anti-sway crane lifting operations.

The test was carried out by inexperienced lab technists as the crane operators, provided with 30 min training. Load sway in offshore operations could occur in three dimensions; however, the sway in the transverse direction of the vessel is the most dominate and dangerous. To simplify the problem for the experiment, the load is given an initial load sway of ±20° in the transverse direction of the vessel with 10 meters lifting wire. External environmental impacts were not included in the simulation model, nor any automated intelligent anti-sway control algorithm. The load sway angle was suppressed by manipulating the crane with and without force feedback using the NHD. The testing results on three individual subjects suggested similar results. According to the simulation results, it took 30 s to reduce the load sway to less than ±2° without force feedback, i.e., Uni-direction control. The amplitude of the sway was reduced to 12° after the first sway cycle. Simulations of anti-sway operations with force feedback, i.e., Bi-direction control, indicated both reduced time and amplitude of the load sway by average, as shown in Fig. 6. However, the effectiveness of the introduction of force feedback in addition to the 3D animation to suppress the load sway is trivial. In the case of 3D visualization unavailable, force feedback could help to prevent problematic operations that would result in accidents, e.g., move the crane in the wrong direction out of panic, and consequently generate more sway of the load.

As shown in Fig. 7, the feedback forces decreased as the sway was reduced until 15 s. From 25 s, load sway was generated intentionally by moving the crane in opposite direction of the load. Consequently, the feedback forces to the operator via the NHD increased. The NHD provides resistance forces to the operator guiding the correct movements of the NHD, hence the crane. In the case of the crane reaches to its limits or collides with other rigid objects, the operation will stop to ensure the safety.

It is also noted that continuous operation with force feedback can be exhausting, especially when the feedback force is big for the operator to hold stable grip of the joystick all the time. According to the recent research and design of flexible haptic devices, such as PHANToM and Force Dimension, the maximum output force is usually set within the range of 10–25 N. The NHD is designed with the maximum force of 12 N and the maximum torque of 0.15 Nm. On one hand, the operator needs to

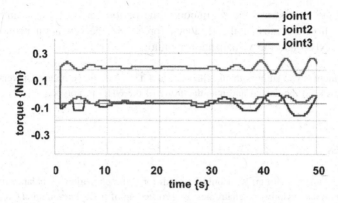

Fig. 7. Feedback forces due to the load sway (Color figure online)

overcome the feedback forces to move the crane. On the other hand, the feedback force cannot be too small to provide sufficient perceptions to the human hand. Improved feedback force algorithms to the operator via the NHD needs to be studied in order to reduce the stress during long period operations.

5 Conclusion

A virtual simulator with a haptic device for marine crane operations is introduced in the study. Simulations in virtual environment provide a flexible and cost effective approach for the testing of crane operations and the training of operators. 3D visualization and force feedback send direct information to the operator during the operations. Haptic device with force feedback adds another sense of feeling to the operator besides the visual information.

Experiments on using the NHD for load anti-sway control showed both the sway time and the amplitude was reduced with force feedback. The experiments were performed in the laboratory by inexperienced users as the crane operators. The results suggested that the introduction of force feedback for suppressing the sway is trivial in addition to the provided 3D visualizations. However, using the haptic device with force feedback helps to prevent problematic operations, which may result in disastrous consequences, especially in the case of visual-blind areas. It is also noted that continuous operations with force feedback can be exhausting for the operators after relatively short periods. On one hand, the NHD is designed with the maximum output force allowing for continuous operations of master-slave mechanisms. On the other hand, small force feedback fails to provide insufficient perceptions for the human hand.

As has been pointed that offshore crane operations are far too complicated in terms of unpredictable factors, the test of using the NHD for training purposes needs a systematic design for the operation scenarios. Quantitive study on the stress induced by the feedback force to the operators during operations is important for the optimization of the force feedback via the NHD. For example, the experiments on the individual subjects could be performed in a larger sample and evaluated by the time used for suppressing the load sway, the continuous time period for operations, and compare these with different scales of the feedback force, and the operation position of the operator, the NHD and the visualization monitor.

Acknowledgment. The authors thank Zhao Lei and Ting Ye with Beihang University for the preliminary work on the design and manufacturing of the NHD prototype.

References

1. Kado, Y., Pan, Y., Furuta, K.: Control system for skill acquisition — balancing pendulum based on human adaptive mechatronics. In: Proceeding of IEEE International Conference on Systems, Man, and Cybernetics, Taipei, Taiwan, pp. 4040–4045, 8–11 October 2006
2. Villaverde, A.F., Raimúndez, C., Barreiro, A.: Passive internet-based crane teleoperation with haptic aids. J. Control Autom. Syst. **10**(1), 78–87 (2012)
3. Sato, R., Noda, Y., Miyoshi, T., Terashima, K., Kakihara, K., Nie, Y., Funato, K.: Operational support control by haptic joystick considering load sway suppression and obstacle avoidance for intelligent crane. In: Proceeding of IEEE Annual Conference of Industrial Electronics, Porto, Portugal, pp. 2301–2307, 3–5 November 2009
4. Farkhatdinov, I., Ryu, J.-H.: A study on the role of force feedback for teleoperation of industrial overhead crane. In: Ferre, M. (ed.) EuroHaptics 2008. LNCS, vol. 5024, pp. 796–805. Springer, Heidelberg (2008)
5. Takemoto, A., Yano, K., Terashima, K.: Obstacle avoidance control system of rotary crane using proposed haptic joystick. In: Proceeding of Eurohaptics Conference, 2005 and Symposium on Haptic Interfaces for Virtual Environment and Teleoperator Systems, 2005, pp. 662–663, 18–20 March 2005. First Joint World Haptics 2005
6. Takemoto, A., Yano, K., Miyoshi, T., Terashima, K.: Operation assist control system of rotary crane using proposed haptic joystick as man-machine interface. In: Proceeding of 13th IEEE International Workshop on Robot and Human Interactive Communication (ROMAN), pp. 533–538, 20–22 September 2004
7. Liang, Y., Li, X., Chu, Y., Li, W.: Kinetostatics and spring static balancing for a novel haptic device. J. Int. J. Adv. Robot. Syst. (2015, submitted)
8. Karnopp, D.C., Margolis, D.L., Rosenberg, R.C.: System Dynamics: Modeling, Simulation, and Control of Mechatronic Systems. Wiley, New Jersey (2012)
9. Chu, Y., Æsøy, V.: A multi-body dynamic model based on bond graph for maritime hydraulic crane operation. In: Proceeding of International Conference on Ocean, Offshore and Arctic Engineering 2015, St. John's, Newfoundland, Canada, no. 41616, 31 May–6 June 2015
10. Bak, M.K., Hansen, M.R.: Analysis of offshore knuckle boom crane - part one: modeling and parameter identification. J. Model. Ident. Control **34**(4), 157–174 (2013)
11. Chu, Y., Sanfilippo, F., Æsøy, V., Zhang, H.: An effective heave compensation and anti-sway control approach for offshore hydraulic crane operations. In: Proceedings of IEEE International Conference on Mechatronics and Automation, Tianjin, China, pp. 1282–1287, 3–6 August 2014
12. Controllab Products B.V. (2015). http://www.20sim.com/
13. Khan, S.: Design and optimization of parallel haptic devices: design methodology and experimental evaluation. Doctoral thesis, Trita-MMK (2012)

14. Ueberle, M., Buss, M.: Design, control, and evaluation of a new 6 DOF haptic device. In: Proceedings of IEEE International Conference on Intelligent Robots and Systems, pp. 2949–2954 (2002)
15. Cruz-Valverde, C., Dominguez-Ramirez, O.A., Ponce-de-León-Sánchez, E.R., Trejo-Mota, I., Sepúlveda-Cervantes, G.: Kinematic and dynamic modeling of the PHANToM premium 1.0 haptic device: experimental validation. In: Electronics, Robotics and Automotive Mechanics Conference (CERMA), pp. 494–501, 28 September–1 October 2010

A Novel Haptic Stylus for Mobile Terminal

Lei Tian, Aiguo Song$^{(\boxtimes)}$, and Dapeng Chen

School of Instrument Science and Engineering,
Southeast University, Nanjing, China
tianleiseu@163.com, {a.g.song,230149546}@seu.edu.cn

Abstract. Haptic interaction is a new interactive function in human-computer interaction of mobile terminal. In this work, we present a novel haptic stylus for mobile terminal, which can achieve haptic display of visual image. The haptic stylus generates force feedback and tactile feedback through electromechanical structure and piezoelectric ceramics respectively. In order to obtain the haptic information of image, we adopt shape from shading (SFS) algorithm to extract height information of image, which is presented in the form of force feedback. And fractional differential method is used to extract edge information of image, which is expressed in the form of tactile feedback. The software system of haptic interaction is developed based on Android system. And the mode of communication is Bluetooth. Finally, the haptic perception experiment is conducted to investigate effect of perception with different haptic stylus and different mode of haptic interaction.

Keywords: Haptic stylus · Mobile terminal · Shape from shading · Image edge extraction

1 Introduction

Haptic interaction technology is a new kind of human-computer interaction (HCI) technology. It expands the mode of HCI and improves the quality of HCI [1]. If it is applied to the mobile terminal (e.g. smartphone or tablet), the HCI interface functions of mobile terminal are no longer limited to audio-visual interaction and simple tactile interaction. In recent years, with the rapid development of mobile terminal, many researchers have done a lot of work in the field of haptic interaction for mobile terminal. Since most of the current mobile terminals interact via touch screen, the design of haptic interactive device is mainly based on stylus and embedded structure.

The stylus-based interactive device basically adopts vibration interaction. Kyung and Park [2] proposed the Ubi-Pen, which is a pen-like haptic interface consisted of a compact tactile display and a vibrating module. They constructed only a 3 × 3 pin array to express texture and vibration stimuli. So the image texture information needed to be compressed and the resolution will be lost a lot. Lee et al. [3] developed a pressure-sensitive tactile feedback stylus. When user operates on the touchscreen with the stylus, pressure signal from user operation can control solenoid to generate tactile vibration. Withana et al. [4] designed a force feedback stylus which can dynamically change its effective length by DC motor and the structure of rack gear and is equipped

© Springer International Publishing Switzerland 2016
F. Bello et al. (Eds.): EuroHaptics 2016, Part I, LNCS 9774, pp. 338–349, 2016.
DOI: 10.1007/978-3-319-42321-0_31

with an accelerometer to calculate its orientation. When a user presses down the nib on touchscreen, the stylus shrinks and a virtual nib appears in the screen. But the volume of the stylus is big and adopts the way of wired connection. Poupyrev et al. [5] developed a tactile interactive device based on a 3 M Microtouch panel which can make the screen generating frequency-controlled electrovibration signal. It can gain a better haptic display for image texture. But the device requires high voltage to drive and the system is more complex.

In order to meet requirements of miniaturization and general for mobile terminals, we have designed a miniature multi-mode haptic pen based on magneto-rheological (MR) fluids damper, linear resonant actuator (LRAs) and piezo-ceramic actuator [6]. The limitation of the haptic pen is that the MR fluids damper is passive and cannot be reset automatically. To receive active and continuous haptic feedback, this paper proposed a new haptic stylus based on electromechanical structure and piezoelectric ceramics. Through the visual image processing and haptic modeling, users can interact with the image by force and tactile simultaneously. Furthermore, three-dimensional visualization scene is established by OpenGL ES library. The stylus is portable because of small volume and wireless transmission.

2 Design of the Haptic Stylus

2.1 Mechanical Design

The mechanical structure of the haptic stylus is shown in Fig. 1. The haptic stylus is composed of capacitance nib, connecting rod, lantern ring, spring, slider, lead screw, motor, encoder and shell. Cylindrical connecting rod is used to connect the capacitance nib with lead screw. Slider is mounted on the lead screw and connected with the lantern ring by a spring. When the slider which is driven by the motor moves linearly, the length of the spring also changes. So the user's fingers holding on the lantern ring will feel the pulling force accordingly. Encoder is installed on the back end of motor. It can count the number of rotations of motor to control the movement distance of the slider.

In this work, we choose Maxon motor. Its rated voltage is 4.2 V and rated current is 0.237A. The diameter of this motor is only 8 mm. So it is very small and suitable for installing in interactive haptic stylus. In order to make the slider moving as fast as possible, the reduction ratio of screw reducer is chose as small as possible. Our choice is 4:1. The piezoelectric ceramic vibrator is produced by Samsung. It is placed in the rear end of stylus with circuit boards (see Fig. 2). Lantern ring and slide block are

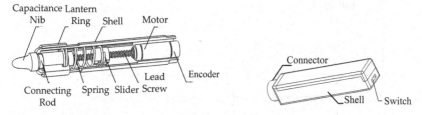

Fig. 1. The mechanical structure diagram of haptic stylus.

Fig. 2. Structure diagram of the rear end of haptic stylus.

machined by brass material. So they have better conductivity and less deformation. The stylus's dimension is 220 × 25 × 22 mm and its weight is 100 g.

2.2   The Haptic Interaction System

Figure 3 shows the schematic of the haptic interaction system. It consists of haptic stylus and mobile terminal. The tasks of the mobile terminal include extraction of the height of image, extraction of the edges of image and sending the information to haptic stylus via Bluetooth. And the position of stylus is obtained by the coordinate information of the stylus sliding on the image, thus achieving the stylus' position tracking. Finally, three-dimensional model of image is established in OpenGL ES three-dimensional space.

The part of haptic stylus mainly consists of power module, communication module, control module (MCU), actuator and attitude measuring module of stylus. HC-05 Bluetooth module is adopted in the communication module. The power module is mainly used for level adaptation. Rechargeable lithium battery (1000 mAh) is used to supply power. It can meet the energy needs of haptic stylus. The control module contains the STM32 microprocessor whose peripheral resources are very rich. Actuator includes height information expression module and piezoelectric ceramics.

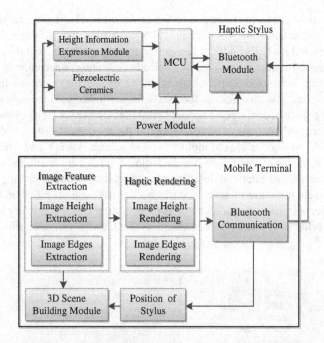

Fig. 3. Architecture diagram of the haptic interaction system.

3 Feature Extraction of Image

3.1 Image Height Extraction

This paper adopts shape from shading (SFS) method for three-dimensional reconstruction of object surface in image. Shape from shading is one of the key technologies of three-dimensional shape recovery problem in computer vision. Its task is to recover the 3D shape of surface by using light and shade change of object surface in a single image [7]. This paper uses the Tsai and Shah [8] algorithm, which is linear method of SFS. The algorithm has the advantages of easy implementation, fast iteration speed and so on.

3.2 Image Edge Extraction

We use the method of fractional differential for edges extraction. Because fractional differential can not only properly enhance the high and moderate frequency part of signal, but also don't sharp attenuate very low frequency part of the signal which is nonlinear reserved to some extent. So fractional differential can extract edges in different smoothness regions of the image, particularly in the smooth area of image edges extraction where the method has better results than other methods.

Fractional differential operation is an extension of the integer-order differential operation. In this paper, we use the G-L definition which is commonly used in digital image processing [9]. For signal $f(t) \in [a, t](a < t, a \in R, t \in R)$, γ-order G-L fractional differential definition is

$$
{}^{G}_{a}D^{\gamma}_{t}f(t) = \lim_{h \to 0} \frac{1}{h^{\gamma}} \sum_{m=0}^{\frac{t-a}{h}} (-1)^{m} \frac{\Gamma(\gamma+1)}{m!\Gamma(\gamma-m+1)} f(t-hm) \tag{1}
$$

Where $\gamma \in R^{-}$, the Gamma function is $\Gamma(n) = \int_{0}^{\infty} e^{-t}t^{n-1}\mathrm{d}t = (n-1)!$.

The continuous range of $f(t)$ is $t \in [a, t]$. And we can get $n = [t-a/h]^{h=1} = [t-a]$ by dividing the continuous range with interval $h = 1$. Then the difference expression of fractional differential can be derived:

$$
\frac{d^{\gamma}f(t)}{dt^{\gamma}} \approx f(t) + (-\gamma)f(t-1) + \frac{(-\gamma)(-\gamma+1)}{2}f(t-2) + \\
\cdots + \frac{\Gamma(-\gamma+1)}{n!\Gamma(-\gamma+n+1)}f(t-n) \tag{2}
$$

We choose the first three items of the difference expression of fractional differential to construct 5×5 fractional differential mask [10]. This choice can make operation easier and not have much error. Finally, we can get edges of the image by subtracting the original image from the image after filtering by mask of fractional differential.

4 Haptic Rendering of Image

4.1 Rendering of Image Height

When fingers grip on the stylus and slide from pixel A to pixel B on the image, we can read the height information of pixel A and pixel B. So force expression of height difference between the two pixels is defined as follows.

$$h_B - h_A = \Delta h \propto F = k(l_B - l_A) = k \cdot \Delta l_{BA} \tag{3}$$

Where h_B and h_A are the height information of pixel B and pixel A, Δh is height difference between the two pixels, l_B and l_A are spring elongation of corresponding pixels, Δl_{BA} is length variation of spring between A and B, namely the displacement of slider.

When slider moves back and forth along lead screw under the microprocessor control, the length of spring will change (see Fig. 4). In addition, the motion of lantern ring can also generate deformation of the spring $\left(\Delta l'_1, \Delta l'_2\right)$. However, this deformation is far less than the deformation simulated by the movement of slider. So it is ignored. If $\Delta h > 0$, it illustrates that the height of image at point B is greater than point A. Microprocessor sends instruction to motor in order to make motor rotate and drive slider upward movement via lead screw. Then deformation of spring increases Δl_1 so that hand feel the damping force $\Delta F = k \cdot \Delta l_1 > 0$. And hand will feel the damping force increases during the sliding from point A to point B, so the user has raising experience. On the contrary if $\Delta h < 0$, it illustrates that the height of image at point B is less than point A. Motor drive slider downward movement via lead screw. Then deformation of spring decreases Δl_2 so that hand feel the damping force $\Delta F = k \cdot \Delta l_1 < 0$. And hand will feel the damping force decreases, so user has sunken experience.

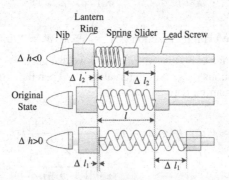

Fig. 4. Force display diagram of image height.

4.2 Rendering of Image Edge

First, it is assumed that the pixel value of a point in the edge image is v. Then the relationship between pixel and piezoelectric vibration can be expressed as follows.

$$v \propto 1/(U,f) \tag{4}$$

Where U denotes the AC drive voltage of piezoelectric ceramics and f denotes the vibration frequency. U is always proportional to v. Vibration frequency f can be adjusted by software to achieve the best tactile sense of vibration.

5   Experiments and Results

5.1   Experiment 1: The Calibration of Force Output of the Electromechanical Structure

This haptic stylus relies on the spring tension to express the height of an image. To verify the performance of the device, it is necessary to design an experiment for the calibration of force output of the haptic device.

Apparatus. Digital force gauge is used to the calibration experiment of force output. It is produced by Addibe. The accuracy and resolution of force gauge are high. Accuracy is 0.5, dividing value is 0.01 N and the range reaches 20 N. It can. meet the test requirements.

Experiment Scheme. Firstly, an iron wire is mounted on the back end of lantern ring and connected with the hook of digital force gauge by string (see Fig. 5). Then the digital force gauge and the haptic stylus are completely fixed to the table plate by tape. And it is ensure that the axis of digital force gauge and haptic stylus on the same line by using a ruler. Secondly, the string on the hook is still in a relaxed state after fixing the position of force gauge and stylus. Then the motor is rotated under the control of software until string is tensioned. When the reading on force gauge is changed from 0 N to less than 0.2 N, the string is just tensioned. And this value is the start point of calibration. Finally, Every time motor rotates four laps under the control of software, the slider can move 2 mm.

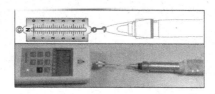

Fig. 5. The calibration of force output of the electromechanical structure

Result. Figure 6 shows the result of calibration. According to the calibration results, at the time of displacement of the slider reaches 1.8 cm, force output of the lantern ring can be up to 3.23 N. After fitting the data by least square method, we got a straight line: F = 1.7791 ∗ x + 0.093818. Where F denotes output force of haptic stylus, x represents displacement of slider. According to the fitting curve, it is calculated that root mean square error is 0.051. So it can be seen that the linearity of the calibration results

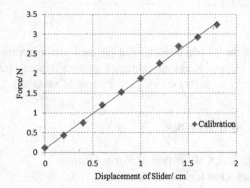

Fig. 6. The calibration results and fitting curve of force output of the electromechanical structure

is good. In other words, according the height of image, motor can control the haptic stylus to generate corresponding haptic interactive effect effectively.

5.2   Experiment 2: Comparison of the Effectiveness of the Two Haptic Styluses in Displaying the Height of the Image

Experimental Images. We conduct haptic experiment with six images (see Fig. 7) to observe the perception effectiveness of the image with different haptic styluses. The six images show different three-dimensional surfaces.

Participants and Apparatus. In this experiment, there are twenty subjects (12 males, 8 females) who range from 20 to 35 years old. None of them had prior experience with virtual haptic display of image on mobile terminal. And all were reported to have no known kinesthetic problems. The devices used in the experiment are two haptic

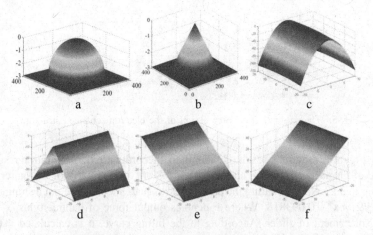

Fig. 7. The six images with different three-dimensional surfaces

styluses and a Samsung tablet computer. The two haptic styluses display the height of the image by the MR fluids damper and the motor/lead-screw system. The haptic interactive software system is developed based on Android system.

Experiment Scheme. There are two types of haptic styluses in this experiment. Before the formal experiment, subjects need to learn how to use the two haptic styluses to perceive the object in image through the menu list. In the formal experiment, the appearance of images is hidden and the order of images is random. The subject moved the haptic stylus across the touchscreen to perform the haptic interaction. Then he or she had to state which image was present in the six experimental images after the experiment.

Result and Discussion. The statistical results of experiment 2 are shown in Table 1. We can see that recognition correct rate of most images with the motor/lead-screw system are higher than the MR fluids damper. To quantitatively analyze the advantages of multi-rendering, we conducted paired T-test analysis of two sets of perception results. Table 2 shows sample statistics for the above experimental data. Paired T-test analysis of recognition correct rate by these two haptic styluses is illustrated in Table 3. When degree of freedom is $df = 5$ and a significant level is $\alpha = 0.05$, the critical value is $t = 2.571$. While $t = 5.000$ is larger than critical value in this T-test. So there are

Table 1. Experimental results of image haptic perception (recognition correct rate %)

Experimental images						
	a	b	c	d	e	f
Motor/lead-screw	100	80	100	90	80	90
MR fluids	80	70	90	60	70	70

Table 2. Paired samples statistics

	Mean	N	Std. deviation	Std. error mean
Motor/lead-screw	90.000	6	8.944	3.6515
MR fluids	73.333	6	10.328	4.216

Table 3. Paired T-test analysis

	Paired differences							
				95 % Confidence interval of the difference				Sig.
	Mean	Std. deviation	Std. error mean	Lower	Upper	t	df	(2-tailed)
Motor/lead-screw– MR fluids	16.667	8.165	3.333	8.098	25.235	5.000	5	.004

significant differences between the mean recognition rates of the two haptic styluses. In other words, the recognition effect of the motor/lead-screw system has significant advantage.

5.3   Experiment 3: Comparison of the Effectiveness of Three Haptic Interactive Modes by Haptic Stylus with the Motor/Lead-Screw System

Experimental Images. We conduct haptic experiment with eight images (see Fig. 8) to observe the perception effect of the image with different haptic interactive modes. Objects have different three-dimensional shape in the eight images.

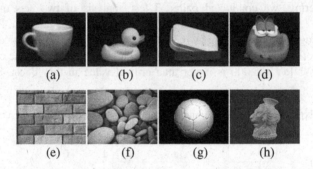

Fig. 8. The eight images with different three-dimensional shape

Participants and Apparatus. In this experiment, there are twenty subjects (12 males, 8 females) who range from 20 to 35 years old. None of them had prior experience with virtual haptic display of image on mobile terminal. And all were reported to have no known kinesthetic problems. The devices used in the experiment are a haptic stylus with the motor/lead-screw system and a Samsung tablet computer (see Fig. 9). The haptic interactive software system is developed based on Android system.

Fig. 9. A subject was exploring on the touchscreen via the haptic stylus with the motor/lead-screw system.

Fig. 10. The height and edge extraction results of experimental images

Experiment Scheme. There are three kinds of haptic interactive mode in the experiment. Mode 1 is display of the edges of an image by piezo-ceramic actuator. Mode 2 is display of the height of an image by electromechanical structure. Mode 3 is display of the height of an image by electromechanical structure and display of the edges of an image by piezo-ceramic actuator.

The height and edge extraction results of experimental images are shown in Fig. 10. The first column shows original images, the second column shows height images and the third column shows edge image. Before the formal experiment, subjects need to learn how to use the haptic stylus to select different haptic interactive mode to perceive image through the menu list.

In the formal experiment, every image needs to be tested alone. Subject chooses one image and must touch this image separately in the three haptic interactive modes. Considering that human touch memory is very short, subject is allowed to touch repeatedly. Finally, subjects are asked to provide a quantitative description for each mode on a scale from 1 to 10 [11]. The maximum value of 10 represents the best mode of haptic interaction of one image among the three modes. The spatial information of this image can be clearly felt. The minimum value of 1 denotes the worst mode of haptic interaction. In each trial, the subject is given a sheet of paper with a horizontal line that contained a visual analogue scale from 0 to 10. When an image is perceived in one mode, they place an "x" on the line according to their feelings. After completing three modes experiments of one image, subject selects second image to continue testing and recording results. The trial is finished until the tests of the whole images are completed. Note that each image is considered to be independent object. Subject can only give the three modes quantitative description on the basis of the same image.

Result and Discussion. The statistical results of experiment 3 are shown in Fig. 11. The ordinate denotes mean value. As can be seen from Fig. 11, the values of mode 1 are lowest and the values of mode 3 are highest. It means that the effect of haptic display

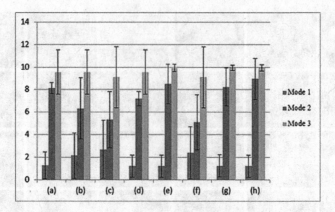

Fig. 11. The statistical results of experiment 3 (Color figure online)

only through the image edge is worst. This because the spatial sense of the image is weakened without the height information of image. In addition, the values of mode 2 are higher than mode 1. It illustrates that we can obtain better interactive effect by display of the height information of image. Obviously, the haptic interactive effect of mode 3 is best. It is worth noting that the values of mode 1 and mode 2 of image (c) and (f) are very close. From image (c), we can see that the display effect of image edge and height are almost the same for the image with simple, regular shape and unobvious height information. And from image (f), it can be seen that the image with more objects of irregular shape almost has the same haptic interactive effect in mode 1 and 2.

6 Conclusions

In this paper, we develop a novel haptic stylus which can interact with image on mobile terminal. The stylus is based on active haptic feedback included force feedback and vibration. The proposed stylus in this paper has a small size, light weights and wireless communication. So it is suitable to carry and interact on mobile terminal. In addition, the software system of this haptic interaction includes extraction and display for the height and edges of image. To verify the performance of the proposed stylus, we carried out three experiments. And the results show that the proposed stylus can express height and edges of an image by force and vibration stimulation effectively.

Because the piezoelectric ceramics can vibrate at different grades of frequency and intensity, it can present other features of an image. In further research, we can try to use piezoelectric ceramics to express the image height, texture, softness and other information. Then the image haptic display on mobile terminal can be improved and the user will have a better haptic experience.

Acknowledgements. This research was supported by the National Natural Science Foundation of China (No. 61272379), the National Hi-Tech Research and Development Program (No. 2013AA013703). The authors appreciate all colleagues in Remote Measuring and Control Laboratory and the anonymous reviewers for their very useful comments.

References

1. Hodges, M.: It just feels right. Comput. Graph. World **21**(10), 48–50 (1998)
2. Kyung, K.U., Lee, J.Y.: Ubi-Pen: a haptic interface with texture and vibrotactile display. IEEE Comput. Graph. Appl. **29**(1), 56–64 (2009)
3. Lee, J.C., Dietz, P.H., Leigh, D., et al.: Haptic pen: a tactile feedback stylus for touch screens. In: Proceedings of the 17th Annual ACM Symposium on User Interface Software and Technology, pp. 291–294 (2004)
4. Withana, A., Kondo, M., Makino, Y., et al.: ImpAct: immersive haptic stylus to enable direct touch and manipulation for surface computing. Comput. Entertainment (CIE) **8**(2), 9/1–9/16 (2010)
5. Bau, O., Poupyrev, I., Israr, A., et al.: TeslaTouch: electrovibration for touch surfaces. In: Proceedings of the 23nd Annual ACM Symposium on User Interface Software and Technology, pp. 283–292 (2010)
6. Chen, D., Song, A., Tian, L.: A novel miniature multi-mode haptic pen for image interaction on mobile terminal. In: IEEE International Symposium on Haptic, Audio and Visual Environments and Games (HAVE), pp. 1–6 (2015)
7. Shimodaira, H.: A shape-from-shading method of polyhedral objects using prior information. IEEE Trans. Pattern Anal. Mach. Intell. **28**, 612–624 (2006)
8. Tsai, P.S., Shah, M.: Shape from shading using linear approximation. Image Vis. Comput. J. **12**(8), 487–498 (1994)
9. Loverro, A.: Fractional calculus: history, definitions and applications for the engineer. Report, Department of Aerospace and Mechanical Engineering, Notre Dame (2004)
10. Yang, Z., Zhou, Z., Yang, J., et al.: Image enhancement based on fractional differentials. J. Comput. Aided Des. Comput. Graph. **20**(3), 343–348 (2008)
11. Wu, J., Li, N., Liu, W., Song, G., Zhang, J.: Experimental study on the perception characteristics of haptic texture by multidimensional scaling. IEEE Trans. Haptics **8**(4), 410–420 (2015)

Texture Rendering on a Tactile Surface Using Extended Elastic Images and Example-Based Audio Cues

Julien Fleureau, Yoan Lefevre, Fabien Danieau$^{(\boxtimes)}$, Philippe Guillotel, and Antoine Costes

Technicolor R&I, Cesson-Sévigné, France
fabien.danieau@technicolor.com

Abstract. A texture rendering system relying on pseudo-haptic and audio feedback is presented in this paper. While the user touches the texture displayed on a tactile screen, the associated image is deformed according to the contact area and the rubbing motion to simulate pressure. Additionally audio feedback is synthesized in real-time to simulate friction. A novel example-based scheme takes advantage of recorded audio samples of friction between actual textures and a finger at several speeds to synthesize the final output sound. This system can be implemented on any existing tactile screen without any extra mechanical device.

1 Introduction

Texture rendering is an active and challenging field of study where many input and output devices have been proposed. In their survey, Chouvardas et al. classified these textures rendering devices into three categories [3]: mechanical, electrotactile and thermal devices. Mechanical devices stimulates the mechanoreceptors within the skin using mechanical actuators. They include pin-based devices applying pressure, vibrating, ultrasonic and acoustic actuators, and devices based on electrorheological fluids. Electrotactile devices use electric stimulation to activate the mechanoreceptors. A matrix of electrodes is a typical example of such devices. Finally thermal devices provide heat or cool stimuli to the skin.

Another way to simulate texture properties without a specific device is to rely on pseudo-haptic feedback. Lécuyer has shown that various haptic sensations can be induced with visual stimuli [6]. This technique may provide sensations of stiffness, friction, mass of objects or haptic textures. Bump and holes have been simulated by varying the speed of the cursor exploring the texture [7]. The elasticity of a texture was also simulated by a deformation of the image and of the cursor [1]. These two approaches require to explore the texture with a mouse. To make the interaction more natural, Li et al. proposed a similar system embedded on a tablet [8]. The user can feel softness of a surface using a pen or a finger. Punpongsanon et al. developed an augmented reality system where the

© Springer International Publishing Switzerland 2016
F. Bello et al. (Eds.): EuroHaptics 2016, Part I, LNCS 9774, pp. 350–359, 2016.
DOI: 10.1007/978-3-319-42321-0_32

user touches an actual object while a projector changes the visual appearance of this object [9]. This visual feedback changes the perception of the softness of the object.

Audio stimuli may also modify the perception of texture. Kim et al. shows that the intensity of the sound changes the perception of roughness with or without haptic feedback [5]. The denseness and ruggedness are also affected by this intensity. Even with actual materials such as abrasive papers, sound modifies the perceived roughness [10].

In this work, we present a texture haptic rendering system based on visual and audio pseudo-haptic feedback. It may have applications in the context of e-shopping to virtually touch different materials of interest associated to clothes or furniture for instance. The user by interacting through a standard tactile screen is able to explore the physical properties of the texture, namely stiffness and friction. In line with the approaches mentioned hereinbefore, we rely on visual and audio illusions to generate haptic sensations. The new contributions involved in this latter system are twofolds:

- First, we propose to rely on the paradigm of elastic images introduced in [1], currently limited to punctual pressure contact with a mouse device. We introduce the features of continuous rubbing interaction and non-punctual contact with a finger on a tablet device. To that end, an underlying viscoelastic law and a new contact model are proposed. During the interaction, the texture is visually and dynamically deformed according to the contact area with the finger and rubbing motions.
- Second, a novel example-based audio synthesis process is proposed to render friction properties. It makes use of real audio samples to create a friction sound synchronized to the user's exploratory movement and consistent with the actual texture and rubbing speed.

Both visual deformation and sound synthesis are on-line processes inducing low-computational complexity. In the remaining of this paper these two key components of the global system are further detailed.

2   Pseudo-haptic Rendering

The first aspect of our work deals with a visual mechanism to render pressure interaction when the user is rubbing the texture displayed on the tablet. In the original elastic paradigm [1], the contact duration with the displayed image is assimilated to the amount of "pressure" applied to the associated texture by the end-user. The image is then radially deformed around the contact point with a dedicated heuristic function (see Fig. 1) to give the illusion of a true deformation.

However, as it is, this paradigm uniquely addresses static and punctual clicks and the case of a user sliding or rubbing the surface continuously with his finger is not handled. To cope with these limitations, two different enhancements are now introduced. First, a new contact model addresses the problem of natural interaction on a tablet with a finger, and second, a viscoelastic mechanical model is proposed to enable dynamic rubbing motions.

Fig. 1. Left: Deformation obtained from [1]. Right: Deformation obtained with the proposed contact model.

2.1 Contact Model

In [1], the interaction between the user and the image is made by means of a mouse device and the maximum "pressure" is applied at the cursor position.

In the context we address here, the end-user is not interacting with a mouse pointer anymore but rather with his finger. The contact area is not punctual anymore and the whole surface of interaction has thus to be taken into account. In the new contact model, we therefore propose to divide the touched area into two main components (see Fig. 2): (i) a first component related to the surface right under the contact location, and (ii) a second component involving the region right around this contact area.

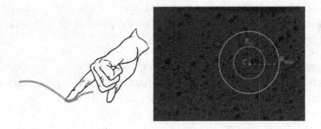

Fig. 2. Left: Schematic representation of a finger touching the surface. The contact surface is divided into two areas under and around the actual contact zone (respectively green and yellow). Right: The two contact areas represented on an image of a sponge texture. (Color figure online)

The maximum amount of "pressure" is now applied on the whole contact surface (and not only a single point) whereas an exponential decrease occurs in the boundary area.

Dedicated heuristic radial functions are also proposed here to quantify the amount of "pressure" applied at a distance d from the contact point after a contact duration t in the two regions defined previously (i.e. $d \in [0, R_{th}]$ and $d \in [R_{th}, R_{max}]$):

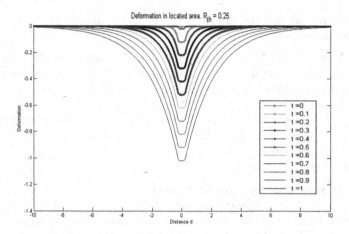

Fig. 3. Plot of the dedicated heuristic radial functions used in the contact model for different contact durations with $R_{max} = 10$ and $R_{th} = 0.25$ (Color figure online)

$$p^1_{deform}(d, t) = \frac{e^{\frac{5(d - R_{th})}{R_{th}}} - 1}{10} - t \text{ for } d \in [0, R_{th}] \tag{1}$$

$$p^2_{deform}(d, t) = -e^{\frac{-5(d - R_{th})}{R_{max} t}} \left(t - \frac{1}{50}\right) \text{ for } d \in [R_{th}, R_{max}]. \tag{2}$$

This analytical expression is plotted for various distances and contact durations in Fig. 3 and a visual comparison of the contact model from [1] and our is given in Fig. 1.

2.2 Viscoelastic Model

The original elastic image paradigm [1] is limited to "static" and punctual pressures and it is not designed for sliding or rubbing interactions. The deformation induced by the finger contact is therefore not managed when the end-user moves the contact-point along the texture surface. To cope with this limitation, the textured image is not considered anymore as a 2D deformable object but rather as a 3D grid where each node is associated with one pixel of the texture image. Each vertex is additionally connected to its 4-connected neighborhood.

A purely vertical mechanical viscoelastic model is then associated to this latter 3D grid. It makes successive contacts of the user spatially and temporally consistent on the whole textured image. In this new context, the contact model described in the previous section is not considered anymore as a deformation field but rather as a vertical force field applied to the 3D grid along the z-axis and given as an external input force to the viscoelastic model. The deformation along the z-axis for each node of the grid is defined by a first order linear differential equation which discrete scheme is given by:

$$P_z[i, j, n] = K E_z[i, j, n] + v \frac{E_z[i, j, n] - E_z[i, j, n - 1]}{T_s} \tag{3}$$

The stiffness K and the viscosity v are the 2 parameters involved in the viscoelastic model and:

- $P_z[i, j, n]$ is the "force" at the sample time n, computed with the contact model described hereinbefore (see Eqs. 1 and 2) and applied to the node located at (i, j) in the image plane. At a sample time n, $P_z[i, j, n]$ is maximal under the contact surface.
- $E_z[i, j, n]$ is the deformation/translation along the z-axis. It is noteworthy that $E_z[i, j, n]$ not only depends on the current force $P_z[i, j, n]$ but also on the previous displacement $E_z[i, j, n-1]$.
- T_s is the sampling period.

In steady state (and for a constant input pressure $P_z[i, j, n] = p_z$), the displacement $E_z[i, j, n]$ converges to the value $E_z[i, j, n] = \frac{p_z}{K}$ which is proportional to the force p_z. For transient state (i.e. increase or decrease of the input force), the displacement reaches its steady state value within a time defined by the viscosity parameter ν. In other words, the higher is K, the lower is the final deformation (the stiffer is the texture) and the lower is ν, the faster the texture reaches its steady state. The final deformation thus ensures a time consistency as well as the integration of the user external interaction while preserving low computational loads. Finally, tuning K and ν makes possible to fit different kinds of texture in order to adapt the visual rendering to simulate different "mechanical properties".

2.3 Details of Implementation

The viscoelastic model presented previously can be easily implemented by means of a regular 3D graphic engine. The textured image is used as a regular 2D texture mapped on a 3D regular square grid. Each node of the grid is continuously updated according to Eqs. 1, 2 and 3. A normal is estimated for each node (on the basis of the local neighborhood) at each sample time which enables the use of a light source to do the shadow rendering, thus increasing the realism of the simulation.

3 Example-Based Audio Synthesis

As mentioned hereinbefore, an audio feedback synchronized to exploratory movements improves the realism of the texture rendering and may change the perception of the roughness. In this context, we now propose a method, complementary to the visual feedback, to synthesize a friction sound when the targeted texture is rubbed by the end-user. The proposed approach is suited for any duration and presents properties which self-adapt with the speed of the rub. Contrarily to [4] and [2] where self-adaptation to speed is proposed on synthesized textures, the proposed method makes use of several real audio recording of the sound generated off-line when touching real samples of the texture of interest at different speed (typically low, medium, high). New sound samples are then synthesized for a given rubbing speed by a combination of the spectral and intensity properties of the initial examples.

The proposed synthesis approach naturally goes through two different steps, namely a learning step and a generation step, that we are going to detail hereafter.

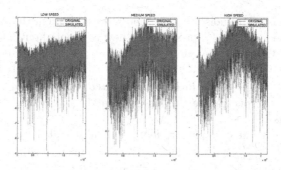

Fig. 4. Original (red) and AR-based estimated (green) spectra of audio samples obtained when recording a user rubbing a sheet of paper at low (left), medium (middle) and high speed (right). (Color figure online)

3.1 Learning Step

The initial off-line learning step aimed at capturing the spectral properties as well as the properties of the intensity of the friction sound made when a texture is rubbed at different speeds. These properties will be then re-used in the generation step. To that end, N audio samples s_i are recorded by means of a dedicated setup when a user is rubbing the texture of interest at varying speed v_i. Each signal s_i is first high-pass filtered to remove the baseline which does not embed the high-frequency spectral properties of the texture we are interested in. The remaining part is therefore a centered audio signal, for which spectrum and energy can be computed, and depend on the rubbing speed (see Fig. 4).

The spectral properties are captured making use of a regular auto-regressive (AR) model but making use of realistic signals. Such a model is represented by an all-pole infinite Impulse Response filter (IIR) which coefficients v_i are optimized (Yule-Walker equations resolution) so that filtering a white noise with this IIR would result in a new signal with similar spectral properties as the example used for the AR fitting (see Fig. 4). The mean power A_i of each temporal sample is also computed to capture the energy properties of the friction sound at each speed.

Eventually, for a given texture, we have N triplets (v_i, F_i, A_i) which characterize its spectral and energy properties at different rubbing speeds. These descriptors are then re-used in the generation step to synthesize the final speed-varying friction sound.

3.2 Generation Step

The synthesis process consists in creating a nth audio sample $y[n]$ consistent with the current rubbing speed $v[n]$ of the end-user as well as with the intrinsic audio properties of the texture. To that end, for each new audio sample to generate at step n:

- N white noises w_i are updated by sampling a new i.i.d. (identically independently distributed) value $w_i[n]$.

- Each of these N white noises w_i are then filtered through the IIR filter whose coefficients are given by F_i, producing a new associated output $y_i[n]$.
- The 2 consecutive indices a and b such that $v_a \leq v_i \leq v_b$ are then computed.
- Under a linear assumption, a first value $u_0[n]$ is computed by $u_0[n] = \frac{(v_b - v[n])y_a[n] + (v[n] - v_a)y_b[n]}{v_b - v_a}$ which is a weighted value of the signal samples which associated spectra are the closer from the one which should occur at the given speed.
- Still assuming a linear behavior, $u_0[n]$ is finally scaled by a scaling factor $\beta[n] = \frac{(v_b - v[n])A_a + (v[n] - v_a)A_b}{v_b - v_a}$ leading to the final new sample value $u[n] = \beta[n]u_0[n]$.

In the end, the new sample is simply a linear speed-based intensity modulation of a linear speed-based combination of the different spectrally-consistent outputs of the auto-regressive models. Figure 5 sums up the different steps of the generation process.

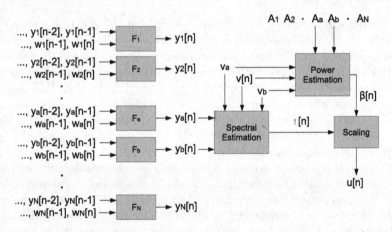

Fig. 5. Block-diagram summing up the different steps involved in the example-based audio synthesis process.

4   Results and Discussion

We conducted preliminary tests to highlight the advantages as well as the drawbacks of the proposed approach. More precisely, our system has been tested with four different texture samples, namely a sponge ($K = 1.4$ and $\nu = 0.1$), a piece of paper ($K = 7$ and $\nu = 0.3$), a paper towel ($K = 7$ and $\nu = 0.3$) and a carpet ($K = 4$ and $\nu = 0.3$). For each of these materials, examples of audio samples (required for the audio feedback synthesis process) have been captured making use of a Senheiser ME66/K6 microphone on a Zoom R16 recorder. Resulting files are wave formatted file sampled at 44.1 kHz with a 24 bits dynamic. The textures were rubbed with the fingertip to produce the sound of friction. Three records per material have been gathered for three different speeds corresponding to slow,

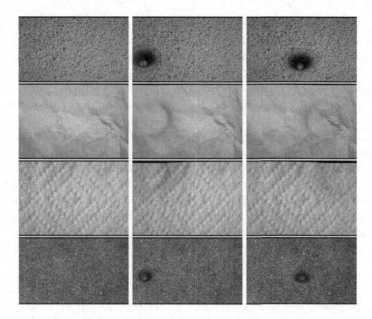

Fig. 6. Examples of textures simulated with the proposed system: sponge, sheet of paper, paper towel and carpet (from top to bottom). The left image is the image of the texture without interaction. The middle image corresponds to a pressure on the left of the screen. The right image is the result of a sliding gesture toward the right.

medium and fast rubbing speed. All the system has been implemented on the Samsung Galaxy S4 tablet with appropriate images for each visual feedback.

Figure 6 depicts screen captures of the four examples introduced hereinbefore. It is noteworthy to mention that the finger is not represented on the images for illustration purposes, but one should have in mind that the contact areas should be covered by the finger of the end-user. Depending on the consistency of the proposed material with the assumption made in the visual and audio feedback processes, realism and quality of the experience may vary.

First regarding the sponge example, the deformation appears quite realistic because this material has elastic properties which nicely match the viscoelastic model. However, the audio feedback is less convincing because the quite high-frequency content captured by the AR model is not sufficient to render the complexity of the friction sound due to the holes covering the material.

On the contrary, the audio feedback is more realistic for the paper which audio spectrum is more compatible with the assumptions of our audio modeling. The texture deformation looks however mode artificial as the intrinsic mechanical behavior of such a material is poorly represent by an elastic model.

The two last examples fit quite well the underlying modeling assumptions. They both present quite regular surface structures which then produce high-frequency friction sounds compatible with the audio model. Besides, the visual deformation, light for the paper towel, stronger for the carpet, are also realistic because each material are quite well modeled by a viscoelastic law.

The video[1] provided with this paper gives to the reader a more representative idea of the visual and audio behaviors of the whole framework in real conditions. As suggested before, materials presenting mechanical properties close to viscoelastic are obviously better rendered. The sheet of paper for which the elasticity is questionable is therefore poorly deformed whereas the sponge or the carpet provide interesting feedbacks. Similarly, as soon as the friction sounds embed complex patterns induced by meso or macroscopic reliefs, the auto-regressive approach does not provide anymore sufficient degrees of freedom to model the friction sounds. For microscopic reliefs, the speed-varying AR approach is quite relevant and one can especially observe the consistent speed-dependent friction sound variations (in terms of energy and spectrum) obtained on the sheet of paper when changing the rubbing speed. These preliminary tests were necessary to roughly understand the limitations of our systems. More rigorous studies will be conducted to finely characterize the perception of those textures.

5   Conclusion

We have proposed a new framework to render texture properties on a tactile screen without using any extra mechanical device. We relied on the elastic image paradigm and proposed a new contact model based on a viscoelastic law to offer to the end-user a pseudo-haptic visual feedback when he is rubbing or pressing the texture with his finger. Additionally, an example-based audio synthesis methodology has been introduced to render texture-specific friction sounds at different rubbing speeds. First qualitative results have been finally proposed to highlight the advantages as well as the limitations of our approach. Indeed, it seems that elastic materials as well as materials with high-frequency audio signature are better suited for the proposed solution. Future works should now focus on the generalization of this framework to more complex textures as well as to the setting up of a more quantitative evaluation of the system performances.

References

1. Argelaguet, F., Gómez Jáuregui, D.A., Marchal, M., Lécuyer, A.: A novel approach for pseudo-haptic textures based on curvature information. In: Isokoski, P., Springare, J. (eds.) EuroHaptics 2012, Part I. LNCS, vol. 7282, pp. 1–12. Springer, Heidelberg (2012)
2. Bianchi, M., Poggiani, M., Serio, A., Bicchi, A.: A novel tactile display for softness and texture rendering in tele-operation tasks. In: IEEE World Haptics Conference, pp. 49–56 (2015)
3. Chouvardas, V., Miliou, A., Hatalis, M.: Tactile displays: overview and recent advances. Displays **29**(3), 185–194 (2008)
4. Culbertson, H., Unwin, J., Kuchenbecker, K.J.: Modeling and rendering realistic textures from unconstrained tool-surface interactions. IEEE Trans. Haptics **7**(3), 381–393 (2014)

---

[1] http://dai.ly/x3pqkwx.

5. Kim, S.C., Kyung, K.U., Kwon, D.S.: The effect of sound on haptic perception. In: EuroHaptics Conference, 2007 and Symposium on Haptic Interfaces for Virtual Environment and Teleoperator Systems. Second Joint World Haptics 2007, pp. 354–360. IEEE (2007)
6. Lécuyer, A.: Simulating haptic feedback using vision: a survey of research and applications of pseudo-haptic feedback. Presence Teleoper. Virtual Environ. **18**(1), 39–53 (2009)
7. Lécuyer, A., Burkhardt, J., Etienne, L.: Feeling bumps and holes without a haptic interface: the perception of pseudo-haptic textures. In: Proceedings of the SIGCHI Conference on Human Factors in Computing Systems, pp. 239–246. ACM (2004)
8. Li, M., Ridzuan, M.B., Sareh, S., Seneviratne, L.D., Dasgupta, P., Althoefer, K.: Pseudo-haptics for rigid tool/soft surface interaction feedback in virtual environments. Mechatronics **24**(8), 1092–1100 (2014)
9. Punpongsanon, P., Iwai, D., Sato, K.: Softar: visually manipulating haptic softness perception in spatial augmented reality. IEEE Trans. Vis. Comput. Graph. **21**(11), 1279–1288 (2015)
10. Suzuki, Y., Gyoba, J.: Effects of sounds on tactile roughness depend on the congruency between modalities. In: EuroHaptics Conference, 2009 and Symposium on Haptic Interfaces for Virtual Environment and Teleoperator Systems. Third Joint World Haptics 2009, pp. 150–153. IEEE (2009)

An IMU and RFID-based Navigation System Providing Vibrotactile Feedback for Visually Impaired People

Claudio Loconsole$^{(\boxtimes)}$, Maryam Banitalebi Dehkordi, Edoardo Sotgiu,
Marco Fontana, Massimo Bergamasco, and Antonio Frisoli

PERCRO Laboratory, TeCIP Institute, Scuola Superiore Sant'Anna, Pisa, Italy
c.loconsole@sssup.it

Abstract. This paper presents the DOVI (Device for Orientation of the
Visually Impaired) system, a new inertial and RFID-based wearable navigation device for indoor environments providing vibrotactile feedback to
visually impaired people for reaching a target place. The DOVI system is
based on sensor fusion techniques, allowing a precise and global localization of the pedestrian thanks to inertial measurements from accelerometers and gyroscope and passive RFID tags. The pedestrian is provided a
haptic feedback through a vibrotactile bracelet, that can guide him/her
through the correct path toward the target. The DOVI system is complementary to both those systems allowing the detection of mobile obstacles
along the path and to other aids, such as the white cane or the guide
dog.

Keywords: Haptic feedback · Pedestrian navigation · Sensor fusion ·
Wearable assistive device · Visually impaired

1 Introduction

Navigation aids can provide information about correct heading direction and
appropriate route selection to pedestrians who are visually impaired through
Personal Digital Assistant (PDAs) and smart phones.

The estimation of user's location and the orientation can be achieved outdoor
with Global Positioning System (GPS) (e.g., [17]), that unfortunately is not reliable enough within indoor environments (e.g., workplaces and public buildings
such as hospital and airports), where degradation and distortion of the GPS
signal are introduced.

In recent years, to overcome the above limitations, alternative solutions
addressing in-door localization have been proposed either based on an *external
infrastructure* or configured as *autonomous* solutions, although none of them
has been effective enough to lead to off-the-shelf navigation systems for visually impaired people. *External infrastructure* solutions are usually based on sensor network technologies (e.g., Ultra Wide Band (UWB), Wi-Fi, Bluetooth and

F. Bello et al. (Eds.): EuroHaptics 2016, Part I, LNCS 9774, pp. 360–370, 2016.
DOI: 10.1007/978-3-319-42321-0_33

Radio Frequency IDentification (RFID), requiring the placement of either sensors or tags in the environment. Their performance can not reach sufficiently high levels of accuracy [12], i.e. lower than 1 m, since it is depending of various factors, such as signal power, interference and number of cells or used antennas. On the other side, *autonomous* solutions are independent of external infrastructures and usually rely on inertial sensors (e.g., Inertial Measurement Unit - IMU) consisting of accelerometers (linear acceleration) and gyroscopes (angular velocity) [6], even if their accuracy is influenced both by drift error due to the integration of signals affected by noise [3] and by the relative (non absolute) estimation of the person position and orientation with respect to the initial value (Dead Reckoning). In the context of assistive devices for indoor navigation of visually impaired pedestrians, several state-of-the-art systems can be found both among the solutions based on *external infrastructure* (e.g., [5]) and among the *autonomous systems* (e.g., [2]).

Analyzing the literature on these systems, it is possible to observe a lack of a comprehensive approach to navigate indoor environments including localization based both on inertial platform (location and orientation tracking step by step) and on low cost external infrastructure (global referencing and drift error reduction), and haptic feedback for accurate navigational instruction (more than two possible directions and possibility to design navigation command protocol). For this reason, in this paper we propose a combined approach based on inertial sensors coupled with passive-tag RFID technologies, including also a vibrotactile feedback to provide navigational commands to the user through an haptic bracelet worn on the wrist and complementing the conventional assistive systems/aids (i.e., white cane, guide dog) and providing information about fixed obstacles, corridors, doors, and specific points of interests (e.g., rooms, toilette, office).

2   System Description

The DOVI system is worn by the visually impaired user (see Fig. 1) and consists of four different units: 1. the *Inertial Navigation Unit (INU)*, based on an Inertial Measurement Unit which allows to estimate the relative user's position and orientation; 2. the *Radio-frequency Identification (RFID) Unit*, which allows to globally locate the user in the environment (both spatially and logically) and to reduce the drift error committed by the IMU; 3. the *Haptic Navigation Unit (HNU)*, which provides the navigation directions to the user by means of vibrotactile feedback at the wrist; 4. the *Wearable Computing Unit (WCU)*, which fuses the data coming from the INU and the RFID and drives the HNU.

2.1   Inertial Navigation Unit (INU)

The sequential nature of human bipedal walking is taken into account in many pedestrian navigation systems, where the IMU is mounted on user's torso, waist, foot or head (e.g., [1]). In this work, we employed a foot-mounted IMU

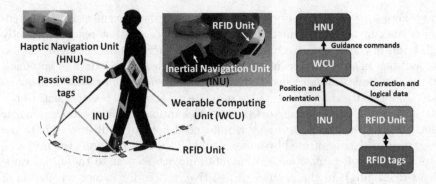

Fig. 1. An overview of the DOVI system.

(see Fig. 1) to take advantage of the consecutive nature of pedestrian movement and to accurately detect stance phases to employ error reduction methods. The positioning algorithm is irrespective of the exact orientation and position of IMU on the user's foot. Considering the IMU requirements and characteristics including sampling rate, dynamic range, size, and bias, we use NavChipISNC01 from InterSense Inc. This IMU is based on a high precision MEMS that is configured to provide inertial data at 200 Hz. The IMU outputs are the output of the three-axis accelerometer $a(t)$, gyroscope $\theta(t)$, and magnetometer $m(t)$. We developed a five-state (15-element) Extended Kalman Filter and five-error reduction method to compensate both the gravity and the sensor biases, and to obtain an accurate estimated position and orientation of the user. An extensive description of the developed approach is discussed in our previous work [3].

2.2   RFID Unit

The RFID module mainly aims to: (i) reduce the drift error committed by the IMU sensor over time (the IMU-estimated position is set to the RFID position which is used as ground truth value); (ii) provide information (both geographical and logical) about the environment; (iii) provide an aid to the path construction and actual navigation. The proposed setup for the RFID unit is based on a wearable active RFID module (reader) and on the environment equipped with modules of passive RFID tags. This strategy presents two main advantages: (i) passive RFID tags allows to reduce costs due to the need of power supply sources, lack of multiple active RFID components and masonry work for installation of the active modules; (ii) in contrast to the systems based on Received Signal Strength Indicator (RSSI) techniques (wearable passive RFID tag and RFID antennas in the environment - e.g., [14]), even if the tag detection is short range, thus appearing a limitation, the DOVI system has been designed to assure the passage close to the tags allowing to obtain a small estimation of position error ($e < 250$ mm) mainly depending on the directivity of the used antennas.

Since not all the points of the environment are within the action field of the RFID infrastructure, we define the concept of a path resulting from a search on the graph of RFID gates as an ideal *tunnel* in which the user can navigate the environment and the methodology to "force" the user to walk in the *tunnel* and passing through a specific sequence of RFID gates. The proposed wearable active RFID module is mainly composed of: (i) two linear polarized high Performance UHF Antennas for PDA; (ii) an OBID i-scan® ID ISC.MU02-CU UHF Short Range Reader (it is used to decode the signal coming from the antennas and forward the code to the Arduino via serial); (iii) an Arduino Pro-Mini board, which allows a preliminary processing of the code coming from the Reader and avoids the transmission of redundant information; (iv) a Bluetooth transponder paired with the WCU.

The modules of passive RFID tags called *gates*, are made of a material resistant to trampling and are used to extract information both from specific Points of Interest (PoIs) in the environment and from Service Points (SPs), which are used for managing the navigation along the path to be followed. The typical information provided by a gate are the spatial position according to a "global" reference framework and a code solvable through software, which can provide more information about the PoI/SP. Each module contains a predefined number of passive RFID tags spatially organized according to a predefined geometrical distribution (e.g., $N \times M$ matrix) and installed in the environment, on the floor, according to a specific strategy. As mentioned above, the strategy proposed in this paper is based on two logical classes of gates: the *gates associated to PoIs*, (such as an office, the bathroom, and etc.) and *service gates* associated to SPs, which are used for managing the navigation along the path to be followed. The user wears the RFID system on the ankle (see Fig. 1), and while walking, this system reads the passive RFID tags contained in the gates.

2.3 Haptic Navigation Unit (HNU)

Navigational directions provided through vibrotactile feedback instead of auditory feedback (e.g., [15]) offer several advantages, as reported in [9] and in [13], including the enhancement of the spatial awareness mainly due to the following reasons: (i) the tactile channel is usually less overloaded than the visual or auditory ones; (ii) the vibrotactile stimulation provides the information without annoying others or drawing their attention; (iii) the stimuli are directly mapped to body coordinates in an intuitive feedback. Although several studies, such as [16], showed that egocentric tactile stimuli reduce the mental effort required for interpreting a navigation information, other body locations have been explored to convey navigational or spatially information through vibrotactile displays, like forearm or wrist (e.g., [10,11]). In particular, Panëels [11] showed that providing simple tactile directional information is a good choice for mobility, because it does not require constant attention and high cognitive effort. On the basis of all aforementioned considerations, the wrist has been identified as a good candidate for receiving vibrotactile stimulation from a wearable device since it is also a comfortable body site already used to wear watches and jewelries avoiding a cyborg aspect, also according to the survey by Golledge *et al.* [8].

The developed wearable vibrotactile feedback device, called Haptic Navigation Unit (HNU), to be worn on the wrist is composed of: (i) the actual *Haptic Bracelet (HB)* (see Fig. 1), which provides, by means of vibrations, guidance directives to the user who is visually impaired; (ii) the *Haptic Control Unit (HCU)*, which is used to command the DC motors, to communicate with the host system and to recharge the on-board battery.

The HB consists of a band of stretchy fabric that can be worn comfortably on the wrist. In order to ensure the most intuitive way to perceive simple guidance commands (start, stop, go forward or backward, and turn left or right) in an egocentric body-fixed frame, the configuration of motor alignment on the user's wrist was designed to cover only four areas. The vibrating motors are distributed over the wristband in order to be in contact with the center of the dorsal (top), ventral (bottom/palm), inner and outer lateral sides of the wrist. This configuration results in a minimum distance between the actuators of about 4 cm that is higher than the two-point discrimination threshold [7], allowing a reliable subjects' spatial detection. Such a low spatial information density around the wrist has a beneficial effect both on the information transfer and on the level of attention in the primary task. The HCU is mainly composed of: (i) a custom-designed circuit board, the MicroController Unit (MCU) equipped with a PIC; (ii) a 2.4 GHz Bluetooth Class 1 module, which is the Wireless Communication Module (WCM); (iii) a 3.7 V battery and a capacity of 1000 mAh (in the worst-case scenario, i.e., all four actuators continuously active, the selected battery has proven to power the system for almost 4 h); (iv) a USB Battery Charger (UBC).

In order to pilot the HCU, command packets (16 bytes length) are sent from the WCU to the MCU. Each command packet is composed of four square wave patterns (one for each motor). For each pattern, four parameters have been defined: (i) pulsing period (T) of the wave; (ii) phase (Φ) of the wave, with respect to the initial time, to indicate if motors have to start all at once or with a certain delay from each other; (iii) duty cycle (DC) of the wave; (iv) number of pulses (N) of the square wave pattern. A typical quadruplet of parameter values used in our experiment for a single motor is $T = 0.15$, $\Phi = 0$, $DC = 40$, $N = 3$. The pattern generation is performed entirely on the bracelet side on the basis of the packet received by the WCU. Though the high computational load, such a solution ensures a powerful parametrization of the vibration patterns and guarantees a precise timing of the wave generation based on the internal bracelet microcontroller timer. The commands to the user are coded through a predefined set of square wave parameters for driving the HNU motors worn on the user's wrist. However, the potential of the system also includes the ability of the HNU to drive two or more vibrators at the same time. In our proposed correspondence protocol, we assumed that the HNU was worn on the right wrist in palm down configuration, but other configurations are available. The vibrational protocol for navigation used for right wrist has been demonstrated to be valid also on the left wrist, thus giving the possibility to discard the customization of the HNU concerning the use of the left or the right wrist.

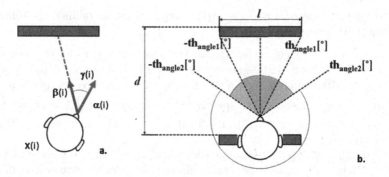

Fig. 2. Illustration of the algorithm of the path thread. (a) Scheme of the variables. (b) Constants. Red rectangle represents RFID gates. (Color figure online)

2.4 Wearable Computing Unit (WCU)

The Wearable Computing Unit (WCU) allows to plan the path to be followed by using a connectivity graph of the RFID gates, the *gate graph*, according to standard graph search algorithms (in our case the *Dijkstra algorithm*). Usually, the end point of the path is identified by a gate associated to a PoI which can be searched and retrieved in the gate table using a vocal command. Besides the path planning, the WCU aims to: (i) receive and perform the data fusion between the data received from the INU and the RFID Unit; (ii) drive (via Bluetooth) the HNU such that the navigation directions are properly conveyed to the user. In order to fulfill these aims, the WCU mainly runs two software threads, the *position* and the *path* threads, respectively. The *position thread* allows to receive via Bluetooth connection and to fuse the data from both INU (synchronous) and RFID (asynchronous) subsystems. Once the position data (ground truth) from the RFID Unit is received, the WCU updates the user's current position on the INU whose estimated position is forced to the ground truth value. Corrected position data is, then, passed to the path thread. The *path thread*, instead, calculates and manages the path (the ideal *tunnel*, i.e., a specific sequence of RFID gates - see Sect. 2.2) to be followed and drives the HNU to provide the navigation directions to the user. The input of the algorithm performed by the path thread is: (i) the user's position provided by the position thread; (ii) the *navigation table* (sorted list of gates), which provides for each instance of time, the position of the upcoming RFID gate (identified as *target(i)*) in the path towards the target RFID gate. For sake of clarity, we assume that the navigation table is calculated before the navigation starts.

The main variables illustrated in Fig. 2a, expressed with respect to the global reference framework and used in the navigation algorithm are: $x(i)$ representing the (x,y) position of the user at time i; $\alpha(i)$ representing the direction (angle in degrees) of the user at time i; $\beta(i)$ representing the desired direction (angle in degrees) that the user should follow at time i to correctly reach the center of the upcoming RFID gate. This direction is calculated using $x(i)$ and *target(i)*; $\gamma(i)$

which is calculated as $\gamma(i) = \beta(i) - \alpha(i)$. Furthermore, we defined the following constants (with reference to Fig. 2b):

- th_{angle1} (> 0) is defined as the angular threshold on $\gamma(i)$ to let the user reach the center of the next RFID gate (green area). This threshold depends on the length of the RFID gate l and on the distance between two consequent gates d (in our case set to 1 and 4 m, respectively) are known: $th_{angle1} = arcsin\left(\frac{\frac{l}{2}}{d}\right)$;
- th_{angle2} (> 0, $th_{angle2} > th_{angle1}$) defined as the "emergency" angular threshold on $\gamma(i)$, such that:
  * if $th_{angle1} < |\gamma(i)| < th_{angle2}$ (light blue area), the user receives Left() or Right() commands properly selected in order to restore the desired direction without stopping his/her motion;
  * if $|\gamma(i)| > th_{angle2}$ (white area), a Stop() command is sent to the user followed by Left() or Right() commands to restore the desired direction. The vibration corresponding to Left() or to Right() command will remain active until the alignment with the desired direction is completed. This HNU pilot strategy allows to solve also particular sub-sequences of non-aligned RFID gates and does not impose constraints on the angle between two consequent gates, as happens in tactile paths for people who are visually impaired, where the standard angle is fixed to 90°. Finally, the variable *timer go* is used to manage both the "live" signal of the system provided to the user each k seconds (in our case $k = 2$ s) and to trigger the (re)initiation of subject walking.

3   Experimental Results and Discussion

3.1   Preliminary Experimental Results of the Haptic Navigation Unit (HNU)

To validate the guidance ability of the HNU and to evaluate the proposed vibrational feedback protocol, we performed a preliminary test involving an on-site

Table 1. An example of command code used by human supervisor to guide the user who is visually impaired. Fwd stands for forward.

Comm.	Cur. state	New state
Go	Stationary	Fwd motion
Go	Fwd motion	Fwd motion
Stop	Stationary	Stationary
Stop	Fwd motion	Stationary (continue along current orientation)
Turn left	Stationary	Rotation of 90° counterclockwise and then Stationary
Left	Fwd motion	Continuing fwd motion, moving slightly to the left
Turn right	Stationary	Rotation of 90° clockwise and then Stationary
Right	Fwd motion	Continuing forward motion, moving slightly to the right

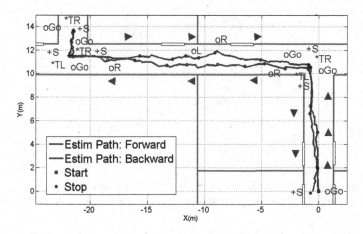

Fig. 3. Estimated trajectory (data processing IMU) followed by the visually impaired guided by a sighted person using the navigation signals imparted through the HNU. (Color figure online)

"manual" HNU piloting. A subject (female, 31 yrs), who is visually impaired from birth, wore the HNU on her right wrist in palm down configuration. To spatially track her walked path in the environment, she wore also the INU on her right foot. A sighted operator followed her from behind without any contact, communicating the walking directives to her only through a "joystick-like" interface running on the WCU. This interface was able to pilot the vibrational commands on the HNU according to the protocol reported in Table 1 along several paths featuring In Fig. 3, the path traveled by the subject (blue indicates forward path, red backward path) with the indication of the commands provided through the WCU (automatic time synchronization between commands and walked trajectory). It is worth to remind that the "Go" directive is sent periodically as a message of "live" from the system to inform the user that he/she is following the correct direction during the navigation and the system is working properly. The test demonstrated the usability of the designed HNU for assisted pedestrian navigation by visually impaired people. The navigation commands were considered clear and immediate by the visually impaired subject, confirming the potential reported in [4], in which faster dynamics related to powered vehicles were involved.

3.2   Experimental Performance of the DOVI System

In order to test the overall usability and evaluate the performance of the DOVI system, we conducted an experimental test on the path reported in Fig. 4. A blindfold subject (female, 30 years old) wore the three DOVI modules (INU, RFID, HNU) and held the WCU (i.e., an Android-based smartphone) in her hand. With reference to Fig. 4, she had to start from the "start" point and to pass through the gates in the following order: 1-2-3-4-3-2-1, by following the navigation commands imparted by the HNU and elaborated by the WCU

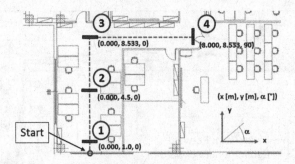

Fig. 4. The experimental path for testing the DOVI system. The subject starts from the "start" point and has to pass through the gates in the following order: 1-2-3-4-3-2-1.

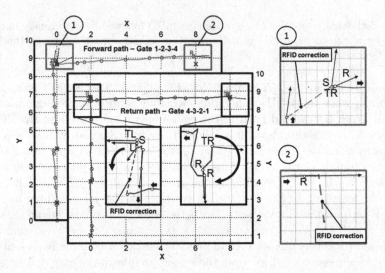

Fig. 5. Estimated trajectory (resulting from the fusion between INU and RFID information) followed by the blindfold sighted subject using the navigation signals imparted through the HNU.

according to the automatic strategy reported in Sect. 2.4. The results of the test are reported in Fig. 5 in which dots indicate that a command was received by the subject through the HNU in that specific position and are labeled as R and TR for right and turn right, L and TL for left and turn left, S for Stop. Dots reported without labels stand for Go command (which is used also as "live" signal). Blue crosses indicate the position of the RFID gates. In the four boxes, we reported the magnified portion of the trajectory involving changes of direction and drift error correction occurring when a RFID gate is passed. The DOVI system correctly guided the subject through the path, opportunely differentiating between slight direction changes (to the left/right) and larger ones (stop followed by TR or TL, and, then, followed by L or R till re-alignment with the correct direction).

4   Conclusion

This paper presented a novel IMU and RFID-based navigation system for indoor environments, the DOVI system, providing vibrotactile feedback to visually impaired people. The system fuses the information coming from the INU and the RFID Unit to locate the user by means of the WCU and provide him/her the navigation directions through the HNU. Two tests were conducted to assess the effectiveness of the vibrotactile feedback provided by the HNU on the wrist and the usability of the entire DOVI system, respectively. The first test conducted on HNU demonstrated the clarity of navigation directives and the easiness in the navigation protocol decoding. The second test conducted on the integration of all DOVI modules, instead, demonstrated the ability of the DOVI system to correctly guide a blindfold person along a articulated path. The experimental results demonstrated the high potential of the entire system according to the aim of developing a new approach for the spatial and logical localization and navigation of visually impaired people, especially in indoor environments.

Future works will deal with a massive experimentation and a component miniaturization of the DOVI system as well as the deployment analysis of the system for visually impaired people affected by comorbidities.

Acknowledgment. This work has been partially funded from the EU FP7 project n. 601165 WEARHAP.

References

1. Alvarez, J.C., López, A.M., Gonzalez, R.C., Álvarez, D.: Pedestrian dead reckoning with waist-worn inertial sensors. In: 2012 IEEE International on Instrumentation and Measurement Technology Conference (I2MTC), pp. 24–27. IEEE (2012)
2. Bagalkot, A.S., Mogali, P.B., Nayak, R.R., Sahana, S.: Blind audio guidance system. IJITR **2**(2), 847–849 (2014)
3. Banitalebi Dehkordi, M., Frisoli, A., Sotgiu, E., Loconsole, C.: Pedestrian indoor navigation system using inertial measurement unit. Int. J. Sens. Netw. Data Commun. **3**, 1–9 (2014)
4. Biral, F., Lot, R., Rota, S., Fontana, M., Huth, V.: Intersection support system for powered two-wheeled vehicles: threat assessment based on a receding horizon approach. IEEE Trans. Intell. Transp. Syst. **13**(2), 805–816 (2012)
5. Chumkamon, S., Tuvaphanthaphiphat, P., Keeratiwintakorn, P.: A blind navigation system using RFID for indoor environments. In: 5th International Conference on Electrical Engineering/Electronics, Computer, Telecommunications and Information Technology, ECTI-CON 2008, vol. 2, pp. 765–768. IEEE (2008)
6. Foxlin, E.: Pedestrian tracking with shoe-mounted inertial sensors. IEEE Comput. Graph. Appl. **25**(6), 38–46 (2005)
7. Gemperle, F., Hirsch, T., Goode, A., Pearce, J., Siewiorek, D., Smailigic, A.: Wearable vibro-tactile display. Technical report, Carnegie Mellon Wearable Group, Carnegie Mellon University (2003)
8. Golledge, R., Klatzky, R., Loomis, J., Marston, J.: Stated preferences for components of a personal guidance system for nonvisual navigation. J. Vis. Impair. Blind. (JVIB) **98**(03), 135–147 (2004)

9. Jones, L.A., Sarter, N.B.: Tactile displays: guidance for their design and application. Hum. Fact. **50**(1), 90–111 (2008)
10. Kammoun, S., Jouffrais, C., Guerreiro, T., Nicolau, H., Jorge, J.: Guiding blind people with haptic feedback (regular paper). In: Frontiers in Accessibility for Pervasive Computing (Pervasive), Newcastle, UK, 18/06/2012–22/06/2012. p. (on line). IST (June 2012)
11. Panëels, S., Brunet, L., Strachan, S.: Strike a pose: directional cueing on the wrist and the effect of orientation. In: Oakley, I., Brewster, S. (eds.) HAID 2013. LNCS, vol. 7989, pp. 117–126. Springer, Heidelberg (2013)
12. Retscher, G., Fu, Q.: Continuous indoor navigation with RFID and INS. In: 2010 IEEE/ION on Position Location and Navigation Symposium (PLANS), pp. 102–112. IEEE (2010)
13. Ross, D.A., Blasch, B.B.: Wearable interfaces for orientation and wayfinding. In: Proceedings of the Fourth International ACM Conference on AssistiveTechnologies, Assets 2000, pp. 193–200. ACM, New York (2000)
14. Ruiz, A.R.J., Granja, F.S., Prieto Honorato, J.C., Rosas, J.I.G.: Accurate pedestrian indoor navigation by tightly coupling foot-mounted IMU and RFID measurements. IEEE Trans. Instrum. Meas. **61**(1), 178–189 (2012)
15. Shiizu, Y., Hirahara, Y., Yanashima, K., Magatani, K.: The development of a white cane which navigates the visually impaired. In: 29th Annual International Conference of the IEEE Engineering in Medicine and Biology Society, EMBS 2007, pp. 5005–5008. IEEE (2007)
16. Van Erp, J.B.F.: Presenting directions with a vibrotactile torso display. Ergonomics **48**(3), 302–313 (2005)
17. Zhu, X., Li, Q., Chen, G.: APT: accurate outdoor pedestrian tracking with smartphones. In: 2013 Proceedings IEEE INFOCOM, pp. 2508–2516, April 2013

Illusion of Wet Sensation by Controlling Temperature and Softness of Dry Cloth

Mai Shibahara[✉] and Katsunari Sato

Nara Women's University, Kitauoya-Nishi machi, Nara 630-8506, Japan
{pam_shibahara, katsu-sato}@cc.nara-wu.ac.jp

Abstract. In order to create a device that produces the sensation of wet cloth, we have proposed a method to augment the wet sensation of dry cloth. This paper investigated whether controlling the surface temperature and softness of a cloth could reproduce the wet sensation or not. Participants scored their feelings after touching the cloth with different temperatures and softness. Results indicated a tendency to perceive a wet sensation equivalent to actual wet cloth by not only decreasing the temperature but also increasing softness of the cloth.

Keywords: Wetness of cloth · Display of wetness · Illusion · Augmented reality

1 Introduction

People perceive wetness in daily life. Examples include sweat from playing sports, taking a bath, and face washing. Perception of wetness has been studied mostly in the textile field for comfort feeling related to wearing clothes [1–3]. Wetness of cloth leads to an uncomfortable feeling, therefore, it is an important factor to evaluate in the performance of cloth materials.

In spite of this important feature, consumers cannot evaluate the wetness factor of cloth materials in stores as soaking the cloth in water can damage them. If it were possible to reproduce the wet state of cloth using virtual reality technology, consumers could evaluate the comfort feeling of cloth materials in their wet state without the need for water and consequently could make better judgments for purchasing the cloth materials. Therefore, we aimed to virtually represent wetness of cloth (Fig. 1).

In order to represent the sensation of wetness, we first had to understand how humans perceive this sensation. Since humans lack hygroreceptors in their skin, it is supposed that the sensation of wetness is perceived through the function of other receptors. Previous studies pointed out that cold, soft (or pressure), and sticky sensations are particularly important to experience wetness [3–8]. For example, Bergmann et al. and Filingeri et al. mentioned that the perception of wetness became more sensitive in the case of dynamic touch (thermal and tactile cues) than in the case of static touch (only thermal cue) [3, 4]. They demonstrated that the wet sensation

© Springer International Publishing Switzerland 2016
F. Bello et al. (Eds.): EuroHaptics 2016, Part I, LNCS 9774, pp. 371–379, 2016.
DOI: 10.1007/978-3-319-42321-0_34

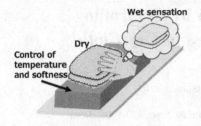

Fig. 1. Conceptual diagram

increased corresponding to a decrease in temperature of samples in static touch, while the sensation did not increase in dynamic touch [4]. This implies that tactile sensation in addition to thermal sensation is important to discern the wetness of cloth. These authors also found that potential sensory interaction between thermal and tactile cues drives the perception of wetness [4, 8]. They examined sensory evaluations for wetness by pressing thermal probes onto the bare backs of participants [7]. Their results showed that cold-dry stimuli evoked wet sensations and that pressure affected this sensation. Interestingly, low pressure resulted in an increase in the wet sensation while high pressure reduced it.

For the purpose of producing a wet sensation of cloth, we have proposed an augmentation method that causes a wet sensation by changing only the surface temperature of dry cloth [9]. We found that participants perceived a similar wet sensation both with wet and dry cloth when the surface temperature of the dry cloth was controlled to reproduce a change in skin temperature after contact with the wet cloth. Furthermore, it is presumed that the softness of cloth affects the augmented wet sensation, as other studies reported applied pressure to the skin as a main factor in wet sensation [6–8]. If the softness of cloth affects the sensation of wetness, there is a possibility that we can more effectively represent a wet sensation using our method.

In this study, we investigated how softness, especially compression characteristics of the cloth, affects the wetness augmentation method we proposed. We evaluated not only wet sensation but also other haptic sensations perceived from dry cloth by controlling not only the temperature but also its softness.

2 Sensory Evaluation

This paper describes the experiment that compared artificially wet cloth (i.e., making dry cloth colder or softer based on the proposed method) with normal dry cloth.

As the index to control the temperature of the cloth, we focused on the change in skin temperature when touching the sample cloth. When humans touch an actual wet cloth, greater heat transfer between the skin and the wet cloth occurs than in the case of dry cloth. If the dry cloth were cold enough to produce the same skin temperature change as in the case of wet cloth, they could feel a wet sensation. We expected that the softness of the cloth would change this illusory perceived wetness. We focused on the factor of compressibility as the index to control the softness of the cloth.

2.1 Participants

Study participants included 21 healthy females, aged between 18 and 24 years. They were monetarily reimbursed for their participation time.

2.2 Materials

Figure 2 shows the experimental setup. The sample cloth was 15 × 30 cm of cotton lawn (Table 1). The surface temperature of the cloth was controlled by a Peltier device (TEC1-12706, AKIZUKI DENSHI TSUSHO Co., Ltd.) with a surface area of 4 × 4 cm that was placed under the cloth (Fig. 2(a), (b)). We placed a thermistor (103JT-025, SEMITEC Corporation) on the Peltier device to measure and control its surface temperature using a proportional-derivative (PD) control method. The Peltier was connected to a motor driver (TA7291P, TOSHIBA. Co., Ltd.) and to a digital-analog conversion terminal, which supported pulse width modulation of an Arduino UNO microcontroller board.

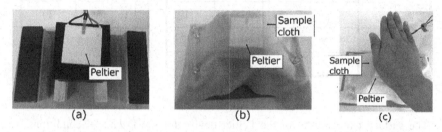

Fig. 2. Experimental setup. (a) peltier device (b) peltier device covered by the sample cloth (c) manner of touching the cloth

Before each stimulus presentation, participants placed their hands on a hot plate (NHP-M30 N, New Japan Chemical Co, Ltd.) to control their skin temperature. The surface temperature of the hot plate was 32° C.

Room temperature and relative humidity (RH) were 23.0 ± 3.8° C and 41.8 ± 11 %, respectively. Participants were blindfolded to avoid confounding the experience by seeing the sample cloths when they touched them.

Table 1. Summary of the characteristics of the sample cloth

Name of sample cloth	composition	thickness (mm)	weight (m g/cm²)	Magnified Photo
Cotton lawn	cotton 100%	0.60	6.8	

500 μm

2.3   Experimental Conditions

There were 18 experimental conditions of the stimuli: dry cloth (D), wet cloth (W), and 16 conditions that differed in surface temperature and number of layers of sample cloth (Table 2).

Table 2. Temperature of Peltier device

Condition		dT_{cold}			
		0	1	2	3
Number of cloth layers	1	27	25	23	19
	2	23	20	17	12
	3	19	16	13	7
	4	16	12	6	2

Condition	D	29
	W	29

The surface temperature for the Peltier device for the D and W conditions was 29° C. This Peltier temperature was lower than skin temperature (32° C) but participants didn't feel a cold sensation because the resistance of the cloth was high. The water content of W was 45–60 %, which was calculated as the comparison between the weight of D and W after the experiment by using a digital scale (0.01 g accuracy) (HT-120, A&D Co., Ltd.). Under these temperature and water content conditions, participants could discriminate wet sensations between the W and D condition. We contained the water in the cloth by sandwiching it between highly hygroscopic sponges.

To produce the illusion of wet sensation from dry cloth, we prepared 16 conditions that were different in their temperature and softness. For the temperature of cloth, we established 4 conditions (dT_{cold} = 0, 1, 2, 3) to control the surface temperature of the Peltier device. These conditions were chosen to cause the same or greater drop of skin temperature than that of the W condition (dT_{cold}). Before the experiment, we measured the change in skin temperature of the author's hand ($dT = dT_{wet} + dT_{cold}$) 8 s after it touched the cloth of all experimental conditions by a Thermistor (P1703, Alpha Technics Inc.) pasted on the palm. As a result, we confirmed that dT_{wet} was approximately 3° C and decided on the 4 temperatures of the Peltier as shown in Table 2. The higher the number of cloth layers, the lower the temperature of the Peltier needs to be, because the thermal resistance of the cloth increases with the number of layers.

For the softness of the cloth, we established 4 conditions by layering sheets of cloth on top of each other. The graphs in Fig. 3 show the compression characteristics obtained from compression measuring equipment (KES-FB3, KATO TECH Co., Ltd.): linearity of compression (LC), work of compressibility (WC) (gf · cm/cm^2), resilience of compressibility (RC) (%), and thickness (T) (mm). We obtained these values leaving the sample cloth for 1 h in the environment for which temperature and humidity were

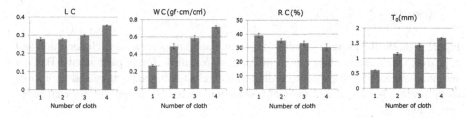

Fig. 3. Characteristic values of compression

$20 \pm 0.5°$ C and 65 ± 2 % RH, respectively. From the graph, we can confirm that WC, which represents softness, increases according to the number of cloth layers.

2.4 Experimental Design

First, the sample cloth was placed on the Peltier device for 60 s to control the surface temperature of the cloth. It was confirmed beforehand that the surface temperature changed enough in 60 s. Simultaneously, the participants' skin temperature was controlled by the hot plate.

After controlling for the temperature of the sample cloth and skin, participants touched the randomly selected experimental stimuli (sample cloth with an experimental condition) and reference stimuli (sample cloth with D condition) with their right and left hand, respectively, for 8 s. The type of touch was static, that is, their palms pressed down onto the sample cloth lightly and did not move (Fig. 2(c)). This is the best way to perceive thermal sensation of an object [10]. We instructed them the way of touch so that the participants touched the cloths by subjectively same force.

After participants disengaged their hands from the sample cloth, we queried their sensation for the cloth touched by their right hand using semantic differential (SD) scales. The scales used 5 adjective pairs and were selected for the basic haptic feelings [11], including wetness and thickness, to investigate possible changes in haptic feelings not only for the wet sensation but also for cold, soft, thick, and rough sensations (Fig. 4). The participants scored each adjective pair based on the feelings perceived by their right hand (experimental stimuli) compared to the left one (reference stimuli). We dried the right palm of each participant with a tissue after every evaluation, as water may have remained on the hand after contact with the W condition.

This procedure was repeated for all 18 conditions. To keep participants focused while in the experiment, after every 5th tested condition, they took a 5 min break. In the sensory evaluation, we did not measure participants' skin temperature.

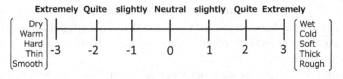

Fig. 4. Adjective pairs and the scale of SD method

3 Results

Figure 5 shows the average scores of all participants' responses for each condition and adjective pair. The error bars represent standard deviations for all participants. The wet sensation appeared to increase according to both change in temperature and number of cloth layers. As expected, the cold sensation increased according to change in temperature.

To evaluate the differences in the scores for each condition from D and W, we conducted a one-way factor ANOVA for every adjective pair. There were significant differences for the wet, cold, thick, and rough sensations (wet sensation: $F(17, 340) = 8.57$, $p < 0.05$; cold sensation: $F(17, 340) = 21.4$, $p < 0.05$, soft sensation: $F(17, 340) = 1.21$, $p = 0.254$, thick sensation: $F(17, 340) = 2.02$, $p < 0.05$, rough sensation: $F(17, 340) = 2.73$, $p < 0.05$). Furthermore, we conducted multiple comparisons of Holm for these four adjective pairs. For the results shown in Fig. 5, the asterisks (*) on the upper left and lower right points represent a significant difference in comparison of the D and W conditions, respectively.

4 Discussion

The relationship between a wet sensation and the actual temperature or softness of the cloth from the experimental results showed that in some conditions, there was a significant difference between the D conditions but no significant difference between the W conditions. We propose that these D conditions clearly produced a similar sensations to a wet cloth (W condition).

When we increased the layers of cloth, more conditions produced a wet sensation similar to the W condition, even if the temperature remained the same. For example, the wet sensation was produced only when $dT_{cold} = 3$ in the case of a single sheet. However, all temperature conditions produced the wet sensation when the cloth was soft (four sheets). Furthermore, we performed multiple regression analysis to evaluate the effect of coldness and softness on the wet sensation. The response variable was the average score of wetness, and the explanatory variables were dT and WC. As a result, regression coefficients were 0.758 and 0.506 for dT and WC, respectively, and the adjusted R-squared was 0.804. These results indicated that increasing the softness of the cloth caused a wet sensation even for dry cloth.

On the other hand, the condition of $dT_{cold} = 0$ with a single piece of cloth, which reproduced the changes in skin temperature after contact with the wet cloth, was not perceived the same as the wet sensation in the W condition. This finding was different from our previous research [9] and implies that for some cloth, the temperature change alone in the case of an actual wet cloth is not sufficient to augment the wet sensation. Our results suggest that with only one cloth layer, it is difficult to augment the wet sensation only by the temperature control method that we proposed in the previous study; however, it is possible to produce a wet sensation by increasing the coldness or softness of the cloth.

The control of softness of the cloth was successful; however, for the design of a device to produce a wet sensation of the cloth, we will try other control methods of

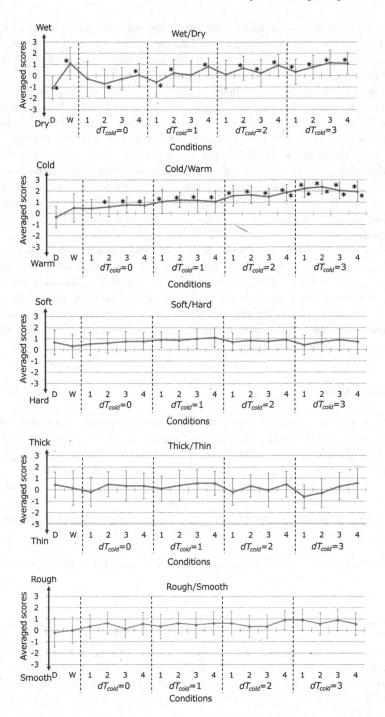

Fig. 5. Results of the experiment *p < 0.05

softness; for example, by placing the cloth on a stage that has a spring or moves up and down. Furthermore, it is known that controlling the contact area for a finger affects the softness sensation [12]. This research shows the possibility that control of the contact area of the cloth also affects the wet sensation.

For the cold sensation, the participants perceived similar coldness as the W condition from the many conditions of $dT_{cold} = 0$, 1, and 2; in addition, five conditions in $dT_{cold} = 2$ and 3 seemed to be perceived as colder than the W condition. The number of cloth layers seemed to have a slight effect, but we suggest that this was due to the setting temperature of the Peltier device. In fact, when we performed the multiple regression analysis to evaluate the effect of dT and WC on the cold sensation in the same way as for wetness, the regression coefficients were 0.928 and 0.0353 for dT and WC, respectively, and the adjusted R-squared was 0.945. This result indicates that increasing the softness of the cloth caused a wet sensation but had little effect on the cold sensation.

In addition, the scores for soft and thick sensations did not show significant differences compared to the D and W conditions in multiple comparisons, although the physical properties were different as shown in Fig. 3. Therefore, although there were physical differences in softness of the cloth that could produce a wet sensation, the participants did not perceive the differences in soft or thick sensations of the cloth. This is an interesting and useful finding because we can augment a wet sensation without changing other haptic impressions of the cloth.

5   Conclusion

We evaluated the wet sensation of dry cloth by controlling its temperature and softness. From the results, we concluded that we could augment a wet sensation perceived from a dry cloth by increasing its softness even if the decrease in temperature of the cloth was not sufficient to create a wet sensation. The results confirmed the efficiency of controlling not only the temperature but also the softness of dry cloth in order to represent a wet sensation in our proposed method.

To realize a device to virtually reproduce a wet sensation of cloth, we need to further investigate other control methods of softness in a future study.

Acknowledgement. This work was supported by JSPS KAKENHI Grant Number 15K12316.

References

1. Bermann, T.W.M., Kosters, N.D., Kappers, A.M.L., Daanen, H.A.M.: Phase change materials and the perception of wetness. Ergonomics **55**(4), 508–512 (2012)
2. Jeon, E., Yoo, S., Kim, E.: Psychophysical determination of moisture perception in high-performance shirt fabrics in relation to sweating level. Ergonomics **54**(6), 576–586 (2011)
3. Bergmann, T.W.M., Kosters, N.D., Kappers, A.M.L., Daanen, H.A.M.: Haptic perception of wetness. Acta Psychol. **141**(2), 159–163 (2012)

4. Filingeri, D., Fournet, D., Hodder, S., Havenith, G.: Why wet feels wet? A neurophysiological model of human cutaneous wetness sensitivity. J. Neurophysiol. **112**(6), 1457–1469 (2014)
5. Bentley, I.M.: The synthetic experiment. Am. J. Psychol. **11**, 405–425 (1900). doi:10.2307/1412750
6. Zigler, M.J.: An experimental study of the perception of clamminess. Am. J. Psychol. **34**, 550–561 (1923)
7. Filingeri, D., Redortier, B., Hodder, S., Havenith, G.: Thermal and tactile interactions in the perception of local skin wetness at rest and during exercise in thermo-neutral and warm environments. Neuroscience **258**, 121–130 (2014)
8. Fillingeri, D., Havenith, G.: Human skin wetness perception: psychophysical and neurophysiological bases. Temperature **2**(1), 86–104 (2015)
9. Shibahara, M., Sato, K.: Illusion of moisture sensation of a cloth by thermal control. Jpn. Res. Assoc. Text. End-Uses **56**(12), 951–958 (2015)
10. Lederman, S.J., Klatzky, R.L.: Hand movement: a window into haptics object recognition. Cogn. Psycol. **19**, 342–368 (1998)
11. Nagano, H., Okamoto, S., Yamada, Y.: Research directions in structuring of tactile dimensions of material textures. TVRSJ **16**(3), 343–353 (2011)
12. Kimura, F., Yamamoto, A.: Effect of delays in softness display using contact area control: rendering of surface viscoelasticity. Adv. Robot. **27**(7), 553–566 (2013)

How Attention Is Allocated When Using Haptic Touch: Shape Feature Distinction and Discrimination Strategy

Torø Graven[(✉)]

Department of Experimental Psychology, University of Oxford,
9 South Parks Road, Oxford OX1 3UD, England
toro.graven@psy.ox.ac.uk

Abstract. This study investigated how attention is allocated by the physical distinction between tactile 2D shape features: Part 1 tested whether certain shape feature distinctions are perceived efficiently (pre-attentively), as opposed to inefficiently (attention dependent). Part 2 explored what discrimination strategies are at use, and with what level of attention (from pre to focused).

It was found (Part 1) that the straight line ↔ angle distinction and the curve ↔ straight line distinction are perceived pre-attentively; the angle ↔ curve distinction attention dependent. Furthermore (Part 2), three discrimination strategies were identified: The figure identity strategy has three levels of attention; it ranks a feature conjunction as the most important target-discriminating feature. The global characteristics strategy and the touch vision strategy have two levels of attention; both rank one separate feature as the most important target-discriminating feature. Despite this, they are equally fast, accurate, and after-decision certain.

Keywords: Attention · Blind · Discrimination strategy · Haptic touch · Shape feature distinction

1 Introduction

Pictures, at least symbols and illustrations, embrace the conventional shape of certain phenomena [1], i.e., the configuration of angles, curves and straight lines. Previous research has found that individuals who are blind recognize tactile pictures of common objects [2, 3] but their recognition fails when the pictured object has to be named [4, 5]. Heller and Gentaz's [2] explanation is that naming requires several cognitive skills, such as perception, categorization, and language. Failure may arise during any of these processes, not only at the recognition stage. Pathak and Pring [5] offer another explanation: all attention is focused on the perceptible features of the pictured object to the exclusion of retrieving the object name. According to Lavie and Cox [6] (cf. also Lavie [7]), sighted individuals cannot reduce the amount of attention paid to visual features – perception is an automatic process: clear physical distinction between the features helps allocate their attention. Currently little is known about the physical distinction and allocation of attention when perceiving tactile 2D shape features, e.g. angles amid curves.

© Springer International Publishing Switzerland 2016
F. Bello et al. (Eds.): EuroHaptics 2016, Part I, LNCS 9774, pp. 380–393, 2016.
DOI: 10.1007/978-3-319-42321-0_35

Haptic touch perceives information serially [8, 9]. Numerous finger pad-sized pieces of information are perceived and linked together in order to recognize, e.g. the picture of some scissors [10] – and with a high quantity of perceived information, perceptual load soon occurs [11]: Selective attention is needed for the perceptual process to proceed [12. Cf. also 13]. Then again, Treisman and Gelade [14] found that certain (visual) features pop out; are perceived automatically – bearing little, or no perceptual load: Popped out features are processed pre-attentively, before selective attention kicks in.

In fact, Treisman [15] suggested a continuum of attention, from pre-attention at one end to focused attention at the other: Pre-attention processes information perceived in parallel about one separate feature [e.g. color (red vs. green)], independent of attention and fast – it calls upon attention. Focused attention, in contrast, processes information perceived serially about feature conjunctions [e.g. color (red vs. green) and orientation (horizontal vs. vertical) [14–17]]. Constant focusing of attention results in attentional load – the information processing system shuts down: Reset only by a feature pop-out [15, 16].

Considering that, haptic touch perceives information serially and that only information perceived in parallel pops out, is pop out not possible by nature when using haptic touch? If this were the case – that pop out is restricted or even impossible –, then individuals who are blind would suffer from constant attentional load. Surely, previous research has found pop out of (tactile) coldness, edges, movement, roughness, surface contour, and vertices, using tasks in which the participants had to search for, e.g. a vertex-target amid sphere-distractors [18–22]. However, none of this research was conducted with 2D shape feature distinctions: The shape features were presented either in 3D objects or in isolation, nor did it include participants with an actual blindness – the most experienced in using haptic touch [23] –, and haptic touch itself was restrained. Experienced participants with no restrains on haptic touch would have used their skills automatically, automaticity possibly reducing any load put on attention [17].

Moreover, Treisman and Paterson [24] suggested that (sighted) individuals may adopt different, even personal, strategies for ranking (visual) target-discriminating features in order of importance – separate features are processed in pre-attention, feature conjunctions in focused attention [14 17]. Graven [25], therefore, investigated how individuals who are blind describe discriminating braille characters, including ranking target-discriminating features in importance – their discrimination strategy[1]. In short, the global characteristics strategy ranks one separate feature (dot location or shape property) as the most important target-discriminating feature, the figure identity strategy a feature conjunction (dot location and dot quantity); the global characteristics strategy lies on the pre-attention end and the figure identity strategy on the focused attention-end of Treisman's [15] continuum of attention [25]. A touch vision strategy was also identified; yet not how it ranks target-discriminating features in order of importance, thus not where it lies on Treisman's [15] continuum of attention [25].

---

[1] "(...) organized, domain-specific, nonobligatory pattern of decisions activated when confronted with (...) problems, and goal directed to attain the solution of the problem" [26, p. 12].

The aim of this study was to go beyond the braille characters and investigate how attention is allocated by the physical distinction between tactile 2D shape features: Part 1 tested whether certain shape feature distinctions are perceived efficiently (pre-attentively), as opposed to inefficiently (attention dependent). Part 2 explored what discrimination strategies (see footnote 1) are at use, and with what level of attention (from pre to focused).

2   Method

2.1   Design

Part 1 was designed as a one-sample experiment, with three conditions of shape feature distinctions: (1) straight line ↔ angle, (2) angle ↔ curve, and (3) curve ↔ straight line[2]. Each experimental condition included two types of trials, with either shape feature serving as the target and the other as the distractors (cf. Table 1).

Part 2 was a mixed design (see footnote 2): Qualitative (think-aloud [28]) data were collected to explore how people describe discriminating, including ranking shape features in order of importance – their discrimination strategy (see footnote 1); quantitative data to examine further on which end of Treisman's [15] continuum of attention each discrimination strategy lies.

2.2   Participants

Nine males and nine females, mean age 48.4 years participated[3]. All were blinded before four months of age: ICD-10 categories 5 and 4; including (cat. 5) total blindness and (cat. 4) light perception, light projection and minimal color perception [27], thus were not influenced; positively or negatively, by previous or current visual shape feature experiences [30, 31]. These individuals participated in Part 1 and Part 2: N = 18.

Because Graven [25] identified a separate discrimination strategy among those who have had, or were still having visual shape feature experiences, seven more individuals participated in Part 2: Two males and five females, mean age 40.4 years (see footnote 3). Three were blinded (ICD-10, cat. 5 and 4) between four and 12 months of age, one was totally blinded less than 25 months before this study, and three were congenitally blinded, ICD-10, category 3; two of whom had light perception in one eye until 10 and 28 years old, now totally blinded in this eye and in both eyes, respectively [27]. N (including Part 1) = 25.

---

[2] A pilot study, with one congenitally and two early blinded females (see footnote 3) [27], assessed the number of trials; the shape feature distinctions (e.g. size); the a priori themes [29] used for scoring Part 2.

[3] They had no cognitive delay or impairment, and no physical disability. They had never before explored the Moon characters (see footnote 4). They were offered a remuneration to compensate for their time.

2.3   Test Materials

Thirty shape feature distinctions were used, ten in each experimental condition, i.e., one per trial. Each shape feature distinction comprised five Moon characters[4], one per shape feature. The five shape features were situated next to each other in a horizontal line; (1) making it possible to explore them simultaneously with the fingers of one hand [8, 9, 14–17], and (2) minimizing the time spent on locating them (cf. Fig. 1).

The shape feature distinctions followed either one or both of two criteria: (a) Two or more shape features had to resemble a global shape [33–35]. EXAMPLE: (Table 1) Trial 1; shape features 2 + 3 = square, or Trial 29; shape features 1 + 2 = circle. (b) The target/target lines had to be oriented in the same direction as two or more distractors/distractor lines. EXAMPLE: (Table 1) Trial 4; both target-angle and distractor-curves on the left (shape features 1, 2, 3, and 5), or Trial 3; diagonal left-to-right and right-to-left lines in angle-target and straight line-distractors (shape features 1, 2, and 3).

Printing size was 24 pt; printed on off-white swell paper. All shape feature distinctions were glued, separately, on foam board: 5 mm thick; 130 mm long; 50 mm wide, and presented in the middle of a blue silicone mat [385 × 275 mm (cf. Fig. 1)].

Table 1.   Shape feature distinctions: some examples

Trial	Experimental condition	Shape feature distinction (TARGET and distractors)	
1	(1) straight line ↔ angle	⌐L ⌐I Γ	angle, angle, angle, STRAIGHT LINE, angle
3	(1) straight line ↔ angle	\ V / –	straight line, ANGLE, straight line, straight line, straight line
4	(2) angle ↔ curve	⊇ ⊏ S ⌐ ⊂	curve, curve, curve, curve, ANGLE
6	(3) curve ↔ straight line	\ S N ⌐o	STRAIGHT LINE, curve, curve, curve, curve
11	(2) angle ↔ curve	< ⊃ V L Γ	angle, CURVE, angle, angle, angle
12	(3) curve ↔ straight line	I \ / U _	straight line, straight line, straight line, CURVE, straight line
13	(3) curve ↔ straight line	∠ ⌐⊃_ ο	curve, curve, curve, STRAIGHT LINE, curve
15	(1) straight line ↔ angle	∧ L ⌐ < \	angle, angle, angle, angle, STRAIGHT LINE
16	(2) angle ↔ curve	Γ ⌐ Ϲ ο ⌐	curve, ANGLE, curve, curve, curve
17	(2) angle ↔ curve	∧ V N < ⌐	angle, angle, CURVE, angle, angle
18	(3) curve ↔ straight line	N Ζ / S ⌐	curve, curve, STRAIGHT LINE, curve, curve
19	(1) straight line ↔ angle	/ – I L _	straight line, straight line, straight line, ANGLE, straight line
24	(2) angle ↔ curve	ο Ο S ⌐L	curve, curve, curve, ANGLE, curve
29	(2) angle ↔ curve	Ϲ ⊃ ∧ U ο	curve, curve, ANGLE, curve, curve

---

[4] Moon were invented in 1845, to allow reading by haptic touch: Straight lines and curves form nine basic shapes, rotated to create the 26 letters of the English alphabet ([32]. Cf. Table 1, e.g. Trial 1: shape features 1, 2, 3 and 5 = Moon "m", "l", "y" and "e", respectively). The Moon "h", "n", "o", "z", "8", and the contraction for "and" all comprise more than one shape feature; however always a curve, thus were included in the test material (cf. Table 1, e.g. Trial 18).

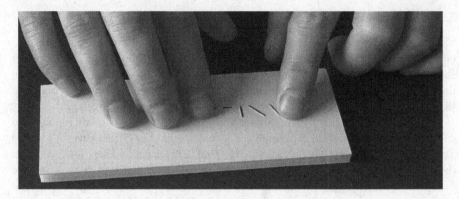

Fig. 1. Test material

2.4   Procedure

The three experimental conditions (and their two types of trials) were presented in random order and the (30) trials were counterbalanced across participants[5].

First, the participant had to make a fist with both hands, to prevent them from taking a peek at the shape features. Guided by the experimenter, the participant had to place both fists in the middle of the test material: the experimenter's hand was on top of the participant's fists. At this point, the participant was asked to explore the shape features: to start when the experimenter's hand was removed and to stop by tapping on the detected target. The participant was not told how many shape features there were in each shape feature distinction, or whether their detected target was correct.

- Task 1: To detect the target, fast and accurately.
- Task 2: To rate own after-decision certainty [36],
- Task 3: To describe what had unified the distractors [28, 37] – how the target was discriminated from the distractors.

In Task 3, the experimenter mirrored back to the participant the essence of what they had thought-aloud; allowing them to correct what was being scored; clarify, add comments and give examples. Part 1 included Tasks 1 and 2; Part 2 included Task 3.

2.5   Scoring

- (Part 1) Task 1: (a) Exploration time and (b) accuracy, i.e., number of (a) seconds from when the experimenter's hand was removed from the participant's fists to when the participant tapped on detected target, and (b) correct target detections.

---

[5] The experiment took place in a quiet room, neutral in color. Distinct light sources, e.g. a specific lamp, were removed to minimize possible visual distractions; the general lighting of the room was lowered to minimize the color contrast between the (off-white) shape feature distinctions and the (blue) silicone mat. Before testing, the experimenter explained both the silicone mat – that it prevented the shape feature distinctions from moving around on the table – and the test itself. The test material was presented directly in front of the participant.

- (Part 1) Task 2: After-decision certainty, i.e. 1 'Not at all sure'; 2 'Unsure'; 3 'Not very sure'; 4 'Fairly sure'; 5 'Sure'; 6 'Very sure' and 7 '100 % sure'.
- (Part 2) Task 3 was scored in two steps. In step one, the participant's thinking-aloud [28] was coded as one of 17 a priori themes [29]; all anchored in Treisman's work [13] and the characteristics of braille [38], and added to by the data from the pilot study (see footnote 2). These a priori themes included the shape features themselves, i.e. angle, curve and straight line, plus the orientation and quantity of these, "angled-curve", "curved-angle", "gap", "orientation of gaps", "quantity of gaps", "global shape", "no unifying feature", and "other things – which?" (cf. Table 2, Code/Themes 01–17). In step two, the participant's clarifications, added comments and/or examples were written down (in exact wording) in a think-aloud protocol [28].

Table 2. Structure of qualitative data analysis: code → theme → combined themes + rich data = templates.

Code	Themes	Combined themes			R	
01	Angle	Named shape feature: codes 01, 04 and 07	"Deductive" name	"Inductive" name	I	
02	Orientation of angles	Orientation of named shape feature: codes 02, 05 and 08			C	
03	Quantity of angles	Quantity of named shape feature: codes 03, 06 and 09			H	
04	Curve	Named shape feature: codes 01, 04 and 07	"Deductive" name	"Inductive" name		
05	Orientation of curves	Orientation of named shape feature: codes 02, 05 and 08				
06	Quantity of curves	Quantity of named shape feature: codes 03, 06 and 09				
07	Straight line	Named shape feature: codes 01, 04 and 07	"Deductive" name	"Inductive" name		
08	Orientation of straight lines	Orientation of named shape feature: codes 02, 05 and 08				
09	Quantity of straight lines	Quantity of named shape feature: codes 03, 06 and 09				
10	"Angled-curve"	Deleted			T	
11	"Curved-angle"				E	
12	Gap				M	
13	Orientation of gaps				P	
14	Quantity of gaps				L	
15	Global shape	Global shape – unnamed (global shape) feature			A	
16	No unifying feature	No unifying feature			T	
17	Other things – which	Deleted			E	
18	Different angle openings	Different angle opening	Spatial relations of named shape features		S	
19	More open angles					
20	More pointed/sharp angles					
21	More open curves	Different curve opening				
22	More pointed/sharp curves					
23	Bent lines	Bent lines				
24	Continuous lines	Continuous lines				
25	Length of lines	Size: codes 25 and 28			D	
26	Orientation of features	Orientation of unnamed shape features			A	
27	Quantity of features	Quantity of unnamed shape features			T	
28	Size	Size: codes 25 and 28			A	

2.6   Analysis

Part 1 was analyzed in three separate (repeated measures) ANOVA tests: (Task 1a) exploration time, (Task 1b) accuracy, and (Task 2) after-decision certainty; to test whether certain shape feature distinctions are perceived efficiently (pre-attentively), as opposed to inefficiently (attention dependent).

Part 2 (Task 3) was approached by Template Analysis [29, 39]: Step one was (a) to read, and (b) to reread the think-aloud protocols. In step two, eleven new themes were discovered: different angle openings, more open angles, more pointed/sharp angles, more open curves, more pointed/sharp curves, bent lines, continuous lines, length of lines, orientation of features, quantity of features, and size (cf. Table 2, Codes/Themes 18–28). Step three was to merge related themes, e.g. different angle openings, more open angles and more pointed/sharp angles into "different angle opening", and delete redundant ones; e.g. those concerning gaps (cf. Table 2, Combined themes). In step four, the think-aloud protocols were read through again, pursuing clarifications, added comments and examples, i.e. rich data. At last, the coded themes and the rich data were unified to identify templates of how people describe discriminating tactile shape features, including ranking them in order of importance – their discrimination strategy.

All (25) participants were assigned to one of the identified discrimination strategies (see footnote 1), based on the quantity of coded themes under each template (i.e. min. 50 %). Finally, the quantitative data were analyzed, using parametric statistics, to examine further on what end of Treisman's [15] continuum of attention each discrimination strategy lies.

3   Results

3.1   Part 1: Efficiency/Inefficiency in Perceiving Shape Feature Distinctions

There was a significant difference in mean exploration time between experimental condition 1 (M = 14.7, SD = 8.60), experimental condition 2 (M = 31.7, SD = 20.43), and experimental condition 3 (M = 16.5, SD = 10.61): $F(1.125, 19.131)^6 = 27.5$, $p = 0.000$, N = 18. Post hoc tests using the Bonferroni correction revealed that experimental conditions 1 and 3 elicited less exploration time than experimental condition 2: $p_{ec1/ec2} = 0.000$; $p_{ec3/ec2} = 0.000$; $p_{ec1/ec3} = 0.183$. The straight line ↔ angle distinction and the curve ↔ straight line distinction are both perceived efficiently (pre-attentively) compared to the angle ↔ curve distinction, which is perceived inefficiently (attention dependent): Did in fact the focused attention required to detect the target in the angle ↔ curve distinction result in attentional load?

Indeed it did: experimental condition 1 (M = 8.9, SD = 1.31), experimental condition 2 (M = 3.4, SD = 1.54) and experimental condition 3 (M = 8.9, SD = 1.11): $F(2, 34) = 115.96$, $p = 0.000$, N = 18. Post hoc tests using the Bonferroni

---

[6] Mauchly's test indicated that the assumption of sphericity had been violated: $\chi^2_{explorationtime}(2) = 24.0$, $p = 0.000$ ($\varepsilon = 0.56$) and $\chi^2_{after-decisioncertainty}(2) = 12.6$, $p = 0.002$ ($\varepsilon = 0.65$), thus the degrees of freedom were corrected using Greenhouse-Geisser estimate of sphericity.

correction revealed that experimental condition 2 elicited lower accuracy than experimental conditions 1 and 3: $p_{ec2/ec1} = 0.000$; $p_{ec2/ec3} = 0.000$; $p_{ec1/ec3} = 1.000$. The mean accuracy for the straight line $\leftrightarrow$ angle distinction and the curve $\leftrightarrow$ straight line distinction was well above 85%; for the angle $\leftrightarrow$ curve distinction, it was less than 35% – barely above chance.

So, did the participants know that their information processing system was shutting down in the angle $\leftrightarrow$ curve distinction? There was a significant difference also in mean after-decision certainty, i.e. experimental condition 1 (M = 6.9, SD = 0.21), experimental condition 2 (M = 6.3, SD = 0.55) and experimental condition 3 (M = 6.9, SD = 0.21): $F(1.295, 22.021)$ (see footnote 6) = 20.412, $p = 0.000$, N = 18. Post hoc tests, using the Bonferroni correction, revealed that experimental condition 2 elicited lower after-decision certainty than experimental conditions 1 and 3: $p_{ec2/ec1} = 0.000$; $p_{ec2/ec3} = 0.002$; $p_{ec1/ec3} = 1.000$. The after-decision certainty was the lowest when the exploration time was the longest and the accuracy the lowest – they certainly did know that their information processing system was shutting down in the angle $\leftrightarrow$ curve distinction.

3.2   Part 2: Discrimination Strategies

Line Analysis → "Inducting" Shape Feature Name. Six males and seven females (mean age 47.4 years) described treating the shape features as lines; in fact counting up the quantity of lines. They clarified that: "An angle has two lines"; "When the shape has more than two lines, then it is a curve; not an angle". Having analyzed line quantity, the shape feature distractors were then named in (186 of 282) 66.0% of all correct target detections [cf. Table 1, e.g. Trial 11 (angle ↔ CURVE distinction); Table 2].

Merely the quantity of lines was reported in 28.4% of all correct target detections, e.g.: [Trials 6 (curve ↔ STRAIGHT LINE distinction) and 15 (STRAIGHT LINE ↔ angle distinction)] "They have more than one line", and [Trial 12 (CURVE ↔ straight line distinction)] "They have less than three lines". Four participants then counted up the quantity of named angles and/or curves; in target and distractors [see e.g. Trials 13 (curve ↔ STRAIGHT LINE distinction) and 17 (angle ↔ CURVE distinction)][7]. See Tables 1 and 2.

In 5.6% of all correct target detections, orientation of features were reported – named [e.g. Trial 15 (STRAIGHT LINE ↔ angle distinction): "Direction of straight lines"] and unnamed [e.g. Trial 1 (STRAIGHT LINE ↔ angle distinction)], and further; size, e.g.: "Length of line", spatial relations of named features, e.g.: "Different angle opening", and "global shape" [e.g. Trials 4, 29 and 24, respectively (ANGLE ↔ curve distinction)]. In three cases the correct target was detected, but with "no unifying shape feature" for the distractors [e.g. in Trial 1 (STRAIGHT LINE ↔ angle distinction). Cf. Tables 1 and 2].

---

[7] For an example of incorrect targeting, see Table 1, Trial 11 (angle ↔ CURVE distinction): "Three figures with two angles and two figures with one angle".

These 13 participants described an identical discrimination strategy, including three levels of attention: *Figure identity*. Level 1: Specific analysis of the line quantity in each shape feature. Level 2: Recognizing and naming the shape features, according to a set of rules. In levels one and two, the ranking of features in order of importance depends on different, even personal, strategy (not on target and distractors): a feature conjunction [i.e. line quantity and ("inducted") shape feature name] is ranked as the most important. Level 3 (if necessary): Analyzing the quantity of named angles and curves in each shape feature. (See Table 3).

Noticing Global Shape → "Deducting" Shape Feature Name. Five males and five females (mean age 46.4 years described treating the shape features as global shapes; one participant clarifying that: "I search for the differences in the global shape: I don't think of them as angles or curves". These participants added comments such as: [Trial 13 (curve ↔ STRAIGHT LINE distinction)] "The others are 'zigzags'", [Trial 16 (ANGLE ↔ curve distinction)] "The others have one short and one long", and [Trial 19 (straight line ↔ ANGLE distinction)] "The others have nothing in another direction" (cf. Table 1). They reported "global shape" in (15 of 216) 6.9% of all correct target detections.

These participants found it necessary to analyse – "break down", in their own words – the global shape in 93.1% of all correct target detections; as one participant clarified it: "When they have too many lines". One participant, for example, broke down "global shape" in Trial 11 [angle ↔ CURVE distinction. Cf. Table 1)]: "One and two are mirror 'thingies'; three and five are curves. (...) A 'thingy' is something messy or indefinable".

Having assessed the global shapes, the distractors were named in 60.7% of all correct target detections. Shape features were named and counted up in 31.8% [e.g. in Trial 18 (curve ↔ STRAIGHT LINE distinction): "The others have more than one straight line"]; named and oriented in 6.0% [e.g. in Trial 17 (angle ↔ CURVE distinction): "Different direction of the angles"]; named and related spatially in 1.5% [e.g. in Trial 4 (ANGLE ↔ curve distinction): "The others have a more open angle". Cf. Tables 1 and 2].

Also these ten participants described an identical discrimination strategy, including two levels of attention: *Global characteristics*. Level 1: Noticing differences in the global shape. Level 2 (if necessary): Specific analyses of the global shape difference(s). In level two, the ranking of features in order of importance depends on different, even personal, strategy (not on target and distractors): one separate feature [i.e. ("deducted") shape feature name] is ranked as the most important. (See Table 3).

Global Shape Association to Regular Print Letters → Analyzing Shape Features. Two females (mean age 37.5 years[8]) clarified that: "I treat them as global shapes". They then associated the global shapes to regular print letters, e.g.: "The regular print 'z' is a symbol for all global shapes that resemble the z" (cf. Table 1, e.g. Trials 4 [ANGLE ↔ curve distinction] and 18 [curve ↔ STRAIGHT LINE distinction]).

---

[8] One was totally blinded about two years before this study and the other was congenitally blinded, with minimal visual shape perception in one eye and light perception in the other [27] until the age of 28; now totally blinded (for more than 20 years).

When an instant association between the global shape and a regular print letter did not occur, then these participants analyzed the global shape; in fact did so in all correct target detections – reporting ("deducted") shape feature name in (23 of 41) 56.1%; combining line quantity and ("inducted") shape feature name in 43.9%: "I recognize them because I count lines."

Indeed, these participants described a third discrimination strategy, including two levels of attention: *Touch vision.* Level 1: Noticing differences in the global shape and associating the global shapes to regular print letters. Level 2 (if necessary): Specific analyses of the global shape difference(s). In level two, the ranking of features in order of importance depends on different, even personal, strategy (not on target and distractors): one separate feature [i.e. ("deducted") shape feature name] is ranked as the most important. (See Table 3).

Table 3. Top three ranking of target-discriminating features

		One separate feature	Feature conjunction	
Global characteristics strategy	1	"Deducted" shape feature name		1
	2	Shape feature name		2
	3		(...) name + quantity	3
Touch vision strategy	1	"Deducted" shape feature name		1
	2		Line quantity + "inducted" (...) name	2
	3	Yet not clear what target-discriminating feature is ranked as no. 3		3
Figure identity strategy	1		Line quantity + "inducted" (...) name	1
	2	Line quantity		2
	3	Orientation of shape feature		3

Exploration Time, Accuracy, and After-Decision Certainty. Before the statistical analyses, one statistical outlier was identified in the figure identity strategy, with mean exploration time almost seven times above that of the others (174.0 vs. 26.0). Following Treisman's work [13], this participant's targeting accuracy should, therefore, be below that of the others; but this was not the case – it was in fact above (M = 24.0 vs. 21.5). This participant clarified, in the think-aloud protocol [28] that: "I'm comparing the trials. There must be a pattern of where it is situated", thus was omitted from all statistical analyses. Furthermore, because only two participants described the touch vision strategy, it would have no statistical power. Then again, the touch vision strategy shows clear similarities with the global characteristics strategy – two levels of attention, treating the shape features as global shapes, and ranking one separate feature [("deducted") shape feature name] as the most important target-discriminating feature (see Table 3). The touch vision strategy therefore joins forces with the global characteristics strategy.

There was no statistically significant difference between the figure identity strategy and the global characteristics/touch vision strategy: Mean exploration time was 26.0 (SD = 17.65. N = 12) and 20.9 (SD = 7.76. N = 12), respectively: t(15.101)[9] = 0.915, $p > 0.05$. Mean accuracy was 21.5 (SD = 1.93. N = 12) and 21.4, SD = 2.84. N = 12),

---

[9] Leverne's Test for Equality of Variances = 0.013.

respectively: t(24) = 0.084, $p > 0.05$. Mean after-decision certainty was 6.8 (SD = 0.27. N = 12) and 6.6 (SD = 0.33. N = 12), respectively: t(24) = 1.127, $p > 0.05$.

4 Discussion

Part 1 found that the straight line ↔ angle distinction and the curve ↔ straight line distinction are both perceived efficiently (pre-attentively); the angle ↔ curve distinction inefficiently (attention dependent): There is a clear tactile physical distinction be-tween straight lines and angles, and between straight lines and curves; but not between angles and curves [cf. 6, 7]. Both the straight line ↔ angle distinction and the curve ↔ straight line distinction allocate attention to the pre-attention end of Treisman's [15] continuum of attention. When it comes to the angle ↔ curve distinction, however, selective attention is needed for the perceptual process to proceed [12, 13]: attention being allocated to the focused attention end of Treisman's [15] continuum of attention – in fact resulting in attentional load [16]. To this end, individuals are aware of any attentional load (at least when processing tactile 2D shape feature distinctions).

Part 2 identified three discrimination strategies, including with what level of attention they are used, i.e. the figure identity strategy, the global characteristics strategy, and the touch vision strategy. The first has three levels, the latter two have two levels of attention; the first ranks a feature conjunction [line quantity and ("inducted") shape feature name], the latter two rank one separate feature [("deducted") shape feature name] as the most important target-discriminating feature. Thus, the figure identity strategy should lie on the focused attention end of Treisman's [15] continuum of attention; both the global characteristics strategy and the touch vision strategy on the pre-attention end. However, there is no statistically significant difference between the discrimination strategies, i.e. on exploration time, accuracy, and after-decision certainty.

As both the straight line ↔ angle distinction and the curve ↔ straight line distinction allocate attention to the pre-attention end of Treisman's [15] continuum of attention, the straight line appears to stand out. Was haptic touch in fact scanning loosely over the angle ↔ curve distinction, in anticipation of a straight line to stand out, or even pop out – to call upon attention [17]? After all, "An angle has two lines" and "When the shape has more than two lines, then it is a curve; not an angle". Furthermore, did too many straight lines call upon attention, causing chaos in attention? If this were the case, then the angle ↔ curve distinction would be problematic because of chaos in attention (and not because of attentional load per se) [cf. 16].

Then again, the load must also have been heavier in the angle ↔ curve distinction than in the two straight line distinctions. Perceiving, e.g. $6 + 3 + 6 + 3 + 2$ ($=20^{10}$) lines put more load on perception, thus inevitably on attention than perceiving, e.g. $1 + 2 + 1 + 1 + 1$ ($=6$ (see footnote 10)) lines [cf. Table 1, Trials 4 (ANGLE ↔ curve distinction) and 3 (straight line ↔ ANGLE distinction), respectively [11, 16]]. Moreover, the angle ↔ curve distinction could also have been problematic because of conjunction illusions and/or conjunction errors, in which the individuals fail to combine, e.g.

---

[10] "An angle has two lines." "When the shape has more than two lines, then it is a curve (…)."

the quantity and orientation of straight lines into angles and curves [14, 16]. Alternatively, did the individuals rather prefer to keep the quantity of straight lines and the orientation of straight lines as two separate features; in order to reduce any load put on perception, and thus on attention [cf. 14, 40]?

The three discrimination strategies identified in this study are quite similar to those identified in Graven's [25] study, suggesting that they are specific to the individuals (and not the task). Indeed, both studies found that the ranking of features in order of importance depends on different, even personal strategy (not on target and distractors [cf. also 24]): The individuals' voluntary control over what is relevant and irrelevant information does not depend on braille character/shape feature distinction [cf. 6]. Angles and curves are treated as straight lines because the individuals do not alter, or are not capable of altering their ranking, e.g. of line quantity as the most important target-discriminating feature. More in this vein, did they not; or were they not capable of altering their discrimination strategy according to shape feature distinction? Although they are amongst the most experienced in using haptic touch [23], they were naive to the Moon characters; and, as such, may not yet have developed a repertoire of appropriate discrimination strategies [cf. 26, 41, 42]. In fact, Graven [41] found that braille readers often continue the discrimination task at hand with a failing discrimination strategy.

On the subject of developing appropriate discrimination strategies. Although the test materials were larger and the number of distractors was higher in Graven's [25] study than in this study[11], both the figure identity strategy and the global characteristics/touch vision strategy[12] were noticeably faster in Graven's [25] study[13]. On the one hand, this could be because the tactile physical distinction between braille characters is clearer than that between 2D shape features [cf. 6, 7]. On the other hand, it could be because individuals who are blind are more experienced in discriminating braille characters than 2D shape features – they have not yet developed an appropriate discrimination strategy for 2D shape features. Surely, with more experience comes more automatic use of achieved skills, automaticity possibly reducing any load put on attention [cf. 17].

Further research is indeed needed to investigate how and why discrimination strategies fail, and also to improve the proficiency in discriminating tactile 2D shape features. Surely mixing up angles and curves makes interpreting pictures, e.g. symbols and illustrations, problematic: the Euro symbol (€) may be mistaken for the capital E and the Pythagorean triangle may have no right angle.

Acknowledgements. Thank you to the Norwegian Research Council and the Norwegian Association of the Blind and Partially Sighed for funding this work; through their schemes for independent projects. A sincere thank you also to Watts Professor of Experimental Psychology, Dr. Glyn Humphreys for his interesting comments on an earlier version of this manuscript.

---

[11] 21 × 21 cm [25] vs. 13 × 5 cm; 11 distractors [25] vs. 4 distractors.

[12] The touch vision strategy was not included in Graven's [25] statistical analyses.

[13] The figure identity strategy used (M) 17.7s [25] vs. 26.0s, and the global characteristics/touch vision strategy (M) 14.3s [25] vs. 20.9s (see footnote 12).

References

1. Oxford Dictionaries (2015). http://www.oxforddictionaries.com/
2. Heller, M.A.: Gentaz, E: Psychology of Touch and Blindness. Psychology Press, New York (2014)
3. Millar, S.: Space and Sense. Psychology Press, Hove (2008)
4. Heller, M.A., Calcaterra, J.A., Burson, L.L., Tyler, L.A.: Tactual picture identification by blind and sighted people: effects of providing categorical information. Percept. Psychophys. **58**, 310–323 (1996)
5. Pathak, K., Pring, L.: Tactual picture recognition in congenitally blind and sighted children. Appl. Cogn. Psych. **3**, 337–350 (1989)
6. Lavie, N., Cox, S.: On the efficiency of visual selective attention: efficient visual search leads to inefficient distractor rejection. Psychol. Sci. **8**, 395–398 (1997)
7. Lavie, N.: Perceptual load as a necessary condition for selective attention. J. Exp. Psychol.-Hum. Percept. Perform. **21**, 451–468 (1995)
8. Lederman, S.J., Browse, R.A., Klatzky, R.L.: Haptic processing of spatially distributed information. Percept. Psychophys. **44**, 222–232 (1988)
9. Millar, S.: Strategy choices by young Braille readers. Perception **13**, 567–579 (1984)
10. Kennedy, J.M., Bai, J.: Haptic pictures: fit judgements predict identification, recognition memory, and confidence. Perception **31**, 1013–1026 (2002)
11. Lavie, N., Lin, Z., Zokaei, N., Toma, V.: The role of perceptual load in object recognition. J. Exp. Psychol.-Hum. Percept. Perform. **35**, 1346–1358 (2009)
12. Lavie, N., Tsal, Y.: Perceptual load as a major determinant of the locus of selection in visual attention. Percept. Psychophys. **56**, 183–197 (1994)
13. Wolfe, J., Robertson, L.: From Perception to Consciousness: Searching with Anne Treisman. Oxford University Press, Oxford (2012)
14. Treisman, A.M., Gelade, G.: A feature-integration theory of attention. Cogn. Psychol. **12**, 97–136 (1980)
15. Treisman, A.: The perception of features and objects. In: Baddeley, A., Weiskrantz, L. (eds.) Attention: Selection, Awareness, and Control: A Tribute to Donald Broadbent, pp. 5–35. Oxford University Press, Oxford (1995)
16. Treisman, A.: Features and objects: the fourteenth Bartlett memorial lecture. Q. J. Exp. Psychol.-A. **40**, 201–237 (1988)
17. Treisman, A., Vieira, A., Hayes, A.: Automaticity and preattentive processing. Am. J. Psychol. **105**, 341–362 (1992)
18. Lederman, S.J., Klatzky, R.L.: Relative availability of surface and object properties during early haptic processing. J. Exp. Psychol.-Hum. Percept. Perform. **23**, 1680–1707 (1997)
19. Plaisier, M.A., Bergmann Tiest, W.M., Kappers, A.M.L.: Haptic pop-out in a hand sweep. Acta Psychol. **128**, 368–377 (2008)
20. Plaisier, M.A., Bergmann Tiest, W.M., Kappers, A.M.L.: Salient features in 3-D haptic shape perception. Atten. Percept. Psychophys. **71**, 421–430 (2009)
21. Plaisier, M.A., Kappers, A.M.: Cold objects pop out! In: Kappers, A.M., van Erp, J.B., Bergmann Tiest, W.M., van der Helm, F.C. (eds.) EuroHaptics 2010, Part II. LNCS, vol. 6192, pp. 219–224. Springer, Heidelberg (2010)
22. van Polanen, V., Bergmann Tiest, W.M., Kappers, A.M.L.: Haptic pop-out of movable stimuli. Atten. Percept. Psychophys. **74**, 204–215 (2012)
23. Sathian, K.: Practice makes perfect: sharper tactile perception in the blind. Neurology **54**, 2203–2204 (2000)

24. Treisman, A.M., Paterson, R.: Emergent features, attention, and object perception. J. Exp. Psychol.-Hum. Percept. Perform. **10**, 12–31 (1984)
25. Graven, T.: How blind individuals discriminate braille characters: an identification and comparison of three discrimination strategies. Br. J. Vis. Impair. **33**, 80–95 (2015)
26. Ostad, S.A.: Strategic competence: issues of task-specific strategies in arithmetic. Nordic Stud. Math. Educ. **5**, 7–32 (1997)
27. ICD-10: International classification of diseases and related health problems 10th revision, Chapter VII Diseases of the eye adnexa (H00–H59). WHO (2010), (2015). http://apps.who. int/classifications/icd10/browse/2010/en#/H53-H54
28. Aanstoos, C.M.: The think aloud method in descriptive research. J. Phenomenol. Psychol. **14**, 243–266 (1983)
29. King, N.: Doing template analysis. In: Symon, G., Cassell, C. (eds.) Qualitative Organizational Research: Core Methods and Current Challenges, pp. 426–450. SAGE Publications Ltd., London (2012)
30. Graven, T.: Seeing Through Touch: When Touch Replaces Vision as the Dominant Sense Modality. VDM Verlag Dr. Müller AG & Co., Saarbrücken (2009)
31. Spence, C., Nicholls, M.E.R., Driver, J.: The cost of expecting events in the wrong sensory modality. Percept. Psychophys. **63**, 330–336 (2001)
32. Moon Literacy: What is Moon? (2015). http://www.moonliteracy.org.uk/whatis.htm
33. Heller, M.A., Clyburn, S.: Global versus local processing in haptic perception of form. Bull. Psychon. Soc. **31**, 574–576 (1993)
34. Lakatos, S., Marks, L.E.: Haptic form perception: relative salience of local and global features. Percept. Psychophys. **61**, 895–908 (1999)
35. Soechting, J.F., Song, W., Flanders, M.: Haptic feature extraction. Cereb. Cortex **16**, 1168–1180 (2006)
36. Persaud, N., McLeod, P., Cowey, A.: Post-decision wagering objectively measures awareness. Nat. Neurosci. **10**, 257–261 (2007)
37. Dienes, Z., Scott, R.: Measuring unconscious knowledge: distinguishing structural knowledge and judgment knowledge. Psychol. Res. **69**, 338–351 (2005)
38. Braille Cell Dimensions (2015). http://www.tiresias.org/research/reports/braille_cell.htm
39. Landridge, D.: Phenomenological Psychology Theory. Research and Practice. Pearson/ Prentice Hall, Harlow (2007)
40. Lavie, N.: Visual feature integration and focused attention: response competition from multiple distractor features. Percept. Psychophys. **59**, 543–556 (1997)
41. Graven, T.: When the discrimination strategy fails: revisiting the figure identity strategy, the global characteristics strategy, and the touch vision strategy. Br. J. Vis. Impair **34**(2), 121–129 (2016)
42. Ostad, S.A.: Cognitive subtraction in a developmental perspective: accuracy, speed-of-processing and strategy-use differences in normal and mathematically challenged children. Focus Learn. Prob. Math. **22**, 18–31 (2000)

It's All About the Subject - Options to Improve Psychometric Procedure Performance

Christian Hatzfeld[✉], Viet Quoc Hoang, and Mario Kupnik

Institute of Electromechanical Design, Technische Universität Darmstadt,
Merckstr. 25, 64283 Darmstadt, Germany
c.hatzfeld@emk.tu-darmstadt.de

Abstract. We investigate the effect of procedure-specific parameters on the performance of three common psychophysical procedures. Methods considered include transformed-staircases, the Ψ-method and the UML method, while performance is evaluated in terms of accuracy, efficiency, precision and robustness. Simple Yes/No- and three alternative forced choice response paradigms were considered. A Monte Carlo simulation was conducted for three different types of test persons and analyzed by analysis of variances. Results show a large effect of the test person on the performance, especially for staircase procedures. No parameter exhibited a relevant effect on accuracy for each analyzed methods, estimation precision can be increased with an increasing number of trials. Only for staircase procedures, efficiency can be influenced by the choice of the progression rule.

Keywords: Psychometric procedures · Staircase · Ψ · UML · Performance analysis

1 Introduction

Psychometric procedures are used to obtain human perception thresholds. The first element of a procedure is a psychometric method, that determines the course of the experiment, in particular the initial stimulus placement (starting rule), stimulus changes during the experiment (progression rule) and the end of the experiment (stopping rule). The second element of a procedure is a response paradigm, that defines the way a subject has to response to a stimulus. Typical paradigms include simple Yes/No-tasks, n-alternative forced choice paradigms (nAFC, [19]), and unforced choice paradigms [7,9].

The selection of a procedure is governed by (1) the required performance of the psychometric procedure, (2) the assumptions and asserted knowledge of the experimenter about the psychometric function of the test persons [6], and (3) the constraints of the experiment. Examples for (3) are the facility to control stimulus intensities or the experience of the test subjects. In the state-of-the-art, several recommendations can be found for selecting a psychometric procedure, for example [2,8,10]. However, works originating from research groups with a

© Springer International Publishing Switzerland 2016
F. Bello et al. (Eds.): EuroHaptics 2016, Part I, LNCS 9774, pp. 394–403, 2016.
DOI: 10.1007/978-3-319-42321-0_36

close focus on psychophysics concentrate predominantly on the performance of procedures. Experimental constraints and typical questions of a system designer are considered to a small extend only. The results of [10], for example, determine a PEST staircase with a 6down1up rule as one of the most efficient procedures. Since it targets detection probabilities of 0.89, results from this procedure will be useful to assert values that are detected by the majority of potential users — but results are probably not usable to attain acceptable error margins for the display of haptic information, that are supposed to be undetected.

On the other hand, the steadily increasing calculation power allows for individual performance analysis for individual experiments. This is alleviated by programs such as *Palamedes*, *Psychtoolbox* and *Psychopy*, allowing researchers and developers of human-machine-interfaces to find the best suited procedure for the planned experiment. Consequently, this development shifts the focus of procedure analysis from statements, which procedure is the best/most accurate/most efficient to the analysis of parameters that affect these characteristics.

In this paper, we present statistical analysis of Monte Carlo simulations of three common psychometric procedures in order to assess the effect of method-specific parameters on performance criteria (Fig. 2). We considered Transformed Staircase Methods with three different progression rules (Sect. 3), the Ψ-method (Sect. 4) and the Updated Maximum Likelihood method (UML, Sect. 5). All methods were simulated with simple yes-no (YN) and three alternative forced choice (3AFC) paradigms. Unforced choice paradigms as presented in [7,9] were not considered because of the comparatively large computation time.

2 Approach and Analysis Methods

In all simulations, we focus on the estimation of the threshold, i.e. the parameter α in (1), since this parameter is more widely used than estimations of other parameters like slope β and lapse rate λ. Monte Carlo simulations are a widely-spread tool to analyze psychometric procedures. Agreement of simulations and human behavior is demonstrated in several studies [9,10,14]. For this paper, we used a framework already presented in [7] for the implementation of psychometric procedures. Simulation was conducted with MATLAB (version 2015a, MathWorks, Natick, MA, USA) on a standard desktop PC. Each parameter combination was simulated for 3000 runs. In all simulations, possible stimulus values x were restricted to an interval of $x \in [0, 100]$. We simulated test persons based on a logistic psychometric function

$$p_c = \gamma + (1 - \gamma - \lambda) \cdot \frac{1}{1 + e^{-\beta(x-\alpha)}}, \tag{1}$$

in which the guess rate γ denotes the percentage correct for chance levels, i.e. sub-threshold stimuli x. For nAFC tasks it is given by $\gamma = \frac{1}{n}$. The lapse rate λ indicates the proportion of stimuli that are not detected by the test person, even though they are above threshold. α is the threshold parameter indicating the center of the dynamic range and β is related to the slope of the function.

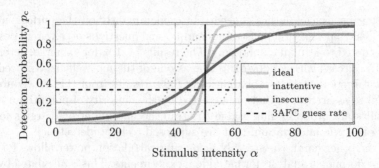

Fig. 1. Simulated psychometric functions for YN paradigms. Subjects were set to a threshold of $\alpha = 50$, the inattentive test person exhibits randomly varying threshold values in the range of $\alpha \in [40; 60]$. Guess rate was set to $\gamma = 0.33$ for 3AFC paradigms. (Color figure online)

As it is known from other simulations, effects like lapses, different slopes and learning have an influence on the performance of psychometric procedures [14]. We therefore selected three hypothetical test persons: ideal (steep slope, steady threshold, no guess and lapse rates), inattentive (medium slope, large guess and lapse rates, varying threshold) and insecure (shallow slope, steady threshold, low guess and lapse rate, Fig. 1). Performance was analyzed using the following performance criteria for each procedure:

Accuracy/Trueness: The difference of the real threshold α_{real}, defined by the simulated test person, and the estimation from the procedure $\tilde{\alpha}_r$ is used as measure for the accuracy of a psychophysical procedure. The mean over R simulation runs, also called 'bias',

$$b = \frac{1}{R} \sum_r (\alpha_{\mathrm{real}} - \tilde{\alpha}_r), \tag{2}$$

is used to quantify this measure. Since α_{real} is not known in a real experiment, the bias b can only be measured in simulations.

Precision: The empirical standard deviation s according to

$$s = \sqrt{\frac{1}{R-1} \cdot \sum_r (\tilde{\alpha}_r - \mu_{\tilde{\alpha}})^2} \tag{3}$$

is used to evaluate the precision, i.e. the ability of a procedure to estimate an identical threshold value in multiple runs R. In (3), $\mu_{\tilde{\alpha}}$ denotes the mean of the estimated thresholds in all considered runs.

Efficiency: Efficiency is assessed by the 'Sweat Factor' K introduced in [18]. This measure weighs the precision of a measurement with the number of trials per run n_r according to

$$K = \frac{\sum_r n_r \cdot (\tilde{\alpha}_r - \mu_{\tilde{\alpha}})^2}{R-1}. \tag{4}$$

Obviously, this measure is related to precision, but allows for the comparison of procedures with different number of trials or other stopping criteria.

Robustness: Robustness is supposed to describe the ability of a procedure to perform reliably, regardless of the properties of the test person. We therefore considered the standard deviations of the above mentioned measures over all six combinations of simulated test persons and paradigms as a measure for this property. They are indicated as b^*, K^* and s^* with regard to the above mentioned measures, respectively.

Analysis. One factor analyses of variance (ANOVA) with Bonferroni correction to account for multiple comparisons were used to analyze the main effects on the performance criteria. They were conducted with GNU R (version 3.2.2). A Welch-correction is used for factors violating the homogeneity of variance criterion [3]. We looked for significant influences with an at least medium effect to identify relevant parameters. Effect sizes were calculated according to

$$\omega^2 = \frac{SS_M - df_M \cdot MS_R}{SS_T + MS_R} \tag{5}$$

for one-factorial ANOVA [3]. Factors with medium and large effect were further analyzed with a Tukey's test at a confidence level of 0.01.

3   Staircase Methods

Staircases are some of the oldest psychometric methods [1]. Experiments start with a super- or below-threshold stimulus and subsequently lower the stimulus intensity following correct or increase the stimulus following false responses (Fig. 2). The progression rule determines the stimulus change depending on the occurrences of correct and false responses and the amount of stimulus change (*stepsize*). Both affect the convergence level of the staircase, as for example determined in [9,13]. Although there are doubts on the performance of staircase procedures [4], transformed up-down-staircases are widely used in the area of haptics — presumably due to their simplicity [12].

Staircase Parameters. We considered transformed up-down methods according to LEVITT [13] with three different progression rules (2down1up, 3down1up and 4down1up). Three different steptypes ([A] fixed, absolute values, [B] random values and [C] values relative to the current stimulus) and three different stepsize vectors $V_1 = [30\ 30\ 30\ 15\ 15\ 15\ 7.5\ 7.5\ 7.5\ 1]$, $V_2 = [40\ 40\ 20\ 20\ 10\ 10\ 5\ 5\ 1]$ and $V_3 = [10\ 10\ 10\ 5\ 5\ 5\ 1]$ were analyzed. These vectors were combined with the steptype factor level: For [A], stepsizes were subsequently taken from V_i, the last value was used for all later changes. For [B], stepsizes were randomly chosen from V_i, while option [C] interpreted the vector values as dB with respect to the current stimulus. Stepsizes were changed after every reversal, i.e. a direction change of the staircase run (Fig. 2). The number of trials is analyzed on three levels (30, 80, 130 trials). Thresholds were calculated as the mean of the stimulus values at the reversal points. The first four values were discarded.

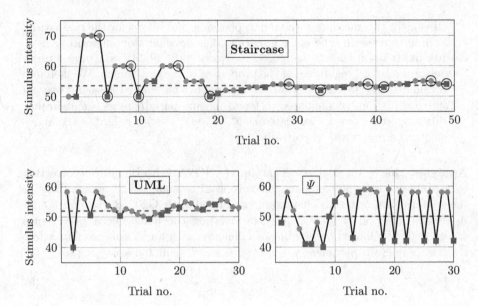

Fig. 2. Simulation of 50 trials of a 3down1up staircase with $\alpha_{\mathrm{real}} = 57.47$ and steptype [C] (top), a UML procedure with $\alpha_{\mathrm{real}} = 50$ (bottom left) and a Ψ procedure with $\alpha_{\mathrm{real}} = 50$ (bottom right), the latter with 30 trials each. Responses are indicated by green circles (correct) and red squares (false), staircase reversals are circled. The dotted line denotes the calculated threshold $\tilde{\alpha}$. (Color figure online)

Results and Analysis. Results were analyzed with respect to the method parameters outlined above as well as the subject type, the guess rate and the variation of the α parameter (Table 1). The bias of staircase procedures is only based on the subject properties in our simulations. This effect seems to be predominantly based on the α-variation exhibited by the inattentive test person. The subjects also reveal relevant effects on both efficiency and precision (Fig. 3).

Efficiency is further affected by progression rule and stepsize, but with much lower impact (small ω^2 compared to subject effects). Tukey post-hoc-tests reveal a significant difference of the 4down1up rule (Sweat Factor mean $\pm$ SD $K_{4d1u} = 3261 \pm 2983$) to the other rules tested ($K_{2d1u} = 1658 \pm 1347$, $K_{3d1u} = 2359 \pm 2054$). Stepsize vector V_2 differs significantly from the other two conditions ($K_{V_1} = 2257 \pm 2024$, $K_{V_2} = 3266 \pm 2863$, $K_{V_3} = 1755 \pm 1658$). Looking into the interactions with the steptype factor, the combination of V_1 with relative stepsizes (dB) yields the lowest sweat factor ($K_{V_1,\mathrm{dB}} = 1456 \pm 1127$), while V_2 with random value selection exhibits the largest sweat factor ($K_{V_2,\mathrm{rand}} = 3846 \pm 2431$).

Precision is only affected by the number of trials with significant differences between each group (deviation $s_{30} = 8.56 \pm 4.68$, $s_{80} = 4.57 \pm 2.69$, $s_{130} = 3.46 \pm 2.21$ stimulus units). The analysis of robustness shows a significant effect of the number of trials on precision. 30 trials exhibit a larger precision variance ($s_{30}^* = 4.03$) compared to 80 and 130 trials ($s_{80}^* = 2.62$ and $s_{130}^* = 2.08$).

Table 1. Main effects on staircase methods. Relevant parameters are marked with ⊛.

Parameter	Test statistic	Sig. p	Effect ω^2
Dependent: Accuracy/Trueness			
No. of trials	$F_{(2,483)} = 1.2$	0.31	0.001
Prog. rule	$W_{(2,299)} = 17$	< 0.01	0.048
Steptype	$F_{(2,483)} = 1.5$	0.23	0.002
Stepsize	$F_{(2,483)} = 6.8$	< 0.01	0.024
Subject ⊛	$W_{(5,221)} = 192$	< 0.01	0.733
Guess Rate	$F_{(1,484)} = 3.3$	0.07	0.005
α-Variation ⊛	$W_{(1,202)} = 857$	< 0.01	0.725
Dependent: Precision			
No. of trials ⊛	$W_{(2,303)} = 78$	< 0.01	0.291
Prog. rule	$W_{(2,315)} = 7.0$	< 0.01	0.022
Steptype	$F_{(2,483)} = 6.6$	< 0.01	0.022
Stepsize	$W_{(2,316)} = 9.2$	< 0.01	0.032
Subject ⊛	$W_{(5,223)} = 83$	< 0.01	0.407
Guess Rate	$F_{(1,484)} = 9.6$	< 0.01	0.017
α-Variation ⊛	$F_{(1,484)} = 114$	< 0.01	0.189
Dependent: Efficiency			
No. of trials	$F_{(2,483)} = 4.0$	0.02	0.012
Prog. rule ⊛	$W_{(2,294)} = 22$	< 0.01	0.074
Steptype	$W_{(2,308)} = 10$	< 0.01	0.023
Stepsize	$W_{(2,309)} = 17$	< 0.01	0.067
Subject ⊛	$W_{(5,219)} = 117$	< 0.01	0.475
Guess Rate	$W_{(1,468)} = 14$	< 0.01	0.027
α-Variation ⊛	$W_{(1,234)} = 159$	< 0.01	0.295

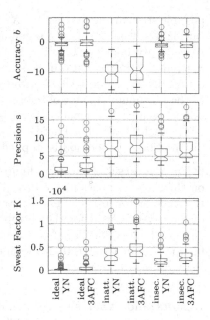

Fig. 3. Performance of SC methods with regard to subject configuration.

Longer runs will therefore compensate the effect of inattentive and insecure test persons on the precision of the estimation. Significant differences of the robustness of precision ($s^2_{2d1u} = 2.33$ vs. $s^2_{4d1u} = 3.44$), accuracy ($b^*_{2d1u} = 3.10$ vs. $b^*_{4d1u} = 6.13$), and efficiency ($K^*_{2d1u} = 1207$ vs. $K^*_{4d1u} = 2552$) can be calculated for the 2down1up-progression rule compared to 4down1up.

From our analysis we conclude, that progression rules such as 2down1up are more efficient and more robust against varying parameters of test subjects than the other ones tested. An increase in trials generally leads to more precise estimations and increases precision robustness. Theoretical limits were not evaluated in this study. Regarding the selection of staircase steps, random or relative steps with medium sizes (1 to 30 % of the stimulus range) seem beneficial.

4 Ψ Method

The Ψ method was proposed by KONTSEVICH AND TYLER [11]. It was developed in the context of visual psychophysics and is able to estimate both threshold (α) and slope parameters (β). Best performance is achieved with YN paradigms [7]. Accurate threshold estimates can be obtained with as little as 40 trials (Fig. 2).

For each trial of a Ψ experiment, the probability of a correct or false response is calculated with Bayes' rule for all combinations of a prior selection of parameters α_l, β_m (γ and λ are fixed) of the psychometric function and a space of possible stimulus intensities $x \in X$. Stimulus placement is based on an entropy calculation, that selects the stimulus $x \in X$ with the lowest entropy over the space of psychometric functions defined by (α_l, β_m). This often leads to larger differences between consecutive stimuli that are supposed to be easier to differentiate by the subject (Fig. 2). Since this rule chooses the stimulus that leads to the maximum amount of information in the next trial, one does not have to select stimulus placement rules for better estimation of α or β. The calculation of the final threshold estimate is based on the mean of the posterior probability distribution. The method is stopped after a defined number of trials.

Ψ **Parameters** Ψ offers only a limited number of parameters when concentrating on threshold estimation. We investigated the effect of the number of trials on the same factor levels as for the staircase methods. Additionally, the sampling of the α-vector used for the entropy calculation is investigated on three levels $N_\alpha \in [50, 120, 200]$. The β-vector was sampled with $N_\beta = 41$ in the range of 0.1 to 0.7. Exact values from the simulated test persons were used for guess and lapse rates.

Results and Analysis. As well as for the staircase method, the test person configuration has a relevant effect on all performance parameters of the Ψ method (Table 2). This is, however, presumably produced by shallow psychometric functions (insecure test person) in combination with nAFC paradigms (Fig. 4). Varying thresholds do not affect the performance of Ψ significantly. Analyzing the precision of Ψ with respect to the maximum trials, the difference between 30 and 130 trials is significant ($p = 0.047$, $s_{30} = 4.633$, $s_{130} = 2.84$). Since no significant difference is found for 80 trials compared to the other two, precision is expected to saturate somewhere in between 30 and 130 trials. The use of 3AFC paradigms induces a significant bias for Ψ procedures. This effect is increased for shallow psychometric functions, as with the insecure test person (Fig. 4, top) and backed by other simulations of the authors [7].

Regarding robustness, post-hoc tests of the α sampling show a slightly significant difference for $N_\alpha = 50$ vs. $N_\alpha = 120$ ($b_{50}^* = 7.15$, $b_{120}^* = 6.75$) in terms of efficiency, but no other significant differences. The deviation of the precision is significantly higher for a small number of trials of 30 ($s_{30}^* = 2.87$, $s_{80}^* = 2.05$, $s_{130}^* = 1.93$) while there is no difference between the other two groups.

5   Updated Maximum Likelihood (UML)

UML originates from acoustic psychophysics [5,6] with recently updated implementations [17]. To our knowledge, it is the only parametric method designed to obtain estimates of threshold α, slope β and lapse rate λ of the psychometric function. As well as Ψ, UML is based on prior distributions of all parameters, but uses a maximum likelihood estimator in order to find the parameter combination with the best fit to the occurred responses of the test person. Stimulus placement is based on minimizing the variance of one of the parameter estimates.

Table 2. Main effects on Ψ.

Parameter	Test statistic	Sig. p	Effect ω^2
Dependent: Accuracy/Trueness			
No. of trials	$F_{(2,51)} = 0.001$	0.99	0.038
α sampling	$F_{(2,51)} = 0.01$	0.99	0.038
Subject	⊛ $W_{(5,19.7)} = 2490$	< 0.01	0.99
Guess Rate	⊛ $W_{(1,26)} = 38$	< 0.01	0.39
α-Variation	$W_{(1,44.2)} = 5.6$	0.02	0.034
Dependent: Precision			
No. of trials	⊛ $F_{(2,51)} = 3.4$	0.04	0.082
α sampling	$F_{(2,51)} = 0.24$	0.79	0.029
Subject	⊛ $W_{(5,20.6)} = 67$	< 0.01	0.725
Guess Rate	$F_{(1,52)} = 1.16$	0.29	0.003
α-Variation	$W_{(1,48.8)} = 2.6$	0.12	0.016
Dependent: Efficiency			
No. of trials	$F_{(2,51)} = 1.5$	0.24	0.017
α sampling	$F_{(2,51)} = 0.75$	0.48	0.009
Subject	⊛ $W_{(5,19.9)} = 147$	< 0.01	0.599
Guess Rate	$F_{(1,52)} = 0.432$	0.51	0.011
α-Variation	$W_{(1,44.5)} = 0.07$	0.79	0.021

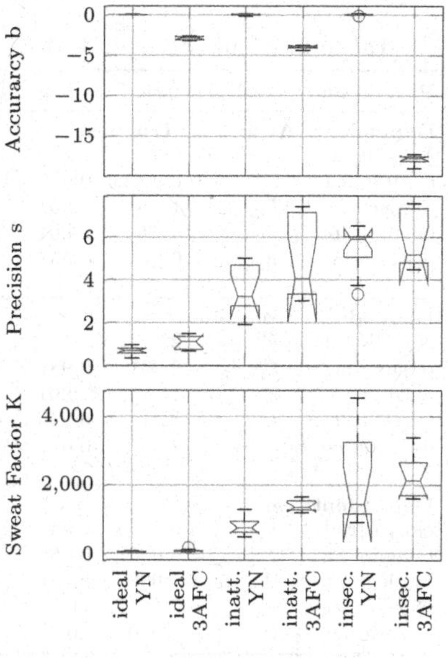

Fig. 4. Performance of Ψ with regard to subject configuration.

The selection of these stimuli, also called 'sweet points', is either random or can focus on a certain parameter. Existing simulations show good estimations for all parameters after about 200 trials and reasonable threshold estimations after about 50 to 70 trials [17] (Fig. 2).

UML Parameters. As with Ψ, we selected the maximum number of trials as well as the α sampling as parameters for the simulation. The range of β-values was selected in the range of 0.1 to 0.7 with $N_\beta = 40$. Guess rates were set based on the paradigm. Lapse rates were analyzed based on a range of 0 to 0.1 with $N_\lambda = 20$ values. For the selection of sweet points, we employed the 3down1up rule proposed in [17] to focus the evaluation on the threshold parameter.

Results and Analysis. Subjects show a strong effect on all performance measures of the UML procedures (Table 3); an increasing guess rate significantly increases the bias for UML, although not as much as for the Ψ-procedure (Fig. 5). The maximum number of trials produces significant differences for precision between 30 and 80 ($p = 0.002$) as well as 30 and 130 trials ($p < 0.001$). Therefore, more than 80 trials are recommended in order to maximize the precision of α-estimates with the UML procedure. Effects of α-variation exist, but are much smaller compared to staircase procedures. Robustness analysis shows an significant effect of the trial number on precision ($s^*_{30} = 5.51$ vs. $s^*_{80} = 3.08$ and $s^*_{130} = 2.34$) but no other effects.

Table 3. Main effects on UML.

Parameter	Test statistic	Sig. p	Effect ω^2
Dependent: Accuracy/Trueness			
No. of trials	$F_{(1,52)} = 0.074$	0.79	0.017
α sampling	$F_{(1,52)} = 0.0002$	0.99	0.019
Subject ⊛	$F_{(5,48)} = 1150$	< 0.01	0.991
Guess Rate ⊛	$W_{(1,30.3)} = 30$	< 0.01	0.337
α-Variation	$F_{(1,52)} = 0.37$	0.55	0.012
Dependent: Precision			
No. of trials ⊛	$F_{(1,52)} = 22$	< 0.01	0.280
α sampling	$F_{(1,52)} = 0.001$	0.98	0.019
Subject ⊛	$F_{(5,48)} = 15$	< 0.01	0.571
Guess Rate	$F_{(1,52)} = 1.41$	0.24	0.010
α-Variation ⊛	$F_{(1,52)} = 4.8$	0.03	0.066
Dependent: Efficiency			
No. of trials	$F_{(1,52)} = 0.60$	0.44	0.008
α sampling	$F_{(1,52)} = 0.0008$	0.98	0.019
Subject ⊛	$W_{(5,19)} = 1000$	< 0.001	0.977
Guess Rate	$F_{(1,52)} = 3.46$	0.069	0.044
α-Variation ⊛	$W_{(1,47.6)} = 8.0$	0.007	0.061

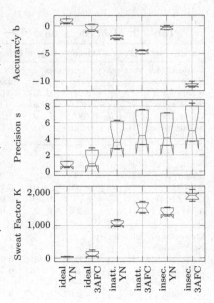

Fig. 5. Performance of UML with regard to subject configuration.

6   Conclusion

The simulation results in this study are in accordance to the findings by OTTO AND WEINZIERL [15] and SHEN ET AL. [16], that simulate comparable procedures, but do not investigate the sensitivity with regard to the procedure parameters. This study shows, that only a small number of parameters can affect performance measures. The number of trials per run affects precision for most psychometric procedures, while accuracy cannot be influenced. For staircase methods, the progression rule can affect the efficiency of the procedure.

Based on the results presented above, staircase methods are relatively robust against different test person types, except for varying thresholds. From the investigated combinations, a 2down1up staircase with relative stepsizes defined by V_1 is the best overall choice.

Parametric procedures such as Ψ and UML generally perform better than staircase-procedures, especially for simple Yes/No-paradigms. If experimental conditions allow for the continuous control of stimulus intensity, these procedures are beneficial, especially for steep psychometric functions. Both of them are robust against varying thresholds and exhibit a low bias.

The simulations analyzed in this work show, however, the strongest dependence of performance parameters of psychometric procedures on the test subject. Therefore, a more thorough analysis of psychometric functions in terms of typical guess- and lapse-rates and base functions for the psychometric function is needed for further optimization of psychometric procedures. Furthermore, the interactions of the different parameters have to be further investigated, as these were not considered in this study.

Acknowledgments. This research was supported by Deutsche Forschungsgemeinschaft (DFG) under grant HA7164/1-1.

References

1. Cornsweet, T.: The staircase-method in psychophysics. Am. J. Psychol. **75**(3), 485–491 (1962)
2. Ehrenstein, W.H., Ehrenstein, A.: Psychophysical methods. In: Windhorst, U., Johansson, H. (eds.) Modern Techniques in Neuroscience Research, pp. 1211–1241. Springer, Heidelberg (1999)
3. Field, A.: Discovering Statistics Using IBM SPSS Statistics. Sage, New York (2014)
4. García-Pérez, M.A., Alcalá-Quintana, R.: The difference model with guessing explains interval bias in two-alternative forced-choice detection procedures. J. Sens. Stud. **25**(6), 876–898 (2010)
5. Green, D.: Stimulus selection in adaptive psychophysical procedures. J. Acoust. Soc. Am. **87**(6), 2662–2674 (1990)
6. Harvey, L.O.: Efficient estimation of sensory thresholds. Behav. Res. Methods **18**(6), 623–632 (1986)
7. Hatzfeld, C., Kupnik, M., Werthschützky, R.: Performance simulation of unforced choice paradigms in parametric psychometric procedures. In: World Haptics. Evanston, IL, USA (2015)
8. Jäkel, F., Wichmann, F.A.: Spatial four-alternative forced-choice method is the preferred psychophysical method for naïve observers. J. Vis. **6**(11), 13 (2006)
9. Kaernbach, C.: Adaptive threshold estimation with unforced-choice tasks. Percept. Psychophys. **63**(8), 1377–1388 (2001)
10. Karmali, F., Chaudhuri, S.E., Yi, Y., Merfeld, D.M.: Determining thresholds using adaptive procedures and psychometric fits: evaluating efficiency using theory, simulations, and human experiments. Exp. Brain Res. **234**(3), 773–789 (2016). doi:10.1007/s00221-015-4501-8
11. Kontsevich, L., Tyler, C.: Bayesian adaptive estimation of psychometric slope and threshold. Vis. Res. **39**(16), 2729–2737 (1999)
12. Leek, M.R.: Adaptive procedures in psychophysical research. Percept. Psychophys. **63**(8), 1279–1292 (2001)
13. Levitt, H.: Transformed up-down methods in psychoacoustics. J. Acoust. Soc. Am. **49**(2), 467–477 (1971)
14. Madigan, R., Williams, D.: Maximum-likelihood psychometric procedures in two-alternative forced-choice: evaluation and recommendations. Aten. Percept. Psycho. **42**(3), 240–249 (1987)
15. Otto, S., Weinzierl, S.: Comparative simulations of adaptive psychometric procedures. In: DAGA. Rotterdam, NL (2009)
16. Shen, Y., Dai, W., Richards, V.M.: A matlab toolbox for the efficient estimation of the psychometric function using the updated maximum-likelihood adaptive procedure. Behav. Res. Methods **47**(1), 13–26 (2014)
17. Shen, Y., Richards, V.M.: A maximum-likelihood procedure for estimating psychometric functions: thresholds, slopes, and lapses of attention. J. Acoust. Soc. Am. **132**(2), 957–967 (2012)
18. Taylor, M., Creelman, C.: Pest: efficient estimates on probability functions. J. Acoust. Soc. Am. **41**(4), 782–787 (1967)
19. Wickens, T.D.: Elementary Signal Detection Theory. Oxford University Press, Oxford (2002)

Does Haptic Feedback Improve Learning and Recall of Spatial Information? A Study Using a Virtual Reality Nasendoscopy Simulation

Greg S. Ruthenbeck[1,2]($\boxtimes$), Michael Tlauka[3], and Andria Tan[3]

[1] The Medical Device Research Institute, Adelaide, Australia
[2] The School of Computer Science, Engineering and Mathematics,
Flinders University, Adelaide, Australia
greg.ruthenbeck@flinders.edu.au
[3] The School of Psychology, Flinders University, Adelaide, Australia

Abstract. In the literature, haptic training has long been regarded as an effective means of acquiring skills that involve force feedback. This is relevant in the context of haptic virtual reality applications that argue that the addition of haptics increases the effectiveness of the training system. Here we describe an experimental investigation which examines whether haptic feedback increases people's spatial knowledge of a simulation. In particular, we address the following question: Is visuo-haptic interaction a more effective way of learning spatial information than purely visual interaction? A comparison of two groups of participants (visual versus visuo-haptic) revealed no significant differences in their spatial knowledge of the simulation. The findings are discussed with reference to potential variables which may affect spatial learning such as cognitive load.

Keywords: Haptic · Spatial learning · Simulation · Virtual reality · Nasendoscopy

1 Introduction

Haptic perception is an important sensory modality, providing cutaneous and kinaesthetic information [6]. Haptic feedback has been shown to enhance force skill learning and haptic guidance (for example, [3,7,10]), tasks which are closely linked to the haptic modality. The question arises as to whether haptic perception also facilitates knowledge which is not directly linked to the haptic modality such as spatial knowledge. This question is addressed in the present paper using a Nasendoscopy Simulation.

Nasendoscopy is used to examine the sinuses using a rigid endoscope. The sinuses are composed of intricate interconnected cavities that are lined with soft mucosal tissue over, sometimes very thin, bone. Moreover, adjacent to the sinuses are delicate and critically important structures (for example, the meninges of the brain, the orbits of the eyes), that are prone to damage if the endoscope isn't

F. Bello et al. (Eds.): EuroHaptics 2016, Part I, LNCS 9774, pp. 404–411, 2016.
DOI: 10.1007/978-3-319-42321-0_37

properly controlled (these danger points are summarized in [5]). Trainee clinicians must learn to control the endoscope safely. Safe control of the endoscope requires spatial knowledge of the sinus anatomy to interpret and supplement the 2-dimensional endoscopic view.

Due to the inherent risks in learning to conduct these examinations, the Flinders Nasendoscopy Simulator was developed [2]. The simulator haptically renders the forces of interaction between the endoscope and the simulated sinus anatomy whilst rendering a realistic simulated endoscope view of the sinuses [9]. The simulation is written in C/C++, DirectX 11, High Level Shader Language (HLSL), and CUDA. Haptic rendering is implemented using NVidia's PhysX[TM]physics engine to constrain a haptic proxy to remain interior to the sinuses, together with a friction constraint that models the forces due to the interaction of the endoscope shaft with the sinus tissues. The simulation was run on a 2.7 GHz Quad Core Intel i7[TM]with 8 GB RAM and a GeForce[TM]470 M graphics processor. The hardware setup used is shown in Fig. 1.

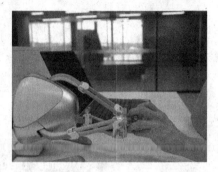

Fig. 1. Experiment hardware setup

To examine the potential benefit of haptic feedback on spatial knowledge acquisition, the performance of two groups of participants was compared (visuo-haptic versus visual). User interaction in the visual group was limited to viewing the screen whilst the view was controlled by a human facilitator according to verbal instructions given by the participant. User interaction in the visuo-haptic group was via a Novint Falcon haptic device. The haptic rendering system of the simulator was modified for this experiment (explained in detail below) to simplify user interaction and remove any significant learning curve normally associated with navigating the sinuses.

2   Methods

2.1   Participants

Forty eight university students participated in this study. Participants were aged between 18 and 46 years (mean: 23 years). Individuals with any prior exposure to haptics were excluded. Included individuals were assigned randomly to each of two groups (visuo-haptic and visual), with 16 female and 8 male students in each group. The experiment was conducted with approval from the Flinders University Ethics Committee.

2.2   Apparatus and Stimuli

The Sinus Model. Inside the nostrils, the sinus cavity is comprised of winding and interconnected cavities. Figure 2 shows a coronal cross-section of the head taken using a computed tomography (CT) x-ray. Black regions are empty space, white is bone, and grey is soft-tissues. Five coloured markers were included in the simulation which were positioned in the simulated patient's right nostril (left side of Fig. 2).

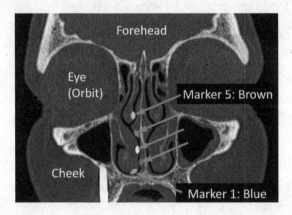

Fig. 2. Sinus model coronal cross-section coloured marker positions (Color figure online)

Markers 1 (Blue) and 3 (White) were positioned on the inferior-turbinate. Markers 2 (Green) and 4 (Yellow) were positioned on the right-side of the sinus cavity on the septum. The simulated endoscope view of Marker 5 (Brown) is shown in Fig. 3. This marker is positioned on the left side of the sinus cavity (on the right side of the middle turbinate anatomical structure). Brown was used instead of red to reduce inferred sequencing (for example traffic lights) and to increase the contrast with underlying pink tissue. All markers were positioned at the same z-depth (where the z-axis is into to screen), and approximately vertically in-line with one-another. Figure 4 shows the relative location of the markers projected to the screen-plane. Markers were positioned such that not more than one marker could be seen on screen at a time during the learning phase.

The five coloured markers were arranged near-vertically in a fixed sequence that was the same for all participants. The marker arrangement is shown in the coronal CT view of the sinuses in Fig. 2 and diagrammatically in Fig. 4. The view

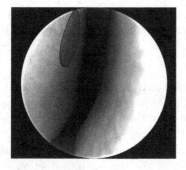
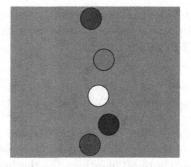

Fig. 3. Simulated endoscope view (Color figure online)

Fig. 4. 2D positions ground truth (Color figure online)

of the markers seen by participants during the learning phase of the experiment was rendered onto the surface of the 3D sinus anatomical model as shown in Fig. 3. The Nasendoscopy Simulation is described in detail in [9].

Haptic Rendering. To reduce the complexity of the interaction (to a level that is more suitable for users with no experience with the sinus anatomy, or with using haptic devices) a horizontal force constraint was used to restrict coarse movements to primarily up and down. The force constraint used was simply the scaled distance from a vertical line through the middle of the markers. This constraint was combined with the surface contact (proxy object with friction) haptic renderer. In this way, the user will experience strong force constraints from the surface, together with the horizontal force constraint up to the maximum force of the Novint Falcon haptic device. The haptic rendering of surface contacts is achieved using a haptic proxy (Virtual Proxy [8]). The in-house simulation engine uses multi-threading to reliably maintain haptic update rates of >1 kHz alongside graphics update rates >40 Hz [9].

2.3 Procedure

The experiment consisted of a learning phase and a test phase. During the learning phase participants were given two minutes to learn the interactive visualization (virtual reality simulation) of a simulated endoscopic view of the sinus cavity. Following a short introduction, the experimenter started the endoscopy simulation software and positioned the haptic device at the start location (just below Marker 1, with Marker 1 clearly in view). The visual group were shown the simulated endoscopy view of the markers with the view being controlled by the experimenter, and hence had no haptic engagement with the learning task. The visuo-haptic group interacted with the simulation. Since the haptic force constraint prevented side-ways movement, and the first marker was at a horizontal part of the anatomy, the only direction that the haptic device could be moved was upwards. In this way, we avoided the need to assign verbal labels to the relative positions to encourage the use of neural pathways associated with tactile interaction and spatial learning without involving language processing of navigation information.

Testing. In the test phase, participants took part in two tasks (up/down task and placement task). In each group (visual and visuo-haptic), half of the participants performed the up/down task followed by the placement task, while the reverse was the case for the remaining participants.

In the up/down task, users were given a computer-based questionnaire consisting of 60 questions. At the beginning of the test an introduction screen was displayed explaining the test and how to provide answers. All tests began with an experimenter present to answer any concerns and ensure that the tests were conducted consistently. During the test, questions were asked of the format, Where is BLUE, relative to WHITE?, and participants answered either Above or Below by pressing the Up or Down key respectively. The participants were told that BLUE and WHITE referred to the coloured markers shown in the simulation. Participants were presented with three blocks of twenty questions. Each block consisted of 10 questions for which Up was the correct answer and 10 questions for which Down was the correct answer. The blocks employed all combinations of up and down relative positions between markers, and there were three orderings of the full set of 20 combinations of Up/Down for the 5 markers (5P2 = 20 permutations). The same ordering of questions was supplied to all participants. The 3 orderings were selected from randomized combinations that had no more than 3 questions in a row involving the same colour, or the same correct responses, in a row. Response times and errors for each response were recorded. A blank rest screen was displayed between all questions for 1500 ms.

In the placement task, each participant was presented with a screen composed of a workspace with a narrow upper section of the screen where the coloured markers were arranged horizontally (see Fig. 5) in a random order that was the same for all participants. Participants were then asked to arrange the markers to match, as near as possible, the marker arrangement from the learning phase

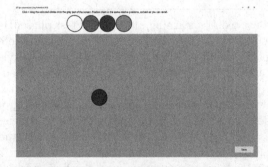

Fig. 5. Placement task screenshot with the green marker placed in the workspace (Color figure online)

(as depicted inside the virtual sinus model). When finished, the screen was saved as an image with a time-stamp to record the time taken to arrange the markers. These images were processed to gain insights into the participant's recollection of the marker arrangement in the simulation. The task was developed in Microsoft™C# programming language using the Dot-Net Framework version 4.5.2 in Visual Studio™2015.

3 Results

The participants' performance in the up/down task (Elevation task) and placement tasks was analysed separately. The up/down test is considered first. This task was analysed employing mixed analyses of variance (ANOVAs) with group (visuo-haptic, visual) as between-participants variable and correct answer (up/down) as within-participants variable. Response latencies (correct responses) and error rates were the dependent variables. For both latencies and error scores (1.4 % of all trials) the analysis revealed no significant difference between the visuo-haptic group and the visual group ($Fs < 1$). Similarly, the main effect of correct answer ($Fs < 1$) and the two-way interaction between group and correct answer ($Fs < 1$) did not reach statistical significance. Table 1 provides a summary of the results for the up/down test.

Table 1. Mean response latencies (in seconds) and mean error scores in the up/down task as a function of group and correct answer. Standard errors are shown in brackets

Group	Response latencies		Response errors	
	Up	Down	Up	Down
Visuo-haptic	2.40 (.20)	2.41 (.20)	4.00 (.99)	4.08 (.97)
Visual	2.38 (.20)	2.41 (.20)	4.33 (.99)	4.37 (.97)

With respect to the placement task, a t-test revealed that the time it took the experimental volunteers to arrange the markers did not differ significantly in the visuo-haptic group (mean latency: 54 s, SE = 4 s) and the visual group (mean latency: 48 s, SE = 4 s), $t(46) = .91$, $p = .36$. The placement of markers was rated for accuracy using two independent raters who evaluated the maps on a 1–5 scale, with higher scores indicating greater accuracy. The raters' evaluations demonstrated strong reliability, $r(46) = .62$, $p < .01$, and were collapsed into a single evaluation score. The analysis of the combined ratings indicated the visuo-haptic group (mean rating: 2.8, SE = .25) and the visual group (mean rating: 2.9, SE = .25) did not differ significantly from each other, $t(46) = -.29$, $p = .77$.

4 Discussion

While haptic training has been regarded as an effective means of acquiring skills that involve force feedback [3,7,10], little is known about the potential effect of haptic feedback on people's spatial awareness of a simulation. This study examined whether visuo-haptic interaction is a more effective way of learning spatial information than purely visual interaction. A comparison of the visuo-haptic and visual group indicated similar spatial knowledge of the simulation in both groups.

How can we account for the similarity in results? It is possible that rather than facilitate spatial knowledge haptic manipulation of the Novint Falcon™device increased visuo-haptic group's cognitive load. Cognitive load is determined by the amount of information processed simultaneously in working memory (for example, [4,11]). Tasks which heavily burden the resource pool of working memory impose a high cognitive load while tasks which are automatic or processed with little effort impose a low cognitive load. Deyzac et al. (2006) [1] tested the ability of participants to learn a spatial description from a route and survey perspective in single and dual task conditions. The researchers found that participants who were distracted by a spatial tapping task demonstrated less accurate recall than participants who were not distracted. These results provide an example of cognitive overload during navigation, in which a high load obstructed spatial encoding. It is possible that in the present experiment, haptic manipulation increased the cognitive load of participants in the visuo-haptic group relative to the visual group who did not interact with the haptic device. This may have detrimentally affected learning in the visuo-haptic group, leading to similar performance in the groups. A future study could reduce this effect by providing a haptic device familiarisation phase.

Can we detect significant differences in the placement of the markers? Recall from Fig. 4 that the markers were not positioned perfectly vertically. A least squares regression line of best fit for this arrangement is oriented 2° counter-clockwise from vertical. A similarly generated line of best fit (LBF) was generated for each participant's marker arrangement. An Angular Error was calculated as the difference between the actual LBF angle (in degrees True North) and the recalled LBF angle. A statistical T-test (assuming unequal variances, two tailed) was performed on the Angular Error of the two groups resulted in $p = 0.1$, with $mean_{VH} = 12°$ and $mean_V = 19°$. This suggests that a larger study, or an improved experiment, may find evidence of haptics improving learning of the orientation of spatial information.

Other error measures were developed to quantify differences in the groups' ability to recall the sequential arrangement of the markers, and the accuracy of the two groups' recollection of the curvature of the sequence, but no statistically interesting results were obtained. Further work is required to better understand the significance of haptic participation in tasks that involve spatial learning. To this end, the authors have designed a new experiment that has better equivalence of tasks, except the experimental variable, between the two groups. This new study tests identical activities with and without feedback forces.

Acknowledgments. This research was supported by a Catalyst Research Grant from the Government of South Australia's Premier's Research Industry Fund and Flinders University.

References

1. Deyzac, E., Logie, R.H., Denis, M.: Visuospatial working memory and the processing of spatial descriptions. Br. J. Psychol. **97**(2), 217–243 (2006)
2. Dharmawardana, N., Ruthenbeck, G., Woods, C., Elmiyeh, B., Diment, L., Ooi, E., Reynolds, K., Carney, A.: Validation of virtual-reality-based simulations for endoscopic sinus surgery. Clin. Otolaryngol. **40**(6), 569–579 (2015). http://dx.doi.org/10.1111/coa.12414
3. Feygin, D., Keehner, M., Tendick, F.: Haptic guidance: experimental evaluation of a haptic training method for a perceptual motor skill, pp. 40–47 (2002)
4. Garden, S., Cornoldi, C., Logie, R.H.: Visuo-spatial working memory in navigation. Appl. Cogn. Psychol. **16**(1), 35–50 (2002)
5. Hosemann, W., Draf, C.: Danger points, complications and medico-legal aspects in endoscopic sinus surgery. GMS Curr. Top. Otorhinolaryngol. Head Neck Surg. 12 (2013)
6. Lederman, S.J., Klatzky, R.L.: Haptic perception: a tutorial. Atten. Percept. Psychophys. **71**(7), 1439–1459 (2009)
7. Morris, D., Tan, H., Barbagli, F., Chang, T., Salisbury, K.: Haptic feedback enhances force skill learning, pp. 21–26 (2007)
8. Ruspini, D.C., Kolarov, K., Khatib, O.: The haptic display of complex graphical environments, pp. 345–352 (1997)
9. Ruthenbeck, G.S., Hobson, J., Carney, A.S., Sloan, S., Sacks, R., Reynolds, K.J.: Toward photorealism in endoscopic sinus surgery simulation. Am. J. Rhinol Allergy **27**(2), 138–143 (2013)
10. Tholey, G., Desai, J.P., Castellanos, A.E.: Force feedback plays a significant role in minimally invasive surgery: results and analysis. Ann. Surg. **241**(1), 102–109 (2005)
11. Vecchi, T., Cornoldi, C.: Passive storage and active manipulation in visuo-spatial working memory: further evidence from the study of age differences. Eu. J. Cogn. Psychol. **11**(3), 391–406 (1999)

Perceived Intensity of Vibrotactile Stimuli: Do Your Clothes Really Matter?

Valérie Duthoit[1,2](✉), Jean-Marc Sieffermann[1], Eric Enrègle[2], and David Blumenthal[1]

[1] UMR GENIAL, AgroParisTech, INRA, Université Paris-Saclay,
91300 Massy, France
valerie.duthoit@renault.com
[2] Renault, 1 av. du Golf, 78084 Guyancourt-Cedex, France

Abstract. Vibrotactile stimuli are of growing interest for everyday interfaces, including car interfaces. For example they can be applied to lane departure warning, collision warning, notifications etc. Yet interfaces that are not directly in contact with the user's skin must take clothing into account. This study investigates whether clothes have a significant effect on perceived intensity of simple vibrotactile stimuli or not, and therefore if they have to be taken into account in the setting of vibrotactile feedback. In this study, we considered a single actuator on the back of a car seat, which was covered by a thin layer of foam, a layer of clothes, and hidden by a black covering. Simple vibrations of 1 s with frequencies ranging from 100 Hz to 200 Hz and three different amplitude levels were triggered. The lowest of them were below several subjects' detection thresholds. We asked 31 subjects to give a score from 0 to 10 to assess the intensity of the stimulus. Results showed that perceived intensity is adversely affected by a thick winter coat but seems to be lightly affected by several thin layers such as T-shirts. We concluded that designers do not have to consider all the variety of clothes to set the vibration parameters, but they must take winter coats into account if final users are expected to wear that type of clothing. Moreover, we demonstrated the ability of naive subjects to score their perception of intensity of simple vibrotactile stimuli.

Keywords: Perception · Intensity · Tactile · Clothes · Seat

1 Introduction

Tactile interfaces. Tactile modality is more and more used for everyday interfaces [2,7,13]. Touch is a proximal sense, i.e., the subject must be in contact with the stimulating device to feel a stimulation. We focused our attention on the seat because it is the only part of the car in constant contact with the driver. Many applications could benefit by using vibrations in the seat to transmit information [8], for instance lane departure warning [16], collision warning [14], hypovigilance alert [3], situation awareness [19], navigation [3,22], notifications [3,18] and even

© Springer International Publishing Switzerland 2016
F. Bello et al. (Eds.): EuroHaptics 2016, Part I, LNCS 9774, pp. 412–418, 2016.
DOI: 10.1007/978-3-319-42321-0_38

relaxing activities [21]. Perception is a critical issue when safety is at stake. Many interfaces such as mobile phones, tactile screens etc. are in direct contact with one's skin while others are not. For example belts [12,22], jackets [10,12], floors [15], seats [9], car pedals [4] have to transmit information through some kind of fabric or shoes, which could affect perception [24].

Other sources of variability. Griffin [6] reported sources of inter-subject variability: body dynamics, body dimensions, body masses, body posture, age, gender, health, experience and training, attitude and motivation, sensitivity and susceptibility. Most of the existing studies investigating the perception of vibrotactile stimuli have considered either the entire body or the fingers in a psychphysics approach. Recent studies show the influence of attention, movement and back pain on tactile sensation in the back [23].

Stimulus parameters. Geldard [5] defined 4 parameters of a simple tactile stimulus to encode information: locus, intensity, duration and frequency. These parameters are the ones commonly used in the litterature although specific authors might prefer related parameters instead for example considering amplitude instead of intensity, or considering timing instead of duration [11,17,20]. The perceived intensity is mostly driven by the amplitude of the stimulus.

2   Method

Apparatus. The study took place in a stationary car (Fig. 1). A voice-coil type actuator was set on the back of the driver's seat with adhesive rubber. It was placed in order to be in contact with the dorsal muscle of 95 % of the tallest women and 95 % of the shortest men according to the database of Renault. A 10 mm thick foam layer was set on the seat back to prevent the subject from feeling its shape. The experimenter then set a layer of clothes. Finally, the experimental set-up was occluded by a black covering. This way the subjects could not be influenced by seeing the clothes. A single subject spontaneously reported a change in his perception of the apparatus.

There were 5 different configurations for the experimental setup: no cloth, 4 thin cotton layers (i.e. two identical T-shirts stacked without folds), 8 thin cotton layers (i.e. 4 identical T-shirts), 2 thicker cotton layers (i.e. one pull-over set without folds) and an extreme cloth (a down jacket). Subjects were also wearing there own clothes, but because test was conducted in summer, those were thin clothes. We did not consider the effect of subjects' clothes because they were constant for each subject.

Stimuli. Stimuli were simple sinusoidal vibrations in the back. Duration was 1 s. There were 3 frequencies (100 Hz, 150 Hz and 200 Hz) which are consistent with the vibrations of commercial mobile phones [24], and 3 modalities of amplitudes (relative scale: 0.2; 0.6 and 1). Those settings were chosen after preliminary experiments with few participants. The stimuli with the lowest amplitude were

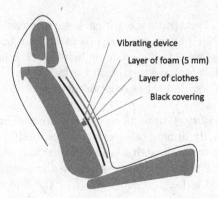

Fig. 1. Experimental setup

below some subjects' detection thresholds. All the frequency and amplitude combinations were tested (9 different stimuli). We triggered twice an intermediary signal (f: 150 Hz, a: 0.6) in order to measure subject repeatability (the tendency to give the same score to the same signal). Moreover, there was a trial without stimulus. Consequently, there were 11 trials, for each clothes modality.

Observers. 31 volunteers were recruited at the Technocentre Renault (Guyancourt, France). There were 19 males and 12 females from 20 to 57 years old (mean: 30; SD: 9). People with different morphologies were recruited, as it is known to be an important source of perception diversity. Body mass indexes $(BMI = weight/height^2)$ varied from 19 to 39 kg/m^2 (mean: 25; SD: 5).

Protocol. Subjects sat on the driver seat without modifying neither the tilt nor upward/downward seat adjustments. We ask them to mimic their driving position: straight forward look, fastened seatbelt, hands on the steering wheel, legs on the floor as if they had set the cruise control, and resting on the seatback as if they were driving. This way we considered the position would be standardized among subjects and constant during the test.

The test was organized in 5 blocks corresponding to the 5 modalities of clothes, to limit manipulation of the setup and movement of the subjects. For each modality the 11 stimuli were triggered in a row. To minimize order bias, the order of 5 blocks was counterbalanced among subjects and the order of the 11 stimuli was counterbalanced among subjects and blocks. The overall duration of the experiment was about 30 min.

Each time the experimenter triggered a signal, even if the subject didn't detect any vibration, he asked the subject to give a score between 0 and 10 (0 meaning they did not feel anything, and the higher the mark is, the more intense the vibration is perceived). Subjects were informed there would be short breaks during the test. During each break, they were asked to stand up and leave the experimental area to wait behind a screen, while the experimenter changed the clothes layer without being seen.

In order to mask the noise of the stimuli, subjects were constantly listening to a monotonous music with earphone and wore an anti-noise headset.

Data analysis. Data was analyzed using repeated measures Analysis of Variance followed by a Bonferroni test at a the 5 % level of significance. The dependent variable was the perceived intensity score and the independent variables were frequency, amplitude, clothes modality and category of body mass index. The known interaction between amplitude and frequency was neglected in our analysis although it might be important.

3   Results

Observers' performance. Four subjects among 31 gave at least one score higher than 0 at a trial without stimulus, each time in the first block, and one gave three scores higher than 0 at trials without stimulus. We explain the fact that subjects failed to detect the absence of stimulus in the first block by a lack reference to evaluate the stimulus. One stimulus (f: 150 Hz; a: 0.6) was triggered twice per block. The absolute mean difference in scores between the two trials is 1 (SD: 1). Considering that subjects were not used to such stimuli, and not trained to evaluate them, this difference is low. We concluded that very naive subjects are able to score their intensity perception of simple vibrotactile stimuli. A familiarization with those kinds of stimuli could improve accuracy. No calibration phase was performed because we were concerned it would mask the interindividual differences.

Influence of stimuli parameters. The three levels of amplitude, whatever the clothes layer, were perceived as significantly different (2 DOF; $F = 586.8$; $p < 0.0001$). Moreover, the stimulus with a 100 Hz frequency was perceived more intense (2 DOF; $F = 138.3$; $p < 0.0001$) but this is consistent with the resonance frequency of the actuators which results in a greater amplitude.

Influence of the clothes layer. The thicker the layer, the less intense the perception of the stimulus, no matter the amplitude or the frequency (4 DOF; $F = 25.7$; $p < 0.0001$). Nevertheless, the difference between perceived intensity is lower than 1, in all configurations but the winter coat (Fig. 2). In short, the perception variability due to the different clothes layers is smaller than the intrinsic variability of the subject. We concluded that clothes do not have an important influence on perceived intensity except for the winter coat.

Influence of subject's morphology. We sorted subjects into 3 groups based on their BMI, roughly corresponding to the groups defined by public health authorities (low: < 20; mid: between 20 and 28; high: > 28). The higher the BMI, the less intense the perception of the vibration (2 DOF; $F = 128$; $p < 0.001$), which is consistent with the litterature [1].

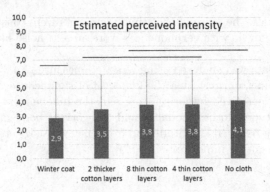

Fig. 2. Influence of a clothes layer on perceived intensity of vibrotactile stimuli regardless of the stimulus'parameters. Sticks correspond to non-significantly different means (5 %)

4   Conclusion and Perspectives

The current study investigates the influence of clothes on the perception of vibrotactile stimuli. Results show that a thick winter coat significantly decreased the perceived intensity. In addition, other layers of clothes lightly adversely affected the perceived intensity of simple vibrotactile stimuli, but this effect was not greater than the difference between two repetitions of the same stimulus. We conclude that designers do not have to take clothes into account when developing vibrotactile feedback unless users are expected to wear thick coats, and if the signal has a safety purpose.

On the other hand, results showed a great influence of body mass index on perceived intensity. Therefore, if the amplitude of feedback is not adjustable by users, designers should tune the amplitude according to the feedbacks given by subjects with different morphologies.

Finally, this experiment also gives us ways to improve future studies. For example, a sample of stimuli should be triggered before the evaluation, in order to familiarize the subjects with the kind of stimuli. Future studies should also be carried out to confirm those results in more realistic environments (i.e. moving cars) and with subjects focusing on a task similar to end-use applications. Then, we will evaluate more complex stimuli (different length, patterns etc.).

References

1. Ajovalasit, M., Jeon, B., Giacomin, J.: Effects of physical body mass on the subjective perceived intensity of steering wheel rotational vibration (2012). http://www.perceptionenhancement.com/docs/papers/ajg2012eop.pdf. Accessed 13 June 2016
2. Benali-Khoudja, M., Hafez, M., Alexandre, J.M., Kheddar, A.: Tactile interfaces: a state-of-the-art survey. In: International Symposium on Robotics, vol. 31. Citeseer (2004)

3. Chang, W., Hwang, W., Ji, Y.G.: Haptic seat interfaces for driver information and warning systems. Int. J. Hum.-Comput. Interact. **27**(12), 1119–1132 (2011)
4. De Rosario, H., Louredo, M., Díaz, I., Soler, A., Gil, J.J., Solaz, J.S., Jornet, J.: Efficacy and feeling of a vibrotactile frontal collision warning implemented in a haptic pedal. Transp. Res. Part F: Traffic Psychol. Behav. 13(2), 80–91 (2010)
5. Geldard, F.A.: Some neglected possibilities of communication. Science **131**, 1583–1588 (1960)
6. Griffin, M.J.: Handbook of Human Vibration. Academic Press, London (1994)
7. Hayward, V., Astley, O.R., Cruz-Hernandez, M., Grant, D., Robles-De-La-Torre, G.: Haptic interfaces and devices. Sens. Rev. **24**(1), 16–29 (2004)
8. Ho, C., Spence, C.: The Multisensory Driver: Implications for Ergonomic Car Interface Design. Ashgate Publishing Ltd., Burlington (2008)
9. Israr, A., Poupyrev, I., Ioffreda, C., Cox, J., Gouveia, N., Bowles, H., Brakis, A., Knight, B., Mitchell, K., Williams, T.: Surround haptics: sending shivers down your spine. In: ACM SIGGRAPH 2011 Emerging Technologies, p. 14. ACM (2011)
10. Jones, L.A., Nakamura, M., Lockyer, B.: Development of a tactile vest. In: Proceedings of 12th International Symposium on Haptic Interfaces for Virtual Environment and Teleoperator Systems, 2004, HAPTICS 2004, pp. 82–89. IEEE (2004)
11. Jones, L.A., Sarter, N.B.: Tactile displays: guidance for their design and application. Hum. Fact.: J. Hum. Fact. Ergon. Soc. 50(1), 90–111 (2008)
12. Krausman, A.S., White, T.L.: Tactile displays and detectability of vibrotactile patterns as combat assault maneuvers are being performed. Army Research Laboratory, Aberdeen (2006)
13. Laycock, S.D., Day, A.: Recent developments and applications of haptic devices. In: Computer Graphics Forum, vol. 22, pp. 117–132. Wiley Online Library (2003)
14. Lee, J.D., Hoffman, J.D., Hayes, E.: Collision warning design to mitigate driver distraction. In: Proceedings of the SIGCHI Conference on Human Factors in Computing Systems, pp. 65–72. ACM (2004)
15. Mégard, C., Repain, D., Anastassova, M.: Exploratory investigation of a haptic floor. In: Workshop at MobileHCI 2010, Tuesday, 7 September 2010, Lisbon, Portugal, p. 38. Citeseer (2010)
16. Navarro, J., Mars, F., Hoc, J.M.: Lateral control assistance for car drivers: a comparison of motor priming and warning systems. Hum. Fact.: J. Hum. Fact. Ergon. Soc. 49(5), 950–960 (2007)
17. Petermeijer, S.M., de Winter, J.C., Bengler, K.J.: Vibrotactile displays: a survey with a view on highly automated driving (2015)
18. Schwalk, M., Kalogerakis, N., Maier, T.: Driver support by a vibrotactile seat matrix-recognition, adequacy and workload of tactile patterns in take-over scenarios during automated driving. Proc. Manuf. **3**, 2466–2473 (2015)
19. Telpaz, A., Rhindress, B., Zelman, I., Tsimhoni, O.: Haptic seat for automated driving: preparing the driver to take control effectively. In: Proceedings of the 7th International Conference on Automotive User Interfaces and Interactive Vehicular Applications, pp. 23–30. ACM (2015)
20. Van Erp, J.B.: Guidelines for the use of vibro-tactile displays in human computer interaction. Proceedings of Eurohaptics **2002**, 18–22 (2002)
21. Van Erp, J.B., Van Veen, H.: Vibro-tactile information presentation in automobiles. In: Proceedings of Eurohaptics, vol. 2001, pp. 99–104. DTIC Document (2001)
22. Van Erp, J.B., Van Veen, H.A., Jansen, C., Dobbins, T.: Waypoint navigation with a vibrotactile waist belt. ACM Trans. Appl. Percept. (TAP) **2**(2), 106–117 (2005)

23. Van Hulle, L., Juravle, G., Spence, C., Crombez, G., Van Damme, S.: Attention modulates sensory suppression during back movements. Conscious. Cogn. **22**(2), 420–429 (2013)

24. Yim, J., Myung, R., Lee, B.: The Mobile Phone's Optimal Vibration Frequency in Mobile Environments. In: Aykin, N. (ed.) HCII 2007. LNCS, vol. 4559, pp. 646–652. Springer, Heidelberg (2007)

Affordable Wideband Sensor Coupled Vibrotactile Actuator Systems for Psychophysical Experiments

Abhijit Biswas[1(✉)], Muniyandi Manivannan[1],
and Mandayam A. Srinivasan[2]

[1] Touch Lab, Department of Applied Mechanics,
IIT Madras, Chennai 600036, India
abhi.tech.2006@gmail.com, mani@iitm.ac.in
[2] The Touch Lab, The Research Laboratory of Electronics,
MIT, Cambridge, MA 02139, USA
srini@mit.edu

Abstract. Generation of high-amplitude high-frequency pure-tone mechanical vibrations over a wide frequency range is required in many applications, such as Vibrotactile (VT) stimulation, material testing and so on. This paper describes development of three different types of actuator systems, pneumatic, electromagnetic and piezoelectric, towards the objective of conducting VT psychophysical experiment above 1 kHz starting from few hundreds of Hz. While the piezoelectric system offers compactness, the 120 W electromagnetic system offers wider bandwidth and is capable of generating suprathreshold stimulus even above 2 kHz. Design and response of the piezoelectric actuator system, including the custom built LVDT coupled with the actuator are detailed in this paper. The frequency response of the tested configuration remains flat over a wide bandwidth till 4 kHz, even at high level of excitation, while generating bursts of 100 μm amplitude sine waves. The developed linear charge-drive is suitable for low-current application ~ 50 mA, maintaining low EMI and small size.

Keywords: Pure tone generator · Pneumatic, electromagnetic and piezoelectric actuator systems · Charge drive · Motion and vibration sensor · LVDT

1 Introduction

Although the study of Vibrotactile (VT) sensitivity began in 19th century [1], it is intensified only at the beginning of 20th century, mainly to train the hearing impaired for interpreting the sound through skin [2] and through bone conduction [3]. VT actuators have different applications in the field of functional response mapping of brain [4], sensory substitution using tactile display [5], rehabilitation [6], robotic surgery [7] and teleoperation [8]. Till date researchers have developed different techniques for conveying speech information through somatosensory channel, yet there are very few attempts to widen the band-width of VT stimulators above 1 kHz towards the upper frequency limit of speech signal. Two major limitations exist in conveying the

F. Bello et al. (Eds.): EuroHaptics 2016, Part I, LNCS 9774, pp. 419–429, 2016.
DOI: 10.1007/978-3-319-42321-0_39

speech signal through somatosensory channel: (1) higher VT Sensitivity Threshold (VTST) and (2) Frequency Discriminability Limen (FDL) above 400 Hz.

Most of the known VTST Characteristics (VTSTCs) are restricted below 400 Hz. However, there are few references of VTST till 1000 Hz and above [2, 9–14]. Among them [10] is possibly an extrapolation of [15], as the characteristics of [15] are actually restricted below 400 Hz and [12] does not mention any primary reference. On the other hand, few researchers claim that human finger-pad is sensitive to vibration even above 3 kHz [14] and till 8 kHz [9]; however they do not provide the complete VTSTC in terms of stimulus amplitude, which can be directly combined with other known sub-kHz VTSTCs. The VTSTC in terms of amplitude as derived from acceleration data of [14] do not follow the profile of the VTSTC, as given in [13] in terms of curvature, slope and absolute value, which also uses full-palm stimulation till 1000 Hz.

The main reason for restricting most of the VTSTCs reported in literature below 400 Hz is the challenges associated with the design of suitable actuator-system which can safely apply a supra-threshold stimulus to the subjects till 1000 Hz and possibly above this frequency. This requires high-power, wide-band, calibrated actuator, which can generate the required amplitude of a pure-tone mechanical vibration, at a desired frequency, under the loaded condition, maintaining its linearity. Such a wide-band low-Q, low noise actuator requires highly customized electro-mechanical design even for lower frequencies [16]. Therefore, in an attempt to quantify the VTSTC from 400 Hz to 3000 Hz, three high-frequency actuator-systems are developed and reported in this paper with electro-mechanical design details. While the developed 120 W electromagnetic actuator offers wide range of VT stimulus with excellent SNR, the piezoelectric system offers portability and good efficiency.

2   Experimental Hardware Design Challenges

2.1   Bandwidth, Power Rating and Actuation Range

Most of the actuator systems used in the psychophysical VT experiments as reported in literature comprise mostly electromagnetic actuators of different forms, besides the piezoelectric ones [17]. The energy dissipated by a vibrating body as present in those actuator systems increases with the square of frequency and amplitude and such dissipated energy mostly gets converted into heat rising the temperature of actuator and skin. Therefore, due to excessive energy dissipation at higher frequency the amplitude of the actuators is constrained to be small which in turn reduces the efficiency.

2.2   Damping and Linearity

Generation of pure-tones in a wide frequency band is always a critical challenge for actuator-system design. Most of the actuator shows a large gain variation in the pass-band due to presence of nonlinearity and under-damped natural frequency. Though the voice-coil based electromagnetic actuators show relatively flat pass-band over the piezoelectric actuators, electromagnetic actuators have very poor efficiency and are not suitable for generating more than 10 km/s^2 acceleration within a compact size. On the other hand, piezoelectric-actuators are capable of generating even 100 km/s^2 accelera-tion within a compact size with significantly high efficiency [18]. However, Piezoelectric-actuator shows high-Q frequency response with a sequential pattern of resonance and anti-resonance, based on the mechanical loading. It also exhibits non-linearity and hysteresis in the open-loop voltage vs. displacement characteristics, which needs proper driver for generation of the desired profile of mechanical output [19, 20]. Nevertheless, charge or current driven piezoelectric actuator can offer better lin-earity over a wider bandwidth when operated in an open loop.

2.3   Skin Decoupling from the Indenter

Another critical challenge to conduct high frequency VT experiment is to maintain a consistent contact between skin and indenter tip as at higher frequency starting from few tens of Hz skin decouples from the indenter over a certain phase angel [21]. The decoupling reduces with the preindentation on the skin as well as if the stimulus amplitude is lower. In any case, bonding skin with the cyanoacrylate adhesive can completely remove such uncertainty. However, it obviously alters the stiffness of the stratum corneum and also deviates from the natural process of sensing vibration through our skin.

3   Details of the Developed Hardware

In the process of development of actuator systems suitable for conducting VT exper-iments till 3000 Hz, three different types of actuation mechanisms are attempted: (1) pneumatic, (2) electromagnetic and (3) piezoelectric. Among these three, pneumatic actuator failed to generate supra threshold stimulus above 1 kHz under mechanical loading, while the others worked as expected - their designs are detailed in the fol-lowing section. It is worth noting that the final VT experiment is conducted with the piezoelectric actuator system, while the others are investigated qualitatively for their functionality and capability to generate significantly supra-threshold stimuli above 1 kHz.

3.1   Pneumatic Actuator Based Setup: Air Motor and Compressor

This setup comprises the Banner-II high speed handpiece generally used for the dental drilling applications powered by a Festo air compressor, as shown in Fig. 1.

A ferromagnetic cantilever is mounted on a sliding shaft driven by a solenoid to adjust the distance from the rotating magnet. The setup was tested with both double pole rare-earth magnet (Fig. 1 Right-Top) and a multipole array of magnets (Fig. 1 Right-Bottom). On no-load or in concentric load, the system can rotate up to a few thousands of RPS. However, on eccentric loading by the magnetic interaction between cantilever and the magnet the speed drops below 1000 RPS even at maximum allowed air pressure.

Fig. 1. Turbine based system showing the cantilever and rotating magnet.

3.2   Electromagnetic Actuator Based Setup: Motor, Sensor and Driver

50 W_{RMS} system: A 40 or 50 W_{RMS} motor unit of commercially available for multi-media application is chosen as the base actuator and modified to suite the purpose of VT stimulation without providing the high level of acoustic coupling with the air medium (Fig. 2). The system is quite similar to the classical design of VT experimental setup [16] except the design specializations of the tensioning and damping elements (Fig. 2 Left) and the sensor integration (Fig. 2 Right).

120 W_{RMS} system: As the 50 W_{RMS} electromagnetic system can generate supra-threshold VT stimulus only upto ~ 1000 Hz, a higher power actuator and electronic driver are developed thereafter. Again a high power audio air compression unit (tweeter) is chosen as the base actuator and modified to suite the purpose of VT stimulation as shown in Fig. 3. The voice coil of this actuator is suspended from Ti foil based spider or annular corrugated spring (Fig. 3 Left). To convert the 120 W_{RMS} tweeter in a VT stimulator, the central part of the diaphragm is removed and a Ti ring is mounted at

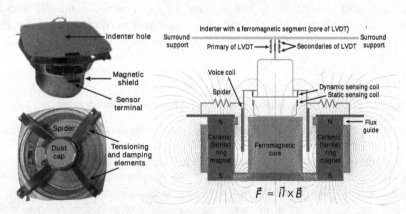

Fig. 2. The developed 50 W_{RMS} electromagnetic VT actuator system. (Left) Mechanical design; (Right) Sensor integration. The simulated image of the magnetic flux in the motor unit of a speaker is adopted from [22].

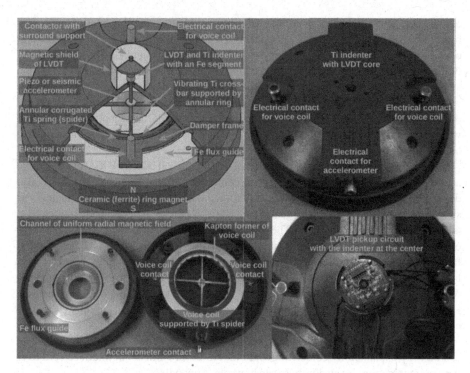

Fig. 3. Mechanical design and sensor integration of the developed 120 W$_{RMS}$ actuator system.

the periphery near the voice coil (Fig. 3 Left-Top). A crossbar of Ti is joined with the Ti ring (Fig. 3 Left) which vibrates as per the motion of the voice coil. The advantage of using a Ti crossbar instead of Ti diaphragm is the reduction of the acoustic coupling with the air medium.

The system has both LVDT and accelerometer coupled with the vibrating parts of the actuator. A piezoelectric disk along with a small seismic accelerometer is mounted at the junction of the crossbar and a Ti indenter is molded on top of them with the help of resin adhesive. While the seismic accelerometer responds to the acceleration of the indenter alone, the piezo-element responds the force and acceleration of the overall indenter column. The ferromagnetic core of the LVDT is fixed on top of the first segment of the indenter matching the height of the coils of the LVDT (Fig. 3). The second segment of the indenter (contactor) is detachable and can be changed as per requirement. Therefore, these three sensors coupled with the indenter offer rich information regarding the micro motion and force variation at the indenter.

Besides the actuators of the VT experimental setups, their electronic drivers are also custom built. The developed digital (Class-D) AC coupled 600 W$_{RMS}$ power amplifier (referred in Appendix) is based on TAS5630 IC from Texas Instruments suitable for driving both the 50 and 120 W$_{RMS}$ systems. The CMOS power stage of the TAS5630 IC is specifically designed for audio application with analog input. The output stage operates based on an internal 400 kHz PWM generator offering an analog bandwidth till 80 kHz which is good enough to operate both the VT actuators in open-loop. The amplifier is designed to support digital input signal too by changing the IC from TAS5630 to TAS5631 with the help of the detachable daughter board of the amplifier, as shown in Appendix. Though the digital input is inherently immune to the noise coupling, the analogue input amplifier also offers high SNR with the help of the differential input. Therefore, in the mono and stereo mode this amplifier is operated with the differential input; thus reducing the noise coupled in the transmission line between the power amplifier and the signal generator.

Apart from TAS5630 based amplifier, DRV8432 dual 5A/50 V CMOS H-bridge and dsPIC33FJ128MC804 digital signal controller based close-loop driver is also developed to drive any high power electromagnetic and piezoelectric actuators, as shown in Appendix. The PWM generator of this system is programmed to operate at 40 kHz with 11-bit resolution. The system is also integrated with two quadrature encoder channels for position measurement and additional analogue channel to interface the analog signals directly to the microcontroller. Most importantly this driver can be connected to the PCI or PCIe slot of any modern desktop or laptop computer through a IEEE 1284 (EPP) interface card. This helps to implement a semi-realtime PC-based close-loop controller for the VT actuator systems. The developed system is capable to drive upto 16 bidirectional and 16 unidirectional actuators simultaneously and independently from any modern personal computer. The system is modular and can be fully expanded by connecting eight motor driver cards to an interface card over the communication expansion bus, as shown in Appendix.

3.3   Piezoelectric Actuator Based Setup: Motor, Sensor and Driver

As generation of a high amplitude in high frequency band requires acceleration above a few thousands of m/s^2 the piezoelectric actuators are preferred for such applications. As shown in Fig. 4, the developed piezoelectric VT stimulator comprises a piezoelectric-stack-actuator APA150 from Cedrat Technologies, as it offers higher efficiency at

Fig. 4. Developed piezo-actuator-system with charge/current drive and the LVDT, along with the calibration probe coupled with the vibrating indenter.

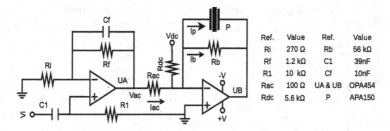

Fig. 5. Simplified schematic of the wide-band linear charge/current driver.

higher frequency within a compact size. The inherent design of the actuator amplifies the range of displacement of the piezoelectric-stack. The actuator is operated in one-side-blocked-mode and its free-side is coupled with a 1 mm diameter indenter to provide VT stimulus to the finger pad (Fig. 4). To avoid decoupling of skin from the indenter tip, it is extended 0.5 mm outside the surround-support for pre-indentation on skin and the finger pad is compressed against the surround-support with a static load applied by the subject.

Piezoelectric-actuators cannot be driven by linear audio amplifiers without proper impedance matching stage, as they have capacitive reactance below first resonance and high-Q frequency response with a sequential resonance and anti-resonance. They also exhibit nonlinearity and hysteresis in input voltage vs. output displacement characteristics [19, 20]. In order use the piezoelectric actuator to generate pure-tone vibrations over a wide frequency band a custom built linear charge/current drive is used (Fig. 5). Such charge or current drive offers good enough linearity in-between the electrical input and displacement output characteristic to operate the stack even in open loop [20]. Such open loop charge drives also offers better stability at higher frequency. Typical choice of the op-amps for this schematic can be OPA454 and LTC6090. As the actuator is coupled with an LVDT for sensing the motion of the indenter, a compact PCB of the LVDT pickup circuit is also developed. The effective on-load motion of the vibrating tip as sensed by the LVDT is digitized using a 10-bit ADC inbuilt to PIC18F4550 microcontroller. The LVDT is calibrated using 1 μm resolution and ±2 μm tolerance Mitutoyo Digimatic® micrometer.

4 Results and Discussions

4.1 Response of the Piezoelectric Actuator-System

As the VT experiments typically require generation of pulsed (short duration) stimulus the actuator-system is tested for generation of the short burst of pure-tones upto its maximum excitation level (above 100 μm amplitude). In the pulsed operation the system can withstand >50 mA current. Such linear charge-drive inherently produces lower EMI compared to the switching charge-drives and also contains less high frequency ripples at the output (Fig. 6 Left). The frequency response of the overall

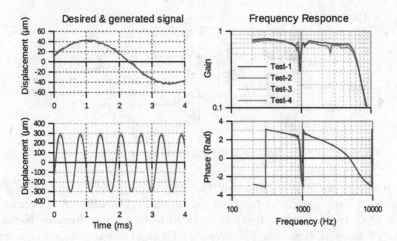

Fig. 6. Response of the actuator-system. (Left) Two typical VT stimuli indicating the level of distortion; (Right) Frequency response of the system. (Color figure online)

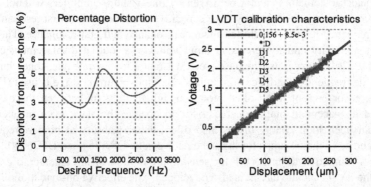

Fig. 7. (Left) Distortion in the output mechanical signal generated by the actuator compared to the intended pure-tone vibration; (Right) Repeatability and linearity of LVDT calibration characteristics estimated from five trials. (Color figure online)

actuator system is shown in (Fig. 6 Right). When the actuator is excited with maximum power at the frequency around 950 Hz a notch is observed in its frequency response (Fig. 6 Right) due to the occurrence of resonance with the overall structure and the presence of an over-current limiter. Such notch effectively vanishes at lower excitation level. Apart from this narrow band around 950 Hz, the open-loop frequency response characteristic remains flat for any excitation level generating a significantly low distortion pure-tone vibration (Fig. 7 Left) across the wide range of amplitude and frequency (100 Hz to 2000 Hz). This whole system consumes less than 5 W power even at the maximum excitation above 1000 Hz.

4.2 Response of LVDT

In order to estimate the distortion of the generated pure-tones (Fig. 7 Left), the random noises e.g., thermal noise and vibration-related artifacts are filtered by synchronous averaging of the LVDT signal. The developed LVDT pickup circuit has 99 % flat bandwidth till 8 kHz and to improve SNR for the synchronous averaging of the stimulus is used. The repeatability of the LVDT calibration is tested five times and the best fit straight line is estimated and used as the calibration characteristic (Fig. 7 Right).

4.3 Limitations and Allied Applications of the Actuator Systems

The pneumatic and the 50 W_{RMS} electromagnetic actuator systems have limited capacity of generating supra-threshold stimulus above 1000 Hz. The drop of the rotational speed of the handpiece is mostly because of the increase of frictional loss in the air bearing of the motor due to oscillatory radial loading of the shaft. However, both the 120 W_{RMS} electromagnetic and the piezoelectric systems can be used for clinical and scientific VT experiments over a wide frequency range, even around 1000 Hz, as the mechanoreceptor Pacinian corpuscle remains sensitive in that range too [23–25]. While the costly APA150 actuator as used in the piezoelectric system offers compactness, the electromagnetic actuators offer affordability as they are based on commercially available audio speakers. The developed electronic drivers have their generic applications for driving various actuators. The multi-channel close-loop control system is suitable for driving different haptic devices, robotic systems, CNC machines and surgical training systems [26] with upto 16 Degrees of Freedom (DOF). While the sixteen bidirectional actuators can be used for generation of controlled motion or vibration over 16 DOFs, the sixteen unidirectional actuators can be used for controlling brake or clutch for each DOF. The developed host and embedded side driver software are compatible with Microsoft Windows and Linux operating systems.

Appendix

See Fig. 8.

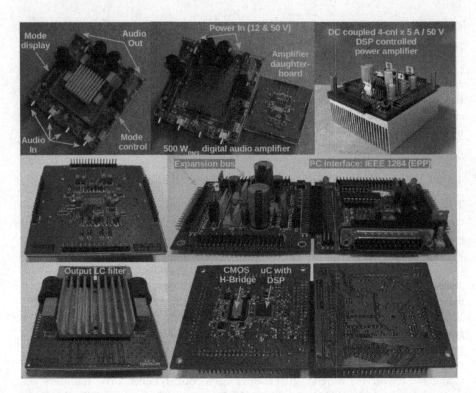

Fig. 8. (Top-Left and Top-Middle) 500 W_{RMS} audio amplifier along with the base board to drive voice-coil based actuator-system; (Middle-Left and Bottom-Left) Top and bottom sides of the amplifier board; (Top-Right) 4-chnl × 50 V/5A driver with digital signal controller for high-power electromagnetic and piezoelectric actuators connected to IEEE 1284 (EPP) interface for PC-based close-loop control; (Middle-Right and Bottom-Right) Top and bottom sides of the driver board connected to the interface board.

References

1. Valentin, G.: Über die dauer die Tasteindrücke. Arch. f. physiol. Heilk. **11**, 438–478 (1852)
2. Knudsen, V.O.: 'Hearing' with the sense of touch. J. Gen. Psychol. **1**(2), 320–352 (1928)
3. Von Békésy, G.: Vibration of the head in a sound field and its role in hearing by bone conduction. J. Acoust. Soc. Am. **20**(6), 749–760 (1948)
4. Briggs, R.W., Dy-Liacco, I., Malcolm, M.P., Lee, H., Peck, K.K., Gopinath, K.S., Himes, N. C., Soltysik, D.A., Browne, P., Tran-Son-Tay, R.: A pneumatic vibrotactile stimulation device for fMRI. Magn. Reson. Med. **51**(3), 640–643 (2004)
5. Benali-Khoudja, M., Hafez, M., Kheddar, A.: VITAL: an electromagnetic integrated tactile display. Displays **28**(3), 133–144 (2007)
6. Biswas, A., Tibarewala, D.N., Biswas, S.: Array based tactile vision for the blind people using multi-directional ultrasonic scanning of environment. Indian patent, 271918. [Application No.: 332/KOL/2008, Issued on: 16 Mar 2016]

7. Pacchierotti, C., Prattichizzo, D., Kuchenbecker, K.J.: Cutaneous feedback of fingertip deformation and vibration for palpation in robotic surgery. IEEE Trans. Biomed. Eng. **63**(2), 278–287 (2016)
8. Debus, T., Becker, T., Dupont, P., Jang, T.J., Howe, R.D.: Multichannel vibrotactile display for sensory substitution during teleoperation, vol. 4570, pp. 42–49 (2002)
9. Goodfellow, L.D.: Vibratory sensitivity: its present status. Psychol. Bull. **31**(8), 560–571 (1934)
10. Kandel, E.R., Schwartz, J.H., Jessell, T.M.: Principles of Neural Science, 4th edn. McGraw-Hill, New York (2000)
11. Muniak, M.A., Ray, S., Hsiao, S.S., Dammann, J.F., Bensmaia, S.J.: The neural coding of stimulus intensity: linking the population response of mechanoreceptive afferents with psychophysical behavior. J. Neurosci. **27**(43), 11687–11699 (2007)
12. Northrop, R.B.: Introduction to Dynamic Modeling of Neuro-Sensory Systems. CRC Press, Boca Raton (2001)
13. Reynolds, D., Standlee, K., Angevine, E.: Hand-arm vibration, part III: subjective response characteristics of individuals to hand-induced vibration. J. Sound Vibrat. **51**(2), 267–282 (1977)
14. Wyse, L., Nanayakkara, S., Seekings, P., Ong, S. H., Taylor, E.: Perception of vibrotactile stimuli above 1 kHz by the hearing-impaired. In: 12th International Conference on New Interfaces for Musical Expression. University of Michigan, Ann Arbor, Michigan, USA (2012)
15. Mountcastle, V.B., LaMotte, R.H., Carli, G.: Detection thresholds for stimuli in humans and monkeys: comparison with threshold events in mechanoreceptive afferent nerve fibers innervating the monkey hand. J. Neurophysiol. **35**(1), 122–136 (1972)
16. Verrillo, R.T.: Investigation of some parameters of the cutaneous threshold for vibration. J. Acoust. Soc. Am. **34**(11), 1768–1773 (1962)
17 Yao, H.-Y., Hayward, V.: Design and analysis of a recoil-type vibrotactile transducer. J. Acoust. Soc. Am. **128**(2), 619–627 (2010)
18. PI Ceramic, Piezo Technology Tutorial: The Piezoelectric Effect (2013). http://www.piceramic.com/piezo_tutorial1.php. Accessed 06 Feb 2013
19. Mahmood, I.A., Moheimani, S.O.R., Bhikkaji, B.: Precise tip positioning of a flexible manipulator using resonant control. IEEE-ASME Trans. Mech. **13**(2), 180–186 (2008)
20. Yi, K.A., Veillette, R.J.: A charge controller for linear operation of a piezoelectric stack actuator. IEEE T. Control Syst. T. **13**(4), 517–526 (2005)
21. Wu, J.Z., Dong, R.G., Schopper, A.W., Smutz, W.P.: Analysis of skin deformation profiles during sinusoidal vibration of fingerpad. Ann. Biomed. Eng. **31**(7), 867–878 (2003)
22. Hoadley, R.: Speaker assembly. Magnet Man (2013). http://www.coolmagnetman.com/gallery/imageset.html. Accessed June 2015
23. Biswas, A., Manivannan, M., Srinivasan, M.A.: Multiscale layered biomechanical model of the pacinian corpuscle. IEEE Trans. Haptics **8**(1), 31–42 (2015)
24. Biswas, A., Manivannan, M., Srinivasan, M.A.: Vibrotactile sensitivity threshold: nonlinear stochastic mechanotransduction model of the Pacinian Corpuscle. IEEE Trans. Haptics **8**(1), 102–113 (2015)
25. Bolanowski, S.J., Zwislocki, J.J.: Intensity and frequency characteristics of Pacinian corpuscles: I. Action potentials. J. Neurophysiol. **51**(4), 793–811 (1984)
26. Prasad, R., Biswas, A., Manivannan, M.: Surgical simulation and education: design and development of a cost effective 5-DOF haptic device for laparoscopic skills training. Int. J. Comput. Assist. Radiol. Surg. **9**(1), S128–S129 (2014)

Going Against the Grain – Texture Orientation Affects Direction of Exploratory Movement

Alexandra Lezkan[(⊠)] and Knut Drewing

Justus Liebig University, Giessen, Germany
{Alexandra.Lezkan,Knut.
Drewing}@psychol.uni-giessen.de

Abstract. In haptic perception sensory signals depend on how we actively move our hands. For textures with periodically repeating grooves, movement direction can determine temporal cues to spatial frequency. Moving in line with texture orientation does not generate temporal cues. In contrast, moving orthogonally to texture orientation maximizes the temporal frequency of stimulation, and thus optimizes temporal cues. Participants performed a spatial frequency discrimination task between stimuli of two types. The first type showed the described relationship between movement direction and temporal cues, the second stimulus type did not. We expected that when temporal cues can be optimized by moving in a certain direction, movements will be adjusted to this direction. However, movement adjustments were assumed to be based on sensory information, which accumulates over the exploration process. We analyzed 3 individual segments of the exploration process. As expected, participants only adjusted movement directions in the final exploration segment and only for the stimulus type, in which movement direction influenced temporal cues. We conclude that sensory signals on the texture orientation are used online during exploration in order to adjust subsequent movements. Once sufficient sensory evidence on the texture orientation was accumulated, movements were directed to optimize temporal cues.

Keywords: Texture · Temporal integration · Sensorimotor control · Perception · Psychophysics

1 Introduction

Moving and sensing mutually influence each other in haptic perception [1, 2]. On the one hand, it is movements that generate sensations during active exploration [3]. On the other hand, humans systematically vary exploratory movements depending on the object property of interest, and, thus, depending on the required sensory input. Texture judgments are typically associated with lateral movements over surfaces [4]. Previously, texture properties were reported to be associated with changes of individual movement parameters, as the exploratory force [5–7] or movement velocity [8]. This study aims to investigate whether movement direction is a parameter, which is adjusted to the texture. We examine how texture orientation influences movement directions used over the course of exploration in a frequency discrimination task.

© Springer International Publishing Switzerland 2016
F. Bello et al. (Eds.): EuroHaptics 2016, Part I, LNCS 9774, pp. 430–440, 2016.
DOI: 10.1007/978-3-319-42321-0_40

As for vision, we know that the direction of eye movements depends on the orientation of depicted textures [9–11]. Although, haptic perception relies even more on presence of movements than vision, haptic research did not focus on the relationship between texture orientation and movement directions so far. Finger movements can be essential for the haptic perception of textures. Striking over the textures produces temporal patterns of stimulation, i.e. temporal cues. Especially for fine-texture discrimination performance is seriously impaired without temporal cues [12]. For less fine surfaces spatial and temporal cues have been reported to be combined [13]. Gamzu and Ahissar [8] demonstrated for a frequency discrimination task that poor haptic performers can improve by using strategies which accentuate temporal cues. In a study of Lamb [14], participants explored textures, which incorporated stripes of raised dots. The spacing between stripes was either modified along the direction of the movement track or perpendicular to the movement track. Discrimination performance was better for manipulations along the track of finger movement than perpendicular to it. This performance increment can be attributed to the additional existence of temporal cues in the case of variations along the movement track. Thus, when exploration generates temporal cues the precision of texture perception can be increased.

It was previously reported that when exploration movements can be chosen freely participants aim to enhance the precision of perception [15]. Consequently, we expect that participants will choose those movements, which generate temporal cues in unconstrained texture exploration. For a spatial frequency discrimination task, haptic textures can be composed of periodic parallel grooves. Here, texture orientation is defined by the groove orientation. In this case, a movement in the direction of the texture orientation does not contain temporal cues. In contrast, every other movement direction produces temporal cues. In the special case of the movement directed orthogonally to the texture orientation, the stimulation is maximized which also leads to maximal differences in the stimulations induced by two different textures. Thus, orthogonal movement potentially optimizes the temporal cues that are useful for texture discrimination. In the present experiment we investigate whether in the discrimination of textures exploration movements are adapted to optimize temporal cues and therefore are directed against the texture orientation.

In order to adjust exploratory movements to texture orientation, sensory information about texture orientation needs to be gathered first. It is, hereby, important to consider that integration of sensory information not only occurs within one movement but also over several movements [16]. Haptic perception has been reported to be more precise with more elongated exploration [17]. Sensory signals are accumulated over the exploration. Consequently, movement adjustments based on the sensory signals are assumed to be more profound at the end of an exploration, as more sensory evidence is captured in that moment. Some studies already demonstrated that exploration movements are adjusted based on previously accumulated sensory signals. Saig and colleagues [1] reported online adjustments of movement parameters induced by sensory processing during exploratory behavior in a haptic localization task. We demonstrated motor adjustment based on sensory signals in softness exploration [2]. Here, participants applied systematically lower forces for softer objects after having gathered sensory signals on the objects softness.

In the present study we will focus on the adjustment of movement direction to texture orientation during a spatial frequency discrimination task. We expect that participants direct their exploration orthogonal to texture orientation, but not before they have accumulated sufficient sensory information from the textures. Thus, we expect that initial movements during the course of exploration are not dependent on texture orientation. In contrast, final exploration movements should be directed orthogonal to the texture orientation and, thus, optimize temporal cues to spatial frequency.

2   Experiment

We created haptic texture stimuli by 3D modeling and printing (Stratasys Objet 30 Pro). Participants explored a standard and a comparison stimulus grating and judged which of the two had a higher spatial-frequency. Standard gratings consisted of a groove pattern following the sine-wave function along one dimension (periods 1.27 and 1.44 mm; see Fig. 1). The texture pattern of comparison gratings consisted of the intersections of two orthogonal sine-wave function patterns (periods: 1.02 to 1.69 mm). A finger movement across a standard in direction of the texture orientation would generate no temporal signals on the texture's spatial frequency. A movement orthogonal to texture orientation would be associated with optimal temporal cues. In this specific case, stimulation and differences between stimulations produced by two different patterns are maximized. Those relationships between movement direction and temporal cues do not hold for comparison stimuli. As a consequence of their construction, movements in orthogonal directions over comparison stimuli would provide

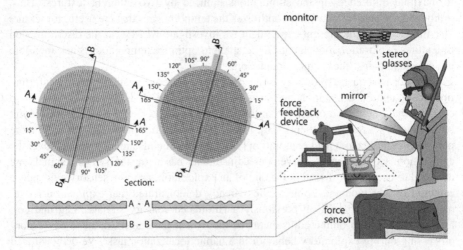

Fig. 1. Sketch of setup and stimuli. Stimulus location and shape were visually represented on a monitor and were seen through a mirror and stereo glasses. The real grating stimuli were placed on a force sensor next to each other. The participant's right index finger was connected to the PHANToM via an adapter. The PHANToM measured the finger position.

similar temporal cues to spatial frequency. We manipulated the orientation of the standard and the comparison in each trial, and measured movement direction for individual strokes. We predict that movements across the standard gratings will be preferentially executed in direction orthogonal to the texture's orientation. We expect to find this effect especially in the final movements of each single exploration, but not in the first movements.

2.1 Participants

The sample consisted of thirteen right-handed participants (average age: 25.4 years, range: 19–32 years; 7 females). All were naïve to the purpose of the experiment and were paid for participating. None of them reported sensory or motor impairments or recent injuries of the right index finger. We tested two-point-discrimination thresholds at the finger pad of the right index finger. All participants had a two-point discrimination threshold of 3 mm or lower. Participants gave written informed consent and the study was conducted in accordance with the ethical standards laid down in the 1964 Declaration of Helsinki.

2.2 Apparatus and Stimuli

Participants sat in front of a custom-made visuo-haptic workbench (see Fig. 1), which comprised a PHANToM 1.5A haptic force feedback device, force sensor (682 Hz, resolution: 0.05 N) and a 22"-computer screen (120 Hz, 1024 × 1280 pixel). The right index finger was connected to the PHANToM via an adapter, which allows for free finger movements having all six degrees of freedom in a 38 × 27 × 20 cm^3 workspace. The PHANToM device was only used to measure finger position. The adapter was connected with double-faced adhesive tape to the nail, which left the finger pad bare. Simultaneously, the participants looked through stereoglasses and via a mirror onto the screen (40 cm viewing distance). The mirror prevented participants from seeing their hand or the real stimuli and enabled spatial alignment of the 3D-visual representation with the haptic display. The participants' heads were stabilized by a chinrest. A custom-made software controlled the experiment, collected responses, and recorded the data from the PHANToM and the sensor with recording intervals of 3 ms. Headphones and ear plugs masked sounds from haptic exploration. The stimuli were presented next to each other in front of the participant. They were placed on the force sensor, which measured the executed finger force. The stimuli were displayed in virtual 3D-scene as three dimensional cylindrical discs with a border. The visual representation did not display the texture pattern or orientation. Position and size of the 'visual' stimuli corresponded to those of the real ones. Outside of the stimulus area present finger position was visible as a small sphere (8 mm diameter).

Haptic grating stimuli were created using the OpenSCAD software and 3D printing. The 3D printer (Objet 30 Pro, Stratasys Ltd., United States) creates arbitrary 3D objects from 3D digital data. In this method 3D objects are build drop wise with support and model photopolymer material (VeroClear) having a build resolution of

600 × 600 × 1600 dpi (x-, y-, z-axis). The stimuli were 4 mm high (z-axis) grating discs with a texture diameter of 90.7 mm and a total diameter including the border of 100.7 mm. A 10 × 5 mm grip indicated the texture orientation for the experimenter (see Fig. 1). We created two types of stimuli, standard and comparison gratings. Standard gratings consisted of a groove pattern following the sine-wave function. Texture height was defined as a sine-wave function with the peak amplitude (A) of 0.3 mm, see Eq. 1, depending only on one of the other two dimensions. We defined two standard stimuli with the periods (P) of 1.27 mm and 1.44 mm. For comparison stimuli, we computed texture height from two overlaid sine-wave functions that were oriented perpendicular to each other. The intersection of both textures defined the comparison. Thus, the texture height was at each point the minimum of the two functions, see Eq. 2. A cut through two orthogonal axes of comparison stimuli would result in identical images (see Fig. 1). We created 5 comparison gratings with periods of 1.02, 1.19, 1.35, 1.52 and 1.69 mm. For each of the two standards we used three comparisons. Two comparisons were defined by ±20 % of the standard's period, because 20 % corresponds to the Weber fraction in active touch (as assessed e.g. from [18]). The third comparison was the same stimulus for both standards (1.35 mm); it has 6 % lower period than the standard of 1.44 mm and 6 % higher period than the standard of 1.27 mm. Consequently, the frequency comparisons should be too difficult for static touch only. Based on the stimulus construction we defined texture orientation in standard gratings as the orientation of the parallel grooves. By definition, comparison gratings had two equal groove orientations. In the following, we will refer to one of them as the texture orientation (see Fig. 1).

Standard grating:
$$z = \frac{1}{2}A\sin\frac{2\pi x}{P} + \frac{1}{2}A \qquad (1)$$

Comparison grating:
$$z = min(\frac{1}{2}A\sin\frac{2\pi x}{P} + \frac{1}{2}A, \frac{1}{2}A\sin\frac{2\pi y}{P} + \frac{1}{2}A) \qquad (2)$$

2.3   Design and Procedure

In each trial a stimulus pair, consisting of one standard and one comparison stimulus, was explored. The participant judged which of the two had a higher spatial-frequency regardless of other differences between the textures. We explained spatial frequency as the number of experienced grooves over a certain distance. Thus, stimuli with a higher period have lower spatial frequencies. We manipulated the standard stimulus (period of 1.27 or 1.44 mm) and the orientation of the stimulus pair on the force sensor (15°, 45°, 75°, 105°, 135°, and 165°; in Fig. 1 depicted in the orientation of 75°). The dependent variable was the movement direction used over standard and comparison grating. We focused on the first, middle and last stroke, as they represent movement adjustments at different moments during exploration regardless of the exact stroke number in a trial.

Each standard was paired with one of three comparisons (standard 12.7 mm with comparisons with periods of 1.02, 1.35, 1.52 mm and standard 1.44 mm with 1.19, 1.35, 1.69 mm). The standard grating was either presented at the right or the left side. Standard and comparison grating were always placed in the same orientation. Note that due to its definition the comparison grating felt the same when being explored along or against its orientation and also stimulation from explorations along oblique axes was only moderately different in temporal frequency (factor below 1.4). Additionally, to keep motivation high over the entire experiment, we introduced the experiment as a game. Participants could earn 10 or 100 points with a correct answer. Overall, there were 2 [standards] × 3 [comparisons] × 6 [orientations] × 2 [standard left or right] × 2 [10 or 100 points] = 144 trials. The order of trials was randomized and trials were presented in 3 successive blocks of 48 trials. Participants were instructed to take a break of at least two minutes between each two blocks. The experiment lasted 2–3 h.

Before starting the exploration of a trial, the screen indicated how many points a correct response would correspond to (10 or 100). The exploration randomly started either with the right or the left stimulus on a random start position at the border of this stimulus (20°–350°, in steps of 30°). Then, participants were free to perform as many strokes and to switch as often between stimuli as they wanted. During the exploration no visual information about the stimulus was given. The basic payment was 16€. An additional euro was gained, whenever the participant accumulated 500 points. A visual and auditory feedback was given 1–3 trials after the points had been accumulated. Pure guessing would have led to a total payment of approximately 23€ and perfect task performance to a total of about 31€.

2.4   Data Analysis

We segmented the exploration behavior on each stimulus into single strokes. A stroke was defined as a continuous movement over the texture in one direction. We analyzed 3 strokes (first, middle, last) of the exploration of each stimulus. In case of even numbers of strokes, the middle stroke was defined by the later one of the two possible. For the definition of a stroke we considered those parts of the exploration, in which the finger was touching the stimulus area with at least 0.1 N of force. We detected strokes as continuous movements either from one texture border to another or between two movement turns, which we extracted by zero crossings in y- or x-velocity. For each stroke we derived its movement direction and duration (restricted to minimum duration: 200 ms). Only those trials entered in the analysis, in which the participant at least performed two strokes on each grating. In order to collapse data over trials, we aligned all stimulus orientations with an orientation of 0°. Therefore, stroke directions were rotated by their corresponding texture orientation in the opposite direction. As strokes differed highly in their duration, we weighted individual strokes with their duration. Technically, strokes were duplicated in accordance to their duration. Based on this data we calculated histograms of movement directions (bin size: 15°) for each participant, grating and exploratory segment. The resulting histograms represented which propor-tion of exploration time one participant followed a specific direction for this stroke (first, middle or last) in this grating (standard or comparison). In an overall participant analyses we computed average histograms to keep statistical power equal with the individual participant analyses. We conducted circular statistics on these binned data separately for each exploratory segment (first, middle, last) and grating type (standard, comparison). For this purpose, we used the V-test, a variant of the Rayleigh test, which tests the alternative hypothesis that the population is not distributed uniformly around the circle but has a specified mean direction [19], 90° in our case. For standard gratings, we predicted that over the course of exploration movement directions should get more and more non-uniformly distributed. Thus, we expect significant values especially for the last stroke in the exploration of the standard.

3   Results

3.1   Exploration and Task Performance

On average, participants performed 3.9 strokes (SD = 1.8) on the standard grating and 3.7 strokes (SD = 1.7) on the comparison grating, and they switched twice between the stimuli (M = 2.05, SD = 0.82): once from first to the second stimulus and then once back to the first stimulus. An average stroke took 1.6 s (SD = 0.6) for the standard grating and 1.7 s (SD = 0.6) for the comparison grating. Participants used more strokes for the exploration of standard gratings, $t(12) = 2.26$, $p = 0.04$, while stroke duration was higher for comparison gratings, $t(12) = -3.04$, $p = 0.01$. On average participants gave 59.2 % correct answers (SD = 8 %), which is significantly higher than guessing (50 %), $t(12) = 3.88$, $p < 0.01$.

3.2   Movement Directions

The angular distributions of movement directions for the first, middle and last stroke exploring the standard or the comparison grating are plotted for all participants in Fig. 2. We calculated the V-test based on the binned data presented in Fig. 2. This test reports V-values, which increase with the deviation of the empirical distribution from a uniform distribution and with the consistency of the empirical mean direction with a predicted one. A non-significant test could either be due to a uniform distribution or a distribution with a mean that deviates from the predicted direction of 90°. For the first stroke V-values were not significant for both gratings (standard: $V = -6.15$, $p = 0.82$; comparison: $V = 0.59$, $p = 0.47$). Also in the middle stroke values were not significant, although Fig. 2 appears to indicate a tendency in the standard stimulus (standard: $V = 6.93$, $p = 0.16$; comparison: $V = -1.23$, $p = 0.57$). As predicted in the last stroke participants showed a significant non-uniformity in their movement directions and moved orthogonally (90°) to the standard grating, $V = 17.85$, $p < 0.01$. For the comparison stimulus this non-uniformity did not reach significance in the last stroke, $V = 7.19$, $p = 0.15$. This result is well reflected in the individual participant analyses. We found significant movement adjustments to the texture orientation for 9 of 13 participants. None of the participants significantly adjusted the first stoke to the texture orientation. Additionally, no one showed more significant adjustments in the comparison than in the standard. The data of two participants revealed the same pattern as the average data. Four participants significantly adjusted their middle and last stroke to the standard and only one of the strokes to the comparison. Three participants showed

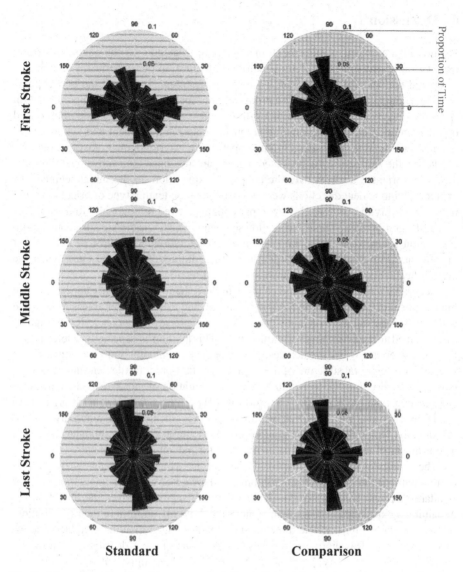

Fig. 2. Movement direction histograms including all participant data for each exploration segment and texture type separately. All textures were aligned to a 0° orientation. Possible movement directions varied between 0–180° and were mirrored on the lower part of the figure.

significant adjustments to standard and comparison (2 in middle and last stroke; 1 in last stroke only). Taken together, adjustments of movement direction were not found in the beginning of the exploration. However, for standard gratings, the last stroke was adjusted to move orthogonal to the texture orientation. So that in this case 25 % of the movements had a direction between 75°–105°.

4 Discussion

We investigated whether movement directions are changed over the course of natural exploration in order to move orthogonally to a texture. In our experiment participants compared the spatial frequency of two types of gratings. For one of the two gratings moving along the texture orientation produced only spatial cues and no temporal cues on spatial frequency. In contrast, moving orthogonally to the texture orientation produced optimal temporal cues. This simple relationship between movement and texture orientation did not hold for the second grating type, where two orthogonal moving directions resulted in the same cues. As predicted, participants changed their movement direction across the oriented textures over the course of exploration. In the initial segments of exploration movement directions were not dependent on texture type or orientation, but rather uniformly distributed. However, participants moved orthogonally to the textures of the first grating type in final exploration segments. Thus, sensory signals about texture orientation seem to be taken into account for the following control of exploration movements. Movements were chosen to produce improved temporal cues, when the availability of cues depended on the movement direction.

According to our data profound changes in movement direction only appeared in the final segment of exploration. In the middle stroke, and therefore after at least one stroke with an average duration of more than 1.5 s., movement directions were not significantly aimed towards orthogonal exploration. This finding is especially interesting in light of a recent study [20], which described that edge orientation is already coded by the intensity and temporal structure of the responses of first-order tactile neurons. However, our result is very unlikely to be attributed to the duration of motor responses, as those were demonstrated to take only 100–200 ms. [21]. Thus, although sensory signals are available early on, we think that within finger movements signal reliability is low. Presumably, temporal signal integration processes are necessary to produce an as reliable estimate of texture orientation as required for movement adjustments.

The results revealed the expected pattern, in which movements were chosen orthogonally to the texture orientation only in the case of a unique orientation (i.e. for standard gratings) and only in the final exploration segments. From the first sight the remaining 5 experimental cases seemed not to look highly uniform in their distribution. In order to control for possible directional preferences other than the predicted one we computed simple Rayleigh tests for these cases. None of the 5 distributions showed a significant non-uniformity, $z \leq 1.80$, $p \geq 0.16$. Correspondingly, our results primarily reflect the expected bottom-up effects on movement direction. However, there are also some hints that chosen movement directions might not only be based on bottom-up stimulus information. In our comparison gratings a movement in $0°$ direction and a movement orthogonal to that ($90°$) generated precisely the same cues. However, as it can be seen from Fig. 2 movements in these two directions ($90° \pm 30°$ vs. $0° \pm 30°$) are not represented equally often (37 % vs. 28 %) during the final stroke. This difference shows a statistical trend, $t(12) = 1.96$; $p = 0.06$ in a paired t-test on the rationalized arcsine transformation of the individual proportional data. Perhaps, the $90°$ direction was chosen more often, in order to move in a similar way as in the standard grating of the same trial. This observation indicates that the task to compare two stimuli has a top-down influence on movement directions and fits well to recently reported results on movement control [22].

As we reported in the results about 25 % of the last movements were at directions ±15° from orthogonality. Even about 48 % of the last movements were at directions ±30° from orthogonality. We assumed that orthogonal movements maximize temporal cues and therefore optimize sensory input. Based on our data we can perform post-hoc analyses to compare whether the movements approximately orthogonal to the texture orientation (±30°) led to better task performance, measured by the proportion of correct responses, than other movements. A paired-sample t-test on the rationalized arcsine transformation of the individual proportions of correct responses reveals significantly better performance for trials with approximately orthogonal movement direction, t (12) = 2.43, p = 0.03 in comparison to other movements. Both groups of trials did not differ in their average number of strokes used, $t(12) = -0.05$, $p = 0.96$. However, it needs to be considered that this experiment was not designed for this analysis. We plan future experiments where exploration length and movement direction are manipulated independently to better address this question. We will also address the question of how much the previous movement direction influenced the following movement.

Our initial expectation of directing movements orthogonal to the texture orientation was based on the idea, that orthogonal movement optimizes temporal cues. However, an alternative explanation for choosing orthogonal movement direction could be that participants tried to avoid exploration movements in line with the texture that generate no temporal cues on spatial frequency. If our system takes into account motor and perceptual noise, than aiming for orthogonal movements would maximize the chance to avoid exploration in line with the texture. In order to distinguish between both possibilities, future research could use more complex virtual textures, in which the movement direction generating maximal temporal stimulation is not orthogonal to the direction generating no temporal cues.

5 Conclusion

This study asked the fundamental question of whether texture orientation influences movement directions used in a frequency discrimination task. We focused on natural and unconstrained exploration of two types of textures, one with and one without a unique orientation. Participants adjusted movement direction over the course of exploration depending on the texture they encountered. In the first exploration segment movements were uniformly distributed along all directions regardless of the texture type. However, in cases in which the texture had a unique orientation, movement directions changed until the final exploration segment. In the last stroke participants moved orthogonally to the texture orientation. This result indicates that sensory signals on texture orientation were accumulated over the course of exploration and influenced motor control. We suggest that the reason for this adjustment is the optimization of sensory cues needed to perform the task. Taken together, this study strongly supports the idea of a sensorimotor control loop. Sensory signals are used to perform those movements, which optimize the sensory feedback itself.

Acknowledgements. We would like to thank Maria Ebsen and Claire Weyel for their help in collecting the data and Steffen Bruckbauer for help with the figures. This research was supported by the German Research Foundation (DFG; grant SFB/TRR135/1, A05).

References

1. Saig, A., Gordon, G., Assa, E., Arieli, A., Ahissar, E.: Motor-sensory confluence in tactile perception. J. Neurosci. **32**(40), 14022–14032 (2012)
2. Lezkan, A., Drewing, K.: Predictive and sensory signals systematically lower peak forces in the exploration of softer objects. In: 2015 IEEE World Haptics Conference (WHC), pp. 69–74. IEEE, June 2015
3. Gibson, J.J.: The Senses Considered as Perceptual Systems. Houghton-Mifflin, Boston (1966)
4. Lederman, S.T., Klatzky, R.L.: Hand movements: a window into haptic object recognition. Cogn. Psychol. **19**, 342–368 (1987)
5. Lederman, S.J.: Tactile roughness of grooved surfaces: the touching process and effects of macro- and microsurface structure. Percept. Psychophys. **16**, 385–395 (1974)
6. Gibson, G.O., Craig, J.C.: The effect of force and conformance on tactile intensive and spatial sensitivity. Exp. Brain Res. **170**, 172–181 (2006)
7. Nefs, H.T., Kappers, A.M.L., Koenderink, J.J.: Frequency discrimination between and within line gratings by dynamic touch. Percept. Psychophys. **64**, 969–980 (2002)
8. Gamzu, E., Ahissar, E.: Importance of temporal cues for tactile spatial-frequency discrimination. J. Neurosci. **21**, 7416–7427 (2001)
9. Wismeijer, D.A., Gegenfurtner, K.R.: Orientation of noisy texture affects saccade direction during free viewing. Vis. Res. **58**, 19–26 (2012)
10. Wismeijer, D.A., Erkelens, C.J., Van Ee, R., Wexler, M.: Depth cue combination in spontaneous eye movements. J. Vis. **10**(6), 25 (2010)
11. Wexler, M., Ouarti, N.: Depth affects where we look. Curr. Biol. **18**(23), 1872–1876 (2008)
12. Hollins, M., Risner, S.R.: Evidence for the duplex theory of tactile texture perception. Percept. Psychophys. **62**(4), 695–705 (2000)
13. Cascio, C.J., Sathian, K.: Temporal cues contribute to tactile perception of roughness. J. Neurosci. **21**(14), 5289–5296 (2001)
14. Lamb, G.D.: Tactile discrimination of textured surfaces: psychophysical performance measurements in humans. J. Physiol. **338**(1), 551–565 (1983)
15. Kaim, L., Drewing, K.: Exploratory strategies in haptic softness discrimination are tuned to achieve high levels of task performance. IEEE Trans. Haptics **4**(4), 242–252 (2011)
16. Henriques, D.Y., Soechting, J.F.: Approaches to the study of haptic sensing. J. Neurophysiol. **93**, 3036–3043 (2005)
17. Drewing, K., Lezkan, A., Ludwig, S.: Texture discrimination in active touch: effects of the extension of the exploration and their exploitation. In: 2011 IEEE World Haptics Conference (WHC), pp. 215–220. IEEE, June 2011
18. Nefs, H.T., Kappers, A.M., Koenderink, J.J.: Amplitude and spatial-period discrimination in sinusoidal gratings by dynamic touch. Perception **30**(10), 1263–1274 (2001)
19. Mardia, V., Jupp, P.: Directional Statistics, 2nd edn. Wiley Ltd., London (2000)
20. Pruszynski, J.A., Johansson, R.S.: Edge-orientation processing in first-order tactile neurons. Nature Neurosci. **17**, 1404–1409 (2014)
21. Johansson, R.S., Westling, G.: Signals in tactile afferents from the fingers eliciting adaptive motor responses during precision grip. Exp. Brain Res. **66**(1), 141–154 (1987)
22. Callier, T., Saal, H.P., Davis-Berg, E.C., Bensmaia, S.J.: Kinematics of unconstrained tactile texture exploration. J. Neurophysiol. **113**(7), 3013–3020 (2015)

An Adaptive Strategy for an Immersive Visuo-Haptic Attention Training Game

Xiaoxiao Yang, Dangxiao Wang[⊠], and Yuru Zhang

Beihang University, No. 37 Xueyuan Rd., Haidian, Beijing, China
hapticwang@buaa.edu.cn

Abstract. Attention training using virtual environments is a promising way to treat mental disorders such as attention-deficit hyperactivity disorder (ADHD). Interactive haptic tasks combined with immersive visual display provide a potential solution for attention modulation and training. In this paper, we introduced a visuo-haptic game consisting of stimulus-response tasks using fingertip pressure control with immersive visual display using the Oculus Rift. Users were required to press a force sensor using either the index or middle finger from either hand. In each trial, users needed to maintain a constant force with an expected tolerance within an allowable response time. An adaptive strategy was proposed to tune the difficulty level of the task to match the force control skill of the user, which may produce an optimal success rate in each trial to maintain users' interest and keep them motivated. Furthermore, a randomized algorithm was adopted to vary the target fingertip, target force magnitude and target tolerance between adjacent trials, which was designed to avoid the boring repetition and thus to keep the users' curiosity on the task. Experimental results on six participants show that the proposed strategy was able to obtain different expected success rates, i.e. either 79.4 % or 50 %.

Keywords: Attention · Visuo-haptic game · Adaptive strategy · Immersive

1 Introduction

Attention is the foundation of neural and cognitive activity, whereas the ability of effective attention control is the foundation of perceiving external information [1, 2]. Our learning capability, social skills and even happiness are closely intertwined with our capacity for controlling our attention focus. Decreased attentional control skill may lead to mental disorders such as ADHD that may prevent people from learning and working efficiently and even cause serious symptom [2].

The study of attention training may innovate new methods for the diagnosis, prevention, and treatment for mental disorders or neurological diseases, such as ADHD patients [2], brain injuries and stroke [3, 4]. Effective and timely attention training may provide significant benefits for these patients [3]. Furthermore, attention training may provide a novel training approach for special professionals under heavy workload, high-pressure and high-paced situations, such as pilots, personnel monitoring in railway and airport control towers etc. [5].

© Springer International Publishing Switzerland 2016
F. Bello et al. (Eds.): EuroHaptics 2016, Part I, LNCS 9774, pp. 441–451, 2016.
DOI: 10.1007/978-3-319-42321-0_41

Various efforts have been explored for training attention. DeBettencourt *et al.* used closed-loop neurofeedback for attention training and they concluded that moment-to-moment feedback about attentional state could enhance sustained attention abilities [6]. Montani *et al.* [7] demonstrated that adaptive video game training improved attentional control and cognitive abilities during play. Franceschini *et al.* [8] demonstrated that playing action video games enhanced the reading speed in children suffering from dyslexia, resultantly improved the attention abilities. Green *et al.* [9] illustrated how video game training enhanced cognitive control in healthy participants with normal attention levels. Anguera *et al.* [10] found that video game training enhanced cognitive control and attention in older adults.

Most of the existing attention training methods rely on visual and/or auditory signals, and there has been little work on using haptic tasks for attention training [11, 12]. It would be interesting to investigate whether intensive activation/utilization of the haptic channel might produce a different attention training effect. Furthermore, low-cost head-mounted display devices (HMD) such as Oculus Rift provide immersive feeling to users, which can eliminate external visual disturbance. To the best of our knowledge, there has been no attention training system combining haptic tasks with the Occulus Rift.

The aim of the present study is to develop a novel adaptive visuo-haptic game for training attention. One important instructional principle common to all adaptive games is to maintain attention and motivation by providing sufficient positive reinforcement. This was achieved by continuously adapting the task difficulty in order to maintain a suitable correct rate for most trials, e.g. 75 % correct rate [15]. In this paper, we proposed an immersive visuo-haptic game using fast-paced stimulus response tasks with variable elements to modulate attention. An adaptive strategy was proposed to tune the difficulty level of the task to match the motor control skill of the user, which may produce an optimal success rate in each trial to maintain users' interest. Six participants performed experiments to validate the effect of the proposed method.

2   Design of the Visuo-Haptic Game

2.1   Design Rationale for Attention Training Games

Useful lessons from action video games were adopted for designing visuo-haptic attention training games [9], including defining clear goal, providing immediate feedback, providing positive reward, and keep curiosity of the user during the gaming process. Rizzo *et al.* developed virtual reality games for the assessment and rehabilitation of ADHD. Their experimental results showed that virtual environments delivered via HMD are well suited for attention training as they provide a controlled stimulus environment where cognitive challenges can be presented along with the precise delivery and control of "distracting" auditory and visual stimuli [13].

In comparison to traditional attention training games relied on visual or auditory channels, design rationale of the proposed visuo-haptic training games include:

- Efferent pathway: The capability of producing an accurate force and/or motion is a unique feature of the haptic channel, while visual and auditory channels can only produce afferent information to the brain. We hypothesize actively "send out" commands through haptic channel may provoke stronger attentional workload for the brain than passively "read in" commands through visual or auditory channels, and thus may produce more effective attention training outcome.

- Uniqueness of fingertip: As fingertips has highly sensitive perception and dexterous force control capability, accurate force control using fingertips might recruit intensive attention, which provides a promising solution to invoke attention and to stimulate the brain.
- Multimodal augmentation: It is possible to integrate haptic channel with visual/ auditory channels for attention training. However, it remains unclear what underlying criteria should be followed to combine haptic channel with visual/auditory channels to obtain more effective attention training outcome.

2.2 Components of the Visuo-Haptic System

As shown in Fig. 1, there are three subsystems in the visuo-haptic attention training system. First subsystem is the stimulus-response task, which consists of visual cues provided by a HMD (Oculus Inc. USA), and fours force sensors (Honeywell Inc. USA) mounted on a mechanical support for measuring pressure force of the user, and an algorithm to produce a sequence of visual cues with randomized parameters. Second is the feedback system, which consists of a feedback generation module, sequences of visual and audio feedback signals, and the earphone and the HMD for providing the feedback. Third is the adaptive controller, which accepts the output from the stimulus-response task system, and then tune the parameters of the visual cue along with producing output for the feedback generation module.

The prototype of the visuo-haptic attention training system is shown in Fig. 1. The details of the stimulus-response task system and feedback system will be introduced in Sect. 2.3, and the adaptive controller will be introduced in Sect. 3.

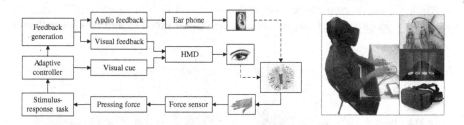

Fig. 1. Components of the attention training system: diagram and experimental scenario

2.3 Stimulus-Response Task

The design rationale of the task is to fully exploit the potential of human visual perception and force control capability, and thus to produce a high attentional workload during the task execution process. Furthermore, immediate feedback could be provided to motivate the user to focus on the training task.

A fast-paced stimulus-response force control task based on Fitts' Law was adopted. In each trial, the user needs to press a force sensor to produce a force magnitude (A) falling within the expected range (W). The magnitude was required to be maintained for a required duration (T_D). The pressing task has to be finished with an allowable response time (T). According to Fitts' Law, the difficulty level of the task depend on the combination of the parameter vector $\{A, W, T\}$. Shannon formulation of Fitts' law is most frequently used, which is defined as [14]

$$T_R = a + b \cdot \underbrace{\log_2(\frac{A}{W} + 1)}_{ID} \qquad (1)$$

where a and b are regression coefficients, and ID is the index of difficulty. It should be noted that the definition of the actual response time T_R is different from the T.

In the task design, we modulate the difficulty level of each trial through the parameter vector $\{A, W, T\}$. The target force (A) was chosen from the set $(1, 2, 3, 4$ N$)$ while the tolerance range (W) was chosen from the set $(0.5, 0.6, 0.7, 0.8$ N$)$. The tolerance range was defined symmetrically with respect to the target force, that is, $(A \pm 0.25, A \pm 0.3, A \pm 0.35, A \pm 0.4)$. Therefore a total of 16 pairs (4×4) of A-W conditions were generated.

Visual cues were provided to show the required A and W. As shown in Fig. 2, there are four gray semi-transparent cylinders in the virtual environment, while each bottom of the cylinder has a color disk. Users can lift the color disk by pressing the corresponding force sensor. The height of the color disk increases along with the force magnitude.

When a visual cue (i.e. a gray disk with varied thickness) pops up in one of the cylinder, users should control the color disk to move into the volume of the gray disk. As shown in Fig. 3, the actual force increased and the three states of the actual force relative to the expected tolerance was displayed by the relative distance between the color disk and the grey disk. For example, when the actual force belongs to the range of the required force tolerance, the color disk overlapped with the grey disk. In order to successfully perform a trial, the duration of the "dwell time" should be greater than a

a) left index fingertip, A = 2N, W = 0.8N.   b) right middle fingertip, A = 3N, W = 0.5N.

Fig. 2. Illustration of the visual cue (i.e. target disk) with varied A and W, and varied fingertip. (Color figure online)

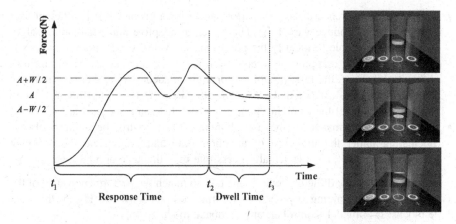

Fig. 3. Illustration of force fluctuation during one trial (Color figure online)

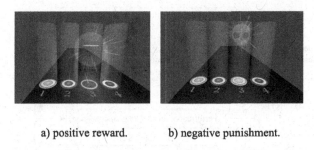

a) positive reward.   b) negative punishment.

Fig. 4. Two types of visual feedback (Color figure online)

predefined threshold T_D (e.g. 100 ms), and the "response time" T_R should be smaller than the allowed response time T of the current trial.

If the current trial was successful, the gray disk disappeared and a reward signal was displayed (audio and visual feedback as shown in Fig. 4(a). Otherwise, the gray disk disappeared automatically, indicating failure and only visual feedback was provided as shown in Fig. 4(b). Along with the visual feedback, audio feedback with a melodious tone was also provided to enhance the reward, which was designed to encourage subjects to get more rewards through multi-modal feedback. The virtual environment was developed using Unity 3D (Unity Technologies, UK). To avoid boring feeling of the user, four fingers were utilized in the task, i.e. the target fingertip in each trial was randomly selected from the index and middle fingertips of either hand.

3 Attention Training Strategy

3.1 Closed-Loop Attention Training Approach

Challenges for adaptive module to tune the difficulty level of the trials to match the capability of the user, and thus to maintain a constant success rate across trials:

- Personalized difference of control performance: for a given $\{A, W\}$, different user may definitely produce varied T_R. Therefore, an adaptive and personalized algorithm should be able to identify the performance level of different users;
- Multi-dimensional mapping between performance (i.e. the success rate) and task difficulty level (i.e. the task variables): for a given success rate, there are multiple combinations of $\{A, W, T\}$ that can obtain the rate. It is necessary to construct an isosurface to model the sampling points that own the same success rate;
- Fluctuating performance of the user: human's force control behavior is always fluctuating under the influence of attention state and fatigue etc. For a given combination $\{A, W, T\}$, the actual success rate may fluctuate around a value.

In order to tune the difficulty level of the task to match the performance level of the user, a closed-loop training approach was introduced. As shown in Fig. 5, there are three blocks: task model, controller, and feedback module.

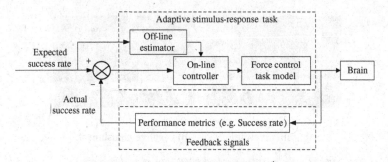

Fig. 5. Closed-loop attention training approach

In the task model, we need to model the dependence of task difficulty on its independent variables. As explained in Sect. 2.3, the Fitts' Law was utilized to model the relationship between T_R and $\{A, W\}$. In Sect. 3.2, we will introduce a multi-dimensional model of the task difficulty, which aimed to model the interaction between the user's performance level and the task's difficulty level.

In the feedback module, the feedback signal was defined as the actual performance level of the user. We measured the performance level of each trial in real time including T_R and the response (i.e. correct or wrong). Based on the response of the latest 20 trials, we computed the actual success rate in the current trial.

Last but not the least is the adaptive controller. The design rationale of the controller is to maintain the difficulty of the training task within the "zone of proximal development", minimizing failure whilst maintaining adequate difficulty, thus providing a presumably ideal level of attention arousal [15]. In this paper, we proposed two steps for the controller: an off-line estimator to construct the performance space of each user, and an on-line adaptive controller to dynamically tune the difficulty level of the current trial. We will introduce the detail of the controller in Sect. 3.3.

3.2 Estimation of the Performance Space

In the off-line estimator, we used an adaptive algorithm to measure the actual performance level of the user. As there are three dimensions of independent variables to modulate the difficulty level of the trial $\{A, W, T\}$, we defined the combination of the three dimensions as a "performance space", which can be described as a cube with the three dimensions as sides. Every trial corresponds to a point within this cube, and every point is associated with a certain probability of success. Higher probability is associated with easy trials and the opposite for the hard trials. Users can be presented with a problem at any point in the performance space, and will have different probabilities of success for tasks at different sampling points.

The purpose of the algorithm is to adapt to the performance of a user in the three-dimensional performance space, maintaining their success rate close to a pre-specified fixed level. This is achieved by estimating the user's current ability of this difficulty, and by using this representation to present the user with problem at the level of difficulty required to maintain the desired success rate.

Each user will be associated with a different probability matrix of success rate, which was defined as the individual "performance space". The task of this algorithm is to estimate what the performance space looks like for each user. Given an expected success rate, we need to find all sampling points that lead to the success rate, and all these points may formulate an isosurface as shown in Fig. 6. Different isosurfaces could be identified to lead to varied success rate.

As proposed in previous cognitive training studies, the success rate in each trial should be optimal because too high or too low may cause frustrated or boring feeling of the user. In order to obtain a constant success rate for each trial, we proposed an adaptive algorithm to search for the isosurface for a given success rate, and this algorithm can be generalized for different users.

For a given $\{A, W\}$, the initial value of the allowable response time T was determined by the Eq. (1). The lower and upper bound of the T were set as T_{lower} and T_{upper} respectively. Based on the score in previous trial, T_{lower} and T_{upper} were adjusted to be a smaller range. In order to accelerate the searching process, the golden cut method was adopted to reduce the range of the T with a constant decreasing ratio. The one-up

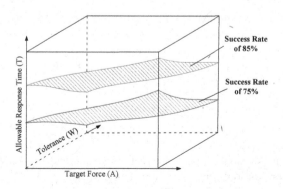

Fig. 6. Examples of two isosurfaces

three-down strategy was used to adjust the range [16]. If the user succeeded for three consecutive trials, the upper bound of the T will be reduced, and this means the increase of the difficulty level of the next trial. If the user failed for one trial, the lower bound of the T will be increased. Otherwise, the lower and upper bound of the T will not change. When the range is smaller than a pre-defined threshold (e.g. 20 % of the initial value of the T_{upper} at the beginning of the searching process), the searching process stopped, and the lower and upper bound of the T was recorded as the range for the allowable response time for the current sampling point $\{A, W\}$.

As shown in [16], the expected success rate for the one-up three-down strategy is 79.4 % and the expected success rate for the one-up one-down strategy is 50 %. These two success rates were used to validate the proposed adaptive algorithm in Sect. 4.

3.3   Adaptive On-Line Controller

As the outcome of the construction session, a range of the allowable response time for each $\{A, W\}$ was recorded. The purpose of this range aimed to account for the fluctuating performance of the user during the on-line attention training process.

An on-line adaptive controller was proposed to dynamically tune the difficulty level of the current trial. In each trial of the validation session, the T is selected as the lower bound if the success rate in the previous trial is greater than the expected success rate. This aims to increase the difficulty level in the current trial. Otherwise, the T is selected as the upper bound if the success rate in the previous trial is lower than the expected success rate. This aims to decrease the difficulty level. Therefore, the actual success rate could be maintained around the expected success rate.

In order to keep the curiosity of the user, a random model for sampling independent variables $\{A, W\}$ in the performance space was adopted, which ensure the variety of the trials during the validation session.

4   Experimental Validation

4.1   Participants

Six adults (4 females, 6 right-handed, mean age = 23 years) participated in the study. All of them were right-handed and had no hearing disorder, visual impairment or somatosensory disorder. All participants gave written consent to participate in the study and each of them received a bonus of ¥ 50 (about \$8) after the whole experiment finished.

4.2   Procedures

The whole experiment includes one construction session and two validation sessions. In the construction session, each user' ability in each pair of $\{A, W\}$ was measured. The searching process introduced in Sect. 3.2 was used to determine the lower and upper bound for each given pair of $\{A, W\}$. During each trial in the searching process, the visual and audio feedback was provided.

In each of the two validation sessions, subjects performed 200 trials with randomized combinations of $\{A, W\}$, and the target finger for each trial was randomized selected from the four fingers. The adaptive algorithm was used to change the T between the upper and lower bound according to users' real-time performance. During each trial in the validation sessions, the visual and audio feedback was provided as explained in Sect. 2.3.

Before the construction session, every participant received a five minutes pilot experiment to get familiar with the system and the stimulus-response task. There was 3 min break between each two adjacent sessions.

4.3 Results

Figure 7(a) show the upper bound and lower bound of allowable response time during the construction session. For all the 16 pairs of $\{A, W\}$, the algorithm effectively found the converged value for the range of the parameter T.

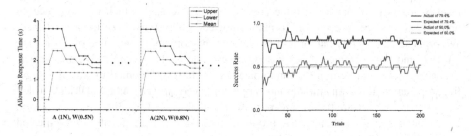

Fig. 7. (a) Convergence process during a construction session. (b) Expected and actual success rate during the validation session of one participant (Color figure online)

Figure 7(b) shows the expected and actual success rate during the validation session of one participant. The actual rate is fluctuating about the expected rate. Figure 8 shows the mean and standard deviation of the actual success rate of all participants during the validation session. The actual success rate is fluctuating about the expected rate, and the largest average error is less than 10 %.

The results show that two different success rates could be achieved by the proposed method. As the previous study [15] pointed out 75 % is the best way to train users, however, there lacks rigorous comparison study on the effect of the success rates for attention training. The proposed algorithm provides a flexible platform for comparing the training effect under different success rates. Based on this platform, we could observe neural signals during the attention process, and thus it is possible to reveal neural mechanism of attentional plasticity under modulation of force-control tasks. Furthermore, the developed system could be used to explore various topics for attention training, such as whether integrating visual and tactile stimuli may result in better performance compared with individual presentations in either modality alone.

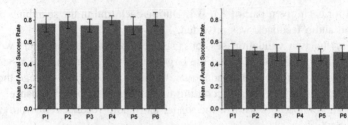

Fig. 8. Mean and std. of the actual success rate of all participants. a) 79.4 %, b) 50 %.

The limitation of the proposed algorithm is that the success rate cannot be adjusted in a continuous scale. Another future research topic is how to make the game more interesting and thus it could be used for training kids with ADHD.

5　Conclusion

In this paper, a visuo-haptic game consisting of stimulus-response tasks with immersive visual display was developed. An adaptive strategy was proposed to tune the difficulty level of the task to match the force control skill of the user, which may produce an optimal success rate in each trial to maintain users' interest and keep them motivated. We proposed an adaptive algorithm to measure the corresponding value of T for each $\{A, W\}$, and thus obtained an expected success rate at the given $\{A, W\}$ in the performance space. Furthermore, a randomized algorithm was adopted to vary the target fingertip, target force magnitude and target tolerance between adjacent trials, which was designed to avoid the boring repetition and thus to keep the users' curiosity. Experimental results validated the proposed method can maintain the two expected success rates.

In the next step, we will use the developed haptic-visuo game to perform multiple-sessions longitudinal studies on ADHD kids to observe the plastic change and retention effect on training sustained attention.

Acknowledgement. This work was supported by the National Natural Science Foundation of China under the grant Nos. 61572055, 61170187 and 61190125.

References

1. Raz, A., Buhle, J.: Typologies of attentional networks. Nat. Rev. Neurosci. **7**(5), 367–379 (2006)
2. Chun, M.M., Golomb, J.D., Turk-Browne, N.B.: A taxonomy of external and internal attention. Annu. Rev. Psychol. **62**, 73–101 (2011)
3. Michel, J.A., Mateer, C.A.: Attention rehabilitation following stroke and traumatic brain injury, a review. Europa Medicophysica **42**, 59–67 (2006)
4. Virk, S., Williams, T., Brunsdon, R., Suh, F., Morrow, A.: Cognitive remediation of attention deficits following acquired brain injury: a systematic review and meta-analysis. Neurorehabilitation **36**, 367–377 (2015)

5. Edkins, G.D., Pollock, C.M.: The Influence of sustained attention on railway accidents. Accid. Anal. Prev. **29**, 533–539 (1997)
6. Debettencourt, M.T., Cohen, J.D., Lee, R.F., Norman, K.A., Turk-Browne, N.B.: Closed-loop training of attention with real-time brain imaging. Nat. Neurosci. **18**(3), 470–475 (2015)
7. Montani, V., De Grazia, M.D.F., Zorzi, M.: A new adaptive videogame for training attention and executive functions: design principles and initial validation. Front. Psychol. **5**, 409 (2014)
8. Franceschini, S., Gori, S., Ruffino, M., Viola, S., Molteni, M., Facoetti, A.: Action video games make dyslexic children read better. Curr. Biol. **23**, 462–466 (2013)
9. Green, C.S., Bavelier, D.: Learning, attentional control, and action video games. Curr. Biol. **22**, R197–R206 (2012)
10. Anguera, J.A., Boccanfuso, J., Rintoul, J.L., Al-Hashimi, O., Faraji, F., Janowich, J., et al.: Video game training enhances cognitive control in older adults. Nature **501**, 97–101 (2013)
11. Dvorkin, A.Y., Ramaiya, M., Larson, E.B., Zollman, F.S., Hsu, N., Pacini, S.: A virtually minimal visuo-haptic training of attention in severe traumatic brain injury. J. Neuroeng. Rehabil. **10**, 9 (2013)
12. Wang, D., Zhang, Y., Yang, X., Yang, G., Yang, Y.: Force control tasks with pure haptic feedback promote short-term focused attention. IEEE Trans. Haptics **7**(4), 467–476 (2014)
13. Rizzo, A.A., Buckwalter, J.G., Bowerly, T., Zaag, C.V.D., Humphrey, L., Neumann, U., et al.: The virtual classroom: a virtual reality environment for the assessment and rehabilitation of attention deficits. Cyberpsychology Behav. **3**, 483–499 (2000)
14. Li, T., Wang, D., Zhang, S., Zhang, Y., Yu, C.: Speed-accuracy tradeoff of controlling absolute magnitude of fingertip force. In: The 6th Joint Eurohaptics Conference and IEEE Haptics Symposium. US, Chicago (2015)
15. Wilson, A.J., Dehaene, S., Pinel, P., Revkin, S.K., Cohen, L., Cohen, D.: An adaptive computer game for remediation of dyscalculia. Behav. Brain Funct. **2**, 1 (2006)
16. Jones, L.A., Tan, H.Z.: Application of psychophysical techniques to haptic research. IEEE Trans. Haptics **6**, 268–284 (2013)

Deaf-Blind Can Practise Horse Riding with the Help of Haptics

Matjaž Ogrinc[1,2(✉)], Ildar Farkhatdinov[1], Rich Walker[2], and Etienne Burdet[1]

[1] Department of Bioengineering, Imperial College of Science,
Technology and Medicine, London SW72AZ, UK
{matjaz.ogrinc,i.farkhatdinov,e.burdet}@imperial.ac.uk
[2] Shadow Robot Company LTD., London N11LX, UK
{matjaz,rw}@shadowrobot.com

Abstract. This paper introduces the first haptic interface to help blind and deaf-blind people to practice horse riding as a sportive, recreational and therapeutic activity. As a form of animal assisted therapy, horse riding has been shown to benefit people with various medical conditions. Among other benefits, horse riding can improve self-esteem and a sensation of independence. However, in the case of deaf-blind individuals a therapist or an interpreter must be present at all times to communicate with the rider by touch. We developed a novel interface which enables deaf-blind people to ride a horse while the therapist is observing and remotely providing cues to the rider, which improves his independence. Initial tests of the concept with an autistic deaf-blind individual received very positive feedback from the rider, his family and therapist.

Keywords: Vibrotactile · Rehabilitation · Navigation · Deaf-blind

1 Introduction

We present a haptic interface which enable deaf-blind individuals to enjoy recreational, therapeutic and sportive horse riding. According to the World Health Organisation the world's blind population is about 39 millions [7]. For deaf-blind, accurate global statistics are not available, although there are around 50,000 deaf-blind individuals in USA only [2]. Assistive technology may remedy the difficulties of the blind and deaf [2,12], and enable them to overcome communication barriers and improve their independence. When two key sensory modalities are impaired as in deaf-blind people, tactile interfaces present a great potential to bridge the interaction difficulties. In recent years, extensive work has been done on assistive haptic interfaces, including wearable and portable devices, such as the *Lorm glove* human-computer interface [5] which enables exchanging of messages using the Lorm alphabet. Similarly, the *dbGLOVE* enables bidirectional communication based on the Malossi alphabet [1].

A number of devices for spatial orientation and navigation based on tactors have been demonstrated in recent years which have potential in applications for

© Springer International Publishing Switzerland 2016
F. Bello et al. (Eds.): EuroHaptics 2016, Part I, LNCS 9774, pp. 452–461, 2016.
DOI: 10.1007/978-3-319-42321-0_42

deaf and deaf-blind users [2]. Nagel et al. developed a compass which presents a directional information using a vibrotactile belt [6]. Another example is the ActiveBelt system which also provides directional cues by delivering vibrations to the waist and employs GPS signals [10]. However, despite the active research in developing interfaces for the blind and deaf-blind, many of the interfaces have never advanced beyond the prototype stage. Commercial solutions are often limited to human-computer communication applications (most commonly Braille interfaces). Though new technologies such as shape memory alloy may facilitate the development of low cost and compact Braille displays [9], for activities such as horse riding a hands free communication interface is required.

Development of novel technologies for deaf-blind users which will enable them to practice various life activities is critical, as the barriers in communication and social interaction caused by deaf-blindness can lead to a number of health-related difficulties, including high risk of depression, cognitive decline, developmental disorder in children and psychological distress [3]. Deaf-blind also affects the ability to achieve autonomous living, independent mobility and social inclusion.

Horse riding is a form of animal assisted therapy known to have positive effects on the physical and mental health of riders who have disabilities. It is widely used in occupational therapy for people with disabilities including the blind and deaf-blind population. Riding improves physical strength and posture, and commanding such a large animal that responds to one's cues also improves self-esteem [4]. Though people with disability can benefit from activities such as horse riding, their disability often prevents them from practicing it, in particular in the case of blindness and deaf-blindness.

To our knowledge there are no technologies available on the market to assist blind or deaf-blind people during horse riding. The high cost of technical solutions for people with disabilities available on the market and interfaces' limited functionality to work mainly with computers makes practice of animal based therapy difficult and inaccessible for the deaf-blind. To address these limitations we propose a novel haptic communication system giving a deaf-blind person an ability to command a horse independently, rather than through physically guidance from the instructor. The interface is conceived to provide tactile stimulation to deaf-blind rider's arms. Next section describes the interface design. Then we present results of psychophysical study to investigate the users reaction time to the tactile stimuli used in the interface. The paper concludes with the results and discussion on field tests with horse riding.

2   Tactile Interface for Horse Riding

2.1   Overview

In the conventional way for deaf-blind horse riding the rider either passively rides the horse while it is guided by the instructor, or the rider controls the reins while the instructor communicates the cues to the rider by touch. An interpreter with the knowledge of sign tactile language is required to facilitate communication between the rider and horse riding instructor, as shown in Fig. 1.

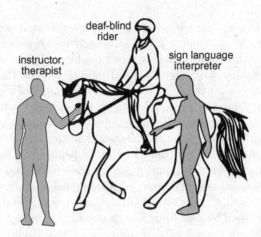

Fig. 1. In traditional therapy the sign language interpreter is required to bridge the communication barrier between the instructor and the rider.

This conventional therapy cannot produce maximal positive therapeutic effect on the rider, who remains dependent on direct proximity of the therapist or interpreter. Thus the rider cannot enjoy the sense of control and independence.

To provide a remote communication between the deaf-blind rider and an instructor or therapist we propose to use a simple set of tactile instructions and simulators attached to the riders arms. Our system includes two vibrotactile actuators (tactors) worn by the rider which are wirelessly controlled by a riding instructor/therapist with the help of a custom designed Android smartphone application. With our system, the deaf-blind rider is able to command a horse based on wirelessly transmitted commands perceived via vibrotactile stimulation. The rider wears the vibration motors on his upper arms. While a motor is active, the rider pulls the reins in a way to direct the horse in the corresponding direction, i.e. continuous vibration on the right arm corresponds to instruction to pull the reins with the right hand. The proposed system enhances the level of control the rider has over the horse as the instructor is not physically interacting with the horse or the rider, but sends only high level commands. The concept is illustrated in Fig. 2.

After consultation with Riding for Disabled Association UK (RDA) we compiled a basic list of commands used by the instructors in horse riding with deaf-blind users. The basic commands are: "go", "stop", "turn left" and "turn right". We defined a tactile stimulation combinations for each of the vibration motors (left and right upper arms) in accordance to selected basic commands. A short simultaneous vibration (1 s) of both actuators instructs the rider to command the horse forwards (command 'go' to start the movement). A long simultaneous vibration (2 s) of both actuators stands for "stop". Vibration on either arm suggests a turn in the respective direction. The rider pulls on the reins accordingly

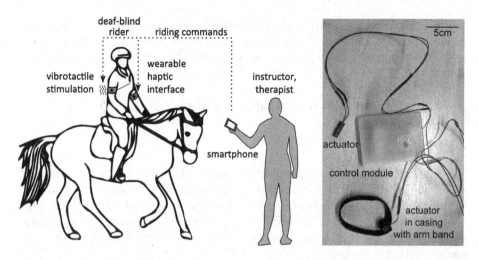

Fig. 2. The instructor communicates messages to the rider remotely using the proposed wireless interface (left). Photo of the interface consisting of a wireless control module and two actuators (right).

as long as the stimulation is present. The mapping of stimulation to command mapping is explained to a deaf-blind user before riding. Based on our experience, learning of this mapping is straightforward as it is sufficient to explain these commands only once.

2.2 Technical Specification

The model 307-100 Precision Microdrives (UK) vibration motors were selected to display haptic instructions to a deaf-blind rider. The actuators were encapsulated in a robust plastic case and attached to wearable textile straps for convenience. The rise and stop times for the selected motors are 34 and 73 ms respectively, which is sufficient for our application. The motors were powered from a control module carried in a rider's pocket. The control module contains the logic and communication electronics. The design of the control module enables simultaneous control of up to six actuator modules. The communication subsystem of the control module connects to a host mobile device (smartphone or computer) via Bluetooth communication protocol using the RN42 bluetooth module (Roving Networks Inc). The device is powered by a 3.7 V LiPO rechargeable battery. The MOSFET transistors operating as switches amplify the PWM signals generated using an Arduino Pro Mini. The data exchange with the host device is implemented with the standard serial communication protocol at 38400 baud rate.

An Android OS application has been developed for controlling the interface. Graphical user interface of the application consisted of buttons which triggered the basic instructions described in previous subsection. Additionally, the application has functionality to set the vibration intensity to a comfortable to a user level. The proposed interface is low cost: excluding the cost of an Android mobile device, the total cost of the prototype is under £50.

3   Experimental Evaluation: Response Time to Stimulation

3.1   Method

We first evaluated the time required to initiate the arm pulling movement as a reaction to vibrotactile cue applied to the subjects upper arm on a group of healthy subjects. This response time is critical for deaf-blind riders who should react fast enough to haptic instructions in order to prevent dangerous situations such as collisions. It is necessary that a rider be able to stop the horse fast enough during dressage.

In the experiment we compared three sensory modalities as triggers for arm pulling movements: visual, auditory and haptic. The visual condition can be seen as riding by a healthy user who plans motion based on visual understanding of the environment. The auditory condition can be regarded as riding by a blind user who receives instructions via voice commands. The haptic-only scenario corresponds to a deaf-blind rider who relies only on vibrotactile cues to perform actions.

For this study we recruited six healthy right handed adults (aged between 27 and 33 years old, with 1 female) without any previous experience with the particular device. The participants seated at a desk with their right arm resting on the desktop. They were asked to pull back their arm as if they were pulling the reins of a horse once they detect the sensory cue.

In the visual condition an LED light was positioned on the desktop in front of the subject wearing audio-cancellation ear plugs and headphones. In the case of auditory condition, the sound was created by the vibration motor sitting on the desktop and was loud enough to be easily detected in the quiet experimental environment. As in the case of the visual condition, during the haptic trials the subjects wore noise cancellation ear plugs and headphones with vibrotactile actuator of the proposed interface attached to the right upper arm. The actuator was driven at the nominal voltage of 3 V.

Ten trials for each sensory condition were repeated during the experiment for each subject. Sensory cue in each trial was triggered by the experimenter at random time instants. The motion of the subjects' upper arm was recorded using a wireless inertial measurement unit (IMU MTw, XSens, Enschede, Netherlands) and was also synchronised with the sensory cue activation signal which was simultaneously recorded with the data acquisition system of the IMU.

3.2   Results

The IMU on a subject's upper arm measured acceleration of the limb in anterior posterior direction. The recorded arm's acceleration was used to detect the time of movement initiation for each sensory cue. The results are shown in Fig. 3. The first three plots show the time series of the arm acceleration of a typical subject for visual, audio and haptic conditions respectively. By comparing the magnitude of the acceleration against a predefined threshold we obtained time instances when the arm movements started. The acceleration threshold was predefined empirically based on the levels of noise and fluctuations in the acceleration measurements when the subjects were asked to keep their arm still. The threshold was set to $0.4\,m/s^2$. The identified movement starting points are shown with thick grey markers in the time history plots of Fig. 3. The right panel of Fig. 3 presents the means and standard deviations of the reaction time over all trials and subjects per condition. We analysed the data over all subject. Small differences were observed in response time per subjects within the same experimental condition. The mean delays were 243 ± 62 ms (mean $\pm$ std), 185 ± 55 ms and 199 ± 57 ms for visual, auditory and haptic modality respectively. Mean delays over all trials and all subjects were compared using an ANOVA test which showed that the means were not significantly different ($p > 0.05$). However, slightly larger delay in the case of vision agrees with previous work, visual perception is known to be slower compared to audition and haptics [11]. The reaction time measurements in haptic case were at similar levels to the visual and auditory conditions which means that usage of simple tactile stimulation for providing instructions will not delay the response time, assuming that the tactile mapping for instructions is easy enough to interpret by the rider. In the next section we show that the proposed tactile mapping of riding instruction can be successfully used in real horse riding.

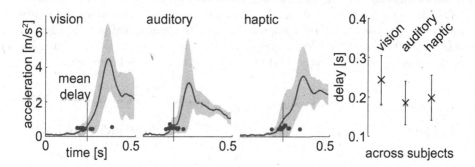

Fig. 3. Time history of recorded arm's acceleration for a typical subject for three conditions. Mean and standard deviation (shaded area) are shown. The thick grey markers represent the time instants the acceleration as it exceeds the threshold for motion detection. The rightmost panel shows the mean and standard deviation across all subjects.

4   A Feasibility Study on Deaf-Blind Riding

4.1   Method

Subjects and Protocol. In collaboration with RDA we tested our tactile guidance system in real horse riding. A healthy subject (female, age 22 years old) and an autistic deaf-blind rider (male, aged 31, complete deaf and blindness since childhood) participated in a study where we experimentally evaluated the performance of riding with the proposed tactile interface. Both subjects were experienced in riding. The tests were performed in a riding arena with the same horse. The subject wore our tactile interface which was remotely controlled via a smart phone by a professional riding coach. The subjects received all required information on the tactile mapping commands and carried out familiarisation trials. The vibration amplitude was adjusted for each participant so that the cues were clear and not uncomfortable. A deaf-blind tactile language interpreter facilitated communication with the second subject. All required safety regulations were observed during the tests and permission from the family of the deaf-blind rider was obtained. An XSens wireless IMU module was attached to the subject's trunk to track their motion (sampling rate 75 Hz) which enabled us to reconstruct their trajectories.

In the first test the healthy subject was asked to ride a horse following tactile instructions sent by the instructor standing approximately 10 m away from the horse. The sequence of commands sent to the rider was: go, right (short duration), right (long duration), stop. The timing between the commands was 3–5 s. This test included 5 trials.

In the second test, the autistic deaf-blind subject was asked to ride the horse following the sequence of commands send by the coach. As this was a feasibility test we did not use a repeatable sequence as with the healthy subject. The goal of this feasibility test was to demonstrate that our tactile communication interface could be safely and efficiently used by deaf-blind to practice horse riding.

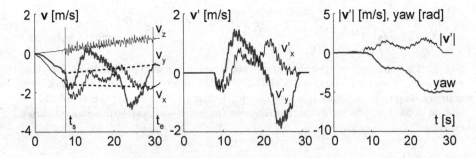

Fig. 4. Position estimation by double integration of acceleration. Integrated accelerometer output (left), compensated velocity as a result of acceleration integration (middle), velocity magnitude and yaw angle (right).

Trajectory Estimation. The Xsens MTx IMU measured translational acceleration, angular velocity and magnetic field which provided angular orientation after internal fusion with angular velocity measurements. It is common practice to obtain the position by double integration of acceleration. However, the bias in the noise present in acceleration measurement introduces drift in the velocity with the integration. This is shown in the left panel of Fig. 4. As the initial and final velocities at t_s and t_e respectively should be zero, we can compensate for this phenomenon. To obtain the drift-free velocity v' we subtract the estimated drift (dotted black lines). The middle panel of Fig. 4 shows the horizontal components of the velocity vector v'. This procedure of drift compensation is commonly used in gait analysis, where the compensation is executed at each step to correct the acceleration measurement during the swing phase [8]. Finally, the position vector is obtained as $p(k) = f_s^{-1} \sum_0^k \|v'(k)\| [\cos(yaw(k)), \sin(yaw(k))]^T$, where f_s is sampling rate, $yaw(k)$ is measured angular orientation, and time at sample k is $t(k) = k/f_s$.

4.2   Results

We reconstructed the movement trajectories for the tests with the healthy (Fig. 5 left) and the deaf-blind (Fig. 5 right) riders. In the left panel of Fig. 5 one can observe the two right turns and the straight path section which correspond to the commanded instructions. As expected, the first right turn (short cue) resulted in a smaller change of direction. The trajectories were smooth and similar to each other which means that the rider was able to interpret and implement the instructions well in all cases. The mean length of the trajectories was $19.2 + 3.4$ m (mean±std). The mean duration of each trial was 21.8 ± 0.9 s. The average velocity was 3.2 km/h.

In the second test the trial consisted of the sequence of left and right turns commanded by the coach and the resulting trajectory corresponded well to the instructions. A photo of the subject during the test is shown in Fig. 5. The movement was smooth and there were no unexpected pauses and faults during the trial. The average velocity was 4.88 km/h which is slightly larger than for a healthy subject. This can perhaps be explained by longer straight sections of the trajectory that allowed for high speed. The results show that with the help of our tactile communication interface a deaf-blind person can command a horse independently.

We interviewed the deaf-blind-autistic subject and his therapist (who is also his horse riding instructor) to obtain their feedback about the usage of the proposed tactile interface. The subject involved in this study has been using the interface for a period of five months, in weekly sessions. He took part in a UK national dressage competition for disabled riders prior the tests and interview reported in this paper. The overall feedback from the subject and the therapist was very positive. The subject was able to learn the tactile mapping quickly from the first use and required no dedicated learning in later sessions. The instructions were easy to understand and to realise. The subject felt confident and safe during horse riding with the help of the tactile interface. Feedback from the

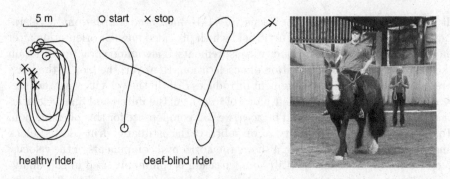

Fig. 5. Estimated trajectories of trials of the healthy (left) and the deaf-blind rider (middle). The photo shows the autistic deaf-blind rider and the instructor using the smartphone interface in the background.

therapist indicated that the subject was enjoying the riding session with the tactile interface more than the conventional one, as he felt to directly control the horse.

5   Conclusion

We have presented a novel haptic interface which enables deaf-blind people to practice horse riding. It is one of the forms of therapy used in deaf-blind and autistic people rehabilitation to improve their mental and physical condition. We have tested the designed tactile communication interface with an autistic deaf-blind rider and the outcome of the tests was very positive. The rider was able to understand the provided haptic cues easily and to control the horse safely and efficiently. The interface has been well accepted by the rider, his family and the therapist.

The results presented in the paper are initial but very promising. In future, we plan to improve the ergonomics of the interface and introduce it to a larger number of users. The presented study suggests that haptic interfaces are the only efficient mean of communication for deaf-blind communities for practising sports as therapeutic and recreational activities.

Acknowledgment. This work is supported by the European Commission under EU-FP7 grants PITN-GA-2012-317488-CONTEST, ICT-601003 BALANCE, ICT-2013-10 SYMBITRON and H2020 ICT 644727 COGIMON. We would like to than Doug Smith from RDA for fruitful discussions and assistance during the tests.

References

1. Caporusso, N.: A wearable malossi alphabet interface for deafblind people. In: Proceedings of the Working Conference on Advanced Visual Interfaces, pp. 445–448. ACM (2008)
2. Caporusso, N., Trizio, M., Perrone, G.: Pervasive assistive technology for the deaf-blindneed, emergency and assistance through the sense of touch. In: Holzinger, A., Ziee, M., Rcker, C. (eds.) Pervasive Health. Human Computer Interaction Series, pp. 289–316. Springer, London (2014)
3. Dammeyer, J.: Deafblindness: a review of the literature. Scand. J. Public Health **42**, 554–562 (2014)
4. Fine, A.H.: Handbook on Animal-Assisted Therapy: Theoretical Foundations and Guidelines for Practice. Academic Press, Cambridge (2010)
5. Gollner, U., Bieling, T., Joost, G.: Mobile lorm glove: introducing a communication device for deaf-blind people. In: Proceedings of the Sixth International Conference on Tangible, Embedded and Embodied Interaction, pp. 127–130. ACM (2012)
6. Nagel, S.K., Carl, C., Kringe, T., Märtin, R., König, P.: Beyond sensory substitution - learning the sixth sense. J. Neural Eng. **2**(4), R13 (2005)
7. World Health Organisation: Visual Impairment and Blindness (2014). http://www.who.int/mediacentre/factsheets/fs282/en/
8. Sabatini, A.M., Martelloni, C., Scapellato, S., Cavallo, F.: Assessment of walking features from foot inertial sensing. IEEE Trans. Biomed. Eng. **52**(3), 486–494 (2005)
9. Sawada, H., Zhao, F., Uchida, K.: Displaying braille for mobile use with the microvibration of sma wires. In: 2012 5th International Conference on Human System Interactions (HSI), pp. 124–129, June 2012
10. Tsukada, K., Yasumura, M.: ActiveBelt: belt-type wearable tactile display for directional navigation. In: Mynatt, E.D., Sno, I. (eds.) UbiComp 2004. LNCS, vol. 3205, pp. 384–399. Springer, Heidelberg (2004)
11. Wolfe, J.M., Kluender, K.R., Levi, D.M., Bartoshuk, L.M., Herz, R.S., Klatzky, R.L., Lederman, S.J., Merfeld, D.M.: Sensation and Perception. Sinauer, Sunderland (2012)
12. Ziefle, M., Röcker, C., Holzinger, A.: Current trends and challenges for pervasive health technologies: from technical innovation to user integration. In: Ziefle, M., Röcker, C., Holzinger, A. (eds.) Pervasive Health. State-of-the Art and Beyond, pp. 1–18. Springer, London (2014)

Perceptual Force on the Wrist Under the Hanger Reflex and Vibration

Takuto Nakamura[1]([✉]), Narihiro Nishimura[1], Taku Hachisu[2],
Michi Sato[1], Vibol Yem[1], and Hiroyuki Kajimoto[1]

[1] The University of Electro-Communications,
1-5-1 Chofugaoka, Chofu, Tokyo, Japan
{n.takuto,n-nishimura,michi,yem,kajimoto}@kaji-lab.jp
[2] The University of Tsukuba, 1-1-1 Tennodai, Tsukuba-shi, Ibaraki, Japan
hachisu@ai.iit

Abstract. The hanger reflex is a phenomenon that accompanies illusory force sensation and involuntary head rotation when the head is fastened with a wire hanger. This phenomenon is also observed on the wrist, and is expected to apply when using small and simple haptic feedback devices. However, issues of slow response and the requirement for large actuators still remain. Here, we discuss the discovery of a new phenomenon: the perceptual force from the hanger reflex is enhanced when a vibration is also presented. If we can control the strength of the perceptual force induced by vibration, a smaller, simpler, and higher response device might be achieved, because a vibrator can be controlled easily. This paper reports details of this phenomenon, and the effect of the frequency and amplitude of the vibration on the strength of the perceptual force. We observed that low frequency (50–100 Hz) vibrations efficiently enhanced the perceptual force, and that participants perceived a stronger perceptual force if the vibration of a greater amplitude was presented. These results suggest that the enhancement of the perceptual force is controllable and can be applied to construct a new type of wearable haptic device.

Keywords: Hanger reflex · Haptic display · Perceptual illusion · Skin stretch

1 Introduction

While haptic cues are considered important in many areas such as sports training, remote control and VR gaming, conventional haptic devices commonly require large and expensive equipment, which limit their potential application areas.

To solve this problem, some methods have been proposed for presenting a "perceptual force" by using perceptual illusions [1–3]. These methods allow the use of compact and inexpensive devices, because they do not need to reproduce an actual force. However, there is a limitation on the strength of the perceptual force induced by these devices.

To produce a strong perceptual force using a perceptual illusion, we focused on the "hanger reflex". The hanger reflex is a perceptual illusion in which the head rotates involuntarily when it is fastened with a wire hanger [4]. During the hanger reflex,

© Springer International Publishing Switzerland 2016
F. Bello et al. (Eds.): EuroHaptics 2016, Part I, LNCS 9774, pp. 462–471, 2016.
DOI: 10.1007/978-3-319-42321-0_43

Fig. 1. Presenting the vibration on the wrist under the hanger reflex: The force caused by the hanger reflex is enhanced, and it induces the wrist rotation

people feel a strong perceptual force, and rotate their heads. Because of its strength of the perceptual force, the hanger reflex has been expected to apply to pseudo force display. However, the device is still too large to control skin deformation, and time response is poor.

While seeking solution to these issues, we discovered a new phenomenon: the strength of the hanger reflex on the wrist is enhanced by additionally applying vibration (Fig. 1). Because the enhancement changes by changing the characteristics of the vibration, this phenomenon might be used to control the strength of the hanger reflex with a simple setup, and the time response of the device might be improved. Based on these experiments, this paper reports the details of this phenomenon, and the basic characteristics of its frequency and amplitude dependence.

2   Related Work

Nowadays, several force displays are commercially available [5–7], which present an actual force to the user through a grounded device. While these devices succeed in producing a high-quality force sense, they have several limitations such as limited workspace and relatively high cost. Several wearable force displays, which do not limit the movement of the user, have also been proposed [8], but these devices typically become complicated.

To achieve small and low-cost devices, techniques that use perceptual force illusions have been proposed. Visually induced haptic sensations, known as pseudohaptics, have been intensively studied [9, 10]. Amemiya and Gomi [2] and Rekimoto [3] used the non-linearity of human perception and produced force sensations by presenting asymmetric acceleration. These devices do not present a physical force, but do induce a perceptual force by stimulating other senses, thereby achieving small and low-cost devices. However, the strength of the perceptual force induced by these devices is limited, and hence, applications using these devices are limited, such as navigation.

To produce a strong perceptual force using a perceptual illusion, we focused on the hanger reflex. The hanger reflex is a perceptual force illusion in which the head rotates involuntary when it is fastened with a wire hanger. Sato et al. [4] found "sweet spots" on the head by measuring the pressure distribution on the head under the hanger reflex and showed that the direction of lateral skin stretch contributes to the direction of the hanger reflex [11]. In addition, the hanger reflex has been observed not only on the head but also on the wrist and waist [12].

Previous studies [13] have reported that skin deformation generates force perception, and this has been used as an interface [1, 14–16]. The hanger reflex might be regarded as one type of such illusion, but it is characterized by its strong force that induces the involuntary head rotation. Sato et al. [4] developed a device that reproduces the pressure distribution of the hanger reflex, and controls the direction of the hanger reflex. Naka-mura et al. [17] also developed a similar device for the wrist, which presses the "sweet spots" on the wrist found by measuring the pressure distribution. However, these devices use actuators that are large in size and poor in response time to present pressure.

3 System for Enhancement of the Perceptual Force from the Hanger Reflex

Our new finding was that a vibration applied to the hanger enhances the hanger reflex. To test this finding, we developed a new device. The device mainly consists of a "hanger device" that generates the hanger reflex on the wrist (Fig. 2), and two vibrators (HaptuatorMark2, Tactile Labs Inc.). The "hanger device" is made of an aluminum bar bent in a U-shape, and it is adjustable to fit to any size of wrist. A urethane sheet is placed inside the device, which directly contacts the skin to protect it (Fig. 2). Figure 3 shows how the hanger device generates the hanger reflex.

1. First, the user mounts the hanger device on their wrist.
2. Second, by rotating the device slightly, the device is deformed elastically, and pushes the "sweet spots" of the hanger reflex found in the previous work [17]. Because the vectors of the pressure from the device do not cancel each other, the device generates rotational moment.
3. The device tries to rotate the wrist, but the friction between the device and the wrist stops the device, and deforms the skin of the wrist.
4. As a result of a perceptual illusion, the user perceives the skin deformation as an external rotational force.

The vibrators mounted on the hanger device are able to vibrate the whole device, so that the user perceives both the vibration and hanger reflex on the wrist. An audio

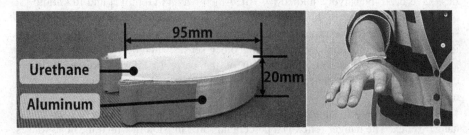

Fig. 2. The "hanger device" that induces the hanger reflex on the wrist

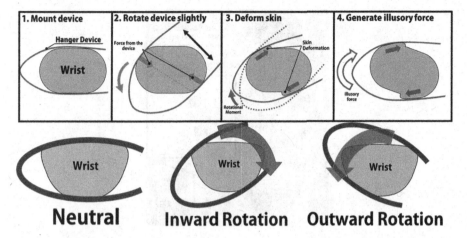

Fig. 3. Mechanism of the hanger device: by changing the direction, the device can induce illusory force in two directions

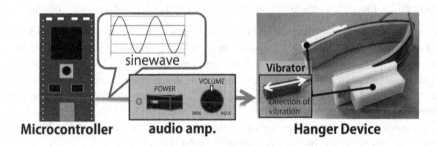

Fig. 4. System configuration of the hanger device used in the experiment

amplifier (RSDA202, RASTEME SYSTEMS Inc.), and a microcontroller (mbed LPC1768, NXP Inc.) are used to generate the vibrations (Fig. 4).

In our preliminary test with several laboratory members, they felt the enhanced force only while the vibration was being presented. They also commented that "when the acceleration amplitude of the vibration is increased, the enhancement rate of the force was also increased". When we turned the vibration on and off periodically, we observed that the participants involuntarily rotated their wrist every time they received stimulation. Based on these comments and observations, we expect that this phenomenon is capable of solving the issues of previous hanger reflex devices.

4   Experiment 1: Effect of Frequency

The purpose of the first experiment was to investigate the effect of vibration frequency on the perceptual force of the hanger reflex. We compared the perceptual strength of force between the hanger reflex only condition and the hanger reflex with vibration

Fig. 5. Participant and mounted devices

condition using the method of magnitude estimation. This experiment has been approved by the ethics committee of the University of Electro-Communications.

Setup. The system described in the last section (Fig. 4) was used to present vibration and the hanger reflex to the participants' wrist. We prepared four sinusoidal waves of different frequencies and the same acceleration amplitude of 0.20G. To standardize the acceleration amplitude of the waves, we used the accelerometer to measure the acceleration and adjusted the value to 0.20G. To measure the posture of the hand during the experiment, we mounted a motion sensor (MPU-9150, InvenSense Inc.), which consists of a 3-axi acceleration sensor, a 3-axi gyro sensor, and a 3-axi geomagnetic sensor, on the back of participants' hand (Fig. 5).

Procedures. The participants were six laboratory members (all male, age range: 21 to 25). Before the experiment, all participants confirmed whether the hanger reflex occurred on their wrist. Only those who experienced the effect of the hanger reflex on their wrist participated the experiment. Before starting the experiment, we instructed the participants to wear the hanger device on their left wrist, and to mount the motion sensor on their back of their left hand. To mask auditory cues, we asked the participants to wear noise canceling headphones and listen to white noise. During the experiment, we instructed the participants to wait while allowing their left arms to sag, to relax, and not to look at their hands. The vibration presentation time was six seconds.

After presentation, we asked the participant to estimate the perceived force as a numerical value. They were asked to assume that the perceived force from only the hanger reflex (initial state) was "100", and to express the perceived force from the hanger reflex superimposed by the vibration as a numerical value. For example, if the participant felt a stronger force from the hanger reflex plus vibration than the force from the hanger reflex alone, the participant would give an answer like "110" or "120". Conversely, if the participant felt a weaker force, they would give an answer like "90" or "80".

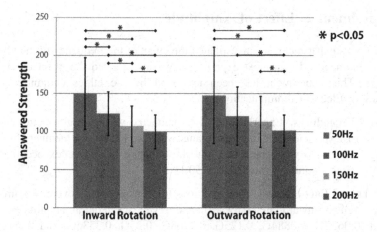

Fig. 6. The average values of answered strength in each frequency

Conditions. There were two directions of hanger reflex (inward and outward), four frequencies of vibration (50 Hz, 100 Hz, 150 Hz, and 200 Hz), and each condition was repeated ten times. Therefore, 80 trials were conducted for each participant. We divided the experiment into an "inward session" and an "outward session", and took at least a two-hour rest interval between each session. In each session, the vibration frequencies were presented randomly. The order of the two sessions was balanced between participants. To prevent adaptation to the vibration, the participants rested for at least 30 s after every eight trials.

Results and Discussion. Figure 6 shows the results of the experiment. The vertical axis represents the average value of the answers, and the horizontal axis represents the frequency of the vibration. The error bar represents the standard deviation. Because of the number of participants, we analyzed the data with non-parametric tests. As heteroscedasticity was observed, we used the Kruskal-Wallis test for this analysis. The results of the test showed a main effect of each session (df = 3, χ^2 = 93.5564, p < 0.01 and df = 3, χ^2 = 36.9429, p < 0.01 for the inward and outward sessions, respectively). Post-hoc tests (Steel-Dwass test) showed that for the inward hanger reflex, there were significant differences between 50 Hz and {100 Hz, 150 Hz, 200 Hz}, 100 Hz and {150 Hz, 200 Hz}, and 150 Hz and {200 Hz} (p < 0.05). For the outward hanger reflex, there were significant differences between 50 Hz and {150 Hz, 200 Hz}, 100 Hz and {200 Hz}, and 150 Hz and {200 Hz} (p < 0.05).

From the results, the answered value was the highest when the frequency of vibration was 50 Hz for both the inward and outward directions. The value became lower and was almost equal to the standard (100) when the frequency was 200 Hz. Several participants also reported that a vibration with a lower frequency gave a stronger perceptual force. Conversely, they reported that a vibration with a higher frequency reduced the perceptual force. These results and reports suggested that a vibration with a lower frequency efficiently enhances the perceptual force from the hanger reflex.

5   Experiment 2: Effect of Amplitude

In the previous experiment, we investigated the effect of the frequency of the vibration on the phenomenon. In the next experiment, we investigated the effect of vibration amplitude. This experiment has been approved by the ethics committee of the University of Electro-Communications.

Setup and Procedures. Experiment 2 was conducted with the same setup and procedures as in Experiment 1. The participants were six laboratory members (all male, age range: 21 to 24) who confirmed that the effect of hanger reflex occurred their wrists. Vibration frequency was fixed to 50 Hz.

Conditions and Participants. The conditions for this experiment were two directions of hanger reflex (inward and outward), and seven acceleration amplitudes of the vibration (0.0625G, 0.0884G, 0.125G, 0.1768G, 0.25G, 0.3536G, and 0.5G). Each condition was repeated five times. Therefore, 75 trials were conducted for each participant.

The same way as in Experiment 1, we divided the experiment into an "inward session" and an "outward session", and the time interval between these sessions was at least two hours. In each session, the order of the vibrations' conditions was random. To prevent the wrist from adapting to the vibration, the participants rested for at least 30 s after every seven trials.

Results and Discussion. Figure 7 shows the results of the experiment. The vertical axis represents the average value of the participants' answers, and the horizontal axis represents the acceleration amplitudes of the vibration. The error bar represents the standard deviation. The data were analyzed using non-parametric tests and heteroscedasticity was observed. The Kruskal-Wallis test showed that the main effect of

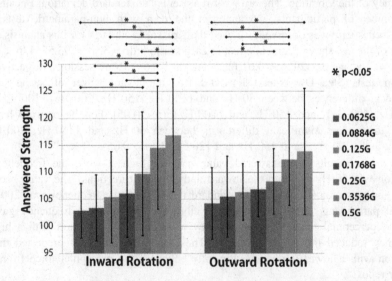

Fig. 7. The average values of answered strength in each acceleration amplitude

acceleration amplitude was significant for each session (df = 6, χ^2 = 58.0891, p < 0.01 and df = 6, χ^2 = 34.7814, p < 0.01 for the inward and outward sessions, respectively). Post-hoc tests (Steel-Dwass test) showed that, for the inward hanger reflex, there were significant differences between 0.5G and {0.0625G, 0.0884G, 0.125G, 0.1768G, 0.25G}, 0.3536G and {0.0625G, 0.0884G, 0.125G, 0.1768G}, 0.25G and {0.0625G} (p < 0.05 for all). For the outward hanger reflex, there were significant differences between 0.5G and {0.0625G}, 0.3536G and {0.0625G, 0.0884G, 0.125G}, and 0.25G and {0.0625G} (p < 0.05 for all).

The graph suggests that the participants perceived a stronger perceptual force if a vibration of a greater amplitude was presented. According to post-experimental questioning, there were some participants who noticed multiple strengths of the perceptual forces and were able to clearly distinguish them. Thus, these results and reports suggest that we can control the strength of the perceptual force by changing the acceleration amplitude.

6 Discussion

In both experiments, the average values were greater than "100", a perceptual force caused by the hanger reflex alone, and it suggests that the vibration really enhances the perceptual force caused by the hanger reflex. In addition, in Experiment 1, the perceptual force increased as the frequency of the presented vibration lower. In Experiment 2, the perceptual force increased as the amplitude of the presented vibration increased. These results suggest both frequency and amplitude can change the enhancement of the perceptual force. Therefore, to change the enhancement more efficiently, the user should change both frequency and amplitude simultaneously. To present greater force, the frequency should be lower and the amplitude should be bigger. Also, to enhance a little, the frequency should be higher and the amplitude should be smaller.

In addition to the discussion of experiments, we will discuss why this phenomenon occurs when both hanger reflex and vibration were presented based on the experimental results above. Nonlinearity of perception is a possible candidate for this illusion. The induction of pseudo-forces using the nonlinearity of perception has been researched by presenting asymmetrical acceleration [2] [3]. In these studies, a strong and short acceleration was perceived as stronger than a weak and long acceleration, resulting in a directional force illusion. In our case, the skin is deformed in one direction by the hanger reflex, which provides a kind of offset. When the vibration is superimposed on the skin, the vibration increases or decreases the offset skin deformation. At this time, the participants might perceive a stimulus that increases skin deformation as stronger, either by perceptual reasoning or via the nonlinearity of skin elasticity. Thus, without using an asymmetric vibration, our method succeeded in presenting a unidirectional force illusion.

The other possible candidate is illusory kinesthesia, which is a phenomenon reported by Goodwin et al. [18]. It is a perceptual illusion that occurs when a vibration of around 70 Hz is presented to the tendon, resulting in a feeling as if the vibrated part of the body was bent, even it was not. In addition, Cordo et al. [19] reported that if people perceive passive motion during illusory kinesthesis, the sensation of the illusory kinesthesis is enhanced. In our study, we presented the vibration to the wrist, not to the elbow that previous studies presented. However, there is a muscle called the "pronator quadratus" in the wrist that twists the arm. Thus, the enhancement of the force from the hanger reflex occurs because of illusory kinesthesia. Furthermore, as reported by Cordo et al., passive motion during the illusory kinesthesis strengthen the illusion. In our case, the hanger reflex might have acted as this passive motion, and enhanced the perceptual force.

7   Conclusion and Future Work

In this paper, we reported the characteristics of the enhancement phenomenon that can be used to control the strength of the perceptual force. This phenomenon enhances the perceptual force induced by the hanger reflex when a vibration is also presented to the wrist. From the results of the experiment investigating the effect of frequency, we observed that a 50 Hz–100 Hz sinewave enhanced the perceptual force the most. The results of the experiment investigating the effect of amplitude suggested that the participants perceived a stronger perceptual force if a vibration of a greater amplitude was presented. These results suggest the possibility of controlling the perceptual force by changing the amplitude of the presented vibration.

In future work, we will develop a device that controls the perceptual force, as well as the direction. Figure 8 shows a sample design of the device using the phenomenon we reported in this paper. To control the user's wrist bidirectionally, we use two hanger reflex devices, and wear them in the opposite direction to counter the effect that each one provides. After that preparation, vibration is presented to only one of these two hanger devices, and the user will perceive the enhanced force and rotate their hand. The validity of this design has already been confirmed in a preliminary experiment.

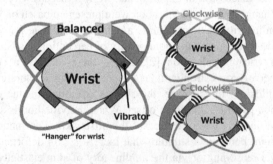

Fig. 8. Description of the conceptual device

Acknowledgment. This work was supported by JSPS KAKENHI Grant Number 15K12079.

References

1. Minamizawa, K., Prattichizzo, D., Tachi, S.: Simplified design of haptic display by extending one-point kinesthetic feedback to multipoint tactile feedback. In: Proceedings of IEEE Haptics Symposium 2010, pp. 257–260 (2010)
2. Amemiya, T., Gomi, H.: Distinct pseudo-attraction force sensation by thumb-sized vibrator that oscillates asymmetrically. In: Proceedings of EuroHaptics 2014, pp. 88–95 (2014)
3. Rekimoto, J.: Traxion: a tactile interaction device with virtual force sensation. In: Proceedings of 26th ACM Symposium User Interface Software and Tech (UIST2013) (2013)
4. Sato, M., Matsue, R., Hashimoto, Y., Kajimoto, H.: Development of a head rotation interface by using hanger reflex. In: Proceedings of 18th IEEE International Symposium Robot Human Interactive Communication (RO-MAN), pp. 534–538 (2009)
5. Massie, T.H., Salisbury, J.K.: The PHANToM haptic interface: a device for probing virtual objects. In: Proceedings of 3rd Symposium on Haptic Interface for Virtual Environment and Teleoperator Systems, pp. 295–300 (1994)
6. Harders, M., Barlit, A., Akahane, K., Sato, M., Szekely, G.: Comparing 6dof haptic interfaces for application in 3D assembly tasks. In: Proceedings of EuroHaptics 2006 (2006)
7. Kadlecek, P.: Overview of current developments in haptic APIs. In: Proceedings of CESCG 2011 (2011)
8. Yang, G., Ho, H.L., Chen, W., Lin, W., Yeo, S.H., Kurbanhusen, M.S.: A haptic device wearable on a human arm. In: 2004 IEEE Conference on Robotics, Automation and Mechatronics, pp. 243–247 (2004)
9. Kuschel, M., Luca, M.D., Buss, M., Klatzky, R.L.: Combination and integration in the perception of visual-haptic compliance information. IEEE Trans. Haptics **3**, 234–244 (2010)
10. Lécuyer, A.: Simulating haptic feedback using vision: a survey of research and applications of pseudo-haptic feedback. Presence Teleoperators Virtual Environ. **18**, 39–53 (2009)
11. Sato, M., Nakamura, T., Kajimoto, H.: Movement and pseudo-haptics induced by skin lateral deformation in hanger reflex. In: Proceedings of SIG TeleXistence 5th Workshop (2014). (in Japanese)
12. Nakamura, T., Nishimura, N., Sato, M., Kajimoto, H.: Application of hanger reflex to wrist and waist. In: Proceedings of IEEE Virtual Reality (VR) 2014, pp. 181–182 (2014)
13. Edin, B.B., Johansson, N.: Skin strain patterns provide kinaesthetic information to the human central nervous system. J. Physiol. **487**, 243–251 (1995)
14. Solazzi, M., Provancher, W.R., Frisoli, A., Bergamasco, M.: Design of a SMA actuated 2-DoF tactile device for displaying tangential skin displacement. In: Proceedings of IEEE World Haptics Conference (WHC 2011), pp. 31–36 (2011)
15. Kuniyasu, Y., Sato, M., Fukushima, S., Kajimoto, H.: Transmission of forearm motion by tangential deformation of the skin. In: Proceedings of 3rd Augmented Human International Conference (2012)
16. Yem, V., Kuzuoka, H., Yamashita, N., Ohta, S., Takeuchi, Y.: Hand-skill learning using outer-covering haptic display. In: Auvray, M., Duriez, C. (eds.) EuroHaptics 2014, Part I. LNCS, vol. 8618, pp. 201–207. Springer, Heidelberg (2014)
17. Nakamura, T., Nishimura, N., Sato, M., Kajimoto, H.: Development of a wrist-twisting haptic display using the hanger reflex. In: Proceedings of 11th Advances in Computer Entertainment Technology Conference (ACE2014) (2014)
18. Goodwin, G.M., Mccloskey, D.I., Matthews, P.B.C.: The contribution of muscle afferents to kinesthesia shown by vibration induced illusions of movement and by the effects of paralyzing joint afferents. Brain **95**, 705–748 (1972)
19. Cordo, P.J., Gurfinkel, V.S., Brumagne, S., Flores-Vieira, C.: Effect of slow, small movement on the vibration-envoked kinesthetic illusion. Exp. Brain Res. **167**, 324–334 (2005)

A Pocket-Size Alphabet Display with Letter Trajectories Presented to Fingers

Koji Tanaka[1(✉)], Keisuke Hasegawa[2], Yasutoshi Makino[1,2], and Hiroyuki Shinoda[1,2]

[1] Graduate School of Information Science and Technology, The University of Tokyo, 7-3-1, Hongo, Bunkyo-ku, Tokyo-to, Japan
tanaka@hapis.k.u-tokyo.ac.jp
[2] Graduate School of Frontier Sciences, University of Tokyo, 5-1-5, Kashiwanoha, Kashiwa-shi, Chiba-ken, Japan
Keisuke_Hasegawa@ipc.i.u-tokyo.ac.jp,
{yasutoshi_makino,hiroyuki_shinoda}@k.u-tokyo.ac.jp

Abstract. We propose a pocket-size device that enables users with no prior long-time trainings to intuitively read text letters using only their haptic sense. The device forces the user's finger-tip to trace trajectories of lowercase roman alphabet characters. In displaying multistroke characters, vibrotactile stimuli are accordingly superposed on fingers so that users can distinguish writing strokes from transient movements of fingers between strokes. Our experiments showed that participants could recognize all alphabet characters. They were able to identify them with an accuracy rate of approximately 80 % when presented at an average rate of 1.4 s/letter. We also showed that the accuracy rate varied slightly depending on holding orientation of the device, and that these identification performances could be obtained after only five-minute training. These results suggest that the access to symbolic information via haptic modalities, which were conventionally considered to be of limited use among people with early blindness, would turn into practical mobile applications for people with late blindness or even people with normal vision.

Keywords: Alphabet display · Mobile haptic device · Human performance

1 Introduction

Many researchers have studied on methods to display characters to readers with only tactile stimuli. Among them, braille is one of the most widely used, which mainly aims to present information to visually handicapped people. There also exist refreshable braille displays [1,2], some of which are designed for mobile use [3]. Thus, indeed braille is a quite valuable method, but it is not common among other than people with early blindness. This is presumably because its learning requires long-term trainings [4,5]. There are still other less-popularized tactile character display techniques such as presenting stimuli of characters' patterns

© Springer International Publishing Switzerland 2016
F. Bello et al. (Eds.): EuroHaptics 2016, Part I, LNCS 9774, pp. 472–482, 2016.
DOI: 10.1007/978-3-319-42321-0_44

to the finger-tip or palm [1, 6–8], which also demand a considerable amount of trainings for their fluent use.

As these examples show, tactual reading has been predominantly regarded as merely a substitute method access to text information for well-trained visually handicapped people. They have not been expected as a practical technique of conveying symbolic information open to people with late blindness or to people with normal vision. On the other hand, if there were such a technique which people with late blindness or with normal vision could use, it would widen the variety of applications based on our tactile modalities. If a mobile device existed, it would allow us to read e-mails in our pockets in a crowded train or during walking, without occupying our visual or auditory modalities.

There are a few examples of such a mobile device. Clarke et al. proposed the one that enables its users to identify a single letter or number in the way that their finger-tip was guided along the character trajectories on a sliding sheet, along the horizontal direction on a tablet [9]. Since this device induced only continuous horizontal motions, multistroke characters were redesigned into singlestroke ones that resembled them. Although the size and time taken to present the characters was not described in this study, it is reported that research participants could identify letters at high (over 90 %) recognition rates. The participants were trained for periods that ranged from 20 min to one hour before the tasks. Correspondingly, this is a good paradigm of reading after a short training. The study also introduced a mobile prototype, with which the reading performance of the participants was not evaluated. In the realm of psychophysical studies, it has been reported in several literatures that people can read letters tactually by being forced to trace them on a smooth surface [10–12].

In relation to these studies, our preceding study found that participants could identified alphabetic characters at high accuracy rates without prior long-term training by means of having their hands guided along three-dimensional letter trajectories with an electronically manipulated stylus held by them [13]. The participants could read 7 mm sized letters presented to them in a pace of 1 s/letter with an accuracy rate of 85 % after a five-minute training. This accuracy rate reached over 90 % in reading letters with a size of 14 mm. These outcomes indicated that sufficient for the readers are letter trajectories confined within approximately $10 \times 10 \, \text{mm}^2$ square with a regular writing speed. Since the displayed characters were not specifically coded symbols such as braille but actual strokes of written roman alphabets in this technique, we expect it to be more suitable for sighted people or people with acquired blindness. These indications backup the feasibility of a mobile device with which users could read letters at the same speed as the speed used for regular writing.

Although the writing motion was presented in the experiments reported in [13] and implemented with a large-sized device, a pocket-size device is desirable for practical uses. This paper describes a prototype of a pocket-size device that enables users to read letters without visual or auditory information by simply using the finger's motion to trace trajectories of letters. We report that in the multistroke characters presented, users can distinguish motion-writing strokes from motion between strokes by the presence of vibration, and that research participants could read letters at an accuracy rate of 81.7 % with our device. The holding orientations of the device was also found to have a little influence over their performances.

2   Device Description

Our fabricated device is shown in Fig. 1. It consists of an electrical stage equipped with a linear actuator, which yields two-dimensional horizontal movements, and a vibrator attached to the stage. Users hold the device in one hand with their finger-tip on the stage. The finger-tip passively traces trajectories of characters, by which users recognize them as individual alphabets. The vibrator is activated when the presented trajectories are supposed to be writing strokes (e.g. the dot and the vertical line under it in writing "i") and is deactivated when they are the transitions between strokes (e.g. the transient movements of a pen tip from the dot to the vertical line under it in writing "i"). The vibration is a substitute for upwards-downwards motion of the pen in [13], and was transmitted to a finger on the stage. The presence of this vibration informs users of the intervals between strokes so that the device can present multistroke characters and sequences of characters. Whereas the users in [13] pinched a stylus in a similar manner to hold a pen, our newly fabricated device is not equipped with it because of the difficulties in finding a proper hand posture which can pinch it while holding the device in one hand. Although in the following experiments the participants were engaged in a reading task where they pinched a stylus attached to the device as one of the variations in experimental conditions, our goal is to offer users to read with the device held in one hand.

The size of the device is small as it can fit inside a box with dimensions of W60 × D70 × H40 mm. Its body is made of acrylic resin, and is composed of orthogonal side faces which allows users to easily identify its spatial orientation using their haptic sense (Fig. 1).

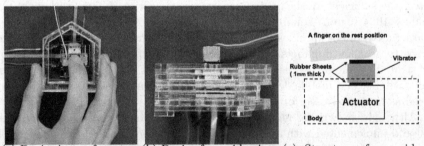

(a) Device in use from top view. (b) Device from side view. (c) Structure from side view.

Fig. 1. Appearance and construction of the fabricated device. Its size is W60 × D70 × H40 mm. It consists of a vibrator and an actuator.

Figure 2 shows the system configuration of the device. The Actuator and vibrator were controlled by a computer. Descriptions of each component follow.

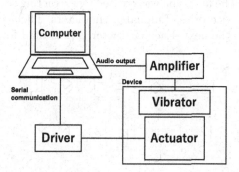

Fig. 2. System configuration. The vibrator is driven by audio output of the computer through the amplifier. The actuator is controlled by the computer.

2.1 Actuator

The actuator for presenting the trajectory is model XYDT70-105 by Technohands. This actuator is driven in the two orthogonal directions. Its in-plane size is $22 \times 22\,mm^2$ and has a height of 17.3 mm. The strokes are 10 mm long in each direction and are assumed sufficient for letter recognition [13]. The actuator's holding power is 250 gf and the maximum velocity is 10 mm/s. The actuator is controlled through serial commands via it's driver. The movement of the actuator was a sequence of linear paths from one point to another. The actuator stopped between each path, which was unavoidable in our current setup. Because of this, it took much more time for the actuator to trace along fine curves than along coarse paths composed of several lines. In order to attain the minimum duration in presenting letters, we set the actuators to move between points quantized by a two-dimensional lattice with an interval of 2 mm.

2.2 Vibration

As mentioned earlier, our device had a vibrator telling users intervals between strokes subject to the presence of vibration. The vibrator is FORCEREACTOR TOUGH (FPC type) from Alps Electric Co., Ltd. installed over the actuator via a natural rubber sheet of $10 \times 10\,mm^2$ square. We put another rubber sheet on top of the vibrator where the fingers are supposed to lie on, so that its vibration propagates to the user's finger directly. The rubber sheets are joined with double-sided tape with a 0.15 mm thickness. The voltage input to the vibrator is a 220 Hz sinusoidal wave generated from the audio output of the computer, and amplified to 6 V through a digital amplifier (TP21, Topping Co.).

All of the participants in our experiment described in Sect. 3 indicated that they perceived the vibration vividly on their finger-tips when they held the device.

2.3 Alphabet Characters

The trajectories of lower-case alphabet characters presented in our experiments are shown in Fig. 3. The font type was created by extracting several sample points from handwritten trajectories of alphabet characters. The actuator moved from one sample point to the next. Each character is presented for 1.4 s on average.

Fig. 3. Alphabetic characters presented by our device. Each square is $10 \times 10\,\text{mm}^2$.

3 Experiments

3.1 Purpose

We conducted several experiments on the recognition of performance with our device under several conditions that should be taken into account in the actual use of the device as a portable gadget.

Since the device was supposed to be handheld, multiple holding orientations are possible, and readability might vary among them. In addition, since users hold the device and trace trajectories with one hand, the counterforce of the actuator would be exerted on the hand. It is unclear, and has not been validated in prior work, on whether users can read in such a situation, and on whether there are any differences in readability in comparison to the device fixed to the ground. In addition, the performance in [13] was assessed in the case when users pinched a pen, which does not directly guarantee a commensurate readability when users put their finger on the stage that was driven horizontally.

Therefore we set the purposes of the experiments to investigate the accuracy rate when the device was held in the following manner: participants held with its face upwards in the air (we refer to it as condition 1), participants held with its face downwards in the air (condition 2), participants held the device fixed on the table laying their finger on the stage (condition 3) and participants pinched the stylus on the stage of the device fixed on the table (condition 4). The device was fixed in comparison between conditions 3 and 4 because it was difficult to hold the body and pinch the stylus in the air using only one hand. With three comparisons between 1 with 2, 1 with 3, and 3 with 4, we can tell how the twist of the wrist, the fixation of the device and the presence of the stylus affect the reading performances. These conditions are showed in Fig. 4.

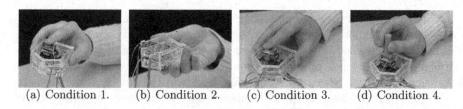

(a) Condition 1.   (b) Condition 2.   (c) Condition 3.   (d) Condition 4.

Fig. 4. Four conditions in the experiments. The device was nonfixed in conditions 1 and 2 whereas fixed in conditions 3 and 4. The device was upwards in condition 1 whereas downwards in condition 2. The participants put their finger-tip on the stage in condition 3 whereas pinched a stylus attached to the stage in condition 4.

3.2 Procedure

In this study, participants received a demonstration of the device and five-minute training at first, followed by the experiments where the device was nonfixed (conditions 1 and 2) and fixed (conditions 3 and 4), each of which comprised 104 trials in total. Half of the participants worked with the device in a nonfixed configuration before the use of the device in the fixed configuration. The other half of the participants worked in the reverse order so that each of the conditions examined was not influenced by extra trainings that occurred in prior experiments. The details of the demonstration, the training, and each of the experiments are described in the second half of this section.

For every trial in the experiments, participants were presented with one character using our device and indicated orally the character they guessed. They were not shown the correct answers. They were instructed that a character would be presented only once for each trial and that they had to provide an answer, even if they did not know the answer. No equivocal answers were permitted. They were also informed that it was possible for a character to be presented multiple times in one experimental set. The presented characters were lowercase alphabetic characters shown in Fig. 3. As mentioned before, the sizes of the characters were within an area of $10 \times 10\,\mathrm{mm}^2$ and the presentation time was $1.4\,\mathrm{s}$ on average.

We tested eight naive participants. All of them were male, right-handed, and with normal vision. Their ages ranged between 22 and 34. They were seated in front of a desk throughout the experiments. They wore earplugs or heard white noise with the use of headphones, and a curtain covered the hand that held the device in order to nullify any auditory or visual cues. They could take a rest whenever they wished during the experiments.

Demonstration and Training. In the demonstration, participants were visually displayed the character font in Fig. 3 printed on paper and were informed of the concept of the device. They were then traced trajectories of each letter once. All of the participants said that they felt vibration on their finger-tip on the stage and could distinguish motions of strokes from transient interstroke movements.

They trained for five minutes after the demonstration. In their training, they asked the experimenter to present specific alphabets. When they did not, the experimenter chose an alphabet and presented it telling them what it was. Throughout the demonstration and training, they did not obtain visual or auditory cues as well as experiments following, and held the device in the air with their elbow on the desk. They could always see the character font during the demonstration and training but they could not in following experiments.

Nonfixed Device Experiment. In the nonfixed device experiment, the participants held the nonfixed device, in the air, and with their elbow on the desk. This experiment consisted of one block that comprised 104 trials.

Participants reversed the hand that held the device every four trials. Thus, they made identifications with the device facing upwards in 52 trials (condition 1) and facing downwards in the remaining 52 trials (condition 2). Holding the device facing downwards meant that the trajectories were horizontally flipped.

An experimenter directed the reversing timings so that the participants did not attend them. The participants were told to keep the device parallel to the ground as far as their concentration was not disturbed.

Fixed Device Experiment. In the fixed device experiment, the participants worked with the device fixed on a desk over multiple trials. This experiment consisted of two blocks. One of the blocks was a trace block in which participants put their index finger-tip on the moving stage and traced trajectories (condition 3). The other one was a pinch block in which they pinched a stylus attached to the stage in the similar manner to pinching a pen (condition 4). Each of the blocks comprised 52 trials.

The participants were told to identify letters with their wrist on the table. The stylus, shown in Fig. 4(d), was made by a 3D printer and its size was the same as the grip size in [13], namely 11 mm in diameter and 30 mm in height. Similar to the order of the two experiments, the order of these two blocks in the fixed device experiment varied from participant to participant.

3.3   Results

The results are shown in Fig. 5. The average accuracy rates and their standard deviations in each condition were 81.7 % (SD = 10.6) in condition 1 (nonfixed/upwards), 70.4 % (SD = 17.5) in condition 2 (nonfixed/downwards), 86.3 % (SD = 10.8) in condition 3 (fixed/trace) and 79.6 % (SD = 16.8) in condition 4 (fixed/pinched a stylus). The paired t-tests between conditions 1 and 2, 1 and 3, 3 and 4 indicated that significant difference ($p < 0.05$) was seen only between conditions 1 and 2, not in the others ($p > 0.05$).

The average accuracy rate of the first 104 trials in all of the 208 trials in total and the latter 104 trials were 76.3 % (SD = 15.6) and 82.7 % (SD = 13.7), respectively. The paired t-test applied to these cohorts resulted in no significant differences ($p > 0.05$).

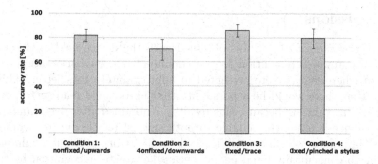

Fig. 5. Performances under each condition. The error bars indicate the standard deviations.

Table 1 shows the confusion matrix in condition 1 (nonfixed/face upwards), which is equivalent to the supposed device orientation in its practical use.

Note that one participant conducted two trials in which the device should have been facing downwards but the device was facing upwards, or conducted the nonfixed device experiment with 54 trials with the device facing upwards and 50 trials with the device facing downwards. We regarded this as negligible bias which should have no significant effect on the statistics.

Table 1. Confusion matrix on condition 1, nonfixed/upwards condition. Each number means the rate [%] at which the presented letter was identified with the answers. The empty cells mean zero. The blue and green cells are correct ones: blue denotes over 70 % and green under 70 %. Yellow denotes 10 % or more.

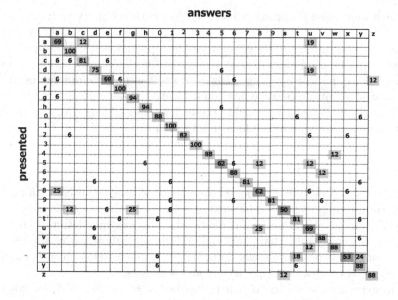

answers

presented	a	b	c	d	e	f	g	h	0	1	2	3	4	5	6	7	8	9	s	t	u	v	w	x	y	z
a	69		12																		19					
b		100																								
c	6	6	81		6																					
d				75										6							19					
e	6								69	6				6												12
f						100																				
g	6						94																			
h								94						6												
0									88											6					6	
1										100																
2		6									82									6					6	
3												100														
4													88									12				
5					6									62	6		12			12		12				
6															88							12				
7			6						6							81								6		
8	25																62			6		6				
9														6		6		81		6						
s		12		6		25		6											50							
t					6				6											81				6		
u			6													25					69					
v			6																			88		6		
w																				12			88			
x														6					18					53	24	
y														6						6					88	
z																12										88

4   Discussions

The accuracy rate of 81.7 % was obtained with the device held in the air and with its face upwards (condition 1, most commonly expected orientation in practical use) where letters were presented in approximately 1.4 s/letter. This fact suggests that there would be a possibility that users could read sentences with our device. In addition, because this result was obtained after five-minute training, the device is assumed valuable to both sighted people and to people with acquired blindness who have not learned braille. Conversely, it might not be beneficial to congenitally blind people because character recognition by tracing it's trajectory might be thanks to their experience of writing. As for the reading speed of people who have learned braille, they read at a pace of 7.5 characters per sec [14], which is superior to that with our proposed technique.

Our current experiments are limited to the evaluation of human performances in reading individual alphabets. As a more practical situation, evaluation of reading speed and usability in reading sequences of alphabets such as words or sentences, would be included as our future work.

The only element which significantly affected the performance was the orientation of the device (conditions 1 and 2), which still limited the degradation to approximately 10 %. The reason for this is considered to be the difficulty in the identification of mirror characters. Thus, the proposed device is concluded to be fairly immune to the changes in holding orientations. It was also verified that there is no need for the device to be fixed to the ground or to contain a stylus to pinch. Note that the statistical test results were not affected by unexpected training since the order of the experiences varied among participants, and there were no significant differences between the first and second half of the conducted trials.

There were some confusing pairs of letters, as shown in Table 1: such as the pairs of "s" and "g", "u" and "q", "x" and "y", and so on. Any of the two letters in these pairs is similar to its counterpart in a partial sense. These pairs were also found to be confusing in prior reports [9,13]. These similar letters would become less confusable by using a new font emphasizing the differences in each pair. Almost all of the participants could identify all 26 alphabet characters at least once. Hence, the letters would become more identifiable with a simple user input such as a switch which allows users to request redisplay.

5   Conclusions

We proposed a prototype of a pocket-size device with which users with no prior long-term trainings could read letters tactually. The users trace passively trajectories of alphabet characters and can recognize the presented letters. Our device can present multistroke characters by superposing vibration on strokes. The device completed presenting each letter in fairly short time, which is expected to enable users to read multiple letters and sentences.

Our experiments concluded that the participants could identify letters at an accuracy rate of 81.7 % when they held the device in the air. The accuracy rates with the device fixed to a desk, or with users pinching a stylus attached to the stage, did not change significantly. These suggested that our technique would work properly in mobile use with a variety of holding orientations. Moreover, these performances were obtained after training for five minutes, showing that our device does not require long-term training and would be valuable to both sighted and acquired blind people.

In the current prototype, what the reader is presented is a random sequence of individual alphabets. We will elaborate it to more refined version that enables users to read multiple sentences. To this end, we think it necessary for the device to be an interactive one allowing users to determine what part of the word or the sentence is to be displayed.

Acknowledgement. This work was partly supported by JSPS KAKENHI (Grant Number 15K12073).

References

1. Benali-khoudja, M., Hafez, M., Alex, J., Kheddar, A.: Tactile Interfaces: A State-of-the-Art Survey (2008)
2. Xu, C., Israr, A., Poupyrev, I., Bau, O., Harrison, C.: Tactile display for the visually impaired using TeslaTouch. In: CHI 2011 Extended Abstracts on Human Factors in Computing Systems, pp. 317–322 (2011)
3. Velázquez, R., Pissaloux, E.E., Wiertlewski, M.: A compact tactile display for the blind with shape memory alloys. In: Proceedings of IEEE ICRA, pp. 3905–3910 (2006)
4. Truan, M.B., Trent, S.D.: Impact of adolescents' adjustment to progressive vision loss on Braille reading skills: case studies. J. Vis. Impairment Blindness **91**, 301–308 (1997)
5. Kauffman, T., Théoret, H., Pascual-Leone, A.: Braille character discrimination in blindfolded human subjects. NeuroReport **13**, 571–574 (2002)
6. Linvill, J.G., Bliss, J.C.: A direct translation reading aid for the blind. Proc. IEEE **54**, 40 51 (1966)
7. Loomis, J.M.: Tactile recognition of raised characters: a parametric study. Bull. Psychon. Soc. **23**, 18–20 (1985)
8. Hoshi, T.: Handwriting transmission system using noncontact tactile display. In: Proceedings of the IEEE HAPTICS, pp. 399–401 (2012)
9. Roudaut, A., Rau, A., Sterz, C., Plauth, M., Lopes, P., Baudisch, P.: Gesture output: eyes-free output using a force feedback touch surface. In: Proceedings of the ACM CHI, pp. 2547–2556 (2013)
10. Heller, M.A., Nesbitt, K.D., Scrofano, D.K.: Influence of writing style and categorical information on identification of tactile numerals and letters. Bull. Psychon. Soc. **29**, 365–367 (1991)
11. Magee, L.E., Kennedy, J.M.: Exploring pictures tactually. Nature **283**, 287–288 (1980)
12. Symmons, M.A., Richardson, B.L., Wuillemin, D.B.: Components of haptic information: skin rivals kinaesthesis. Perception **37**, 1596–1604 (2008)

13. Hasegawa, K., Sakurai, T., Makino, Y., Shinoda, H.: Character reading via stylus reproducing normal handwriting motion. IEEE Trans. Haptics (in print). doi:10.1109/TOH.2016.2517625
14. Legge, G.E., Madison, C.M., Mansfield, J.S.: Measuring braille reading speed with the MNREAD test. Vis. Impairment Res. **1**, 131–145 (1999)

Haptic Rendering of Thin, Deformable Objects with Spatially Varying Stiffness

Priyadarshini Kumari[(✉)] and Subhasis Chaudhuri

Vision and Image Processing Laboratory, Department of Electrical Engineering,
Indian Institute of Technology Bombay, Powai, Mumbai 400076, India
{priydarshini,sc}@ee.iitb.ac.in

Abstract. In real world, we often come across with soft objects having spatially varying stiffness such as human palm or a wart on the skin. In this paper, we propose a novel approach to render thin, deformable objects having spatially varying stiffness (inhomogeneous material). We use the classical Kirchhoff thin plate theory to compute the deformation. In general, physics based rendering of an arbitrary 3D surface is complex and time consuming. Therefore, we approximate the 3D surface locally by a 2D plane using an area preserving mapping technique - Gall-Peters mapping. Once the deformation is computed by solving a fourth order partial differential equation, we project the points back onto the original object for proper haptic rendering. The method was validated through user experiments and was found to be realistic.

Keywords: Haptic rendering · Deformable thin surface · Spatially varying stiffness · Kirchhoff's thin plate theory · Gall-Peters projection

1 Introduction

Haptic perception becomes more realistic when we incorporate physical and material properties of an object. For kinesthetic rendering of rigid objects, it is sufficient to calculate only the force as they do not undergo any deformation under the applied force. But rendering of deformable objects is more complex since we need to calculate the force as well as the deformation. If the stiffness of the object varies over the surface, there is further complications as the rendered force is a function of both local deformation and local variation in stiffness. The continuity of deformation and a smooth movement of the proxy on the deforming surface are some of the key concerns while rendering a deformable object having a variable stiffness.

In the last two decades, haptic rendering has found several applications on interactions with virtual environment such as virtual museum [17], dental surgery simulation [11] and force modeling for needle insertion [14]. However these interactions cannot handle skin or bowel simulator which requires the object to

Funding supports from Bharti Centre for Communication, NPPE Project from DeitY and The Indian Digital Heritage Project are gratefully acknowledged.

© Springer International Publishing Switzerland 2016
F. Bello et al. (Eds.): EuroHaptics 2016, Part I, LNCS 9774, pp. 483–492, 2016.
DOI: 10.1007/978-3-319-42321-0_45

be both deformable and have variable stiffness. The proposed method tries to achieve this special type of rendering.

We propose a method to render a point cloud data representing a thin deformable objects having spatially varying stiffness such as skin and elastic sheets. First, the point cloud in the neighborhood of the proxy is locally fit into a hemispherical surface and using the parameter of the fitted sphere these points are then projected on a plane using Gall-Peters projection [8]. This being an area preserving mapping, preserves the stiffness variation on the projected 2D plane. Subsequently, we use the Kirchhoff's thin plate theory [18] to calculate the deformation due to an applied force at the proxy and for a given stiffness pattern. The solution is obtained by solving a fourth order non-homogeneous Partial Differential Equation (PDE). Once the deformation map is estimated, it is back projected on the original 3D surface for proper rendering.

Most of the work done in the field of deformable object rendering can be classified into two categories: geometry based deformation and physics based deformation. Geometry based models are fast but do not necessarily focus on the physics involved in the deformation. On the other hand physics based rendering model is computationally expensive as the simulation of physical and material properties of the object is complex. In geometry based modeling most of the methods use Gaussian [12] or a polynomial function to move the surrounding vertices around Haptic Interaction Point (HIP). Another widely practiced method is spline based in which control points are assigned on the object and these control points are manipulated to effect a smooth deformation [5].

An FEM based method such as [3,6] provides the most accurate rendering. However, this is computationally very demanding for haptic applications, requiring specialized hardware. It has been shown in [10] that by sacrificing the accuracy marginally the computations can be speeded up by a factor of 10 by using a mass-spring model. However, the choice of dampers is very critical to ascertain the desired dynamic behavior and usually they are chosen heuristically. The purpose of the proposed method is to avoid these heuristics by solving a proper PDE over 2D plate. In smoothed-particle-hydrodynamics (SPH) approach [4], authors have introduced a technique which renders the object in different possible states (fluid, elastic and rigid) in the same scene. But in this technique, the stiffness of the entire object is varied as opposed to spatially varying the stiffness. Moreover in [4], a volume model of the object is used, while we use a 3D surface model which is comparatively much faster than the volume model.

The key contribution of our work is the development of an alternate, stable, physics based haptic rendering method for an inhomogeneous, elastic deformable object.

2   Proposed Method

The input for our method is point cloud representation of the 3D object. Since there is one-to-one relationship between point cloud and mesh data [7] (albeit the rendering process is a bit different), the algorithm can be extended to other

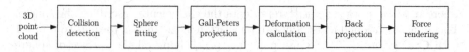

Fig. 1. Various steps involved in haptic rendering of a deformable object with variable stiffness.

form of data representation. The point cloud is given by 4-tuple point $P_i = \{(x_i, y_i, z_i), d_i\}$, where (x_i, y_i, z_i) is the location of the ith point and d_i is the corresponding stiffness. The overall algorithm can be broken into several stages as shown in Fig. 1. The various stages of algorithm are described in the following subsections.

2.1 Collision Detection

With point cloud data, we do not have surface normal defined at a point. In order to provide the appropriate force feedback to the user, we need the normal information at the collision point. We follow a proxy based technique proposed in [16] for computation of normals. In this method, the normal is computed from radial overshoot of each point inside the spherical proxy. Once the collision occurs, HIP penetrates the object and the proxy is constrained to lie on the surface by using a dynamic function as defined in [16]. A collision is detected when the condition $(\mathbf{v}_n \cdot \mathbf{v}_h) < 0$ is satisfied, where $\mathbf{v}_n$ is the computed surface normal at the point of collision and $\mathbf{v}_h$ is the vector joining the proxy to HIP as shown in Fig. 2. Once the collision point is detected, we select the point cloud in the neighborhood of the point of collision for fitting a sphere locally.

2.2 Spherical Facet Modeling

We use the algebraic distance based method proposed in [15] to fit the surface points in the neighborhood of the proxy. Let $f(x, y, z)$ be an equation of sphere in the algebraic form

$$f(x, y, z) = u_0(x^2 + y^2 + z^2) + u_1 x + u_2 y + u_3 z + u_4 = 0$$
$$\text{subject to } u_1^2 + u_2^2 + u_3^2 - 4u_0 u_4 = 1 \tag{1}$$

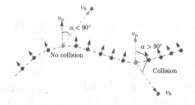

Fig. 2. Illustration of collision detection. The proxy and the HIP is shown in green and red colors, respectively. The point cloud is shown in blue. Blue arrows show the computed outward surface normals. (Color figure online)

where $\mathbf{u} = [u_0\ u_1\ u_2\ u_3\ u_4]^T$ represents the coefficients describing the sphere. The above mentioned constraint can be written in the matrix form as $\mathbf{u}^T\mathbf{C}\mathbf{u} = 1$ with $\mathbf{C}$ as given in (2). So any point (x_i, y_i, z_i) lying on the surface of sphere will have an algebraic distance equal to zero. We minimize the sum of squared algebraic distances to estimate the best possible spherical fit $\mathbf{u}$. Although several possible constraints have been suggested in [1,2], we use the constraint $\mathbf{u}^T\mathbf{C}\mathbf{u} = 1$, as Pratt [15] has shown that such a constraint has only one point of singularity of being a zero radius sphere. The resulting cost function can be expressed by introducing a Lagrangian multiplier λ as:

$$\underset{\mathbf{u}}{\text{minimize}}\ (\|\mathbf{D}\mathbf{u}\|^2 - \lambda(\mathbf{u}^T\mathbf{C}\mathbf{u} - 1)) \tag{2}$$

$$\mathbf{D} = \begin{bmatrix} x_1^2 + y_1^2 + z_1^2 & x_1 & y_1 & z_1 & 1 \\ \vdots & \vdots & \vdots & \vdots & \vdots \\ x_n^2 + y_n^2 + z_n^2 & x_n & y_n & z_n & 1 \end{bmatrix}, \ \mathbf{C} = \begin{bmatrix} 0 & 0 & 0 & 0 & -2 \\ 0 & 1 & 0 & 0 & 0 \\ 0 & 0 & 1 & 0 & 0 \\ 0 & 0 & 0 & 1 & 0 \\ -2 & 0 & 0 & 0 & 0 \end{bmatrix}$$

where $\mathbf{D}$ is an $n \times 5$ matrix derived from n points from the point cloud data, selected in the neighborhood of the collision point. The solution is given by solving the generalized eigenvalue problem $\mathbf{D}^T\mathbf{D}\mathbf{u} = \lambda\mathbf{C}\mathbf{u}$, which can be solved using QZ algorithm developed by Moler and Stewart [13]. The center and the radius of the sphere can be calculated using an expression, $\mathbf{c} = -\frac{1}{2u_4}[u_1 u_2 u_3]$, $r = \sqrt{c^T c - \frac{u_0}{u_4}}$ as given in [9]. Once we get the center $\mathbf{c}$ and the radius r of the sphere, all the points are locally projected on to a 2D plane as discussed in the next subsection.

All points, however, need not lie on the surface of the best fit sphere as shown in Fig. 3a. In order to approximate the object surface by an area preserving planar patch, we need to project all points on the surface of the fitted sphere. We use a projection technique in which we join all the points (which are not lying on the surface of the sphere) from the center. The joining line intersects the sphere at two points. The intersecting point nearest to the object point is chosen to be the projection of the corresponding point on the sphere. Figure 3b shows the best fit sphere to a set of object points near the proxy.

As it was mentioned earlier that deformation due to an arbitrary variation in material properties is easier to compute for a thin sheet, the fitted sphere is mapped onto a 2D plane. For an equi-curvature surface (like a sphere), the amount of energy required for deformation is proportional to the surface area when the stiffness is constant. Hence we require a projection operator $g : \mathbb{R}^3 \to \mathbb{R}^2$ which is area preserving so that deformation computation is a function of stiffness alone. Gall-Peters projection [8] used in cartography is one such operator that preserves the area. Hence we use Gall-Peters projection in a way so that the proxy position lies at the center of the unfolded globe. While fitting the sphere, if there are points on the western hemisphere, these points are not visible at the proxy and hence they are rejected and only a hemispherical facet is considered. This is illustrated in Fig. 3a, where D is the proxy on the surface, AB corresponds

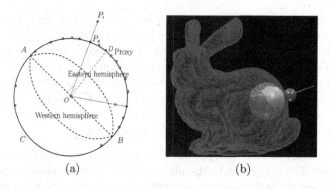

(a)   (b)

Fig. 3. (a) Illustration of projection of points on the surface of the best fit sphere and employing the constraint of hemisphere fitting. The object points P_i are shown in red and the projected points P_s are shown in blue. (b) Illustration of the best fit sphere to the set of object points near the proxy. The proxy is shown with a red ball and the green line points to the direction of normal at the collision point. (Data Courtesy: http://graphics.stanford.edu/data/3Dscanrep/) (Color figure online)

to the plane joining the north pole (A) and the south pole (B) and the point D corresponds to $(0,0)$ latitude and longitude of the sphere. Points lying on the western hemisphere (shown as the arc ACB) are discarded.

2.3 Area Preserving 3D to 2D Projection

Since Gall-Peters projection describes a technique to project the globe onto a plane, we have used it for a sphere to plane projection. The longitude and latitude of each point on the sphere is calculated from polar coordinates of the points. Considering the z-axis to be perpendicular to the computer screen, each point on the sphere is projected onto the x-z plane using (3).

$$x = \frac{r\alpha}{\sqrt{2}} \qquad z - r\sqrt{2}sin(\beta), \tag{3}$$

where α and β are longitude and latitude of the point in radians respectively and r is radius of the sphere. While using the Gall-Peters projection some issues emerge, when points lie either near the pole region or near the 180° longitude.

1. A point lying on the north/south pole gets stretched to a line on the plane after projection.
2. Points on 180° longitude get mapped on both the extreme of the 2D plane.

We avert such problem by shifting the coordinate axis of sphere so that our proxy (point D in Fig. 3a) falls in the region of zero latitude and zero longitude. After shifting the axes, we discard the points on the other half of the sphere opposite to the proxy (arc ACB in Fig. 3a). In this way, all neighborhood points around the proxy fall near the center of the plane, which would be very useful while employing an infinite horizon boundary condition in Sect. 2.5. Once the points are projected on a plane, we compute the deformation of each point using Kirchhoff thin plate theory [18]. As mentioned earlier, computation of deformation on the planar sheet is easier than directly computing on the object surface. Therefore we compute the deformation of each point on 2D plane and subsequently project the points back on the original 3D object.

2.4   Deformation Computation on a Planar Sheet

In Kirchhoff theory of plate [18, pp. 29–37], the thickness of the plate is assumed to be very small as compared to the planar dimensions. In addition, some more assumptions are made to reduce the three dimensional problem to two dimensions. These assumptions are summarized as follow

1. The line normal to the neutral axis remain straight after deformation.
2. The normal stress in the direction of thickness is neglected.
3. Thickness of the plate does not change during bending.

Let s, w and t be the displacements of a point along x, y and z directions, respectively, and $|\mathbf{F}|$ is a distributed load on the planar sheet.

Since the planar sheet is on the x-z plane, we can write the variation of s and t across thickness in terms of displacement w as $s = -y\frac{\partial w}{\partial x}$, $t = -y\frac{\partial w}{\partial z}$.

Taking all the assumptions into account, the deformation of a point is governed by the following PDE as explained in [18, pp. 29–37].

$$\frac{\partial^4 w}{\partial x^4} + 2\frac{\partial^4 w}{\partial x^2 \partial z^2} + \frac{\partial^4 w}{\partial z^4} = \frac{|\mathbf{F}|}{D}, \ \ or \ \ \nabla^4 w = \frac{|\mathbf{F}|}{D}, \tag{4}$$

where ∇^4 is the biharmonic operator and D is flexural rigidity of the object. Interestingly, this equation was first obtained by Lagrange in 1811. The flexural rigidity is a material property of the object and is defined as

$$D = \frac{Eh^3}{12(1 - v^2)}, \tag{5}$$

where E, h, v are the modulus of elasticity, thickness of the plate and Poisson's ratio (usually $0 < v < 0.3$), respectively. Equation (4) is valid only if material property D of the object is constant. In this case, computation of deformation also becomes easier as the governing differential Eq. (4) is a standard biharmonic equation. However in real world, there are numerous objects which have spatially varying material properties when E and v are functions of x and z. Equation (4) cannot be applied to compute deformation for such objects. Hence we move to the next stage where stiffness of the object is allowed to vary over the surface. In order to compute the deformation in variable stiffness object we use the extended Kirchhoff thin plate theory [18, pp. 93–95]. The deformation of each point in such cases is governed by the following equation

$$D\nabla^4 w + 2\frac{\partial D}{\partial x}\frac{\partial}{\partial x}(\nabla^2 w) + 2\frac{\partial D}{\partial z}\frac{\partial}{\partial z}(\nabla^2 w) + \nabla^2 D(\nabla^2 w)$$
$$-(1-v)\left(\frac{\partial^2 D}{\partial x^2}\frac{\partial^2 w}{\partial z^2} - 2\frac{\partial^2 D}{\partial x \partial z}\frac{\partial^2 w}{\partial x \partial z} + \frac{\partial^2 D}{\partial z^2}\frac{\partial^2 w}{\partial x^2}\right) = |\mathbf{F}|. \tag{6}$$

The detail derivation of (4) and (6) is explained in [18]. Unfortunately finding an analytical solution of this form of PDE is extremely difficult. Hence we solve the equation in discrete domain by using Jacobi iterative method for a given boundary condition. As the Gall-Peters projection uses non-linear mapping function (3), points are not projected evenly on a plane. Therefore we first sample the projected points on the uniform grid and subsequently we discretize all the variables and parameters of (6) by using central difference. The value of D at a grid node is taken as the value of D of the closest projected point from the grid node. Our initial condition on deformation is $w(i,j) = 0$. The final expression for iterative updating can be written in the form of a function $L()$:

$$w^{n+1}(i,j) = L(|\mathbf{F}|, \mathbf{D}(i,j), w_{\mathcal{N}}^{n}(i,j)) \tag{7}$$

where the superscript n denotes the nth iteration and $w_{\mathcal{N}}^{n}(i,j)$ refers to the various lattice entries in the neighborhood of the central lattice (i,j), while $\mathbf{D}(i,j)$ is the given flexural rigidity map and its all derivatives (upto second order) at the lattice (i,j). In each iteration, we update the w matrix and compare it with w matrix of previous iteration. We stop the iteration when the Frobenius norm of difference between current and previous w matrices becomes very small. The final w matrix gives the deformation at the grid point. However, one needs the deformation value at the location where the 3D point was originally projected using (3). The deformations at projected points are computed using bi-linear interpolation.

2.3 Boundary Conditions for PDE

As we mentioned earlier, in order to obtain the solution of the PDE given in (6), we need suitable boundary conditions. For simplicity, we assume edges of the projected plane to be parallel to the coordinate axis X and Z. We need two boundary conditions at each edge. In our work, we assume all four edges of projected plate to be fixed (i.e. deformation at infinite horizon is zero). Hence the deflection and the first order derivative become zero at all four edges. After getting the deformation locally on the projected plane, we project back the points to compute the deformation on the original object for proper rendering. Points on the object are displaced in the direction of the force $\mathbf{F}$ using the governing equation, $\hat{P}_i = P_i + w_i \frac{\mathbf{F}}{|\mathbf{F}|}$, where $\hat{P}_i$ is the final position of the ith point on the deformed surface and P_i corresponds to the position before deformation with w_i being the deformation at the point.

3   Force Rendering

In order to haptically render the object, we first detect the collision of HIP with the object as discussed in Sect. 2.1 and compute the force if a collision is detected. Once the collision is detected, the force needs to be fed back by the haptic device to provide the sensation of touch. Two important factors for force computation are its magnitude and its direction. The magnitude of force should be proportional to the penetration depth of HIP from the surface and its direction should be in the direction of the normal at the point of collision. Hence the reaction force is calculated using the expression, $F = -\frac{EA}{h}(|X_h - X_p|)$. Here X_h is the HIP position, X_p is the proxy position, A is the area of the plate and E is the modulus of elasticity at that location.

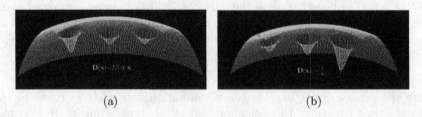

(a)   (b)

Fig. 4. Computed deformations on the object surface with different flexural rigidity functions under the same amount of applied force: (a) Linear, (b) Hyperbolic (x in cm). Deformation at various locations are superimposed together for ease of visualization.

4   Results

The proposed method was implemented in Visual Studio 2010 in a Windows 7 platform with a Core(TM2) Quad CPU Q8400 processor @ 2.66 GHz clock speed with 8 GB RAM. We use OpenGL 2.0 for graphic rendering and HAPI library for haptic rendering. We experimented with 3D point cloud model using Falcon haptic device from NOVINT. In order to make the rendering faster we segregate the tasks of deformation computation, proxy updation and force computation through three different threads while programming. We observed that the deformation thread, as expected, runs relatively slowly due to iterative solution for Eq. (6). The average time required to run the deformation thread once is around 160 ms. We have set $v = 0.2$ in the study.

We initially use a simulated elliptical object consisting of 40000 points. The 3D grid used to sample the point cloud is of size $200 \times 200 \times 200$ with inter-node space of 0.025 cm. Figure 4 shows the deformations at several points on the object surface with different flexural rigidity functions. In Fig. 4a, flexural rigidity is varied gradually along the horizontal direction while in Fig. 4b it is varied rapidly. We applied the same amount of force on the object surface and observed that deformation decreases as flexural rigidity increases as shown in Fig. 4a. It may be noted that the deformation is restricted to the neighborhood only due to the choice of boundary conditions. To explain this further, we experiment on a real object model and show the deformation at the ear lobe of a bunny in Fig. 5a. One may expect the ear lobe to be bent due to the applied force like a cantilever. Instead one observes a dip within the ear lobe, exact shape of which would depend on the size of the chosen neighborhood.

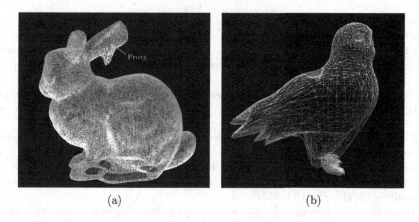

(a)   (b)

Fig. 5. Deformation shown on the object models: (a) Bunny, (b) Bird

We also verify the performance of the proposed algorithm in terms of user experience while interacting with various object models. We set up an experiment in which ten participants were asked to interact with an object model (say Fig. 5) and rate the experience on a scale of $1 - 5$, with 1 being very poor to 5 being excellent. Out of ten, eight of the participants rated the experience as very good (rating 4) remaining two gave the rating of 3. When asked if they are able to perceive the change in stiffness, nine participants responded positively.

5   Conclusion

We have proposed a numerical method to solve the haptic rendering problem of elastic deformable objects with spatially varying stiffness. It is a physics based rendering technique and gives realistic feeling of touching the object. We have not observed any divergence issue in computation of the deformation map or the movement of proxy over the deforming surface. In order to mathematically handle any object, an area preserving map projection technique is used to transform an arbitrary 3D surface to a planar one following which Kirchhoff's thin plate deformation propagation model involving a fourth order PDE is used to compute deformation in case of spatially varying stiffness. We also tested with some subjects and observed that hapto-visual rendering technique using the proposed algorithm greatly augmented the user's experience. Our future work will involve the choice of alternate boundary conditions and extension to dealing with volumetric data. Further an implementation in GPU is required for real-time rendering.

References

1. Albano, A.: Representation of digitized contours in terms of conic arcs and straight-line segments. Comput. Graph. Image Process. **3**(1), 23–33 (1974)

2. Bookstein, F.L.: Fitting conic sections to scattered data. Comput. Graph. Image Process. **9**(1), 56–71 (1979)
3. Chan, S.C., Blevins, N.H., Salisbury, K.: Deformable haptic rendering for volumetric medical image data. In: World Haptics Conference (WHC), pp. 73–78. IEEE (2013)
4. Cirio, G., Marchal, M., Otaduy, M., Lécuyer, A., et al.: Six-dof haptic interaction with fluids, solids, and their transitions. In: World Haptics Conference (WHC), pp. 157–162. IEEE (2013)
5. Coquillart, S.: Extended free-form deformation: a sculpturing tool for 3D geometric modeling **24** (1990). ACM
6. Courtecuisse, H., Allard, J., Kerfriden, P., Bordas, S.P., Cotin, S., Duriez, C.: Realtime simulation of contact and cutting of heterogeneous soft-tissues. Medical image analysis **18**(2), 394–410 (2014)
7. Fabio, R., et al.: From point cloud to surface: the modeling and visualization problem. Int. Arch. Photogrammetry Remote Sens. Spat. Inf. Sci. **34**(5), W10 (2003)
8. Gall, J.: Use of cylindrical projections for geographical astronomical, and scientific purposes. Scott. Geogr. Mag. **1**(4), 119–123 (1885)
9. Guennebaud, G., Gross, M.: Algebraic point set surfaces. ACM Trans. Graph. (TOG) **26**, 23 (2007)
10. Hammer, P.E., Sacks, M.S., Pedro, J., Howe, R.D.: Mass-spring vs. finite element models of anisotropic heart valves: speed and accuracy. In: ASME 2010 Summer Bioengineering Conference, pp. 643–644. American Society of Mechanical Engineers (2010)
11. Heiland, M., Petersik, A., Pflesser, B., Tiede, U., Schmelzle, R., Höhne, K.H., Handels, H.: Realistic haptic interaction for computer simulation of dental surgery. In: International Congress Series, vol. 1268, pp. 1226–1229. Elsevier (2004)
12. Luciano, C.J., Banerjee, P.P., Rizzi, S.H.: GPU-based elastic-object deformation for enhancement of existing haptic applications. In: IEEE International Conference on Automation Science and Engineering, pp. 146–151. IEEE (2007)
13. Moler, C.B., Stewart, G.W.: An algorithm for generalized matrix eigenvalue problems. SIAM J. Numer. Anal. **10**(2), 241–256 (1973)
14. Okamura, A.M., Simone, C., Leary, M.: Force modeling for needle insertion into soft tissue. IEEE Trans. Biomed. Eng. **51**(10), 1707–1716 (2004)
15. Pratt, V.: Direct least-squares fitting of algebraic surfaces. ACM SIGGRAPH Comput. Graph. **21**(4), 145–152 (1987)
16. Sreeni, K., Chaudhuri, S.: Haptic rendering of dense 3D point cloud data. In: Haptics Symposium (HAPTICS), pp. 333–339. IEEE (2012)
17. Sreeni, K.G., Priyadarshini, K., Praseedha, A.K., Chaudhuri, S.: Haptic rendering of cultural heritage objects at different scales. In: Isokoski, P., Springare, J. (eds.) EuroHaptics 2012, Part I. LNCS, vol. 7282, pp. 505–516. Springer, Heidelberg (2012)
18. Ventsel, E., Krauthammer, T.: Thin Plates and Shells: Theory: Analysis, and Applications

An Eight-Legged Tactile Sensor to Estimate Coefficient of Static Friction: Improvements in Design and Evaluation

Wei Chen, Han Wen, Heba Khamis, and Stephen J. Redmond$^{(\boxtimes)}$

Graduate School of Biomedical Engineering,
UNSW Australia, Sydney, NSW 2052, Australia
s.redmond@unsw.edu.au

Abstract. According to the laws of friction, in order to initiate a sliding motion between two objects, a tangential force larger than the maximum static friction force is required. This process is governed by a material constant called the coefficient of static friction. Therefore, it is of great utility for robots to know the coefficient of static friction between its gripper and the object being manipulated, especially when a stable and precise grip on an object is necessary. Furthermore, it is most useful if the robot can estimate the coefficient of static friction upon touching an object at the very beginning of a manipulation task, instead of having to further explore the object before it tries to move the object. Motivated by this issue, we have designed (and in this paper, further improved) a novel eight-legged tactile sensor to estimate the coefficient of static friction between a planar surface and the sensing components of the prototype sensor (which will also serve as the gripper). While the basic principle of the sensor is still unchanged, here we highlight some improvements to the sensor's design and evaluation, including more robustly controlled frictional angles (vital for the accurate sensing) and the use of a programmable xyz-stage during evaluation. The coefficients of static friction between the sensor and nine different materials were estimated and compared to a measurement obtained via traditional methods as a reference. For all testing materials, the estimated ranges cover the corresponding reference values. Good conformance with the reference coefficients is also visually indicated from a least-square fitted line of the estimated coefficients, which has a gradient close to one and an r^2 value greater than 0.9.

Keywords: Friction · Sensor · Tactile

1 Introduction

Without question, the ability to manipulate an object without dropping or crushing it is vitally important for both human hands and robotic grippers. As the coefficient of static friction (μ_s) is one significant factor that determines the minimum grip force required to lift a given object, it is therefore believed that accurate knowledge of μ_s will allow improved dexterity for robotic manipulators. Although μ_s can be measured under laboratory conditions [1], these methods are not practical for real-time robot manipulation, especially in unstructured environments. While an estimate of the friction

© Springer International Publishing Switzerland 2016
F. Bello et al. (Eds.): EuroHaptics 2016, Part I, LNCS 9774, pp. 493–502, 2016.
DOI: 10.1007/978-3-319-42321-0_46

coefficient between known materials can be obtained from published tables, large variations usually exist due to changes in surface texture, cleanliness, moisture, etc. [2]. Therefore, it is desirable to equip robot grippers with tactile sensors that can estimate the coefficient of static friction in real-time during object manipulation.

A variety of techniques have been proposed in recent decades aiming to improve grip security. However, most of these methods focus on either gross or incipient slip detection – identifying that the object has slipped or is about to slip and then trying to recover a secure grasp on the object before it falls. Such sensors often detect micro-vibrations during slip or onset of slip using accelerometers or polyvinylidene fluoride films [2–8], or directly use the force information (normal force and tangential force) when slip is detected to estimate μ_s for later use [9, 10]. However, they all require the gross sliding of the grasped object, and thus there is little time to adjust the grip force before the object drops. In addition to the above slip-based methods (either gross or incipient slip), Shinoda *et al.* [11, 12] developed a tactile sensor using an acoustic resonant tensor cell to estimate μ_s, and Maeno *et al.* proposed a method for estimating friction by pressing an elastic finger-shaped sensor against a planar surface [13, 14].

For the purpose of estimating μ_s during real-time object manipulation, previously published by our group in [15], an eight-legged tactile sensor was developed (dubbed the *spider*) which can estimate μ_s between a planar surface and the sensor itself when pressed against the testing material. Although the experimental results indicated that the spider sensor produced consistent estimates with reference values which were given by traditional methods, there were certain limitations in both the sensor design and the way that experiments were conducted. For example, due to how the stoppers for the legs were assembled, it was difficult to fix the frictional angles (explained again later in this paper) at the exact predefined angles, such as $10°$ for the innermost sensor legs. Also, the sensor legs were not restricted to movement in the plane where they should rotate; as they were on a narrow hinge which was loose in order to minimize friction in the hinge, there was some small motion in and out of the intended plane of motion. In addition, the platform we used for experiments was not automatic; that is to say, normal forces were manually and gently applied to the spider sensor, meaning the force waveforms varied among testing repeats. All of the above problems may give rise to errors in the estimation of μ_s, and this paper details our efforts to address these problems.

In this study, another eight-legged tactile sensor (now dubbed the *spider2*) that can estimate μ_s when brought into contact with an object was designed, constructed, and evaluated. The spider2 also has eight straight rigid legs, each making a different predefined angle with the vertical (termed the *frictional angle* here) and a corresponding μ_s (refer to Sect. 2 explaining how each frictional angle corresponds to a value of μ_s). Theoretically, a range of potential values for μ_s can be estimated by simply detecting which of the legs have slipped when a normal load (corresponding to a grip force if used in a griping task) is applied to the spider2. This version solves some of the existing design problems of the last version and has a smaller size. We validate the performance of the spider2 by pressing it against a number of planar materials (with different μ_s) and increasing the contact force.

2   Physical Principles of the Sensor

The spider sensor is based on simplified theoretical principles of friction. An illustration of one of the eight sensor legs in contact with a planar surface is shown in Fig. 1. Assuming static equilibrium, we have the following equalities:

$$F'_n = F_n \tag{1}$$

$$F'_n \cdot d_1 = F_f \cdot d_2 \tag{2}$$

where F_n is the normal force applied to the sensor, F'_n is the reaction force from the surface in contact with the leg, and F_f is the friction force. Therefore, we can obtain the relationship between μ_s and the frictional angle, θ, as below:

$$\mu_s = \frac{F_f}{F'_n} = \frac{d_1}{d_2} = \tan \theta. \tag{3}$$

Thus, for a leg to slip, the coefficient of static friction, μ_s, should follow:

$$\mu_s < \tan \theta. \tag{4}$$

On the contrary, for a leg to remain stuck (i.e., not slip), the opposite condition should be satisfied:

$$\mu_s \geq \tan \theta. \tag{5}$$

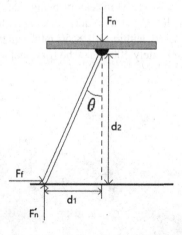

Fig. 1. Illustration of forces acting on one leg of the spider, pressing down against a planar surface. The leg is at an angle θ to the vertical, and connected to the body of the sensor via a hinge joint at its top.

Supposing that we have two legs with friction angles θ_1 and θ_2 ($\theta_1 > \theta_2$), when a normal force is applied to the sensor, if the first leg slips and the second one does not slip, we can make the following conclusion:

$$\tan \theta_2 \leq \mu_s < \tan \theta_1. \tag{6}$$

Theoretically, when the difference between the frictional angles of adjacent legs becomes small enough, we can acquire an accurate estimate of the coefficient of static friction.

3 Methodology

3.1 Sensor Redesign

The spider2 prototype was built out of 3D-printed parts (ABS plastic), nuts, stainless steel shafts, ball bearings, and some electronic components. Ball bearings are added to reduce the friction between sensor legs and the shaft that those legs rotate around. The finished structure of the sensor is shown below in Fig. 2. For the new spider sensor, we designed a friction sensor with eight legs in total (two symmetric sets of four legs on each side). Ordered from outermost to innermost, each pair of legs is vertically lower down than the next pair (i.e., closer to the surface to be tested) and has a larger frictional angle, which prevents any of the inner legs from interfering with the sensing ability of the outer legs which have yet to slip. The frictional angles (θ) of each leg are predefined so that the corresponding coefficients of static friction are 0.2, 0.4, 0.6, and 0.8 respectively. In this way, we obtain five ranges, 0–0.2, 0.2–0.4, 0.4–0.6, 0.6–0.8, and 0.8–∞, which the estimated coefficient of static friction may occupy.

Furthermore, in the spider2 design, the four sensor legs on each side of the sensor now rotate along the same axis (shaft) instead of being distributed separately (see the old spider in Fig. 2(b)), which makes the spider2 sensor smaller. The dimensions of the spider2 sensor are approximately within a 70×50 mm^2 square, while the length of the previous version was approximately 100 mm. The frictional angles of each leg are now

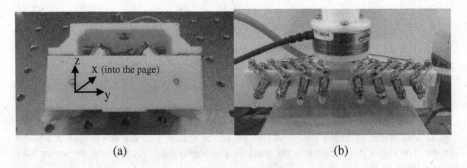

(a)   (b)

Fig. 2. (a) Photo of the new spider2 sensor. The coordinate frame is defined in accordance with that of the ATI force/torque sensor. (b) The old spider sensor [15].

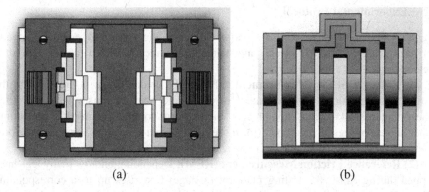

(a)   (b)

Fig. 3. (a) Top-view (Solidworks screenshot) of the spider2 sensor (the upper mount is hidden to show the structure of sensor legs more clearly). The part in blue in the top view is the sensor housing, while the parts in white are the eight sensor legs (four in each side). (b) End-view. The housing in the end-view is hidden to show the shape of sensor legs (now in light blue). (Color figure online)

structurally fixed by using a specially-designed housing which limits the range of rotation allowed (see Fig. 3(a)).

The stair-like cutting on the top side of the housing acts as stoppers for each sensor leg so that their frictional angles or corresponding coefficients of static friction are unchangeable and exactly equal to a predefined value (e.g., the tangent of friction angle is 0.2 for the innermost pair of legs). What we refer to as sensor legs, in reference to the previous design, are now more of a rectangular frame, which helps prevent the sensor legs move outside yz-plane (in terms of the coordinates in Fig. 2). Small elastic bands are used to return the legs back into their default positions after each test; although this is necessary, the elastic bands introduce a measurement bias expected to cause an overestimation of μ_s (they make it more difficult for the legs to slip).

There is a small metal plate glued onto each sensor leg, and eight plates on the housing, serving as contact switches. Each leg is wired to a regulated five volt supply via a pull-down resistor. When the legs slip, the contact switch is opened, and the voltage changes from 5 V to 0 V, indicating that the leg has slipped.

The sensor was mounted on an ATI Mini40 six-axis force/torque sensor (ATI Industrial Automation, NC, USA) which was itself mounted on the upper beam of a testing rig which consists of a large metal baseplate with a metal frame (including the beam to which the sensor is attached) (Newport, CA, USA), and a xyz-stage (PI M-605.1DD, Physik Instrumente, Germany) (see Fig. 4(a)). The xyz-stage is driven by three linear stepper motors, which were programmed to control the test movements.

Nine materials were used for testing: aluminum, glass, polycarbonate, cardboard, wood, paper, cotton cloth, leather, and rubber (see Fig. 4(b)). The data was collected (with a sampling rate of 1000 Hz) using PowerLab 16/35 and its corresponding software LabChart 8 (ADInstruments, Dunedin, New Zealand). All analysis was conducted using MATLAB version 2013b, 64-bit (MATLAB, Natick, MA, USA).

3.2   Experimental Protocol

The experiment consisted of two parts: (1) using the sensor to estimate μ_s, and (2) measuring μ_s from normal and tangential forces using a more traditional methodology.

(1) Sensor Friction Measurement (SFM): The spider sensor is pressed into the testing material (along z/vertical-axis) so that some pairs of sensor legs slip while others remain stuck. During this process, the platform continues rising at 5 mm/s until either all sensor legs have slipped (for those most slippery materials) or a normal force limit of 25 N is sensed by the ATI force/torque sensor.

(2) Reference Friction Measurement (RFM): Depending on how many legs have slipped during SFM, the testing platform (z-stage) first rises up to a corresponding height. For example, for wood, three pairs of legs have slipped, so the platform is programmed to rise to a level at which exactly three outer pairs of legs slip and the remaining pair of legs is still in the air above the test material. Then, while maintaining the same z-axis position, the xy-stage moves along negative x-direction (refer to Fig. 2(a) and Fig. 4(a), out from page).

Each of the nine testing materials was tested using the test sequence described above. This was then repeated ten times for each of the nine materials tested. The estimated μ_s ranges obtained from the spider sensor legs slipping (or not) during the sensor friction measurement (SFM) part of the protocol were then compared against the calculated μ_s values obtained from the normal and tangential forces measured by the ATI force/torque sensor at the moment the spider2 slips during the reference friction measurement (RFM) part of the testing protocol.

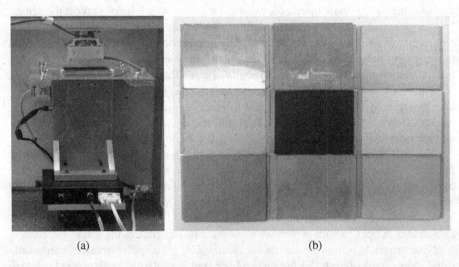

(a)   (b)

Fig. 4. (a) Photo of the whole testing rig. The spider2 is mounted to the ATI force/torque sensor, which is mounted onto the metal frame (top of image). Testing materials are inserted in a 3D-printed slot which is glued on a horizontal platform. The spider2 is fixed while the platform is driven by programmable stepper motors. (b) Photo of the nine testing materials (aluminium, polycarbonate, wood, cotton cloth, leather, paper, cardboard, glass and rubber in the order from upper left to lower right). All the materials are glued on a wooden baseplate.

3.3 Data Analysis

During SFM and RFM, voltage signals of eight channels (corresponding to eight sensor legs) and force signals of three channels (forces along x, y and z-axis) were recorded, respectively. A 2 Hz, second-order, low-pass Butterworth filter was applied to the ATI force signals to remove noise at frequencies greater than those of interest in this experiment. The 0–5 V slip detection voltages for each leg were converted to a binary variable by rounding. Any events which occur after the normal force reaches 25 N are disregarded, as we expect that large forces above what occur during normal object manipulation will eventually violate the idealized laws of dry friction, upon which the operation of the spider2 is based. Understanding the sensor's behavior at for larger forces will require further investigation.

As described earlier, the sensor provides a range for μ_s, which is given by the frictions corresponding to the leg at the largest angle which does not slip, to next smallest angle that slips. The sensor friction estimate is referred to as $\hat{\mu}_s$. In the RFM, experiment, to obtain a reference measure of friction, the maximum tangential force is found from the magnitude of the x- and y-axis data (F_x and F_y). This is then divided by the corresponding normal (z-axis) force (F_z) to obtain a reference measure of μ_s for each iteration. The reference friction is referred to as $\bar{\mu}_s$.

4 Results and Discussion

4.1 Experimental Results

Table 1 reports the $\hat{\mu}_s$ and $\bar{\mu}_s$ for all nine testing materials: the same legs slipped for all ten repeats for each material, hence one range is shown. Figure 5 shows a comparison of $\hat{\mu}_s$ and $\bar{\mu}_s$. Vertical lines demonstrate the range of $\hat{\mu}_s$ (from SFM experiment), and horizontal lines indicate $\bar{\mu}_s$ (from RFM experiment). A least-squares linear fit was performed on the center (midpoint) of the $\hat{\mu}_s$ range and the mean $\bar{\mu}_s$, and the fitted line is also shown in Fig. 5.

Table 1. Results of estimated ($\hat{\mu}_s$) and reference ($\bar{\mu}_s$) coefficient of static friction. #L means #th leg from outside on the left side and #R means #th leg from outside on the right side. Results are from ten repeated experiments.

Testing material	Which legs slipped?	$\hat{\mu}_s$	Mean ± standard deviation of $\bar{\mu}_s$
Aluminium	All legs	0–0.2	0.1893 ± 0.0023
Glass	All legs	0–0.2	0.1277 ± 0.0024
Polycarbonate	All legs	0–0.2	0.1495 ± 0.0150
Cardboard	3L, 2L, 1L, 1R, 2R, 3R	0.2–0.4	0.2316 ± 0.0149
Wood	3L, 2L, 1L, 1R, 2R, 3R	0.2–0.4	0.2378 ± 0.0170
Paper	3L, 2L, 1L, 1R, 2R, 3R	0.2–0.4	0.2504 ± 0.0056
Cloth	3L, 2L, 1L, 1R, 2R, 3R	0.2–0.4	0.2760 ± 0.0071
Leather	2L, 1L, 1R, 2R	0.4–0.6	0.4822 ± 0.0144
Rubber	1L, 1R	0.6–0.8	0.7609 ± 0.0775

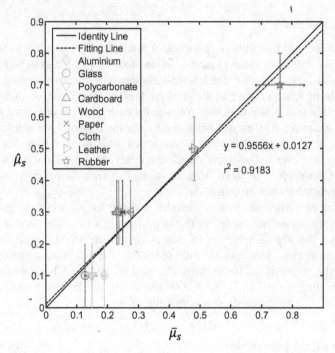

Fig. 5. Estimated ($\hat{\mu}_s$) and reference ($\bar{\mu}_s$) coefficient of static friction. Vertical lines indicate the range of $\hat{\mu}_s$, and horizontal lines indicate the interval centred at the mean of $\bar{\mu}_s \pm$ one standard deviation from ten measurements. Note that the horizontal lines for aluminium, glass and paper are not observable due to the extremely small standard deviations of these reference friction measurements, $\bar{\mu}_s$.

4.2 Discussion

From the testing, it can be seen that the estimated $\hat{\mu}_s$ is consistent with $\bar{\mu}_s$ for all testing materials; although for aluminum, the reference value is quite close to the upper boundary of the estimated range. In our previous work [15], that underestimation also occurs for several materials. A reason for such underestimation might lie in the dynamics of how the sensor legs made contact with the surface of testing materials. Since, if the leg will slip at all, it actually slips immediately after contacting the surface (the sensor is never actually static for us to measure static friction), and what it detects may be closer to the coefficient of kinetic friction, rather than μ_s. Here this problem has been somewhat mitigated by setting the velocity of the platform to rise at 5 mm/s.

For the old spider sensor, there was another factor that might have resulted in the underestimation, which was the sensor legs being slightly inclined out of the yz-plane. Ideally, the sensor legs should lie in the yz-plane (refer to Fig. 3) or be perpendicular to the xy-stage. However, a small angle (about five degrees) was observed for the old spider sensor. This problem does not exist for the spider2, and this is reflected by better performance. More specifically, the reference value for cloth (0.287) is above the estimated range (0.176–0.268) [15], while reference values for all testing materials lie in the corresponding estimated ranges. In addition, the least-square fitted line in this study is closer to the line of identity than that in previous work.

Overall, the spider2 friction sensor prototype demonstrates an ability to measure μ_s and this is shown by the least-squares linear fit (of the measured $\hat{\mu}_s$ compared to the reference $\bar{\mu}_s$) which has a gradient close to one and an r^2 value greater than 0.9 (Fig. 5). The novelty of the sensor is in its ability to measure μ_s by applying a normal force to the sensor, rather than dragging it across the test materials. Furthermore, *no knowledge of the forces involved is required*; we must only sense which legs have slipped. The accuracy of the estimation could be improved if more legs are constructed, with smaller differences in the frictional angle between adjacent legs. In contrast, the elastic finger-shaped sensor by Maeno *et al.* [13, 14] has a relatively poor error of 0.1, and more importantly it cannot distinguish between different values of μ_s above 0.5.

5 Conclusion and Future Work

We have proposed a novel friction sensor for tactile applications that is based solely on idealized physical principles of dry friction. The coefficient of static friction (μ_s) can be estimated by pressing the sensor against the surface of an object and detecting the slip or stick conditions of each sensor leg. This sensor provides an estimate of μ_s without the need for delicate measurement devices (strain gauges, for example) as most other tactile sensors contain, or sophisticated signal processing algorithms. In particular, this paper has demonstrated the resolution of some problems which existed with both the previous version of the spider sensor and its evaluation. The performance of the sensor is reasonable. Better robustness is achieved by using frame-shaped sensor legs, instead of the previously-used bar-shaped legs. Specifically, in terms of the contact interface, a rectangular area (the 2D convex hull around two contact lines from two sensor legs against a surface) rather than a line (between two contact points from two older legs) is formed when the new spider2 is pressed against a surface, which is more appropriate for gripping objects. In addition, since each set of sensor legs rotate around the same shaft, the size of the new spider is smaller than its previous version. Also, the dimension of the sensor will not increase dramatically as more sensor legs are added; in contrast, adding additional legs to the old spider design would require the sensor to be longer. Although the proposed sensor is currently limited to applications in which manipulated objects have a planar surface, such problem might be readily solved when more advanced manufacturing makes the sensor smaller so that the curvature of the contact interface could be neglected.

Future work will mainly focus on three areas of interest. Firstly, the effect of elastic bands will be considered and the estimated friction ranges will be corrected accordingly to undo the interfering effects of these bands. The second focus will be on the application of the sensor to dynamic testing scenarios – that is, a robotic gripper controlled by a force control system. The sensed coefficient of static friction of the manipulated object will be an input to the control system to assist it in adjusting the grip force of the robotic gripper. Finally, efforts will be made to further miniaturize the sensor to make it useful for real tactile applications.

Acknowledgments. The authors are indebted to Mr. Yuanyou Wang, who offered support in making the electronic instrumentation components of the sensor. This research was supported by an Australian Research Council Future Fellowships grant (FT130100858).

References

1. Blau, P.J.: The significance and use of the friction coefficient. Tribol. Int. **34**(9), 585–591 (2001)
2. Tremblay, M.R., Cutkosky, M.R.: Estimating friction using incipient slip sensing during a manipulation task. In: Proceedings of the IEEE International Conference on Robotics and Automation, vol. 1, pp. 429–434 (1993)
3. Patterson, R.W., Nevill, G.E.: The induced vibration touch sensor–a new dynamic touch sensing concept. Robotica **4**, 27–31 (1986)
4. Dornfeld, D., Handy, C.: Slip detection using acoustic emission signal analysis. In: Proceedings of the IEEE International Conference Robotics and Automation, vol. 4, pp. 1868–1875 (1987)
5. Howe, R.D., Cutkosky, M.R.: Sensing skin acceleration for slip and texture perception. In: Proceedings of the IEEE International Conference on Robotics and Automation, vol. 1, pp. 145–150 (1989)
6. Canepa, G., et al.: Detection of incipient object slippage by skin-like sensing and neural network processing. IEEE Trans. Syst. Man Cybern. B Cybern. **28**(3), 348–356 (1998)
7. Fujimoto, I., et al.: Development of artificial finger skin to detect incipient slip for realization of static friction sensation. In: Proceedings of the IEEE International Conference on Multisensor Fusion and Integration for Intelligent Systems, pp. 15–20 (2003)
8. Chuang, C.-H., Liou, Y.-R., Chen, C.-W.: Detection system of incident slippage and friction coefficient based on a flexible tactile sensor with structural electrodes. Sens. Actuators A Phys. **188**, 48–55 (2012)
9. Bicchi, A.: Intrinsic contact sensing for soft fingers. In: Proceedings of the IEEE International Conference on Robotics and Automation, vol. 2, pp. 968–973 (1990)
10. Bayrleithner, R., Komoriya, K.: Static friction coefficient determination by force sensing and its application. In: Proceedings of the IEEE/RSJ/GI International Conference on Intelligent Robots and Systems, vol. 3, pp. 1639–1646 (1994)
11. Shinoda, H., Sasaki, S., Nakamura, K.: Instantaneous evaluation of friction based on ARTC tactile sensor. In: Proceedings of the IEEE International Conference on Robotics and Automation, vol. 3, pp. 2173–2178 (2000)
12. Nakamura, K., Shinoda, H.: A tactile sensor instantaneously evaluating friction coefficients. In: Proceedings of the 11th IEEE International Conference on Solid-State Sensors and Actuators, pp. 1430–1433 (2001)
13. Maeno, T., Kawai, T., Kobayashi, K.: Analysis and design of a tactile sensor detecting strain distribution inside an elastic finger. In: Proceedings of the IEEE/RSJ International Conference on Intelligent Robots and Systems, vol. 3, pp. 1658–1663 (1998)
14. Maeno, T., Kawamura, T., Cheng, S.-C.: Friction estimation by pressing an elastic finger-shaped sensor against a surface. IEEE Trans. Robot. Autom. **20**(2), 222–228 (2004)
15. Chen, W., et al.: An eight-legged tactile sensor to estimate coefficient of static friction. In: 37th Annual IEEE International Conference Engineering in Medicine and Biology Society, pp. 4407–4410 (2015)

Tactile Vision Substitution with Tablet and Electro-Tactile Display

Haruya Uematsu[1](✉), Masaki Suzuki[2], Yonezo Kanno[2],
and Hiroyuki Kajimoto[1]

[1] The University of Electro-Communications,
1-5-1 Chofugaoka, Chofu, Tokyo, Japan
{uematsu,kajimoto}@kaji-lab.jp
[2] EyePlusPlus, Inc., Shinsagawa Bldg. 201, 1-27-1,
Ishihara, Sumida-ku, Tokyo, Japan
{suzuki,kanno}@eyeplus2.com

Abstract. We developed a device that converts visual information on a tablet into tactile information on the fingertip. To achieve this we mount optical sensors and a tactile display on the fingertip. Our first prototype using a vibrator for each finger revealed that it was difficult to recognize the information of the display, mainly because of its low resolution. We addressed this limitation in our second prototype by using electro-tactile stimulation. From our preliminary experiment with a mechanical pin matrix, we decided to use a single index finger. In a subsequent alphabet recognition experiment, we confirmed that it is possible to recognize relatively complex shapes on a tablet with the device. Furthermore, we observed that the learning curve is quite steep, which implies the potential of the device.

Keywords: Electro-tactile · Tactile vision substitution · Visually impaired

1 Introduction

Understanding information on a computer screen is a challenge for visually impaired people. When the character-based user interface (CUI) was dominant, it was relatively easy to convert the information to voice or braille display. Then, the era of the graphical based user interface (GUI) arrived, where the presented information cannot be easily translated to a temporal sequence. Today, tactile graphics displays that incorporate numerous mechanical pins are widely used to present graphical information.

Now we live in the era of personal portable computing devices. Of these, the tablet has perhaps the ideal user interface for non-blind users because it is "what you see is what you touch". However, for visually impaired users, information has once again become difficult to access. Tactile graphics displays can be connected but the portability is sacrificed.

This paper addresses this issue, by developing a portable tactile vision substitution system for a tablet. The device is composed of an array of optical sensors and an electro-tactile display for one finger. The optical sensors capture the brightness of the display, and the electro-tactile display presents it directly to the finger. This device is a

© Springer International Publishing Switzerland 2016
F. Bello et al. (Eds.): EuroHaptics 2016, Part I, LNCS 9774, pp. 503–511, 2016.
DOI: 10.1007/978-3-319-42321-0_47

direct descendant of previous SmartTouch system [1], but it has four times more electrodes, which greatly improves its resolution. This enables numerous functionalities. For example, by using the tablet's camera, visually impaired users can take a picture of the surrounding environment and determine its contents by their finger, enabling them to go sightseeing.

The contribution of the paper is twofold. First, we demonstrate that shape recognition using a single optical sensor and vibrator on one finger is quite difficult, but multiple fingers are not required. Second, we use the developed system to perform a relatively complex shape recognition task using alphabets.

2 Related Work

A tactile vision substitution system (TVSS) was first proposed by Collins [2]. They used a video camera and vibrators or electrodes on the abdomen or back to let users feel the surrounding environment. This type of TVSS for the 3D environment has numerous descendants, such as the Forehead Retina System [3], which used electrical stimulation on forehead, and the HamsaTouch [4], which used a smartphone camera to capture images and selected the palm as a display site.

TVSS for the 2D desktop environment also has a long history. Optacon [5] was the most successful product, which let users touch written information on paper using a handheld camera and a mechanical pin matrix. Although a mechanical display still requires a large setup, SmartTouch uses electrodes and an optical sensor matrix to shrink its size.

TVSS are now being used with tablets to allow users to feel the information on the surface of the display. Giudice and Palani [6] detect finger position on the tablet and vibrate the whole surface. Burch and Pawluk [7] used a combination of an optical color sensor and a vibrator mounted on each finger to enable users to feel the surface of the tablet. However, although the latter work achieved the perception of textures and simple shapes, recognition of complex information remains a challenge.

In the following we describe two prototypes. The first is composed of an optical sensor and a vibrator unit for each finger, similar to previous approaches [7, 8]. The second is composed of a matrix of optical sensors and an electrode unit, similar to the SmartTouch device [1]. While the SmartTouch was composed of a relatively limited number of sensing and display units, and it did not validate the accuracy of the presented information, the system was much improved and evaluation using alphabet recognition task was conducted.

3 Prototype Using Vibrator Unit and Sensor Unit on Each Finger

As a first prototype, we developed a device that uses a vibrator and an optical sensor on each finger. We used a linear resonant actuator (LRA) (LD14-002, Nidec Copal Corporation) that can vibrate at 150 Hz with 20 ms latency, and a phototransistor (PT19-21C, Everlight Electronics Co., Ltd.), which has a peak wavelength of 940 nm.

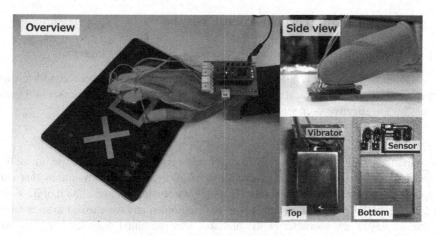

Fig. 1. Overview of the prototype using a vibrator and a sensor unit for each finger.

The unit was mounted on each finger so that it reacted to the brightness change of the tablet. A microcontroller (mbed NXP LPC1768, ARM Holdings) was used to control the whole system (Fig. 1). This system is similar to the structures developed by Burch and Pawluk [7] and Ando et al. [8]. While the primary purpose of the optical sensor–vibrator pair was to present texture information, we also examined whether it is possible to convey more detailed shape information.

We conducted a preliminary experiment to verify whether it is possible use the device to recognize the shape displayed on the tablet. We attached the units to all five fingers but we did not explicitly ask participants to use them all. However, we found that it was quite difficult to recognize the shape of the figure with the device, although the LRA responded quickly and the texture was presented to the finger.

We believe that there were two possible causes for this uncertainty. First, there was a size mismatch between the sensor and the actuator. The size of the vibrator was 14.0 mm × 11.2 mm, about 100 times larger than the size of optical sensor (1.6 mm × 0.8 mm). Therefore, users might not have been able to identify the relationship between the sensor position and the display position. Second, there was a lack of local information on the fingertip. In the situation when a bare finger strokes on a relief shape, the relief generates a line or dot pattern on the finger, giving users local directional information. However, the whole finger vibration cannot provide this information, and so the user must scan the whole surface to identify presented shapes.

To resolve these issues, it is necessary to reduce the sensor stimulation area and use multiple stimulators–sensor pairs on a finger to let users feel local shape on the fingertip. This can be achieved with an electro-tactile display that can stimulate with a higher density while keeping the device thin.

We observed that frequency of use of each finger is different among fingers. After getting used to the device, the participants mainly used the index finger and middle finger and the thumb and little finger were barely used. Therefore, the number of fingers to be used will be examined before constructing the next system.

4 Prototype Using Electro-Tactile Display

4.1 Experiment 1: Identification of Necessary Number of Fingers

To develop a TVSS for a tablet using an electro-tactile display, we conducted an experiment using a mechanical tactile graphics display to identify the number of fingers necessary for effective user sensing.

4.1.1 Procedure

Six participants, all male, aged from 21 to 25 years, participated in this experiment; the authors were not included. We used a DotView DV-2 (KGS Corporation) that can display the graphic as mechanical relief in a pin matrix with a pin resolution of 32 × 48 and a pitch of 2.4 mm. The participants were blindfolded and were asked to sit in front of the display. Each character of the alphabet was presented once randomly on the display, making 26 characters displayed in total. The participants were asked to identify the displayed alphabet relying on the sense of touch of their bare fingers, as fast and accurate as possible.

There were three finger conditions: index finger only (I), index finger + middle finger (I/M), and index finger + middle finger + ring finger (I/M/R). There were two font size conditions: large (about 52 mm in height) and small (about 20 mm in height) (Fig. 2). There were 26 × 3 × 2 = 156 trials for each participant. We fixed the condition pairs and repeated 26 trials for each condition. The order of conditions was randomized to avoid anticipation bias.

4.1.2 Results

Figure 3 (left) and (right) show the median answer time and the average correct answer rate for each finger condition, respectively. We performed a two-way within-participants repeated-measure analysis of variance (ANOVA). The within-participants factors were the number of fingers used and the size of the character.

Regarding answer time, the number of fingers was significant ($F(2, 930) = 3.00$; $p < 0.05$). The relation between the number of fingers and the size of the character

Fig. 2. Displayed character on the tactile display; (left) large condition, (right) small condition.

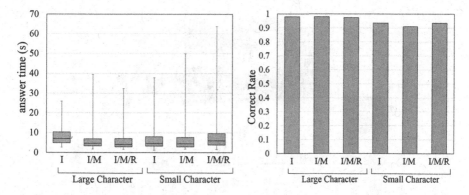

Fig. 3. Answer time (left) and correct answer rate (right) for each finger condition; I: index finger, M: middle finger, R: ring finger.

identified was also significant (F(2, 930) = 3.00; p < 0.01), as was the relation between the size of the character and the correct answer rate (F(2, 35) = 3.31; p < 0.01).

The number of fingers used made no difference to the percentage of correct answers. The participants identified the character with a high degree of accuracy in all finger conditions. Wrong answers were often observed for particular character pairs, such as O/C and Q/G. Using multiple fingers tended to give shorter answer times for the large character condition, but this tendency was reversed in the small character condition. These results suggest that for shape recognition tasks, the number of fingers only has a small effect on the correct answer rate, and the optimal number of fingers for recognition time depends on the character size. Craig [9] suggested that a searching task with two fingers gives lower performance than with one finger. Lappin and Foulke [10] pointed out the poor performance with multiple fingers. Our results are generally consistent with these studies.

4.2 High-Density TVSS for Finger

Based on the preliminary experiment, we developed a high-density TVSS for a tablet using an electro-tactile display and a matrix of optical sensors for one finger (Fig. 4). Although the electro-tactile display still has some disadvantages, such as stability and quality of sensation, it is also thin, high density, clear, permits localized sensation and is low cost [1, 4, 11, 12].

The electro-tactile display is composed of 63 (7 × 9) electrodes with 2-mm center intervals. The sensor is composed of the same number of optical sensors (PT19-21C, Everlight Electronics Co., Ltd.), arranged just beneath the electrodes (Fig. 5). As the two-point discrimination threshold of the finger is known to be 1.5 mm at the fingertip and 3 mm at the finger pad [13], the electrode intervals of 2 mm are sufficient for the finger pad. We used a 10.1-inch tablet (T100TA-DK32G, ASUS) for all experiments. The optical sensors detect the brightness distribution of the tablet and the electro-tactile stimulation is actuated when the brightness reaches a certain threshold. The control loop was 68 Hz, pulse frequency was 35 µs, maximal pulse height was 10 mA, which

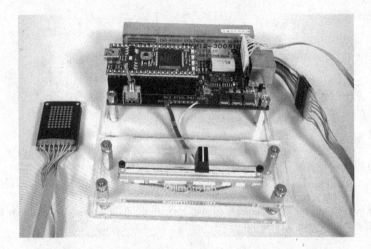

Fig. 4. Electro-tactile stimulation device for a single finger.

Fig. 5. High-density TVSS. (Left) electrodes, (center) sensors, (right) combined, side view.

could be freely adjusted by participants using a slide volume; most participants chose a pulse height of less than 5 mA. For these settings line direction could be clearly determined. For the next experiment, we set the thickness of the line displayed on the tablet to around 2 mm so that it could be recognized by the optical sensor.

4.3 Experiment 2: Alphabet Identification Task Using High-Density TVSS

4.3.1 Procedure

Six participants, all male, aged from 21 to 25 years, participated in this experiment (Fig. 6); the authors were not included. Each character was displayed on the tablet randomly, making 26 trials in total to complete the alphabet. The participants were blindfolded and asked to respond to the displayed character as fast and accurately as possible. There were two character size conditions, large (52 mm) and small (20 mm), as per Experiment 1. The index finger was used in all recognition tasks in the

Fig. 6. Overview of the experiment.

experiment. There were 52 (26 × 2) trials for each participant. Three participants conducted the large character condition first, followed by the small character condition, and the others conducted the experiment in reverse order, to avoid order bias.

4.3.2 Results

Figure 7 shows the median answer time and the average correct answer rate. Figure 8 shows the median answer time for each trial number from 1 to 52, where the character size was mixed. We performed a *t*-test on the data. There was a significant difference in answering correctly for the two character sizes ($p < 0.05$).

The correct answer rates were 76.2 % for the large characters and 56.4 % for the small characters, which are significantly higher than the chance rate (1/27 – 3.8 %) but lower than the answer rates in the previous experiment using mechanical tactile display. The answer time was also longer than in the previous experiment. However, we observed a learning curve in this experiment; answer time was 50 s at the beginning but dropped to 30 s by the end of the experiment (Fig. 8). Some participants commented that they came to recognize the character clearly in the second half of the trials. We also conducted a preliminary experiment with a participant who carried out the experiment

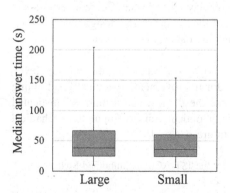
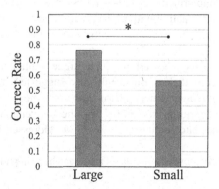

Fig. 7. Results of the alphabet identification task for the two character sizes.

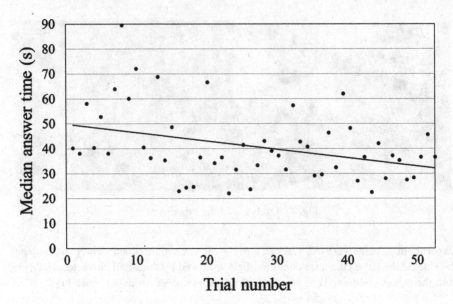

Fig. 8. Answer time for each trial number.

using the electro-tactile display on a daily basis. His answer rate was 94 % and his median answer time was 12.4 s, which was comparable with the results from the mechanical display. From these observations, we submit that further training with the device will improve recognition accuracy. In our current algorithm, we simply stimulated based on display brightness. However, a more sophisticated algorithm, such as with edge enhancement, could be used to simulate mechanical interaction between skin and the relief.

5 Conclusion

We developed and evaluated a tactile vision substitution system for people with visual impairments. Employing an electro-tactile display, the device can convert optical information with high density to a small area of the fingertip. The design was based on preliminary experiments with a mechanical pin matrix, which demonstrated that a single finger device is sufficient for shape recognition. The experiment with the new device showed a much higher character recognition rate than the chance level. Nonetheless, our results also suggested areas for improvement. Specifically, a training regimen is needed for the user to learn to use the device, and a more sophisticated algorithm is required for the conversion from optical sensory input to mechanical actuator output. These will be addressed in future work.

Acknowledgements. This research is supported by the JST-ACCEL Embodied Media Project.

References

1. Kajimoto, H., Inami, M., Kawasaki, N., Tachi, S.: Symposium on haptic interfaces for virtual environment and teleoperator systems, HAPTICS 2003 (2003)
2. Collins, C.C.: Tactile television–mechanical and electrical image projection. IEEE Trans. Man Mach. Syst. **11**(1), 65–71 (1970)
3. Kajimoto, H., Kannno, Y., Tachi, S.: Forehead electro-tactile display for vision substitution. In: EuroHaptics 2006, Paris (2006)
4. Kajimoto, H., Suzuki, M., Kanno, Y.: HamsaTouch: tactile vision substitution with smartphone and electro-tactile display. In: The ACM CHI Conference on Human Factors in Computing Systems (2014)
5. Linvill, J.G., Bliss, J.C.: A direct translation reading aid for the blind. In: Proceedings of the IEEE (1966)
6. Giudice, N.A., Palani, H.: Learning non-visual graphical information using a touch-based vibro–audio interface. In: Proceedings of ASSETS (2012)
7. Burch, D., Pawluk, D.: Using multiple contacts with texture-enhanced graphics. In: World Haptics (2011)
8. Ando, H., Miki, T., Inami, M., Maeda, T.: SmartFinger: nail-mounted tactile display. In: ACM SIGGRAPH (2002)
9. Craig, J.C.: Attending to two fingers: two hands are better than one. Percept. Psychophys. **38**(6), 496–511 (1985)
10. Lappin, J.S., Foulke, E.: Expanding the tactual field of view. Percept. Psychophys. **14**(2), 237–241 (1973)
11. Kaczmarek, K.A., Tyler, M.E., Bach-y-Rita, P.: Electrotactile haptic display on the fingertips, preliminary results. In: Proceedings of the 16th Annual International Conference of the IEEE Engineering in Medicine and Biology Society, pp. 940–941 (1994)
12. Bach-y-Rita, P., Kaczmarek, K.A., Tyler, M.E., Garcia-Lara, J.: Form perception with a 49-point electro-tactile stimulus array on the tongue. J. Rehabil. Res. Dev. **35**, 427–430 (1998)
13. Jones, L.A., Lederman, S.J.: Human Hand Function. Oxford University Press, Oxford (2006)

Augmentation of Thermal Sensation on Finger Pad Using Stimuli for Finger Side

Katsunari Sato[✉]

Nara Women's University, Kitauoya Nishi Machi, Nara City 630-8506, Japan
katsu-sato@cc.nara-wu.ac.jp

Abstract. This paper proposes a thermal display that can present a virtual thermal sensation to the finger pad using thermal stimuli on the finger side. The author developed the prototype device and evaluated the perceived strength of the thermal sensation on the finger pad after the pad makes contacts with an object. The results confirm that users perceive hot or cold sensation even if there are no thermal stimuli on the finger pad by presenting stimuli to the finger side. Furthermore, the proposed method successfully improves thermal sensation by applying the same thermal stimuli to the finger side as the sensation on the finger pad.

Keywords: Thermal display · Thermal perception · Virtual reality · Augmented reality

1 Introduction

Presentation of the thermal sense, by which a human can perceive an object's temperature and material, has been a great challenge in the development of haptic displays. Because it has been revealed that the thermal sense is one of the important properties in human texture perception [1, 2], many haptic displays that can present not only skin deformations or vibrations, but also temperature change, have been developed [3–5]. These displays mainly place thermal devices on a finger pad because users can perceive haptic sensation on their finger pad.

The aim of this study is to develop a thermal display that does not have thermal devices on the user's finger pad, but can present thermal sensation on the pad. If there is no thermal device on the finger pad, the author expects mainly two advantages compared with conventional thermal displays. First, we can realize a thermal augmentation haptic device, such as a vibrotactile augmentation device, that uses a vibrator on the fingernail [6]. We can change the thermal sensation when a user touches real objects in order to perceive them as being made from a different material. For example, when the user touches with the finger pad an object made from wood, the cold sensation presented from the thermal device could cause the user to perceive the object as though it were metal. Second, the thermal device can be easily integrated with other haptic devices, such as vibrators and electrotactile displays, in order to realize haptic groves that represent various sensations. For example, when we integrate conventional thermal displays with vibrators, we have to place the thermal display on the vibrators, and such display then disturbs the quality of the vibrotactile sensation. In another case,

© Springer International Publishing Switzerland 2016
F. Bello et al. (Eds.): EuroHaptics 2016, Part I, LNCS 9774, pp. 512–520, 2016.
DOI: 10.1007/978-3-319-42321-0_48

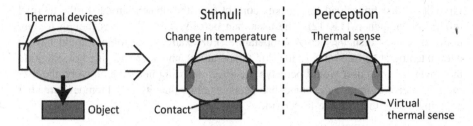

Fig. 1. Conceptual diagram for proposed thermal display

when thermal and electrotactile displays are integrated, perceiving the thermal sensation becomes difficult because the electrodes are placed between the thermal display and the pad. Placing thermal devices outside the pad can solve these problems.

In order to develop such thermal display, the author focuses on the spatial characteristics of thermal perception. Many studies [7–9] have shown that the spatial resolution of thermal stimulus that causes changes in skin temperature, especially hot, is not high and humans tend to perceive the thermal sensation at the position where there is no thermal stimuli. Some studies [10–14] have investigated the thermal referral phenomenon. They have applied thermal and tactile stimuli to different fingers or arm sites simultaneously and confirmed that illusory thermal sensation occurs at the site of tactile stimulus. Another study [15] reported the possibility of thermal phantom sensation that causes thermal sensation on the skin surface at the midpoint of thermal stimuli. The author considers that when this phenomenon is applied to the device's design, the thermal display that augments thermal sensation to the finger pad where there is no actual stimulus (Fig. 1) can be achieved.

In this study, the author proposes a thermal display that presents thermal stimuli to the side of the fingertip, and evaluates how users perceive thermal sensation from an object that makes contact with their finger pad by presenting thermal stimulation on their finger side.

2 Presentation of Augmented Thermal Sense

2.1 Thermal Stimuli to Finger Side

The author focuses on the side of the fingertip as the position for thermal stimulation. Previous studies [11, 12] on the thermal referral phenomenon have shown that the distance between tactile and thermal stimuli affect the perceived thermal sense on the tactile site: short distance is suitable for this phenomenon. Furthermore, the heat phantom sensation [15] can be expected by "sandwiching" the fingertip with thermal stimuli from both sides. From these studies, the author considers that when the thermal and tactile stimuli are presented to both the side and pad of the fingertip, respectively, the thermal sense is virtually perceived on the finger pad.

Figure 1 shows the proposed thermal presentation method. When the user's finger pad makes contact with an object, thermal stimuli are applied to both sides of the fingertip. Then, the user perceives thermal sense not only on the finger side, but also virtually on the finger pad that makes contact with the object, similar to the thermal referral phenomenon [11, 12]. The user then perceives the object as though it were hotter or colder than the actual temperature. For example, the object could have a neutral temperature (the same as the skin temperature), and after applying hot stimuli to the finger side, the user would perceive the object as being hot. Alternatively, the user might perceive as though the object had become colder than its actual temperature after applying cold stimuli to the finger side.

2.2 Prototype Implementation

Figure 2 shows a prototype of the proposed thermal display. The author places two Peltier devices (8.3 mm × 8.3 mm × 2.4 mm; TEFC1-03112; Nihon Tecmo Co., Ltd.) on each side of the fingertip. The Peltier devices create a heat flux between the two sides of the devices by applying a voltage. The Peltier devices work as either a cooler or heater depending on the voltage polarity, and the rate of temperature change can be controlled by adjusting the voltage. Furthermore, the Peltier devices can easily be attached to the fingertip because they have a relatively small body.

The proposed method requires the temporal response of the thermal display to present the thermal sense at the moment when the finger pad makes contact with an object. Therefore, two Peltier devices are used for hot ("a" "d," as shown in Fig. 2) and two for cold ("b" "c," also shown in Fig. 2) stimuli only. In a previous study [16], the author confirmed that this spatial configuration is efficient for virtually improving the temporal response. The author places thermistors (P1703, Alpha Technics Inc.) between the front surface of two of the Peltier devices ("b" and "d") and the user's skin to measure the boundary temperature. Heat sinks (19 mm × 14 mm × 5 mm; made from aluminum) are attached on the back surface of the Peltier devices to improve their stability. The Peltier devices are attached to the heat sink using a double-coated heat transfer tape. These devices are then fixed to the user's fingertip using Velcro tape in order to arrange the Peltier devices between the finger's tip and first joint.

The controller for the Peltier devices consists of a laptop, microprocessor board (Arduino Nano; Arduino Inc.), and two motor servo driver chips (TA7291P; Toshiba Co., Ltd.). The Peltier devices are connected in series of two to the driver chip ("a" "d" and "b" and "c," as shown in Fig. 2). The laptop calculates the voltages applied to each

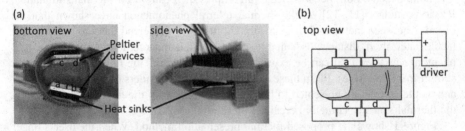

Fig. 2. Constructed prototype. (a) Picture of the device. (b) Schematic diagram that represents an example of serial connection of Peltier devices "a" "d."

Peltier device, and sends these values to the Arduino Nano through a serial connection. The voltage is output from the conversion of two digital signals to analog (DA); pulse-width modulation (PWM) output pins are connected to a driver chip that is in turn connected to the Peltier devices. The power supplies for the motor drivers are two DC adapters (9V2A; Akizuki Denshi Tsusho Co., Ltd.). The voltages applied to the Peltier devices are updated at 200 Hz.

In the next section, the author evaluates the following hypothesis using this prototype: whether the proposed method can augment the thermal sensation of an object.

3   Experiment

3.1   Objective

In this section, the author examines the thermal sensation perceived with the finger pad when presenting thermal stimuli to the finger side after the finger pad makes contact with an object: the object produces a neutral or the same thermal sensation of stimuli. The evaluation is based on the magnitude estimation method.

3.2   Materials and Methods

Participants. Nine females aged 18 to 21 years, and who did not know the hypotheses being investigated participated in the experiment. Prior to the experiment, all participants were instructed on the experiment procedures. There was no visual or audio restriction through the experiment.

Equipment and Environment. Figure 3 shows the setup for the experiments. The author prepared a hot plate (NHP-M20, NISSIN Co., Ltd.) in order to adjust the initial temperature of the skin and the objects to be used for touch; the objects were then placed on the hot plate. Two Peltier devices ("e" "f", as shown in Fig. 3) on green-colored aluminum were the target objects used for touch in this experiment. Black aluminum was used as the platform on which to rest the participant's fingertip during an interval in the experiment.

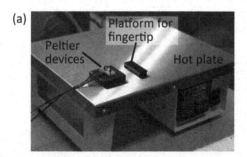

Fig. 3. Experiment equipment. (a) Hot plate and target object (Peltier devices) used for touch. (b) Method used to touch target object.

The surface temperature of the hot plate was set to 32.5 °C in order to increase the temperature of the Peltier devices and platform to approximately 31.5 °C in a room where the temperature and humidity were approximately 22 °C and 35 %, respectively.

Conditions. The experiments were separated into two parts: hot and cold. For the hot part, the participants perceived only hot stimulus, and answered how they perceived the strength of the hot sensation. For the cold part, the participants answered how they perceived the strength of coldness after experiencing the cold stimuli.

For each part, there are six conditions for stimuli, where each condition of consists of one stimuli pattern and strength. There are three patterns in total (Fig. 4). The first stimuli pattern is "Both," where the participants perceive thermal stimuli from the Peltier devices on the pad ("e" "f") and fingertip side ("a" "d"). In the "Pad" and "Side" patterns, the participants perceive stimuli from the finger pad and sides, respectively. For each "Pad" and "Side" pattern, the author selected two Peltier devices to equalize the energy applied to the fingertip from the Peltier device. Prior to the experiment, the author confirmed that the "Pad" pattern does not affect the temperature of "Side," and vice versa. Furthermore, the participants trained to touch the Peltier devices ("e" "f") with the center of the finger pad, and the author adjusted the position of the Peltier devices on their finger side ("a"–"d").

The author prepared different stimuli strength in order to prevent the participants from noticing the experiment design. Strong and weak stimuli were defined as the rate of temperature change in the fingertip: they were approximately 3.5 °C/s and 2.5 °C/s, respectively, fpr the hot part of the experiment. For the cold part, the change rates were 3 °C/s and 2 °C/s, respectively. These strengths were selected for the participants to clearly perceive the stimuli. Because humans are more sensitive to cold stimuli than hot [17], the hot stimuli produce larger changes in temperature compared with the cold stimuli. The experiment stimuli were applied for 2 s and there was no thermal stimulus from the Peltier device to the skin before and after the experiment stimuli. The duration of the stimulus was determined in order to present a clear thermal sensation based on a preliminary experiment.

Procedures. Prior to the experiment, each participant placed their right hand directly on the hot plate for longer than 5 min in order to adjust their surface temperature. The prototype device was also placed on the hot plate. Subsequently, they wore the prototype device on the index finger of their right hand. Afterward, the temperature of the participants' finger pad increased to approximately 32 °C, whereas that of the finger side increased to approximately 31 °C because of the low room temperature.

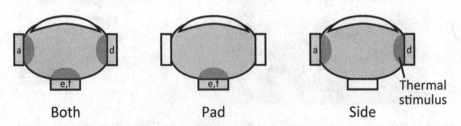

Fig. 4. Patterns for thermal stimuli

In the first part of the experiment (hot or cold was selected randomly), the participants placed their finger pad on the platform for 30 s. Subsequently, they touched the target object without stimuli. The author indicated that the strength perceived from the target object was "zero." Then, the participants touched the target object again with thermal stimuli where the condition was Pad-Strong; this is used as the standard stimuli, and it represents strength of "100." The timing of the thermal stimuli started immediately after contact, and such timing was executed by the author with a click of the mouse. After the standard stimuli, the participants touched the target object with a randomly selected condition, and indicated verbally the perceived strength compared with the standard strength. Between each condition, the participants returned their fingertip to the platform, and adjusted the fingertip skin temperature for 30 s. The participants executed each of the six conditions, and answered questions after each condition. This process was repeated three times. Therefore, the participants evaluated each of the six conditions three times. After completing the first part, the participants rested for five minutes, and continued with the second part.

It should be noted that the author instructed the participants to indicate the strength of the sensation perceived on their finger pad regardless of their perception on the finger side.

3.3   Results

The graphs shown in Fig. 5 indicate the results for hot and cold stimuli. The horizontal and vertical axes represent the pattern and perceived strength of the stimulus, respectively. The bars and error bars represent the average and standard deviation, respectively, of all participants. The dark and light bar colors represent the strength of the stimuli. For the strength perceived by each participant, the author calculated the average of the three evaluations per stimulus condition.

One-factor ANOVA shows significant differences in the results for both hot [$F(5, 53) = 17.48$, $p < 0.05$] and cold [$F(5, 53) = 12.86$, $p < 0.05$] stimuli. Furthermore, multiple comparisons using Ryan's method show that there are significant differences ($p < 0.05$) between some conditions. The "*" shown in Fig. 5 represents the

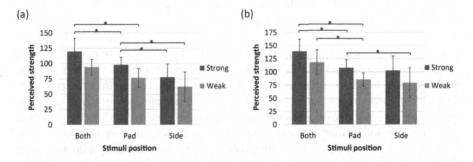

Fig. 5. Average perceived strength for each condition. (a) and (b) indicate hot and cold conditions, respectively. * represents $p < 0.05$. (Color figure online)

pairs of conditions that show significant differences compared with the "Pad" conditions. For the results of the hot stimuli, there are significant differences between "Both" and "Pad," and between "Pad" and "Side" for the strong stimulus. The weak stimulus for "Pad" and strong stimulus for "Side" do not show significant differences. In the case of cold stimuli, there are also significant differences between "Both" and "Pad," regardless of the strength of the stimuli. However, there is no significant difference between "Pad" and "Side" per stimuli strength.

The participants appear to perceive the thermal sensation on their finger pad in the "Side" condition equivalent to that in the "Pad" condition for the cold stimuli. For the hot stimuli, the perceived strength in the "Side" seems to be smaller than "Pad," but the participants also perceive thermal sensation in this case. Furthermore, the "Both" condition presents stronger thermal sensation than the "Pad" for both warm and cold stimuli.

3.4 Discussion

The results of the experiment indicate that the participants could perceive the virtual thermal sensation from the stimuli to the finger side when the object in contact with the finger pad has a neutral temperature. Furthermore, when the object is hot (or cold), the hot (or cold) stimulus to the finger side appears to increase the thermal sensation. Therefore, the author concludes that thermal augmentation on the finger pad using the proposed method is possible.

The author expects that the proposed method could diminish the thermal sensation on the finger pad when presenting the opposite thermal stimuli to the finger side. For example, applying cold stimuli to the finger side could eliminate the thermal sensation on the finger pad when the latter makes contact with a hot object. The author will investigate this in future works.

When the author develops a thermal display using the proposed method, the perceived strength will become an important parameter. Based on the results of the thermal referral study [13], the perceived strength on the site of the tactile stimulus appears to become smaller than the perceived strength of the actual stimulus because the thermal sensations on surrounding sites appear to combine and redistribute to both sites of the thermal and tactile stimuli (finger side and pad). The results of the hot stimuli agree with this hypothesis. However, the perception of the cold stimuli on the finger side is the same strength as that on the finger pad. The author believes that this is caused by the lower skin temperature on the finger side. When the skin temperature was cold, the participants could more easily perceive the cold stimuli, but it became more difficult to perceive the hot stimulus [18]. This difference seems to affect the thermal sensation on the finger pad. In addition, the environmental temperature could affect the perceived thermal sensation. In the future, the author will investigate the perceived sensation more clearly in order to design an application for this thermal device. For example, using the proposed method, the author will evaluate the sensation on the finger side or finger pad without making contact with an object. The findings in this paper also clarify the mechanism of human thermal perception.

4   Conclusion

In this paper, the author proposed a thermal display that can present thermal sensation on the finger pad using the thermal stimuli applied to such finger pad. The author experimentally confirmed that thermal stimuli on the finger side can change the perception on the finger pad: such stimuli could make an object of neutral temperature appear hotter or colder, and enhance the hot or cold sensation after making contact with a hotter or colder object.

The author expects the findings of this study to facilitate the development of haptic displays, and realize a thermal augmentation device. The author will investigate the characteristics of perceived strength using the proposed method for these applications.

Acknowledgement. This work was supported by JST ACCEL Embodied Media project.

References

1. Yoshida, M.: Dimensions of tactual impressions (1). Jpn. Psychol. Res. **10**(3), 123–137 (1968)
2. Shirado, H., Maeno, T.: Modeling of human texture perception for tactile displays and sensors. In: The First Joint Eurohaptics Conference and Symposium on Haptic Interface for Virtual Environment and Teleoperator Systems, pp. 629–630 (2005)
3. Kammermeier, P., Kron, A., Hoogen, J., Schmidt, G.: Display of holistic haptic sensations by combined tactile and kinesthetic feedback. Presence MIT Press J. **13**(1), 1–15 (2004)
4. Sato, K., Shinoda, H., Tachi, S.: Design and implementation of transmission system of initial haptic impression. In: SICE Annual Conference 2011, pp. 616–621 (2011)
5. Kurogi, T., Nakayama M., Sato, K., Kamuro, S., Fernando, C.L., Furukawa, M., Minamizawa, K., Tachi, S.: Haptic transmission system to recognize differences in surface textures of objects for telexistence. In: IEEE Virtual Reality 2013, pp. 137–138 (2013)
6. Niwa, M., Nozaki, T., Maeda, T., Ando, H.: Fingernail-mounted display of attraction force and texture. In: Kappers, A.M., van Erp, J.B., Bergmann Tiest, W.M., van der Helm, F.C. (eds.) EuroHaptics 2010, Part II. LNCS, vol. 6192, pp. 3–8. Springer, Heidelberg (2010)
7. Vendrik, A.J.H., Eijkman, E.G.: Psychophysical properties determined with internal noise. In: Kenshalo, D.R. (ed.) The Skin Senses, pp. 178–193. Charles Thomas, Springfield (1968)
8. Cain, W.S.: Spatial discrimination of cutaneous warmth. Am. J. Psychol. **86**, 169–181 (1973)
9. Nathan, P.W., Rice, R.C.: The localization of warm stimuli. Neurology **16**, 533–540 (1966)
10. Green, B.G.: Localization of thermal sensation: an illusion and synthetic heat. Percept. Psychophys. **22**, 331–337 (1977)
11. Green, B.G.: Referred thermal sensations: warmth versus cold. Sens. Process. **2**, 220–230 (1978)
12. Ho, H.-N., Watanabe, J., Ando, H., Kashino, M.: Somatotopic or spatiotopic? Frame of reference for localizing thermal sensations under thermo-tactile interactions. Atten. Percept. Psychophys. **72**(6), 1666–1675 (2010)
13. Ho, H.-N., Watanabe, J., Ando, H., Kashino, M.: Mechanisms underlying referral of thermal sensations to sites of tactile stimulation. J. Neurosci. **31**(1), 208–213 (2011)

14. Watanabe, R., Okazaki, R., Kajimoto, H.: Mutual referral of thermal sensation between two thermal-tactile stimuli. In: Haptics Symposium 2014, pp. 299–302 (2014)
15. Oohara, J., Kato, H., Hashimoto, Y., Kajimoto, H.: Presentation of positional information by heat phantom sensation. In: Kappers, A.M., van Erp, J.B., Bergmann Tiest, W.M., van der Helm, F.C. (eds.) EuroHaptics 2010, Part II. LNCS, vol. 6192, pp. 445–450. Springer, Heidelberg (2010)
16. Sato, K., Maeno, T.: Presentation of rapid temperature change using spatially divided hot and cold stimuli. J. Roboti. Mechatron. **25**, 497–505 (2013)
17. Stevens, J.C., Choo, K.C.: Temperature sensitivity of the body surface over the life span. Somatosens. Mot. Res. **15**, 13–28 (1998)
18. Kenshalo, D.R.: Correlations of temperature sensitivity in man and monkey, a first approximation. In: Zotterman, Y. (ed.) Sensory Functions of the Skin with Special Reference to Man, pp. 305–330. Pergamon Press (1976)

Modal Superimposition for Multi-fingers Variable Friction Tactile Device

Sofiane Ghenna$^{(\boxtimes)}$, Christophe Giraud-Audine, Frederic Giraud,
Michel Amberg, and Betty Lemaire-Semail

Univ. Lille, Centrale Lille, Arts et Metiers ParisTech, HEI, HeSam,
EA 2697 - L2EP - Laboratoire DElectrotechnique Et DElectronique de Puissance,
59000 Lille, France
{sofiane.ghenna,frederic.giraud,michel.amberg,
betty.semail}@univ-lille1.fr, christophe.giraud-audine@ensam.eu

Abstract. In this study, we develop and implement a method for superimposing two vibration modes in order to produce different tactile stimuli on two fingers located in different positions. The tactile stimulation is based on the squeeze film effect which decreases the friction between a fingertip and a vibrating plate.

Experimental test have been conducted on a 1D tactile device. They show that it is possible to continuously control the friction on two fingers moving independently. Then, we developed the design of a 2D device based on the same principle, which gives rise to the design of a two-fingers tactile display. Evaluations were conducted using a modal analysis with experimental validation.

Keywords: Ultrasonic · Vibration modes · Tactile stimulation · Multitouch

1 Introduction

The Variable Friction Devices (VFD) modulate the friction between a user's fingertip and a surface to create tactile stimulation. Electrostatic forces can be used to attract the finger and thus to increase the friction [2]. Friction reduction based tactile devices use an ultrasonic vibration to modify the contact mechanisms between a user's fingertip and a vibrating plate [10]. Many implementations of this principle have been proposed, to create 2D tactile displays. For instance [3] uses a circular patch glued on the screen of a tactile display. In order to free the touched surface of non-transparent piezo-electric material, [5] proposes to produce the vibration with exciters glued at the periphery of the display. Finally, recent optimization in the design helps to improve the efficiency and limit the amount of power requested by the tactile stimulator [11], thus allowing implementation into handheld devices.

These implementations are using a single Rayleigh vibration mode [7]. In order to prevent a user's finger from crossing or feeling a stationary nodal lines, the distance between two nodal lines of vibration – that is half a wavelength – should

F. Bello et al. (Eds.): EuroHaptics 2016, Part I, LNCS 9774, pp. 521–530, 2016.
DOI: 10.1007/978-3-319-42321-0_49

be comparable with the finger 's contact length. In practice, for a light touch exploration [1], this leads to a maximum length of 12 mm. An other approach consists in switching between two vibration modes, the nodal lines of which have orthogonal directions [9].

These approaches however are limited to a single touch interaction. Indeed, they do not allow to precisely control the vibration amplitudes at two or more different positions simultaneously. To cope with this issue, [4] proposed to super-impose two vibration modes, and to control the vibration amplitude of each mode according to the position of two fingertips. This principle take advantages of modal superimposition by using two modes which half wavelength is higher than 12 mm.

So far, the principle has been validated in static operation and for 1D tactile display. In this paper, we further validate the proposal in the case of tracking two fingers, and we extend the principle to 2D displays. In the first part, we briefly recall the principles of the modal superimposition. We then present the validation with a tracking of two fingers with a psychophysical study. In the last part, we show evidence that the approach is also valid for 2D.

2 Presentation of the Multimodal Approach

Vibrations of a plate can be written as a combination of an infinite number of modes, determined by the equilibrium equation [7]:

$$DV^4w(x,y,t) + \rho h \frac{\partial^2 w(x,y,t)}{\partial t^2} = 0 \tag{1}$$

where $w(x,y,t)$ is the flexural vibration, ρ, h and ∂ are respectively the density and the thickness of plate and the partial derivative. D is the flexural rigidity of the plate in bending defined by

$$D = \frac{Eh^3}{12(1-\mu^2)} \tag{2}$$

E and μ are the Young module and poisson's ratio of the plate.

Together with the kinematic boundary conditions.

For a steady state and monochromatic vibration at angular frequency ω, one can write the solution using complex notations using $\underline{w}(x,y,t) = \underline{W}(x,y,t)e^{j\omega t}$ as follows:

$$\underline{W}(x,y,t) = \sum_{n=1}^{\infty} \underline{W}_n(t)\phi_n(x,y) \tag{3}$$

with $\phi_n(x,y)$ are the modal shapes, in the sequel, $\underline{W}_n$ is called the vibration amplitude of mode n.

Hence, theoretically, the vibration shape $w(x,y,t)$ can be controlled at the condition that the vibration amplitude of each mode $\underline{W}_n$ is controlled too.

Therefore, if we consider m different positions on the plate namely (x_i, y_i) where $i = \{1..m\}$, where the deformation must be controlled to render different tactile stimulations, we can select at least $p \geq m$ modes of vibration to write the problem as follows:

$$
\begin{bmatrix} \underline{W}(x_1, y_1) \\ \underline{W}(x_2, y_2) \\ \vdots \\ \underline{W}(x_m, y_m) \end{bmatrix} = \begin{bmatrix} \phi_1(x_1, y_1) & \phi_2(x_1, y_1) & \cdots & \phi_p(x_1, y_1) \\ \phi_1(x_2, y_2) & \phi_2(x_2, y_2) & \cdots & \phi_p(x_2, y_2) \\ \vdots & \vdots & \ddots & \vdots \\ \phi_1(x_m, y_m) & \phi_2(x_m, y_m) & \cdots & \phi_p(x_m, y_m) \end{bmatrix} \begin{bmatrix} \underline{W}_1 \\ \underline{W}_2 \\ \vdots \\ \underline{W}_p \end{bmatrix} \tag{4}
$$

This can be written in matrix form as:

$$
[W_f] = [\Phi_f] \cdot [W_M] \tag{5}
$$

where $[\Phi_f]$ is a $m \times p$ matrix. It is possible to find a vector of modal deformation amplitude $[W_M]$ which can be set in order to obtain the required deformation of the plate at the positions of the fingers $[W_f]$:

- if $m = p$, $[W_M] = [\Phi_f]^{-1} \cdot [W_f]$ if $det\,[\Phi_f] \neq 0$ [4],
- if $p > m$, a solution can be found either using the pseudo inverse of $[\Phi_f]$ which is equivalent to the least square approximation, or by using more elaborated optimization to introduce technological constraints for example.

In the rest of the paper, we consider two fingers and two vibration modes. For the specific case of $2D$ and 2-fingers VFD, they are denoted by $\phi_{k,X}$ and $\phi_{k,Y}$, where k is an integer. For the purpose of demonstration, and without loss of generality, we can approximate the modal shapes by simplified equations as follows:

$$
\phi_{k,X}(x, y) = W_X \sin(\lambda_k x) \quad \text{and} \quad \phi_{k,Y}(x, y) = W_Y \sin(\lambda_k y) \tag{6}
$$

with $\lambda_k = (2k+1)\frac{\pi}{2}$. Therefore, the problem of controlling the amplitudes under the user's fingers at positions (x_1, y_1) and (x_2, y_2) is stated by :

$$
\begin{cases} W_X \sin(\lambda_k x_1) + W_Y \sin(\lambda_k y_1) = W_1 \\ W_X \sin(\lambda_k x_2) + W_Y \sin(\lambda_k y_2) = W_2 \end{cases} \tag{7}
$$

where the amplitude of the modes X and Y are denoted W_X and W_Y respectively. The problem has a solution for the modes amplitude W_1 and W_2, as long as the determinant is not nil, which gives rise to the condition:

$$
\sin(\lambda_k x_1) \sin(\lambda_k y_2) - \sin(\lambda_k x_2) \sin(\lambda_k y_1) \neq 0 \tag{8}
$$

At the positions where the condition 8 is not fulfilled, the solutions for W_1 and W_2 doesn't exist. This defines a set of loci, for a given position of one of the finger, where amplitudes can not be controlled, like the ones depicted on Fig. 1 for the position $x_1 = 0.25$ and $y_1 = 0.5$. This loci creates a limitation of the method, because the dual touch interaction cannot be obtained at any position. To avoid this limitation, one solution could be to use more than 2 modes. This solution has not been evaluated in this paper.

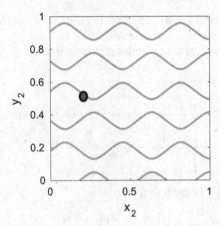

Fig. 1. Loci of the position of the second finger in the x_2, y_2 plane where amplitudes can not be set. These loci depends on the position of the first finger (symbolised by the ellipse)

3   Validation in the 1D Case

3.1   Experimental Setup

A $6 \times 6 \times 350$ mm^3 aluminium beam is actuated by two Langevin transducers. Two aluminium horns have been designed and manufactured in order to be able to transmit the vibration to the beam. The whole system is fixed on a rigid support, which is mobile to measure vibration velocity at several points. A laser interferometer (OFV-525/-5000-S) is used for that purpose. The control algorithm is implemented on a DSP (TI 2812) and two amplifiers (HSA 4051) supply power to the transducers.

For the experiment, the boundary condition is free-free; the two vibration modes 16 and 17 are selected with regards to the half-wavelength, which is approximately equal to $20, 5$ mm. The working frequency is arbitrarily chosen between the resonant frequency of the two modes, that is $27, 7$ kHz.

A Linear Variable Differential Transformer (LVDT) is attached to the user's right hand index. By this way, we track its position and generate the references $[W_M]$ in the modal space. A closed loop control as described in [6] calculates the required voltage amplitude on each transducer. To simplify the set-up, the fingers are not tracked independently, but we considered that the second finger is located at a fixed position apart from the first one. In our experiment, we chose 3 cm as a convenient distance for the participants.

Figure 2-left shows the desired and measured vibration amplitude under each finger as a function of the position on the beam. To perform the measurements, the LVDT was manually moved and the amplitudes were measured at the planned positions. The systematic error observed is small (less than 0.1μ m), and may by due to the errors in the identification of the deformation mode shape.

Moreover, as it can be seen, it is actually possible to achieve in most cases the desired amplitudes, except at some points where the determinant of $[\varPhi_f]$ is close to zero. In these cases, the actuator's voltage reference exceeds the maximum voltage amplifiers (300 V peak to peak). Figure 2-right illustrates an example of the calculated and measured modal amplitude references as a function of planned positions of the two fingers on the beam.

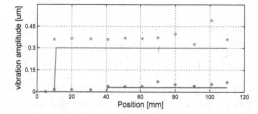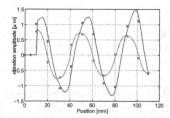

Fig. 2. Comparison between references (−) and measurements (∗); left: vibration amplitude under the fingers as a function of the right finger (blue: left finger, red: right finger); right: modal amplitudes (blue: left actuator, red: right actuator (Color figure online)

As it can be seen, the modal amplitudes and their references are in good agreements. However, a systematic error occurs on the vibration amplitude at the location of the two fingers. It has been observed a systematic lag of 1 mm on the nodes that may be attributed to an error in the identification of the modal shape ϕ_n. However, the error remains under sensitivity threshold.

3.2   Experimental Procedure and Results

Seven volunteers participated to the following experiment: 3 females, 4 males, all right handed, aged from 25 to 30 years. Two of them were familiar with VFD. Their hand was guided to explore the beam after washing. Three stimuli were presented. The first one was the beam without excitation. In the second one, the beam was activated with a standing wave of 1μ m, in order to create friction reduction. The subjects could explore the device with one finger. After this first part of the experiment, they were asked to qualify and to rate the friction reduction in their personnal scale.

In the second part of the experiment, the subjects could explore the beam using two fingers of left and right hands, separated by a constant distance. Here, the multi-finger control was activated to present an node of vibration under the right finger, and a vibration amplitude of approximately 1μ m on the left one. They were then asked to rate the friction reduction on each fingers, according to their personal scale. The normalized results are summed up in Fig. 3.

3.3   Discussion

As a result of the experiment, the subjects felt the beam on the left finger more "slippery" or "smoother" than the friction on the right finger. This is consistent

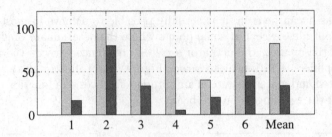

Fig. 3. Normalized perceived friction reduction for each participant (from 1 to 6) and average; light: left finger; dark: right finger.

with the multifingers algorithm, which produced a node under the right finger and approximately 1μ m of vibration under the left finger. Since the finger's position is tracked during the experiment, the node is sliding with user's finger. If a stationary wave would have been set on the beam, then the users would have felt nodes and antinodes of vibration successively on each fingers, and would not have detected a finger smoother than the other [4].

Moreover, 5 subjects found the beam more slippery for the left finger compared to the beam without any vibration. This highlights the fact that the plate vibrates on both side of the node. As a consequence, even though a node is always placed under the fingertip, there is still friction reduction. This reduction is however 48 % (average, Standard deviation 24%).

These results show that it is possible to create independent friction reduction under two fingertips, on a $1D$ VFD, with an appropriate tracking of the finger, and the multi-finger algorithm of Eq. 5. The next part of the paper presents the prototype for $2D$ and 2-fingers VFD.

4   Towards 2D

4.1   Design Considerations

In a first attempt to extend the previous study to the case of plate, a second set-up has been realized. It was chosen to use two similar modes since in the case of square plates, two orthogonal modes with a same wavelength and theoretically a same frequency can be excited. In the case at hand, the 8th modes in the X and Y directions were selected based on the half-wavelength. Also, the working frequency should be above the audible spectrum, thus, the design was a 140 $\times$ 140 $\times$ 4 mm^3 plate. This results in a rather thick plate as a consequence of the large required wavelength. Hence, this method may be more suitable for large tactile devices, where volume constraint should not be a problem. Figure 4 presents the plate and its actuators.

The placement of the actuators, which consists in piezoelectric patches glued on the surface of the plate, is also critical. Theoretically, two actuators would have been enough to excite the two modes. But to preserve the symmetry of the

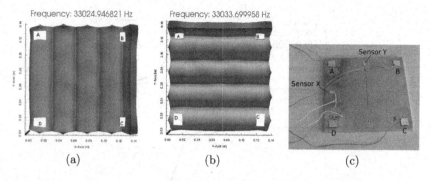

Fig. 4. Vibration modes and mode shapes using FEM with the position of the actuators (in white in a and b), and the prototype (c).

device, four actuators were used, denoted A, B, C and D in the sequel. Their location and the direction of their polarization is crucial for the application :

- A and D are placed on a antinode of vibration of mode X, while B and C are on an opposite antinode of vibration (Fig. 4a)
- C and D are placed on a antinode of vibration of mode Y, while A and B are on an opposite antinode of vibration (Fig. 4b)
- the two pairs of actuators A and D on one hand, and C and D on the other hand, are placed in such a way that their polarization direction are opposite.

These considerations have the following advantages:

- the four actuators have the same contribution to each mode, but can be additive or destructive,
- by connecting A and C to the same supply denoted V_{AC}, and B and D to V_{BD}, the contribution to mode X is given by $V_{AC} + V_{BD}$, while the contribution to mode Y is given by $V_{AC} - V_{BD}$. This allows to continuously mix both modes, and not to switch between them as in [9]

The device is supposed to work in closed loop, in order to control the amplitudes of the modes. Hence, in addition to the actuators, two aditionnal piezoelectric patches are used as sensors. In order to measure the actual amplitude of each mode, they have to be precisely placed. Ideally, they should be at the position of an antinode of one mode and a node of the other one [8].

4.2   Experimental Results

Figure 5 shows the measured deflection as a function of frequency on the manufactured prototype. The two modes have similar resonant frequency ($f_x = 33010$ Hz, $f_y = 33064$ Hz), and the actuators have the same contributions since the amplitudes are similar.

We also show in Fig. 6 the deformation mode shapes of the two modes. They are close to the calculated one presented Fig. 4.

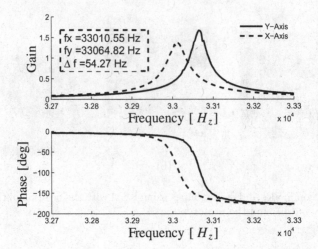

Fig. 5. Vibration amplitude of the 2 vibration modes as a function of frequency

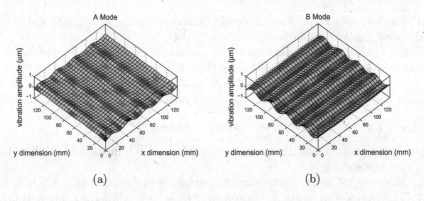

Fig. 6. Deformation mode shape; (a) X mode, (b) Y mode

The working frequency chosen for the experiment was equal to the median frequency of the modes. In this way, a mode is not promoted compared to the other one. However, as a consequence of the high quality factors of the resonances, the phase rotation is very stiff. It is thus necessary to adjust the voltages amplitude and phase, in order to compensate for the gain discrepancy and the phase shift.

The Figs. 7 presents simulation and experimental measurements for different combinations of modes X and Y which confirm the possibility to control the spatial pattern of nodes and antinodes.

For example, the point P_1 in Figure 7 is located on a node of vibration when $W_X = W_Y$, and becomes an antidone of vibration when $W_X = -W_Y$. Conversely, P_2 is an antinodde of vibration for the first case and a node of vibration for the second one.

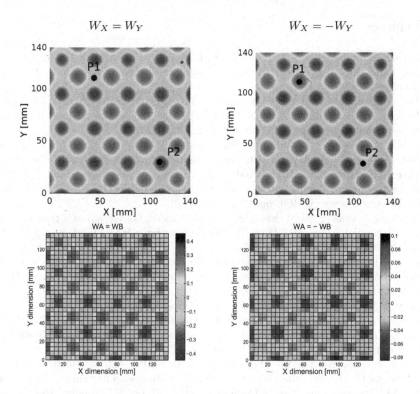

Fig. 7. Plate's deformation for several combinations modes X and Y; top: simulation, bottom: experimental measurement. (Color figure online)

5   Conclusion

This paper presents a Variable Friction Device which can independently control the friction reduction under two fingertips. First, the approach has been validated on a $1D$ device. During the experiment, a beam was controlled in such a way that a node was continuously presented under a fingertip, while a second finger was moving over an antinode of vibration. Subjects have found that the sliding node is 48 % less slippery than the sliding antinode of vibration. We then present the design of a $2D$ device. The vibration control of the X mode according to the Y one allows to change smoothly and continuously the position of nodes and antinodes of vibration.

Future work will be dedicated to the introduce the tracking of the two fingers on the $2D$ device. Moreover, introduction of a third vibration mode may be necessary in order to be able to control the friction over the whole display.

Acknowledgement. This work has been carried out within the framework of the project StimTac of IRCICA (institut de recherche sur les composants logiciels et matériels pour la communication avancée), and the Mint project of Inria.

References

1. Adams, M.J., Johnson, S.A., Lefèvre, P., Lévesque, V., Hayward, V., André, T., Thonnard, J.L.: Finger pad friction and its role in grip and touch. J. R. Soc. Interface 10(80) (2012)
2. Bau, O., Poupyrev, I., Israr, A., Harrison, C.: Teslatouch: electrovibration for touch surfaces. In: Proceedings of the 23rd Annual ACM Symposium on User Interface Software and Technology, UIST 2010, pp. 283–292 (2010)
3. Chubb, E., Colgate, J., Peshkin, M.: Shiverpad: a glass haptic surface that produces shear force on a bare finger. IEEE Trans. Haptics 3(3), 189–198 (2010)
4. Ghenna, S., Giraud, F., Giraud-Audine, C., Amberg, M., Lemaire-Semail, B.: Preliminary design of a multi-touch ultrasonic tactile stimulator. In: 2015 IEEE World Haptics Conference (WHC), pp. 31–36, June 2015
5. Giraud, F., Amberg, M., Lemaire-Semail, B., Casiez, G.: Design of a transparent tactile stimulator. In: 2012 IEEE Haptics Symposium (HAPTICS), pp. 485–489, March 2012
6. Giraud, F., Giraud-Audine, C., Amberg, M., Lemaire-Semail, B.: Vector control method applied to a traveling wave in a finite beam. IEEE Trans. Ultrason. Ferroelectr. Freq. Control 61(1), 147–158 (2014)
7. Graff, K.F.: Wave Motion in Elastic Solids. Dover Publications, Mineola (1991)
8. Nadal, C., Giraud-Audine, C., Giraud, F., Amberg, M., Lemaire-Semail, B.: Modelling of a beam excited by piezoelectric actuators in view of tactile applications. In: Mathematics and Computers in Simulation (2015)
9. Son, K.J., Kim, K.: The use of degenerate mode shapes in piezoelectric variable-friction tactile displays(the 12th international conference on motion and vibration control). Dynamics and Design Conference 2014(12), pp. 1–7, August 2014
10. Vezzoli, E., Ben Messaoud, W., Amberg, M., Giraud, F., Lemaire-Semail, B., Bueno, M.A.: Physical and perceptual independence of ultrasonic vibration and electrovibration for friction modulation. IEEE Trans. Haptics 8(2), 235–239 (2015)
11. Wiertlewski, M., Colgate, J.E.: Power optimization of ultrasonic friction-modulation tactile interfaces. Trans. Haptics 8(1), 43–53 (2014)

Author Index

Printed in the United States
By Bookmasters